Middle East Encounters

Extracts from letters home
&
selected articles published in
'The Age' and 'The Sydney Morning Herald'
1977-1984
(by courtesy of Fairfax Media Syndication)

Also by David Balderstone

A Road from Damascus

'Balderstone's novel is about people, land and displacement. It traces the lives of one-time Jerusalem friends and neighbours, the Palestinian Habeebs and the Jewish Avrahams as war, politics and ideology separate them, and then makes their paths cross again. Balderstone has the cadences and the speeches they enwrap just right too….above all he gets the people of the region right.'

The Age, Melbourne

The Baghdad Chameleon

'Like its predecessor, *A Road from Damascus,* this adventure is centred in the Middle East and sows a triangle of intrigue between Cyprus, Syria and Iraq…. When our Middle Eastern News diet is primarily pictures of violence and Islamic extremism, The Baghdad Chameleon provides the counter-image of complex interrelated cultures united by the pragmatism of doing deals.'

The Australian

Shining the Boot of a Nation: A Portrait of Egypt after Nasser

For an understanding of the Egyptian political mood and events juxtaposed with the concerns of the man in the street following the death of Nasser, this cannot be bettered!

Kindle e-book review

DAVID BALDERSTONE

Middle East Encounters

THE
POPPY
PRESS
AUSTRALIA

© Susan Balderstone 2015

ISBN 978-0-9943464-3-8

All rights reserved. No part of this publication may be reproduced without the prior permission of the publisher and copyright owner except for brief excerpts for the purpose of fair criticism and comment acknowledging both author and publisher.

Cover photograph
David Balderstone 1992

National Library of Australia
Cataloguing-in-Publication entry
Creator: Balderstone, David, author
Title: Middle East Encounters/ David Balderstone.
ISBN: 9780994346438 (paperback)
Subjects: Balderstone, David- -Correspondence
    Middle East- -Politics and government
    Middle East- -Social conditions
    Middle East- -Social life and customs
Dewey Number: 956.04

Published by
The Poppy Press AUSTRALIA
(Australian business name registration number 1064567K)
P.O.B. 850, Parkville, Victoria, 3052, Australia
Poppypress@bigpond.com

Contents

Preface by Susan Balderstone 11
Note re style and transliteration 14
List of illustrations 15
Map 16
1977 17
False dawn: Turkey still in dark 17
We back Arab homeland 21
Egypt jets blast Libyan air base 22
Hussein's subtle shuttle 23
   Amman July 30, 1977 26
Hussein: the remarkable Middle East survivor 30
Bridge over River Jordan gives Middle East some hope 35
Time no healer for Jerusalem 38
Blow for peace hopes 43
   Amman October 4, 1977 46
Past keeps its grip on Lebanon 48
   Amman November 1977 53
The next move is up to Begin 54
A hero's welcome home for Sadat 58
Wanted – another Act of Grace for hero's widow 60
3000 years before Moses 62
Sideshowing the way 69
Mid-East talks open 73

Honeymoon is over: time for hard words 75
Egypt is key to peace 79
1978 82
    Amman January 1978 82
Arabs ban our firms 83
Words fail to ease ache for Palestine 87
Turkey caught in a quicksand of compromise 90
    Amman January 6, 1978 93
Assad set for a new term 95
Dispute splits front against Sadat 96
Clashes shake Lebanon hope 99
Hawke gets a welcome in Jordan 102
Hawke wants ban on PLO visitors 105
    Amman February 1978 106
    Amman February 27, 1978 109
Shadow over Middle East 111
Israeli 'solution' solves nothing 115
Crusaders' castle still under siege 119
UN force enters southern Lebanon 123
Give lands for peace: Israel rally 126
....And who are the Arabs? 128
    Amman April 11, 1978 132
Israel mood gives hope: prince 134
A city fighting for its life 136
    Amman May 1978 144
Learn from mistakes, Hussein tells Arabs 145

A terror campaign against Syria's ruling sect 148
Miss Liza becomes a queen 151
    Amman June 1978 153
Israeli stall kills peace hope 155
The veil begins to lift 159
    Amman June 30, 1978 162
Lebanon: a war that won't stop 164
Living with war in the street 168
Syrians angry at Camp David talks 172
The city of waters goes thirsty 174
World's eyes are on Hussein now 180
A new life for the Bedouin 182
Australian digs for key to old puzzle 185
Palestinians closing ranks 188
    Amman October 24, 1978 191
Peals of peace from Bagdad 193
    Amman November 21, 1978 196
President's coma leaves Algeria in limbo 199
New image from Bagdad, and it's not so smug 201
1979 205
Guns still for now. 205
Dominoes now the game in Mid-East 209
Iran's turmoil shakes the neighbors 211
Iran's revolution turns things Arafat's way 214
    Amman, March 1, 1979 217
Yemeni war 'a threat to Gulf stability' 218

Iranians to examine our killing methods ... 220
City of bunkers ... 222
Women and zealots in Iran battle ... 225
A nation in the hands of the mob ... 227
The true crucible of peace ... 232
Talk peace, Begin urges Arabs ... 238
Arabs buy our TV shows ... 240
'A treaty of war' Syria hits Egypt deal ... 242
Lebanon a hostage to war ... 244
Another dawn ... 249
Moslem group 'plotting to overthrow Assad' ... 251
Arab former enemies find unity in common fears and problems . 252
Separatist violence poses growing challenge to Iran ... 256
Iran: will anarchy be the next step ... 258
Baktiar back on stage ... 265
Threat to peace as old foes fall out ... 267
    Amman, August 18, 1979 ... 269
    Amman August 21, 1979 ... 271
Peace at all costs ... 272
Sadat set for autonomy tussle ... 276
Calm before crunch on autonomy ... 278
Swing low, sweet Syria ... 280
Iran leaves Gulf of strained relations ... 283
Clergy lose a scapegoat ... 287
Kurds' lonely fight continues ... 290
Arab unity unlikely over PLO ... 294

Saudis retake Mecca shrine	295
Iran's echoes rattle the Saudis	297
Revolt, Saudis urged	301
Army battles Tabriz rebels	303
The man against Khomeiny	306
Secrets from the embassy in Teheran	310
1980	315
Iranians vote to elect President	315
Once again the West carves up the East	317
Australians find ancient 'riches'	322
Bleak omen in Teheran	325
Time to take a risk for peace: Hawke	328
Saudis face up to a changing world	330
The enigma of the Ayatollah	335
No tension in Teheran's life	341
Hammer and sickle flies at the Caspian	343
A problem to haunt Iran	346
Mullahs to decide fate of hostages	349
High tension on the Left (sic) Bank	354
Middle East no closer to peace	357
Terrorism endangers Turkish democracy	362
Arafat: enigma of the PLO	366
Amman July 18, 1980	370
The time for travel	372
Sadat the successful	374
Amman, August 8, 1980	380

Turkish forces stage a reluctant coup 382
Cues for conflict 384
Big guns amid Bagdad's trees 387
A man who sees no borders 391
Rubble pile 22km inside Iran 393
After 12 days, war leads to nowhere 395
Iraqi clergy back Hussein 397
King steps up word war with Iranians 403
Peace in the streets of a city at war 404
Bazaaris flex muscles 408
A tenuous grasp of justice 411
Jordan-Syria border tense 415
    Amman December 6, 1980 417
    Amman December 11, 1980 418
    Amman December 14, 1980 419
It's business of war as usual in the Holy Land 420
1981 422
Holy war? Not exactly 422
Syria 'sent soldiers to kill Jordan PM' 424
Lebanon's barbaric 'saviour' 426
An unlikely alliance 429
Yemen troops crossed border: Oman 431
Begin's opponents have a big start 432
Rival powers shun peace for Lebanon 436
Iran slow to reopen 'hotbeds of dissent' 440
A bad deal after all 443

Syrians down Israeli aircraft 445
A human statistic in futile fighting 447
Palestinians brace for attack 450
Israeli raid dashes US peace hopes 453
Stay out of Sinai force, Arabs say 457
More of the same 459
More martyrs for Iran's revolution 461
Gulf war goes on…..a child dies 464
At the front line 466
Suicidal zeal fuels Iran war effort 471
Divided opposition a Khomeiny asset 474
Regretful Ghali criticises Israelis 478
Death of a President 481
Sadat plot linked to arrests 486
Spectre of fanaticism 488
Anthony wooed on Sinai force 490
Sadat death opens new path to peace 492
Parliament vote shows split in Iran leadership 495
Saudis arm PLO, Iraq, says Israel 498
Sinai 1982: Will the Diggers be back? 501
Summit failure lifts tension in Mideast 508
Long distance battle for Iran 512
Golan move puts peace in danger 515
Bahrain, a land of problems 519
1982 521
Persecuted people 521

Divided by peace 523
Jordanians heed king's call to fight for Iraq 526
A war just waiting to happen 528
Israelis join West Bank protest 531
Palestinian rights key issue: Street 533
Australia-PLO contact encouraged 535
Israeli raid near, Lebanon fears 536
Millions strike over killing of Moslems 538
M-E peace a mirage after Sinai handover 540
PLO keeping the peace 544
'Jerusalem offensive' gives Iran initiative in Gulf war 547
Gulf victories 'according to plan' 550
Opposition lives on in the Majlis 553
News Diary 556
Israel invades Lebanon: Tanks roll over border for strike at PLO 561
Syrians bring in more armor 564
War casualties cram hospital 567
Beirut about to fall: Israel 569
Israel looks set for a long stay 572
Israeli armor traps PLO in Beirut 575
Israel guns batter PLO 580
Blood and mystery follow Israel's drive to Beirut 584
Westerners warned to quit Beirut 589
PLO evacuation hitch 591
Arafat plays a game of brinkmanship 593
Guns open up again in Lebanon 596

Begin peace pact plan gets rebuff 598

News Diary 600

Hussein's reputation for survival tested 605

Arabs share Beirut blame 609

Israel accepts US Beirut peace plan 612

Come and see for yourself, Begin challenges Fraser 614

Israel threatens to shell Syrians 616

Israeli peace treaty gets Beirut rebuff 618

Begin's coalition still far ahead in popularity polls 619

Inside the refugee camps of Lebanon 621

News Diary 626

New offensives in a forgotten war 630

New opportunities open up for PLO after defeat 633

News Diary 636

Concession may follow PLO talks in Jordan 639

A semblance of security returns to Beirut 640

1983 644

Sharon resigns post, but stays in the Cabinet 644

Jordan king may try to climb the minaret 647

News Diary 651

New hope of a solution to Cyprus problem 655

Carter raps Israel over Palestinians 657

PLO divided on mandate for Jordan 659

M-E Plan still alive 660

War clouds darken Lebanon's summer 662

News Diary 666

Another milestone on the road to nowhere ... 670
   Amman May 14, 1983 ... 674

PLO chief faces military revolt ... 675

Mid-East: new tack needed ... 676

PLO leader appeals for backing ... 680

Where to from here? ... 682
   Kakopetria, Cyprus July 4, 1983 ... 694
   Kakopetria, Cyprus July 12, 1983 ... 696
   Kakopetria, Cyprus August 25, 1983 ... 698
   Heslington, York October 9, 1983 ... 699
   Heslington, York October 27, 1983 ... 700
   Kakopetria, Cyprus Christmas Day 1983 ... 701

1984 ... 703
   Heslington, York February 28, 1984 ... 703
   Heslington, York June 20, 1984 ... 704
   Heslington, York, September 5, 1984 ... 706
   Gasthof Drachenwand, near Mondsee, Austria September 12, 1984 ... 707

Postscript ... 708

Other books by David Balderstone ... 711

Preface by Susan Balderstone

In 1977 my husband David Balderstone, having researched conditions and calculated a budget, persuaded Greg Taylor, then Editor of Melbourne newspaper 'The Age', that it was high time 'The Age' had an Australian journalist in the Middle East, writing for Australians, rather than relying on British and American correspondents. 'The Sydney Morning Herald' agreed to join the deal. He took up the post from July 1, having arrived in Amman, Jordan which was to be our base for the next six years, on June 30, 1977. Announcing the imminent opening of the new overseas post, 'The Age' recorded that:

"Balderstone joined 'The Age' as a cadet journalist in 1965 and then transferred to 'The Times' in London. Later he served as a correspondent in Cairo. Balderstone returned to Australia in 1971 and recently has been Melbourne correspondent for 'The Bulletin'."

As reviewers of David's books have noted, he developed an intimate knowledge of more than merely the politics of the area. He knew the people, and developed an understanding of their traditions, customs, family ties and way of life. While he met and interviewed several prominent leaders, he was interested in the ordinary people of the area, with whom he established friendly relationships. As Cameron Forbes noted in his review of David's novel 'A Road from Damascus' – "he gets the people of the region right". His accounts of encounters with the people of the region as recorded in his letters home from June 1977 to December 1984 illuminate in small part why this was so. The conversations he had with people stayed in his memory, and coloured his depiction of events. The descriptions and conversations sometimes found their way into his articles published in 'The Age' and 'The Sydney Morning Herald'.

This collection of some of his published articles interspersed with extracts from his letters home gives a picture of the area as it was at that time from his own unique perspective; picking up on local attitudes and eccentricities while homing in on the issues.

His first articles covered the political chaos in Turkey in the wake of a recent election – we drove through Turkey in June 1977 on our way to Amman from London. Soon after we arrived he flew off to Cairo to cover Libyan-Egyptian skirmishes over their shared border area, with Egyptian air attacks extending as far west as Tobruk. His early articles include a profile of King Hussein as he celebrated 25 years on the throne; attempts by Cyrus Vance, then US Secretary of State and President Carter's envoy, to advance Middle East peace; an account of crossing to the Israeli-occupied West Bank via the Allenby Bridge, and the situation in Jerusalem and Lebanon.

He went on to cover the historic visit by Egyptian President Sadat to Jerusalem in November 1977 and subsequent peace talks; Israeli incursions into southern Lebanon in response to Palestinian raids in March 1978; Iran after the fall of the Shah in 1979 and the subsequent American hostage crisis; ongoing troubles in Beirut, the siege of Beirut and expulsion of the Palestinians in 1982; the Iran-Iraq war from both sides; the military coup in Turkey; the Mecca mosque siege in Saudi Arabia; and Arab summits in Cairo, Baghdad and Morocco. In the process he interviewed political and religious leaders as well as ordinary people from communities on all sides of the conflicts.

In general the articles have been selected to provide an overview of the period he covered and follow the threads of the main stories – Israel-Arab peace moves, the ongoing troubles in Lebanon, and post-revolution Iran. They provide background to the lively descriptions of the personal encounters he had while travelling in the region. His bailiwick stretched from Morocco in the west to Iran in the east; from Turkey in the north to Sudan in the south and involved more-or-less constant travel. Amman proved to be a good base for obtaining visas and had the advantage that Israel, Syria, Turkey, Lebanon, Iraq and Iran could all be reached overland if necessary. In between trips it provided a stable and peaceful haven, although not without its own frustrations as he records.

The seeds of recent and current movements for change in the Middle East – the so-called "Arab Spring" across North Africa and Egypt; the rise of ISIS in Syria and Iraq; the Houthis in Yemen and flares of insurgency in the Arabian Gulf States and Saudi Arabia can be detected in these accounts. They trace the events of an earlier period of upheaval growing out of the Israeli-Palestinian conflict, the civil war in Lebanon and the Islamic revolution in Iran. Summing up his six years covering the area, David made some chilling predictions that have proved remarkably prescient.

In his final article from Amman on 27 June 1983, he concluded that "the consequences of failure to resolve the Palestinian problem could be grim indeed – both for the Arab States neighboring Israel, Western interests, and Israel itself". He predicted that "young Palestinians and other Arabs, disillusioned at the failure of the existing forces, are likely to turn to Islam as a liberator," noting that "already this has begun to happen amongst young Palestinians on the West Bank, where pro-PLO students have clashed with Islamic fundamentalists". He foresaw that "this would not only destabilise the Arab regimes, but also could infect Israel's own Arab population," and noted that "in view of Israel's limited Jewish population growth, this could exacerbate widespread Israeli fears that they will be outnumbered in their own State by considerably faster breeding Arab Israelis. Some statistics show this could happen within 50 years". He predicted that "Arab States ruled or heavily influenced by Islamic fundamentalism would never recognise Israel's right to exist, and could back track on the implied recognition already demonstrated by Syria and Jordan".

In the end, after six years he felt he had had enough. He said he needed a change. So he resigned from his arrangement with Fairfax and we moved initially to Cyprus, into a small mountain village house, which I had bought and restored over the previous year or so. Later we moved to York, UK where I undertook a Masters course in architectural conservation and David wrote the first draft of his novel 'A Road from Damascus'. He had intended to write an anecdotal book about the preceding years in the Middle East and to that end had kept copies of his letters home, and the newspaper cuttings of his articles. He had begun to think about such a book again before he first became ill in 2010 and before he died in 2013 had marked the letters and articles he planned to use.

The articles were selected from his almost daily reports as published in 'The Age' and 'The Sydney Morning Herald' over the period, representing perhaps fifteen per cent of his total output over that time. They are usually what he would have called "situationers", providing background and analysis of the situation as he saw it. These form the basis of this book.

Note re style and transliteration

The style and transliteration as published in 'The Age' and 'Sydney Morning Herald' is not always consistent. The same articles were often published in each newspaper but with different headlines, and different style and spelling. In general the 'The Age' articles have been used in preference to the 'Sydney Morning Herald' for the sake of consistency. The style and spelling as published has been followed throughout, but the reader will note that the transliteration of Arab words and names into English varies. For instance Irak changes to Iraq in 1981; Akaba changes to Aqaba, and American spelling is used for some words. On the other hand, the letters use Australian English.

An index to this print edition has not been provided. Readers are referred to the Kindle e-book edition (May, 2015) for detailed reference purposes.

List of illustrations

Ill. 1. In the office, Amman, August 1977............................29

Ill. 2. Interviewing Basil Hennessey at Teleilat Ghassul, December 1977..68

Ill. 3. At Mena House, Cairo: Sadat-Begin talks, Christmas 1977..72

Ill. 4. Baqaa Camp, Jordan, January 1978............................89

Ill. 5. Interviewing Bob Hawke (left) at the Allenby Bridge, February 1978..104

Ill. 6. Three-handed icon Madaba, February 1978.................108

Ill. 7. South Lebanon, Beaufort Castle, March 1978...............122

Ill. 8. Cairo Stock Exchange, May 1978.............................143

Ill. 9. Roman Theatre Amman, September 1978...................179

Ill. 10. At Salalah Oman, February, 1979............................210

Ill. 11. Basil Hennessey at Pella, February 1980....................324

Ill. 12. In the Greek Islands, August 1980...........................381

Ill. 13. Najaf, Iraq, October 1980.....................................402

Ill. 14. Fez, Morocco, November 1981..............................511

Ill. 15. Clearing the North Theatre, Jerash, 1982...................560

Ill. 16. In the kitchen, Kakopetria house, July 1983................695

Ill. 17. Main street of Old Kakopetria, Cyprus.....................697

Ill. 18. Petunia display, Heslington, June 1984.....................705

Map

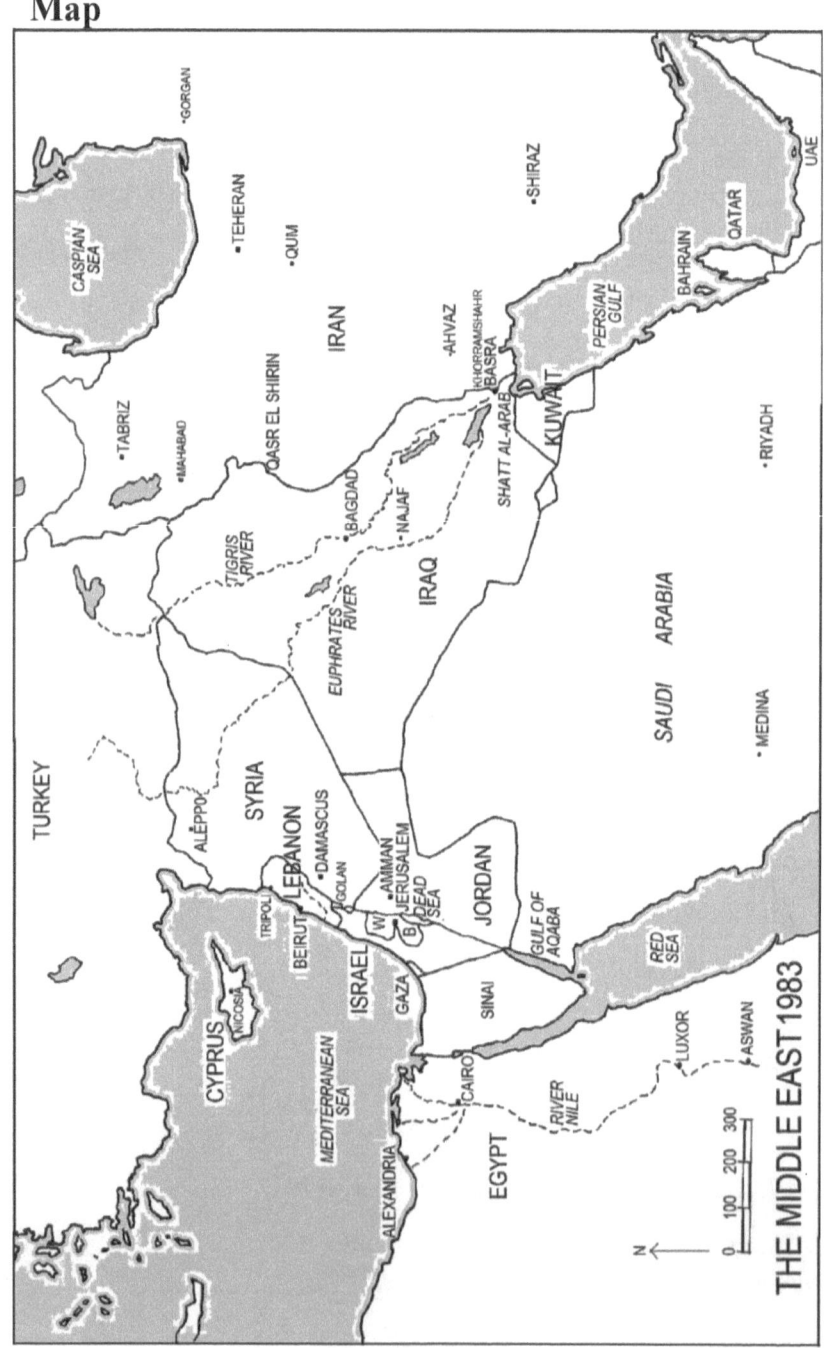

1977
False dawn: Turkey still in dark.
Second of a two-part report from DAVID BALDERSTONE our Middle East correspondent – a newly created post. Balderstone visited Turkey on his way to Amman, where he will be based.

'The Age', Amman, July 8, 1977

The main road from Europe to the Arab world chokes up in the Gulek Pass through the Taurus Mountains in southern Turkey.

For about 40 kilometres through the rugged pass heavy trucks carrying the number plates from every country from Britain to the Gulf States, travel bumper-to-bumper at a snail's pace. From dawn to dusk, this isolated road resembles the worst of the world's peak-hour traffic jams.

The pass provides something of a change for the mainly suicidal truck drivers who provide the trade link between Europe and the Arab world – and play their own brand of Russian roulette on the way. It is their rule to travel at breakneck speed and overtake on hills – and especially on blind curves in the road.

I drove through the pass the other day. Especially up the rugged-sided hills along the road, the trucks would move 10 metres or so and then stop again. The old Austin truck in front of our car had doubtful brakes. Every time it stopped a small boy jumped from the passenger seat with a block of wood and placed it behind the rear wheel. This, thank goodness, did the trick the brakes could not do.

The traffic through the Gulek Pass underlines that Turkey is literally a crossroads of the world. Its geographical position – straddling the eastern-most portion of Europe and Asia Minor – explains many of the difficulties facing a Turkish Government.

Turkey has a long northern border with Russia, it controls the Bosphorus – the Soviet fleet's only link between the Black Sea ports and the Mediterranean, but it is a member of NATO.

Ninety-five per cent of Turks are Moslems, but the country has cool relations with its southern Arab neighbors – Irak and Syria – and maintains diplomatic links with Israel.

It has a continuing dispute over Cyprus with its neighbor Greece and maintains a 30,000-strong garrison on the island.

Also, the discovery of oil in the Aegean Sea around the Greek and Turkish islands has done nothing to improve the jealously tense relationship between the two countries.

Although Turkey is a member of NATO, the US Congress slashed military and economic aid to Turkey following the 1974 Cyprus crisis. In response, Turkey seized most of the key American military installations in the country.

Foreign Affairs priorities of a new Turkish Government will have to be improving relations with Greece and the United States.

The Turkish people are extremely nationalistic – and this is one main reason the country is now facing such massive economic problems.

Because of this nationalistic sentiment, Turkey has discouraged foreign investment. But at the same time, successive Governments have pressed ahead with grand industrialisation projects.

According to observers, many of the projects could easily have been financed through private foreign investment but the Government has had to raise the money itself.

This, coupled with a big trade imbalance, has resulted in a gigantic short-term debt. It has been estimated that close to $100 million in short-term loans falls due for repayment by the end of this year.

Undoubtedly Kemal Ataturk did much to modernise Turkey after the crushing defeat of the Ottoman Empire during World War I.

Certainly he moved the capital from Istanbul to the then small trading village of Ankara, changed the alphabet from Arabic to Latin characters, and launched social programmes to help villagers who had been virtually forgotten by the vast Ottoman administration.

But Turkey remains a country of enormous contrasts in wealth and opportunity. There are the wealthy landowners and businessmen, and the illiterate villagers who scratch out a living – many of them working for the tenant farmers who in turn rent their land from wealthy landlords.

Because of the plight of many villagers, the cities, especially Ankara, have large populations virtually camping around them. The people have come to the cities in the vain hope of employment and more money.

This has led to Ankara's services being greatly overtaxed (electricity blackouts are common).

But while Turkey has economic and social problems there is a good deal to be hopeful about.

Driving across the country it is impossible to be unimpressed by the rich agricultural land – especially in the coastal areas bordering the Aegean and the Mediterranean.

Agricultural exports are growing annually. Oil has been discovered in limited quantities, and there are rich deposits of other minerals including copper, chrome and coal.

It had been expected that the election four weeks ago would give Bulent Ecevit's Republican People's Party a chance to govern in its own right. Then some of the economic, social and foreign relations problems could have been tackled without the limitations imposed by the extreme Right-wing minority parties – principally the National Salvation Party.

Instead, these small parties again hold the balance of power. Again they will be in a position to block Government initiatives.

The People's Party won 213 of the 450 Assembly seats in the election to 189 seats by the Justice Party, the main partner in a right-of-centre coalition which governed until the election.

But Mr Ecevit failed early this week to gain a vote of confidence from the Assembly to form a minority Government. And new President Koruturk has asked former Prime Minister Suleyman Demirel, leader of the Justice Party, to try to form a Government.

Only a supreme optimist could be confident that another Demirel-led coalition could tackle the country's problems effectively.

It is all reminiscent of an incident over dinner in an Ankara restaurant the other night. One of those small boys they still employ to help the waiters, spilt a drop of water. The reprimand was an immediate slap across the face by the head waiter.

The recent election gave a hopeful Turkey a big slap across the face.

We back Arab homeland
From DAVID BALDERSTONE

'The Age', Amman, July 14, 1977

Australia's Minister for the Capital Territory, Mr Staley, has stressed during meetings with Syrian President Hafez Assad that a newly created Palestinian homeland alongside Israel would have the support of the Fraser Government.

Mr Staley is leading a five-member Australian parliamentary delegation which has arrived in Amman after talks in Egypt, Lebanon and Syria.

The delegation's visit has received prominent coverage in the Arab Press.

While in Jordan, the delegation will have talks with King Hussein, Crown Prince Hassan, and the Jordanian Prime Minister Mr Mudar Badran.

In Egypt, the delegation was reported to have declined an offer of discussion with senior representatives of the Palestine Liberation Organisation.

Mr Staley has stressed these main points of Australian Middle East policy during talks with Arab leaders.

Australia supports United Nations Resolutions 242 and 338, which specifically call for the withdrawal of Israel's armed forces from territories occupied in the 1967 Six Day War.

Australia views Israel's right to exist as beyond question.

Australia would support a Palestinian homeland alongside Israel, if there was agreement on the establishment of such a homeland following negotiations between Arab States, Palestinian representatives, and Israel.

Egypt jets blast Libyan air base
From DAVID BALDERSTONE, Our Middle East Correspondent

'The Age', Cairo, July 24, 1977

Egyptian planes today destroyed anti-aircraft rocket posts and six Libyan jets in an attack on the Libyan air base at El Adem, the Middle East News Agency reported.

The agency quoted a military spokesman as saying Egypt used "a great number of planes in the attack".

The Libyan jets were destroyed on the ground, the spokesman said.

The attack followed a brief lull in three days of air and ground fighting between Egypt and Libya as Arab peace makers attempted to finalise a ceasefire.

Two Egyptian Sukhoi-20 planes were shot down by Libyan air defences, the spokesman said.

An Egyptian pilot landed safely inside Libyan territory, he said.

The spokesman denied a Libyan claim that Egyptian jets raided Kufra Oasis inside Libyan territory during which an Egyptian jet was shot down.

"Our air activity today was limited to Adem air base," the spokesman said.

It was the second time in three days that Egyptian planes had pounded the Adem air base, near Tobruk, some 120 kilometres west of the Egyptian border.

Egypt said the first raid was in retaliation for three Libyan air force raids over the Salloum area, just inside Egypt's western desert border, during which three Egyptian soldiers were wounded.

Hussein's subtle shuttle
From DAVID BALDERSTONE

'The Age', Amman, July 25, 1977

Around 20 kilometres out of Amman on the road to Damascus is the Baqaa refugee camp. The past few nights the Palestinians have crowded round the television sets drinking their Arab coffee and sweet minted tea.

"We like to see what Begin and Carter are up to," said one.

With around 500,000 refugees in camps, another one million or so Palestinians registered as refugees with the United Nations, and other Palestinians spread throughout the world, the Palestinian lobby has considerable clout in moderate and extreme Arab capitals.

And yet, while the peace proposals of Israel's new Likud-dominated Government will not even whet the appetite of Palestinian demands, there continues to be talk in Cairo, Amman and Damascus – and particularly Cairo – of reconvening the Geneva peace conference.

Egypt's President Sadat has welcomed the new Israeli Prime Minister's willingness to go to Geneva, and has talked for the first time in terms of recognising Israel "as one of the Middle East States".

To cap it off, he has invited Jews who have left Egypt since 1948 to return to Egypt.

Now Mr Begin, the Israeli Prime Minister, has completed his talks with President Carter and announced major aspects of his proposals for getting the Arab States and Israel together, there is certain to be Arab criticism, initially at least.

The Arab criticism will underline for the world the major differences remaining between the Arabs and Israel. Mr Begin talks of no preconditions to Geneva, but everyone knows the Arabs are publicly demanding return of all occupied territories, and that the

Israeli Government wants to keep the West Bank while giving up parts of the Golan Heights and Sinai.

"Mr Begin's proposals hardly provide a starting point for discussion," one Jordanian put it.

But once the initial Arab criticism of Mr Begin's proposals has died down, there is certain to be renewed talk of Arab willingness to take part in peace talks.

It is difficult to doubt that Sadat, Jordan's King Hussein and Syria's Hafez Assad would sincerely like peace. Equally it is clear that every senior official in these so-called confrontation States knows peace cannot come without a solution for the Palestinian problem.

So why should Arab talk of reconvening the Geneva peace conference continue?

The most widely put view amongst diplomats and political observers in Arab capitals is that Sadat and Hussein particularly, plus Saudi Arabia's King Khalid and Syria's President Assad, believe they have the Israeli Government on the run – diplomatically speaking.

Following visits to President Carter, Sadat, Hussein and Khalid are convinced Carter is capable of taking a stronger line with the Israelis than any other President.

Therefore the more moderate the Arabs can look at present, the better.

They are teasing the new Israeli Prime Minister into negotiation. They are making use of the poor Press coverage Mr Begin has received since his election.

Unless the new Israeli Government is seen to be making meaningful concessions to the Arabs in the coming months, the Arabs believe the much-publicised description of Mr Begin – Right wing and former guerilla – will be cemented in the mind of the American Administration.

During the past few weeks King Hussein has been carrying on a Kissinger-style diplomatic shuttle around Arab States. In the words of the Jordanian newspapers, he is briefing the Arab leaders on the current Middle East situation. But in addition, he is almost certain to be stressing the need for Arab restraint if the policy of putting pressure on Mr Begin is to be successful.

There are very good reasons for Egypt, Jordan and Syria wanting peace at present. They are economic and military.

Jordan and Egypt particularly have embarked on major economic programmes, which would be disastrously affected if there was another war.

President Sadat has not been as successful as he had hoped in attracting Arab capital. But the Suez Canal is operating again and earning foreign currency for the sick Egyptian economy.

At the very least, another war would put an end to this income, which amounts to around $456 million annually.

On the military side, the Arab States are not in a good state of preparedness at present. Equipment is getting old, and they are short of it anyway.

Egypt's split with the Soviet Union has left the Egyptian forces short of spare parts. While the Saudi Arabians have pledged to develop the armed forces, this will take some time.

While Syria's armed forces are in a better condition – at least equipment-wise – much of their strength is being milked by Syria's peace-keeping presence in Lebanon.

A great fear of the leaders of Syria, Jordan and Egypt is that the continuing fighting in Lebanon could prompt the Israelis to strike into southern Lebanon, claiming self-defence.

Amman July 30, 1977 *(To Mother and Aunt Ethel)*

We received your letter of July 23 today. I was particularly interested in your comments that "they truly miss you" and that you "truly think". I know we are now living in the Bible lands, but verily I say unto you it is not necessary to use the jargon.

Thank you for your prompt work with Canon Holt and the Merton Hall chaplain. (*Ed: This was in reference to his request for proof of being Christian, required for obtaining a visa for Saudi Arabia.*)

It is just over a week now since I wrote to you last – and of course, another war. Oh what a lovely war that it should break out when the jasmine is out. (*Ed: This was a series of air attacks by Egypt and Libya over their common border.*) At least the fragrance does something to break down the human zoo smell of central Cairo. I decided to go to Cairo on Saturday morning last week and amazingly not only did my universal air travel plan card work, but I got a seat on Alia, the Royal Jordanian Airline. A Jordanian friend says that ALIA stands for "always late in arrival". It was a jumbo jet and full, mainly with Italian tourists. It is only three hundred miles as the crow flies from Amman to Cairo, but airliners don't fly as the crow flies because of the hawks sitting on the other side of the Jordan River. The flight took two hours. It was really a very good flight and I am sure Arab airlines service their planes as well as anyone else, so I thought it was a bit rude of the Italians to clap so vigorously when the aircraft landed safely.

I did not have a hotel booking in Cairo so I asked the tourist official if the Semiramis had any vacancies. No, he said they are full up because it is under renovation. So I caught a cab to Sheppard's Hotel, right next door to the Semiramis. But the Semiramis is more than under renovation; it has been pulled down and there is a big hole in its place. So there went my chance of a rooftop dinner watching belly dancers. Sheppard's did have rooms but did not take Diners Club cards. So I tried the Hilton and the Sheraton but they were full. I had to go to the old Cosmopolitan in what they like to call 'downtown Cairo'. It doesn't take Diners Club either, but is so cheap it didn't matter. It was fashionable in the days of the British, and the bar is timber-panelled like an English bar. But the rooms, although they all have baths, need a good clean. Actually it is the most convenient place for me to stay in Cairo as it is only five minutes' walk from Reuters and the Middle East News Agency.

And the people are very nice… "Velcome Velcome very nice to see you. First time in Cairo?...... so you lived here? Well that is very good. Velcome Velcome….. English? Deutsch? Oh Australian dinky di that is very good. You would like to see my brother's shop. He likes Australians very much."

After two days of this I could tell my English was going to pot, and I couldn't express myself properly. I checked out of my room – they let me stay in the room until 4 pm because I think I was the first person to say he would be back at the Cosmopolitan Hotel within a month – but I didn't have to catch the plane back to Amman until 10 pm. After checking out, I said:

"Is the hotel full or do you have rooms tonight?"

"Now you want to stay, Mr David," said the puzzled man who had helped me check out.

"No, I was just thinking if there was no room on the plane for me, I might have to come back."

"No, Sir. You don't mean no room on the plane for you. You mean no seat on the plane for you."

*****

Naturally I had financial affairs to straighten out after I got back from Cairo. So I went to the British Bank of the Middle East, which is manned mainly by Jordanians of course. I went to the counter and said I had had money from Australia paid in the last couple of days and wondered exactly how much was deposited.

"I'm sorry," said the bank official, shaking his head slowly. "I don't remember exactly."

It's not quite the C.B.A. (*Commercial Bank of Australia*), but after some considerable questioning of the officials I was relieved to find they do not commit everything to memory. I was able to find out how much was deposited.

Middle East Encounters 29

Ill. 1. In the office, Amman, August 1977

Hussein: the remarkable Middle East survivor
From DAVID BALDERSTONE, our Middle East correspondent

'The Age', Amman, August 15, 1977

The name is on the Sergeant's clipboard. So he waves, and the three guards with automatic rifles and Arab headdresses allow the car to pass.

The car climbs up the wide tarmac drive out of the bustle of Amman. Suddenly the dusty, crowded city has been replaced by the serenity of a pine-covered hill. This hill is centre-stage of one of the most remarkable – but also tragic – family stories.

It is the main royal palace complex of the Royal Hashemite Kingdom of Jordan. It is where King Hussein has his office within the Basman Palace.

"Whoever would have thought 25 years ago – given the turbulent nature of the Middle East – that the 17-year-old king would have survived to see his silver jubilee?"

It was the comment of a diplomat. Undoubtedly it sums up what a lot of people are thinking.

Against what must be a stack of odds King Hussein, now aged 41, has celebrated his silver jubilee. His reign has covered three Arab-Israeli wars, a civil war in Jordan, three Egyptian Presidents, six Israeli Prime Ministers and more Syrian leaders than most people can remember.

He has survived several assassination attempts.

"I still think of myself as a relatively young man but when I realise that I have been directly involved in the Middle East conflict longer than any other leader in the area or the world time loses much of its meaning," commented the King at a Washington lunch earlier this year.

"I can assure you it is not a fact to be envied but it does provide a continuity and a perspective which at times has been useful. Measured individually it has spanned six American Presidents, seven Secretaries of State, and, I am told, eight directors of the CIA."

The Hashemite Kingdom gets its name from Hashem who was prominent in the decadent pre-Mohammedan days of Mecca, then the capital of the Hejaz. Hashem's great-grandson married Fatima Al-Zahra, a daughter of the prophet Mohammed. Therefore, today, King Hussein and his family claim direct descent from the prophet Mohammed who was born in 571 AD.

But it is necessary to skip generations to reach the period from which emerged King Hussein's great-grandfather, Hussein of Hejaz, who was Sherif of Mecca from 1908-1918 and King of Hejaz from 1918-24.

Hussein of Hejaz led the Arab revolt on the side of the British which ended the Ottoman Turks' domination of Arabia, during the First World War.

Although Hussein himself had wanted to throw off the Ottoman yoke, it was not until the British gave assurances of Arab freedom that Hussein rallied his forces under the command of his sons, Abdullah and Feisal.

But once the First World War was over the idea of Arab freedom disappeared. Instead, in general terms, one imperial power had been replaced by another: Britain and France had designs on the Middle East.

Hussein of Hejaz was to lose out again a few years later under pressure from Arabian warriors led by Ibn Saud, the founder of today's Saudi Arabia.

In 1924 Hussein of Hejaz abdicated as King of Hejaz, and went into exile in Cyprus. Briefly his eldest son Ali became King of Hejaz.

But it was two other sons of Hussein who were to receive the rewards for the help the Arabs gave the British Allies during the war. Abdullah was appointed Emir of Trans-Jordan in 1921 and Feisal became King of Irak in 1923.

In 1948, Abdullah became King of independent Jordan, which was formed in the partition plan which also generated Israel and Arab Palestine.

During the war which broke out immediately Israel became an independent State, King Abdullah's troops annexed Arab Palestine – the West Bank.

In the wake of this annexation, King Abdullah was assassinated by a Palestinian in 1951 as he was leaving a mosque in Jerusalem after Friday prayers. King Abdullah's 16-year-old grandson was with him that day and narrowly escaped injury. The grandson is today's King Hussein.

Following King Abdullah's assassination, Abdullah's son Talal became king. But because of ill-health, King Talal was deposed only a year later.

On August 11, 1952, Hussein Bin Talal – the son of King Talal – was proclaimed King of the Hashemite Kingdom of Jordan. However because he was only aged 17, a regency council was appointed until his formal accession to the throne on May 2, 1953.

Only a month before he was proclaimed king, Egypt's King Farouk had been deposed. After the brief Egyptian presidency of General Neguib the Nasser era came into full swing. Arab nationalism swept the Middle East.

The young king was not immune to this Arab nationalism: this Arab desire to be master of the Arab house. In 1956, King Hussein dismissed Sir John Glubb, the British Chief of Staff of the Jordanian armed forces.

King Hussein's relations with Arab neighbors have seen highs and lows. In the late1950s Syrian fighters tried to shoot down the king's aircraft as it was flying over Syria en route to Europe.

King Hussein has been married three times – the first two marriages ended in divorce and the third ended in tragedy when Queen Alia died in a helicopter crash in February this year.

Although his first wife, Queen Dina (now called Princess Dina) lives in Egypt, she returned to Jordan last month for the wedding of their daughter, Princess Alia.

Recently, when the king moved into his new palace, the Hashemiya Palace, which is in the hills 18 kilometres from Amman with a distant view of the Dead Sea, he left his former residence, the Hummar Palace to his second wife, Princess Muna, and their children.

Princess Muna was Antoinette Gardiner, the daughter of an Englishman who had come to Jordan as a senior army officer – and stayed. Because she was British, Princess Muna was never proclaimed Queen.

The king and Queen Alia had two children, Prince Ali and Princess Haya.

If anything has ever underlined to the king the precariousness of a Middle East monarch's survival, it must be the news he received in July 1958. A coup had taken place in Irak, and his distant cousin King Feisal of Irak (grandson of King Abdullah's brother, Irak's first King Feisal) had been murdered.

King Hussein has two brothers, Prince Mohammed and Prince Hassan, the kingdom's 30-year-old crown prince. Prince Hassan and his wife are the only members of the royal family who live in the palace complex on the pine-covered Amman hill.

However the king uses one of the palaces in the complex, the Basman palace, as his administrative headquarters.

Crown Prince Hassan is no prince out of some modern-day fairy tale. While the king tends to concentrate on foreign relations, the crown prince takes a deep interest in the country's economic problems.

But it isn't all heaviness of affairs of state. Beside Prince Hassan's office is fixed a large poster given to him by his wife, Princess Tharwat. The poster reads: "Remember. Even Superman was Clark Kent most of the time."

The crown prince gives King Hussein's strong leadership as the main factor contributing to the stability of the monarchy.

"Our background is one of 1000 years of responsibility and a very direct involvement in the early beginnings of the Arab renaissance for which members of my family have either been expelled or assassinated. Regardless of trial or tribulation, my family has been able to keep the evolutionary commitment going.

"We have never really wavered from our belief that stability in the area is best served by a middle path policy. We have never associated ourselves with an extreme attitude, either Left, or Right."

Bridge over River Jordan gives Middle East some hope
From DAVID BALDERSTONE

'The Age', Jerusalem, August 27, 1978

There are about 60 in the group - mainly Palestinians. Under the sun shelter the benches are crowded. Hardly a word is spoken. Two Israeli soldiers with automatic rifles slung over their shoulders stand guard.

Atop a building 10 metres away a pile of sandbags partially hides another Israeli soldier. The black barrel of his gun stares down.

Back in the crowd, a blind Arab who has shuffled along all morning with his white stick and a few kind hands guiding him reaches into his pocket. He swings open the top of his silver pocket watch. He rubs his fingers slowly over the Braille face. It is 8.45 am. The sun is already hot.

We are about a kilometre from the Allenby Bridge, having crossed the Jordan River. The barbed wire, the mine fields, the heavily armed soldiers are reminders that this is a border on the brink of war. It is Israel's front-line border with Jordan.

"There is no border between Jordan and Israel," the Jordanian official in Amman had been at pains to point out. "There is only a crossing. You understand there is no border because it is our territory on the other side of the river."

Then it is a border by another name.

This border crossing is a bone of contention among many Arabs. For it provides a link between Israel and the Arab world. It is one reason the Palestine Liberation Organisation sometimes refers to the "Jordanian-Israeli West Bank conspiracy".

Hundreds of Arabs, and a growing number of tourists, pass across the Allenby and two other Jordan River bridges each week. Truck loads of West Bank fruit and vegetables – plus crates of the

Latroun wines from the Trappist monks' vineyards near Jerusalem – move across the bridges each week to the Jordanian market.

There is no trade from Jordan to the West Bank, according to Jordanian officials. The high Israeli customs charges, plus the Israeli security searches which would inevitably take place, are the main reasons.

The little-publicised trade is a symbol of hope in the Middle East that one day perhaps Israel and its Arab neighbors could live in peace with a workable – if not friendly – relationship.

The initiative behind the opening of the bridges between Jordan and the occupied West Bank is generally credited to Israel's Foreign Minister, Moshe Dayan. After the 1967 Israeli occupation of the West Bank during the Six Day War he was concerned that the territory would become something of a pressure-cooker of tension. So he proposed the opening of the bridges as a safety valve.

Although the border across the Jordan River is open, it is a laborious process getting permission to cross – especially for Arabs.

Jordan is the only Arab country that permits its nationals to cross the bridges. The other Governments say it is a gesture of recognition of Israel to cross the 1967 ceasefire line.

The residents of the West Bank hold Jordanian passports. It is not possible for Israelis to cross to Jordan.

For a Jordanian living in Jordan to cross, he or she must get a friend or relative living in the West Bank to apply for permission from the Israeli military authorities. Once this permission has been granted, the Jordanians have to seek permission from Jordan's Interior Ministry in Amman.

It is easier for tourists to cross as they only need Jordanian permission, which can be obtained in about 24 hours in Amman. But tourists can only cross from Jordan to Israel and back to Jordan. Tourists in Israel cannot cross to Jordan and then return to Israel.

The Jordanian argument for this regulation is that the West Bank is Jordanian territory. They will allow tourists to visit "their" West

Bank. "If we allowed tourists in Israel to come to Jordan we would be showing recognition of Israel," a Jordanian official said.

It was 7 am when the taxi picked me up for the 55-kilometre drive from Amman to the Jordanian police station near the Allenby Bridge. The road winds down off the hills around Amman through the parched countryside where the Bedouin scratch out a living.

Slowly through the haze the green ribbon of the River Jordan and the fertile belt around Jericho became visible. It's Moses' Promised Land.

After formalities at the police station, an Arab bus is boarded for a breakneck speed drive a few kilometres to the bridge. Again the Jordanians check documentation, and then the bus crosses the 30-metre bridge. Under the Star of David Israeli soldiers check documentation. Then the bus drives on a kilometre to the main Israeli checkpoint. It is 8.45 am by the blind man's watch.

Then there is the drive through Jericho, up the Road of the Good Samaritan, to Jerusalem. Before 1967 the trip from Amman to Jerusalem took about one and a half hours. Today it takes about three hours.

But it is something of a journey of hope. There is something hopeful about seeing the green, white, red and black Jordan flag and the blue Star of David fluttering 30 metres apart across the trickle they call the Jordan River, across this border by another name.

Time no healer for Jerusalem
From DAVID BALDERSTONE our Middle East correspondent

'The Age', September 9, 1977

Ten years after the victorious Israeli soldiers tore down the wall which cut Jerusalem in two, the city remains divided. Time has been no great healer.

On the West Bank, the Arabs are as resentful towards the Israelis today as they were immediately after the Six Day War.

The children of the war, who were just five, six and seven when the Israelis took over, are turning to the underground Communist Party. They are disillusioned with the ability of the traditional forces in Middle East politics to liberate "their" land

The resentment against the Israelis is so great in some areas, particularly in the town of Nablus, that Israelis rarely visit, except on army duty.

"I certainly wouldn't go to Nablus and I don't think any of my friends would go. We would be running too much of a risk of being attacked," a young Israeli commented.

"I remember a friend of mine did go and his car was pelted with stones. It is just not safe for Israelis. When we go during army service we never go alone and the army makes us carry arms."

Because of this tension many Israelis say they would like to give the land back to the Arabs: "if the security of Israel wasn't involved; if we didn't have a need for the secure military borders, I think most Israelis would like to give up the land," one Israeli said.

"Of course there are the extreme Jews who have settled on the West Bank who would object. But they say it is so important to stay in these parts of Judea and Samaria that they would stay even if the land was returned to the Arabs. But that might be a bit unrealistic, I think."

Every Arab has been affected by the occupation. Allegations of torture of Arabs in Israeli prisons have been well documented. Stories of Arabs being woken early and taken by Israeli soldiers and dumped into Jordan across the Allenby Bridge are common.

What is often forgotten is the day to day humiliation of living under the rule of an occupying "foreign" force. The day to day regulations and procedures contribute a lot to Arab resentment.

"I work in this hotel, and I have to go home late some nights," one Arab told me. "Every few nights the Israelis stop me on my way home and ask me where I am going and a lot of other questions.

"The other night I was stopped and they made me hold my hands above my head for one hour for no reason. I told them to contact the hotel and check that I was just going home from work, but they wouldn't. It is just not fair."

Such incidents cause soul-searching among Israelis.

"From time to time I read in the newspaper here that Israeli soldiers have bashed up Arabs," said an Israeli who emigrated from the United States. "Of course it is terrible and the newspapers are full of condemnation. But what surprises me is not that it happens, but that everyone is so surprised it happens. Like every other country, Israel has its share of cranks. Israelis don't like to admit that."

Under the occupation Jordanian municipal infrastructure and laws govern the day to day life of the Arabs on the West Bank, although "security" offences are dealt with by the Israeli military authorities, who are also in charge of jails.

Interestingly, under Jordanian law the death penalty is still carried out, whereas under Israeli law it is not. There have been cases where Arab judges have sentenced murderers to death. The Israeli military authorities have commuted the sentences to jail terms.

The recent fuss over Israeli proposals for extending Israeli public services to West Bankers arose because it involves extending the law of Israel – at least laws governing welfare services – to the

West Bank Arabs. It has been described as annexation in a humanitarian disguise.

Although the Government of Israel still considers the West Bank and the Gaza strip as "occupied territories" which come under military administration, Israel annexed east Jerusalem and its environs shortly after the Six Day War.

On the hills around east Jerusalem, which was administered by Jordan until the war, the Israelis have built a number of apartment blocks for Israelis. In many cases the land was compulsorily acquired from Arab land owners who continue to challenge the level of compensation paid.

In this way the divided city is being united. For a tourist, the city is united; Arabs, Israelis and foreigners can freely travel throughout Jerusalem.

But under this united facade the story is different. The Arab shopping areas remain unmistakeably Arab.

The Arab taxi driver who collected me at the Allenby Bridge took me to the Arab-run hotel in east Jerusalem, the Ambassador.

The switchboard operators in Arab-run hotels will invariably call Arab taxi drivers, Arab tour operators, and, when I wanted to rent a car, called the Arab Hertz agent in east Jerusalem rather than the Hertz head office in King David Street.

This is not prompted purely by anti-Israeli feeling. They continue their pre-1967 business habits.

Of course there is business between Arabs and Israelis. Neither Arabs nor Israelis are averse to making money.

So the barriers come down, albeit reluctantly – sometimes. Travelling through the West Bank – more specifically Samaria – I stopped for lunch at the grand Lod Hotel which reeked of British influence from the time of the Palestine mandate. Under the pine trees the Amstel beer was so pleasant I asked the hotelkeeper whether Israelis stayed very often.

"Never," he replied. "When they telephone to book a room I tell them the hotel is full."

The same question put to a hotel manager in east Jerusalem drew a paranoid reply:

"We discourage Israelis because they are not good. They only come here for prostitution purposes. They bring their girls here and it is not good for the image of the hotel."

Political meetings are banned in occupied territories. But the underground Communist Party is attractive to the young people – partly because members of the Communist Party of Israel have been critical of Israel's occupation policy and have exposed allegations of torture in Israel's jails.

But the Palestine Liberation Organisation remains the most powerful force among the Arabs. In the West Bank municipal elections last year, pro-PLO mayoral candidates stood for election in 20 of the 25 municipalities – and all won.

Ironically, these elections are the only elections even resembling Western-style free elections which have been held in this part of the Arab world in recent years.

Therefore, when West Bankers and Palestinians call for their own Palestinian homeland with the right of self-determination are they not asking for something their Arab brothers in Egypt, Syria and Jordan don't have?

"We Palestinians are a very democratic people. We want to have elections," Aziz Shihadeh, a lawyer from Ramallah, answers.

Shihadeh was the first to suggest the idea of a West Bank State for Palestinians. "When I first suggested the idea I was described as a traitor. Now it is an acceptable idea."

Some Arabs will admit that public services such as roads, water, electricity and even telephones have been improved greatly since the Israeli occupation. Others will not even give the Israelis credit for these improvements, saying they were only done for defence reasons.

Karim Khalif, the mayor of Ramallah and the strongest pro-PLO force on the West Bank, says the Arabs want a Palestinian State within the pre-1967 borders with east Jerusalem as the capital.

"It would be a free city where Jews, Moslems and Christians can move freely."

But after 10 years of occupation, no one thinks it will come easily. Some will fight for it – and terrible terror attacks will continue.

Others will be like an Arab friend: "Don't ask me about these things. I just want to go to work, and come home each night; I just want to live here and earn enough money to send my children to school."

Blow for peace hopes
From DAVID BALDERSTONE in Beirut

'The Age', September 23, 1977

The stage is some lush fields and villages in southern Lebanon. The audience is a group of Middle East Foreign Ministers assembling in Washington and New York.

The fierce fighting in southern Lebanon this week has cost many lives, caused considerable damage, and seems to have shattered the chance of early Lebanese peace. But the implications of the fighting extend far beyond Lebanon.

Whatever chance there was of the Carter Administration dragging some kind of formula out of the Foreign Ministers from Israel and the so-called Arab confrontation States, to enable a resumption of the Geneva peace conference must have gone out the window because of the current fighting.

Eye-witness reports from northern Israel and southern Lebanon indicate Israel has dramatically stepped up its military support for Lebanese Christians in southern Lebanon.

There have been reports over the past few days of Israeli army half-tracks and armored patrols seen returning to Israel from Lebanon, increased overflying of Lebanon by Israeli fighters, and a continuation of the Israeli artillery bombardment of Leftist and Palestinian strongholds – something which the Israeli Prime Minister himself admits takes place.

In return, shells have landed around Israel's northernmost village Metulla, which is at the tip of a tongue of Israel sticking north into Lebanon. On the one hand the so-called Christian Rightists are getting support from Israel and on the other the Leftist forces and Palestinians have called for support from Arab heads of state. Palestinian Liberation Organisation leader Yasser Arafat sent messages to Arab leaders requesting them to "assume their historic responsibilities".

The implications of this current southern Lebanese fighting – the fiercest since peace came into force in the rest of the country 10 months ago – are twofold.

First, it makes it very difficult to see any compromise being worked out on the key question blocking resumption of a Middle East peace conference in Geneva – Palestinian representation.

Secondly, it dramatically increases the risk of a direct confrontation between Israeli and Syrian forces which are in Lebanon as the main part of the Arab peace-keeping force.

The thorny question of Palestinian representation at Geneva is high on the agenda of talks President Carter and Secretary of State Cyrus Vance are having with Israel's Foreign Minister Moshe Dayan, and Arab Foreign Ministers this week and next week. The Arab Governments insist – some more enthusiastically than others – that there must be PLO representation at Geneva. Israel rejects any participation of the PLO and indeed any separate Palestinian delegation at Geneva.

The US State Department gave the Palestinians some cause for optimism last week when they said there should be Palestinian representation at Geneva, although the Department said the Palestinians would have to accept Israel's right to exist.

It was enough encouragement to prompt certain key moderate members of the PLO's 55-member Central Council to work on a formula which would soften the PLO's stand towards Israel. The PLO has the chartered aim of eliminating Israel.

In particular, Egypt and Saudi Arabia have urged the PLO to at least tacitly approve Israel's right to exist. This, they have argued, would lead to PLO-United States talks, which could lead to pressure being put on Israel to accept PLO representation at Geneva.

A special PLO Central Council meeting was scheduled for last weekend. There was considerable speculation the moderates might make their move, but Yasser Arafat had to cancel the meeting due to the seriousness of the fighting in southern Lebanon.

The current fighting and the extent of Israeli involvement against the Palestinian forces virtually rules out any softening of the PLO line against Israel for some time. The risk of a direct clash between Syrian and Israeli forces has developed because the fiercest fighting has taken place around the Litani River.

Israel has set the river as the southernmost line at which it will tolerate the presence of Syrian peace-keeping forces. The river is only about 20 kilometres from the Israeli border at the closest point, near Metulla.

Two weeks ago when I was in Metulla, Israeli army officers pointed to a hill on the other side of the river. They believed the Syrians were dug in there.

In an explosive situation like the present one in southern Lebanon, 20 kilometres isn't far.

Amman October 4, 1977 *(To Mother and Aunt Ethel)*

I must start off by telling you about poor Mr Junerious, a keen young American in Amman on a rushed trip. His first big break. All was going fine. He had an appointment with the chairman of Jordan's most ambitious project, the Arab Potash Company, and he was all set to pull off a big deal – all unbeknownst to me.

All would have worked out for poor Mr Junerious had I not unwittingly got his appointment. I wanted to see someone at Arab Potash and had gone to the press centre in the Intercontinental Hotel to try to get them to get me an appointment. True to form, the press centre couldn't even raise the company on the phone for some time, and it took them some more time to find out where the company was. Eventually they told me and I set off with the name of the chairman.

I found the company's office and asked for the chairman's secretary. The chairman's secretary, a man, greeted me like a long lost friend. He took my card, which he called "your ticket", looked at it quickly and said: "Welcome, Welcome Mr Junerious….your appointment is not until 11am." He had added that "they" had rung him from the Intercontinental Hotel to tell them I was coming.

How pleased I felt that the press centre should have been so kind as to arrange an appointment! They must have telephoned between me leaving them and arriving at the company. It didn't occur to me that there was a man named "Mr Junerious". I thought it was just a variation on the much-used expression "Mr David". This time it was "Mr Journalist".

It was an hour until 11 am so I went home. When I arrived back, another man was sitting waiting. The secretary was trying to explain something to me about "my ticket". First I was shunted off to someone else's office, but he was so impressed that the Crown Prince had told me Arab Potash was interested in Australian co-operation, that he arranged for me to see the chairman immediately. Mr Junerious was last seen disappearing down the passage. A rather surly man I thought…….

*****

Susan and I were to have gone away last Friday, but at the last minute the Palace – one says "Palace" when one wants to convey the impression that one is close to King Hussein and Crown Prince Hassan – suggested I go with the Crown Prince and his party to Aqaba last Saturday for the opening of a road of all things. Roads are much the same anywhere, but one must be seen at these things. So I went. I had to be at the airport at 7 am for the flight down, which turned out to be the regular 8 am service to Aqaba. Once at Aqaba we drove by bus sixty kilometres up the road (and along the Israeli border) to the road-opening ceremony. The Taiwanese had built the road and had put a Chinese pagoda at this point. Very attractive really, but as one Jordanian commented, the pagoda will confuse archaeologists in around 2000 years.

We all travelled in an air-conditioned bus and as we approached the opening site – about half a mile away in fact – there were about fifty Bedouins on camels on either side of the road. The bus slowed down as it passed the camels and the Bedouins clapped the prince. As soon as the bus passed, the camels started running after us so they could get a good position at the opening ceremony. They all lined up and sat there quietly. Their Bedouin riders smoked non-stop during the opening. Later the Crown Prince approached them and they all moved forward with their camels, he gave them a quiet greeting and a wave, and they all charged off into the desert. The prince then greeted local leaders for around an hour and the Bedouins – quite obviously sick of racing each other around the desert came back to join the celebration again. They yelled as they charged their camels around the crowd. It was quite hilarious.

As we drove back to Aqaba airport, the prince shouted to me a few rows back: "Do you think Australia will help us make this country green?" I then moved up and had quite a long talk with him. He is going to Australia this weekend, and is interested in Australian help in dry land farming. ALIA had special aircraft down for us and depending on the strictures of one's faith we drank orange juice, Pepsi cola or Champagne on the 45 minute flight back to Amman.

Past keeps its grip on Lebanon
From DAVID BALDERSTONE our Middle East correspondent in Amman

'The Age' October 27, 1977

The poster catches today's Lebanon exactly. Drawn at the height of the fighting, in which 25,000 15 to 20-year-olds died, it is more poignant now than it was then.

Under a picture of a blood-stained youth the poster cries out: "We Die for You to Stay".

Lebanon's problems stayed. The big men of the Christian establishment – notably Camille Chamoun and Pierre Gemayel – are still there guarding their lot along with the Leftists wanting more of a say; the religious bigots stirring the pot, and around 400,000 Palestinians keeping the situation on the boil.

The year-old Government of President Sarkis and Prime Minister Selim Al-Hoss has just unveiled its recovery-oriented budget for 1978, and is bravely working on a six-year recovery plan.

But the political and social problems behind the civil war have not been solved. The year-old peace in most of the country has been achieved by the brute force of 25,000 Syrian peace-keeping soldiers.

There are two factors blocking Lebanon's recovery. Firstly, political insecurity has placed a brake on the flow of investment and directed financial grants.

Secondly, since the civil war broke out the Middle East has got used to doing without the business hub of Beirut. Amman, Bahrain, and Athens have attracted businesses previously based in Beirut. It is ironical that the future of Lebanon – never a major participant in the Arab-Israeli dispute – is now inextricably tied to the outcome of current United States sponsored Middle East peace moves.

Although the presence of so many Palestinians on Lebanese soil was an irritant only to the basic social causes of the civil war –

Christian and Moslem power and wealth sharing – it is hard to see a permanent peace being achieved while the Palestinian problem remains so heavily on Lebanon's shoulders.

While the large Palestinian presence exists, it is highly doubtful the leaders of the Christian establishment will agree to compromises which would set the system of power-sharing right.

All along the Christian establishment leaders have claimed the Palestinian presence was the cause of the civil war and, rightly or wrongly, this thesis is not going to change now.

"This is our country....we made it," says a senior official of Chamoun's National Liberation Party. "Lebanon cannot recover while there are so many Palestinians here."

In the Middle East any prediction is risky, but there are two main thrusts of opinion regarding the future of the Palestinians in Lebanon – one involves Middle East war and the other a Middle East settlement.

In the unlikely event of a Middle East peace settlement being achieved which would involve the creation of a Palestinian State, then Palestinian pressure would be taken off Lebanon.

But if the peace moves break down and the situation degenerates towards war, Lebanon will be in a more vulnerable position than she has been in previous Middle East wars.

Lebanon has always been careful not to give Israel any excuse for attack and today the Lebanese border facing Israel is the only Arab border with Israel which has remained unchanged since before the State of Israel was created.

The situation might not be the same again. There are 25,000 Syrian troops in Lebanon making up most of the Arab peace-keeping force. Their presence would dramatically increase the chance of a full-scale Israeli assault on Lebanon if another war should break out.

There has been considerable speculation about the degree of Israeli help for the Lebanese Christian forces during the civil war –

and Israel openly admits it gives help, both military and social, to the Christians in the south.

So it would be conceivable that there would be co-operation between Lebanese and Israeli forces against the Palestinians during another Mid-East war. After all it would be in the interests of both parties.

If Lebanon's problems are not solved the much-talked about option of partition cannot be discounted. The idea of a Christian Lebanese State has a precedent in Ottoman times, and the creation of a Christian State would mean the position of a Jewish State in the Middle East would cease to be an anomaly.

Anywhere but in Lebanon such scenarios would seem fanciful, but Lebanon is a country of private militias, where the law remains the gun, where the Government is virtually forced to act as referee rather than leader.

President Sarkis, a former banker and one-time political whiz kid, has an impossible job. He has legal but little physical power.

For example, the new Lebanese army has recruited about 3000 men – but as few as 300 are considered battle hardened – professional enough to do their job.

Because of this the planned move of the Lebanese army into southern Lebanon to keep peace between the Leftists, Palestinians and the predominantly Christian Right-wing forces has been delayed time and time again.

The Lebanese army cannot move in to keep the peace until peace has been achieved.

Compare this situation with the power of the militias. Former President Chamoun's National Liberal Party displayed its militia a couple of weeks ago and recruited 1000 Lebanese youths.

"Within 24 hours we can raise a militia of 4000-5000", a party official said.

The Chamoun militia together with the bigger and better armed Falangist militia of Pierre Gemayel and the Cedar Guards make up the Right-wing predominantly Christian forces.

Militarily, the militias of the Lebanese Right wing are stronger than those of the Left, but this is more than made up by the fact that the Leftists are supported by Palestinian commando groups.

If it were not for the sheer resilience of the Lebanese there would not even be the facade of recovery in Lebanon.

From Tripoli to Tyre street stalls have been set up. In many places a damaged building is no excuse for stopping business. In Beirut a flourishing stall market has grown up in the shadow of the ruined skeletons of once luxurious hotels and business empires.

But it will take more than resilience to rebuild Lebanon. It has been estimated that the civil war cost the industrial sector $A1500 million in capital losses alone. The tourism sector lost 13 first class hotels.

Lebanon's problems are not purely financial though. An estimated 350,000 people – mainly skilled – have stayed outside the country despite the ceasefire at the end of last year. This plus the fact that 6 per cent of the workforce was killed during the fighting, has left the country in a critical manpower situation.

It is no secret that the Lebanese Government is disappointed at the small amount of financial aid which has come from the country's oil-rich neighbors. In early October, the Lebanese Government had received only $A15 million from Saudi Arabia, $8 million from Kuwait, $4 million from the United States, and $5 million from the United Arab Emirates.

This month negotiations for loans from the European Economic Community and the Arab Fund for Economic and Social Development are continuing.

Power in Lebanon is divided between Christians and Moslems on the basis of a census taken 45 years ago which revealed the communities were evenly balanced.

Today it is estimated that the Moslem community is bigger than the Christian community with the Shi'ite Moslem community said to be considerably larger than the Sunni community.

And yet the old ranking stays. The President is a Christian, the Prime Minister is a Sunni Moslem and the Speaker of Parliament is a Shi'ite. This system of power sharing permeates the whole society.

Strictly, the problem isn't religious, but rather that the people who are Christian are generally better off than those who are Moslem. Also, the Moslems generally embrace Pan-Arab and Palestinian ideas more enthusiastically than the Christians.

But Chamoun and Gemayel can count Moslems among their supporters. And so, of course the Leftists, who may be better called Liberals, can count Christians among their supporters.

Lebanon is in a mess. During lunch at a coastal restaurant north of Byblos, the waiter threw our empty beer cans out of the window. Perhaps he does not believe Lebanon has a future. Certainly, a lot of people are waiting before making up their minds.

Amman November 1977 *(To eldest brother John)*

Susan and I have just returned to Amman today after about nine days touring Syria and Lebanon. It was great fun, but it is tiring driving and crossing borders. Arab bureaucracy is really incredible. I feel a bit like a Western diplomat who left Libya after two years and was asked what he had learnt during his time in Libya. "I have learnt to wait", he replied.

We spent the last two nights in Damascus. When we arrived we went to the hotel where we had stayed previously called the New Omayyad, which is really good. But it was fully booked – like all the decent hotels in Damascus – but they offered us the Presidential suite at a knockdown price of $40 a night instead of $100 a night. This was still quite a bit more than the usual double room rate of $18 a night but there was little we could do about it. "President Sadat of Egypt", the man at reception said "had the same suite a few years ago".

It is all very well them slashing the price of the suite, but no one tells the legion of Arab waiters, maids, door-openers and door-closers etc that one is not really rich and that one is only sleeping in President Sadat's bed because there is nowhere else to stay. So by the time we arrive by lift at the floor a whole platoon was there to help us into the suite. Doors are opened, shutters swung back, extra towels brought in, lights switched on and off, telephone tested…. It goes on and on and there is only one way to stop it.

Tipping, some people erroneously think, is paying someone for a service he or she has performed. Tipping is in fact something one does because he or she is worried about what they will think if one doesn't. It cost me dearly to move two small cases and a typewriter from reception to the suite. But pride was intact. I saw one nodding to another with a knowing wink to his friend: "Ships," I thought I heard him say – although waterless Damascus is perhaps an unlikely place to find a shipping magnate.

The next move is up to Begin
From DAVID BALDERSTONE our Middle East correspondent

'The Age', Jerusalem, November 21, 1977

Egyptian President Anwar Sadat has done what the Arab armies could not do. He has put enormous pressure on Israel to make concessions in the cause of Middle East peace.

For the first time in the 29-year history of Israel, an Arab Head of State has begun a visit to the Jewish State. What was impossible just a few days ago has happened.

President Sadat has described his visit as "sacred" to experience the emotion of hope of the Israelis – and, of course, many Arabs – it is tempting to believe the visit marks the end of hostilities in the Middle East.

But the angry reactions from many parts of the Arab world are testimony to the fact the visit is fraught with problems.

Anwar Sadat – a man dubbed as "stop gap" when he took over from President Nasser in 1970 – is too experienced a politician not to have known what the reactions from certain sections of the Arab world would be.

One visit to Israel by an Arab leader cannot eradicate a whole generation of carefully nurtured anti-Israeli feeling, the suffering caused by four Arab-Israeli wars, and the plight of the Palestinian people.

Sadat, who was the officer chosen to announce on Egyptian radio the 1953 Egyptian revolution which ousted King Farouk, has a penchant for surprise.

In 1973 he dealt a heavy blow to Israel by sending the Egyptian army across the Suez Canal on the most holy day in the Jewish calendar (*Yom Kippur*).

Now, undoubtedly, his acceptance of the Israeli Prime Minister's formal invitation had something of an element of surprise about it also. Unlike the Sadat offensive of 1973 this diplomatic gesture cannot be repelled with the might of the Israeli armed forces.

His visit has put enormous pressure on Israel to make some concessions towards peace.

Plagued by chronic economic problems and a genuine weariness of war at home, Sadat has staked his survival on peace.

The vehemence of criticism from some quarters of the Arab world; the muted criticism of the visit from Saudi Arabia, a major sponsor of Egypt, and the resignation of senior Egyptian Ministers, is a clear indication Sadat hasn't got a lot of time on his hands.

If nothing is achieved from this historic visit, it is hard not to see the Egyptian President being forced back into staking his survival on a more militaristic stance towards the Arab-Israeli dispute.

President Sadat's stated willingness just a week ago to visit Israel – and Menachem Begin's formal invitation – follow almost a year of effort by the Carter Administration to bring about a resumption of the Geneva Middle East peace conference.

The Carter Administration initiatives have stalled on the thorny issue of Palestinian representation at the conference.

Since the brief formal session of the conference in December 1973, Arab leaders – meeting in the 1974 Rabat Arab summit – have decided that the Palestine Liberation Organisation is the sole representative of the Palestinian people. With varying degrees of enthusiasm, Arab leaders have abided by that decision.

However the Government of Israel has repeatedly said it will not deal with the PLO, an organisation with the chartered aim of eliminating Israel.

It is understood that Rumanian President Nicolai Ceausescu has played a big part behind the scenes in arranging the Sadat visit to Jerusalem. Rumania is the only Eastern bloc country with diplomatic relations with Israel.

Menachem Begin and Anwar Sadat have recently made State visits to Rumania. It is understood Ceausescu conveyed Begin's desire for a direct meeting to the Egyptian President.

Over the past few months there has been growing concern in Syria – and to a lesser extent Jordan – that Egypt was heading towards a separate peace agreement with Israel.

Sadat's decision to go ahead with the visit has heightened this concern. But such an agreement is virtually out of the question simply because it is neither in Egypt's nor Israel's interests.

The economic benefits of peace with Israel on such a basis would be completely outweighed by the economic consequences of Arab isolation which would automatically follow. Egypt cannot do without the sponsorship of the oil-rich Arab states.

For Israel, the signing of a peace agreement with Egypt would dramatically increase the anger of the other Arab states.

Sadat is a master of public relations. His visit is the clearest indication the world has ever had that an Arab leader wants peace.

Amongst Sadat's guests on the historic flight from Ismailia to Lod airport were American media personalities Walter Cronkite and Barbara Walters. It is clear Sadat is speaking to Israel's sponsor during the current visit in the hope of pressure being applied by Washington.

But more than this, the goodwill shown towards Sadat by the Israeli people is a clear indication the Begin Government will be under increasing domestic pressure to make concessions.

The very fact that the Egyptian Government has decided to give the visit maximum coverage in the government-controlled Egyptian media indicates the Egyptian President is pretty certain the people at home will appreciate his peace initiatives.

What can be achieved by the visit?

The mere arrival in Israel of the Egyptian President has had one tangible and significant result. For the first time since the establishment of the State of Israel, a direct dialogue has been established publicly between Israel and an Arab government.

Although nothing has been officially announced, it is widely expected Sadat will invite Mr Begin to visit Cairo before he leaves for home.

On the key issues blocking peace, it is difficult to predict in which areas there could be a narrowing of views.

When the Israeli and Egyptian delegations began their talks in Jerusalem shortly after Sadat's arrival the two sides were a long way apart on the key issues – Palestinian representation at Geneva; Israeli occupation of territory won in 1967, and the Arab demand for the establishment of a Palestinian State in the West Bank and Gaza Strip.

Israel believes withdrawal from the occupied territory and particularly the establishment of a Palestinian State would jeopardise security.

Menachem Begin deserves a great deal of credit for picking up the chance for this visit when offered by Sadat in a speech to the Egyptian Parliament. The very fact both leaders have agreed to the scheduling of a joint press conference on the last day of the visit is a good indication both the Egyptians and the Israelis have reason to believe some real moves towards peace will be achieved.

However it is a high risk operation.

Just a week ago, I asked a Jordanian journalist when Anwar Sadat was going to Jerusalem.

"We have a saying in Arabic," he replied. "When the donkey climbs up the minaret."

The impossible of a few days ago has happened. The donkey has climbed the minaret.

A hero's welcome home for Sadat
From DAVID BALDERSTONE

'The Age', Cairo, November 22, 1977

President Anwar Sadat received a hero's welcome when he arrived back in Cairo late yesterday after his historic visit to Israel.

The 30-kilometre route from the airport to the city was lined with many thousands of placard-carrying and chanting Egyptians.

Applause broke out as the presidential jet landed after a 50-minute flight. After brief official welcomes on the tarmac and inspection of the military guard, Sadat drove in an open car past the crowds who had been waiting at the airport for several hours.

For two days Egyptians have been watching Sadat's visit live on television.

During the visit the government-controlled Egyptian Press had staunchly defended President Sadat against critics of the trip in other Arab countries.

Sadat, who is the first Arab leader to visit Israel in its 29-year history, will report on his mission in a televised address to the Egyptian National Assembly on Saturday.

His use of an open car returning to Cairo seemed something of a gesture of defiance to Arab critics who have called for the toppling of the Sadat regime.

There is speculation in Cairo that the President will announce a new Government within two weeks. A reshuffle is virtually necessary because of the resignation of two Ministers on the eve of his departure for Israel.

A Government spokesman said today that the trip had prepared the ground for resuming Middle East peace talks in Geneva.

The spokesman, who accompanied Sadat to Israel, said the visit was "100 per cent successful. The purpose was to make real preparations for the Geneva conference and this has been completed".

He gave no hint when the conference – which met briefly in December 1973, after the last Middle East war two months earlier – might be reconvened.

Sadat will receive another morale boost with a visit from Sudan's President Jafar Nimeiry today.

The Sudanese Government has already issued a strong statement in support of the Egyptian leader.

Meanwhile, Sadat has been showered with gifts from Israel. They include a huge portrait of a dove and ancient poetry from the time of the Jewish and Arab forefather Abraham.

Three clay jugs came from President Ephraim Katzir as part of an Israeli effort to stress the common heritage of the two peoples.

Prime Minister Menachem Begin gave Sadat nine candlesticks from the time of the Jewish uprising against Greek rule of Palestine in the second century BC.

Wanted – another Act of Grace for hero's widow
From DAVID BALDERSTONE, in Khartoum

'The Age', December 3, 1977

The death of an almost forgotten Australian hero, Frederick Hamilton March, in Khartoum early this month has left his wife facing destitution.

March, a veteran of two world wars and a George Cross winner, was granted an "Act of Grace" pension by the Australian Government in 1975.

This pension, which amounted to $1500 a year at the time of his death, enabled March and his wife, Teresa, an Italian-Eritrean by birth but virtually stateless, to just make ends meet in their humble mud-floored home in Khartoum.

They were still hard up. To save the electricity bill they pulled the plug out of the refrigerator each night before going to bed.

But this "Act of Grace" pension stopped when March, aged about 95, died early this month. Now his wife Teresa faces destitution. It is understood Australia's Ambassador in Cairo, Mr C R Ashwin, has made the Australian Government aware of Teresa March's plight.

But so far no action has been taken by the Government on the case.

It is believed the Australian Embassy in Cairo, which looks after Australian interests in the Sudan, has recommended to the Australian Government, an investigation into the possibility of Mrs March being granted her own "Act of Grace" pension.

Before his death, March had explored the possibility of getting Australian citizenship for his wife, who speaks only Arabic and Italian.

He did not ever consider they would return to Australia, but rather was concerned about his wife's financial plight after his death. He thought she may have been entitled to a pension in her own right if an Australian citizen.

During his dramatic career, March served in two world wars, was a member of the Cairo Police Force, and served in Sudan's Agriculture Ministry.

During the Anzac campaign at Gallipoli, March swam the Dardanelles at night with General Freyberg VC, cutting minefield anchor wires to enable troops to land.

Also, he was chauffeur to Sir Lee Stack, Governor-General of Sudan and Commander in Chief of Egyptian Armed Forces, when Stack was assassinated in 1924.

Since March's death, Teresa March has been living on around $600 raised by the Air Force Association in Victoria. But that won't last forever. Who says old soldiers never die?

(*Ed: On Christmas Eve 'The Age' reported that Mrs March had subsequently been awarded a $1200 annual ex gratia pension by the Australian Governmen*t.)

3000 years before Moses
DAVID BALDERSTONE reports from Amman

'The Age', December 17, 1977

Almost 3000 years before Moses saw the Promised Land from Mt Nebo, around 4500 years before Jesus, and about 5000 years before the birth of the Prophet Mohammed, the people of Teleilat Ghassul lived well off the land in the Jordan Valley.

An Australian archaeological team – led by world renowned Australian archaeologist Professor Basil Hennessey, of Sydney University, has just completed a season digging in the area which has provided a fascinating insight into these little known ancient Ghassulian people.

They discovered and recovered a wall painting dating back more than 6000 years – the second oldest wall painting ever recovered.

The wall painting at Teleilat Ghassul was discovered on the collapsed walls of a building which has been dated, by radio carbon tests, to about 4300 BC.

The only older wall paintings known anywhere are the paintings discovered at Catul Huyuk, in Turkey.

Not far from the foot of Mt Nebo and just northeast of the Dead Sea in what today is Jordan, the people of Teleilat Ghassul lived in mud brick houses and farmed the land which was much more lush than it is today.

They lived well.

The painting, which was found about eight feet below the surface under one of the series of mounds on the site, depicts three human figures; two of them wearing masks, standing to the right of a larger, hooded figure holding a curved sceptre in his left hand.

"All three figures appear to be grouped to the left of a main central figure which is possibly representative of a shrine or religious area," comments Professor Hennessey. "The decoration is in black, red, white and yellow and the colours are quite brilliant.

"The paintings will be a very important addition to our information on ritual practices in the early Chalcolithic (4500-3500 BC) period."

The intial lifting and cleaning of the painting was completed during the "dig" season which has just ended. An expert from the British Museum, Miss Ann Searight, spent a month working with the Australian team consolidating the painting.

Experts from UNESCO's School of Conservation in Rome are expected in Jordan shortly to do the final restoration and mounting of the painting for exhibition in Amman Museum.

During this year's "dig" a painter's workshop was isolated. Lumps of red, yellow and white ochre were found in association with stones used to pound the ochre into a powder. Nearby there was a polished palette made from the shoulder blade of an animal.

Teleilat Ghassul is a large settlement site of the late Neolithic and Chalcolithic periods (approximately 4500-3500 BC). From the site, the view west is across the Israeli-occupied West Bank territory to Jerusalem. The lights of Jerusalem can be clearly seen at night.

Teleilat Ghassul is near the foot of Mt Nebo. After 40 years leading the Jews in the wilderness, Moses is said to have seen the "promised land" from Mt Nebo, shortly before his death.

The settlement, a series of mounds on the site which is around 300 metres below sea level, was first rediscovered in the early 1920s and was initially excavated by the Pontifical Biblical Institute of Rome between 1930 and 1936.

"These intial excavations demonstrated that the settlement represented a new culture in the history of Palestine, but it was some years before it was realised the settlement was pre-Bronze Age (approximately 3000-1200 BC)," Professor Hennessey says.

In 1960 the Pontifical Society carried out more excavations on the site.

While Director of the British School of Archaeology in Jerusalem, Basil Hennessey began the present series of excavations in January 1967.

But the Six Day War in the middle of the year put a stop to the project. With the Israeli armed forces dug in only a few kilometres from the site on the other side of the Jordan River, the area was considered military territory by the Jordanians. In fact a minefield still borders the site.

It was not until 1975 that the Jordanian Government gave Basil Hennessey, who by then was at Sydney University, permission to recommence excavations on the site.

The season of digging just completed was the third successive – and last – season on the site.

This year's season, which cost about $20,000, was funded mainly by the Australian Research Grants Committee, Sydney University, the British Museum, and the Metropolitan Museum of New York.

"The major problem of Teleilat Ghassul, its stratification and the sequence of settlements, was solved during the 1967 season when it was established that the site had been destroyed on a number of occasions by seismic activity," Professor Hennessey says.

"The results of earthquakes, subsidence, tilting and the cracking of the site have made it one of the most complicated of stratigraphical problems, but once these problems were recognised it was comparatively simple to establish the full sequence of events."

In 1967 nine separate phases of building were recognised – but excavations over the past three years have revealed that there were 15 phases of building on the site.

Today the area is hot, bare and dry, with summer temperatures regularly over 50 deg. Centigrade. Water is available about 50 metres below the surface. The local people carry on market gardening.

However a pedological (*soil science*) survey carried out in 1967 suggested the conditions were somewhat different at the time of the original settlements, which appear to have been made on sand banks in the midst of slow moving fresh water. The plant life was abundant, the survey suggested.

"There is evidence that during the period of occupation of the site there was a considerable lowering of the water table, a factor which probably led to the ultimate desertion of the settlement," Professor Hennessey says.

The excavations have revealed that the normal method of construction throughout most building phases of the site's occupation was a single foundation course of heavy river stones with mud-brick superstructure.

The mud bricks are bun shaped and sun dried. They were laid in a mud mortar.

Entrance to a dwelling was through a single doorway. Roofs appear to have been pitched and constructed of reeds and a mud capping over a heavy timber frame.

"The reed and mud capping roof is identical with the type still in use in the Jordan Valley today," Professor Hennessey says.

"Stone-lined hearths and fire pits occur inside houses and in courtyards. From these has come a large quantity of animal bones. The majority appear to be of goat, sheep, deer, wild pig and cattle.

"The domestic areas have also produced large quantities of grain and seed...wheat, barley, legumes, lentils and olives. There is little doubt that the population of Teleilat Ghassul lived well."

One of the most interesting finds has been a complete flint factory. Fine examples of stone tools – chisels, axes and hammers – were found in the courtyard of a house.

"The periodic destruction of the settlements at Teleilat Ghassul by earthquake has meant the preservation of a great deal of such evidence as the occupants were forced to flee their houses.

"It is perhaps pleasant to note that no one seems to have been caught by collapsing walls," Professor Hennessey says.

No adult skeletons have been found. However, many well preserved skeletons of newly born children have been found beneath the floors of houses, normally in a corner of a room in a large earthenware jar.

Professor Hennessey says it is not known whether or not the children were slain as a foundation sacrifice for the house.

Basil Hennessey, who studied at Sydney University and Oxford, was the first Australian to become a director of one of the prestigious British Schools of Archaeology.

Interestingly, Dr Tony McNicoll, also of Sydney University, who was field director of the "dig", was the second. He joined Sydney University this year, after a period as Director of the British Institute of Afghan Studies in Kabul.

Basil Hennessey was Director of the British School in Jerusalem from 1965 to 1970, when he became a visiting professor at Sydney University. In 1973 he was appointed Edwin Cuthbert Hall Professor in Middle Eastern Archaeology at the university.

It is the only Australian university specialising in Middle Eastern archaeology.

What relevance is Mideast archaeology to Australia? "It seems a long way away of course, but Middle Eastern archaeology is just as much part of our history and philosophy in Australia; just as relevant to people in the West as it is to these people here," Professor Hennessey says.

"Almost everything we do – our technology, agriculture, religious beliefs and practices etc. – you can refer back to what has happened here."

Although often forgotten in Australia, a number of the world's most famous modern archaeologists have been Australians.

There was the late JRB Stewart, who was Professor of Archaeology at Sydney University, and the late Professor Grafton Elliot Smith, who was long before as Professor of Anatomy at Sydney University, one of the first to become interested in the comparative physical anthropology of the early societies of the near east.

"And we have to remember the late Professor Gordon Childs, who was regarded by many as the father of modern archaeology. He was director of the British Institute of Archaeology," Professor Hennessey notes.

"Childs was the first archaeologist who most ably suggested that archaeology should be more than just digging up things; that archaeology should be used to show social development.

"It is only really since the end of the Second World War that people have realised archaeology should be used to determine social developments, how people lived, agriculture of the period, and climate conditions of the period under study."

Ill. 2. Interviewing Basil Hennessey at Teleilat Ghassul, December 1977

Sideshowing the way
From DAVID BALDERSTONE in Cairo

'The Age', December 19, 1977

Although it became apparent shortly after the official opening last Wednesday that the Cairo conference was little more than a sideshow to real Middle East peace moves, the mere staging of the conference has helped pave the way to peace.

Aside from work done during informal discussions and one working session held so far on narrowing legal differences between the Arabs and Israelis, it has in three ways reinforced the view that a Middle East settlement could really be on the way.

First, it has been a major tool for maintaining the peace momentum – and direct Egyptian-Israeli contact – generated by President Sadat's visit to Israel.

Secondly, the presence in Cairo of a large number of Israelis – officials and journalists – has provided a significant litmus test by which the Egyptian leadership has been able to judge domestic, popular support for the Sadat initiatives.

Thirdly, the invitation to the Palestine Liberation Organisation to attend, which was rejected, has been used to push the PLO towards concessions to Israel or, as is more likely, to get moderate Arab leaders off the hook forged by the 1974 Rabat Arab summit decision appointing the PLO as the sole representative of the Palestinian people.

President Sadat called the Cairo conference five days after returning home from Israel. He invited all parties to the Middle East dispute, the United Nations, and the United States and the Soviet Union as chairmen of the stalled Geneva peace conference.

Only Egypt, Israel, the United States and the United Nations are attending the conference, which is being held at the historic Mena House Hotel beside the pyramids outside Cairo.

The very fact that the delegations are headed by senior civil servants, who need to refer anything significant back to their political masters, means that there is a limit on what can be achieved.

It is quite obvious the talks in Washington between Israel's Prime Minister, Mr Begin, and President Carter and the telephone calls between Washington the Egyptian President's palace have been considerably more important to the peace process.

Nevertheless, the significance of the Cairo conference should not be underestimated.

Without positive concessions from Israel early after Sadat's visit, the Egyptian President convened the conference to keep up the momentum lest the chances of peace fade away leaving his tenure on the Presidency seriously at risk.

The warm welcome given the Israelis in Cairo has strengthened Sadat's hand against his Arab critics by providing strong indications that most Egyptians are behind his peace initiatives.

"It is clear that 98 per cent of Egyptians are all for Sadat's peace moves," a senior Western diplomat said.

"Anyone contemplating a coup against the President would have to take into account they would probably receive no popular support."

Not only has the Israeli presence provided a litmus test to judge the leadership's popularity, but it has somewhat softened up the attitude of the Egyptians in readiness for the visit of the Israeli Prime Minister, which is expected to take place sometime this week.

The 1974 Rabat decision appointing the PLO as the sole representative of the Palestinian people has proved a major stumbling block to peace.

Although supported with varying degrees of enthusiasm by all Arab States, it was a decision which was pushed for mainly by Arab League members with no direct involvement in the Arab-Israeli dispute.

While the decision forces Egypt, Jordan and Syria into demanding PLO representation at a reconvened Geneva conference, the Israelis have consistently refused to deal with the organisation, which has the chartered aim of destroying Israel.

Despite Egyptian and Saudi Arabian pressure on the PLO to moderate its stand, the hardliners in the badly split organisation have successfully blocked any such concession.

If the PLO had accepted the Egyptian invitation to attend the Cairo conference it would have put Israel in a very difficult position.

Of course acceptance of an invitation to attend a conference which could have been attended by Israel would have amounted to some concession on the part of the PLO towards recognition of Israel.

Following the PLO's failure to attend the Cairo conference, President Carter said it had disqualified itself from the peace process.

At a weekend Press conference President Sadat followed up the Carter statement by saying the PLO's participation in the anti-Sadat Tripoli summit decisions and non-attendance at Cairo had cancelled the 1974 Rabat decision – although he said he would give the organisation another chance to join the peace process.

The Cairo conference may have changed the Middle East ball game, particularly with reference to the PLO.

Unpalatable as it may be to the organisation, bedevilled as it is with problems, it is facing the squeeze.

Ill. 3. At Mena House, Cairo:
Sadat-Begin talks, Christmas 1977

Mid-East talks open
From DAVID BALDERSTONE

'The Age', Ismailia, December 25, 1977

President Sadat of Egypt and the Israeli Prime Minster, Mr Begin, today began talks on proposals for a Middle East peace settlement.

Mr Begin, the first leader of the Jewish State to be welcomed by an Arab country, was warmly greeted by President Sadat when he stepped from a helicopter which brought him to Ismailia.

He had flown by plane earlier this morning from Israel to Egypt's Abu Suweir air base, 15 kilometres from Ismailia.

He was greeted at Abu Suweir by Egyptian Vice-President Hosny Mubarak, the Prime Minister, Mr Salem, and other Egyptian officials. Within minutes of arrival at Ismailia, Mr Begin went with Mr Sadat into the latter's rest house where they are to hold their talks on trying to shape a comprehensive Middle East settlement.

As their delegations filed in behind, the two leaders posed inside the conference room for photographs. Around the house was the tightest security operation ever mounted in Egypt.

Although Mr Begin was originally due to return to Israel today, the sources said the two leaders might decide to hold further talks tonight or tomorrow. A joint news conference – scheduled for today – might then be postponed until tomorrow.

President Sadat, 59, today had awaited Mr Begin sitting in a wicker chair in the grounds of the villa, enjoying the bright winter sunshine.

Mr Begin was leading a large delegation, including his Foreign Minister, Mr Dayan, and the Defence Minister, General Weizman.

During talks with the Egyptian leader, Mr Begin was expected to give full details of Israel's peace proposals.

Kept secret by Israeli officialdom, these are said by Israeli Television to include a bilateral settlement with Egypt over Sinai and a solution to the Palestinian and Jerusalem issues.

An Israeli official said yesterday that the plan – originally consisting of six main points which Mr Begin presented to Mr Carter in Washington last week – now includes 19 topics.

The Israeli Press reports said Mr Begin was ready to hand over most of the Sinai Desert back to Egypt provided the area was demilitarised and Israel retained two enclaves – in the Rafa approaches and Sharm el-Sheikh.

Sharm el-Sheikh situated on the southern-most tip of the Sinai and controlling the entrance to the Gulf of Aqaba, was one of the reasons for the 1967 Arab-Israeli war when the late Egyptian President Gamal Abdul Nasser closed the strait to Israeli shipping.

Israeli officials said Mr Begin was taking two peace plans to Egypt, one dealing with a bilateral Israeli-Egyptian settlement and the other concerning the Palestinian issue.

President Sadat had maintained a hardline public stand on the eve of today's talks in Ismailia.

He told a delegation of West Bank Arabs yesterday that Egypt was insisting on complete Israeli withdrawal from occupied territories on the West Bank and Gaza Strip.

Egypt was determined to "alleviate the grievances" of the Palestinian people, he said. This hardline statement was seen as being aimed as much at President Sadat's Arab critics as at the Israeli delegation.

Mr Sadat accused Arab critics of his peace initiatives of hiding behind the Soviet Union.

As final preparations were being made for the talks, a new Egyptian Foreign Minister was appointed yesterday. He is a career diplomat, Mr Mohammed Ibrahim Kamel, who is Egypt's former Ambassador to West Germany.

Honeymoon is over: time for hard words
From DAVID BALDERSTONE

'The Age', Cairo, December 29, 1977

The honeymoon is over. Egyptian President Anwar Sadat and Israel's Prime Minister Menachem Begin have had talks in each other's country. Now the hard grind of Ministerial-level negotiations begins.

After the five weeks of euphoria in Egypt and Israel that followed Mr Sadat's visit to Israel, the Ismailia Sadat-Begin summit meeting was something of a disappointment.

Despite the statements by the two leaders expressing optimism, there was little released publicly to indicate Israel and Egypt have progressed far towards a comprehensive Middle East peace settlement.

Mr Sadat confirmed that Israel and Egypt still disagreed on the crucial Palestinian question, but said progress had been made on Israeli withdrawal from Arab territories occupied in 1967.

Few would disagree with Mr Begin that after 29 years of conflict peace is not made in a day. However, Egyptian officials are disappointed that Israel did not bring enough concessions to the summit to vindicate Mr Sadat's decision to visit Israel.

Such concessions would have reduced hardline Arab criticism of Mr Sadat.

But the Egyptian President's own confirmation that Israel and Egypt differed on the Palestinian question merely prompted another round of criticism.

So what has been achieved? President Sadat's statement that progress had been made on the question of Israeli withdrawal dovetails with his earlier statement that the occupied Egyptian territory of Sinai was not a problem.

It is understood that Israel's proposals made at Ismailia covered, among other things, an offer of almost total withdrawal from Sinai, but with early warning defence systems strategically placed and a continued Israeli presence at Sharm el-Sheikh guarding the entrance to the Aqaba Gulf.

Mr Sadat has consistently maintained he is not interested in a separate Egyptian-Israeli peace agreement. Instead he has been working for a comprehensive Middle East settlement.

Israel's plans for withdrawal from Sinai do not go far enough to satisfy this aim.

On the Palestinian question, Egypt insists on the establishment of a Palestinian State on the West Bank territory and in the Gaza Strip.

Israel's plan for limited self-rule – covering municipal and domestic affairs – for Palestinian Arabs in these territories falls a long way short of what could be seen even by the Egyptians, to amount to the establishment of a Palestinian State.

The hopeful part of the Ismailia summit was the decision taken to keep the peace-making going. Among the Egyptian and Israeli officials the in-word at present is "momentum".

The decision to raise to Ministerial level the Cairo conference, which has been attended to date by Egypt, Israel, the United States and the United Nations, and to create two Ministerial-level working committees will maintain momentum – at least for a while.

One of the working committees is to be political and led by Israeli and Egyptian Foreign Ministers. The other is to be military and led by the Defence Ministers. They will convene in January and are expected to sit for at least six weeks.

Judging from their public appearances, there is considerable rapport between Mr Sadat and Mr Begin. Also, it seems, there is good will.

For the first time in 29 years there is, perhaps, even some Egyptian and Israeli understanding of each other's problems. Mr Sadat's critics would not have missed his reference at the Ismailia

Press conference to "Judea and Samaria" – the Biblical names Mr Begin prefers to use to describe the West Bank.

Apart from the goodwill that the Egyptian people have shown visiting Israelis, there are signs that the Egyptians now understand the problems of Israel considerably better.

"Peace is going too slowly for my liking," an Egyptian who had a lot to do with the Israelis told me. "Mr Begin should have given more in Ismailia, but they have problems too. They are concerned their security will be jeopardised if they give back territory."

Israel has a strong military case for not withdrawing from the West Bank, which was formerly controlled by Jordan, or the Golan Heights, which were Syrian territory.

Total withdrawal from the West Bank would return Israel to the pre-1967 situation of having major population areas within conventional artillery range and a width of 15 kilometres at the narrowest point.

Israel learned in the run-up to the 1967 war not to rely on international guarantees of demilitarisation when the United Nations peace-keeping forces were withdrawn at President Nasser's request.

The 1973 war proved the importance to Israel of distance between population areas and borders. Fought on pre-1967 lines, a surprise advance of the kind achieved by the Syrians and Egyptians early in the 1973 war would have cut Israel in two.

Faced with criticism from Syria and the Palestine Liberation Organisation, it would be strange if Mr Sadat didn't just fleetingly ask himself: "How can Israel be expected to trust them when I face all this trouble?"

Mr Sadat says the "core and crux" of the Middle East dispute is the Palestinian problem. This does not merely encompass Palestinian Arabs within Israel's military borders. There are the Palestinian refugee camps in Jordan, Syria and Lebanon. There are the settled Palestinians throughout the world – particularly in Arab countries – who ache for free access to visit Israel.

It is not sheer altruism which prompts the Arabs to push for a solution to the Palestinian problem. The refugees, whom Arab leaders used at least partly as a political weapon in the early years of Israel, have become a problem.

The Jordanians became convinced of this during the run-up to their civil war. There has long been strife associated with the Palestinian presence in Lebanon, and the Syrians have had a taste of the problems in their role as peace-keepers in Lebanon.

Although it is hard to see that a small Palestinian State in only part of what used to be Palestine would solve the Palestinian problem, some peace formula going a long way towards this needs to be found for there to be a comprehensive settlement.

But solution of this problem is something of a vicious circle. Can the Israelis be asked to make concessions towards the establishment of a Palestinian State which could jeopardise security when the PLO maintains in its charter the aim of eliminating Israel?

"The organisation called the PLO is bent on the destruction of Israel. It is written in its charter. From our point of view everything is negotiable except the destruction of Israel," Mr Begin told the Ismailia Press conference. It had been hoped in Egypt there would be sufficient Israeli concessions made during the Ismailia summit to allow Jordan to join the peace process without offending Syria. But this seems unlikely.

Mr Begin says he believes a solution to the Palestinian problem can be achieved during negotiations in the political and military working committees. The Israeli proposals put forward at Ismailia can be considered a first bid.

Egypt is to put counter proposals during the working committee stage of peace negotiations. Some movement towards a solution to the Palestinian question will have to be seen by Syria and the Palestinians to have been made early in the working committee stage. Otherwise, not only will the chances of reconvening the Geneva peace conference and a comprehensive settlement drift away – but maybe also the good will and understanding between the Egyptians and Israelis.

Egypt is key to peace
From DAVID BALDERSTONE in Cairo

'The Age', December 31, 1977

It is difficult to take an optimistic view of peace prospects in the Middle East during 1978.

Egypt is the key to war and peace in the area, as President Anwar Sadat pointed out this week.

Certainly it is hard to see that any other Arab leader but Sadat could have made the decision to visit Israel after 29 years of conflict. Undoubtedly any Arab war effort against Israel would be greatly hampered while Egypt does not want to fight.

However the Middle East is a mesh of jealousies and intrigue. Even if there is a major breakthrough during the coming Egyptian and Israeli peace negotiations, this will provide only the chance of Middle East peace – not peace itself.

It would be hard to doubt that Israel's Prime Minister, Menachem Begin, and the leaders of the Arab confrontation states neighboring Israel want peace, but it remains to be seen whether the Arab and Israeli leaders can make the necessary compromises needed to achieve it.

It is not because anyone is bloody minded, but because the problems are immense.

Can Israel make the necessary territorial concessions and concessions to the Palestinians without jeopardising security? Can Syrian President Hafez Assad make moves towards peace with Israel – even if concessions are made – without jeopardising his leadership of the divided ruling party?

Can King Hussein move – even with Syrian agreement – without facing hostility from his Iraki neighbors and Palestinian nationals? Can war-torn Lebanon do anything without agreement from the confrontation states?

The irony of the hardline criticism of President Sadat's initiative is that it is pushing Egypt towards what critics fear most – a separate Egypt-Israel peace agreement.

Unless some significant breakthrough in Egypt-Israel peace negotiations leads to a healing of the rift in the Arab world caused by Sadat's visit to Israel, it is difficult to be optimistic about the possibility of a lasting peace.

There are four main developments on the horizon if the current peace moves stall. First the criticism of the initiatives from Palestinian groups is certain to escalate into terrorist action.

The murder this week of a Palestinian official in the West Bank town of Ramallah indicates this process is already underway.

When the world failed to take notice of the Palestinian cause in the late 1960s, Palestinian elements stepped up terrorist activity – particularly against Israel. The terror activities subsided as the Palestinians became more widely recognised.

Secondly, although the Saudi Arabians are a moderating influence in the Arab world at present, this does not rule out the possibility of further oil embargoes being imposed in support of the Arab cause.

Senior members of the Saudi Arabian leadership have said recently Saudi Arabia would not hesitate to use the oil weapon, if the need arises.

Thirdly, after a period of diminishing Soviet influence in the Middle East the hardline Arab states could increase their reliance on Russia. This could divide the Middle East clearly again into pro-Soviet and pro-American blocs.

Fourthly, the fact Egypt is not about to go to war with Israel does not rule out war being waged on the Syrian front by a combination of hardline Arab armies.

It would not be as damaging to Israel as a multi-fronted war, but could still cause considerable damage.

President Sadat's visit to Israel has prompted a tremendous feeling of goodwill between Egyptians and Israelis. But statements by President Sadat and Mr Begin following their Ismailia summit indicated that little progress has been made towards a comprehensive settlement.

It remains to be seen whether the Israeli-Egyptian goodwill and the chance of Mid-East peace was merely a passing phase.

1978
Amman January 1978 *(To Mother and Aunt Ethel)*

Mohammed, our loyal servant, insists on coming in while we are away to air the house, clean, and water the plants. He comes once a week and cleans very well, but he also likes to be involved in all his clients' lives. So at least one other morning each week, he comes and sweeps the courtyard, and if we are home, comes in and puts the dishes away from the drying rack. Now he says we have to pay too much for meat, so he buys us steak downtown. It's very good meat. He always stays and has a cup of coffee in the kitchen and a cigarette before moving on to his next client. When we had a party in November while the Australian archaeologists were here, he came in a white coat and served drinks. It was a disaster for Mohammed though because – so used to diplomatic parties – he thought the dress of some of the archaeologists quite unacceptable. And made his feelings known – in a nice way.

When everyone was due to arrive, he went outside and stood at the foot of the stairs waiting to greet people. But it was Professor Basil Hennessey who offended his sense of decency most. Hennessey was at the opposite end of the room to the drinks so was running two glasses of beer at the same time. They both became empty so I asked Mohammed to bring over two beers. He brought them and Basil took them. Mohammed looked at me and asked: "Two, Sir?" I said it was OK.

Mohammed is Palestinian and we talk politics, but only in a small way because his English is not much better than my Arabic. He calls Susan "Lady", and me "Sewer".

Arabs ban our firms
DAVID BALDERSTONE reports from Amman

'The Age', January 4, 1978

Seventy-three Australian companies and organisation have been blacklisted by Arab States because of their dealings with Israel.

The organisations are named in a five-page list – officially kept secret by the Central Boycott Office in Damascus and by Commerce Departments in Arab capitals

Blacklisted organisations are prohibited from operating in most of the Arab League's 22 member States.

Crown Prince Fahd of Saudi Arabia is on record as saying that the boycott will continue until a comprehensive Middle East settlement has been achieved.

A company can be blacklisted for:

- Having a main office, agency or assembly plant in Israel;
- Granting Israeli companies manufacturing licences;
- Participating in Israeli companies or supplying technology to Israeli manufacturing plants;
- Being agents or principal importers of Israeli goods;
- Mineral prospecting in Israel;
- Failing to answer a Boycott Office questionnaire.

Although there have been indications that some Arab States, particularly Egypt, have taken a more liberal attitude to blacklisted companies, the deep rift in the Arab world caused by President Sadat's dialogue with Israel means the Arab boycott is far from over.

The blacklist includes Australian off-shoots of American companies, such as Ford, a whole range of smaller companies, plus organisations such as the Jewish Board of Deputies.

The Arab boycott is designed to prevent Arab States and interests – and discourage non-Arabs – from contributing to Israel's economic and military strength.

Although the boycott was born in the years immediately before modern Israel was created in 1948, it has only been during the past five years that is has become a force in international commerce.

Soaring Arab oil revenues prompting massive development in the Arab world, and the importance of Arab finance, have given muscle to the previously limp boycott.

In a number of countries, including the United States, moves have been made to legislate against foreign boycotts – including the Arab boycott.

On October 12, 1976, Senator Cotton told the Senate that the Australian Government did not have a list of Australian companies affected by the boycott.

"Even if such information was available, it would not be appropriate for the Government to publish any information of a kind that could adversely affect the standing of particular Australian companies," Senator Cotton said.

The Australian section covers only a small part of the Arab blacklist. For example, more than 1000 United States organisations are listed.

Originally in the mid-1940s the boycott was established to stop Arab States and interests from dealing with Zionist interests.

Officially all Arab League members ban Government trade, or trade by their people or companies with Israel. This is dubbed the "primary" boycott.

After Israel was created in 1948 the boycott was extended to ban Arab trade with non-Arab countries and organisations which were considered to contribute to Israel's economic and military strength. This is commonly called the "secondary" boycott.

Six Arab States do not adhere to the secondary boycott but follow the primary boycott. These countries are Algeria, Mauritania, Morocco, Somalia, Sudan and Tunisia.

There is an additional boycott, called the "tertiary" boycott in the West, which stops companies trading with Arab States from using the services of blacklisted firms while fulfilling their Arab contracts.

But this is the most vague and most frequently ignored boycott procedure.

In most of the Arab countries which apply the secondary boycott, companies selling goods have to provide a "negative certificate of origin" – a document saying no part of the goods was made in Israel.

Some countries accept a "positive certificate of origin", for example that the goods were made in Australia.

The Central Boycott Office in Damascus has no direct power. It compiles advisory blacklists which it sends to the commerce departments in Arab capitals.

Some Arab States which apply the secondary boycott make special exemptions or additions. Therefore there is no universal blacklist.

Government-to-Government sales – including significantly, military equipment sales and tourist operations – are not subject to boycott procedures.

It is not clear exactly how the Central Boycott Office in Damascus goes about the job of compiling the blacklist. It is assumed the office scrutinises newspapers, particularly the Israeli business press, and gets help from Arab embassies overseas.

Questionaries sent to companies are used to clarify a company's relationship with Israel.

It has been alleged in the United States and Europe that companies have supplied information to the Central Boycott Office about their competitors in a bid to get them out of the running for Arab contracts.

Special exemptions are made as the need arises.

For example, although RCA has been blacklisted, Jordan extensively uses RCA global communications, which are also used by Israel, and Saudi Arabia continues to import RCA spare parts for the television network the company set up before it was blacklisted.

"When British Leyland went on the blacklist (it has since been removed)", commented a Jordanian official, "we remembered the army in Jordan was equipped with a great number of Land Rovers …so we decided all Rovers except Land Rovers were blacklisted."

The two most famous cases of companies being blacklisted involve Coca Cola and Ford. Coca Cola was blacklisted in 1966 after licensing a bottling plant in Tel Aviv.

Ford was blacklisted after licensing an assembly plant in Israel.

Both these companies have made extensive investments in Egypt recently.

Ford of the US has signed an agreement to establish a joint venture to make medium-sized trucks. Coca Cola has invested in a citrus growing venture.

Both investments are seen as a move by the companies to pave the way for their removal from the blacklist.

Although the procedure is long, companies can be removed from the blacklist by proving to the satisfaction of the boycott office they no longer have "objectionable" interests in Israel, or by making comparable investments in Arab countries and stopping investment in Israel.

When faced with criticism over their boycott, Arab governments usually cite United States and other countries' boycotts, particularly during the Cold War period and the Korean and Vietnam wars.

The Arabs point out they are officially at war with Israel.

Words fail to ease ache for Palestine
From DAVID BALDERSTONE

'The Age', Amman, January 5, 1978

For three days it had rained. Everywhere there was mud in Baqaa Palestinian refugee camp near Amman. But nothing dampens the people's ache for Palestine.

On television they watched President Carter and President Sadat in Aswan yesterday. The leaders' diplomatic words, which correspondents used to hang stories about the US and Egypt being close to agreement on the Palestinian issue, mean little here.

Most of the 70,000 people in Baqaa – like other Palestinian refugees – gave up hope for a solution to their problem years ago.

"The Zionists don't want peace. They want land. They will refuse to give any land back to the Arabs," declared a man named Mohammed, aged about 26.

"The Palestinian people know this. That is why for Sadat to go to the Knesset is not right because we know they will not give back the land."

While some members of the Palestinian leadership say they would settle for a Palestinian State in the West Bank and Gaza Strip, the refugees are divided on this issue.

"Begin is a Jew from Poland. You are a Christian from Australia. There are Muslims in Turkey, but they are Turkish and they want to stay in Turkey.

"Religion is not nationality," said Mohammed, adding the long-term solution was the establishment of a democratic and not a religious Palestinian state.

But his brother thinks a West Bank and Gaza Palestinian State would be a solution. "It will be satisfactory. This is my opinion, but others may not agree. But if Israel withdraws from the West Bank and Gaza Strip it will be satisfactory."

There are almost 600,000 Palestinian refugees in camps organised by the United Nations Relief and Works Agency.

Before the Six Day War in 1967, many of the people in Baqaa, a collection of leaking huts on the Damascus road about 20 kilometres from Amman, lived in the West Bank near Jericho.

Now in the mud, the leaking huts, through the blackouts and the misery, the village bonds from the days in Palestine remain dominant.

Ill. 4. Baqaa Camp, Jordan, January 1978

Turkey caught in a quicksand of compromise
From DAVID BALDERSTONE in Amman

'The Sydney Morning Herald', January 5, 1978

Turkey, embroiled in massive economic and law and order problems, is at a crossroads unless Mr Bulent Ecevit succeeds in leading a Government which can survive to tackle the problems. Democratic government could be jeopardised.

Almost exactly six months ago Mr Ecevit failed to gain a vote of confidence from Turkey's National Assembly after the country's elections. Last Saturday, the Government of Suleyman Demirel fell after 12 of his Justice Party deputies defected.

After the mid-year elections Mr Ecevit, whose Republican People's Party won 213 of the 450 National Assembly seats, idealistically tried to form a minority Government.

He was trying to avoid government-by-compromise, but he failed.

After the weekend fall of the Demirel Government, Mr Ecevit spent this week scraping up the numbers to form a coalition Government with defecting members of the Justice Party and members of two small right-wing groups, which between them hold three National Assembly seats.

He is paying a high price for the loyalty of his new coalition partners. According to reports, Mr Ecevit is offering these small groups eight seats in a 29-member Cabinet.

And the coalition will still have a majority of only one, two or three seats in the National Assembly. Such a slim majority does not inspire confidence about stability, especially in Turkey.

If the Ecevit Government fails to survive it cannot be assumed that senior army officers, who have remained influential since the military junta of the early 1960s, and their intervention in 1971, will continue to tolerate the government-by-crisis situation which has bugged Turkey in recent years.

Although it is understood military leaders would be extremely reluctant to take over, their reluctance could be overshadowed by the need to get the country moving again. Turkey's problems are as bad as that.

On the economic side, Turkey is $300 million behind in short-term loan repayments, has unemployment of 20 per cent and worsening, and an inflation rate of 35-40 per cent.

The International Monetary Fund is demanding stringent financial measures, including devaluation of up to 20 per cent to bring the currency to its real value against major currencies, before it clears the way for future bank loans.

In the meantime, manufacturing businesses in Turkey which depend upon imported basic materials are being forced to wind down their operations, further increasing the unemployment problem.

In the past year, clashes between right-wing and left-wing extremists have left 250 people dead. On polling day of the recent municipal elections, three people died.

As well as these economic and law and order problems there are difficult foreign affairs issues – two of which exacerbate problems with neighboring Greece.

These two are the unresolved Cyprus issue, and problems arising from sovereignty claims in areas of the Aegean Sea in which oil has been discovered.

Suleyman Demirel was unable to effectively tackle any of these problems because of the continuous compromises he had to make to satisfy his coalition partners, particularly the National Salvation Party of Mr Erbakan.

Under the Turkish constitution, another election cannot be held until four years after the mid-year election last year.

The recent municipal elections indicate Mr Ecevit's Republican People's Party would win handsomely if an election could be held now.

Of 67 provincial capitals contested in the December 11 poll, the RPP won 42, the Justice Party 15, the Nationalist Action Party five, the National Salvation Party three, and Independents two.

Although there had been disenchantment within Justice Party ranks before this, these election results can be seen as a major contributing factor to the party's 12 defections.

In turn, the election result and the defections led to the RPP censure motion which led to Mr Demirel's fall.

However, the Justice Party's poor performance in the municipal elections and the defections can be sheeted home to the Demirel Government's failure to deal adequately with the economic problems, which have not only left the country facing bankruptcy, but the working person's fight with inflation virtually intolerable.

Mr Demirel has said economic problems would have been significantly eased if it were not for a world glut on the wheat market. Turkey's rich agricultural land produced five million tonnes of wheat last year, most of which Turkey has been unable to sell. This, Mr Demirel says, would have earned Turkey $500 million.

Mr Ecevit served as Prime Minister from January, 1973 until September, 1974, which includes the period of the major Turkish invasion of Cyprus.

The question now is: can a new Ecevit Government last?

Amman January 6, 1978 (*To Susan's Aunt Margot in New Zealand*)

It might surprise the average newspaper reader to know how foreign correspondents go about their job, particularly, it seems to me, at something like the Cairo conference or the Ismailia meeting. The problem is that no one knows what the hell is going on, but equally no one is prepared to admit that to his editor who may be thousands of miles away.

So rumours abound – some I am sure enlightened (leaked by the governments involved), and others not. As the days dragged by during the Cairo conference short-wave radios would quietly come out of bags on the hour and the distinctive signature tune of the BBC World Service would waft across the garden bar areas of the Mena House Hotel. No-one would admit to listening. But a few minutes after the news ended, the newspaper men would quip: "Glad I'm in print rather than audio…I'm told the BBC was running a remarkable story about Begin coming here on Christmas Day. Can't be true." It was. And we print men had it in good time for the full story for our editions.

Quite remarkably the Egyptians did a very good job on communications. About fifty telex machines were laid on and telephone calls to any part of the world could be got within about ten minutes. The telex operators, whom I got to know particularly well because they all seemed to have cousins or brothers living in Sydney or Brisbane and are mad about Australia, became quite enthusiastic with all this talk of peace…………

The first night in Cairo I stayed at the old Cosmopolitan Hotel. Before retiring, too late I must admit having got caught up with some journalists who like the taste of beer, I said to the man at reception that I wanted an early morning reminder call at 5.55 am. "No, Sir, why don't you say 6 am", he replied. I scttlcd on 5.45 telling him I had to go to work, but not telling him I actually wanted to hear the 6 am BBC news. I also slipped the all-night servant half a pound, telling him to wake me at 5.45 am with a cup of tea "because I have to go to work".

At 5.45 am on the dot the man and the tea arrive with a cheery "Time to get up Sir, remember, you have to go to work." I settle back and listen to the news. At 6.15 am there is a loud banging on my door. I lean out and open it (situation made worse by the fact I couldn't get out of bed, having left pyjamas in Amman), and cheery face has become a bit more serious.

"Now Sir," the face says, "don't go back to sleep.... Remember have to go to work early today." It was no use explaining that listening to the wireless was work for me.

Arrive in the lobby for breakfast finally at 7.15 am. The man behind Reception from the night before is still there and he says to me: "You say you must be woken at 5.45 because have to go to work." He gives me a doubting smile as I say: "I was working in my room."

All the shops had put banners across the streets hailing "Sadat, hero of war and peace" or something similar. I particularly liked a banner near the Cosmo hotel erected by a shoe shop calling itself Eccentric House. It read: "Eccentric House supports President Sadat".

Assad set for a new term
From DAVID BALDERSTONE

'The Age', Amman, February 8, 1978

As Syrians went to the polls today to confirm a second seven-year term for President Assad, the man Mr Assad overthrew in a bloodless coup in 1970 remained in detention.

The former Head of State, Dr Nuredin al-Attassi, is understood to be one of Syria's political prisoners Irak wants released if reconciliation between the rival Syrian and Iraki leaderships is to be achieved.

After years of instability, Mr Assad overthrew Dr Attassi, the leader of a rival faction in Syria's ruling Baath Party, in November, 1970. He became President four months later.

President Assad's second seven-year term has already been approved by the Baath party and Syria's People's Council. He was unopposed.

Around 4.2 million Syrians are eligible to vote in today's referendum.

President Assad, who is considered a moderate in Syrian politics, has provided Syria with a period of unusual stability following a series of bloody coups since Independence in the early forties.

Dispute splits front against Sadat
From DAVID BALDERSTONE in Amman

'The Sydney Morning Herald', February 9, 1978

Attempts by Arab States opposed to Egypt's peace initiatives to form a powerful hardline Arab front have been stymied by the failure so far of continuing moves to reconcile differences between Syria and Irak.

Geographically, Irak is the only staunch Arab critic of President Sadat's initiatives – apart from Syria – which can add any real clout to a military front threatening Israel.

But Irak refused to attend last weekend's hardline Arab summit meeting in Algiers, mainly because no progress had been made in the on again, off again reconciliation moves between Damascus and Bagdad.

This left Algeria, which is closer to London than to Tel Aviv; Libya, which could help with money but only in a small way with arms; South Yemen, which has neither money nor arms to spare; and the Palestine Liberation Organisation.

They were able to offer strong words indeed, pledge support for Syria and the PLO, but not able to pose any real threat to Israel – at this stage.

Borders between Syria and Irak are closed because of the continuing dispute, which stems from rivalries between the ruling Baath parties in both Damascus and Bagdad.

There are specific problems which make reconciliation difficult. Irak has been very critical of Syria's role in the Lebanese civil war, initially in opposition to Palestinian forces, and later Syria's continuing peace-keeping role.

Also Irak wants Syria to renounce its support for United Nations Security Council resolutions 242 and 338, which, in effect, provide for a negotiated settlement of the Arab-Israeli crisis based on Israel's withdrawal from Arab territories occupied during 1967.

Syria has blamed Irak for many bomb attacks in Damascus and more than one assassination attempt on Syria's Foreign Minister, Abdel Halim Khaddam. Iraki and Syrian jails hold a considerable number of the other's supporters and this is a continuing cause of friction.

So, for reconciliation to take place, Irak would have to acquiesce to Syria's support of resolutions 242 and 338, which the Syrian leadership has given no indications of wanting to abandon, and to Syria's role in Lebanon, which can't be abandoned without the serious risk of full-scale civil war breaking out again.

Some agreement would also have to be reached on political prisoners.

But the leaderships in Bagdad and Damascus have so much distrust of each other that it is hard to see that a reconciliation at this stage would be anything but what one diplomat described here this week as a "papering-over exercise".

Certainly, there is mutual interest in a reconciliation now that the Syrians firmly believe President Sadat's visit to Israel was wrong and will lead nowhere. The Irakis share this view, but in any case they belong to the "rejectionist" Arab camp which rejects the idea of a negotiated settlement with Israel.

There are three main reasons why Syria has been pushing for reconciliation with Irak, albeit on its own terms.

First, Syria obviously does feel isolated in a desire for effective opposition to President Sadat's initiative – especially with its only "confrontation" neighbor with any potential military muscle, Jordan, sitting on the fence and tending to support Sadat.

Second, a reconciliation with Irak would strengthen Syrian President Assad's position with Irak-leaning members of his ruling Baath Party.

Third, a reconciliation with Irak and the firm establishment of a strong military hardline front would greatly enhance President Assad's stature in the Arab world.

Syria recently concluded a new arms agreement with the Soviet Union and substantial arms reinforcements are reportedly already arriving in the country. If a reconciliation took place between Syria and Irak, which together have fighting forces of close to 300,000 men, the hardline Arab front would pose a substantial threat to Israel – even if it were only on the northern flank.

Clashes shake Lebanon hope
From DAVID BALDERSTONE in Amman

'The Age', February 16, 1978

The renewed fierce fighting in Beirut – after 15 months of relative calm – has done a great deal to damage the credibility of the new Lebanese Army. This army was designed to be one of the major tools for reasserting Lebanese national control over the war-torn country.

The new army was gradually being built up as a force reflecting national Lebanese interests. It has been working with the predominantly Syrian Arab peace-keeping force – from which, ideally, it would one day take over.

But after the fighting between Syrian peace-keeping forces and a small group of the Lebanese Army, which broke out around the Fayyadiyeh barracks and sparked several days of bitter clashes between the Syrians and Rightist forces, Syrian President Hafez Assad has reportedly called for the disbandment of the new army.

The Fayyadiyeh Lebanese army barracks were commanded by a Colonel Antoine Barakat, who had led one of the Right-wing splinter-groups militias which emerged from the civil war collapse of the regular Lebanese Army. To many people it was a surprise that an officer with such partisan leanings was in a position of authority within the new army.

The fighting around the barracks broke out when Syrian peace-keeping forces tried to establish a checkpoint outside the barracks. But the checkpoint incident merely sparked the fighting and resentment against the Syrian presence has been building up for some time in Lebanon – particularly within the predominantly Christian Right-wing community.

The Syrian obstacle has become particularly hard to bear for some members of the Christian hierarchy because they have seen their opportunity to reassert influence. They have summed up the

Moslem community as being demoralised, divided, and plain sick of the strains of a divided community.

However the Christian hierarchy has also grown alarmed at the rapprochement between the Syrians and Palestinians, which has been helped greatly by Egyptian President Anwar Sadat's peace initiatives with Israel.

When Syrian troops arrived in April, 1976, they brought relative peace to war-torn Lebanon by supporting the Christian forces and restoring an uneasy balance of power. The Syrian support for the Christians drew much criticism in the Arab world and brought about a severe cooling in Syrian-Palestinian relations. But thrown back together in opposition to the Sadat initiatives, Syrian-Palestinian relations have improved significantly.

The Sadat initiative has had another important effect on the Syrian presence in Lebanon. It can be seen as important to the Syrian leadership to be in Lebanon at present. The leadership does not have the influence it would like and the presence in Lebanon increases Syria's sphere of influence.

The Arab League mandate for Syria's peace-keeping role in Lebanon is due for renewal in April. There are two main problems.

First in the wake of divisions within the Arab League caused by the Sadat initiatives, it may be difficult for it to legally renew Syria's peace-keeping mandate.

Secondly, some Western diplomats argue that even if it is possible to get a meeting convened legally, some powerful members may oppose a mandate renewal. While Syria has championed the cause of the hardline Arab States, she has annoyed the moderates with her opposition to Sadat. There are other Arab elements who just don't like Syria's sphere of influence including Lebanon so directly.

Conspiracy theories run rife in Syria and Lebanon. Since the fighting broke out in Lebanon last week, it has been said the United States, Egypt, and Israel – individually or together – had stirred up trouble to divert attention from the Egyptian-Israeli dialogue.

More likely, of course, it is merely the reappearance in Lebanon of the ferment beneath the surface, which was never removed but merely quelled by the presence of 25,000 Syrian troops.

Hawke gets a welcome in Jordan
From DAVID BALDERSTONE

'The Sydney Morning Herald', February 21, 1978

Watched by Israeli and Jordanian soldiers, the ACTU president, Mr Hawke, walked across the 30-metre-long Allenby Bridge across the River Jordan from Israeli military territory today to begin a visit to Jordan.

He was farewelled by a friendly "Shalom" from Israeli officials standing under a fluttering Star of David on the west bank of the river and met on the other side by a greeting in Arabic.

"Ahlan wah sahlan" (welcome), the president of the Jordan Trade Union, Mr Sami Mansour, said.

Mr Hawke replied: "I am very interested to be visiting Jordan, particularly at this time when expectations for peace in the Middle East are rising."

Mr Hawke was invited to Jordan by Crown Prince Hassan, King Hussein's brother.

After leaving the bridge the first stop on the busy three-day schedule was a visit to Karameh, a Palestinian refugee camp destroyed by Israeli forces shortly after the 1967 war.

The Israelis alleged that guerillas had been operating against Israel from the camp.

The Jordanians are out to woo Mr Hawke. They have taken the unusual step of arranging private accommodation – a real honour in the Arab world – for him in Amman.

He is to be the house guest of one of Jordan's most prominent and wealthy businessmen, Mr Raouf Abujaber. Among other things, Mr Abujaber is general manager of Jordan brewery Co. Ltd, which makes Amstel beer under licence.

Jordanian officials are fully aware that Mr Hawke is a supporter of Israel. One official who has seen statements by Mr Hawke on the Middle East quipped yesterday: "They sound like the Israeli Prime Minister speaking."

However, during his visit Mr Hawke will get a heavy dose of Jordanian thinking on the Middle East situation.

Reports from Australia that Mr Hawke has been dubbed "Public enemy No 1" by the Arab Information Bureau in Melbourne have bewildered Jordanian officials rather than concerned them. Certainly the reports have cast no shadows over the visit.

Ill. 5. Interviewing Bob Hawke (left) at the Allenby Bridge, February 1978

Hawke wants ban on PLO visitors
From DAVID BALDERSTONE

'The Age', Amman, February 23, 1978

The ACTU president, Mr Hawke, said today that the Palestinian Liberation Organisation representatives should not be allowed to visit Australia, while the PLO held on to the aim of eliminating Israel.

"I have always been unequivocal in my support of Israel's right to exist," Mr Hawke said. "There has been no change in my opinion on this."

Mr Hawke said he had "no doubt at all" about Jordan's sincere desire for peace in the Middle East.

He said his three days of talks in Jordan had given him greater perception of the Arab position and the Palestinian problem.

Mr Hawke was speaking before departing for Geneva after three days of talks in Jordan. There is no doubt that the Jordanians took the visit extremely seriously.

For a foreign visitor, he spent an unusual amount of time with Jordan's Crown Prince Hassan. He had three meetings and a total of more than four hours talking with the prince about the Middle East situation.

During the visit, Mr Hawke proposed co-operation between the trade union movements in Australia and Jordan.

Amman February 1978 (*To niece Cathy*)

Bob Hawke was in Amman and I had breakfast with him yesterday. I have a lovely photograph of me and him taken on arrival in Jordan from Israel. Tomorrow Dr David Owen, Foreign Secretary of Britain is arriving so I will have to get up early to get to the airport – not that I expect to be having breakfast with him.

Also this week I am meant to be getting an interview with King Hussein, but it has been on and off so many times that I will believe it when it happens. And next weekend Susan and I are probably going across to Israel You might remember we were to go to Jerusalem for Christmas, but the Muslims and the Jews conspired to wreck Christmas for the Christians and we spent it in Ismailia, Egypt.

I have spent most of the past week getting through the bureaucratic process here to get our residence permits extended. They need all sorts of references, documents, health certificates, and enough photographs to run a one-man exhibition. After hours and hours we had success yesterday, and we got slips of paper to keep in our passports. On mine my name is given as "David Robert" (no Balderstone) and on Susan's the name is "Susan Mary Balder".

While the bureaucracy is somewhat inefficient, the farming certainly isn't – and I think they could teach Australian farmers and graziers something. For example, if a shepherd wants to move a flock of sheep he jumps on his donkey, has some green grass sticking out of the saddle, and rides off up streets, through traffic lights, and the sheep follow along happily. If I could tell them of the business my brothers go on with – horses galloping around in circles; shouting and swearing at dogs – I am sure they would either laugh or cry.

*****

A miracle occurred near here the other day. I wrote a story for 'The Age' about it, but I don't think it appeared so I will tell you about it. It happened during a Sunday service at the Greek Orthodox church in Madaba, around 30 kilometres from Amman. According to the story, during the service a bright light suddenly appeared on a small painting of the Virgin Mary and Baby Jesus. When the light went, a third adult hand had appeared on the painting. Certainly the hand is there, but I don't know whether to believe it appeared, or has always been there, or that the painting was switched. Madaba is near to Mt Nebo from where Moses is said to have first seen the Promised Land. Some people are said to have been healed after rubbing oil which was blessed in front of the Icon into their trouble spots. For example, a man who could only walk with crutches can now walk without help – according to local Christians.

Whether or not the miracle was faked, I think it has something to do with Christian and Muslim jealousy in the town of Madaba. Before Israel was established causing many thousands of Palestinians to cross the Jordan River into Jordan, the town was mainly Christian – about 90% in fact. Now, with the influx of Muslim Palestinians, the town is only 60% Christian. At dinner with Crystal Bennett at the British Institute of Archaeology the other night, some French priests were saying that often or usually miracles occur in places where there is some religious jealousy. They left open an opinion on whether the local community was responsible or whether God picks such places out because there is scope for influence – and of course, the Muslims and Christians supposedly have the same God, or at least believe there is only one God. Scientists of course, as you will find out, often use their test tubes and fancy descriptions for water and other things to prove such happenings are not miracles at all. But I prefer the thought of a Christian in Madaba who told me "It depends whether you believe or not."

Ill. 6. Three-handed icon, Madaba, February 1978

Amman February 27, 1978 (*To niece Sally*)

Thank you for your recent letter. We, like you, were "so sorry" you had not written since September – but as I don't think I have written you anything but post cards, I can't complain too loudly.

Two mornings ago I had to go to the airport early because Dr David Owen, Britain's Foreign Secretary was arriving.

Because I got there early, I was invited to coffee in the officers' mess. The Turkish Ambassador, who is also the dean of the diplomatic corps here, arrived and I was talking to him about Turkish and Arabic and the interrelation thereof.

When the British diplomats arrived, he turned to me quietly and said: "You Australians understand English?"

"Yes" I said, "it's our language."

"Very interesting," he added. "You speak English and can understand the British? You speak English like they do?"

"We have different accents", I said.

"But you can understand each other. Well that is very good…."

*****

I have had a most distracting time recently. The landlord has hired an elderly man to dig the garden, which in itself is very good. The distracting part is that the man is a devout Muslim, and insists on praying at noon and three in the afternoon. He has adopted the bit of pavement outside my office window to pay his respects to Allah. Every day at noon there is a great deal of murmuring as he prays and bows towards Mecca. It goes on for about ten minutes. Problem is I don't like to do any typing during that time in case it could be thought irreverent. I have been meaning to write to you for some time. But it was always noon.

I still have some trouble with the bureaucracy here. For example the other day, Bob Hawke was arriving in Jordan from Israel and I had gone through days of work to get a special permission for me and a photographer to go to the Allenby Bridge (across the Jordan River). We arrived at the police post about an hour before time and showed our letter of permission to the police officer.

"This says you and the photographer can go to the bridge but it does not say you can take photographs."

The Jordanian photographer rightly pointed out that it was logical that if a journalist and photographer were given special permission to go to the bridge that they would want to take photographs. Eventually logic prevailed and the officer rang police headquarters and cleared the photographs.

Shadow over Middle East
DAVID BALDERSTONE reports from Jerusalem

'The Age', March 14, 1978

Pale, drawn and looking exhausted, his eyes bloodshot, Israeli Prime Minister Menachem Begin entered the conference room in his Jerusalem office suite to answer questions.

The Palestinian terrorist raid the previous evening, which left 37 Israelis dead and more than 70 wounded, had probably given him the most harrowing night of his 10-month Prime Ministership.

He was controlled, outspoken in a measured way, and polite, but did not resemble the effervescent Israeli leader of the Ismailia summit in Egypt less than three months ago.

President Sadat's visit to Israel last November has brought the Middle East so much hope, so much hate – and the promise of continuing bloody reprisals and instability.

Asked whether Israel would retaliate in the wake of the deadliest terrorist attack in its history, Mr Begin said: "I suppose you will understand that such a question cannot be answered."

He then added: "What I can say is that those who kill Jews in our time cannot enjoy immunity."

With six (and as it subsequently turned out nine) of the 11 guerillas already dead, and two held prisoner, it was doubtful whether the Prime Minister was just stating the obvious – that the two held prisoners would face, as he called it, "justice".

It seems he meant more. Several times Mr Begin used the phrase "we will not forget", and it seemed likely then that Israel will strike back at Al Fatah and the Palestine Liberation Organisation. Al Fatah, the military wing, had claimed responsibility for the attack.

There are two main points somewhat in doubt about the raid, which was launched north of Tel Aviv as Israel was coming alive again after the Sabbath last Saturday evening.

First, two rubber boats were found on the beach near Kibbutz Ma'agan Michael, and Israel says the guerillas used them to enter Israel from Lebanon.

But Al Fatah says the attack was the work of a guerilla unit operating from within Israel.

Seas were rough that day, which would have made a voyage of at least 70 kilometres from Lebanon extremely hazardous.

On the other hand, the bad weather and poor visibility would have helped the raiders to evade Israeli surveillance forces, something that would have been nearly impossible on a clear day.

Second, Mr Begin's own statement raised the possibility that most of the deaths in the attack may have been the unfortunate result of Israeli forces taking action against the guerillas.

"Unfortunately, the bus was burnt as a result of an explosion – probably a hand grenade thrown by one of the killers," Mr Begin said.

Twenty-five bodies were found burned beyond recognition in the bus which had been hijacked by the guerillas.

Mr Begin's use of the word "probably" cast some doubt on whether the explosion was the result of a terrorist grenade, or the result of Israeli action against the terrorists still in the bus.

Revenge has been the Israeli pattern after previous terrorist attacks. In this case revenge would probably cost Israel a great deal of sympathy from the West at a time in the peace process when it needs it most.

Also, it would make it more difficult for Egypt and Jordan and even Syria – none of which has been immune from Palestinian annoyance – to move slowly towards peace.

Most important, there is considerable danger that Israeli retaliation would escalate into something far worse. Even soon after the terrorist attacks, observers in Israel were predicting that Israel would retaliate against Al Fatah and other Palestinian strongholds in southern Lebanon.

The risk is that such retaliation might inadvertently involve at least some of the 25,000 Syrian peace-keeping troops in Lebanon.

Although it seems certain that Syria – in no shape for a major clash with Israel despite recent Soviet arms supplies – would not relish involvement at this stage, Middle East political development might force it to become involved.

The closest Syrian troops are within about 30 kilometres of Israel's most northern town, Metulla. They are north of the Litani River.

Last year the Syrians were careful not to get involved when Israeli and Palestinian forces clashed in southern Lebanon. But is the situation different now? Since President Sadat's visit to Israel, Syria and the PLO have come back closer together, and both are Arab hardliners against the Sadat initiative.

It was no coincidence that the attack took place on the eve of Mr Begin's scheduled departure for Washington, for talks with President Carter which could have helped Middle East peace moves. The talks – when they take place – could push Egypt and Israel closer to agreement.

Ironically perhaps, Al Fatah and the PLO had a vested interest in stopping the peace moves. With the PLO at a complete loss about how to involve Palestinians in negotiations without itself losing stature and face, the moves had to be halted – at least temporarily.

It seems clear that Al Fatah's aim was to underline the point that no Middle East peace could be achieved without Palestinian involvement or without restoration of Palestinian rights. Al Fatah wanted to block any chance that President Carter might succeed in persuading Israel to make concessions to the Arabs which could allow the Egypt-Israel dialogue to continue.

Also, more cynically, it could be said that part of the aim of the attack was to bolster the position of Al Fatah and PLO leader Yasser Arafat. In the past few months his position has looked shaky and he has been seen by hardline elements in the Palestinian movement as being too compromising.

Mr Begin has not missed the opportunity to make political capital out of the attack.

First, he described the PLO and Al Fatah – which, admittedly, have the chartered aim of destroying Israel – as "one of the meanest and basest organisations since the days of the Nazis".

Certainly he was speaking under extreme provocation, but the attack and his comments will make it easier for Israel to resist pressure to compromise on PLO recognition in the wake of predicted rapprochement between moderate Jordan and the PLO.

By coincidence, the day before the attack the 'Jerusalem Post' carried an editorial in its Thirty Years Ago column criticising Zionist guerilla groups. The editorial criticises an act of terror carried out by one of these groups as "an act of which only the disciples of Hitler are capable". Menachem Begin – Britain's most wanted man in Palestine at the time – was the leader of the main group, the Irgun.

Secondly, Mr Begin stressed that the attack might make more people realise why Israel opposed the establishment of an independent Palestinian State on the West Bank and Gaza Strip territories. The Arabs, including Egypt, demand such a State.

Finally, Mr Begin condemned the Soviet Union for supplying weapons to the Palestinian guerilla groups. His criticism coincides with moves – particularly by King Hussein of Jordan – to bring the Soviet Union back into the peace process.

Mr Begin says the attack should not block the Egypt-Israel peace dialogue – if Egypt sincerely wanted to continue. But the attack and its aftermath have cast a dark shadow over the already slim hopes of Middle East peace.

Israeli 'solution' solves nothing
DAVID BALDERSTONE, our Middle East correspondent reports from Jerusalem.

'The Age', March 17, 1978

Just before 10 o'clock on Tuesday night – as Israeli forces in northern Israel were getting their final briefing as it turned out – the soloist completed his Beethoven concerto in the Jerusalem theatre. He announced he was to play what on other occasions would have been called an encore.

There was no applause. He played a funeral march.

The Israeli audience seemed to expect it. The Government, the newspapers, the radio and television – all of Israel – had been full of outrage for three days. As on the other similar occasions, the nation had been tearing its heart out over the Palestinian guerilla attack north of Tel Aviv on Saturday.

Israel is a small country in area and population – about 3.7 million people. Despite divisions between European and Oriental Jews, there is great camaraderie – partly due to the almost universal military service. It is united in the need for survival. After the weekend trajedy, more than a funeral march was wanted.

And the Israelis – as expected – got more. But it is doubtful whether the massive Israeli drive into southern Lebanon, launched at midnight on Tuesday, will solve any of their real problems.

If the operation goes as planned, it will make northern Israeli villages and settlements safer from Palestinian guerilla rocket and artillery attacks from across the Lebanese border.

But on the negative side for Israel, it will not stop Palestinian terror attacks. And, almost certainly, it has destroyed any surviving hopes of a comprehensive peace settlement with the Arabs.

With close to 600,000 registered refugees living in discontent-breeding camps in Lebanon, Syria, Jordan, the Gaza Strip and the

West Bank, terror attacks will continue. In fact the Israeli raid – and temporary occupation of southern Lebanon, will not be a symbol of defeat for the Palestinians. It is more likely to strengthen their determination to continue.

And if Egypt's President Sadat decides that the Israeli-Egyptian dialogue should continue, it will look more and more as if he is prepared to head towards a separate peace with Israel – exactly what his Arab critics predicted all along.

The raid makes it seemingly impossible for Jordan – 60 per cent of whose population is Palestinian – to join in any peace talks, at least for some time.

Syria, equally, would find it difficult to talk about peace – even if the format was changed to a wider Geneva-style peace process with the Soviet Union as co-chairman with the United States.

Since President Sadat visited Israel, Syria's President Assad has emerged as the leader of the hardline Arabs. It is hard to see him pursuing peace and sacrificing that status. Instead he is more likely to use the Israeli attack as an indication that he was right all along, that he and not Sadat is the most prominent leader among the Arab confrontationist States.

Israel's Prime Minister Begin says he wants agreement with all parties – except the Palestinian Liberation Organisation, with which Israel refuses to talk – guaranteeing security in southern Lebanon. He says Israeli forces will not withdraw from Lebanon until such a security agreement, which would halt Palestinian guerilla rocket and artillery attacks into Israel, is achieved.

Israeli forces look like being in southern Lebanon for a long time.

Lebanon's Government admits it cannot control the south in the wake of the civil war. The Lebanese army is inadequate for the task.

Peace in the rest of the country – despite occasional outbursts of fighting in Beirut – has been maintained only through the brute force of the 25,000 Syrian soldiers who make up the major part of the Arab peace-keeping force in Lebanon.

For Israeli security reasons, it is impractical for Syrian forces to control the border area. At present, Israel does not tolerate their presence south of the Litani River, which at the closest point is about 30 kilometres from the border.

The aim of the Israeli advance is to provide a secure buffer zone, 10 kilometres wide, along the border. This strip will link up already established – and Israeli supported – Christian Falangist strongholds in the border area. There are indications that these strongholds helped the Israeli advance.

In addition, Israeli air and naval forces have been attacking supply ports used by the Palestinians, including Tyre. The aim is to eliminate bases in southern Lebanon.

The implications of the Israeli drive could be considerable for the Lebanese Christian forces.

Recently, I talked to a spokesman for former Lebanese President Camille Chamoun's National Liberal Party. He said at the time words to the effect that Palestinian presence had to be dramatically reduced or eliminated before the basic power-sharing problems in Lebanon could be resolved and recovery from the civil war achieved.

He did not know how this would be done, but thought it might be with the help of Israel – although of course, he was careful to point out the Lebanese Christians would prefer it some other way.

Did Israel provide this opportunity this week? Certainly it would not be surprising to see Christian Falangist-inspired fighting breaking out in other parts of Lebanon in a bid to eliminate Palestinian power in Lebanon once and for all. If this happened, perhaps Mr Begin would get a Lebanese Government strong enough to cope with controlling the south – a government based on the old and unjust power-sharing arrangement which would not have to contend with the Palestinian irritant.

Although the Palestinian presence was not the cause of the Lebanese civil war, it is widely believed that the fundamental issues could have been resolved much sooner and much more successfully without them.

Yet the Israeli advance seems in some ways to have played into the hands of the PLO. It was no coincidence that last weekend's bloody raid north of Tel Aviv by Al Fatah – the biggest Palestinian guerilla group , which is led by Yasser Arafat – came on the eve of Mr Begin's scheduled departure for Washington. The aim was to jeopardise any moves President Carter might have in mind which would bring about Israeli concessions allowing the Israeli-Egyptian dialogue to continue.

Certainly the Israeli drive into southern Lebanon, which was triggered by the attack, has made it more difficult politically for Egypt – as a part of the Arab world and a depender on favors from oil-rich States – to compromise.

On the other hand the terrorist attack has reinforced Israel Government thinking that withdrawal from the occupied territories other than Sinai is impractical for security reasons.

All along, President Sadat has demanded a declaration of principles which includes provision for Israeli withdrawal from all occupied territories.

So either the Israelis or the Egyptians or both have to compromise. And the events of the past week make compromise on either side unlikely.

Crusaders' castle still under siege.

DAVID BALDERSTONE, 'The Age' Middle East Correspondent, has just returned to Israel after a visit to the southern Lebanon war zone where invading forces are trying to crush Palestinian guerillas. He filed this report.

'The Age', Metulla (Israel) March 21, 1978

"Keep the car moving," the Israeli army escort said. "We keep moving on this road. It makes it more difficult for them."

As the car continued up the bare ridge-top road to the southern Lebanon town of Marjayoun, the Israeli pointed left. Out about six kilometres across the Litani River stands the hill-top Beaufort crusader castle.

Despite heavy Israeli bombardment, it remains a Palestinian guerilla stronghold. The road to Marjayoun is well within range of Palestinian 25-kilometre-range 130-millimetre cannon and Katyusha rockets.

"I think the Christian crusaders would never have expected their castle would be bombed by the Jews to get out the Moslems," the Israeli said.

Then he adds, almost nonchalantly: "Beautiful isn't it. Almost like Switzerland." To the right across the rich pastures of the Marjayoun Valley, was the snow-covered Mt Hermon range, in Syria.

Dairy cows were grazing beside the road. Beaufort Castle looked serenely beautiful.

With a French and German correspondent and the Israeli escort, I had left Israel's northernmost town Metulla, for a tour of Lebanon villages.

The night before, six Palestinian shells had fallen around Metulla. There had been no casualties, but a house had been damaged. The people had gone to the air-raid shelters for several hours.

Certainly, the Palestinian guerillas have caused the undoubted might of the Israeli defence forces continued problems. This is because of political-geographic restraints on the movement of Israeli ground forces but, probably more significantly, because Israeli defence forces are conventional armed forces. Unlike previous wars in which they fought conventional Arab armies, this time they were fighting guerillas.

The guerillas could never defeat Israel. But by hiding by day and moving and operating by night, they have caused problems for Israel since the Israeli drive into Lebanon was launched just after midnight last Wednesday morning.

The road to Marjayoun passes through two small villages. In the second village, Klea, two Christian Falangist Sherman tanks, which the Israelis gave the Lebanese Christians, were parked beside the road. Smooth young faces of boys who looked little older than 15 or 16, poked through the hatches in the armor. Although the Falangist forces have some very experienced senior officers, it is in some ways a boys' army.

Makram is 17. He is wearing an army uniform which is identical to Israeli army issue. He is a Falangist.

"For the past two years there has been no school in Marjayoun," he said as he leant against a shop window in Marjayoun's main square. "I have not gone to school for two years. I don't go to work. I am a Falangist. Yes I carry a gun."

Many of the buildings in Marjayoun have been damaged during the past two years of fighting between Christian and Palestinian forces. Small-arms fire has scarred most buildings, and many have been damaged by artillery and rockets.

It must have been beautiful, though. Most of the stone buildings were built 30-60 years ago and are French in style.

In the main square, a few shops were open and the people of Marjayoun were buying vegetables. The Lebanese traders will never lie down for long, and one man was selling tax-free cigarettes. They were proving a temptation for the tax-slugged Israelis.

Certainly it is no myth that the Israelis are extremely popular with the southern Lebanese Christian villagers. The Christians make it plain they welcome the Israeli advance into Lebanon. After fighting Palestinian guerillas for two long years, they are glad to see the Palestinians on the run.

"Well we are very happy, but we don't want the Israelis to stay here. We are Lebanese," Archbishop Sharer, the resident Greek Catholic archbishop, said.

After the Israeli advance last week Palm Sunday was something special for the Christians of Marjayoun. The Maronite and Greek Orthodox priests left some time ago, but the Greek Catholic archbishop had been holding regular services in a small chapel.

Christmas service could not be held because of Falangist-Palestinian fighting.

On Palm Sunday, a small candle procession was held through the streets of Marjayoun. But the service still had to be held in the small chapel, because the church windows have been broken by bullets.

On the archbishop's balcony, the burnt-out shell of a Katyusha rocket is lying. It had hit the roof of the building and caused considerable damage.

The archbishop said 1800 people lived around Marjayoun. About 500 Christians had been killed during the past two years of fighting.

Ill. 7. South Lebanon, Beaufort Castle on distant ridge, March 1978

UN force enters southern Lebanon
From DAVID BALDERSTONE

'The Age', Metulla (Israel), March 22, 1978

Iranian soldiers of the United Nations peace force moved into southern Lebanon today after threats of opposition from Lebanese Christians.

About 150 of the Iranian troops drove across the Israeli border in a convoy of about 20 trucks, to applause from Moslem villagers.

Falangist Christian militiamen posted at a roadblock inside the border let them through, despite earlier threats that they would resist the UN forces.

The Iranian troops formed the advance guard of the UN interim force for Lebanon, called into being by last Sunday's Security Council resolution.

The force's mission is to take over policing duties in southern Lebanon from the Israeli forces which invaded the area a week ago to stamp out Palestinian guerilla activity.

Earlier in the day the commander of the Falangists in southern Lebanon, Major Haddad, said his men would block the entry of Iranian troops.

"United Nations forces are not friendly to us," Major Haddad said. "In the past they have informed on us to the Palestinians".

The unilateral ceasefire proclaimed by the Israelis last night appeared to have held in most places.

In the early afternoon a burst of Katyusha rocket fire fell on northern Israel but caused no casualties or damage.

During the morning two UN officers in a car driving to an observation post were stoned by Christian militiamen near the village of Klea and forced back across the border into Israel.

A party of UN observers belonging to the newly established UN interim force in Lebanon will arrive in the area tomorrow from Nepal and Norway.

Although the area has remained quiet so far for the first time since Israeli forces moved into the area just after midnight last Wednesday morning, serious doubts are held here about how long the Palestinian guerillas will continue to hold their artillery and rocket fire.

Israel's Defence Minister, Mr Weizman, said last night Israel would return the fire if the UN-sponsored peace was violated by the Palestinian forces.

It is assumed here that the Palestinians' observation of the ceasefire so far has been in response to Syrian pressure on the Palestinian Liberation Organisation.

About 25,000 Syrian troops make up the major part of the Arab peace-keeping force sent into Lebanon to stop the bloody civil war.

Spokesmen for Christian Falangist forces in southern Lebanon, which have received considerable help from Israel during the past two years of continued Palestinian-Christian fighting, today expressed deep anxiety about probable Israeli armed force withdrawal from Lebanon.

The southern Lebanese Christians fear Palestinian guerillas will return to the area and attack them again if the Israelis withdraw.

In Metulla, Israel's northern-most town, the local council chairman, Mr Bialik Bielsky, a hotel owner, warned today that residents of the northern area would take steps to stop Israeli withdrawal from Lebanon.

"We will even consider lying down in front of the tanks and will not rest until we have 100 per cent security so that the murderers' shells will not be able to hit our settlements," he said.

The Metulla area again came under attack from Palestinian rockets and artillery yesterday before the ceasefire came into effect.

Metulla is only six kilometres from the Litani River – the line beyond which Israeli ground forces have not penetrated into Lebanon.

The UN force in southern Lebanon will total 4000 soldiers.

Give lands for peace: Israel rally
From DAVID BALDERSTONE

'The Age', Tel Aviv, April 2, 1978

Thousands of Israelis gathered in Tel Aviv's main square yesterday and called on the Prime Minister, Mr Begin, to moderate his policy for Middle East peace.

About 35,000 people took part in the demonstration which was held under the slogan "Peace is preferable to an enlarged Israel".

It was one of the biggest demonstrations ever held in Israel.

It demonstrated the huge and growing groundswell among ordinary Israelis who feel that a unique chance for Middle East peace, initiated by President Sadat's visit to Israel last November, is being lost by Israel.

It was not just a rally of young people and students. Old people and young people took part – many arriving by bus and truck from all over Israel.

Although many demonstrators said they were losing faith in the ability of any Israeli Government to cope with peace, the size of the demonstration has to be seen as an embarrassment for the Government.

The rally was organised by a group of reserve army officers who have formed the "Peace Now" movement.

The demonstrators have heard speeches from young army officers – no politicians were invited to speak – standing on a huge stage adorned with the banner "Shabbat Shalom" – Sabbath for Peace.

Most of the demonstrators were convinced Israel should make territorial concessions in the occupied West Bank territory – something Mr Begin's Government has so far steadfastly resisted.

Although he might try, Mr Begin will find it difficult to ignore the rally because the demonstrators were not a young, radical fringe, but people from all walks of life, most of whom have served and are serving in Israel's armed forces.

Israel's Cabinet went into regular Sunday session today to discuss Israel's next peace moves in the wake of Defence Minister Mr Weizman's visit to Cairo late last week.

Although there seems little prospect of the formal Egypt-Israel military and political peace committees being reconvened, there are strong indications that Mr Weizman and the Egyptians agreed to a continuing direct dialogue.

The emphasis will be on quiet – and, if possible secret – meetings between Egyptian and Israeli officials in contrast with the glare of publicity which has surrounded previous Egypt-Israel meetings.

There seems to be agreement in Cairo and Jerusalem that a direct dialogue, rather than United States mediation is the best way to break the deadlock.

....And who are the Arabs?
From DAVID BALDERSTONE in Amman

'The Sydney Morning Herald', April 4, 1978

'It is important for Palestinians to have a political, psychological, and legal link to a Palestinian State. For Palestinians it would be a focal point, a centre."

These are the views of Mr Rami Khouri, the American University-educated editor of the English language 'Jordan Times'.

Mr Khouri is one of four million Palestinians, by conservative estimates, which include 500,000 living in Israel and about 600,000 living in refugee camps.

Although the PLO and extreme Palestinian groups such as the Popular Front for the Liberation of Palestine officially hold to the view that Israel should be eliminated, it is difficult to find Palestinians – those not involved directly with these organisations – who do not favor the establishment of a Palestinian state.

There have been many indications that the moderates within the PLO's ruling council could be successful in removing the aim of elimination of Israel from the organisation's charter.

However – especially with Israel refusing to deal with the PLO – moves in this direction have been stymied because removal of this charter aim would involve recognition of Israel. But certainly it cannot be taken that the PLO would not accept a Palestinian state in part of Palestine and recognition of Israel.

Although such a state is strongly opposed by Israel, which argues it would be a security risk and could become a Cuba-style state on its back doorstep, it is a concept which is becoming widely accepted throughout the world.

"I have nothing tying me down. I have a good job, I am well paid, I have good friends, but I am living in an alien country. I would be the first one back if a Palestinian state were established," Mr Khouri says.

The most common proposal now is that a Palestinian state should be established in the West Bank and Gaza Strip territories occupied by Israel in the Six Day War of 1967.

Who are the Palestinians?

They range from professional people and wealthy entrepreneurs living in the Middle East and throughput the world, including Australia, to the refugees in the camps in Israel-occupied territory, Jordan, Syria and Lebanon.

Almost all Palestinians – rich and poor, educated and uneducated – support the Palestinian Liberation Organisation, although they naturally vary in their acceptance of terror tactics used by Palestinian guerilla groups. In 1974, the Arab summit meeting in Rabat appointed the PLO as the sole legitimate representative of the Palestinian people.

"We support the PLO because it provides a focus for our aspirations. The PLO is working for the restoration of the legitimate rights of the Palestinian people," a Palestinian academic living in the West Bank says.

"One doesn't necessarily approve of the killing of innocent people, but innocent people are innocent people all over the world." He was making the point that he considers the Palestinian people are innocent people harmed and exiled by the emergence of the modern Israel.

Palestinians vary in their views about whether a Palestinian state, if established in the West Bank and Gaza Strip, would satisfy their ambition to return to Palestine.

After all, a majority did not come from the occupied territories originally, but from territory inside the Israel borders set out in the 1947 UN partition plan, and land which Israel took over during its war of independence with the Arabs.

Mr Khouri says: "It is pretty clear that the Jews are not going out – not going to be sent back to Europe and other places from where they came. This is a historical reality. The Arabs have accepted the facts on the ground have been changed.

"What the Arabs and Palestinians would like in the long term is not the physical displacement of the Israelis, but a redrawing of the structures that govern all of Palestine. This is a long-term goal.

"In the short run there has to be devised a goal – a Palestinian state. In the long term Palestinians would like a democratic secular state in the whole of Palestine."

By their comments, it seems all Palestinians – West Bankers included – seem to view the establishment of a Palestinian state quite idealistically.

A teacher from Ramallah, near Jerusalem, says initially the state would have to be independent completely, but would then work closely in trade and other matters with Jordan and Israel.

He, like an apparent majority, does not favor an early link with Jordan in a federal system.

It is pretty clear that Palestinians feel alien in the Arab countries – even though most have employment, some are extremely wealthy, and many are in extremely important jobs, particularly in the rapidly developing oil-rich states. But they remain Palestinians.

In Jordan 60 per cent of the 2.8 million population is Palestinian. They hold key jobs and ministerial positions – although the number of Palestinian ministers has been reduced for political reasons since the 1974 Rabat decision.

About 90 per cent of big business in Jordan is controlled by Palestinians, according to a senior businessman.

All Arab states support the concept of self-determination for the Palestinian people. Although all Arab states flamboyantly indicate they want a Palestinian state established in the West Bank and Gaza Strip, their rhetoric can be misleading. For instance it is pretty clear the Jordanian Government would prefer the West Bank to become a Palestinian state federally linked to Jordan – rather than a national entity in its own right.

Part of the reason the Palestinians feel alien in Arab countries is that while Arab leaders vocally champion their cause, their actions have not always been so pro-Palestinian.

For example Jordan is the only country to have freely given Palestinians passports. Most West Bankers and refugees in Jordan carry Jordanian passports.

Obviously, West Bankers and Palestinians living outside Palestine – especially those in the refugee camps – have different problems, different views – although they all seem to want a Palestinian state.

The West Bankers have the problems, the humiliations of military occupation. The refugees in the camps live in poor conditions – although not at starvation levels – and have to live with the humiliation of being exiled.

"I think most Palestinians in the West Bank and Gaza Strip would be against the creation of a West Bank – Gaza Palestinian state if the Palestinians outside the occupied territories are not for it," says Dr Nafez Nassal, who is director of the Middle East Studies Centre of Birzeit University, near Ramallah.

"For this reason, Palestinians in the occupied territories have not formed a political leadership which could negotiate with the Israelis for a Palestinian state.

"The issue is Palestine and the Palestinians. We are inseparable from the Palestinians outside. We are inseparable from the PLO, which is the representative of the Palestinian people."

Although Palestinians want the establishment of a Palestinian state, all Palestinians would not necessarily want to live there.

Some, particularly those well established in Arab and other countries, merely want free access to all parts of the old Palestine: they want to visit the areas in which they grew up.

Amman April 11, 1978 (*To Mother and Aunt Ethel*)

Life throughout the fighting in Lebanon was quite normal in Jerusalem, Tel Aviv, Amman, and Damascus. They were all a long way from the fighting which was quite limited in area anyway. We spent the whole three and a half weeks in Jerusalem and the city was as beautiful and normal as ever. Only on two days did we go to Metulla on the border. Susan came to drive (insisted) because I had been working until 1 am both nights previously and had to leave on the four hour drive at 3 am.

The first day in Metulla there were a few rockets falling around the town. Of course, it is not a nice sound, but we were inside most of the time. That was the second day of Israel's invasion and the Israelis were going to take journalists into Lebanon that day, but they changed their minds because they said it was too dangerous. The second time in Metulla all was quiet, although the town had been hit a couple of times the night before. I did go into Lebanon that day. Luckily I met an Israeli soldier I had met previously in September in Metulla and he took me in. He is actually a management consultant but was called up because of the fighting. I drove in the Hertz car we had hired and another car with a French and German correspondent followed.

We got back to Amman a week ago yesterday. Everyone was concerned that we had been away so long and half thought the Israelis must have kidnapped us. Mohammed said he had been "very afraid" the Palestinians had got us. Curious that he, a Palestinian, should think the Palestinians rather than the Israelis might harm us. But I don't think he likes power brokers of any kind. For example he doesn't ever intend going on the pilgrimage to Mecca and Medina because he says how terrible it is that the Saudi Arabians make so much money out of it.

I was to see Crown Prince Hassan at 8.30 this morning but after I got to the Palace the prince rang and asked if it could be put off until this afternoon. He had more time then and wanted to have a longer talk. But just now, our neighbor who is also Prince Hassan's press secretary rang and asked me if I was free at lunch time, because the prince wanted me to join a lunch he is having and then have a talk afterwards.

After the interview part of the talk with the Crown Prince I said to him: "by the way, I don't know if I should ask you to help on this matter, but I have been having a lot of trouble arranging an interview with His Majesty." I said it seemed that if one was resident in Jordan it was a disadvantage because the officials could always say: "Well if you are resident you can wait until next week", which became next month. I am yet to find out whether it did the trick, but he said he would try to arrange it, and told his press secretary that "this is important, fix it." After his visit (*Ed: Crown Prince Hassan visited Australia in October 1977*), he is very interested in Australia.

After that he said: "By the way, I understand your wife is building a dig house for Hennessey in the Jordan Valley and is planning to use a wind generator." He said he was hoping to use a wind generator at his new "bungalow" near Petra and asked me to get Susan to pass on any information she had. I said she would and that she now thought it would be too expensive for the archaeologists, but that it might not be for him. He laughed and said: "Maybe if we order two they will give us a discount."

Israel mood gives hope: prince
From DAVID BALDERSTONE

'The Age', Amman, April 12, 1978

Jordan's Crown Prince Hassan has welcomed the growing groundswell of ordinary Israelis who want Israel to make territorial concessions in exchange for peace with Arab neighbors.

"The recent peace initiatives within the Israeli society appear to be quite heartening," the prince told me today.

"The concept of security plus compromise as a means of achieving peace is certainly one we all adhere to and certainly one hopes such realistic thinking can spread in Israel."

The prince was referring to the Peace Now movement in Israel which organised a "peace-in-exchange-for-territory" rally, attended by 35,000 people in Tel Aviv two weeks ago.

But Crown Prince Hassan, King Hussein's brother and effectively Jordan's No. 2 man – said he was gloomy about progress in the Egypt-Israel peace dialogue, which he said had hardly reached a starting position". He also said there was a "chronic need" for an Arab summit meeting.

The intransigence of Israel's Prime Minister, Mr Begin, had served the Arabs in a sense by showing the world how "narrow-minded" the Israeli Government was on the question of Israel's security. The military strength of Israel was superior to the combined military strength of Egypt, Syria and Jordan.

The prince said Israel's invasion to the Litani River in Lebanon made one wonder whether Israel expected to continue its water-resource planning by brute strength. He said Jordan's Yarmuk River basin had always been a cherished objective of Israel.

Like the Litani River, the Yarmuk River basin, in northern Jordan, was included in early Zionist plans for a Palestinian homeland for Jews.

"In the late '60s a statement by Israel's Foreign Minister Dayan said future generations would not forgive him unless he secured the heights overlooking the Yarmuk basin," the prince said.

"It is always the case of the next hill looking more attractive than the one they are currently sitting on.

"I think they probably have plans on the shelves for all these projects as the recent incursion into Lebanon showed."

He said that whether or not Israel's expansionist rhetoric became a real design probably depended on the success or failure of current peace moves.

"It has been characteristic of Israel to be very over-sensitive in terms of its water resource requirements," he said.

The prince said: "The recent Lebanese incursion, I think, was a very clear example of the fact that security for Begin – and Mr Begin's generation – is really a matter of keeping ahead of the Arabs in terms of use of physical strength as opposed to accepting to become part of this area."

A city fighting for its life
From DAVID BALDERSTONE in Cairo

'The Age', May 13, 1978

Cairo's Valley of the Dead is coming alive as the grand city of the Nile – choked by unrelenting population growth – fights its own drawn-out death.

From the Citadel Hill – on which stands the Mohammed Ali mosque – there is a commanding view of a slight valley running between Cairo itself and the Mukattam hills. Along this valley are streets of sandy coloured mausoleums and tombs.

From the height of the citadel it is not clearly apparent that the valley is alive – not with the ghosts of Saladin's Cairo, Ottoman Cairo, Napoleon's Cairo, or Mohammed Ali's Cairo – but alive with the poorest of the poor of today's Cairo.

South of this valley, King Farouk of Egypt got his final wish. It says a lot for the nationalistic revolutionaries led by President Nasser that after Farouk died in exile, they agreed his body could be placed in a family tomb in El Imam El Shafi'i mosque.

Ironically, now near the tomb of the king the 1952 revolution overthrew to place Egypt in the control of the Egyptian people – for the first time since the Persian conquest of 525 BC – the children playing are a constant reminder of the problems faced by today's Egypt.

In 1948, Cairo's population was 1.5 million. By 1966 it was more than four million, and how it houses more than eight million.

Cars have choked the city's roads; the telephones have failed, sewers and drains are constantly bursting. The elaborate buildings remain, crumbling, as a constant reminder of the grand Cairo of old.

It remains a remarkable and cosmopolitan city. The old families of European, Turkish and Egyptian origin, who made their fortunes before the 1952 revolution, continue to live in their large mansions in Heliopolis, Dokki, and on the Nile island of Zamalek.

Seven years after the death of President Nasser, many of the restrictions of the Nasser era have gone. The city is more relaxed – but more crowded – and the shops have come alive again with foreign and imported goods.

Tourism is booming. There is a shortage of first class hotels and it is almost impossible to get into the Nile-side Hilton, Sheraton or Meridian if one arrives without a booking. Most of the people staying in these hotels are businessmen – frustrated by an over-manned bureaucracy – or tourists who stay just a few days.

They see the tourist sites, are usually horrified at the decaying downtown area, and more than a little frustrated by Egyptian organisation.

But Cairo is what it is. I remember seven years ago going to the television centre beside the Nile when a friend was broadcasting over a radio circuit to London. After a two-hour wait and a disconnection immediately after contact was made, the frustrated broadcaster stormed to the control room and shouted: "You people talk about fighting an electronic war. You couldn't open a bottle of coca cola without spilling it."

The inevitable fuss which followed resulted in the foreign press chief saying: "You must be kind to these people."

One has to be kind and tolerant to Cairo to enjoy it.

Because of the hotel accommodation shortage, I have often stayed in the 70 year-old hotel, the Cosmopolitan, just off Kasr el Nil, in the business area. No one ever recommends the hotel, but it has some of the fading charm of old European Cairo about it. It was never in the class of old Shepheard's, which was burnt down by the nationalists as a protest against continued European – and particularly British – influence, or the continental Savoy.

The Cosmopolitan Hotel has a marvellous wood-panelled, English-style bar. Right next door to the stock exchange, near the major business houses, and only a short walk from the barracks which stood around the site of the Nile Hilton, it attracted a wide cross-section of Europeans and well-to-do Egyptians in its heyday.

There were businessmen, journalists, lawyers and army officers, although according to one aging Egyptian with an eye for rank, senior non-commissioned ranks usually outnumbered officers.

Any repertory theatre wardrobe would be delighted with the Turkish-influenced galabias the servants – and in view of the pittance they are paid they remain virtually "servants" – wear around the hotel.

But service remains service. Explaining I had to go to work early I slipped half a pound to the porter the other night with instructions to wake me at 5.45 am with tea. True to form, he arrived at my shabby room at 5.45 on the dot. I settled back to listen to the 6 am BBC news.

At 6.10, there was loud banging on the door. "Now don't go back to sleep, sir, remember you have to go to work early today," he said with a frown-furrowed brow.

After going through the elaborate procedure of checking out – inevitably in Egypt, in triplicate – I asked the Nubian reception man whether there were any rooms left tonight.

"Now sir," he exclaimed in horror. "Now you want to stay tonight?"

"No," I replied. "My plane leaves very late and if there is no room on it for me I might have to come back."

"No sir, you don't mean no room on the plane for you. You mean no seat on the plane for you."

Around the corner from the Cosmopolitan, past an Arabic food stall which competes with the putrid puddles from the broken underground drains for the dominant smell, is the stock exchange.

There are eleven stockbrokers operating five days a week at the Cairo stock exchange – and four brokers operating at the Alexandria exchange. The Cairo stock market has never recovered from the company nationalisations which followed the 1952 revolution.

Six months ago, 65 companies were registered on the Cairo exchange. Until the early '60s, when nationalisation became widespread, more than 300 companies were listed.

But the brokers – sitting around the round-tables and pillared operating chamber – are hopeful. President Sadat's open door investment policy is resulting in new companies being registered. Twenty-five new companies are expected to be listed in the next few months.

The 1952 revolution did not cause a slump on the exchange. "In fact, prices rose after the revolution and the market remained strong for several years," says one broker who has been operating on the exchange since 1928. "People didn't think so many companies would be nationalised."

Another haunt of old is the Cecil bar in Talat Harb Street. The brass railing around the bar has been kept sparkling mainly due to the efforts of a Greek barman who has worked there for 40 years. The British "Raj" has gone, but the place does well with a clientele of Egyptians, Sudanese, Saudi Arabians, and a few Europeans.

Cairo, which was something of a den of vice before 1952, became quite restrained and sedate after the revolution, mainly due to the almost puritanical and religious nature of some of the young officers, particularly Gamal Abdul Nasser. Most of the brothels closed, and the once erotic belly dancers restrained themselves to a sort of revolutionary code of respectability.

But, alas, you can't have increased foreign investment, westernisation and more tourists, without the habits of old reappearing. Now some of the belly dancers are throwing off their revolutionary restraint.

Someone always wants to sell you something. After leaving the Cecil late one night with another journalist, we jumped into a horse-drawn cab and as the cab went down Talat Harb towards the

Cosmopolitan, a man jumped from the gutter onto the running board. "Please sir, excuse me sir, like a nice clean girl?"

Neither the man's soiled Galabia nor the stench from the gutter from which he had emerged were any advertisement for a nice clean girl. Anyway, the tired old horse, who had seen it all before, had just kept walking and the man had fallen back into darkness.

Groppi's coffee parlour, chocolate shop and restaurant is still doing well on Talat Harb Square, although it is in need of a coat of paint. And Lappas, its main competitor 100 yards away, still has a delicious display of cakes in the window each day. They'll survive come revolution or revival. The only thing which could hurt them is the unlikely demise of the incredibly sweet Egyptian tooth.

The Turf Club lives on at a new location near the American University and New Shepheard's Hotel. The old Turf Club, which was in the grand old European quarter near Opera Square, suffered the same fate as old Shepheard's.

On January 25, 1952, it was burnt down in a spate of anti-monarchy and anti-European riots which preceded the revolution. When the rioting broke out, about 25 members stayed on drinking against the urging of the secretary. Ten members were burnt alive or killed.

But the spirit of a minority of members lives on in the new premises of the club. "Very good really. It needs a bit of work done on it here or there, but it is almost a second home for me here in Cairo," one of the English members told me quietly the other night.

"We try and limit the number of Egyptian members we let in. Now don't get me wrong. This is not racist. Just as there are Englishmen and Englishmen and Australians and Australians, there are Egyptians and Egyptians. After all, it is a club."

Sadly, the small but grand Opera House on Opera Square, which survived the pre-revolution rioting, was burnt down a few years ago. Its shell remains, but it is beyond repair. In 1970, I went to see a Russian ballet company performing at the Opera House. For two or three nights, the elegant Cairo of old was back, with women in long dresses and men in dinner suits. It might have been the last grand night for the sweet little French-influenced Opera House.

The open-door investment policy has attracted considerable foreign investment, but the factors not associated with financial regulation place a brake on foreign investment.

The instability of the area is a factor, but foreign investment is limited mainly by the fact that foreign businessmen find it difficult to operate in an environment in which the telephones hardly work, and where the bureaucracy is frustrating.

To its credit, the Egyptian Government is spending considerably more of its budget this year on completing half-finished projects. Previously, the emphasis was on starting new grand projects which took years and years to complete – if they were ever completed.

The extensive work on Cairo's telephone system is scheduled for completion late this year.

It is doubtful whether the increased foreign investment has helped the majority of poorer Egyptians who scratch a living cleaning shoes, guarding cars, making coffee, opening doors, and generally doing small jobs for small returns.

The main result of more investment flexibility coupled with soaring oil revenues in oil-rich Arabia, for these poor people, has been staggering inflation. This inflation, among other things, caused the food riots of a year ago, during which 60 people died.

Inflation is real. Six years ago I rented a small one-bedroom flat overlooking the Nile from Zamalek and thought the 15 Egyptian pounds expensive. Today, a similar flat costs around 700-900 Egyptian pounds a month – if one's lucky. That works out to about $A900 to $1200 a month.

Taxi meters are switched on usually, but unlike a few years ago when they were religiously followed, the sum which appears on the meter bears no relation to what you are asked to pay.

The proud Egyptians, full of fun, often show initiative – even when you would least expect it. Mohammed shines shoes just off

Kasr el Nil Street. He has fixed an electric bell to his blackened shoe box.

Unlike other shoeshiners, who tap the brush on the side of your boot when they want feet changed, Mohammed pushes the button and the bell rings out. But initiative doesn't come cheaply. Almost mimicking the rich men of Cairo who flamboyantly wear a silk handkerchief in their top pockets, Mohammed wears a 25 piaster note as an indication of the outrageous sum he expects.

As shoes are shined, donkeys – with their strap-worn haunches making them resemble some toy animal passed down to many generations in a family – walk past. They fight with hundreds of tooting taxis and cars for space on the road.

On the corner of Kasr el Nil and Sharia Sherif, a blind man stands selling lottery tickets, and a beggar sprawls on the broken and spit-spattered pavement, displaying the horror of his leg cut off above the knee.

Mohammed has seen it all before. He rings the bell and I weakly hand over 25 piasters. Mohammed smiles and his weathered old friend, who never misses the chance to tell you he knew Australians during the two world wars, says: "Dinky di bloody Aussie." And then with a look of feigned reluctance, he requests: "Cigarette?"

Ill. 8. Cairo Stock Exchange, May 1978

Amman May 1978 (*To brother-in-law Don*)

Don Dunstan was here about two weeks ago – another person following up invitations extended by Crown Prince Hassan during his visit last October. Quite a change actually, for his previous guests have been Rockman (a Jew) and Hawke (an Israeli supporter). We went to the Crown Prince's house for dinner during the Dunstan visit. I was asking him about the house and when it was built (it is in the same palace compound where Hussein's main office is although he doesn't live in the compound). The prince said it was built for the British Ambassador during the reign of Abdullah, "but I was fortunate to get it when it became inappropriate for the British Ambassador to be living so close to the Palace."

Learn from mistakes, Hussein tells Arabs
From DAVID BALDERSTONE in Amman

'The Sydney Morning Herald', May 30, 1978

Disputes between Arab and Palestinian leaders have become an accepted part of the quest for a Middle East settlement.

Now both sides may be able to resolve some of their differences if they heed the advice given in an essay written by King Hussein of Jordan.

The essay, a refreshing break from the continuous stream of propaganda from both sides, is an introduction to a new English language edition of the memoirs of King Hussein's grandfather, who was assassinated by a Palestinian's bullet outside the Al Aqsa Mosque in Jerusalem in 1952.

The memoirs are to be published by Longman's.

Although basically historical, the essay – read with developments in Middle East peace moves – gives a rather detailed view of past Arab mistakes which Arab and Palestinian leaders should heed in making decisions today.

Nothing in the essay is direct advice to Arab or Palestinian leaders in "do" and "don't" terms. Nevertheless, published as it is at the present crucial time in Middle East negotiations, King Hussein's historical comments provided strong lessons for the present.

On the Palestinian question the main point the king makes is that the Palestinian leadership in the past did a disservice to their people by failing to comprehend the reality and strength of Zionism.

He makes the point that failure to accept the fact of Zionism meant that the Palestinian leadership rejected early partition plans that would have left most of fertile Palestine in Arab hands.

In a comment with a lesson for today, the king says: "The extremist elements within the Palestinian leadership rejected it outright and since they possessed the gun, their counsel prevailed.

"It is often said that the Palestine question is a chronicle of missed opportunities. This is partly true, though not entirely.

"For judging in retrospect, it is my considered opinion, as it was my grandfather's, that the Zionist thrust and avalanche could have been blunted, but not entirely thwarted; morality and power politics do not in most instances match.

"The tragic undoing and dismantling of the Palestinian people, to which their leadership unwittingly contributed, was that they adamantly refused to understand or accept this unpleasant but elementary fact of life."

On his grandfather's assassination (King Hussein, then 16, was standing next to Abdullah when the bullet struck) the king is particularly bitter.

"And what pretext was used by those who were behind the assassin's bullets? That he had betrayed the Palestine cause. When things reach such an abyss of ugly wickedness, I sometimes wonder whether blind irrationality is not a more predominant trait in politics than rationality," he says. "Let me set the record straight, clearly and categorically. No country in the world likes to be partitioned and Palestine is no exception. King Abdullah was as opposed to the alienation of any part of Palestine as anyone else.

"But to him, moral judgement and personal beliefs were an exercise in futility unless backed by viable and adequate power, in the broad meaning of the term.

"The tragedy of the Palestinians was that most of their leaders had paralysed them with false and unsubstantiated promises that they were not alone, that 80 million Arabs and 400 million Muslims would instantly and miraculously come to their rescue.

"To me, as to King Abdullah, there is a golden rule in evaluating policy and in taking decisions. The first is to know thyself for this is pivotal in assessing your capabilities and your limitations.

"The second is know the enemy, for failure to do that can spell disaster. This is precisely what happened to the Palestine people and their rightful cause."

In his essay, it seems that King Hussein is arguing that historically it would be correct for the Palestinian homeland to be linked to Jordan.

"As is well known to those familiar with the Middle East, Palestine and Transjordan (as Jordan was known until 1948) were one entity, which in turn, constituted southern Syria," he says.

On splits in the Arab world, the king says: "I have struggled with all the means at my disposal to continue on the path of Arab unity.

"It is with profound regret that I find myself impelled to state that the same forces of negativism, disarray and selfishness which had obstructed the efforts of earlier generations are still very much evident and active.

"Persons and personalities have in many instances changed, but erroneous orientations and malicious machinations have not."

Later he adds: "Is it any wonder then that the Arabs over the past quarter of a century, and in spite of their considerable potential, have not achieved anywhere near what they should have achieved?

"With a disunited Arab world in the real and meaningful sense, with instability more often the rule than the exception, and with regimes changing with rapidity and regularity, how could any nation go very far?"

The overriding impression gained from King Hussein's essay is that the Arabs and Palestinians should learn from past mistakes if they are to be realistic in finding a solution to the Middle East crisis.

A terror campaign against Syria's ruling sect
from DAVID BALDERSTONE in Damascus

'The Sydney Morning Herald', June 7, 1978

Syria's Alawite community – the small and secretive Moslem sect to which President Hafez Assad belongs – is being shaken by a continuing terrorist campaign against its influential members.

In the past two years at least 15 members of the sect have been assassinated. The latest victim – a relative of President Assad – was gunned down on the doorstep of his Aleppo, North Syria, home about two weeks ago.

Although there is little doubt the campaign is directed against President Assad's leadership, there are no outward signs the terrorists are succeeding in undermining his position.

However the campaign is causing grave concern obviously, both to the leadership and the Alawite community.

Although there are divisions and deep jealousies between the religious groups and tribes in Syria, which to a lesser extent than neighboring Lebanon remains somewhat feudal, there is more behind the terrorist campaign than the fact the President is an Alawite.

The Alawites are his protection. Although no observer would ever rule out the possibility of President Assad being overthrown, it is generally conceded it would be extremely difficult.

This is because the President is surrounded by three circles of protection. The first two circles – the presidential guard and Damascus security – are almost exclusively made up of Alawites. The third circle – the armored divisions around Damascus – is not under the command of the Alawites but Alawites make up a significant number of the officers.

Of course, more than this, there are no signs of popular opposition to President Assad. He is the first man to have provided

Syria with any stability since it gained independence in 1946. In the 24 years between independence and Assad's bloodless coup in 1970, there were 21 successful and unsuccessful coups.

Although in the past two years Syria – in common with many countries – has gone through an economic pinch following two years of financial boom, there is no widespread criticism of the President.

The last victim of the anti-Alawite campaign was a warrant officer, Jaber Suleiman Issa, a relative of President Assad. He was hit by five bullets in the stomach and two in the head as he was leaving his Aleppo home.

Two days later, according to an unconfirmed report, the Alawite father of the commander of the People's Army was also shot at outside his Aleppo home – but the gunman missed.

Although Jaber Suleiman Issa was a warrant officer, who according to stories in Damascus had significant business interests on the side, he held a key intelligence position.

A Syrian Government official laid the blame for the anti-Alawite campaign squarely on Iraq. Iraq and Syria have extremely poor relations because of a dispute stemming out of jealousies between the two countries' ruling Baath parties. Therefore Iraq is an easy target for blame.

Others put the blame for the campaign on the Soviet Union, which – although Syria's arms supplier – has an uneasy relationship with the independent Assad regime, and Right-wing Lebanese groups, who now oppose Syria's post civil war peace-keeping role in Lebanon.

Almost every Middle East development is officially described in Syria as a "conspiracy" – for example Sadat's peace initiative was a conspiracy between the United States, Israel and Egypt to undermine the Palestinians and Arab unity. Therefore it is reasonable for the anti-Alawite campaign to be blamed on external forces.

But judging by the Syrian authorities' lack of success in stopping the assassinations, it is rather clear the authorities have not got to the bottom of the problem. And it is more likely the campaign is the work of Syrian opponents of the President.

Whoever is behind the campaign it is clear they are exploiting old religious divisions in Syria.

The Alawites come from the fertile coastal strip in Syria, north of Lebanon. The area takes in the port city of Latakia, Baniyas, and Hama. Their geographical position has led to many ties between the Alawites and the Lebanese Maronite Christians, and their religious practices include many Christian elements.

The Alawites were nurtured by the French when they ruled Syria – partly on a divide-and-rule basis and partly because the Alawites were considered an intelligent minority which could be trusted.

They have been traditionally looked down upon by the Sunni Moslems, who make up 80 per cent of Syria's population of eight million. (Although Assad is an Alawite, most Syrian Cabinet Ministers are Sunni Moslems.)

Generally there have been two main thrusts of Alawite development in society – through the armed forces, particularly the Air Force, and in teaching and the universities.

Almost all the Alawites assassinated have been either academics or military personnel – and most have had close connections with the President.

Miss Liza becomes a queen
From DAVID BALDERSTONE

'The Age', Amman, June 16, 1978

King Hussein and his new American-born queen are spending a few days in Jordan's resort city of Aqaba before flying to a quiet honeymoon in Europe following their marriage yesterday.

In a four-minute Moslem ceremony, King Hussein, 42, married 26-year-old Miss Liza Halaby and immediately proclaimed her queen. The wedding – the king's fourth marriage – was held in the Zahran Palace, the king's mother's Amman residence.

Following their engagement last month, Miss Halaby took the Arabic name Noor Halaby. She is now Queen Noor of Jordan.

King Hussein's second wife, English-born Princess Muna, attended the reception in the palace garden yesterday.

She was not proclaimed queen because their marriage coincided with the height of Nasserist Arab nationalism and it was thought inappropriate to have a non-Arab as queen of an Arab kingdom.

Princess Muna stood only about a metre away from Hussein and his bride when the couple cut their seven-tiered wedding cake.

Watched by about 500 guests and pushed by dozens of photographers, the king cut the cake with a regimental sword. Under the weight of the sword and the pushing of photographers, the cake rocked on its table.

Queen Noor, a Princeton University-trained architect, worked in Sydney in 1974-75. She came to Jordan 15 months ago and worked as a design manager for the Royal Jordanian Airline, Alia.

She is the daughter of Mr Najeeb Halaby, who was the US Federal Aviation authority administrator in the Kennedy Presidency.

Mr Halaby's father came from Aleppo, Syria, before emigrating to the US. It is thought this Arab connection had a bearing on the king's decision to proclaim his new wife queen.

King Hussein divorced his first two wives. His third – the Palestinian Queen Alia – died in a helicopter crash 16 months ago.

Amman June 1978 (*To eldest brother John*)

H.M., as those in the know call His Majesty King Hussein, and Queen Noor had just cut the wedding cake. About fifty photographers – mainly French, Italian and American who all crave after royalty having none of their own – were in something resembling a rugby scrum in a bid to capture the happy couple on their films. They had already knocked over a wheelbarrow decked with flowers and looked like taking on the wedding cake. There I was under the oak tree and coasting, as you would have said, on my fifth glass of Pepsi cola. The Crown Prince, Prince Hassan, caught my eye and waved. I waved back with a slight break at the waist and a reverent nod of the head, as one does in such circumstances. Thinking little more of it, I continued coasting. Next the well-groomed head of palace protocol pushed through the scrum and said to me that the Crown Prince wanted to see me. I followed him back through the scrum; the Crown Prince took me by the arm, and immediately we were next to H.M....

"Your Majesty," as the Crown Prince oddly calls his brother, "I would like you to meet the only Australian journalist in the Middle East."

Already high on Pepsi and dazed at having to become so involved in the wedding cake ceremony I thought frantically that I must not call H.M. "Your Highness", which as you would know, would be something resembling indignity.

"Your Majesty," I said confidently. "Congratulations."

I left the palace feeling what a wonderful family wedding it had been. It all ran so smoothly. It seemed it may have been rehearsed one, two or three times before.

I was, let me point out from the start, not an invited guest. I was there to capture the event for my newspapers. More than 100 journalists and photographers had flown in especially and were asked the day before to wear as dark suits as possible. The Jordanians always get the press ready for such events so early one feels exhausted before the fun starts. This time we had to wait outside the garage for about an hour and a half before we were let in. The press looking, as it turned out, as elegant if not more elegant than the invited guests stood around outside for a while and then, under pressure of the hot sun, sat down on the gutter of the road. It was the first time I had sat in a gutter in my new blue suit, so the day was quite an experience all round. Then we were ushered in and after a photographer session we were roped off in a corner of the garden. Rather nice really. Our side of the party seemed to be going much better partly because the drinks and savouries had to pass us on the way to the invited guests. After a while security became more relaxed and we could move into the invited section and pass the odd "Your Excellency", but most found it more relaxed on our side and retreated behind the deep red rope.

*****

Two days before Menzies died, Mohammed our loyal servant said to me: "you know Robber Menz."

"Yes," I said.

"Prime Minister of Australia wasn't he. Well when Nasser take Suez Canal the French and the British were much talking and shouting, and Robber Menz goes to Cairo to talk to Nasser. Of course, he didn't say it in Cairo, because there would have been much trouble, but when he got London he said he would like ring Nasser neck. Then Nasser much laughing."

Two days later I told him Menzies had died, and Mohammed then much laughing, not I think because the poor man had died, but because he was so pleased with himself knowing so much about Australian prime ministers.

"Perhaps," I said, "Menzies and Nasser will meet again up there." I pointed upwards.

Mohammed pondered a long time and then said: "Nasser was good man; I don't think he would have travelled down."

The inference seemed to be that he thought Menzies might have.

Israeli stall kills peace hope
From DAVID BALDERSTONE, our Middle East correspondent, in Amman

'The Age', June 23, 1978

Despite the statement by Egypt's President Sadat that Middle East peace moves will continue, Israel's vaguely non-committal response to American questions on the future of the West Bank and Gaza Strip seems to rule out any possibility of progress towards a comprehensive settlement during current peace efforts.

Furthermore, the Israeli response probably rules out the small chance there was of Israel securing something resembling a separate peace with Egypt under the guise of a framework towards a comprehensive settlement.

In Jordan, the reply serves to confirm King Hussein's view that he was right not to join the Sadat initiative.

In Damascus, the Palestine Liberation Organisation headquarters, and hardline Arab capitals it serves to confirm leaders' views that they were right and President Sadat wrong all along.

In the moderate Arab capitals, it will go a long way to persuading leaders that Sadat must renounce his initiative, for the sake of Arab unity.

In Cairo, it will increase tensions in the army and the community – especially coming as it does, after President Sadat's crackdown on political freedom.

In short, peace seems to most observers in the Arab world to be further away now than it was before Mr Sadat visited Jerusalem last November.

Now it seems that the only hope of getting the peace show back on the road is a miraculous breakthrough during shuttling by the US assistant secretary of State, Mr Alfred Atherton, which is expected to resume shortly, or during visits to the area by Secretary of State Cyrus Vance and Vice-President Mondale.

And as Arab officials concede, with US House of Representatives and Senate elections in November, there is little chance of anything that could be construed as pressure being put on Israel to force a move towards meeting Arab demands.

President Sadat and Israel's Prime Minister, Mr Begin, are widely seen as playing the same game: procrastination, a contest about as tortuous as marathon dance contests.

Mr Begin is motivated by his unwavering desire for Israel to hold on to the West Bank – for Biblical and security reasons. "Between the sea and the Jordan there will be Israeli sovereignty alone," said the Likud Party's platform for the last election.

Mr Sadat, it seems, keeps talking about peace – and about his initiative being more dramatic than man landing on the Moon – because he can't afford not to.

The question that arises is: does Mr Sadat believe his position would be jeopardised if he declared his initiative a failure, thereby allowing moves to resume towards a Geneva-style peace process, involving the Soviet Union, Syria and Jordan?

After his crackdown on political freedom, his warlike comments placating an obviously restive army, and his difficulties with critics including two former Foreign Ministers, a still-prestigious former editor, and now a senior diplomat, no one could be blamed for thinking he does.

Israel's vague statement on the future of the West Bank came in reply to two questions put by the US.

First, Israel was asked to clarify whether at the end of the proposed five-year local self-rule period it would be prepared to resolve finally the issue of West Bank sovereignty.

Secondly, it was asked how it proposed allowing West Bank residents to participate in the determination of their future.

The reply was in three parts.

First: "The Government of Israel considers it vital to continue the peace-making process between Israel and her neighbors."

Second: "The Government of Israel agrees that five years after the application of administrative autonomy to Judea, Samaria (Biblical names for the West Bank) and Gaza, which will come into force upon the establishment of peace, the nature of relations will be considered and agreed upon at the suggestion of the parties."

Third: "For the purpose of reaching agreement the parties will conduct negotiations between them with the participation of representatives of Judea, Samaria and Gaza, as elected under the administrative autonomy plan."

The kindest thing that can be said about the statement itself is that it "avoided" giving a clear indication of Israel's long-term intentions on the West Bank and Gaza, occupied areas which all Arabs – including Mr Sadat – demand must be returned to Arab sovereignty under a comprehensive peace settlement.

But it also raised the question of when the five-year period would start and therefore end. Does the term "come into force upon the establishment of peace" mean that the Arabs have to sign peace treaties five years before their land claims will even be considered? This is a question being asked in Arab capitals.

Also, who are the parties – apart from Israel and West Bank and Gaza representatives – deemed to have the right of negotiation after five years? Do they include some representatives of Palestinians in the Diaspora?

If they don't, it is hard to see any solution to the Palestinian problem, and therefore the Middle East dispute.

The Israeli Cabinet approval of the reply, which was reached 14 to one with four abstentions, was regarded as a victory for the hardliners. Significantly, the one vote against approval was that of Defence Minister, Mr Weizman, who favored a more positive reply. The four abstentions were by Democratic Movement for Change Ministers.

After 30 years punctuated by war, Israel would face security risks if it accepted the Arab demand and withdrew to the pre-1967 borders, which give it a width of 15 kilometres at its narrowest point.

But the point a growing number of Israelis, including the Peace Now Movement, are making is that Israel needs to be more flexible in negotiations. The Israeli reply to the Americans merely played into the hands of Arab hardliners and opponents of President Sadat.

So where should peace efforts be directed now?

King Hussein of Jordan, who could hardly be called an Arab hardliner or pro-Soviet, has for several months called for the involvement of the Soviet Union, which, in effect, would mean a return to moves towards a Geneva process.

Because the Soviet Union supplies arms to Syria, the PLO and Irak, it is hard to see any peace moves proceeding unless the Soviets feel themselves to be fully involved. The chance that an early breakthrough after the Sadat initiative would draw in Israel's other Arab neighbors has long since gone.

The problem with the Egyptian-Israeli dialogue (excluding other Arab neighbors) was that neither side was in a position to take risks, to play their cards in negotiations.

Maybe Mr Sadat's initiative was, as he says, more dramatic than man's landing on the Moon. But the astronauts came back to Earth – a planet, Mr Begin and Mr Sadat should remember, on which the Soviet Union plays a large part and on which the Palestinian sore remains festering.

The veil begins to lift
From DAVID BALDERSTONE

'The Age', Amman, June 1978

A chronic labor shortage in Jordan and some other countries is providing considerable impetus towards equality of women in Arab society.

A seven-day regional conference for Arab women, held under the auspices of the economic commission for Western Asia – has just finished in Amman. During the conference a regional plan of action for the integration of women in development was drawn up.

The conference dealt with wide-ranging problems facing women in Arab countries.

The fact that their recommendations will get attention by many Arab countries is not so much a reflection of official recognition of the injustice of the unequal position of women, but rather economic considerations.

Women are needed in the labor force.

This is the case in Jordan. High salaries in the oil-rich Gulf States and Saudi Arabia have lured a considerable proportion of Jordan's skilled manpower.

"In 1973, the Arab world faced a third war with Israel, which was followed by the well publicised increase in world prices of oil," Jordan's Crown Prince Hassan, honorary chairman of the conference, told the delegates.

"In the labor market, for example, demand for Jordanian manpower began to increase in such a way as to nullify the tremendous efforts that went into its training.

"We have therefore concentrated on the principle of increasing supply, which means a greater integration of women in development activities."

Not only, the Crown Prince said, were women less likely to emigrate to the oil-rich Arab states, but also the added income they provided the family in Jordan could significantly reduce the incentive for the man to seek employment outside the country.

The conference made no attempt to set priorities for action when drawing up the regional plan. The plan is essentially a long checklist of things which should be done to improve the status of women in the area.

Illiteracy is a major problem highlighted in the report. In the region, the average illiteracy rate is around 47 per cent of the total number of males aged 15 and above, but exceeds 70 per cent among women.

"One study of the literacy situation reveals the relatively slow progress being made in female compared to male education in Arab states in general," the report says.

"However efforts made to promote girls' education are clearly reflected in the increased proportion of girls enrolled at various educational levels in the Arab countries. These rose from around 14.3 per cent in 1960 to around 25 per cent of the total in 1975."

The report says Arab history give many examples of women prominent in the fields of science, politics, law and literature but "there is a residue of spurious values and attitudes that has accumulated during the periods of decline and stagnation of the region's culture".

Arranged marriages are still widespread – particularly in less developed Arab countries.

The report proposes Governments implement laws specifying a minimum marriage age, and setting down men's and women's rights to choose freely their partners.

Also the report urges that a programme should be carried out in the area to educate boys and girls "towards their equal responsibility in the household, in child care, and in other family matters requiring the participation of couples in decision-making".

There was little doubt about the interest of Jordan's Crown Prince in the conference. He was present at almost all sessions and took an active part.

But whether such interest will be shown in the development of women's role in other Arab capitals remains to be seen.

Amman June 30, 1978 (*To Mother & Aunt Ethel*)

I was in Beirut two weeks or so ago and was taken by the PLO (*Palestinian Liberation Organisation*) to see the "Zionist aggression" at Damour about 20 minutes south of Beirut. They wanted me to go to the south but a taxi all day to the war zone is expensive and anyway I have seen the "Zionist aggression" many times before and it all tends to look the same. Broken building after broken building. Anyway at Damour, we picked up a PLO militiaman with his rifle to guide us up the hill. My guide wanted to introduce me and said:

"What is your name again?"

"David."

"Jewish name."

"Yes, and Christian name."

"Second name?"

"Balderstone."

"Another Jewish name."

"No, I said, BaldersSTONE."

"Same thing. Stein in German, Stone in English.

"Maybe, BUT I DON'T THINK SO."

"Yes but not matter. The Revolution has many Jewish friends."

*****

About two months ago when I was in Cairo, I had one taxi driver on and off for three days. On the way to the airport, I saw a little boy with a badly mangled arm and with half his face missing. So to stop him pestering with his poor terrible head being poked into the window, I handed out some piasters very quickly.

"You have a very big heart, Mr David," said the driver. He then asked how many children we had. I said: "None."

"You not only have a very big heart, but also a very big head. You are very wise Mr David. I have six and every night they wake me up crying."

He was the first Arab I have ever heard say anything like that.

Lebanon: a war that won't stop
DAVID BALDERSTONE, our Middle East Correspondent, reports from Amman

'The Age', July 11, 1978

Behind the current crisis in Lebanon, which threatens to spark a direct clash between Israeli and Syrian forces, lies the re-emergence of the ambition of the Maronite Christian minority to reassert its control over the feudal country.

This ambition is in direct conflict with the objectives of the Syrian Government, which sees its aim of exerting influence over the country best served through a stable and balanced government in Lebanon.

For six days last week Syrian forces, which entered Lebanon as the major part of the Arab peace-keeping force less than two years ago and brought the bloody two-year civil war to an end, pounded the main Christian militias around Beirut in an attempt to bring the Maronite political leadership back into line.

The fighting drew a warning from Israel that it would not stand by and watch the Syrians crush its Maronite Christian allies, whose influence in Lebanon is seen as crucial if Lebanon is not to become a potential confrontation State on Israel's northern border.

After Israel reinforced its warning by flying two warplanes low over Beirut and Lebanon's President Sarkis threatened to resign, the fighting subsided.

But nothing has been solved so far as the Christians and the Syrians are concerned. The risks remain high of full-scale fighting erupting again.

No one is taking lightly the risk of a clash between Syrian and Israeli forces. Throughout the weekend the Syrians were on high alert, and the Israelis built up troop strength along their border with Lebanon.

Ironically, Syria brought an end to the main civil war less than two years ago by fighting on the side of the Maronite Christians, who looked like being defeated by the Leftist Moslem-Palestinian alliance.

At that stage, the Syrians feared a Christian defeat would pave the way for a radical Palestinian-Moslem State, which could jeopardise the position and influence of Syrian President Assad's regime and increase the risk of Syria being involved in a war with Israel at a time not of its own choosing.

Now the situation has reversed. Spurred on by low morale among the Moslem political leaders and the feeling that the Palestinians have been weakened by their March struggle with Israel, the Maronites are pushing to reassert their pre-war dominance.

During the civil war the Maronites talked about the Palestinians as an occupying force in Lebanon, but now they direct their accusations about occupation at the Syrian peace-keepers.

Since he became President in 1976, with the approval of the Syrians, Elias Sarkis has been very much the man in the middle.

Under the Lebanese system, the President must be a Christian, the Prime Minister a Sunni Moslem, and the Speaker a Shi'ite Moslem.

Sarkis, a former banker and bureaucrat, is a Maronite without a wide political base of his own. Without a strong army in a land of private militias where the gun remains the law, he has been a President without much power.

His threat to resign came after two years of desperately seeking to steer a middle course through Lebanon's political jungle and at the same time take directions from Damascus.

In an attempt to rebuff accusations that they are occupying Lebanon, the Syrians insist that it is President Sarkis who directs the operations of the peace-keeping force.

For Sarkis, discouraged enough by the lack of progress towards national reconciliation, last week's fighting was almost the last straw.

No wonder. There he was, a Maronite, but supposedly in charge of the peace-keeping force that was fiercely pounding the Maronite militias.

For some time the Syrians have been annoyed with the two main Maronite leaders, former President Camille Chamoun and Falangist chief Pierre Gemayel. They consider they have not shown enough gratitude for the Syrian help at the end of the civil war.

When the Government of Prime Minister Selim Al-Hoss resigned two months ago, Chamoun and Gemayel were instrumental in blocking efforts to form a government of politicians representing the main power groups in Lebanese politics.

The main tactic used by the Christian establishment during the period following the resignation of the technocrat Al-Hoss Government was to call for an all-parliamentary government.

That sounds fine in principle. But elections have not been held in Lebanon since 1972 – and have been put off until 1988 – because of the civil war and none of the Leftist leaders is in Parliament.

The attempt to form a politicians' government failed, and the Al-Hoss Government was reinstated.

For their part the Syrians, after bringing the civil war to an end, let their contacts with the Maronite leadership slip. Their main contact remained with the third main political Maronite force, former President Suleiman Franjieh and his son Tony.

Coinciding with the re-emergence of their aim to regain control of Lebanon, Mr Chamoun and his National Liberal Party, and the Falangists led by Mr Gemayel, took an increasingly anti-Syrian public stand. The Syrians, who had saved them in the war, had become an obstacle to their ambitions.

Suleiman Franjieh, however, refused to join the other Maronite leaders against Syria, and this caused a deep rift in the Right-wing Christian Lebanese Front.

Franjieh has long been considered pro-Syrian. Once after shooting dead a number of people during a political feud, he had to seek refuge in Syria and stayed much of the time with the family of Hafez Assad, who was to become President of Syria.

The crunch in the Syrian-Maronite crisis came last month when Falangist militiamen murdered Tony Franjieh, a good friend of both President Assad and his brother Rifaat Assad.

Although the Maronites have long feuded among themselves, the murder seems to have been at least partly in reprisal for Suleiman Franjieh's refusal to join the other Maronites in their anti-Syrian stand.

The murder was the final straw for the Syrians. They were determined to teach the Maronites a lesson. Hence last week's fierce fighting, and with it the threat of a direct Syrian-Israeli clash.

Living with war in the street
From DAVID BALDERSTONE in Beirut

'The Age', July 17, 1978

On Rue Hamra in West Beirut shops are full of local and Paris fashions. The aroma of fresh pastry, Turkish coffee and cognac surrounds pavement cafes and young men walk up and down admiring their reflections in shop windows.

Here, in daytime Beirut, only the presence of Syrian troops manning checkpoints, Palestinian and Leftist militiamen loosely handling their Kalashnikov automatics, and the occasional rat-tat-tat of fire from somewhere not too far away, reminds you Beirut is a divided city.

A few kilometres away, in the predominantly Christian East Beirut suburbs of Ain Remmaneh and Ashrafiyeh, no reminder is necessary.

Although there was relative calm in Ashrafiyeh late last week after the bloody six days of Syrian-Christian clashes of the previous week, nothing resembled normal.

Shutters were down on the scarred and burnt-out buildings; almost the only people to be seen were jeans-clad teenage Christian militiamen, and the silence was often broken by long bursts of machine gun fire.

It is difficult to telephone across the divided city and nearly impossible to persuade a West Beirut taxi man to drive across the "green line", which divides the city, into East Beirut.

"Not for a million dollars will I drive to Ashrafiyeh. For nothing I will go. I will never come back," said one driver. However by weekend, a trickle of Christians from the eastern suburbs had begun to come out of the safety of cellars and basements to brave the crossing to work in West Beirut. Such is the resilience of the Lebanese.

But talk to anyone in Beirut – politicians, and Palestinian officials – and they all say last week's relative lull in Christian-Syrian fighting was only a respite, the calm before another storm.

While President Elias Sarkis' weekend decision to withdraw his threat to resign may prolong the period of relative calm, and ease tension, it is nothing like a guarantee that trouble will not break out again. The problem is that the underlying issues which prompted him to resign have not been solved.

The overall leader of the Christian militias, Mr Bashir Gemayel, son of the Falangist leader, Sheik Pierre Gemayel, said last week: "Whether President Sarkis resigns or not is no consequence whatever. The truth is one doesn't give up powers one doesn't have."

Ironically, the Syrians, who ended the main civil war by fighting with the Christian militias to balance the power of the Leftist-Palestinian alliance, are now lined up against the Christian militias, whose leadership has thrown the fragile political balance out of kilter by trying to exert their pre-war influence over the country or else seek the country's partition.

The Syrians, who now have more than 30,000 troops in Lebanon as part of the Arab deterrent force, fear partition because it would lead to the establishment of a Christian State. This could be allied to Israel and with a Moslem Palestinian state in the south, could embroil Syria in a war with Israel at a time not of Syria's own choosing.

How much influence Syria wants to exert over Lebanon is an unknown quantity – and an issue of much argument in the Middle East. Although Syria believes that historically Lebanon is part of Syria, there is no concrete evidence to suggest Syria's involvement in Lebanon is anything but designed to restore stability and balance to the war-torn country.

Israel has already warned it will not stand idly by and see her Christian allies crushed by Syrian might. However, most diplomats in Beirut tend to the view that if – as could easily happen – Christian- Syrian fighting breaks out again in earnest in the next days or weeks, Israel will be reluctant to do any more than carry out a token warning or operation.

These diplomats argue that Israel would be reluctant to interfere in a major way for fear of prejudicing the renewed peace talks with the Egyptians.

However, Israel has almost certainly taken the past week's respite to help re-arm the two main Christian militias. These are the Falangists and the Tigers militia of the former Lebanese President Camille Chamoun's National Liberal Party.

Senior Western diplomats in Beirut have joined Lebanese newspapers in stating that Israel has been sending arms to the Christians through the port of the "Christian capital" Junieh, which is 16 kilometres north of Beirut. The supplies have been mainly small arms with some anti-tank weapons.

The bitter clashes of the past fortnight were the third major Christian-Syrian armed encounter this year. After each battle the morale of the Christian militiamen has remained high, and their leaders in no way consider the last bout to have been a defeat.

It is unlikely the Syrians will continue to tolerate this situation, although any further Syrian involvement may be tempered by Syria's concern about a direct clash with Israel.

The last bout ended when President Sarkis threatened to resign and the Israelis sent fighters low over Beirut at supersonic speed in a warning to the Syrians.

In spite of the decision by Mr Sarkis to stay on as president, it is hard to see that any of the root causes prompting his resignation threat have been resolved. It really will be something if, in Lebanon's political jungle, Mr Sarkis secures effective control of the Syrian troops; persuades the Christian leaders to go anywhere towards disarming their militias, allows Lebanese army personnel to take up positions within their strongholds, and restricts the Palestinian armed presence to certain areas of the country.

But then, the country has waited long enough for a miracle.

Certainly the eeriness of East Beirut is no cause for optimism. Although the taxi driver would not go to East Beirut for a million bucks, he did agree to take me to the "green line" so I could get to an appointment at the offices of Mr Camille Chamoun in Ashrafiyeh.

"Walk over to those taxis and they will take you – they know the way," the taxi driver said after a quick U-turn had pointed his car back towards the safety of West Beirut.

It was a lonely walk to the taxis on the other side. A driver who was used to making his money out of taking risks said he would go to the Chamoun headquarters.

After passing the burnt-out former headquarters of the National Liberal Party and an office of the Tigers militia, the driver was suddenly waved down by two militiamen behind sandbags who had their guns aimed up the street away from the taxi.

As the driver reversed quickly around the corner, bursts of automatic machine gun fire could be heard coming from up the street. The two militiamen returned the fire.

The driver willingly agreed to turn back. This calm before the storm was not at all calming – and a warning of what is expected to come.

Syrians angry at Camp David talks
From DAVID BALDERSTONE

'The Age', Cairo, August 11, 1978

Hopes of gradual moves towards rapprochement between Egypt and Syria have been undermined by the decision of the Egyptian President, Mr Sadat, to attend the Camp David summit next month.

The Government-controlled Syrian press has reacted angrily to President Sadat's decision to attend the summit with President Carter and Israel's Prime Minister, Mr Begin, beginning on September 5.

Accusing the Egyptian President of "high treason", the Syrian press says Egypt is heading towards a separate peace agreement with Israel.

Saudi Arabia's Crown Prince Fahd – effectively the ruler of the oil-rich kingdom – last week visited Egypt, Syria, Jordan and Irak in a bid to heal the rift in the Arab world which developed after President Sadat visited Israel last November.

Although little has been said publicly about the degree of success of the mission, it is understood senior officials – particularly in Jordan and Syria – felt progress had been made towards rapprochement between Egypt and Syria.

It was believed in Jordan that Syria – preoccupied with its problems in Lebanon – has qualified its demand that President Sadat renounce his initiative as a failure.

Also, President Sadat's reluctance for further meetings with Israel following the Leeds Castle talks had been welcomed by senior officials in Jordan and Syria who believe Arab unity cannot be achieved while Egypt continues negotiations with Israel.

It is understood the Egyptian Foreign Ministry is planning to send envoys to several Arab capitals in the next week to explain the reasons behind President Sadat's decision to go to Camp David.

Foreign Ministry officials believe President Carter's decision to invite President Sadat and Mr Begin to a summit indicates that the United States is prepared to do more than act as a mediator.

The Egyptians want the United States to put forward its own suggestions on how peace can be achieved.

"We view this step as an expression of the role of America as a full partner in the peace process and realise that the next step will be the start and not the end of the road," Cairo's semi-official daily, Al Ahram, said today.

The US special Middle East envoy, Mr Alfred Atherton, arrived in Saudi Arabia last night for meetings with the Foreign Minister, Prince Saud.

The city of waters goes thirsty
From DAVID BALDERSTONE in Amman

'The Age', September 16, 1978

In the Old Testament, Amman is described as a "city of waters". It is ironical because one of the major problems bugging the rapidly expanding Jordanian capital in recent years has been a shortage of water.

Unlike Cairo on the Nile, Baghdad on the Tigris, and Damascus on the legendary Barada, Amman is built on seven hills on the edge of the Arabian desert. Because of this, it is more a truly Bedouin city than other great Arab capitals.

Until after World War I when Emir (late King) Abdullah – King Hussein's grandfather – made Amman the capital of Transjordan, it was a village of 2000 people. Now the population is 850,000.

Even today, most of Amman's water supply comes from the same springs which were used by the Ammonites (around 1200 BC) and by the Romans. It is not surprising that the springs which made it a "city of waters" in Biblical times have not been able to provide enough water for the present-day population.

But for the Ammonites and Romans – just two of the major occupations of the site – the pure spring water plus the hilly terrain made the principal hill, Jebel Qala, an ideal site for a defensible city.

In the Old Testament, Amman is called "Rabbah" or "Rabbath Ammon", and during the Roman period it was "Philadelphia" – one of the great cities of the Decapolis.

Rabbath Ammon was the scene of drawn-out battles between the armies of King David and the Ammonites, who were often assisted by Syrian forces. Perhaps it is not surprising in this area where history repeats itself, but modern Amman's population expansion has been due considerably to the Arab-Israeli dispute.

Before the establishment of Israel in 1948, Amman had a population of around 200,000. With the influx of Palestinian refugees and natural expansion, the population had more than doubled by the mid-1960s. The Six Day War in 1967 pushed more people across the River Jordan to Amman and the refugee camps in Jordan.

The last major unnatural population growth was due to the civil war in Lebanon. An estimated 100,000 Lebanese have made Amman their home.

Although Rabbah or Rabbath Ammon is first mentioned in the Bible in Deuteronomy, it is in the Second Book of Samuel that the fascinating intrigue of Biblical times comes alive in Amman.

Shortly after King David came to the throne around 1000 BC, King Nahash of Ammon died. David sent servants and messengers to console the new King Hanun on the death of his father.

However Hanun's advisers persuaded him that David was sending the servants and messengers as spies before attacking the city. So David's men were seized and given most humiliating treatment. Half their beards were cut off and the bottoms of their garments were cut away.

David was incensed and sent Joab with an army to avenge the insult. Eventually, after several drawn-out battles, David's armies captured the city.

According to the Bible, most of the Ammonites were burnt alive by King David's men.

Amman was occupied by the Nabataeans for a short time in the first century BC. However they were driven out about 30 BC by Herod the Great. After the Roman conquest the city was replanned on a grand scale.

After a period of flourishing Islamic development during the seventh and eighth century AD the population gradually declined and the city was finally abandoned.

Around 1880, the Turks, who used the nearby city of Salt as their capital of the area, settled a small community of Circassians in Amman. But Amman did not flourish again until Emir Abdullah made it his capital after World War I.

Little remains in Amman today of the pre-Roman occupations. There are two rather crumbling Ammonite watch towers, but little else. The Ammonites had 13 of these towers around their city to warn of attack.

The most impressive of the Roman monuments still standing is a 6000-seat Roman theatre in the downtown area beside Jebel Qala – or the citadel.

It is still used occasionally and is a favorite spot for today's Ammanites. However, the dank smell of urine on the higher tiers prompts the question whether the Romans had a better public toilet system than exists today.

The hilly terrain which made the area so attractive a position for the early occupations has caused havoc for traffic planners in Amman.

During peak hours, traffic jams can be as bad as could be expected in a city three times the size. Consequently, there is growing movement of businesses away from the downtown area to the flat, long hill-tops, which remain predominantly residential.

Although it has a stark desert attractiveness about it, Amman is hardly a beautiful city. It is very much a desert-edge city and rapid development has scarred the surrounding landscape.

But it is a rather comfortable, although expensive, city in which to live. Western goods are freely available and supplement the excellent locally grown fruit, vegetables and meat.

In common with most Arab capitals, the bureaucracy can drive the most patient person to despair. To collect a parcel air-mailed from Australia the other day, I had to go to five counters at the post office – each had a function in clearing the parcel. The whole operation took more than one hour.

To be fair, all the Jordanian Government departments have highly skilled and efficient people. But often they are hard to find.

Telephones, international telex and the electricity system work reasonably well and shortly – with water soon to be pumped from the just-completed King Talal Dam – the water problem should be eased.

To cope with the water problem, each house in Amman has one or two cubic metre tanks on the roof, which are filled from the mains twice a week. For the rest of the week the houses rely on this tanked water – and there are problems if it runs out.

However, the Lebanese civil war fired rapid development and a lot of new buildings – although connected to the mains – cannot draw water because the pressure is too low. Water has to be trucked.

The Lebanese influx sent rents sky high and caused a great deal of uncontrolled development.

However, the mayor of Amman, General Ma'an Abu Nuwar, who was installed in the job two years ago to smooth development of the city, is confident about the future. He believes the city services, which have been severely strained in recent years, have been upgraded sufficiently. With the help of US experts, the municipal administration and the Government are working on development plans.

Amman is around 60 per cent Palestinian – although official figures are hard to come by because of the sensitivity in the Hashemite kingdom.

According to a senior businessman about 50 families control free enterprise in Jordan. "Some might say 100 but I think it would be closer to 50."

Of these families, he estimates 90 per cent would be of Palestinian origin.

Although rapid expansion has meant the growth of several areas of extremely poor residential accommodation, it is a reasonably modern and clean city.

It is proudly Arab. Arab kaffiyehs or headdresses usually top off Western clothes. The smell of Arabic food pervades the downtown area. But what Amman is not today is a "city of waters".

Middle East Encounters 179

Ill. 9. Roman Theatre Amman, September 1978

World's eyes are on Hussein now
DAVID BALDERSTONE in Amman

'The Age', September 20, 1978

Around mid-afternoon on Monday a young American woman diplomat delivered to Jordan's Crown Prince Hassan the texts of the agreements signed by Egypt and Israel at the end of the Camp David summit.

Soon afterwards the worried-looking Crown Prince, with the texts in his satchel, took the wheel of his Mercedes and drove to the airport to meet his brother, King Hussein.

After the royal Boeing landed the two brothers embraced briefly and then set off, accompanied by senior officials, for long discussions – talks at which perhaps some of the hardest decisions of Hussein's 26-year reign would have to be considered.

Both the King and the Crown Prince would have been aware that all eyes were on their reactions to the Camp David agreements.

From the United States there would be pressure to join in negotiations with Israel towards a Jordan-Israel peace treaty. From Jordan's northern neighbor, Syria, from the Palestine Liberation Organisation and from much of the Palestinian community in Jordan, would come pressure against.

The Camp David outcome has drawn angry Syrian and Palestinian reaction – and increased speculation about a major Syrian-Israeli clash in Lebanon.

And, given the timing of previous outbursts of increased Palestinian guerilla activity, there are considerable risks of a build-up of guerilla attacks against Israel in a bid to stymie the agreements.

This might seem an unduly pessimistic view of events which could follow the summit, which was all about peace and preventing war, but it is too easy to impose Western rationale on Arab politics.

What makes the coming weeks so difficult for King Hussein is that he not only has to consider his own reactions but also the reactions of Syria and of the Palestinians who make up 60 per cent of his country's population.

Also, while the summit resulted in a declaration of principles for a comprehensive Middle East peace, there are a number of areas in which the agreements fall short of long-held Arab demands.

Leaving aside the expected angry reactions from Syrian and PLO officials, the agreements were greeted with pessimism in the Arab world. The resignation of Egypt's Foreign Minister, Mr Kamel, did nothing to alleviate this.

Jordanian leaders are weighing up whether the guidelines for peace go far enough for Jordan to risk the economic penalty of its border with Syria being closed and hostile Palestinian reaction.

"The last thing the King wants is to find himself negotiating with Israel while at the same time West Bankers demonstrate with placards saying he doesn't speak for them," said one Jordanian.

A new life for the Bedouin
From DAVID BALDERSTONE in Amman

'The Sydney Morning Herald', September 23, 1978

Traditionally the nomadic Bedouin of Arabia saw themselves as far superior to the settled villagers they traded with and plundered.

More and more, however, drawn by the unrelenting pressure of Arab development and pushed by lack of health and education services and diminishing income, the Bedouin are opting for a settled lifestyle.

A survey just published in Jordan reveals that the heads of most Bedouin households in the country don't, ideally, want their children to have to follow them in scratching a living in arid areas.

These fathers have realised that the best future for their children would be gained by moving closer to the modern urban centres, where their children would be educated and prepared for jobs outside the traditional Bedouin lifestyle.

Both by design and by the seemingly irresistible forces of modernisation, the Bedouin of Jordan are being drawn into a new, settled lifestyle so quickly that, before long, the truly nomadic tribes will be a thing of the past, according to the survey.

The survey is the work of four academics, including the Dean of Jordan University's economics faculty, Dr Kamel Abu Jaber, a former Government minister. Some 20 academics and 60 university students helped.

The survey is based on questionnaires completed in more than 35 locations throughout the country.

Although there have been many Government attempts in Jordan and other Arab countries to settle the Bedouin, they have often met resistance.

Today, economic considerations are making inroads where Governments failed.

The process has been spurred on by the fact that the gravitation of settled peasant villagers from rural areas to the large cities has left the Bedouin without his traditional trading partner. He has been left with little choice, and has followed suit by moving to the cities or establishing small permanent settlements throughout the Badia – the area he inhabits traditionally.

The Bedouin make up about 7 per cent of Jordan's population of three million. There are eight main tribes, some of whose descendants wandered to Jordan from Iraq and the Hejaz area of Saudi Arabia. One tribe claims descent from the prophet Mohammed.

Today's Bedouin population has been severely affected by the migration to the urban areas of young men. Although these men return to their families part of their income, this migration has resulted in labor shortages, leaving women and children to do the work.

The survey reveals marriage to be almost universal for women, the average marriage age being 17.8 years. Each woman produces an average of seven children, but 15 per cent of all Bedouin children born alive die before they reach their first birthday.

The report says that the average life span for the Bedouin is 50 years. This compares quite unfavorably with that of Jordan's population (not including the West Bank population) which is 64 years.

Thus, the principal conclusion which can be derived from the survey data is that the recent improvements in the health of the East Bank (Jordan, not including the West Bank) population has not been shared by the Bedouin population living in the desert regions.

Men appear to be a good deal healthier than women, possibly because of the better health care provided through the armed forces, or because of better nutrition during infancy and adulthood.

"Considering the scarcity of sources of assistance – doctors, health clinics, social service centres and other rural assistance agencies – it is a tribute to the resilience of the Bedouin community that is as large as it is today, and in moderate physical shape," the report says.

The bulk of the diet for both adults and children consists of cereals. Protein and mineral-rich foods are not common.

As would be expected, the education standard of the Bedouin is well below Jordan's average national standard: "in addition, it seems that the upcoming generation will not attain very much higher education levels than those reached by its parents because of the low school-attendance figures, particularly for young adolescents."

Lack of nearby schools – particularly schools which take girls – is a major reason for the low standards.

Another reason quoted in the report is that some parents so not consider that schools teach skills required for Bedouin life. Also some parents fear that if their children are educated, they will be lost to the Bedouin workforce.

Australian digs for key to old puzzle
From DAVID BALDERSTONE in Amman

'The Age', September 30, 1978

World-renowned Australian archaeologist, Professor Basil Hennessey, of Sydney University, is hopeful excavations he is to begin in Jordan this year will produce a library of tablets throwing considerable new light on the middle and late Bronze Ages.

Professor Hennessey has been in Jordan making final preparations for excavations at Pella – locally called Tabbaqat Fahl – in the Jordan Valley.

"Pella is one of the most important sites in the Near East. There is evidence of continuous occupation from the Neolithic Ages (8000-4500 BC) to the medieval period," he says.

"The site is mentioned sufficiently in Egyptian records of the middle (2100-1650 BC) and new kingdoms (1580-1075 BC) to lead one to hope that Pella will produce a library of tablets."

Professor Hennessey, who is Edwin Cuthbert Hall Professor of Middle Eastern Archaeology at Sydney University, led an excavation which discovered and recovered wall paintings dating back more than 6000 years at another site in the Jordan Valley last year.

They are the second oldest wall paintings recovered.

During Roman times, Pella – on a knoll overlooking the Jordan River – was famous as one of the cities of the Decapolis. Although little excavation has taken place at the site, it is considered to be at least as large as the city of Jerash, one of Jordan's best restored tourist attractions.

The excavations at Pella are to be the joint project of Sydney University and Wooster College Ohio. Professor Hennessey says the project, expected to last at least five years, will keep Australia in the forefront of world archaeological research.

"Probably it will be the first time there has been co-operation between two major institutions on a major site," Professor Hennessey says.

"We are rapidly approaching the time when to tackle a major site is becoming beyond the resources of any one institution."

The combined budget – of which the Australians are raising half – is around $120,000 for the first year of excavations. The Australian funds have come from the Australian Research Grants Committee, the Australian National Gallery and Sydney University.

"Sydney University has had long experience of archaeological exploration in the Near and Middle East. The Pella project will mean the addition of a great deal of material to Australian museums and universities," Professor Hennessey says.

"The site is huge and has the remains of a great many impressive buildings of the Hellenistic (332-63 BC), Roman (63 BC-324 AD) and Byzantine (324-640 AD) periods.

"In conjunction with the Jordan Department of Antiquities, the joint expedition is hoping that some of these buildings can be reconstructed during and after the excavations." The Jordanian authorities are hoping the site will one day become a major tourist attraction.

Professor Hennessey will begin excavations shortly after Christmas. Twenty-five experts from the university will work on the site for an initial season lasting until March, 1979, when a team from Wooster College will take over for a season of similar length.

Professor Hennessey's Australian co-director on the dig is Tony McNicoll, who joined the university last year after a period as director of the British Institute of Afghan Studies in Kabul, Afghanistan.

The Wooster College expedition will be led by Professor Robert Smith, who carried out two brief seasons of pilot excavations on the site in 1967 and 1968. One of the main reasons the site has not been touched since 1968 is that the Six Day War of 1967 put it in a militarily sensitive area of Jordan.

"Although each university will have its own season and areas of excavation, the explorations are designed to complement each other leading to joint publication of the work under the aegis of both institutions," Professor Hennessey says.

Professor Smith and Professor Hennessey have made final plans with Jordan's Director of Antiquities, Dr Adnan Hadidi. They visited the site to inspect the construction of the permanent dig headquarters, which have been designed for Professor Hennessey by Melbourne architect Susan Balderstone (my wife). The Jordanians plan to turn the building into a museum after excavations have finished.

"From the time of the middle Bronze Age, Pella is known to us from a great many historic references," Professor Hennessey says. "It was known to the Egyptian pharaohs of the 12th and 18th dynasties as Pihilu, the capital of an important principality. Its history continued unbroken through the Iron Ages and it was renamed as Pella by the followers of Alexander the Great."

Professor Hennessey says a major aim of the excavation will be to produce a totally reliable historical sequence of events during the different occupations of the site. Also, he hopes a full environmental survey of conditions existing at the time of each settlement will be compiled.

Palestinians closing ranks
From DAVID BALDERSTONE in Amman

'The Age', October 3, 1978

Ironically, in the two weeks since the Camp David summit, the accords have proved the catalyst for strengthening and unifying the very organisation that they omit to mention – the Palestine Liberation Organisation.

For the first time since the 1970-71 civil war in Jordan, King Hussein has told PLO leader Yasser Arafat that he is prepared to renew relations with the organisation on a "sound basis", according to PLO officials.

The radical leader of the Popular Front for the Liberation of Palestine, Dr George Habash, has moved towards reconciliation with the mainstream of the PLO and with Syria.

And the two weeks have brought a multi-million dollar contribution to the PLO from Algeria and Libya.

But it is the next two weeks which many observers see as the time for concern.

With Egyptian and Israeli officials due to begin hammering out details of a peace agreement next week, the risk of Palestinian groups dramatically stepping up guerilla activity is being taken seriously in the Middle East.

It is understood that extra security measures are being taken in Israel, Egypt and Jordan, which fears that guerilla activity across the Jordan River could prompt Israeli retaliation.

Extreme Palestinian officials have also indicated that US installations in the Middle East could be at risk.

The chairman of the Palestine National Council, Mr Khalid Fahoum did not rule out this possibility when I talked to him in Damascus.

Mr Fahoum, a diplomat and politician, is not a member of any of the Palestinian guerilla groups. "They (the guerilla leaders) don't consult me. I don't know whether there will be any action against American installations. But, of course, if the US continues to ignore the Palestinians then anything can be expected," he said.

The obvious cause for concern within the PLO about the Camp David accords is that it is not given any role.

This in itself is not surprising, as Israel has long refused to deal with the PLO. Even if the PLO removed its chartered aim of eliminating Israel, it is hard to see a change in Israeli attitude – at least for many years.

But more than this, PLO officials are angered by the accords because they see them as leading towards a separate Egyptian-Israeli peace treaty, but not towards a solution to the Palestinian problem or the establishment of a Palestinian State.

They fear a separate Egyptian-Israeli peace treaty because it would neutralise a major chunk of Arab military and negotiating muscle.

The accords have left the PLO's leaders in something of a dilemma, however. Initial reaction indicated that the more moderate leaders would be forced into hardline positions, but this is by no means considered certain now.

It is being argued in some quarters that the accords are an irreversible step along the negotiating path which will require Palestinian leaders to moderate their positions if they are to benefit. This would be especially so if Jordan decided to join negotiations with Israel and Egypt on the future of the West Bank.

Dr Habash, a Christian Arab, resigned from the PLO's executive committee in 1974 over the very question of whether the Palestinians' future was negotiable.

A rejectionist, Dr Habash had already brought the Palestinian cause to world attention – it was his Popular Front that introduced airliner hijacking as one of the weapons in the struggle.

Dr Habash quit the PLO executive committee when a 10-point phased political programme was adopted giving Yasser Arafat the right to negotiate for the setting up of a Palestinian State on any part of Palestine.

Although the programme rejected negotiations on the basis of UN Security Resolution 242 (which treats the Palestinian issue as a refugee problem), it was too much for Dr Habash. It amounted to a compromise because it meant that the PLO could aim at a State not covering all of Palestine.

Dr Habash has been out of favor in Syria, where he was jailed in 1968. But moves towards reconciliation with Yasser Arafat and Syria gained momentum at the hardline Arab summit in Damascus two weeks ago.

According to officials at the summit, the meeting was not bugged by the usual animosity between Arafat and Habash. And Habash stayed on after the summit for meetings with Syria's President Assad and other officials in order to cement a new relationship with the Syrian regime.

But although the Habash-Arafat and Habash-Syria reconciliations are important, the Iraqi-based Palestinian groups still remain outside the PLO mainstream.

Khalid Fahoum said Algeria and Libya committed something less than $1000 million, which would go mainly to the PLO and Syria, at the hardline summit.

"In my opinion Algeria and Libya could have participated in a bigger financial way, but sometimes in politics you have to take the longer path," he said.

Amman October 24, 1978 (*To Mother*)

I was pleased you liked my story on Amman, City of Waters, but surprised you should ask if there was a good research library in Amman. The inference seemed to me that how would David, a moderate scholar at best, have known all those biblical references? As you said you wrote that part of the letter at 6.30 am I conclude that my godmother (*Aunt Ethel*) was still asleep. She would have been shocked with you. After all, why do you think I used to call her the reading machine? It was because she always used to read me the Bible. As she said to me in those days: "Know thy facts and verily, verily I say unto you, you will find a place in the Holy Land one day." Over the past 18 months I have sometimes regretted she was so correct.

I am not infallible though, and checked my references at the British Council Library. They have a very good two volume dictionary of the Bible, which gives every city's biblical references – amongst other things. Bit of a fag for those like me who know the Bible though, because with this book anyone can look a scholar. I wouldn't be at all surprised if Mr Begin and President Carter – those biblical scholars on the world stage – seek out the same volumes at the British Council in Jerusalem and Washington.

I expect to be going to Baghdad next week for the Arab summit conference. I went to the Iraqi Embassy yesterday about a visa, but typically the first man I saw wasn't very helpful.

"I am an Australian journalist based in Amman and I want to go to Baghdad to cover the Arab summit."

"Fine," he said. "The visas take 21 days to get."

"Well thank you very much for your help but in 21 days the summit will be over."

Much thinking on his part. I then suggested that I see the ambassador. In the event I didn't see the ambassador but the counsellor, who was very helpful. He expects to be able to give me a visa tomorrow – but I will believe that when I see it. But with, as they say: "that capitulationist Sadat playing into the hands of Zionist imperialism in the current phase", I think they will be handing out visas to journalists. What with all those "children, political dwarfs and pygmies" meeting in Baghdad it could be quite interesting. I sometimes wonder how well Arab political leaders get on together, that is of course, when they are getting on together.

*****

Mohammed asked me about my mother and father the other day. I told him my father had died when I was small and he said: "Very bad." But in an effort to cheer me up said: "Robber Menz dead too." Then he asked about you:

"Is she strong?"

"Yes."

"Stronger than Lady (Margot – Susan's aunt who had recently been staying with us)?"

"Yes."

"Good. So she can do much walking."

Peals of peace from Bagdad
From DAVID BALDERSTONE in Bagdad

'The Age', November 10, 1978

It could be that the Arab leaders – back home in their palaces and presidential residences – are laughing at the obscurity of their Bagdad summit's final communiqué. If they're not, they should be.

Here in Bagdad they managed to agree on some significant decisions without appearing really to do so. The moderates, led by Saudi Arabia's Crown Prince Fahd – hardened their attitude to Egyptian-Israeli peace, and the hardliners became more moderate.

For example Irak, a leader of those Arab states previously opposed to any negotiated settlement with Israel, and PLO leader Yasser Arafat have put their names to a communiqué which is widely seen as implying the summit's de facto recognition of UN Security Council Resolution 242.

This key Middle East resolution affirms the right of every State in the area – including Israel – to exist. Passed after the 1967 war, it also calls for the withdrawal if Israeli forces from occupied Arab territories.

Although accepted by Egypt, Jordan, Syria and Lebanon, it has not been publicly accepted by the rejectionist states, including Irak, nor by the PLO. The PLO's main objection to resolution 242 has not been that it recognises Israel's right to exist – albeit on the pre-1967 borders – but that the resolution treats the Palestinian issue a refugee problem rather than a political problem.

The moderate view also prevailed on the question of condemnation of President Sadat and the United States. Neither were criticised in the final communiqué – and, more than this, neither were mentioned by name.

But the hardliners did not come out the losers.

They secured the summit's agreement "not to approve" the Camp David agreements and the Palestinians' right to their own State.

The summit agreed to reaffirm the 1974 Rabat summit decision appointing the PLO the sole legitimate representative of the Palestinians.

Also, the summit agreed to punitive economic measures being taken against Egypt if a peace treaty is signed with Israel. Although details have not been made public, Western diplomats in Bagdad believe this includes Saudi Arabia's agreement to withdraw aid to Egypt if a peace treaty is signed.

In short, while deciding "not to approve" the Camp David agreements, all Arab governments have decided to face the fact that the Camp David agreements have seemingly irreversibly altered the Middle East equation.

With Egypt preparing to sign a peace treaty with Israel, the rest of the Arab world has been forced to agree on a strategy designed to make the best of the bad lot of losing Egyptian military and negotiating muscle.

The summit's apparent de facto recognition of Resolution 242 adds strength to moves by Jordan and Syria to get the question of an overall settlement to the Middle East crisis resolved through a Geneva-style conference.

The summit's feeling on Resolution 242 is interpreted from a short passage in the communiqué which states; "The summit confirmed the Arab nations' obligation towards a just peace based on full Israeli withdrawal from all Arab territories occupied during 1967...."

Can this mean anything else but that the rejectionists have agreed not to be rejectionists anymore? The fact that they agree "a just peace" can be based on full Israeli withdrawal from all Arab territories occupied in 1967" can hardly mean anything other than they accept a negotiated settlement; that they accept Israel's right to exist on pre-1967 borders.

However the communiqué does not state in words that the summit agreed to accept Resolution 242.

But if Yasser Arafat builds upon this communiqué and gets full PLO agreement to recognise the UN resolution, it will remove the main objection the United States has against formal relations with the organisation. In effect, such recognition would supercede the PLO's chartered aim of eliminating Israel.

The PLO's formal acceptance of Israel's right to exist would also remove Israel's main public objection to negotiating with the PLO.

Although all leaders did not attend the summit, all Arab states except Egypt were represented. The only leaders not present who were important to the Arab-Israeli equation were Saudi Arabia's King Khalid and Libya's Moammer Gaddafi. But King Khalid was represented by Crown Prince Fahd – effective ruler of the oil-rich kingdom – and Libya sent a delegation.

There are two main conclusions to be drawn from the summit. First, by deciding "not to approve" the Camp David agreements, the summit has made it considerably more difficult for Jordan to agree to negotiating the future of the West Bank.

These negotiations were envisaged in the "framework" for overall peace in the Camp David accord.

Second, if the communiqué prompts further action then a Geneva-style peace conference seems the obvious outcome. And, if the PLO builds upon the communiqué and formally accepts Resolution 242, Israel could be fighting an uphill battle if it continues to refuse to deal with the PLO.

Amman November 21, 1978 (*To Mother and Aunt Ethel*)

I returned almost two weeks ago from Baghdad and the Arab summit. It was a very cheap trip because the Iraqis paid all hotels, telex, drinks, and international telephone calls for the 600 journalists who attended. They must have more oil than sense. I was going to stay with the Australian ambassador (at his invitation), but my plane didn't arrive until 3.30 am and with late night meetings etc. I decided it would be easier to stay in a hotel.

After lunch a day or so later I went across the road (to the embassy) and spent a couple of hours with the commercial counsellor, then got back to my hotel about 7.30 pm wanting to do some work. I was fairly tired because Yasser Arafat had given a press conference the previous night at 2-3.30 am and then I had to get up early to write a story on the end of the summit. But when I entered the hotel, my guide rushed over to tell me "some good news".

"Mr Sweden and Mr Kenya - we have sent them to another hotel, so now you are the only journalist staying with us," he said.

"How nice," I said. The Kenyan and the Swede had been the only people speaking English.

"Yes, I thought they were a bit imperialist," I said, making a joke of the Iraqis' constant allegations of Zionist-imperial plots and conspiracy. They got the joke, and there was much laughing. I was about to go upstairs to start work.

"Now you are the only one left so hotel is putting on special dinner for you and us." The other Baath Party officials, with their moustaches turned down around their lips, nodded in excited anticipation. It was an invitation I could not refuse. The dinner started at 10pm. It seemed to me that they had wanted me to come to dinner so they could order Scotch, beer, brandy and charge it to the government. And they did.

"Who is the best Arab leader?"

"Which is the best Arab country?" I don't see why it should be me who is chosen to make the Iraqis see sense, so I gave them the answers they wanted. After each satisfactory answer, one of the five would come around the table – already charged with half a bottle of brandy – and shake my hand elaborately.

But it was my observation that if the Shah was overthrown Israel's supply of oil from Iran might be cut off that did the trick. The official opposite, who I didn't realise spoke English, nodded slowly and said: "You are very clever, Mr David."

I was one of them. They offered me Marlboro cigarettes, but I said I couldn't smoke those American imperialist cigarettes.

At 1.30 am, the man drinking brandy started singing in Arabic. He then stopped and said:

"Now you sing Australian song."

"I don't think so."

"Yes you must," they said in chorus.

"No."

"Yes."

"If you sing another Arabic song, I will sing an Australian song." Of course he sang.

So at 1.45 am in the Sahara Hotel, Baghdad, before an audience of Baath Party officials, I took my feet. I sang two verses of Waltzing Matilda. There was much applause. "Now it is very simple. The words are just Waltzing…."

"'alzing."

"Good, now Matilda."

"'ilda." Then we all sang "'alzing "'ilda together.

Then at 2 am as we said goodnight, I asked what time the bus tour was leaving for Babylon the next morning. They told me I must be downstairs at 6.30 am. I knew it would be running a bit late so got down at 7 am. No one to be seen. Most likely they were all still nursing their sore heads. The bus finally left the hotel at 9.30 am.

*****

I spent quite a bit of time with the Kenyan journalist, who told me his father didn't think it was very good him being a journalist. Journalists spend too much time in bars etc. It seemed a bit familiar and I concluded this was a multi-racial prejudice about journalists. He lives in Nairobi and has a holiday farm beside Lake Victoria. He said the swimming was very good now because they have got rid of most of the crocodiles on the Kenyan shore. "Mingusa, I inquired, "what do you do if a crocodile comes along while you are swimming?"

"What do you mean what do you do! Nothing. They just eat you".

President's coma leaves Algeria in limbo
From DAVID BALDERSTONE our Middle East Correspondent

'The Age', December 22, 1978

For more than a month Algeria's President Houari Boumedienne has been in a deep coma with two blood clots on his brain. And the question is: what happens now?

President Boumedienne's failure to appoint either a Vice-President or a Prime Minister – as provided for under the 1976 national charter and constitution – has left Algeria without an heir apparent.

Government of the country is being carried on by the remaining eight members of the Revolution Council. It has been predicted this council could continue to provide stability – in the short term at least.

Colonel Boumedienne, 51, a leader in Algeria's fight for independence from France, came to power in 1965 in a bloodless coup which overthrew Algeria's first President, the national hero Ahmed Ben Bella.

Under the constitution a Presidential election must be held within 54 days of the death or resignation of the President. In the interim, the head of the National Assembly, who cannot be a Presidential candidate, acts as Head of State.

Middle East observers have been wondering how long the present limbo period can last. Clearly the President is not able to resign.

Although there is no heir apparent, the Foreign Minister, Abdul-Aziz Bouteflika, 41, must have a chance of being a future President. He is the only Algerian politician – other than Boumedienne – of any international stature.

The council now ruling is made up of six civilians and two military officers. They are all that is left of Boumedienne's original

26-member Revolution Council. The others have either died or faded from politics. Boumedienne, an austere, determined, and secretive man, has fiercely pursued a policy of making Algeria a modern industrial State. He has never been linked with any scandals of corruption or graft.

Algeria, which is rich in oil and natural gas, has developed rapidly since independence in 1962. But there is still a lot to be done. Nearly 30 per cent of the population of 18 million remains unemployed.

Boumedienne's fault has been to take on too many responsibilities personally. His Government has been very much a one-man band. He has been Head of State, President of the Revolution Council, President of the Council of Ministers and Defence Minister all at once. It is unlikely any one man would assume all these positions in future.

A fierce nationalist first, an ideologue second, Boumedienne adopted a foreign policy which was more pragmatic than his rhetoric indicated. It is based on the view that the country is Arab, African and Mediterranean. Algeria is a hardliner in the Arab-Israeli conflict, a supporter of developing countries, and it maintains strong links with European countries, particularly France.

Although it has strong ties with the Soviet Union, it also has healthy trade links with the United States. Relations were broken off for several years at the time of the 1967 Middle East war, but Algeria now sells nearly $1000 million worth of natural gas to the US each year.

Observers consider any dramatic shift in foreign or domestic policy unlikely. Algeria has poor relations with neighboring Morocco and Mauritania – mainly because of its support for the Polisario Front fighting for the liberation of the former Spanish colony of Western Sahara.

As with Boumedienne's support for the Palestinian Liberation Organisation, at least part of the support for the Polisario Front has been prompted by his old freedom-fighter instinct. He has always tended to identify with liberation movements.

New image from Bagdad, and it's not so smug
From DAVID BALDERSTONE our Middle East Correspondent

'The Age', Amman, December 23, 1978

Behind the blatantly self-righteous façade that Irak has presented for so long, small cracks are developing. Bagdad is no longer uncompromising in the belief that friendly relations are something to be had on Irak's terms only.

A new wind is blowing through sprawling Bagdad – a city of brick villas, domed mosques, red London buses and palm and gum trees. Even young Baath Party officials often ask: "which is the best Arab country?" It is almost as if they are seeking reassurance.

A major factor behind this change in Iraki attitude is concern about the Shah's troubles in Iran. Irak, like Iran, is pushing ahead rapidly with oil-financed development.

The predominantly Sunni Moslem Government in Bagdad is concerned that Shi'ite Moslem fanaticism will spread across the border into Irak's Shi'ite majority population.

Irak is a lucky country. As well as being potentially the second largest oil producer in terms of estimated reserves, the Tigris and Euphrates rivers provide what the other oil-rich Arab States don't have – water.

But the regime of President Ahmed Bakr is undoubtedly repressive.

It seems inconceivable that any moderate liberal Westerner could visit Bagdad without prejudice against the regime. Memories linger about the 10-year-old "revolution's" first Premier, gunned down in London four months ago; the gun battle outside Irak's Paris embassy, and at least 21 "communist" army officers executed early this year.

But the price paid for the stability provided by President Bakr's 10-year rule is repression. There is no free Press, and plans for a National Assembly have been shelved.

After all, Irak is a patchwork of minorities that have been suspicious and hostile to the concept of a national entity ever since imperial powers drew the country's illogical borders after World War I.

The central Government's dispute with the Kurds is the most dramatic example of the divided country. Although the situation in the Kurdish north is reasonably quiet at present, it could flare up at any time. The regional autonomy plan has not satisfied Kurdish demands.

President Bakr came to power in a bloodless coup 10 years ago. Not only is his predominantly Sunni Moslem regime ruling a Shi'ite majority population, but Bakr, his personally selected strong man deputy, heir-apparent and relation by marriage, Saddam Hussein, and many other leading members of the Revolution Command Council all come from the same small town.

This is Tikrit, which is beside the Tigris, north of Bagdad. It is within Irak's so-called Sunni Moslem triangle made by joining Bagdad, Mosul in the north, and Rutba, near the Jordanian border.

Sunni Moslems provide Irak's elite, but more than 50 per cent of the population of 12 million is Shi'ite. The Sunni grip is further reduced by the two million or so Kurds, and the sizeable Christian – mainly Assyrian – community. Also, there are other small groups such as 200 Jews – remnants of the once large Jewish community.

True to Baathist doctrine, the Government is fanatically pan-Arab, socialist, and – ironically in view of Irak's friendship with the Soviet Union – fiercely independent.

Because it is not on the front line in confrontation with Israel, it has been in a position to maintain a rejectionist stance towards any negotiation with the "Zionist entity", as Israel is always called.

But the Leftist coup in Afghanistan and the Shah's troubles are considered to be among the factors that have forced Bagdad to look closely at its foreign policy.

Irak's only port, Basra, is on the Arabian Gulf, which is why Bagdad is extremely concerned about Gulf security.

If security in the Gulf deteriorated, religious fanaticism could spread and threaten the ruling families in Kuwait, Saudi Arabia, Bahrain, Qatar and the United Arab Emirates.

The old radicals from Tikrit are worried indeed. It is all very well for them to be radical, but radicalisation of Irak's neighbors is another thing altogether.

The situation has caused a perceptible moderation of Irak's foreign policy. Bagdad is making strenuous efforts to get on with the Arab neighbors.

Less than a year ago, Irak considered itself too hardline to even stay in the "steadfastness front" of Arab nations and the Palestine Liberation Organisation opposing President Sadat's peace initiative.

But last month it hosted the Arab summit. It was prepared to go along with other Arab leaders in endorsing a communiqué implying Israel's right to exist – within pre-1967 borders.

Another sign of Bagdad's conciliatory attitude is the reconciliation with the rival ruling Baath Party leadership in Damascus.

Oil wealth has enabled Irak to maintain its independent policy in the past, and to pursue long-term development and social programmes. Foreign observers give the Government credit for churning oil money back into development programmes.

But military expenditure is high. According to the International Institute for Strategic Studies, Irak spent around $1500 million in 1977-78 on defence.

Irak's oil policy, which makes it a price-rise hardliner within the Organisation of Petroleum Exporting Countries, is based on the realisation that oil is a finite resource. The strongman deputy, Saddam Hussein, said recently that of the last two barrels of oil taken from the earth, one would come from Irak.

Irak is making major drives to improve health and education services, improve roads and electricity supplies, and dramatically boost the industrial and agricultural sectors of the economy.

But the Mukhabarat – the general intelligence – is unrelenting in its pursuit of anyone suspected of being an opponent to the regime. Detention without trial is widespread.

During the "revolution's" tenth anniversary, 3000 prisoners were given amnesty. The Interior Minister, Izzat Ibrahim, announced that this included 266 out of 317 political prisoners. While it was an interesting admission that there were political prisoners, the total given is considered to be conservative to say the least.

From the age of seven or eight children get "national" training in the Young Pioneers – a group something like a military Boy Scouts. It is virtually compulsory for teenage youths to belong to the Vanguards, who get around in a brightly mottled camouflage uniform. From the age of 20, they do national service for two years, although this can be deferred for study.

In Irak, Big Brother could be your neighbor. Irakis are encouraged to report to the Mukhabarat anything suspicious about the people around them.

But it is a land of contradictions. People with grievances are encouraged to ring or write to Saddam Hussein, who acts as an ombudsman. People get through to him on a special "hot line" and he usually asks that the problem be written out for him. He promises to look into the problem. It is evidently no gimmick.

1979
Guns still for now...

The crisis in Iran has brought a spark of urgency to Egypt-Israel talks. Even if the talks succeed, many hurdles bar the way to Middle East peace. DAVID BALDERSTONE reports.

'The Age', January 2, 1979

Surface-to-air missiles bask in the sun, tanks lurk in man-made hollows, and antiaircraft guns point towards the sky. The toys of war are clearly visible as the road from Amman heads across the basalt plain to Damascus beyond the Syria-Jordan border.

In the past 18 months there has been a considerable build-up of Syrian weaponry along the road behind the UN-policed Golan Heights. Not far away, deep into Jordanian airspace, Israeli fighters scream high overhead two or three times a week in a flagrantly aggressive gesture against the moderate regime of King Hussein.

According to Western military officials in Amman, Jordanian aircraft get up behind the Israeli fighters regularly. The Jordanian pilots radio back to base, but are instructed not to fire. Rather than risk retaliation, Israeli overflight is something Jordan puts up with.

Increased tension in the Middle East has led to considerable talk in the area about the possibility of another war within the next 12 to 18 months – whether or not Egypt and Israel sign a peace treaty. The point is that while the Camp David summit peace formula may still lead to peace, however shaky, between Egypt and Israel, this formula will not lead to an overall peace settlement.

The present drive for peace began when President Sadat of Egypt visited Israel in November 1977. Mr Sadat demanded full Israeli withdrawal from Arab territories occupied in 1967 and called for the restoration of Palestinian rights.

After 14 months of stop-start negotiations, the signing of an Egypt-Israel peace treaty is again bogged down. Although both Egypt and Israel have compromised considerably, the problem now boils down to the Egyptian demand for a link from an Egypt-Israel peace to an overall settlement.

The real hope of the Sadat initiative and the Camp David summit agreements was that Jordan would agree to join negotiations and that Saudi Arabia would lend its support. But things haven't gone that way.

The Shah's troubles in Iran provide a constant reminder to the Arab regimes of the danger of religious fanaticism and political radicalisation.

There is no more emotive issue to the Arabs than the Arab-Israeli dispute. Nothing could be more calculated to fire the exploitation of political and religious extremes than a unilateral move by King Hussein, the Saudi monarchy, or even the Syrian president.

Therefore it is important for Saudi Arabia, Jordan, and Syria that all parties to the dispute move together. For this reason they have the long-term aim of a return to a Geneva-style or all-party negotiating process.

Although the regimes respect the Soviet Union and the Palestine Liberation Organisation with differing degrees of enthusiasm, they face the fact that both must be involved in the negotiating process.

For the PLO and the Soviet Union not to be involved would be to invite the exploitation of radical and fanatical feeling. "The Soviet Union has to be involved because they have an enormous capacity for making mischief," a senior Jordanian comments.

The legacy of the Sadat initiative is that all Israel's neighbors, the PLO and Saudi Arabia realistically face the prospect of a negotiated settlement with Israel. The recent Arab summit in Bagdad affirmed the Arabs' obligation towards a negotiated settlement.

The stability of the Arab regimes is conducive to a negotiated settlement. King Hussein has ruled for 26 years; the Saudi monarchy is secure under the effective leadership of Crown Prince Fahd, and President Hafez Assad has brought unprecedented stability to Syria.

Although the Arabs other than Egypt have refused to negotiate within the Camp David framework, all Israel's neighbors – Egypt, Jordan, Syria and Lebanon, plus Saudi Arabia – support the principle of a negotiated settlement based on UN Security Council resolution 242.

This resolution calls for the withdrawal of Israel's armed forces from territories occupied in 1967. It emphasises the "inadmissibility of the acquisition of territory by war".

Also, at the Arab summit in Bagdad in November, all Arab nations except Egypt (which was not represented) and the Palestine Liberation Organisation accepted the principle of a negotiated settlement based on full Israeli withdrawal from the occupied territories.

But there is a need for urgency. The Arabs are extremely concerned about the turmoil in Iran. Unless there is some unexpected let-up to the crisis, there could be two major implications for the Arab-Israeli dispute.

First, if the Shah should fall, the Arabs would become less willing to join any Arab-Israeli negotiation for fear a move on this emotive issue would encourage Islamic fanaticism to jump the Persian Gulf.

Secondly, whether or not the Shah falls, Iranian Governments in future are almost certain to have to take greater heed of Shi'ite Muslim extremism, and Israel could find her supplies of oil from Iran in jeopardy.

More than 70 per cent of Israel's oil comes from Iran.

Although the US has an agreement with Israel to make good any oil loss, such action in the wake of the Shah's demise and amidst the risk of religious fanaticism jumping the Gulf could prompt the Arab oil producers to use the oil weapon against the West.

Then Israel could find her worst – and often expressed – fear close to realisation. The US and Western Europe could find the whim of the Arab regimes more important to their economic interests than Israel's demands.

Therefore, whether or not Egypt and Israel sign a peace treaty, the Arabs are likely to gain support from the West in the coming months for their bid to get peace negotiations moved to an all-party arena.

Dominoes now the game in Mid-East
From DAVID BALDERSTONE

'The Age', Muscat, February 9, 1979

The turmoil in Iran has turned talking politics in the Arab Persian Gulf States these days into a nostalgic trip back into the Australian foreign affairs debate of the 50s and 60s.

The catch-phrase is the domino theory – the belief that one State after another could fall under communist domination. Here they are not talking about South-East Asia but the countries on which Western economies depend – the oil-rich Arab countries.

"Absolutely……the Soviet Union wants to control at least half the world," the Under-Secretary of Oman's Foreign Affairs Ministry, Mr Yousus al-Alawy said today.

In Oman, formerly known as Muscat and Oman – the strategically important Gulf State which literally controls the entrance to the Gulf – the commonly expressed view is that the Soviet Union has the clear-cut objective of progressively undermining pro-Western leadership in the Middle East.

The view is held also in United Arab Emirates, Qatar and Kuwait.

Mr Al-Alawy, like other senior Gulf officials, does not stick his neck out and say the Soviet Union was behind or directly exploiting the situation in Iran.

"I don't know the extent of the role type they are playing. But what is certain is that the Soviet Union has shown interest in Iran. And they have proved in the past they don't hesitate to interfere in such situations," he said.

"We are in the middle of the storm."

With the domino theory becoming a passionately-held fear, the Gulf States are increasing co-operation in Gulf security, particularly in the area of internal intelligence.

Ill. 10. At Salalah, Oman, February 1979

Iran's turmoil shakes the neighbors
From DAVID BALDERSTONE, our Middle East correspondent

'The Age', February 15, 1979

The rapid pace of Iran's revolution has sent a tidal wave of concern across the Persian Gulf. For the Arab oil monarchs, whose countries fuel the Western world's economies, the warning lights are flashing.

The so-called policeman of the Persian Gulf, the Shah of Iran, has gone, leaving a power vacuum in the area.

The underlying concern is that the revolution's factions – united until now by a passion to get rid of the Shah – will split, paving the way for massive Soviet exploitation of the country.

The Ayatollah Khomeiny's aim of an Islamic republic in Iran in itself does not unduly concern the Arab Gulf States and Saudi Arabia. Given that communism and Islam are poles apart, such a republic – if stable and united – would be an effective brake on Soviet expansion in the area.

But the fear is that the coming weeks and months will reveal that a united and stable Islamic republic was a fantastic dream; that the factions will divide, and widespread fighting will erupt.

"What is feared is that Iran will become an ulcer of shooting and lawlessness like Lebanon," an adviser to the Sultanate of Oman says.

The domino theory of Soviet expansion is a passionately held concept in the Arab Gulf States. And they don't have to look far to point out examples to anyone sceptical of their hardline vision of Soviet ambitions. They point to South Yemen, Ethiopia and Afghanistan. But how vulnerable to instability are the Arab States on the Persian Gulf?

All these countries – excluding Irak, which has its own problems – are capitalist economies ruled by royal families. All –

excluding Irak – have been transformed by oil revenue into modern States. Irak, potentially the biggest Arab oil producer after Saudi Arabia, has special problems stemming from the Iranian revolution. The regime of President Ahmed Bakr is predominantly Sunni Moslem, but more than 50 per cent of the population is Shi'ite Moslem, the Islamic branch to which most Iranians belong.

Also, although the Bakr regime has rapidly developed careful health, education and development programmes, big contrasts remain between the rich and poor. In addition, the country is a patchwork of religious groups held together within illogically drawn borders.

And although the regime is cautious about its relationship with the Soviet Union, Irak is the only Gulf State with a friendship treaty with Moscow. So, while the possibility of the Soviet Union wanting to tighten its grip on Irak cannot be discounted, most observers believe that the real threat could come from Shi'ite fanaticism jumping the border from Iran.

The other Gulf States are vulnerable to instability in a different way. While not discounted, the risk of religious fanaticism jumping the Persian Gulf to Kuwait, Qatar, Saudi Arabia, the United Arab Emirates and Oman is not considered a serious threat – at present at least. In Saudi Arabia particularly, the leadership could almost be said to have written the rules for modern but doctrinaire Islamic States.

These States have comparatively small populations – which is both an advantage and a disadvantage. They range in size from Qatar, which has a population of about 200,000 to Saudi Arabia, with about eight million.

The advantage of the small populations is that the oil revenue has been able to be spread more evenly than in Iran, with 34 million people, and Irak, with 12 million. But the small populations are also a disadvantage because the rapid development and government expansion has had to be manned largely by skilled outside labor.

"The problem is particularly bad in Kuwait, where the royal family has opted out of governing their country to a great extent.

They prefer to jet around Europe and leave the Government to be run by Palestinian immigrant workers," one senior official in the area said. The fear of divisions within the Gulf States' populations is paramount. "In other parts of the world we have seen the Soviet Union create, or pretend there are, dissident groups in a bid to undermine the current leadership," he said.

For this reason, the Arab Gulf States are said to be at a last making real progress in co-operating in internal intelligence. Visas to most States are becoming harder to get, and checks are being carried out more systematically.

The going of America's close ally, the Shah of Iran, has jolted the Arab Gulf leaders into the realisation of the need to co-operate more closely to protect each other.

Iran's revolution turns things Arafat's way
From David Balderstone, our Middle East Correspondent

'The Age', February 22, 1979

Just over a year ago President Carter's national security adviser, Dr Zbigniew Brzezinski, declared: "Now, bye-bye PLO."

The Palestine Liberation Organisation's leader, Yasser Arafat replied during a Beirut rally: "Somebody called Brzezinski says 'Bye-bye PLO'. To him I say, 'Goodbye to America in the Middle East'."

It is some understatement to say these days that Mr Arafat's words were more prophetic than Dr Brzezinski's.

While the US Administration was still pondering how it could have so badly underestimated the power of the Iranian revolution, Arafat this week became the first Arab political leader to be received in Iran by Ayatollah Khomeiny.

Given head-of-state status by the new Iranian leaders, Arafat – the political acrobat – picked up the keys of the door of Israel's Teheran mission, which had been left vacant by Iran's expulsion of all Israelis in the country.

Admittedly, the comment by Dr Brzezinski which I quoted above was made soon after Egypt's President Sadat had visited Jerusalem when it looked as though a major breakthrough in the 30-year Middle East deadlock had been achieved.

Angered by the PLO's refusal to compromise on its aim of eliminating Israel, he said: "We have done everything possible to urge moderation on the PLO. We have made every possible overture to them. They did not respond. Now, bye-bye, PLO."

But things have changed. The Carter Administration's drive for Middle East peace – already undermined by the decision of the Bagdad Arab summit last November "not to approve" the Camp David agreements between Egypt and Israel – has been dealt a heavy, maybe fatal blow by the swift success of the Iranian revolution.

Prospects of a comprehensive Middle East peace eventually stemming from the Camp David agreements – which were received with such euphoria in Washington, Cairo and Jerusalem – now look very bleak.

The Iranian revolution has undoubtedly strengthened the hand of Yasser Arafat, and his organisation.

Like the ageing Islamic theologian Ayatollah Khomeiny, Arafat is not everyone's picture of a charismatic leader. But his ability to survive for more than 10 years as the PLO leader is as remarkable as his ability to maintain a two-day beard every day of the week.

A question now being asked in the Middle East is whether the US can afford to continue to talk publicly with the PLO and risk being overtaken in the broader Middle East conflict – as it was so badly in the Iranian revolution.

Until now, the US has refused to publicly deal with the PLO because of its chartered aim of eliminating Israel.

Although the aim remains on the PLO's charter, Arafat is reported to have told at least one US congressman that the organisation was ready to recognise Israel if Israel agreed to the establishment of a Palestinian State in the occupied West Bank and Gaza Strip.

Congressman Paul Findley, an Illinois Republican who advocates a US-PLO dialogue, told the Beirut weekly 'Monday Morning' that he saw a link between the Iranian revolution and the Palestinian cause.

"I recognise the link myself and because of the enormous importance of Iran to the United States it is my hope that developments – however distressing they are – may have the good result of causing the US Administration to take a more thoughtful and a constructive attitude towards the Palestinian problem," he is reported to have said.

"I believe that true peace in the Middle East cannot come until the Palestinian problem has been solved by the establishment of a Palestinian State. I believe a US-PLO dialogue is possible. I think it is essential."

The point is that even if it were possible to discount the importance of the PLO to the Middle East equation a year ago – as Dr Brzezinski obviously thought it was – it certainly is not now. Few people in the Arab world ever thought it was. Arafat and the PLO have got much more than the key of the door of Israel's Teheran mission in the wake of the revolution.

In addition to the possibility of the US being forced to rethink its relationship with the PLO in favor of a dialogue, there are three other main advantages for the PLO.

First, the mere fact that it has picked up another – potentially rich – sponsor gives the PLO more manoeuvrability.

Second, the Palestinian "revolution" has been given a morale boost in two ways. It has not gone unnoticed in the Palestinian refugee camps how successful the Islamic revolution was against the Shah's guns. Also, the fact that Iran is no longer Israel's oil supplier has boosted morale.

Third, the Arab leaders – who always face the risk of Islamic fanaticism threatening their regimes – will be even more reluctant to act independently of the PLO. In the wake of events in Iran, acting independently now on such an emotive and religion-linked issue as the Arab-Israeli conflict could be courting disaster.

It has been reported that some guns in the hands of the Iranian revolution came from the PLO, but the full extent of the help provided by the organisation will probably never be known. What is certain is that the PLO will be looking for an adequate return on any help given.

Amman, March 1, 1979 (*To Richard Z*)

I was sorry to have missed your father-in-law and certainly we would have invited him to our place had we been here at the time. Anyway I hope he enjoyed the trip.

I am off to Teheran in two days amid rumours abounding here that the lid is about to blow off the revolution. That might give me a chance to recover some ground lost by being the Middle East correspondent away from the area when the Shah fell. Of course everyone was too polite to say anything to me in Melbourne, but unless newspapers have changed I can imagine the comments made out of earshot.

Claude Forell and Bruce Wilson were through Amman last week having just been to Saudi Arabia as guests of the government. Apart from them, I haven't seen an Australian journalist in the Middle East since Christmas 1977. So perhaps this area isn't as important as the Arabs and Israelis love to think.

Yemeni war 'a threat to Gulf stability'
From DAVID BALDERSTONE

'The Age', Amman, March 1, 1979

Fears are growing that the week-old border war between North and South Yemen will threaten the stability of the Gulf States and Saudi Arabia.

Some senior Arab officials believe the Soviet Union is exploiting the conflict in a bid to unsettle further the West's oil supplies following the Iranian revolution.

The Soviet Union provides military aid and advice to the Marxist regime in South Yemen.

It has been alleged that Cuban military personnel are stationed in South Yemen,

Saudi Arabia's Defence Ministry yesterday cancelled all leave in the armed forces and ordered a partial mobilisation.

Saudi Arabia made what is seen as an attack on the Soviet Union for its support of South Yemen.

It said the conflict threatened Saudi Arabia and the Gulf States.

"The Yemen border conflict and the support given to rebel forces endanger not only the security and stability of the kingdom, but also the countries of the Arabian peninsula," a Government statement said.

"It is feared the conflict may spread to other parts of the Arab world with unforeseen consequences."

Reports that Saudi Arabia has withdrawn its forces from the Arab force in Lebanon because of the crisis have been denied.

In Washington, the State Department announced yesterday that the US was speeding arms supplies to pro-Western North Yemen because of the crisis.

Frantic Arab mediation efforts aimed at bringing an end to the conflict have so far failed.

The Arab League will hold a special council meeting on Sunday to consider the crisis.

North Yemen has alleged that forces of South Yemen have captured three border towns since the fighting started last Friday.

Both North and South Yemen accuse the other of starting the fighting.

Iranians to examine our killing methods
From DAVID BALDERSTONE

'The Age', Teheran, March 8, 1979

Iranian officials – plus a special representative of the spiritual leader Ayatollah Khomeiny – are expected to visit Australia shortly to inspect Islamic killing methods in abattoirs.

The visit will be part of moves already underway aimed at reversing or modifying the ban on frozen meat imports imposed by the Ayatollah last week.

Australia stands to lose multi-million dollar frozen meat contracts unless the ban is reversed.

Already Australian officials have met senior government and meat industry officials in a bit to convince the new Iranian authorities that meat imported from Australia has been killed in accordance with Islamic rites and under Islamic supervision.

This week, Australia's commercial counsellor in Teheran, Mr Karas, and a representative of the Australian Meat and Livestock Corporation showed key officials an 18-minute film on Islamic killing in Australian abattoirs.

They were the new Agriculture Minister, Dr Izadi, and the three new board members of the Iranian Meat Organisation.

It is understood they were extremely impressed by the film. It is expected the film will be shown to Iran's full Cabinet, including the Prime Minister, Dr Bazargan, within the next few weeks.

There are also moves to have the film shown to Ayatollah Khomeiny and his aides in a bid to change his opinion that all imported frozen meat is religiously unclean and forbidden. He has said existing stocks should be turned into fertiliser.

The Ayatollah's ban, which came in the form of a directive to the Government, has left the Government in an awkward position.

If the ban continues, there will be a serious shortage of meat – particularly in Teheran. The next shipment of Australian frozen meat is not due until late this month.

Australia is Teheran's biggest supplier of frozen meat. Last financial year more than 50,000 tonnes was exported to Iran, Australia's biggest frozen meat market in the Middle East.

City of bunkers
From DAVID BALDERSTONE in Teheran

'The Age', March 10, 1979

By 7 am, Teheran's wide boulevards are jammed with traffic as Iranians edge to work bumper to bumper.

But the capital's notorious traffic problems are nothing compared with the political problems as Teheran drags itself back to work after the two months of turmoil which unseated the Shah.

Along the footpaths women in boots and leather coats outnumber their counterparts in the modest scarves and veils preferred by the ageing fathers of this country.

There are small children with black veils partly covering their faces, reminding the city that the forces of Islam are at work.

A few at least, while waiting for a school bus, scribbled more slogans on a wall. It was a reminder that the revolution is not yet over.

Also, there are the sandbagged bunkers, most abandoned by 7am after skirmishes pushing the same message somewhat more forcefully.

Of course, Teheran isn't Iran, but the sight of the capital's large Westernised middle class commuting to work in their European cars and clothes, provides more than an inkling of the problems to be faced as the country moves towards becoming an Islamic republic.

Add to this the "Leftist" groups – most notably, the People's Fedayeen – and their Rightist counterpart, and a shadow passes over hopes of a peaceful few months for Iran and the Government of Prime Minister Bazargan.

While the Ayatollah Khomeiny said at the weekend that it was Islam and faith which felled the Shah and corruption "not you, not me", the problem is that the Leftists believe their arms and their cohesive support gave the revolution, at the very least, a heavy nudge. United with the forces of the spiritual leader in the aim of getting rid of the Shah, they are irked now that they have no voice in the Bazargan Government.

And they are still heavily armed. Every night armed skirmishes break out around Teheran, particularly around the "Leftist" focal point, Teheran University.

One political observer said yesterday such skirmishes had to be expected until "the ammunition runs out." But this is probably a naïve view if one compares Teheran with the shattered Lebanese capital, Beirut. The ammunition hasn't run out there.

Prime Minister Bazargan has acknowledged he is not in control of these militias, nor of the Ayatollah Khomeiny's special revolutionary council.

Prime Minister Bazargan does not appear to have too much more control of the country than does Prime Minister Hoss of Lebanon.

Certainly, the thousands of foreigners who wanted to leave Iran, the last of which were evacuated last week, feared the worst.

"Everyone seems to expect that only phase one of the revolution has taken place," a British archaeologist in Amman told me. "Most people expect phase two, when Leftists clash with Rightists, to be worse than anything we have seen yet.

It is widely believed in Teheran that because of the speed with which the revolution succeeded, it was too much to expect that all power could be vested in this or any Government. There are too many forces wanting a say.

So an umbrella organisation to co-ordinate activities has been advocated.

A leading Iranian columnist puts the blame for the polarisation of political views in Iran squarely on the Bazargan Government.

In the 'Teheran Journal' at the weekend, he compared Bazargan, with reservation, with the Shah's last two Prime Ministers.

The crux of the problem today is that the people are not getting a say on the type of government they want, and the prospect of a one-question referendum: "Are you for an Islamic republic?" late this month increases frustration felt by many people.

"Why is everyone talking of a second revolution, instead of talking of reconstruction and rebuilding?" the columnist, Fariborz Atapour, asked. His own explanation was directed at Dr Bazargan. "The reason is that you are not giving the people the total democracy for which they fought.

"What is going wrong with the revolution? Bazargan says that the majority of the people do not want Iran to become a second Lebanon. We would like him to elucidate what he exactly means by that, because the gun-toting militias, which he has so boldly denounced as illegal parallel governments, are the armed wing of the very revolution which he is officially leading."

It is not only the problems of political leadership which leave one wondering about Iran. Since the Ayatollah returned, pop music has gone from the radio and all frozen meat is to be destroyed because the Ayatollah maintains it was not killed Islamic-style.

The Ayatollah says: "We shall reform the Press. We shall reform the radio. We shall reform the television. They must all conform to Islamic norms." The problem is that as with the proposed Islamic republic, nobody knows exactly what is meant. Ignorance on such important matters produces enormous concern, and considerable anger.

But despite the uncertainties, there is a Brave New World excitement about Teheran. Iranians overseas are taking every available seat aboard incoming aircraft to be part of the adventure. This is despite regulations which make it difficult for many Iranian men to leave again.

When I flew in from Amman at the weekend, the undercarriage had hardly touched the soil of Iran when the chorus went up: "God is truly great."

Women and zealots in Iran battle
From DAVID BALDERSTONE

'The Age', Teheran, March 12, 1979

Stone-throwing Moslem zealots carrying knives and knuckledusters clashed with thousands of women demonstrators in Teheran yesterday.

Revolutionary militiamen fired automatic weapons into the air to break up the clashes which left many women injured. The violence was the worst seen on the streets of Teheran since the Shah was overthrown.

But the women, undeterred, were gathering this morning for a rally outside the Foreign Ministry. And preparations are under way for a massive march through the capital tomorrow.

Several hundred women, who chanted slogans and shook their fists, occupied the Justice Ministry for several hours yesterday. It was the third successive day that women had taken to the streets in protest against the erosion of women's rights since the revolution that ousted the Shah.

Yesterday's clashes occurred when women marchers converged on the Justice Ministry from several parts of Teheran. The worst violence occurred near the British Embassy when hundreds of Moslem zealots threw stones and manhandled women to stop them getting to the Justice Ministry.

An American television crew had equipment damaged as they were filming the clash.

Outside the Justice Ministry, I watched as several hundred women chanted slogans because the revolution in which they had taken part was taking away hard-won women's rights.

"Freedom is not Western. Freedom is not Eastern; freedom is freedom," they chanted. The slogan was an angry rebuttal for

Ayatollah Khomeiny, who has said Iran must shed Western customs and return to life under Islam.

Since the revolution, the Family Protection Law introduced by the Shah to free women from cruel Islamic divorce and marriage customs has been suspended. Abortion has also been banned and women directed to wear modest non-Western clothing in line with Islamic custom. Many women have taken this to mean they are being forced to wear the traditional veil, but this has been denied.

The Ayatollah Teleghani, Khomeiny's chief representative in Teheran, said that the directive women should wear Moslem dress did not mean they must wear the chador, which leaves only the eyes, nose and mouth uncovered.

"We mean dignified dress, the veil of dignity, the veil of personality – that is what an Islamic veil means," he said.

The weekend clashes were a startling example of the deteriorating order in Iran as the embattled provisional Government struggles for control of the country.

Gun battles between rival factions of the Iranian revolution raged in several parts of Teheran into the early hours of today.

A nation in the hands of the mob
DAVID BALDERSTONE, summing up after a week's visit to Iran, says the country has fallen into anarchy

'The Age', March 15, 1979

Iran is gripped by anarchy and in danger of plunging into civil war.

Ruled until so recently by a repressive monarch, it is now a country of a thousand committees in the hands of a faceless mob.

There is fear, uncertainty and doubtful justice. The Provisional Government, which lacks the clout of either a police force or an army, is yet to demonstrate its ability to control the country.

Even the uniting force of the revolution, Ayatollah Khomeiny, 78, has been issuing contradictory statements and is considered by a growing minority to be out of touch with the needs and aspirations of the Iranians.

In almost all Government departments and organisations, the top one or two, and often more, people have been purged, leaving previously lower-ranking officials in charge.

These men have to contend with their own inexperience and the problem of operating under the watchful eye of a revolutionary committee.

In every small town and provincial capital there is a revolutionary committee, which has put hasty justice into its own mainly closed Islamic courts, and successfully keeps most power away from Government officials.

These committees supposedly work under the umbrella of Khomeiny's Central Revolutionary Council, whose members have not been disclosed.

For anyone who did well under, or loyally served and supported the Shah, Iran is under a reign of terror.

It has been announced that about 50 former senior military and intelligence officers, a pro-Shah Majlis deputy, and two national television executives have been executed.

In view of the poor state of communications in Iran, it would not be surprising if the execution toll were far higher.

In Teheran alone, another 200 people are said to be under arrest, and there are other lists of people who are being closely watched and barred from leaving the country.

The uncertainty leads successful businessmen still in Teheran to ask journalists: "What have you heard about the lists?"

Islam is at work. Women's rights have been eroded. Alcohol, while not officially banned by the Government is hard to get apart from at major hotels.

Adulterers have been flogged, and people involved in prostitution shot.

But let's stop here a minute. After all, it is only four weeks since the Shah's last government fell to the revolution.

A vindictive and revengeful transition it has been, certainly, but probably this was inevitable in view of the upheaval.

Although there have been nightly gun battles between rival factions of the revolution in Teheran, little blood has been shed.

The revolutionary militiamen, although clumsy and raw, seem to be doing their best to keep Iran under control.

During a women's protest rally outside the Justice Ministry in Teheran last weekend, I saw militiamen doing an efficient job protecting the women from Moslem zealots out for a clash.

Elsewhere in Teheran, according to other correspondents, the militiamen were doing their best, but the situation got out of control because of the number of zealots with knuckledusters and knives.

The danger is the militiamen's inexperience. The way they handle their weapons, they make the various groups of Beirut militiamen look like crack troops.

With illiteracy more than 50 per cent, there is little doubt that most of Iran's 35-million population ("The Shah killed a million, so now there are 34 million," a Kurd quipped to me) are behind Khomeiny's call for an Islamic republic.

While the proposed one-question referendum – "Are you in favor of an Islamic republic?" – is obviously unfair, any referendum, however fairly it took account of different community ideas, would almost certainly lead to an Islamic State.

The hope for Iran is that the Shi'ite Moslem establishment will prove to be more compromising and more enlightened than some of the Ayatollah Khomeiny's statements would suggest.

This is not a vain hope. Members of the religious hierarchy, notably Teheran's religious leader, Ayatollah Teleghani, express views considerably more moderate than those of Khomeiny, who only a month ago ended 15 years in exile.

Even Khomeiny's contradictory statements, which have justifiably angered women and the Westernised middle class, may be aimed at testing public opinion, rather than merely being doddering, as his age might suggest.

Although the middle class desires a representative democracy immediately, this is probably unrealistic in view of the illiteracy and class division.

But the middle class desire may be fulfilled in another way – and if one listens only to the Khomeiny utterings, an unexpected way.

The Shah used to tell the West he was the only force which could unite the country and protect its oil supply. The West believed him.

This "uniting force", which under the Shah was based on military might rather than popularity, has gone to the religious establishment, but not exclusively to Khomeiny.

It could turn out that the Shi'ite hierarchy could move the country towards a representative system of government far more conscientiously than the Shah.

Certainly, unlike the Shah, they are allowing the call for democracy to be heard loud and clear.

Under the Shah, demonstrations were officially banned and the Press censored.

But in the past weeks thousands of women have taken to the streets to protest at the erosion of women's rights since the revolution. They have been protected by pro-Khomeiny revolutionary militiamen.

The Press is full of criticism of the Government and constantly advocates establishment of a democratic republic. This is hardly discouraging.

To be fair, there is a certain amount of Press self-censorship and criticism of Khomeiny's statements is carefully handled. But the newspapers report opposing comments factually.

The Governed-controlled national radio and television is selective in its news coverage. But the only formal censorship in past weeks I am aware of affected foreign television broadcasts.

Foreign television networks satelliting coverage of Moslem zealots clashing with women found their transmission abroad cut off.

But even this should not be seen in too sinister terms. It is likely that the new Iranian Government is being over-zealous in its efforts to induce Western confidence in post-revolution Iran.

Although the Government is fiercely nationalistic, it realises Western confidence and business are needed if it is to maintain its independence.

While everything is not black in Iran, and there is reason for hope, there is an undeniable risk.

This is that the upheaval which has wracked Iran for the past few months will continue. This would prevent the Government gaining control and block recovery.

Then food would become scarce – already there is a meat shortage after Ayatollah Khomeiny's ban on frozen meat – and civil war could break out. Islam is a powerful force, but hunger is almighty.

Even limited civil war would create a situation ripe for communist exploitation or the emergence of a Right-wing, military-dominated regime.

And Iranians might find themselves no better off than under the Shah.

The true crucible of peace
From DAVID BALDERSTONE in Jerusalem

'The Age', March 28, 1979

A young Israeli soldier stands on a knoll beside the road listlessly glancing at his watch. His automatic rifle pans across the windscreens of the waiting cars.

Other members of the Israeli Army section are on the road, which leads from Jerusalem to Nablus, checking identity cards of drivers and passengers.

Cars are banked up for 200 metres. Tempers get hot. Arab drivers and Israeli soldiers shake their fists at each other every few minutes.

"Shalom," the Arab drivers utter without much sincerity. "Shalom," comes the reply.

Since 1967 there have been permanent Israeli roadblocks on this highway. But they are more frequent at present and queues have become longer as increased tension brings more stringent checks.

This is the West Bank, the disputed territory on which most hopes of real, lasting Middle East peace depend.

It is in the West Bank – and in the Gaza Strip – far from the euphoria of the Egyptian-Israeli peace treaty signing, that the reality of political rhetoric about the treaty being a first step towards a solution of the Palestinian problem will be tested.

Further negotiations have to take place, but an autonomy plan for West Bankers and Gaza Strip residents is due to start.

An administrative council replacing the Israeli military Government will be elected by the Palestinians to run local affairs.

Departments of education, religious affairs, finance, transport, housing, agriculture, health and others are envisaged. But security and public order will remain the responsibility of the Israelis.

Although the autonomy plan does little for Palestinians living outside the Israeli-occupied Arab territories, it could be, if accepted, a first step to solution of the 30-year-old Palestinian problem.

But West Bank leaders reject the autonomy plan, seeing it as merely formalising and legalising Israeli occupation of the area and the Gaza Strip.

Most people in the West Bank seem to agree with this and attempts to impose autonomy and elections for the envisaged council are likely to be boycotted.

However some West Bankers, it is impossible to judge what proportion, do see good points in the Egyptian-Israeli peace treaty. They hope it will lead to negotiations between Israel and particularly Jordan, but also Syria and the Palestinian Liberation Organisation.

I have been to the West Bank many times in the past two years, and have not come across a Palestinian who does not want a Palestinian State. But hope is another thing to expectation.

The mayor of Ramallah, Karim Khalif, who with most West Bank mayors won election in 1976 by standing as a supporter of the PLO, sees autonomy as an American and Israeli ploy to undermine the PLO leadership.

"America is one of your Western countries which does not recognise the PLO. Now their game is to create a new Palestinian leadership through the so-called autonomy plan to replace the PLO," Mayor Khalif says.

"If they establish this leadership, we will lose our recognition for the PLO at the United Nations.

"Ramallah is Palestinian. The West Bank is Palestinian. President Carter has often talked about human rights. Here Palestinians have suffered torture, confiscation of land, the blowing up of houses, and the erection of Jewish settlements. Where are the human rights in this?

"Ramallah is surrounded by Israeli settlements and camps."

The West Bank, which the Israeli Government refers to as Judea and Samaria, was taken from Jordan by Israeli troops in the 1967 war.

The United Nations' partition plan of 1947 envisaged the West Bank as part of a Palestinian State. But Jordan took over the area during the war after Israel's creation in 1948, and later annexed it.

About 600,000 Arabs live in the West Bank, which cuts into Israel proper to within 15 kilometres of the Mediterranean.

There are stoney rises, fertile valleys and plains, and desert hills falling into the below-sea-level Jordan River Valley.

It includes the old city of East Jerusalem (Israel is alone in claiming that East Jerusalem, which it has unilaterally annexed, is not part of the West Bank), Hebron, Bethlehem, Nablus and Jericho.

Driving from Jerusalem to Nablus is like flipping through a picture-book Bible. The road is flanked by terraces of olive groves. Arabs till the fertile pockets within the terraces with horse-drawn, single-prong ploughs. Shepherd boys play cane flutes as they watch their sheep.

But the cultural complexion of the land is changing. Since 1967, more than 30 Israeli settlements have sprung up stirring anger among Arabs already distraught at the occupation.

There are about 7000 Jewish settlers on the West Bank.

About 10 kilometres from Ramallah, the Jericho road which is lined with charming Arab stone houses; some grand, some more modest, suddenly passes the Jewish settlement of Ophra.

Its pre-fabricated yellow buildings and caravans make it look more like a road camp than the home of 200 settlers.

Menucha Nathan, whose husband, Geoff, migrated to Israel from Melbourne, works in the silk screen printing plant at the settlement, one of several small "factories".

"I think we all live here for ideological reasons," she says.

The settlers believe they have the right to settle on the West Bank because it was part of Biblical Israel.

This God-given right does not come cheaply in modern Israel.

As well as being scorned by many Israelis as trouble-makers, religious fanatics, and a block to real peace, the settlers face a cost of living which is considerably higher.

"Previously we lived on a kibbutz, one which had been established 30 years, and we found we were stagnating," Menucha Nathan says.

"We don't have unfriendly relations with the Arab community. But we don't have friendly relations. We do a lot of shopping in Ramallah, but I don't think any friendships have developed. We belong to two different cultures."

The two cultures clashed three weeks ago when students from Birzeit University near Ramallah, demonstrated during President Carter's visit to Israel.

Four students were shot by Jewish settlers from the area.

From the Ophra settlement is a 15-minute drive to the Grand Hotel, Ramallah, where a group of students was drinking beer or Coca-Cola under the pine trees.

"We are against autonomy. It is just another shape of Israeli occupation," says Hisham, self-appointed spokesman of the group.

"If we agree with autonomy, we will show the world that this was what we were fighting for. Autonomy is a step in the wrong direction. It is an Israeli plan."

The seven students, three of whom have been in Israeli jails, declare that they are all communists. They are rather vague on the meaning of the word.

"The students don't have a clue what communism means," comments a West Bank Arab, a moderate who holds a senior position with the UN.

"At this stage, most people are united against Sadat because they believe the peace is not honourable. It is seen as a separate Egyptian-Israeli peace," he says.

"At this stage hotheads prevail and there is no real alternative to the PLO. This is partly because people don't know what is coming. People don't know what the autonomy plan really means.

"But what are the Arabs going to do? So they will impose sanctions on Egypt and expel her from the Arab league. What will that do for us?"

He sees three main advantages in the peace treaty for the Palestinians.

First, it would mean no more major wars because the other Arabs would not want to fight and lose without Egypt.

Secondly, Egypt has proved Israel was prepared to return to 1967 borders along Sinai. This provided hope they might also agree to withdraw to 1967 borders in the West Bank in exchange for peace.

Thirdly, the Egyptian-Israeli treaty could lead to trust between Egyptians and Israelis and moderate Israeli attitudes to the Arabs.

However, he was adamant that the autonomy plan would not be accepted.

"Now we have to go to the military governor to get an identity card.

"It would be so much worse if we had to go to an Arab but knew there was still an Israeli on top."

Asked his reaction to Palestinian terrorism, he said: "Most moderate people would say they don't like violence, but condone it because it keeps the Palestinian problem before the world."

Karim Khalif, tall, impressive, and a dapper dresser, believes no Palestinian representatives will be found for the forthcoming negotiations on the autonomy plan.

He believes any elections will be boycotted.

"Now, 95 per cent of West Bankers are behind the PLO leadership. I am 100 per cent sure no one will take part in the negotiations.

"If somebody did get involved, we would consider him a traitor."

Karim Khalif offers Turkish coffee and smokes Kent cigarettes. Friends sit in his mayoral office and listen to every word.

"I am not working against peace. But I am not ready to give up my country, shake hands with you, and say 'That is peace'.

"Peace to the Israelis is spelt PIECE. They want our piece of land, not peace."

Talk peace, Begin urges Arabs
From DAVID BALDERSTONE

'The Age', Cairo, April 3, 1979

Israel's Prime Minister, Mr Begin, last night appealed to Arab States hostile to the Egyptian-Israeli treaty to join the peace process.

Mr Begin, the first Israeli Prime Minister to visit Cairo, made the appeal at a dinner in his honour given by President Sadat.

"We appeal to those who for the time being took or were misled to take a negative attitude to relinquish this futile negativism," he said.

The Arab States "should join us in the peace-making effort for their benefit as much as for ours.

"I am convinced that in God's good time they will do so."

Mr Begin said today that Egypt and Israel would declare their common border along the Sinai Desert open on May 27.

He and Mr Sadat had also agreed to meet in Al Arish, capital of Egypt's Sinai Peninsula, on the same day, one day after Israel withdraws from the coastal city.

Most Arab ambassadors have left Cairo following the weekend decision of 19 Arab States meeting in Bagdad to impose political and economic sanctions against Egypt.

These States oppose the Egyptian – Israeli peace treaty because they see it as a separate peace that will not lead to comprehensive Middle East peace.

In a short speech, Mr Sadat said Egypt would continue fighting for peace.

Mr Begin, on the first day of his mostly low key two-day trip, visited the pyramids, laid a wreath on the Unknown Soldier's tomb, and prayed in Cairo's main synagogue yesterday.

Only about 30 members of Cairo's once large Jewish community were at the synagogue.

But there were tears in the eyes of several as the Prime Minister entered the synagogue after 30 years of war with Egypt.

The synagogue is one of 19 in Cairo which once served a community of 150,000 Jews.

Officials here have done nothing to encourage Egyptians to turn out on the streets to welcome Mr Begin.

But a crowd of several hundred Egyptians waited outside the synagogue to get a glimpse of their former enemy.

"President Sadat is the greatest, President Carter is number two and Mr Begin number three," one Egyptian told me.

Similarly, a crowd of about 300 Egyptians crowded around the gates of the Kubbeh republican palace when Mr Begin arrived for the dinner last night.

Arabs buy our TV shows
From DAVID BALDERSTONE in Amman

'The Age', May, 12, 1979

Jordan seems an odd place to find a television station chief talking enthusiastically about Australian television programmes.

But the director-general of Jordan Television, Dr Mohammed Kamal, does – and he has put his money where his mouth is.

Jordan television broadcasts three Australian programmes – the wartime drama 'The Sullivans', 'Bluey, and 'Against the Wind'.

"They are very good indeed and very popular," Dr Kamal says.

"If we can get other good Australian programmes in the future we will be very happy."

Jordan television has two channels and claims a nightly audience of up to six million viewers in Jordan, Israel, South Lebanon, Syria and northern Saudi Arabia.

While the two Crawford productions, 'The Sullivans' and 'Bluey' are popular, it is 'Against the Wind' which is really making an impact.

This Pegasus production made in co-operation with the Channel 7 network is about a young Irish woman, transported to NSW in one of the early convict ships.

The station's programme director, Mr Faruk Jarrar, who has just returned from a television executives' conference in the Caribbean, says that in American and European markets 'Against the Wind' has been dubbed "the white Roots".

"They think it is as important as 'Roots'," he says.

Jordan television bought the three Australian series through London distributors. The station does its own Arabic subtitling.

Unlike some other government-controlled Arab television stations which are heavy on propaganda, Jordan television runs news reasonably straight and has a reputation for showing latest release British and American programmes.

Jordan's demand for the latest programmes is partly political.

"People in Israel and Syria watch our television and we watch theirs," Dr Kamal says.

"Therefore we can't afford to be inferior. We can't afford to be second.

"If we lost our viewers to Israel, for instance, it would be a national disaster.

Jordan television has an advantage. Israel rarely screens in colour. Jordan switched to colour in 1972.

It seems odd to think of the Arabs settling down with a cup of Turkish coffee at night to watch 'The Sullivans'.

But, given Jordan's position at the centre of the Arab-Israeli dispute, it was even stranger switching on Jordan television last year to watch the British-produced series 'Disraeli'.

A local television executive said: "'Disraeli' was historical. We can't change history.

"If the English had a Jewish Prime Minister, that's their problem."

'A treaty of war' Syria hits Egypt deal
From DAVID BALDERSTONE

'The Age', Damascus, May 18, 1979

Syria's Foreign Minister, Mr Khaddam, has accused Israel of planning to annex southern Lebanon.

In an interview with 'The Age', Mr Khaddam criticised the massive military aid the United States was providing Israel in the wake of the Egyptian-Israeli peace treaty.

"It would be appropriate to say the Egyptian-Israeli peace treaty is a treaty of war and aggression and not a peace treaty," he said.

Mr Khaddam's comments came just hours before Israel launched another attack against a Palestinian guerilla base in southern Lebanon early this morning.

Israel's latest raid made today the ninth day in just over three weeks when Israel's defence forces have launched attacks against "Palestinian targets" in Lebanon.

"Israel's objective is to tear Lebanon apart and to occupy and annexe South Lebanon to Israel," Mr Khaddam said.

An early Zionist plan for a proposed Jewish state in Palestine included southern Lebanon as far north as the Litani River. Most of this part of Lebanon is controlled today by Israeli-backed Christian militias, who have declared the area Independent Free Lebanon.

Mr Khaddam said the Soviet Union had made gains in the Middle East because of Arab hostility to American efforts to secure the Egyptian-Israeli peace treaty. Most Arab nations, including Syria, Jordan and Saudi Arabia, oppose the treaty because they say they do not believe it will lead to comprehensive Middle East peace.

"It is natural that when a superpower commits an error in a certain area the other superpower will benefit and take advantage of the error," he said.

"The US stands on the side of the enemy of the Arabs and provides them (Israel) with aid and assistance to enable them to continue their aggression."

Lebanon a hostage to war
From DAVID BALDERSTONE in Amman

'The Age', May 22, 1979

Lebanon, trampled upon by Israel and engulfed in sectional fighting and blood feuds, is hostage to the continuing Arab-Israeli dispute.

The unsolved Palestinian problem stands as a major hurdle in the path of Lebanon's recovery from the 1975-77 civil war.

The battered country is a monument to the 31-year-old Middle East dispute. It is where the American hope of the Egyptian-Israeli peace treaty being a "cornerstone" of comprehensive Middle East peace is seen as a dream.

Lebanon is also a time bomb. Unless a political Palestinian solution is found, a stable Lebanon is virtually out of the question. And instability in this once prosperous and beautiful place could spark a Middle East war.

In the meantime, the continuing crisis in Lebanon will further erode the chances of the Egyptian-Israeli peace treaty enduring.

Lebanon is the battleground now for five "wars".

First, there is the running battle in the south between the Palestinian guerillas and the Israeli-Christian alliance.

Second, there are regular clashes – mainly around East Beirut – between the two main Maronite Christian militias and the Syrian forces that make up the "peace-keeping" force in Lebanon.

Third, there is a fierce blood feud raging between the Falangist militia of Pierre Gemayel and the militia of another Christian political leader, Suleiman Franjieh, a former Lebanese President. Mr Franjieh is out to avenge the life of his son Tony, a former Lebanese Minister and businessman, who was murdered by the Falangists last June.

Fourth, there has been fighting in Beirut recently between the Falangists and the Armenian community. This dispute between two rival Christian communities stems from Falangist anger at the Armenians' desire to take a neutral course in the web of Lebanese political intrigue.

Fifth, there is a simmering battle between the various "Leftist" militias, mainly over areas of control in the capital. This is fought out on an occasional basis after dark in previously safe West Beirut.

The Christian-Christian, Falangist-Armenian, Leftist-Leftist, and Syrian-Christian disputes could be wound down, at least partly controlled, and lived with, if authority was restored to the central Government, its army and police force.

That leaves "war number one", between the Israel-Christian alliance and the Palestinians. This cannot be solved until a solution to the Palestinian problem is found.

In the past four weeks Israel has used planes, artillery and gunboats to bombard "Palestinian targets" in continuing war against Palestinian guerillas.

The bombardment began on April 22, just hours after four Israelis, including two children, died in a Palestinian suicide mission against the northern Israeli resort town of Nahariya.

Lebanese Government and Palestinian sources estimate that many more than 50 Palestinians and Lebanese died in the bombardment, which also destroyed many homes. Another 40,000 people fled north from southern Lebanon, Israel's main target.

Although it is common for the 1975-77 civil war to be viewed as merely domestic, it was the participation of the Palestinian guerillas, fighting on the side of the predominantly Moslem Leftists that made it so bloody.

The failure to find a Palestinian solution blocks Lebanese reconciliation in two ways.

First, the Palestinians will continue to use the country as a political and military base for action against Israel.

Second, while the Palestinians use Lebanon as a base, the dominant Maronite Christian politicians, former President Camille Chamoun and Pierre Gemayel, will not agree to political compromises essential for the restoration of the authority of the central Government.

Power in Lebanon is divided between Christians and Moslems on the basis of a census taken 47 years ago which showed the communities were evenly balanced,

But today it is estimated that the Moslem (Sunni and Shi'ite) community is bigger than the Christian community, with the Shi'ite community believed to be considerably larger than the Sunni community.

And yet, the old ranking stays. The President is a Christian, the Prime Minister a Sunni, and the Speaker of parliament a Shi'ite. This system tends to permeate the whole society.

While this unfair power (and wealth) sharing remains a root cause of Lebanon's problem, the influx of Palestinians following the creation of Israel in 1948 has added dramatically to the trouble.

There are more than 190,000 United Nations-registered Palestinian refugees in Lebanon. Just over 100,000 of these live in camps, according to the United Nations Relief and Works Agency for Palestinian Refugees.

Obviously, a refugee problem of this size is a real burden on a country of 3.3 million. But it is made worse because Lebanon is the main political and guerilla base for the various factions of the Palestinian revolution.

The strength of the Palestinian guerillas on the side of the Moslem Leftist militias almost led to the defeat of the Christians in the civil war.

The Christians were saved by the intervention of the Syrian forces, which fought on their side when they entered Lebanon in 1977.

The Syrians' objective was to balance power and set the stage for the restoration of central authority. They were concerned that a Palestinian-Leftist victory could lead to a radical Palestinian-dominated Lebanon which could draw Damascus into a war with Israel at a time not of Syria's choosing.

Equally, Syria does not want the country to be dominated by the Maronite Christians, who have become close allies of, and receive arms supplies from, Israel.

Ironically, the men who benefitted from the Syrian intervention – Mr Chamoun and Mr Gemayel – now want the Syrians to leave Lebanon, and dub them "occupying forces". Not surprisingly, the Syrians are irked that the Christians have such short memories.

In Lebanon, as in all of the Middle East, no one has a monopoly on right or wrong. The Christians – partly through church-organised education and because they were favored by the French – did have a lot to do with building Lebanon's pre-civil war prosperity and style. They have become victims of the Palestinian influx and the higher birth rate of the impoverished Shi'ite community.

But the truth is rather different from the picture that might be conjured up by newspaper headlines such as "Syrians Pound Lebanese Christians" and by Israeli propaganda about Israel standing behind the Christians to save them from Syrian annihilation.

In short, that is rubbish. Mr Chamoun and Mr Gemayel have consistently blocked political compromises proposed by President Sarkis, a Maronite Christian.

They are at war with other sections of the Christian community, demand protection money from their own supporters, and are scorned by many prominent Christians who just want to live in peace.

Israel's Prime Minister, Mr Begin, has proposed peace talks between Israel and Lebanon. In the same speech to the Knesset he seemed to acknowledge that the Palestinian presence was a stumbling block to recovery. He suggested that the Palestinians could be resettled in Saudi Arabia, Syria, Irak and Libya.

This suggestion fails to take account of Palestinians' desire to return to their homeland, or part of it, or receive compensation – in line with numerous UN resolutions.

However, Mr Begin reiterated recently that Israel would not consider the establishment of a Palestinian State and would not return to the 1967 borders which would give the Palestinians the West Bank.

The Israelis are like ostriches with their heads in the sand. Their solution is either to have the Palestinians resettled or bomb the living daylights out of the Palestinian "war machine".

Judging by Arab policy over the past 31 years – and also the feelings of the Palestinians – the first suggestion is unrealistic. And the policy of bombardment is futile.

It is futile because bombardment merely increases Palestinian desperation and drives more young Palestinians towards volunteering their lives to the guerrilla organisations.

Also, bombardment carries with it the high risk of a direct Israeli clash with Syrian forces in Lebanon – a clash which could spark another major Middle East war.

Another dawn
From DAVID BALDERSTONE in Al Arish, Sinai

'The Age', May 28, 1979

With the jubilation of President Sadat's return to Al Arish at the weekend no one could blame the people of the Sinai capital for forgetting a welcome they gave another "liberating force" 63 years ago.

But just after dawn on December 21, 1916, the people of Al Arish enthusiastically welcomed Australian troops who had taken the town from the Turkish army.

It was an "excited demonstration of delight" with the Arabs "crowded around the Light Horsemen, grasping their stirrups and kissing their boots", according to the official history of Australia in the War of 1914-18 (Vol. 7, Sinai and Palestine).

In 1916 Al Arish was an "old mud-built village", but the Australian troops were happy to reach the town after the terrible hardship of the Sinai desert.

"Al Arish with all its squalor was to Australian eyes a pleasant, civilised town," the war history records.

Today, concrete has replaced mud as the main building material. But just a touch of squalor remains as an odd reminder that this is the same town mentioned in the Australian war history.

Bullet holes remain from when it fell to the Israelis during the Six Day War of 1967. But at the weekend, banners proclaiming Egypt's President Sadat as a hero of war and peace distracted visitors from the remaining squalor and damage.

Al Arish was handed back to Egypt on Friday. It was Israel's first instalment of the complete handover of Sinai, phased over three years, under the Egyptian-Israeli peace treaty.

It was dawn on December 21, 1916 when the First and Third Light Horse brigades, the Camel Brigade, and New Zealanders surrounded the town.

"The dramatic appearance of the Anzac horsemen encircling the town caused the helpless time-serving Arabs to greet the Australian horsemen with an excited demonstration of delight," the war history records. They were "time serving" Arabs because they had been occupied by the Turks – one occupation was being replaced by another. The history notes that Al Arish had enjoyed prosperity under the Turks.

Set behind palm trees on the edge of the Mediterranean, the Egyptians are already talking about pouring vast sums of money into Al Arish. They are considering building a tourist resort on the edge of the beach.

Although the residents of Al Arish are glad to see the town back in Egyptian hands, many residents have become used to, and even dependent on, the economy of Israel.

Many of the residents previously worked in Israel or on Israeli settlements in northern Sinai. Any change brings concern and some people express fears about not being able to work in Israel and shop in Tel Aviv.

But at the weekend, Al Arish forgot any slight fears and welcomed Anwar Sadat. And doubtless, none remembered the dawn of December 21, 1916.

Moslem group 'plotting to overthrow Assad'
From DAVID BALDERSTONE

'The Age', Beirut, June 24, 1979

The extreme Right-wing Moslem Brotherhood blamed by Syria for last week's artillery school massacre is plotting an uprising to topple the Syrian Government, according to informed sources.

The sources said the Brotherhood was smuggling weapons into Syria from Turkey and Lebanon, and buying automatic rifles from dissidents and gun-runners inside Syria.

They said the brotherhood aimed to overthrow the Syrian leadership, which is drawn mainly from the minority Alawite Moslem sect, and to install a Right-wing military Government more representative of the Sunni Moslem majority.

A massive manhunt is underway in Syria for the ringleaders of a terrorist group which massacred at least 50 Syrian army cadets. The cadets were mown down by machine-guns and hand-grenades at an artillery school in Aleppo, northern Syria, just over a week ago by opponents of President Assad of Syria.

Syria's Interior Minister, Brigadier Adnan Dabbagh, disclosed details of the massacre at the weekend. He said 32 cadets had been killed immediately. But reliable reports say that other cadets badly wounded in the attack have since died, bringing the death toll to at least 50. A leading Jordanian newspaper says the death toll has reached 63.

Many arrests have been made, but it is believed the alleged ringleader of the terrorist group, a Captain Ibrahim Youssef, is still at large. Brigadier Dabbagh has blamed the Moslem Brotherhood for the massacre, and a wave of political assassinations in recent months.

Sources close to the Brotherhood claim the movement plans to step up the terrorist campaign in Syria.

Arab former enemies find unity in common fears and problems
From DAVID BALDERSTONE

'The Age', Amman, July 5, 1979

It was coming on lunchtime when Jordanian air traffic controllers picked up three unidentified aircraft approaching Jordan from Bagdad.

As far as the controllers were concerned the three aircraft did not have clearance to enter Jordanian airspace.

On board one aircraft was Irak's strongman Vice-Chairman, Mr Saddam Hussein, who is effective ruler of the hardline Arab regime. He was on an urgent visit to Amman arranged at less than two hours notice.

So hastily organised was the visit that most officials in the Basman Palace, King Hussein's office complex in Amman, did not know of the visit until Mr Hussein's plane had taken off from Bagdad on the one and a half hour flight.

Telephones in the pine-treed Basman Palace enclave were going mad as officials contacted Ministers and royal household members.

By the time Saddam Hussein's aircraft touched down, full protocol was being observed by the Jordanians. King Hussein and his brother, Crown Prince Hassan, had made it to the airport on time.

Mr Hussein's arrival in Amman last Saturday was just one incredible incident during the extraordinary past fortnight during which Amman has been the stage for Arab political intrigue.

It has been a fortnight during which King Hussein has played host to two former enemies – Saddam Hussein and Libya's Colonel Gaddafi.

After the 1970-71 civil war in Jordan – during which King Hussein's army expelled the Palestinian armed presence from the country – Irak and Libya regularly called for the king's overthrow.

Now they have reasonably good relations because they are all opposed – with varying degrees of enthusiasm and vehemence – to the Egyptian-Israeli peace treaty.

The Jordanians are being extremely tight-lipped about both visits and senior Jordanians have been sworn to secrecy about details. The official Jordan newsagency was forthcoming enough only to say that Saddam Hussein and King Hussein discussed "Middle East developments and bilateral relations". The agency added that the leaders discussed "matters of mutual concern and reviewed all aspects of the Arab stand".

They gave a similar explanation for Colonel Gaddafi's visit.

But just why did Mr Hussein and Colonel Gaddafi find it important to visit Jordan last week? After endless cups of Turkish coffee and sweet Arab tea – and just occasionally something stronger – three main reasons have emerged.

First, after the Syrian-Israeli dogfight over South Lebanon last week during which at least four Syrian aircraft were shot down, the Arabs fear they will become embroiled in a war with Israel at a time when they are under-equipped to fight.

Secondly, Irak particularly fears that domestic problems in Syria could topple President Assad.

Thirdly, Colonel Gaddafi seriously fears a border war with Egypt, and embarked on a tour of Arab States at least partly designed to demonstrate to the West that, after all, he really is loved by the other Arabs – including King Hussein and the West's oil suppliers.

Rightly or wrongly, there is a sincerely-held fear in Amman, Damascus and Bagdad, that Israel is deliberately escalating tension in Lebanon. It is feared that last week's Syrian-Israeli clash could lead to a full-scale war from which Jordan and Irak would find it difficult, in view of their alliance against President Sadat's peace treaty, to remain aloof.

None of the Arab air forces has fighters capable of standing up to the sophisticated aircraft supplied to Israel by the United States.

For this reason, Jordan has decided to buy Mirage F-1s, which, while not a match for Israel's F-15s, are a lot more sophisticated than their current fighters.

Senior Jordanians have confided that they were hopeful Colonel Gaddafi would make available to Jordan at least some of the 38 Mirage F-1s being delivered to Libya.

Although nothing official has emerged, I believe the Jordanians remain hopeful that Colonel Gaddafi will provide the aircraft. In return, Jordan has committed itself to provide limited military training for Libya's over-equipped but under-trained, forces.

"We will send a few officers," one official said. It has agreed also to provide training in Jordan for Libyan police.

The Irakis have expressed concern to the Jordanians about President Assad's position.

There is considerable tension in Syria because of a terrorist campaign against the minority Moslem sect of Alawites – the sect to which Mr Assad belongs. Although the campaign has been underway for three years in an attempt to undermine Mr Assad, it escalated recently with the massacre of at least 50, mainly Alawite Syrian army cadets in Aleppo, northern Syria.

Syria has blamed the Moslem Brotherhood and executed 15 people last week.

Less than a year ago, Irak and Syria were at loggerheads. But because of events in Iran and the Egyptian-Israeli peace moves, the two regimes patched up their differences and say they are committed to political union between Irak and Syria.

Although the Irak leadership has been less than happy with Mr Assad as a partner, it is now concerned that he might be toppled at a time when it (Irak) is seen to be identified with him and his regime.

It is also concerned that Mr Assad might be right in blaming the fanatical Islamic movement, the Moslem Brotherhood. Already in trouble with its eastern neighbor, the Islamic Republic of Iran, it does not want to see the emergence of a fanatical Islamic regime in Syria.

The Government in Bagdad has a particular reason for concern. Although the government is predominantly Sunni Moslem, the majority in Irak is Shi'ite Moslem. Shi'ite Islam is predominant in Iran and the Government is believed to be concerned about Iran's revolution jumping the border into Irak.

What came out of at least part of the Jordanian-Irak talks was not so much that Mr Assad might fall, but that Irak did not want to be caught with its pants down.

Separatist violence poses growing challenge to Iran
From DAVID BALDERSTONE

'The Age', Teheran, July 15, 1979

Iran's Government faced a serious challenge today after Kurds routed revolutionary guards in the north and sabotaged the crucial southern oil pipeline system for the third time.

Revolutionary guard reinforcements were being flown to Kurdistan today after autonomy-seeking Kurds took over the border town, Marivan, in bitter clashes yesterday.

At least 22 people were reported dead when a ceasefire was arranged last night.

Tanks were also being moved in to back up the guards, according to Kurdish Democratic Party officials in Teheran.

In the main oil-producing province, Khuzestan, saboteurs succeeded in damaging the pipeline system for the third time in a week.

A group calling itself "Black Wednesday", which is believed to be fighting for autonomy for the Arab majority in the province, claimed responsibility for the first two acts of sabotage.

Production at the world's biggest oil refinery at Abadan has had to be cut because of damage to the pipelines.

Iran's unofficial Head of State, Ayatollah Khomeiny, said at the weekend that Iran was passing through its most sensitive time since the revolution ousted the Shah almost six months ago.

In a speech in the religious capital Qum, he warned Iranians about conspiracies aimed at undermining the Islamic revolution.

"At this moment, which is more sensitive than any other and when the fate of the country must be set out, and the foundation of the country must be laid, there are conspiracies in the process of being implemented," Ayatollah Khomeiny said.

Fighting between Kurds and revolutionary guards broke out early yesterday when the guards attempted to disarm Kurds taking part in a demonstration in Marivan.

During eight hours of fighting, the Kurds took over the offices of the local revolutionary committee, according to the Kurdish Democratic Party.

A spokesman for the party said today the town of Marivan, which is near the border with Irak, was in the hands of the Kurds.

It is believed that leaders of the Kurds in the north and the Arabs in the south have had meetings recently in a bid to co-ordinate their attempts to achieve autonomy.

Iran: will anarchy be the next step
From DAVID BALDERSTONE, our Middle East correspondent who visited Teheran

'The Age", July 28, 1979

A small lane leads to an unpretentious villa near central Teheran. It is early still and a couple of revolutionary guards are just waking as the hot morning sun edges the shadow away from the large rug in the garden.

Israeli-made sub-machine guns are out of sight under the pillows. Another two guards are washing in the fountain at the centre of the garden. Tea is being brewed.

A servant leads the way to the upstairs reception room. It is empty except for two large Persian rugs and a few cushions around the wall. A telephone on the floor rings, but is ignored.

Ayatollah Ali Khamenai, a tall, bearded man in his early forties, enters and sits on one of the cushions. He touches his black turban, lights his pipe and apologises for being late.

Ayatollah Khamenai, a former student and close confidant of Iran's unofficial Head of State, Ayatollah Khomeiny, is a member of Iran's supreme governing body, the Revolutionary Council.

He is a member of Iran's new power elite – the Islamic clergy.

In secret conclave in the religious capital, Qum, the clergy-dominated revolutionary council holds the reins of government – to the regular humiliation of the Provisional Government led by the Prime Minister, Mr Bazargan.

Since the last of the Shah's governments fell in February, decision-making has been divided between the Ayatollah Khomeiny, the Revolutionary Council, the Provisional Government and the revolutionary committees.

The Government and the committees take directions from the Revolutionary Council

The humiliation of working with this cumbersome system has brought Mr Bazargan to the brink of resigning several times.

With Iran staggering from one crisis to another Iran's religious and political leaders hammered out a formula last week aimed at unifying decision-making.

Five members of the Revolutionary Council – four of them, including Ayatollah Khamenai and senior clergy – will join the Government. A number of Government Ministers will join the Revolutionary Council.

But while this shake-up may give Iran a more unified and central system of government, it is clear the clergy have tightened their grip on decision-making – at the expense of Mr Bazargan's Government.

"The Revolutionary Council sees that at this time of the revolution the Government has not used its existing authority to do everything as fast as was needed," Ayatollah Khamenai told 'The Age'.

"After the revolution there was an urgent necessity to act fast and the Government was always slower than it should have been."

There is little to indicate that the clergy have any intention of relinquishing power to the Government. Instead, intentionally or unintentionally, power has been manipulated on a divide and rule basis which effectively has made certain power resides in Qum rather than Government offices in Teheran.

"The Revolutionary Council is acting like a Parliament. So the Government is carrying out the orders of this Parliament. Also revolutionary committees are obeying the orders of the Revolutionary Council – and helping the Government," Ayatollah Khamenai says.

"Because the Government has not acted as fast as it should have acted, the gaps have been filled by the committees. These committees have been satisfying the immediate needs of the revolution."

But this divided and disunifed rule has failed to cope with the problems besetting Iran. Certainly the clergy have gained control of the decision-making process. But they are losing control of the country.

Five months after the revolution achieved what was seen then as an incredible final victory – the removal of the Shah – Iran's leaders have failed to fill the vacuum left by the absence of the Pahlavi dynasty.

There is anarchy in much of the country; basic food prices have risen 20 per cent and a large question mark hangs over the oil industry, which is crucial to Iran's economy.

These days it is common to hear sincere, but almost certainly unrealistic talk of the Shah returning to Iran.

The shambles in which Iran finds itself leads to constant talk of a coup d'état.

Ironically, the problems are due to the unstoppable force unleashed by the revolution. As a reaction against the repressive rule of the Shah, the revolution unleashed expectations among workers and ethnic minorities in the provinces that they would play a role at last in their own government.

But most importantly, the revolution unleashed the political aspirations of the Shi'ite Moslem clergy which had been repressed during monarchic rule.

Suddenly the clergy – strengthened by the crucial unifying role they played in bringing down the Shah – have found the power to impose the 1300-year-old laws of the Koran, the Moslem holy book, on Iran's 36 million people.

Ayatollah Khomeiny has banned alcoholic drinks, banned mixed swimming (at the Teheran Intercontinental Hotel women swim in the morning and men in the afternoon), banned music ("the people's opium") and abandoned the Shah's progressive marriage laws in favor of the traditional Islamic laws.

The minimum marriage age for women has been lowered from 15 to 13 years, which the old men of Qum have interpreted as being the Prophet Mohammed's "age of maturity" for women. Since the law was changed two months ago, 1700 girls between 13 and 15 have sought permission for marriage in Teheran alone.

Outside Iran, Ayatollah Khomeiny and the clergy tend to be seen as one. But the reality is that Khomeiny is losing influence to other leaders, such as the more flexible and moderate Ayatollahs Teleghani and Shariat-Madary, whose power bases are considered to be considerably larger than Khomeiny's.

Outside official buildings in Teheran it is more common these days to see pictures of Ayatollah Teleghani than those of the 79-year-old leader of the revolution.

Also there are indications that the younger members of the religious hierarchy intend to play a dominant role in future and relegate Ayatollah Khomeiny to a symbol of the revolution.

With power already in the hands of the clergy, it seems likely a member of the Islamic hierarchy will stand for the Presidency – but not necessarily Ayatollah Khomeiny.

"We have outstanding political people in our young religious men," Ayatollah Khamenai says.

"When I say young I mean not somebody of the age of the Imam (Khomeiny) or somebody like him.

"The Imam Khomeiny is leader of the whole Moslem world. He is the outstanding revolutionary leader of the past 50 years; he should remain as a leader of the revolution and not be bound and limited as President of Iran."

It is argued sometimes that in a country where 56 per cent of the population is illiterate, the return to Islamic laws will not be challenged.

But the imposition of Islamic law has quickly bred discontent among Iran's middle class which, although a minority, are the people on which the Iranian economy – including the oil industry – depends for management and specialist skills.

After years of being projected forward into the 21st century by the Shah, Iran is facing the traumatic experience of returning to the days of the Prophet Mohammed.

The middle class is not taking the change well. It has led to a mass exodus of Iranians from the country.

Every airliner leaving Teheran is booked out for the next two months – and many of the passengers have no intention of returning.

Since the heady days after the Shah left, when foreigners were seen as tools of the corrupt Pahlavi dynasty, the Iranian attitude to foreigners has changed remarkably.

"American?" a young Iranian shouted to me in Teheran the other day.

"Americans are very good you must all return to Iran. So you are not American but Australian. Australia is a very good country – I want to go and live there."

Such exchanges are common.

With the breakdown of law and order, the exodus of foreign experts and middle-class Iranians, uncertainty over industry nationalisation, and the proliferation of in-house company revolutionary committees, the economy is in bad shape.

Iran depends on oil. This year the Government expects to earn $22 billion from oil exports. Iran is producing around four million barrels a day from onshore and offshore rigs.

But can this continue?

"The revolution is a fiasco. The oil industry is running on inertia. Unless foreign experts are brought back, there will be breakdowns in the system," an official in the oil industry said.

Last year Iran had more than 70 oil rigs operating. Late this year it is expected there will only be 10 in action. Each rig directly employs around 100 workers.

Already the National Iranian Oil Company (NIOC) is quietly attempting to lure foreign workers back to the oilfields. Foreign experts are necessary particularly in exploration, which has virtually stopped since the revolution.

Another problem is that most of the oilfields are in Khuzestan Province, where the Arab majority is fighting for independence.

The oil pipeline system has been sabotaged three times in the past three weeks. An Arab guerilla group calling itself "Black Wednesday" has claimed responsibility for the sabotage, which cut production at Abadan refinery – the world's largest – by 100,000 barrels a day.

Unless sabotage is checked, oil exports – and therefore Iran's economy – could be jeopardised.

Elections are to be held early next month for an assembly of experts to study the draft constitution for the Islamic Republic. Although the draft provides for a 270-member Parliament, sweeping powers are given to the President.

The strong hand of the clergy has made it difficult for democratic-thinking liberals of the middle and upper class to see any chance of real democracy in the near future.

For this reason they now talk of a process of evolution towards democracy. For them, the revolution is not over.

"One has to look at things with a revolutionary eye," the head of the National Democratic Front, Mr Hadyatollah Matine Deftary, told 'The Age'.

"After years of corrupt, repressive rule, the country is trying to rise. There is no alternative to going through a proper revolutionary process. What happened last winter (when the Shah was forced to leave) was just a landmark of the revolution."

Mr Deftary, a prominent lawyer, says: "Anarchy is not something to be afraid of." Mr Deftary in fact sees hope of responsible democratic government emerging from a period of anarchy.

"Responsible forces must not get involved in the anarchy. The danger would come if responsible forces become irresponsible."

After five months with a power vacuum – and a leadership which has achieved little more than the imposition of Islamic laws – Iran is ripe for anarchy. The armed forces remain divided and under strength. Local committees and Right and Left-wing militias appear to hold more power than the military.

Without strong central authority, corruption has broken out. Local committees extract pay-offs from sly-grog merchants and others dealing in merchandise banned under Islamic law. At the airport, a young man approached me and said my baggage would not be opened if I paid.

Without order, corruption has been democratised. Just a week after three women had been executed for operating brothels, Teheran's red light district – called the New City – was operating.

"The revolution is facing two major problems," Ayatollah Khamenai says. "The Pahlavi dynasty's corrupt influence on the country was very deep, and remains. We want to cure society.

"Secondly, we are attacked by countries which gained so much benefit from the ex-regime."

Because of the lack of central authority and the absence of a strong army and police force, Western military sources in Teheran do not rule out the possibility of a military coup succeeding. However the thought of the Shah returning is not seriously entertained.

But there is no escaping the fact. The Shah's shadow looms large over Iran.

Baktiar back on stage
 - *DAVID BALDERSTONE*

'The Age', Amman, August 4, 1979

After five months in hiding, Shapur Baktiar – the former Iranian Prime Minister who persuaded the Shah to leave Iran before himself being overtaken by the revolution – emerged this week as the man to watch in Iranian politics.

With turmoil throughout much of Iran, growing hostility towards the imposition of Islamic laws, and the Provisional Government's failure to cope with economic problems, support for the mysterious missing Baktiar has grown considerably in Iran in the past month.

And, almost as if on theatrical cue, Dr Baktiar emerged in Paris this week and accused Iran's unofficial Head of State, Ayatollah Khomeiny, of establishing a religious dictatorship.

"I am a religious man, but religious leaders should not interfere in affairs of State. The mullahs should return to their mosques," he said.

While Dr Baktiar did not go into details about his political plans, it is clear he intends to be to Khomeiny what Khomeiny was to the Shah – a critic using the international media from Paris.

In the hope of stemming the revolutionary tide by replacing the military government with a civil administration, the Shah appointed Dr Baktiar, a long time Opposition politician, as Prime Minister in early January.

Later in the month the Shah tearfully left Iran on "holiday" after Dr Baktiar had stalled Ayatollah Khomeiny for several days. The revolution's leader returned to Teheran to a triumphant welcome on February 1.

In the face of mounting clashes between the army and demonstrators – and widespread defection from the armed forces –

the army withdrew to barracks and the short-lived Baktiar Government fell on February 11.

And Dr Baktiar went into hiding.

At the time, Ayatollah Khomeiny described Dr Baktiar as a person who has neither friends nor supporters. But his ability to evade capture by revengeful revolutionaries, and slip the country sometime during his five months in hiding indicate he had both.

Support among educated Iranians has grown dramatically for Dr Baktiar, who was intent on cracking down on corruption and steering the country towards a republican system of government or a least a constitutional monarchy.

Instead Iran has been left with an impotent Provisional Government operating under the strong arm of Ayatollah Khomeiny's Revolutionary Council.

The point about Dr Baktiar is that he cannot be dismissed as either a Shah's man or a politician with the support merely amongst the middle and upper class.

He is a leading member of one of the largest and most powerful tribes in Iran, the Baktiaris (from which his name is derived) and has spent time in jail because of his long time opposition to the excesses of the Shah's regime.

It is difficult to see how Dr Baktiar is going to make the transition from being an exiled critic to a participant in the mainstream of Iranian politics. But, then, we were all saying that about the Ayatollah Khomeiny a year ago, weren't we?

Threat to peace as old foes fall out
From DAVID BALDERSTONE IN Amman

'The Age', August 15, 1979.

A dramatic cooling in relations between Syria and Irak has cast a shadow over moves by Arab States and the Palestinian Liberation Organisation towards Middle East peace.

While the Arabs, including the PLO, are not poised to embrace the peace initiative of the United States and Egypt, they seemed to be edging towards a more conciliatory posture.

But the Irak-Syria rift threatens Arab unity, which has been nurtured so carefully since President Sadat of Egypt visited Jerusalem in November, 1977.

Without this unity, any Sate, or the PLO, seen to be moving towards peace will be condemned for selling out to the Egyptian-Israeli-American approach. In Arab politics there is safety in numbers.

The cooling in Iraki-Syrian elations comes at a time when the PLO needs to be seen to have the moral, diplomatic, and financial support of a united Arab camp behind it in its stepped-up quest for top-level relations with West European countries – and eventually, the United States.

Also, there are signs that Egypt – depressed about lack of progress in the talks with Israel over autonomy for West Bank and Gaza Strip Palestinians – is becoming more conciliatory towards its Arab opponents and the Soviet Union.

The cooling has taken place because of some alleged Syrian involvement in the "conspiracy" against Irak's new leader, President Saddam Hussein.

At least some of the 21 senior Iraki officials executed for their part in the conspiracy are said to have had close links with the Syrian Baath Party.

Arab officials confirm that the Iraki leadership believed the Syrians were involved, but it is not thought that the Damascus Government played a direct part.

Instead, it is believed the links were latent – a hangover from a previous long period of hostile Syrian-Iraki relations.

King Hussein of Jordan is understood to have spent much of the past week urging President Hussein and Syria's President Hafez Assad to act with restraint.

The danger for the PLO at this stage is that its drive for Western recognition could be threatened by the cooling of relations between Syria and Irak.

Amman, August 18, 1979 (*To niece Sally*)

Although as you know from regular reading of the newspaper, I am an expert on most of the countries in this part of the world, I was puzzled when the Ayatollah Khomeini banned music in Iran and called it the people's opium. After all I thought, if I had his permanently sad and serious face I would have liked a bit of music to cheer me up. It took all of the recent fortnight I spent in Teheran to find out the real reason he banned music. As you will remember, Ayatollah Khomeini spent 15 years exiled from Iran, and then three months in Paris before leading the revolution against the Shah and returning to Iran this year. Well, as a close friend of the Ayatollah told me, he became extremely lonely during this time away from home and looked forward to any contact with his friends and relations.

His niece was very good early on and used to write a lot. He even sent her a special gift because she had written when others had not bothered. But as time passed she spent more and more time playing the lute and there was time no more for writing letters. Ayatollah Khomeini has never forgotten this and, according to his friend, unreasonableness took over his normally rational mind a month ago when he woke up with pins and needles in his neck. And he banned music. Having not received a letter from you for several months, I'm wondering whether there isn't a little bit of Ayatollah Khomeini in me.

It is the holy Muslim month of Ramadan during which all good Muslims fast from dawn to dusk. Smoking is banned in the streets and restaurants and bars are closed during the day, alcoholic drinks are banned altogether. The Muslims wake up at around 2 am and have a gigantic meal and then go back to sleep until its time for work and then don't eat again until dusk. Last year during Ramadan I was in Egypt, and travelling one day in a taxi I asked the driver whether he would mind if I had a cigarette. He said he didn't mind at all and that he would have one (of mine, of course) too, because he was "a Christmas".

Some friends of ours have got a pet donkey. They saw it standing beside a main road in Amman for several days abandoned. On about the fourth day children were throwing stones at it, so Sue stopped the car and bundled the donkey into the back seat. It is only about two months old and is about 18 inches tall. Its ears seem about the same length and it is very sweet. They are hoping to take it home to England when they finish in Jordan at the end of the year.

Amman August 21, 1979 (*To cousin Balfour*)

I was in Iran about a month ago. In spite of the fact a double round of cold teas or Pepsi cola is not exactly what I like to drink before dinner, it is really quite fun over there. At least the story is quite good and obviously not the Arab-Israeli peace moves, which one finds hard to take too seriously when believing Middle East peace is out of the question. I find it hard to see either side making the compromises necessary for enduring peace. Unlike President Carter, who less than a year ago thought the Shah was safe, I reckon I know the Arabs and Israelis pretty well. They both have a natural distrust and hatred of each other and it is hard to see that changing.

But, back to Iran. I had a stroke of luck because I met one of the Ayatollahs who went to Australia and New Zealand to inspect abattoirs to make certain they were killing Islamic style. Well, he is very friendly; loved Australia, and was a great help. He took me to see his friend who is on the Revolutionary Council, which is the most senior decision-making body in post-revolution Iran. Although the country is in a hell of a mess with the army and police forces divided and the economy shaky, this meeting with the clergy made me feel a bit sorry for them. Undoubtedly they are misguided, but they seem sincere. Suddenly they have found they have power but don't know how to handle it. I have never been for a more soaring drive than with Ayatollah Mahdavi – the one who visited Australia – who drove me to see his friend early one Friday morning. He drives very fast; ignores red lights, and toots endlessly when caught in traffic jams. It crossed my mind that I should say to him that he may be a Muslim and believe in predestination but that I wasn't, and didn't.

Peace at all costs
From DAVID BALDERSTONE in Beirut

'The Age', September 4, 1979

There was nothing unsoldierly or undisciplined about it, but an unmistakeable air of bitterness surrounded the Fijian lines in South Lebanon last week.

Three Fijian soldiers, who were part of Fiji's 500-strong contingent attached to the UN peace-keeping force, had been ambushed and murdered in cold blood by gunmen believed to be Leftist Lebanese or Palestinian.

The incident raised to about 30 the number of UN troops who have died since the United Nations Interim Force in Lebanon was sent to the area by the Security Council 18 months ago.

The 6000-odd UNIFIL force has the most difficult UN peace-keeping task in the Middle East. It is operating in the hottest area.

UNIFIL has been given the job of keeping the peace on a 30 by 45 kilometre chequerboard in South Lebanon on which Israel, Christian militias, Lebanese Leftists, and Palestinians have played Arab-Israeli war in deadly earnest – albeit in miniature – for the past two years.

It has never been easy, but UNIFIL had just gone through the most difficult 10 days of its term in Lebanon, the force commander, Major General Emmanuel Erskine of Ghana, said when 'The Age' visited the UN lines.

Six days of mounting tension led up to four days of extremely heavy artillery and rocket duels between the Israeli-backed Christian militias and Leftist Lebanese and Palestinians before the fighting was brought to a shaky ceasefire.

The stillness of the rolling biblical hills was punctuated by the occasional blast of artillery and small arms fire.

It was 10 days of crisis, which left three UN soldiers wounded and cast a long shadow over the future of UNIFIL.

"We regret the loss of the three Fijian soldiers very much. Of the 13 wounded, one is paralysed – we don't know whether it is permanent or temporary. What makes it worse is that he was married only two months ago," Major General Erskine said.

"We are a peace-keeping force. We are not here at war with anyone. If we have to fight every day with people getting killed or paralysed then the contributing countries are going to say: 'Well that's enough'."

If UNIFIL had to be abandoned because governments failed to see any domestic political advantage for them in providing cannon fodder for the Middle East war game, then it would not be in the interests of the area or the Lebanese.

Why is South Lebanon the hottest spot in the Middle East? Why was UNIFIL sent to the area?

For several years the border between Israel and Lebanon has been the only land crossing available to Palestinian guerillas wanting to infiltrate and attack Israel.

Jordan has not tolerated Palestinian armed presence since King Hussein's army routed the Palestinians in the 1970-71 civil war in Jordan. The Syrian and Egyptian borders with Israel have been manned by UN forces for several years.

After the bloody 1975-77 years of the Lebanese civil war, some border areas with Israel were left in the control of Christian militias led by a renegade Lebanese army officer, Major Sa'ad Haddad.

After the main civil war, a fierce struggle developed between the border Christian militias, supplied and supported by Israel, and the Palestinians (and their Leftist Lebanese allies) who found the Christians an obstruction in their war against Israel.

There is one other ingredient in the recipe of South Lebanon's disaster. This is Israel's potential ambition for territory between the

Israel-Lebanese border and the Litani River in Lebanon. The river flows between four and 30 kilometres from the border.

An early Zionist plan envisaged the Litani River as the proposed Jewish State's northern border. In view of Israel's shortage and hunger for water, it is widely believed by the Arabs that the Israelis continue to covet the river.

Whether or not that is true, Israeli forces invaded South Lebanon in March last year after the most serious Palestinian raid into Israel. The stated intention of the invasion was to establish a buffer zone north of Israel's border to prevent Palestinian infiltration.

UNIFIL was formed to fill the vacuum left by Israel's withdrawal from South Lebanon. The force was to patrol between the border and the Litani River in a bid to stop Christian-Palestinian fighting and Palestinian infiltration into Israel.

The Israeli withdrawal was in three stages. The first two went according to UN plans and Israel handed over positions to UNIFIL.

However, in the third stage of troop withdrawal, Israel handed over border positions to Major Haddad's Christian militias rather than UNIFIL. Haddad declared this area "independent free Lebanon".

This has left UNIFIL with a wedge of territory between the Christian militias in the south and the Palestinians and Leftists in the north.

In addition to being caught in the middle of a war between the Israeli-backed Christians and the Palestinians, UNIFIL has to attempt to prevent Palestinian infiltration into Israel.

The area involved is so small that all groups – Israel, Palestinians, Christians and Lebanese Leftists – have artillery and rockets capable of hitting each other.

"When there is action by one group, there is reaction by the other," Major General Erskine said.

"I have been wondering whether groups in the area – the Palestinian Liberation Organisation, the Leftists and the groups in the south (Israel and the Christians) know what UNIFIL is here to do.

"We have been accused by Israel and the de facto Lebanese forces (UN shorthand for the Christians) of co-operating with the PLO and other groups. "When we go to Beirut, we are accused (by Lebanese and Palestinian interests) of co-operating with Israel and the de facto forces.

"Well that's okay. That's fine. But let everybody understand that we are a peace-keeping force here to assist the people of Lebanon and to bring peace to the area. "Our mandate may not be in line with other groups' interests but we are not here to make war."

Major General Erskine said the border area held by the Christians would have to be handed over to UNIFIL if the UN mandate was to be carried out. This would have to be done by force or through diplomatic channels.

"The basic attitude of Israel towards the UNIFIL mandate must change or it will be very difficult for us.

"We know they have some presence in the Christian enclaves. But whether they are firing from the enclaves I don't know. I cannot confirm or deny.

"We are fighting on all fronts. In the north we are fighting infiltration (by the Palestinians) and in the south incursions." (Israel has made incursions into UNIFIL lines allegedly in "hot pursuit" of Palestinian guerillas.)

Major General Erskine, a man with a seemingly impossible job, was speaking with the controlled frankness of an elite officer. But it was frankness fuelled by frustration, and perhaps bitterness.

Then he talked with some relief about the ceasefire, which seemed to be holding. "But what is going to happen in the next hour, or tomorrow, I don't know."

Sadat set for autonomy tussle
From DAVID BALDERSTONE

'The Age", Haifa, September 4, 1979

President Sadat of Egypt arrived here today on his third visit to Israel set to press Israel into giving Arabs in East Jerusalem the right to vote in proposed autonomy elections for the West Bank.

The move seems certain to be resisted by the Israeli Prime Minister, Mr Begin, because Israel has unilaterally annexed East Jerusalem and no longer considers it to be part of the West Bank territory.

President Sadat arrived in Israel's main port, Haifa, on board an 80-year-old Presidential yacht, which once belonged to King Farouk of Egypt.

The Egyptian President, his wife and daughter, were met at the port by President Navon of Israel and Mr Begin.

President Sadat said on arrival that Egyptians were "determined to spread the umbrella of peace to include the Palestinian people".

Mr Sadat was speaking in a response to a welcome from President Navon. Mr Navon said he was confident President Sadat's talks with Mr Begin in Haifa would remove some of the "impediments that lie in the path of peace".

It is President Sadat's eighth summit meeting with Mr Begin.

Three topics seem certain to dominate discussions between the leaders.

First, Israel wants Egypt to sell Israel the total annual production of the Alma oil fields in Sinai, after the fields, which have been developed by Israel, are handed back to Egypt in November.

Egypt has agreed to sell Egypt three quarters of the annual production, but insists the other quarter be sold by international tender.

Second, the leaders will discuss what type of international force should police Sinai disengagement – an issue stemming from the disbandment of the United Nations emergency force in Sinai in July.

It is the third topic – the slow moving talks between Egypt, Israel and the US on proposed autonomy for West Bank and Gaza Strip Palestinians – which is likely to prove the most difficult issue.

Calm before crunch on autonomy
– DAVID BALDERSTONE

'The Age', Amman, September 15, 1979

United States Middle East envoy, Mr Robert Strauss, concluded another brief visit to Egypt and Israel this week saying that he had struck "the spirit of renewed confidence and renewed determination" to conclude successfully Palestinian autonomy negotiations.

But despite this confidence which was echoed by Cairo and Jerusalem, it seems difficult to envisage how a crunch in negotiations can be avoided.

For by the end of March next year Egypt and Israel will have had to resolve major differences over the question of autonomy for West Bank and Gaza Strip Palestinians.

Most of this week's confidence seems to be based on the growing – apparently sincere – friendship developing between President Sadat of Egypt and Israel's Prime Minister, Mr Begin, a relationship strengthened at last week's summit in Haifa.

But it is a friendship that has not been strained by talking about the really thorny issues. In fact, the friendship has been able to develop because both Mr Sadat and Mr Begin have agreed to disagree on the thorny issues.

But this situation cannot continue if Egypt and Israel are to conclude negotiations on autonomy within the specified one year after the peace treaty signing last March.

There are two major differences between Egypt and Israel.

Egypt believes East Jerusalem, which was administered by Jordan before the 1967 war, should be included in the West Bank autonomy scheme. However Israel has unilaterally annexed East Jerusalem, considers it an indivisible part of Israel's capital, and no longer considers it a part of the West Bank.

Secondly, Egypt wants autonomy to include political, economic, legislative and judicial powers while Israel is offering only limited, administrative rights.

The question being asked widely in Israel – and indeed the Arab world – is whether Mr Sadat is playing for time. There are three reasons why time might be on his side. First, three months before the autonomy negotiations must be completed Israel will have completed interim withdrawal from Sinai. This entails withdrawal from two-thirds of Sinai, including the Alma oil fields.

Secondly, unity amongst Egypt's Arab opponents is fraying rapidly at the edges. The recent major slump in relations between Syria and Irak could, with time, make it more simple for Jordan, the Palestinian Liberation Organisation, and Saudi Arabia to move closer to the peace process.

Thirdly, the Palestine Liberation Organisation is moving slowly towards getting recognition by the West.

Fourthly, by agreeing to disagree with Mr Begin on thorny issues, Mr Sadat is further enhancing his good image amongst Israelis – and probably in the West.

With progress on these four points, Mr Sadat may believe he will be in a strong position internationally and in Israel to drive a hard bargain in a few more months.

Swing low, sweet Syria
From DAVID BALDERSTONE in Amman

'The Age', September 29, 1979

The sun sinks behind the Ante-Lebanon Ranges leaving Damascus engulfed in the dusty dusk of late summer. Fluorescent tubes light up the minarets on the mosques, and the muezzins chant across the city.

In the Hamdiyeh souk, parallel to the Biblical "Street called Straight" in the Old City, is a mixture of stalls selling everything from Persian carpets to kitchen utensils.

In the modern shopping area around the National Assembly, chic Syrians browse among Western electrical goods and clothes from Paris and Rome.

Apparently Damascus is a city at peace with the job of living.

But standing in the shadows or patrolling the streets is a legion of fawn Range Rovers with automatic rifles hidden not too discreetly beside the passengers – members of Colonel Rifaat Assad's Damascus Security Forces.

They provide a constant reminder that a security problem exists in Damascus – and Syria generally.

Colonel Rifaat Assad, brother of Syria's President Hafez Assad, spearheads Damascus security. Like the Presidential guard, his men are almost exclusively recruited from the minority Muslim breakaway sect of the Alawites – the sect to which the President belongs.

Although the Alawites make up about 10 per cent of Syria's population, which is predominantly Sunni Muslim, they hold key positions around the President and in the military. They protect the President, and in return – according to a growing number of Syrians – rake in the spoils of government.

For more than two years there has been a growing terrorist campaign against prominent Alawites – a campaign almost certainly aimed at undermining the Assad regime. The Syrian authorities blame the fanatical Islamic group, the Muslim Brotherhood, for the campaign.

But what has changed recently is that the terrorist campaign has drawn a backlash from the Alawite community and brought sectarian fighting on to the streets. Three days of fighting between Sunni Muslims and Alawites took place in Latakia, a stronghold of the Alawites, after a prominent Alawite sheik was assassinated.

Although calm was restored by Syrian troops and tension has eased in the port city, the fighting was a turning point which broadened the base of resentment in both communities.

Add to this the country's economic problems, criticism that the Government is focusing too much attention on foreign issues, weariness with Syria's "peace-keeping" intervention in neighboring Lebanon, and you come up with the classic recipe for instability in Middle East countries.

And instability in Syria could push the Middle East closer to another war – a possibility made more real by the recent dogfight between Syrian and Israeli fighters over Lebanon.

Although a staunch opponent of the Egyptian-Israeli peace treaty, President Hafez Assad has been a stabilising influence in the Middle East since he came to power in a bloodless coup in 1970.

As well as being by far Syria's longest serving President (there were 21 successful and unsuccessful coups in the previous 24 years of independence), he has shifted Syria's foreign policy away from rejecting any settlement with Israel.

After the 1973 war which Syria launched with Egypt against Israel, President Assad's Syria accepted UN Security Council Resolution 338, which calls for immediate implementation of the key Resolution 242. Western diplomats in the Middle East take this as Syria accepting Israel's right to exist because Resolution 242 acknowledges the sovereignty, territorial integrity and political independence of every State in the area.

Also, although there is weariness in Syria over the fact that its "peace-keeping role" in Lebanon has achieved little towards a long-term solution to the neighbor's problems, the Syrians' initial intervention in Lebanon almost certainly saved the Christians from defeat in the civil war.

As events in Iran have proved, it is extremely difficult to assess whether internal strife is coming close to toppling a Middle East leader who appears to derive considerable support from the armed forces. But the Syrian authorities acknowledge they have a serious problem, and it would be fanciful to suggest President Assad is not under threat.

Although comparison with the situation in Iran last year is hardly valid, a Syrian Sunni Muslim religious leader, Isam Attar, preaches rebellion against the Assad regime from exile in Europe. But there the similarity with Ayatollah Khomeiny ends – Isam Attar's sister is the Minister for Culture in President Assad's Government.

"There is urban terrorism in Spain, Italy, Germany and Turkey", a close aide of the president told me at the weekend. "That doesn't mean there is widespread opposition to the Government."

Although President Assad's regime is often dubbed an Alawite regime, the President's aide underlined the fact that only four Cabinet Ministers are Alawites. There are 29 Sunni Muslims, two Christians and one Druze in the Cabinet.

However Alawites hold key positions in internal security. In common with most Middle East leaders, President Assad surrounds himself with people of unswerving loyalty.

The consensus among diplomats and Syrians sounded out this week was that they did not believe President Assad was about to fall. But there was the view that unless the President made major changes in government posts, devoted more attention to domestic affairs, particularly the economy, and was seen to be curbing excesses of corruption, he would not last.

Iran leaves Gulf of strained relations
From DAVID BALDERSTONE in Amman

'The Age', October 10, 1979

Mounting tension between Iran and her Arab neighbors, which has degenerated into a flexing of military muscle, is further eroding security in the Persian Gulf area – source of 40 per cent of the West's oil.

The ominous deterioration in Iranian-Arab relations comes at a time when the Arab States have failed to agree on a security arrangement aimed at filling the vacuum in Gulf security left by the fall of the Shah of Iran, alias policeman of the Gulf.

Put simply, the Iranians and the Arabs each believe the others are trying to meddle in their internal affairs. But that belies a complex situation stemming from historical Iranian-Arab distrust.

This distrust has been laced on the one hand with the Arabs' concern about the Islamic revolution spreading across their borders and on the other with the Iranian revolution's failure to get to grips satisfactorily with the problems of running the country – particularly the oil industry.

Such is the complexity of the situation that several unrelated developments over the past fortnight have come together to spell concern for the oil-hungry West.

So much so that the decision in July by the insurance underwriters Lloyds of London, to declare the Gulf a war zone looks more and more every day as much like prophecy as hard-headed business decision making. (At a London meeting two weeks ago the Gulf States failed to persuade Lloyds to remove their war zone surcharge on shipping insurance in the Gulf.)

The success of the Iranian masses in toppling the Middle East's most militarily powerful man, the Shah, sent an immediate shock around the Arab world – and particularly the Gulf States, including Irak and Saudi Arabia.

The implications of the success of the Shi'ite Moslem revolution were particularly disturbing to Irak and Bahrain – two countries where Sunni Moslem minorities rule over Shi'ite majorities.

Despite the fact that the Shah's relations with the Arab world in his later years as Persian king of kings was more workable than friendly, the revolution's success was only marginally less disturbing to other Gulf States.

It was disturbing because it spelt uncertainty. But more importantly it forced Arab leaders to come to grips with their own potential vulnerability. All Gulf States except Irak employ a high proportion of potentially disruptive expatriate expertise and labor, have limited defence capabilities and are led by privileged groups who are seen to lavish too much of the oil riches on themselves.

Therefore the success of the Iranian revolution raised two problems for the Arab leaders.

First there was the fear that it would spread over Iran's borders and threaten them.

Secondly there was the question of how best to reach some agreement on coping with Gulf security in the wake of the policeman's demise. Although this is threatened most from within at the moment, it is the external threat that has been the traditional concern.

The big bogey among most leaders of Arab Gulf countries, whose penchant for casinos, fast cars, and fleets of executive jets makes them certain loyalists to Western free enterprise, is Soviet expansionism

Just how the Soviets plan to move from their Aden stronghold in hopelessly troubled South Yemen is never fully explained, but to doubt it would be akin to preaching sedition in a Gulf mosque.

Sedition preached from mosques is exactly what Bahrain and Kuwait have had to cope with since the Shah's fall. Both countries recently have expelled Shi'ite Moslem preachers who, despite disclaimers from Iran's Foreign Minister, Dr Ibrahim Yazdi saying

Iran has no intention of exporting revolution, have been attempting to sow the seeds of revolution among Shi'ites.

This brings us to the past fortnight.

Coinciding with a bid by the Sultanate of Oman, which was rejected by other Gulf States, to arrange a security pact financed by Western Europe, Japan and the United States, the Iranian navy – for the first time since the revolution – upped anchors and carried out manoeuvres in the Gulf.

The Iranians claimed – almost certainly legitimately – that they were testing their ability to protect their own oilfields and terminals.

But, although the Arabs claim Iran is not carrying out her responsibilities towards Gulf security, the explanation was not accepted entirely.

The reason is that a senior Iranian clergyman, the Ayatollah Rouhani, has just renewed his claim – based on Iran's occupation of Bahrain in the 18th century – that Bahrain is part of Iran. The Shah relinquished Iran's claim in 1971.

The claim was denied by the Iranian Government and described as the personal view of the Ayatollah Rouhani. But as far as the Bahrain authorities were concerned, the damage had already been done. The message had been heard by the Shi'ite Moslem majority on the island State.

This led to Bahrain's Information Minister being quoted by the English-language 'Gulf Mirror' newspaper as saying troops moved regularly between the Saudi mainland and Bahrain. This also was denied, but the Saudis did make it clear that they would be prepared to supply troops to Gulf States whose territorial integrity was threatened.

The Ayatollah Khomeiny, Iran's revolutionary leader, heightened distrust among the Arabs last weekend in an address to Iranian pilgrims about to leave for Mecca.

"Now that Moslems are going to Mecca, they should in addition to worship, benefit from the political and social aspects of the pilgrimage," he said. "One of your duties is to form a front of the oppressed and, with the help of unity of expression and the slogan 'There is no god but Allah', get rid of domination by satanic powers."

He also said the Islamic world was in the clutches of the United States.

Although the Ayatollah Khomeiny was not specific about whom he saw as satanic powers, the comment immediately made the Arabs edgy. All the more so because his close confidant, the head of Iran's television and radio network, Sadeq Qotbzadeh, had just warned that all "despots, petty kings, emirs and sultans who maintained luxurious living standards at the expense of the masses must heed the Iranian revolution".

Then the tables suddenly turned and Iran was on the defensive. Guerillas, almost certainly Arabic-speaking Iranians fighting for autonomy in Iran's main oil producing province, Khuzestan, blew up a microwave telecommunications centre in the province.

Irak has been accused previously by the new Iranian authorities of aiding the rebels and within a few days the predictable accusation was forthcoming: "An Arab country" was blamed for plotting against the revolution.

While the Iranians may be correct, it is difficult to discount the view that the accusation, the Ayatollah Rouhani's claim to Bahrain, and the Ayatollah Khomeiny's pep talk to pilgrims, may be aimed at diverting the attention of Iranians from mounting problems at home.

It is far more simple to preach revolution than to run a country like Iran.

Both the Iranians and the Arabs are suffering from post-Iranian revolution jitters. The danger is that the implications of Gulf instability extend far beyond the States involved and into the fuel tanks of the West.

Clergy lose a scapegoat

By DAVID BALDERSTONE, our Middle East correspondent, who has just been to Iran

'The Age', November 9, 1979

With the resignation of Prime Minister Mehdi Bazargan's Government, Iran's unofficial Head of State instructed the clergy-dominated Revolutionary Council to run the country. While this was a victory for the Islamic clergy, the success could turn out to be hollow.

The resignation has robbed the clergy of the secular scapegoat for problems besetting post-revolution Iran.

Now Ayatollah Khomeiny and the senior clergy will be increasingly vulnerable to criticism about such earthly problems as unemployment, housing shortages and inflation.

Since the fall of the Shah's last Government in February, opposition to the strong hand of the clergy has been growing steadily among the middle class and educated people who have seen their dreams of a democratic Iran evaporating.

The Kurds and the Arabic-speaking Iranians in Khuzestan – two of the main minority groups wanting autonomy – have no liking of the power brokers among the Shi'ite Moslem leadership in Qum, the religious capital.

Add to this the concern among the Christian and Jewish communities and you come up with a growing movement against the clergy.

Of course, 60 per cent of Iran's 34 million people are illiterate, and Ayatollah Khomeiny undoubtedly has massive popular support. But the risk of growing erosion of this support cannot be discounted.

For Mr Bazargan, the occupation of the United States Embassy in Teheran by fanatic Islamic students was the straw that broke the camel's back. In name he was Prime Minister but in practice he was powerless to prevent the occupation or remove the students.

Since the revolution, power in Iran has been divided between Ayatollah Khomeiny, the Revolutionary Council, the secular Government and the revolutionary committees.

The frustrations of working within this cumbersome power structure placed Mr Bazargan continually on the brink of giving up. He has tendered his resignation several times.

Now his departure has fuelled speculation that the embassy occupation was part of an elaborate plot aimed at further humiliating the Government and that Khomeiny, or at least some close confidants, knew about it in advance.

Since Mr Bazargan took on the job, there has been a running battle between the secular government and the clergy. Some senior members of the clergy, who for the first time were enjoying the taste of power after decades of repression under successive Shahs, criticised the Government for not being revolutionary enough. In other words it was too conventional.

In July, the Revolutionary Council tightened its grip on the power structure at the expense of the Bazargan Government. Under the pretext of unifying the decision making of the Revolutionary Council and the Government, three council members – all senior clergy – joined the Government as junior Ministers.

Now, this Revolutionary Council, whose full membership has never been disclosed, will be running the country. It is still not known exactly how it works.

While the clergy is in firm control now, some senior members of the Islamic hierarchy have expressed criticism about the path Iran is taking. They are fearful that not only the clergy but Islam itself will suffer if Iran's problems are not seen to be resolved.

One of the most respected senior clergymen, Ayatollah Shariat-Madary, whose power base is centred on the north-western city of Tabriz, last week scolded people who dubbed critics of post-revolutionary Iran as "counter revolutionary".

"Criticism should be heeded and, if correct, acted on," he said.

Criticism there is, in post-revolutionary Iran. In Teheran recently the unemployed shouted slogans accusing the Government of being fascist. Women have renewed demonstrations against the erosion of their rights. Food prices have risen more than 25 per cent since the revolution. Minority groups such as the Kurds are stepping up their drive for autonomy.

In the face of these problems it is common to hear Iranians saying that Ayatollah Khomeiny and other senior members of the clergy have had to keep up criticism of the US and the Shah to try to divert attention from domestic problems.

"Survival for the present regime is increasingly becoming a matter of touch and go," a columnist in the English language weekly 'The Iranian', wrote last week.

"The economy is not picking up. Despite the regular inflow of oil money, the administrative paralysis of the country has prevented any effective Government investment plans for creating productivity and jobs; a growing section of the country is disaffected," he wrote.

Ayatollah Khomeiny has said women should wear the chador about their heads and expressed abhorrence of Western music. But already on the streets of Teheran, pavement stalls pump out Western music, such as tapes of Pink Floyd and The Rolling Stones. Every month sees fewer women bothering to wear a chador.

While these deviations are superficial, they are indications that more and more people are failing to follow Ayatollah Khomeiny's advice.

Kurds' lonely fight continues
DAVID BALDERSTONE, our Middle East correspondent, talks with Kurdish guerillas in Iran for autonomy

'The Age', November 10, 1979

It was dark by the time the jeep pulled up outside a villa near the centre of the Kurdish "capital" Mahabad. From the iron gate in the brown brick front wall, two guards – one with an M-16 and the other carrying a Kalashnikov – approached.

After checking credentials, they led the way through the gate into a courtyard garden. It had become overgrown since the previous owner – a Kurdish sheik who had sold out the Kurds to become an agent of the Shah's dreaded secret police, Savak – left during the Iranian revolution.

Now, ironically, this former Savak house is used by the Mahabad military committee of the Pesh Merga, which is the military wing of the Kurdish Democratic Party (KDP). The KDP is battling the new Iranian Government for the Kurds' right to run their own affairs.

In the main room, a group of guerillas are sitting around a table smoking and drinking sweet tea. With just a touch of amusement, they are listening intently to a brother commando named Mo' Alassam who is standing at the end of the table. It seems to be a briefing.

"The Islamic Republic of Iran is not Islamic in practice at all. It is anti-Islamic because Islam is a peaceful religion." Then Mo' Alassam breaks into a chant: "The Kurdish people are alive....."

Mo' Alassam, the Kurdish revolutionary, is aged 13, but his smooth face and fine black hair make him look younger.

Events in the recent fierce fighting between the Kurds and Iranian forces and revolutionary guards destined this small boy, who wears a dagger in his cummerbund, to become a Kurdish guerilla leader.

An Islamic court sent his father to death by firing squad; his brother was killed in fighting, and his mother committed suicide. The notorious Ayatollah Khalkhali, Iran's hanging judge, made this boy an orphan and a revolutionary.

Now Mo' Alassam is looked after by the Pesh Merga. After he sang a patriotic song about Kurdistan, a guerilla in his late twenties with hand grenades on his belt and an M-16 by his side, drew Mo' Alassam back into his arms and hugged him. Mo' Alassam, the revolutionary, was once again a little boy.

For centuries the Kurds have fought for an independent Kurdistan – a homeland roughly centred on the junction of the borders of Iran, Irak, and Turkey. There are also large pockets of Kurds in Syria and the Soviet Union.

The Kurdish cause has rarely been sincerely embraced by outsiders other than romantic travellers captivated by their incredible hospitality, fierce independence and determination, their flamboyant national dress, and the rugged mountains and lush plains of Kurdistan.

However, because of their strategically important position, they have been helped and used by countries playing for bigger stakes.

Just after the Second World War, the Soviet Union – coinciding with its troop withdrawal from north-western Iran – established a Kurdish republic with Mahabad as its capital.

But it was a short-lived dream.

The Shah sent in his troops and the Kurdish President, Zaki Mohammed, who remains a hero today, was hanged in Mahabad's main square. The quest for an independent Kurdistan lived on.

The Iranian revolution unleashed in the Kurds expectations that at last they would have an opportunity to run their own affairs. Now the stated political objective of the Iranian Kurds is to achieve autonomy within a democratic Iran. In essence, they want a federal system of government. They want to run their own affairs, but leave foreign and defence policy to Teheran.

For the past five months, amid dwindling hopes of achieving autonomy, the Kurds have been battling the Iranian army and the revolutionary Islamic guards for control of the major cities, including Mahabad. The number of deaths is well into the hundreds.

The Kurds control Mahabad, Bukan and Beneh. In the other main cities such as Saqqez and Kermanshah, revolutionary guards patrol the streets.

Because all the hotels were closed because of the trouble, we were the guests of a young teacher and his wife, who lived in a modern brick house in a new development on the outskirts of the town.

Just a few days earlier our hosts had been forced to sleep in the basement because the army had been firing into the estate from their hilltop positions. Bullets had penetrated the walls, and a glass-walled vestibule had been badly damaged.

My host, Ali, believes that Kurdish women are reasonably free compared with women in much of the Muslim world. His wife was also a university graduate and worked as a teacher.

The Kurds' call for autonomy is a thorn in the side of the new Iranian authorities. If autonomy was to be given to Iran's 5.5 million Kurds, other minority groups such as the Baluchis in the south-east and the Arabic speaking Iranians in oil-rich Khuzestan would be certain to intensify their campaigns for autonomy.

Unlike most Iranians, who are Shi'ite Muslim, most Kurds are Sunni Muslims. Their spiritual and political leader is Ayatollah Sheik Ezzadin Hosseini, who, since being described as "satanic" by Iran's unofficial Head of State, Ayatollah Khomeiny, has gone underground.

The Kurdish Democratic Party, led by Abdul Rahman Ghassemlou, an intellectual socialist, was banned under the Shah. The party emerged again after the revolution, but was soon outlawed by the Ayatollah Khomeiny.

What sort of autonomy do the Kurds envisage? "A democratic council would make decisions about the internal affairs of

Kurdistan. This would include policies on development programmes, education, local government and transport. But decisions about defence and foreign affairs of Iran would be taken by the central Government of Iran," Karim Husami, a KDP central committee member, told me.

Mr Husami, who spent 20 years in exile under the Shah, mainly in Eastern Europe, is said to be one of the main political brains behind the KDP and the deputy leader of the party.

"If we achieve autonomy, this will inspire the Kurds in Irak and Turkey to see that autonomy in the framework of the existing country is possible. It will strengthen the struggle to get independence within the existing Government framework," Mr Husami said.

A three-man Ministerial committee appointed by the Iranian Government is touring the Kurdish areas to negotiate a settlement. After intial talks in Mahabad, a member of the delegation, Provincial Affairs Minister Mr Dariush Forouhar, told Kurds: "Your legitimate rights will be met."

But whether the Government's view of the Kurds' legitimate rights goes far enough for the Kurds remains to be seen.

The Kurds will resume their centuries' old struggle unless the Government satisfies their demands.

Mo' Alassam, the little boy, will exchange his dagger for a gun as he grows up. And there are thousands of others like him. Iran's hanging judge, Ayatollah Khalkhali, has helped see to that.

Arab unity unlikely over PLO
From DAVID BALDERSTONE

'The Age', Amman, November 20, 1979

Renewed fighting in southern Lebanon has underlined problems faced by Arab leaders at a summit conference in Tunis this week.

President Hussein of Irak said that the Palestinian and Lebanese people were united. Arab countries were committed to help Lebanon "face up to Israeli aggression as often as necessary".

But the summit comes at a time when the Arab world has failed to stop President Sadat of Egypt signing a peace treaty with Israel and when Arab leaders are facing growing domestic criticism for adopting a negative approach towards the Arab-Israeli crisis.

Therefore it seems unlikely that Arab leaders will agree on such a touchy issue as tying the hands of the Palestinian guerillas.

Arab Foreign Ministers, who met in Tunis last week to prepare for the summit, failed to agree on a Lebanese plan.

The plan calls for a reduction in Palestinian armed presence in the south and their movement away from populated areas. It is also believed to call for a halt to Palestinian attacks into Israel from southern Lebanon.

After several weeks of relative calm in southern Lebanon, fighting erupted late on Sunday after Christian militiamen, who are supported by Israel, tried to move from their border enclaves into a village controlled by the United Nations Interim Force.

More than three hours of heavy rocket and artillery exchanges between the Christians and the Palestinians and their Lebanese Leftist allies followed. The situation remains tense.

The Lebanese Government wants a reduction in Palestinian activity in the south to remove Israel's excuse for continuing heavy air and sea bombardment.

Saudis retake Mecca shrine
From DAVID BALDERSTONE

'The Age', Jeddah, November 25, 1979

Saudi Arabian security forces have regained control of Mecca's Grand Mosque, according to Riyadh Radio.

Early today they dislodged the last of 400 gunmen who seized the mosque last week.

But Saudi authorities were slow to confirm today that the five day siege was finally over.

The Imam of the mosque, Sheik Mohammed Ibn Sabeel, said last night that security forces had taken control of the ground and upper floors of the mosque.

But a few remaining gunmen were still holding a small section of one floor of the mosque yesterday.

The gunmen, who included young boys, were described as Karmathians by one newspaper today. The Karmathians are believed to be a breakaway Moslem sect with a long history of rebellion.

The mosque was seized during dawn prayers on Tuesday and the gunmen demanded that Moslems in the mosque recognise their leader, who has been named as Johaiman, the awaited Mahdi or Messiah.

After a virtual blackout of news for five days, Saudi newspapers today published accounts of the siege, which has been sharply condemned by Islamic leaders throughout the world.

Witnesses gave the first details of what happened in the holy city of Mecca last Tuesday.

But the witnesses' accounts would have been approved by Saudi authorities before publication and do not say how many people were killed in the siege.

Sheik Sabeel said there were 300-400 gunmen. They had shouted "Allah O Akbar" and fired shots into the air as they attacked.

He said more than 100,000 pilgrims were performing rites in and around the mosque when the gunmen struck.

The Imam had escaped through a secret tunnel after the gunmen had locked all entrances to the mosque.

After prayers, pilgrims were surprised to see the door of the mosque being closed.

"We ran to the doors and found there were several people closing them with iron chains and big locks," a pilgrim said.

"A policeman tried to stop the gunmen shutting the King Abdul Aziz gate, but they shot him. Then I saw three people taking policemen out of an office. They shot the policemen.

"I sat down with some of the pilgrims and we heard shooting going on all around us. There were boxes of arms near one entrance."

The authorities have said that most of the gunmen are Saudi Arabians who will be harshly dealt with.

The witness accounts support reports that the gunmen were well armed and well trained.

Although there are no details on casualties, it is believed that non-critical patients were sent home from the Jeddah general hospital last Tuesday and Wednesday in case of casualties.

Iran's echoes rattle the Saudis
From DAVID BALDERSTONE in Amman

'The Age', November 28, 1979

Not without reason, the 400 guerillas who launched the bloody six-day siege of the Grand Mosque in Mecca have been compared in Saudi Arabia to California's Jim Jones sect.

For once they launched their assault on the mosque – Islam's holiest shrine – there was scant chance any of them would survive.

Those gunmen who did not die in the ensuing and quite predictable battle with Saudi security forces could have expected nothing less than gruesome execution as Islamic justice took its swift course.

They followed their leader, a man named Johaiman, whom they evidently saw as the awaited Mahdi, or Messiah, into the mosque. The mosque is something of a fortress, twice as easy to defend as to fight your way out of.

Johaiman has been identified as Mohammed Abdul Kahtani, 27, a former student of Mecca University, who holds conservative Islamic beliefs and wants radio and television banned and further restrictions placed on women.

When they stormed the mosque, the gunmen demanded at gunpoint that the thousands of pilgrims completing dawn prayers should recognise their leader as the Mahdi. The problem was no one recognised Johaiman as such.

Although full details are yet to emerge, the affair highlights security difficulties faced by Saudi Arabia – custodians of Islam's holiest places, and the Western world's biggest oil supplier.

And, in view of the fact that most, if not all the gunmen were Saudi Arabians, it raises with new force a question the oil-hungry West would rather not face: could Saudi Arabia become another Iran?

It is not the first time the Grand Mosque in Mecca – towards which all good Moslems face to pray – has seen violence. There are three notorious precedents.

Around 150 years after the death of the prophet Mohammed in 632 AD, a man from Taif, a hill city near Mecca which is today Saudi Arabia's summer capital, led an attack on the mosque. His name was Al Hajaj Bin Yusuf Al Fakathi.

Historically, the most celebrated case occurred in the twelfth or thirteenth century, when a tribe called the Karmathians from near Riyadh desecrated the mosque.

An attempted assassination of King Abdul Aziz, founder of modern Saudi Arabia, took place at the mosque in the early 1930s.

According to the Imam of the Grand Mosque, Sheik Mohammed Ibn Sabeel, there were about 100,000 pilgrims in or near the mosque when between 30 and 400 gunmen struck last Tuesday.

Pilgrims in the mosque at the time said the raiders, who included young boys, were well armed and had boxes of arms. This adds credence to reports that arms were already inside the mosque when the attackers arrived for morning prayers.

The gunmen are said to have been well trained, which has raised the frightening prospect for the Saudi Arabians that they could have received training outside the kingdom.

It is believed the arms could have been spirited inside in a truck used by builders, who are renovating part of the mosque.

Yesterday, a week after the attack, a few gunmen were still holding out in the mosque basement against security forces.

In view of the harshness of Islamic justice, there was little incentive to surrender.

On Sunday a newspaper in Mecca printed a picture of the mosque with smoke billowing out. It seems unlikely that damage was superficial.

Apart from the fact that the gunmen were well armed and trained, the Saudi authorities had two major problems: they had to diffuse the situation while minimising loss of life among the pilgrims trapped inside, and an all-out military action against such a holy shrine could not be undertaken lightly.

Although the Koran, Islam's holy book, says fighting must not take place in a mosque, it adds that if one is attacked in a mosque he may fight the attackers back because they are nonbelievers.

Saudi Arabia's King Khalid met Islamic leaders to seek agreement for the security forces to use arms against the gunmen. They issued a *fatwa*, a religious decree, which in effect gave the forces approval for heavy action.

Although there was mention of a *fatwa* being issued early in the siege, it was not until the last day that it was given heavy publicity inside Saudi Arabia. It is believed there was not full agreement amongst the Islamic leaders on the justification for force early on in the siege.

The question of whether Saudi Arabia could become another Iran is not new and has tended to be answered in the negative.

It is usually said that Saudi Arabia, a country of 5-7 million people cannot be compared with Iran, a country of 34 million. In Saudi Arabia the oil wealth does filter down – directly and indirectly – to the people much better than it ever did in the Shah's Iran.

Certainly, an armed siege of the Grand Mosque in Mecca is no way to gain control of a fiercely Islamic country. In that sense the Saudis are right to describe the events as criminal rather than political.

It is true that it is difficult to compare Saudi Arabia with Iran, but Saudi Arabia does have security problems.

As custodian of Mecca and Medina, it is host to around a million foreign pilgrims each year.

With Islam rearing its political head throughout the world, this presents a risk of Saudis brushing with foreign political ideas. (Scuffles broke out earlier this year when Iranian pilgrims started praising the Ayatollah Khomeiny.)

Whereas the vast majority of Iranians are Shi'ite Moslems, the Saudis are mainly Sunni. However, there is a significant minority of Shi'ites in the oil-field area on the Persian Gulf. It is said that Shi'ites hold a disproportionately high number of jobs in the oil industry.

The dramatic build-up of security plus the nervous way the Saudis were handling official statements about whether or not the siege was over, indicated the Saudi authorities were not so certain the kingdom could not become another Iran.

After all, it is only 55 years since King Abdul Aziz drove the Hashemites out of the Hejaz area, which includes Mecca and Medina. And it was not until 1932 that the monarch was able to finally proclaim the Kingdom of Saudi Arabia.

That was seven years after Shah Reza the Great – the Shah's father – seized power in Iran and founded the Pahlavi dynasty.

Revolt, Saudis urged
From DAVID BALDERSTONE

'The Age', Teheran, December 6, 1979

Relations between Iran and Saudi Arabia hit a new low today after Iran's Oil Minister delivered a strong personal attack on the Saudi Oil Minister, Sheik Yamani.

Iranian students called on Saudis to revolt against the monarchy and the US.

Students holding 50 Americans hostage said in a communiqué directed to the people of Saudi Arabia that it was a Godly duty to rise up against the US.

The attack on Sheik Yamani followed his refusal to go along with a Syrian and Libyan proposal earlier this week that Arab oil producers support Iran in its struggle against the US.

Instead Sheik Yamani walked out of the meeting of the Organisation of Arab Petroleum Exporting Countries in Kuwait saying that OAPEC was an "economic not a political organisation".

Iran's Oil Minister, Dr Moinfar, criticised Sheik Yamani yesterday for believing oil should be kept separate from politics.

"I am surprised that a person like Zaki Yamani, who knows economics and who has been unchallenged director of OPEC, should now claim that oil economics and politics are apart," he said.

"Maybe he would consider oil exports to Israel as being purely an economic activity. Well such personal suggestions are not new to us for the ex-Shah – like Zaki Yamani – declared he did not have political relations with Israel, but at the same time exported to Israel."

Dr Moinfar also said that world-wide oil production must be slashed drastically.

"The production of 35 million barrels a day by OPEC is far too high and has to come down," he said.

Iran would push for dramatic production cutbacks and also a switch in oil payments out of US dollars at the December 7 meeting of OPEC in Caracas, he said.

Addressing Saudi Arabians, the students' communiqué said: "Your land is where Islam rose. But the US easily plunders your oil and sucks your blood. Rising up against the US is a Godly duty."

The communiqué follows reports of anti-American demonstrations in the oil field area of eastern Saudi Arabia near Dhahran.

A Beirut newspaper has reported that Saudi authorities rushed 20,000 troops to the area to crush the demonstrations.

The communiqué said Saudi Arabians had "lived under repression and suppression.

"The US oppresses you with the help of weapons bought at the expense of your oil income."

Although most Saudi Arabians are Sunni Moslems, a significant minority of Saudis in the oil fields belong to the Shi'ite branch of Islam – the branch to which the majority of Iranians belong.

Meanwhile, a thousand followers of Iran's dissident Ayatollah Kazan Shariat-Madary set up barricades outside his house in Qum today to protest against the killing of two people in clashes with supporters of Ayatollah Khomeiny.

The demonstrators shouted "Death to Khalkhaly", a reference to the extremist Islamic judge, Ayatollah Khalkhaly, whom they blamed for yesterday's violence.

Army battles Tabriz rebels
From DAVID BALDERSTONE

'The Age', Teheran, December 10, 1979

After a night of fierce fighting, control of key Government buildings in the north-western city of Tabriz is divided between the Iranian army and rebel Azerbaijanis today.

The army, using units from Teheran, were in control of the television station, but the militant Azerbaijanis still held the Governor-General's Office early this afternoon.

The army and supporters of Ayatollah Khomeiny yesterday regained control of the station, which had been held by the militants for more than three days.

Thousands of people were attending a funeral in Tabriz today for the Azerbaijanis killed in the fighting.

There were widespread fears that renewed violence could be sparked by emotions of the mourners.

The central Government's decision to use force rather than entering into negotiations with the Turkish-speaking Azerbaijanis almost certainly means clashes will erupt again between the rival groups.

At least seven people died and 30 were injured in last night's fighting, which was centred on the television station and the Governor-General's Office.

At one stage pro-Khomeiny protesters marched on the International Hotel and demanded that it be surrendered within two hours, otherwise they would set it on fire.

Most foreign correspondents in Tabriz are staying in this hotel.

However, the management turned off the lights and the demonstrators did not go ahead with their threat.

Trouble broke out in Tabriz on Thursday when about 30,000 Azerbaijanis marched through the streets in protest against the new constitution giving sweeping powers to the Islamic clergy and Ayatollah Khomeiny in particular.

A Government peace mission led by a former Prime Minister, Dr Bazargan, was scheduled to arrive in Tabriz today.

However, it was due in the city two days ago and there was speculation this morning that its arrival might once again be postponed because of last night's fighting. After seizing the radio and television stations, the Azerbaijanis broadcast criticisms of the constitution and demands for autonomy in Azerbaijan.

The religious leader of the Azerbaijanis is Ayatollah Shariat-Madary, who until Khomeiny's return to Iran, was the country's senior ayatollah.

The rebellion in Tabriz, which is believed to have been widely supported by the people of East and West Azerbaijan provinces, presented the central authorities with their gravest crisis since the revolution.

The rebellion has stolen the limelight from the crisis in US-Iranian relations over the 50 Americans held hostage by Iranian students.

Iran has decided not to send a representative to the International Court in The Hague, which is scheduled to consider a US complaint against Iran today.

Iran's Foreign Minister, Mr Qotbzadeh, has said Iran does not recognise the competence of the court to hear the complaint.

About 10,000 supporters of Ayatollah Khomeiny marched through Tabriz yesterday and took back the television station without a bullet being fired.

Earlier, Ayatollah Khomeiny said in a broadcast speech that the rebellion in Tabriz had been caused by "elements of imperialism".

"These acts are committed by plotters who receive their orders from America and elsewhere," Khomeiny said.

"The people of Azerbaijan must be careful not to be influenced by those people so as not to bring disgrace on Azerbaijan forever."

In an interview published in the English language 'Teheran Times' today, Ayatollah Shariat-Madary was quoted as saying he supported the "popular demand" for self-rule in the two Azerbaijani provinces.

Central authorities face demands for autonomy from the Kurds, the Baluchis, the Arabic-speaking Iranians in oil-rich Khuzestan and the Azerbaijanis.

The man against Khomeiny
From DAVID BALDERSTONE in Teheran

'The Age', December 14, 1979

It was very easy, Ayatollah Shariat-Madary said, to accuse someone of being an agent of imperialism or Zionism. It was much more difficult to be fair.

The previous day Ayatollah Khomeiny, the man whose life Shariat-Madary is said to have saved in the early sixties, had blamed a rebellion by supporters of Shariat-Madary on agents of "imperialism".

Ayatollah Shariat-Madary, 74, was sitting cross-legged on the floor at his home in the city of Qum. Slowly rocking backwards and forwards, his hands gently wrestling each other, the old man was talking about his people, the Azerbaijanis of north-west Iran, and how they had got into conflict with the central authorities.

Although now there was a lull in fighting, the Azerbaijanis in Tabriz, capital of East Azerbaijan province, had been through four days of battle with supporters loyal to Ayatollah Khomeiny.

For three days, the Azerbaijanis held the television station; they broadcast demands for greater autonomy for East and West Azerbaijan provinces and echoed Shariat-Madary's criticism of Iran's new constitution which gives Khomeiny sweeping powers.

The trouble did not begin in Tabriz, but in Iran's religious capital Qum, south of Teheran last week. It was sparked when a sniper's bullet pierced the heart of Shariat-Madary's young guard, who had been standing on the Ayatollah's bedroom roof while the old man slept.

"When we objected to the constitution, some people started to demonstrate against us and shout slogans against me," Shariat-Madary said slowly.

"When they heard of this, some of our supporters discussed the point, and ultimately some of them fought against these other people. As a result, one person was killed in the street."

The old man then hesitated, and his eyes looked down to the rug on which he was sitting. "Another one, a young boy, a pious person who was not doing anything but guarding my house, he was shot.

"When this news reached Tabriz, the Azerbaijani people discarded a demonstration against the constitution. When a person is annoyed, he does whatever he likes; so they captured the television station and the Governor's house."

Shariat-Madary lives in a modest, traditional court-yarded house in central Qum's maze of alleyways, a maze symbolic of the political jungle.

According to his aides, Shariat-Madary has 15 million Shi'ite Moslem followers in Iran and more than 40 million worldwide. Before Ayatollah Khomeiny returned to Iran early this year, Shariat-Madary was Iran's senior ayatollah.

In the early 1960s, Khomeiny made a damning speech against the Shah and was being pursued with vengeance by the authorities. But Shariat-Madary secured Khomeiny's elevation to grand ayatollah, so the future revolutionary would benefit from the convention that grand ayatollahs were not to be executed. Soon afterwards, Khomeiny went into exile.

Now Khomeiny, as the country's leader, and Shariat-Madary, religious leader of the Azerbaijanis, are seen to be in conflict.

Not only is Shariat-Madary a critic of the constitution, but he has sharply criticised the central authorities' handling of the trouble in Azerbaijan. He says that when the trouble broke out, members of the Revolutionary Council visited him and asked his advice.

It was agreed a peace mission to the area would include his own representatives as well as members of the Revolutionary Council. But his representatives were not included.

He said this week: "If the executive makes mistakes again, disturbances will continue in Azerbaijan, people will start to kill each other and civil war will take place."

When I visited Ayatollah Shariat-Madary with three other journalists, he explained that the Azerbaijanis, as Iran's biggest minority, wanted a greater say in the running of their own affairs – but not autonomy.

One of the main demands is that senior officials, including the Governors and police chiefs of both Azerbaijani provinces, should be accepted by the people.

The problem in Azerbaijan comes at a critical time for the central authorities, who are already facing demands for autonomy from the Kurds, the Baluchis in south-east Iran, and the Arabic-speaking Iranians in oil-rich Khuzestan.

But there is an extra dimension to the Azerbaijan problem. The Azerbaijanis are something of an elite group in Iran. Tabriz University has had an extremely good reputation and many of Iran's intellectuals and merchants come from the area.

After World War II, they had the brief experience of self-rule. After the Soviet occupation of north-west Iran, the Soviet Union backed a short-lived republic with Tabriz as its capital.

"Fifty years ago, Azerbaijan was the most important province in the country," Shariat-Madary said. "But the Azerbaijanis stood against the regimes of the Shah and his father Shah Reza. Therefore they faced difficulties and were weakened. Other cities and provinces progressed.

"This is the root of the grievance. Now they want to be given more importance by the revolution in which they played a major part. But they have not been given their deserved importance so they are agitated."

Shariat-Madary did not vote "yes" in last week's constitution referendum because he says the constitution contains contradictions. "Articles 6 and 56 give power to the nation, but article 110 takes power away from the nation again," he says.

Article 110 deals with the "duties and responsibilities" of a *velayat faghih* – "the eminent theologian who is just, pious, informed, brave, enterprising and respected by the majority of the people as their undisputed leader."

Under this article, Ayatollah Khomeiny as *velayat faghih* will have for life the duty and responsibility of appointing leading members of the judiciary and the commander of the armed forces, and approving candidates for the second-ranking post of elected president.

Iran's political Opposition has been driven underground; Shariat-Madary and his supporters in Azerbaijan have in a sense taken its place.

Secrets from the embassy in Teheran
From DAVID BALDERSONE in Teheran

'The Age', December 24, 1979

"According to personal data in your passport you are single, were born in Antwerp, Belgium, 08 Jul 34, have blue eyes, have no distinguishing characteristics, and are approximately 1.88 metres tall. Your cover occupation is that of a commercial business representative.

"It is not uncommon to find a Belgian whose native language is Flemish, living in a nominally French-speaking section of Belgium such as Jette. You can say you were born in Antwerp, began work with a company with a regional office in Antwerp, then was transferred to the main offices in Brussels.....

"To activate this passport you will have to register ostensible entry and exit cachet impressions into the passport."

The words are not those of John Le Carre or Frederick Forsyth. Instead they are part of one of more than 20 documents released by the Iranian students who occupied the US Embassy in Teheran on November 4. The students say they are authentic American documents.

While the Iranian authorities' failure to prevent and halt the continuing occupation of the American Embassy violates international conventions of which Iran itself is a signatory, the affair has highlighted equally how nations, in this case the US, violate the spirit of the same conventions.

The students have released documents which they claim were found in the compound, indicating that the embassy was used, in part, for Central Intelligence Agency work.

The documents indicate that entry visas for the US were sometimes given in exchange for "intelligence information useful to the United States Government". Also, it seems, the embassy was not above issuing false passports and could enter fake Iranian entry and exit stamps into the passports.

The US State Department has not denied the authenticity of the documents. However, there are some spelling and grammatical errors in the documents.

Under Vienna conventions governing diplomatic and consular relations between countries, the inviolability and freedom of communication of embassies, diplomatic residences and diplomats is established.

Although there is sometimes seen to be a thin line between legitimate diplomatic political reporting and espionage, governments have found no difficulty discerning the difference when it has suited them. This is indicated by the frequency with which alleged diplomats get expelled from countries for spying.

A widely respected manual on diplomacy, 'Diplomatic Ceremonial and Protocol', by John R Wood and Jean Serres, published by Macmillan, makes clear there is a difference between diplomacy and espionage.

In a chapter defining diplomacy, the book says: "diplomatic agents and consuls are not, in the traditional nature of their duties, spies.

"All action tending to influence by indirect means the internal politics of the country, such as seeking secret information, may be considered a grave dereliction of duty.

"The government of the country of residence has the right to insist on the recall of diplomats who behave in this manner."

Since the embassy was seized, Western attention has been focused on the plight of the 50 Americans held hostage and the fact that a superpower has been held to ransom – the price in this case being the return of the Shah.

The Iranians have been able to generate very little outrage at the fact the US Embassy may have been used for espionage for two reasons. First, the Iranians were able to gain access to secret documents only by violating international conventions.

Secondly, it was widely assumed that the Americans were carrying out espionage activity because most major powers indulge in spying, particularly in the Middle East, and host countries accept it and play the same game.

Even so, little attention has been given to questioning whether the US Embassy was carrying out activities which would outrage ordinary Iranians, ordinary Australians, and ordinary Britons – if they were found to be taking place in their countries.

The Iranian authorities are planning to mount an international "grand jury" to investigate American crimes in Iran since 1953, when, after briefly fleeing the country, the Shah was restored to the throne with US help.

The documents found by the students will be used as evidence at the grand jury hearings.

The sentences quoted at the beginning of this article are from a document marked "Secret", which the students claim was found with a Belgian passport in the embassy office of the narcotics control officer, Thomas Leo Ahern. They claim Ahern is a CIA man.

"To activate this passport, you will have to enter ostensible entry and exit cachets into the passport. First you must ascertain which calendar system was in use for your ostensible entry and-or exit dates. Wolock has seen three versions: one, using the Persian calendar; 2, using the Moslem calendar, but with the last two digits of the year only, and 3, using the Moslem calendar and using the full four digits of the year."

After giving instructions about which stamps and ink pads should be used, the document marked "Secret" says: "Your cachet impressions should be fairly legible. Practice on the enclosed paper until you feel able to enter the cachets into the passport.

"NB: Since Mehrabad (airport) entry and exit cachets each have a different inspector number and it would be most unlikely that a traveller would have the same cachet numbers for consecutive trips, the attached cachets should be used only once in the passport."

Another document released by the students is addressed to all USDAO (US Defence Attaché Office) Teheran staff and marked "Confidential – not releasable to foreign nationals".

It appears to be signed by Thomas E. Schaefer, Colonel, US Air Force, Defence Attaché, dated September 18, 1979. The subject is "visa referrals".

"Visa referrals by USDAO personnel will be limited to immediate family members of: A. Iranian military, gendarmerie and police officers equal to the rank of field grade or above; B. the civil aviation organisation, and C. senior Iranian or foreign diplomatic officials who have direct association with the Defence Attaché Office.

"Visa referrals will only, repeat only be handled to gain intelligence information useful to the United States Government," the memo says.

"The visa referral service can be very valuable to the Defence Attaché Office for gathering information not normally accessible through other means, but it should not be abused. Contacts are important, but only if they provide us information or open doors that will lead to valuable intelligence.

"I expect quid pro quo from these contacts and information that will show up in intelligence reports."

Another document specifically mentions CIA activity. It appears to be a cable marked "Secret" from the embassy's Charge d'Affairs, Bruce Laingen, to Secretary of State Cyrus Vance.

"I concur in assignments Malcolm Kalp and William Daugherty as described reftels," it says.

"With opportunity available to us in the sense that we are starting from a clean slate in SRF coverage at this mission, but with regard also for the great sensitivity locally to any hint of CIA activity, it is of the highest importance that cover be the best we can come up with.

"Hence there is no question as to the need for Second and Third Secretary titles for these two officers. We must have it."

The students claim William Daugherty, who is being held hostage, has confessed to being a CIA officer. It is not known what 'reftels" or "SRF coverage" means.

But it seems Mr Laingen is arguing the need for two officers, who are not diplomats, to be given titles as diplomatic political officers.

The passages quoted above are from photocopies of alleged embassy documents given to 'The Age' by the students. People familiar with diplomatic documents and cables have been shown the documents and say they appear to be genuine.

1980
Iranians vote to elect President
From DAVID BALDERSTONE

'The Age', Teheran, January 25, 1980

Iranians trudged through the snow enthusiastically today to vote in Iran's first free Presidential elections.

"A year ago who would have imagined we would have been voting in a democratic presidential election?" an engineer in wealthy north Teheran near the former Shah's palace told me.

"Now, if the President can get on with the job and is a strong man, we will get rid of our problems and Iran will be a good country."

Of the three front-runners in today's election, the Finance Minister, Dr Bani-Sadr, who returned to Iran with Ayatollah Khomeiny a year ago, seemed to be the favorite in polling stations this morning – particularly in the poorer areas of south Teheran.

But the former navy chief, Admiral Madani, who as Governor-General of oil-rich Khuzestan Province got credit for his handling of unrest in the province, and the Revolutionary Council member Mr Hassan Habibi, were also polling well.

An estimated 22 million of Iran's 36-million population were eligible to vote.

With two other reporters, I visited four polling stations – two in south Teheran and two in the north – this morning. The most impressive aspect was that despite problems caused by an illiteracy rate of more than 50 per cent in Iran, the authorities were conducting the poll efficiently and honestly.

But in south Teheran, where the illiteracy rate is high, there was no secret about who was voting for which candidate. Although the majority of votes we saw cast were for Bani-Sadr, Admiral Madani received a few votes, indicating that voters were enjoying a free choice.

In one south Teheran polling station, in the courtyard of a mosque, two parallel queues led to the registration. One queue was for men and the other for women, who were all wearing full-length chadors.

After registering, voters' identity cards were marked with a small rubber stamp to prevent the person voting again. Voters were then given an official slip of paper on which to write the name of their candidate before slipping it into a ballot box.

Illiterates went to a separate table where young officials wrote in the candidate requested. Although this procedure is hardly in the best traditions of secret ballot, the authorities had a problem.

There were 66 candidates in the election, making it difficult for a symbol system to be used.

In north Teheran the women were wearing fashionable Western clothes rather than chadors, and because almost everyone could read and write, there was no clue on how the voting was going.

Ayatollah Khomeiny cast his vote in a Teheran hospital, where he was admitted two days ago with a heart problem.

The President will be the country's chief executive, whose position is sandwiched between the religious guardian, Ayatollah Khomeiny, and the Prime Minister. It will take time to see how much authority the President really enjoys.

Once again the West carves up the East
From DAVID BALDERSTONE in Amman

'The Age', February 11, 1980

Western strategists, pre-occupied with a possible Soviet threat to the Persian Gulf, seem in danger of overlooking the lesson of Iran: the major recent disruption to oil supplies has been caused not by a superpower or by military might, but by a clergy-led people's revolution.

Despite Iran's economic problems – unprecedented unemployment and food shortages – Ayatollah Khomeiny can still mobilise the support of the majority of Iranians.

A major reason is that he has been seen to rid Iran of American influence, and overseen, perhaps surprisingly, a significant move towards democracy. Although this democracy remains about as fragile as the Ayatollah's health, and is still to be proved anyway, he has – in the view of the vast majority – put power back into the hands of that majority's representatives.

And while Ayatollah Khomeiny is scorned and feared by Arab leaderships, he has gained enormous support among the ordinary people of the Arab world.

What is more, his stand on the occupation of the American Embassy in Teheran and the United States' failure to counter the move effectively, have won him backing even among the middle classes who would abhor the idea of living in an Islamic republic. Clearly they like to see the superpower squirming.

The real danger for the West is that, in its concern about Soviet aggression and intentions, it will forget that sitting upon the Gulf oil fields, the source of around 45 per cent of the world's oil, are not only oil sheiks and rulers, but also millions of people. And many of these people happen to be potential revolutionaries.

It is perhaps more simple to work out a military strategy to counter a possible Soviet threat to the West's Persian Gulf oil than it is to devise a strategy for today, to counter, or more importantly, to take account of the risks of revolution spreading from Gulf State to Gulf State.

This is especially so because such a strategy would have to take account of the fastest growing seed of discontent among the Arabs – the West's failure to solve the Palestinian problem. A solution to this problem is not possible without difficult, and perhaps dangerous, territorial compromise by Israel.

How vulnerable is the Gulf to revolution? In the past four months there have been riots amongst Shi'ite Moslems of Bahrain and in the oil-rich area of Saudi Arabia, plus November's siege of the Grand Mosque in Mecca. At the very least this has awakened the Saudi and Bahraini leaderships to the fact they cannot rule out revolution against their regimes.

In Kuwait only around 50 per cent of the population was born in the country and around two-thirds of the workforce is non-Kuwaiti. Much of the middle and senior management of the country is Palestinian.

In Irak, Saudi, Qatar, United Arab Emirates and Oman the literacy rate is not much better than 50 per cent.

Irak, where more than 50 per cent of the population is Shi'ite Moslem is ruled by a predominantly Sunni Moslem regime. However, at least if the regime of President Saddam Hussein was toppled it would be likely to be replaced by a leadership whose political complexion was not too much different.

But this would not be so if any of the family-led Gulf States or Saudi Arabia fell to revolution.

The West's preoccupation with global strategy rather than a "people policy" is not new to the Arabs, and is unlikely to become any more attractive.

The tragedy has been played out since the British persuaded Amir Hussein of Hejaz (covering Mecca and Medina) to lend his support to the battle against the Ottomans in World War I.

(Hussein's sons, Faisal, later King of Irak, and Abdullah, later King of Jordan, fought with Lawrence.)

Poor old Hussein (great-grandfather of today's King Hussein of Jordan) thought Britain intended to grant the Arabs independence as a reward for helping crush the Ottomans. Instead Britain and France carved up the area, drew borders with an incredible lack of sensitivity, and paved the way for the creation of Israel on the area's prime land (which is something, presumably, the Ottomans would never have done.)

Since the Soviet invasion of Afghanistan, the main thrust of President Carter's doctrine (enthusiastically supported by the Australian Prime Minister) has been about militarily countering possible Soviet moves which might threaten "the West's" oil fields or oil lanes in the Persian Gulf area. Once again the West is carving up the Middle East.

It would not be so bad if the West did not appear to be presuming that the Persian Gulf was its area merely because of its colonial links with the rulers and the fact the West's oil has traditionally come from the area.

But the great flaw in the West's approach is that it neglects to base its presumption on the valid facts that communism is alien to Islam, and that Arab traditions of free enterprise go back further than the West's.

Any strategy designed to maintain the West's interests in the Middle East, and the Gulf particularly, should be based on the assumption that all the Gulf leaders are vulnerable to revolution.

Therefore, while it might be best to try to preserve the rule of the present leaders, this should be done carefully because blatant support could increase the leaders' vulnerability by making them appear wealth-plundering stooges of the West.

There are three issues which cannot be ignored if a successful "people policy" is to evolve. They are the Palestinian question, self-restraint on doubtfully needed exports to the area, and being careful that any military strategy for the protection of the Gulf is not seen by the people of the area as a threat to independence.

Real moves towards a solution to the Palestinian problem are important because it is modern Islam's most tangible grievance against the US and other supporters of Israel.

While it can be legitimately argued that the Arab leadership missed its opportunity to test Israel's willingness to live in peace with the Arabs on Israel's pre-1967 borders – by failing to support and follow up the initiative of Egypt's President Sadat – this is not the way it is seen by the Arab masses.

To them it seems inconceivable that their leaders could have said after Sadat visited Jerusalem: "OK Sadat, you made the wrong decision but we will join you for a short while to gauge or expose Israel's intentions."

This did not happen, and Israel's peace enthusiasm was not tested to the extent of having to make difficult decisions on withdrawing from the West Bank and Gaza Strip – territories occupied in 1967.

But that does not in any way remove the Arabs' view of the West's obligations to pressure Israel into thinking again.

Unless movement towards a solution of the Palestinian question is achieved, Western inaction will be exploited by Palestinians working in the Gulf, and by the Palestinian political machine based in Beirut.

While the Soviet invasion of Afghanistan has been condemned by most Arab Governments, it is an irritation that the US makes such noisy demands for the Soviet withdrawal from Afghanistan when her ally, Israel, continues to occupy territories taken in the 1967 war.

Although Australia is in the fortunate position of selling mainly wheat and meat to the Middle East, other western countries have been involved in multi-million-dollar deals of doubtful necessity to the people of the area.

Did Iran, the Middle East's largest potential producer of oil and gas, need to embark on a deal costing up to $US14,000 million on two nuclear reactors?

While the argument is often put forward that an exporting country cannot help it if a ruler or his Government wants to buy, it is interesting to note that the former Shah himself once wondered aloud whether the Americans were supplying so many arms to Iran for the protection of their strategic interests, or for the sake of their arms industry.

Australians find ancient 'riches'
From DAVID BALDERSTONE

'The Age', February 21, 1980

A burial tomb containing more than 100 pottery objects made around 3500 years ago has been discovered by Australian archaeologists working in the Jordan Valley.

The tomb, which is dug into a steep hill about seven kilometres from the Israel-Jordan frontier in north-east Jordan, is considered to possibly be the richest tomb of the Late Bronze Age discovered in the area.

And, even more significant than the wealth of the tomb itself, the discovery supports previously unproved evidence that the site being excavated by the Australians is the missing city of Pihilu mentioned in documents of the twelfth Egyptian dynasty.

"I can think of no larger tomb containing more pottery of this period found in this area," the leader of the dig, world-renowned archaeologist Professor Basil Hennessey of Sydney University, said yesterday.

But the jubilation of the Australian archaeologists was dampened this week as they continued the exacting task of documenting and drawing the pottery and the position it was found within the tomb.

Thieves, who were obviously aware of the value of the antiquities on the black market, broke through the main tomb into an adjoining tomb and raided the contents.

Jordanian police are investigating the theft which took place on Monday night as the Australians slept at their site headquarters about 500 metres from the tomb.

"Unfortunately, after one chamber was excavated, a small subsidiary chamber that opened off it was completely robbed," Professor Hennessey said.

The team of archaeologists from Sydney University was completing its second annual season of excavations at the site, called Pella, this week.

The village beside Pella is called Tabbaqat Fahl.

During Roman times, Pella was famous as one of the cities of the Decapolis. Until 14 months ago, when the Sydney University team began major excavations, little work had been carried out at the site.

Although Pella is known to contain remains of a great many impressive buildings of the Hellenistic (332-63 BC), Roman (623BC-324 AD), Byzantine (324-640 AD), and Umayyad (650-750 AD) periods, earlier occupation of the site has been shrouded in mystery.

However, the discovery of the tomb provides a pretty clear indication that there was a major Late Bronze Age (1550-1450 BC) occupation of the site.

"The wealth of the tomb – and there should be many others like it – give added hopes of finding a flourishing Late Bronze Age city at the site," Professor Hennessey said.

As well as the pottery objects, the tomb contained imported Egyptian alabaster, a gold dress pin and an Egyptian scarab of the early eighteenth Egyptian dynasty.

The excavations at Pella, a joint project of Sydney University and Wooster College, Ohio, are carried out in co-operation with Jordan's Department of Antiquities.

The Sydney University and Wooster College teams carry out excavation at different times of the year and on different areas of the site.

In 1977, Professor Hennessey, who is Edwin Cuthbert Hall Professor of Middle Eastern Archaeology at Sydney University, led a team which recovered from a settlement in the Jordan Valley, a 6000-year-old wall painting – the second oldest wall painting ever recovered.

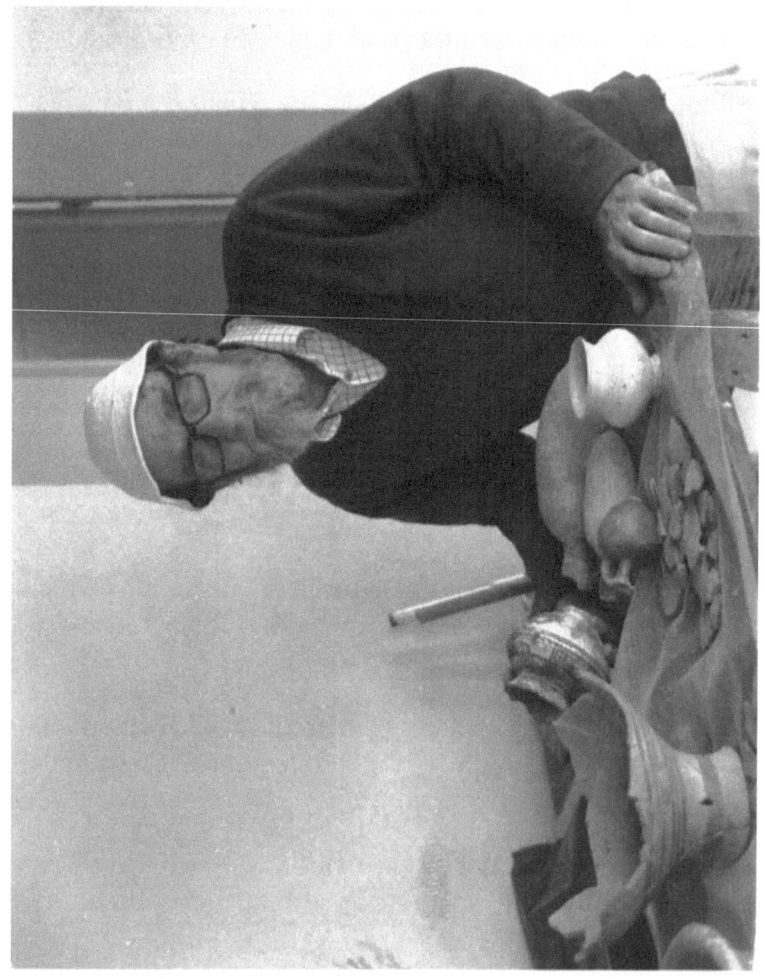

Ill. 11. Basil Hennessey at Pella, February 1980

Bleak omen in Teheran
From DAVID BALDERSTONE in Teheran

'The Age', February 26, 1980

It had been snowing all morning, and was drizzling on and off. But well over 100,000 Iranians turned out in the bitter cold to shout slogans against America and in favor of the revolution.

There were boys in battle fatigues carrying wooden guns. There were revolutionary guards with red carnations in their C-3 rifles. There were women in chadors. There were young and old men shaking their fists towards the American Embassy as they marched.

And there were the slogans: "America – with whom do you want to fight? One million? Two million? Or with 20 million battle-ready men and women?"

This was the scene on Monday afternoon outside the US Embassy in Teheran when Iran's National Mobilisation Headquarters called a march in support of Ayatollah Khomeiny's call for a 20 million-strong people's army.

The fact that the American Embassy was chosen as the focal point of the demonstration, and the fact that Iran's new President took part outside the embassy gates was no good omen for the estimated 49 American hostages held inside the embassy since November 4.

The size of the demonstration and the vehemence of the anti-American slogans did not support the contention that President Bani-Sadr was trying to slowly move public opinion towards accepting the hostages' release. If indeed he was trying to do that, it was a funny way to go about it.

For almost two hours, Abolhassan Bani-Sadr, the French-trained economist, stood almost motionless atop the gatehouse of the American Embassy on Teleghani Avenue, Teheran, and reviewed the passing parade. He didn't look uncomfortable, nor comfortable either. There were no Castro-style clenched fists above the shoulders, just occasionally a gentle wave.

Late last week, after UN Secretary-General Kurt Waldheim was able to announce finally the UN commission to investigate Iran's grievances against the deposed Shah, it looked as if the hostage crisis was on the brink of being solved. The formation of the commission, which is made up of five international lawyers from Algeria, Venezuela, France, Syria and Sri Lanka, seemed to provide a formula which was likely to lead to early release of the hostages. That was until last Saturday, just hours after the Commission arrived in Teheran from Geneva.

Ever since the American Embassy was seized the crux of the problem has been the lack of any unified central authority in Iran with which the US could negotiate directly, or through third parties. Instead, the militant students have consistently declared they will only follow the directions of Ayatollah Khomeiny, who – partly because it served his vendetta against the Shah and the US – has supported the students.

Frustrated, Prime Minister Bazargan and his Government resigned, and later Abolhassan Bani-Sadr was removed as Foreign Minister, partly because he was seen to be too compromising on the Iran-US crisis.

Then, when Dr Bani-Sadr won by a landslide last month's Presidential elections, the US Administration felt, and hoped that at last Iran had a central authority with whom they could negotiate.

Indeed, President Bani-Sadr's early post-election statements looked hopeful. Among other things, he said it was time for the students to go back to their universities. But his statements have become significantly less hopeful. This, according to Western diplomats, could be because he has found the job of achieving some kind of consensus within Iran's inner circle more difficult than anticipated.

However, Dr Waldheim and the US Administration felt the establishment of the International Commission – a longstanding demand of the Iranians – would be a major step towards a solution to the crisis. It would enable Iran to air publicly its grievances against the Shah and the US.

But just before the Commission arrived in Teheran, Ayatollah Khomeiny, in a statement issued from his Teheran hospital, put a decision on the release of the hostages, and concessions to be gained in return for their release, in the hands of Iran's new Parliament.

As the yet-to-be-elected parliament will not sit until early April, and has to decide upon its procedures, a decision on the hostages could not be expected until the middle of April.

Also, the parliamentary elections are being fought keenly and there is no certainty that supporters of President Bani-Sadr will win a majority of seats. Therefore, even if Bani-Sadr and his Government manage to get the necessary majority vote of confidence, a decision on the hostages – and the concessions to be gained in return for their release – could be much more difficult to achieve.

Dr Bani-Sadr has consistently laid down publicly three conditions for the release of the hostages. He wants the US to agree never again to interfere in Iran's internal affairs; to accept Iran's right to seek the Shah's extradition, and to recognise its guilt in being involved in events during the Shah's reign.

These conditions could have been achieved through some compromise if Dr Bani-Sadr was the final authority. But achieving agreement to the release of hostages from the Parliament could be far more difficult.

Time to take a risk for peace: Hawke
From DAVID BALDERSTONE

'The Age', Amman, March 16, 1980

ACTU president Mr Bob Hawke said at the weekend that current opportunities for progress towards Middle East peace "may not return".

Therefore it was time to take risks in the cause of peace, he said.

He said Israel must look more closely at returning to its pre-1967 borders in the context of growing Arab and world opinion that Israeli withdrawal was not merely a one-sided deal but had to be coupled with guarantees about Israel's security and right to exist.

Mr Hawke made his comments before leaving Jordan for meetings in Israel with the Prime Minister, Mr Begin, the Defence Minister, Mr Weizman, and the Opposition Leader, Mr Peres.

During top-level discussions in Egypt and Jordan, it is understood Mr Hawke sounded out his idea of a "penalty clause" being written in advance into any peace treaty providing for Israel's withdrawal from the occupied West Bank.

The Hawke plan, which he first mentioned in the ABC Boyer Lectures last November, is envisaged as a means of reducing the possibility of a West Bank Palestinian State or entity being used as a launching pad for aggression against Israel.

Under this plan, Israel would have the right to its present borders if, after withdrawing to the 1967 lines, another war was sparked by aggression from a West Bank Palestinian State or entity. The plan assumes Israel's ability to win another war.

In Egypt, Mr Hawke met the Vice-President Mr Mubarak and the Prime Minister, Dr Khalil.

In Jordan, he had a lengthy meeting with Crown Prince Hassan.

Mr Hawke said he favored a Middle East settlement based on the controversial United Nations Security Council Resolution 242, which he interpreted as meaning restitution of the 1967 borders with "not substantial" variations.

Although he said resolution of the issue of the walled city of Jerusalem (which was administered by Jordan before 1967) was a major problem, he believed it could be solved.

"In some sense, the opportunity for peace may not return and there must be a taking of risks on both sides," he said. "Israel has taken risks in war and must take risks in peace."

Saudis face up to a changing world
From DAVID BALDERSTONE in Amman

'The Age', April 4, 1980

A long row of large fawn armchairs looked out across the desert racecourse. Wooden coffee tables in front of every two chairs were bare except for a box of Kleenex on each. TV monitors faced the chairs. Military stewards moved up and down the row serving tea and light brown Saudi coffee.

With a cream-coloured telephone beside his lounge chair and a doctor close by, King Khaled's eyes moved slowly from the distant rising dust caused by the 2000 racing camels to the TV monitor giving close-up action of the 22 kilometre race.

King Khaled's step-brother by another of his father's 17 wives, Crown Prince Fahd, sat a few yards away in an identical chair with an equally commanding view of the race. His index finger resting against his lower lip, the Crown Prince listened intently to his neighbor, another of Saudi Arabia's 5000 princes.

It was the annual $10,000 Janadariya camel race last month. King Khaled was making his first major public appearance since his recent bout of serious heart trouble.

After presenting the prizes, King Khaled headed back to Riyadh, the Saudi capital. The royal limousine passed the extreme of poverty, a community living in packing case shelters, on the way to the lavish, oil-financed development in the desert city. But it was dark, and the contrast between wealth and poverty could not be seen.

Thirty-eight years have passed since the old warrior, King Abdul Aziz, was able at last to proclaim the Kingdom of Saudi Arabia, after driving the Hashemites out of Mecca and Medina and uniting the warring tribes of Arabia.

Since King Abdul Aziz's death in 1953, the throne has passed to three of his 35 sons – King Saud (1953-64), King Faisal (1964-75), and King Khaled, who came to the throne as a compromise candidate after Faisal's assassination.

Although oil was discovered in Saudi Arabia in 1938, the country did not become an oil exporter until 1950, and King Saud managed to keep the country close to bankruptcy until his brothers overthrew him in 1964.

So it is only since 1964, when Faisal took over, that Saudi Arabia has really found its feet economically. It is only seven years – since the massive OPEC rises in 1973 following the Arab-Israeli war – that much wealth, development and change has come to the desert kingdom.

Saudi Arabia, a country with a population of about six million is now the world's biggest oil exporter, earning about $265 million a day.

The oil wealth has brought modern education, clean housing, improved roads, subsidised air fares, health services, modern telephone communications and job opportunities. But the change has brought challenge.

Senior members of the royal family have never been unaware of modernisation. However the seizure by Moslem fanatics (the authorities call them deviants) of the Grand Mosque of Mecca – Islam's holiest shrine – last November, and serious clashes between security forces and Shi'ite Moslems in the oil-rich east of the country late last year sent shock waves through the corridors of power.

Already facing pressure from the young educated elite and the middle and upper class business community, the flare-up of religious violence was enough to persuade the King and Crown Prince that it was time for change. It provided the catalyst needed to make the regime look seriously at broadening the base of the decision-making process in the country.

Last month the Royal Cabinet announced the formation of a committee to draw up plans for a new system of government.

Chaired by the Interior Minister, Prince Naif, a full brother of the Crown Prince and step-brother of the King, its first task will be to draw up plans for an appointed consultative council, which one day could be democratically elected.

The Arab view of democracy is not ours. Therefore moves by Arab governments to set up consultative councils can be viewed with scepticism. But the fact remains that whether or not a democratic system emerges the intial impetus is always taken because the leaders, feeling threatened, recognise that the decision-making process has to be broadened.

That realisation on the part of the Saudi regime is the significant part of the move.

For the Royal House of Saud, the problem of religious fundamentalism is a matter of reaping what it has sown. About 1740, Mohammed Bin Saud, Sheik of Dariya, near Riyadh, entered an alliance with Mohammed Bin Abdul Wahhab, who even then was obsessed by the need to return to the basic simplicity of Islam.

Through triumph and adversity the Saud family has co-operated with the followers of Wahhab, who have knitted themselves into a fundamentalist sect of Sunni Moslems. It can be argued that without the co-operation of the Wahhabis, King Abdul Aziz – leader of the Saud family's revival this century – would never have been able to unite the country.

Today the Wahhabis lead the fight against the erosion of traditional Islamic values.

Because it is the Wahhabis who are seen to be behind startling moves against mixed bathing in Western hotels (costing $100 plus a night), women trying on clothes in boutiques, women's beauty salons etc., it could be thought their fundamentalist ideas are the only pressure on the monarchy.

But the Royal family faces increasing pressure from the young educated elite – many of whom have been educated in the US on generous Saudi scholarships – and the middle and upper class business community. Members of the business community have for some time been concerned about the disproportionate number of large contracts going through the network of princes.

Both the educated elite and the business community want a bigger say in the running of the country's affairs. They want an improvement on the present majlis system under which the Crown Prince and other senior princes listen personally to grievances of the people and allot money to satisfy demands and mollify criticism.

The big problem is that the fundamentalists, the educated elite and the business community want changes which to a great extent are irreconcilable with each other.

Under Saudi Arabia's third five-year development plan, which is due to be unveiled in May, the Government plans to spend about $260,000 million. With the major infrastructure projects complete or nearing completion, the emphasis will be on urban improvement, rural development, social services and manpower training.

Manpower is a real problem. Up to 70 per cent of the work force is made up of imported labor – mainly from Arab countries, Pakistan, India, Taiwan, South Korea and The Philippines. The theme of the manpower drive under the five year plan will be the replacement of a foreigner by a Saudi national.

But the problem is not just training. Saudis do not like doing work which could be considered servile. Saudis drive taxis because they are then small businessmen, but are rarely found in anything but top management positions in hotels. They object to waiting on guests and therefore most hotels are staffed by foreigners.

Saudis are often considered arrogant by other Arabs and Westerners. Abroad, the example of the ugly Saudi, who has more money than sense, is not too hard to find. But at home the ordinary Saudi is usually friendly, usually wants to talk, and seems to want – as some kind of reassurance – even fleeting friendship with Westerners.

Because of the country's manpower shortage, there are moves to attract more women into the work force. But in a country where women are forbidden to drive cars, broadening their horizons is carried out as a form of apartheid – the separate development of men's and women's activities.

In the debate over women's roles, suggestions being tossed around could lead to the following situation. A Saudi woman typist would travel to work on a new system of segregated buses, enter work through a separate door, type in a room barred to men and bank in an all female bank just opened in Jeddah.

But to be too critical is to forget the rapidity with which modernisation has come.

Since the Grand Mecca Mosque siege there has been a reshuffle in top National Guard and army positions. In another shake-up last week four princes were appointed as governors in sensitive areas.

Often the princes were educated exclusively within the royal court which has left them with no formal education qualifications that can be quoted by newspapers when they take up new appointments.

For example Prince Majed who was appointed governor of Mecca last week, was described in 'Arab News' to have had an education covering religion, economics, and public administration. "He is said to have a knack with foreign languages and speaks English and French quite well," the newspaper added rather condescendingly.

But many of the third generation princes, such as Foreign Minister Saud Al Faisal, have been highly educated in the US and Europe.

In the wake of the Mecca Mosque siege, trouble among the Shi'ite Moslem minority and the inevitable strains as modernisation continues, they just might need everything they have learned.

The enigma of the Ayatollah
From DAVID BALDERSTONE in Amman

'The Age', April 12, 1980

There was just a flicker of emotion in the old man's voice, but his words touched those listening. Ayatollah Ruhollah Khomeiny was leaving hospital and apologising for having "caused trouble".

"I thank you very much, the employees of the hospital, and thank all the respected doctors who during this period were very kind – like a son who is looking after his old father – and cared for me."

He then went on to urge Iranians to unite in the face of "plots" against the country, adding that he would continue to serve – despite his heart condition and age. "In these last few days of life, I will pray for you all and whatever service I can perform, despite my condition, I will do in the service of all."

Outside the Mehdi Rezai hospital, Teheran, a crowd was chanting Allah Akhbar (God is great) – the same words crowds often used to shout in thanks to Iran's previous leader, Shah Mohammed Reza Pahlavi.

Few admit that now of course. But, the point is, that Iranians en masse are so often as enigmatic in character as their revolutionary leader still appears to be 14 months after he returned triumphantly to Iran.

There he was, just over a month ago, being humble after treatment for a heart condition – treatment carried out with the assistance of West European-based Iranian doctors. This week he was once again the *bete noir* of the West – and America in particular – pursuing his hatred of the deposed Shah.

He vetoed transfer of the American hostages held at the US Embassy from the militant students to Revolutionary Council control and then, when the US retaliated, poured scorn on President Carter.

"If Carter has done one thing in his life which it can be said is to the best benefit of the oppressed, it is this very cutting of relations between a nation risen from liberation from the grip of international plunderers and a world predator plunderer," he said.

They were brave words for the leader of a country – potentially OPEC's second largest oil exporter – whose income now is possibly insufficient to pay Government bills, and whose international credit has been eroded by continuing domestic turmoil.

They were brave words indeed for the leader of a country where up to 30 per cent of the workforce can't find real work and instead of welfare payments is expected to live on Islam and a hatred of America and the deposed Shah.

On Mossadegh Avenue (previously Pahlavi Avenue), revolutionary portraits of Khomeiny jostle for space with posters of Western pop stars, whose music he condemns. Here in a post-revolution street market on one of the poshest drags in town, Western rock is played only yards from vendors with tapes of the Ayatollah's speeches.

From here the view of Khomeiny is contradictory. Among the youths in jeans and American University sweat shirts and the women bare of his favorite chador, he is reduced to being any Middle Eastern leader – respected, but not followed to the letter.

He scorns foreign influence over Iran but did not hesitate to use the sophisticated Western media in Paris during his ride to power and continues to use television to communicate. His revolution said Iran did not need Western expertise, but he rode out the stifling hot summer in Qum, Iran's religious capital, last year with the help of an American-designed air-conditioner.

Behind that solemn face is a man who laughs with his family – especially his grandchildren, and relies heavily for help on his sole surviving son, Ahmad. His elder son, Mostafa, was killed in Irak in 1977 when Khomeiny was building up his opposition to the Shah. In Iran it is commonly thought he died at the hands of the Shah's secret police, Savak. The Ayatollah eats a traditional Parsian diet as he sits cross-legged on the floor. When in Paris he sometimes used to watch on television, soccer – a game he played as a child.

Ruhollah Khomeiny was born in 1900 into an Iran in ferment, a country in which the clergy and the liberals were gearing up to win a dramatic constitutional battle with the then Shah. At Khomein, between Isfahan and Arak and only a little more than 100 kilometres from Qum, he came of a clerical family and therefore was thrust into the midst of the constitutional battle.

His grandfather was a respected Shi'ite Islamic clergyman named Mirza Ahmad who evidently enjoyed the esteemed title Imam – a title his grandson does not now reject. Imam Mirza Ahmad did quite an unusual thing by going to India and studying mysticism.

Both Khomeiny's father and the eldest of his five brothers were considered ayatollahs. It is presumed they gained a great deal of experience from his grandfather, the clergyman and mystic.

Therefore, while a great deal of his experience in later life can be seen to have moulded the Khomeiny of today, his birth into a sufficiently respected family of clergymen gave him an immediate advantage in the closely knit Islamic hierarchy.

Of course he could have toed the line, accepted the status quo, and not become a "revolutionary", but equally his rise within the clerical "opposition" to the monarchy is no case of lift driver to managing director.

A question asked by Iranians is whether Khomeiny's refusal to show any emotion in public – unlike other mullahs – is at least partly a result of his grandfather's embrace of mysticism.

Khomeiny's father, Ayatollah Mostafa Moussavi died in suspicious circumstances shortly after Khomeiny's birth. Khomeiny is tight-lipped about his family. (This is not important he says. What is important is his understanding and belief in the Koran.) He has never openly dispelled the belief that his father was killed by the monarchy. This has led Iranian revolutionary fervour to throw up two versions of his father's death. These are that either his death was ordered by the ruling Qajar Shah, or that somehow the now exiled Shah's father, Reza Khan, who was aged 22 and did not become Shah for another 25 years, had something to do with it.

In fact the death seems to have been somewhat more ordinary and certainly no "anti-monarchy" credential for the family. It seems he died in a fight with another landlord over irrigation rights.

Khomeiny had a traditional Islamic education, first under his eldest brother, Ayatollah Moussavi, and then in seminaries in Isfahan, Arak, and Qum. Important, if not paramount, in Shi'ite Islamic learning is the battle for leadership of Islam in 675 AD. At that time trickery in mediation between the rival contenders led to the split between the Shi'ite and Sunni sects. The Shi'ites lost. Hence Khomeiny as a Shi'ite – believing that sect was right and should have won - now has no faith in third party intervention.

In 1907 Britain and Russia signed an agreement dividing Iran into spheres of influence, and Khomeiny's teenage years saw "neutral " Iran being used as a World War I battleground.

Khomeiny moved to the Qum alleyways of Shi'ite Islamic tradition and intrigue in 1927, when progress – following the discovery of oil – was beginning to threaten the power and influence of the mullahs. Improved communications and the building of schools and hospitals began to loosen their grip.

The new Shah (the exiled Shah's father and founder of the Pahlavi dynasty) banned traditional dress in 1928 and, in 1936, the chador.

In 1941, Khomeiny began his public opposition against the Pahlavis with publication of his 'Discovery of Secrets', a fierce attack on the regime. Publication coincided with the abdication of Shah Reza – after Soviet and British invasion during World War II – in favor of his son, the now exiled Shah.

Despite his fierce opposition to the Pahlavis, which was to later land him in jail four times and eventually send him into exile, Khomeiny stood aloof from the nationalist uprising of premier Mohammed Mossadegh in the early fifties. During this period the

Shah was sent briefly into exile and the oil industry was nationalised.

Khomeiny suspected the influence of the Tudeh (communist) Party during the Mossadegh era. His suspicion and aloof behaviour then could provide a clue to why he tends to overrule secular politicians these days. It is interesting to note that in 1963, when Khomeiny was at the forefront of opposition to the Shah's "white revolution", agrarian and social reforms, many secular political liberals stood aloof. Was there then, and is there now, a mutual distrust of the clerical and liberal politicians?

Despite Khomeiny's consistent and long opposition to the Shah, he was – up until his move from Irak to Paris in 1978 – just one strand in the battle for change in Iran. Another main strand was made up of constitutionalist politicians, many of whom had played a part in the Mossadegh era.

In 1977, during a brief period of liberalisation by the Shah, these constitutionalists were building up opposition but their emphasis, at least at that stage, was towards making Iran a constitutional monarchy.

But once Khomeiny was in Paris, there was no doubt about who was leading the revolution. Suddenly he had access to the mass media and knew exactly how to use it. No longer did he have to rely on taped messages being smuggled into Iran and played in mosques. Instead his calls for revolution could be heard on any shortwave radio in Iran.

In Paris, Khomeiny did not have the traditional constitutionalist politicians of Iran around him. Instead he had a new group of secular advisers whose names were little known inside the country. These included Abolhassan Bani-Sadr, the French-trained economist who is now President, and Sadegh Qotbzadeh, who is now Foreign Minister.

Although there was contact between the constitutionalist politicians and Khomeiny's camp, it was not until the final months before the Shah left Iran in January 1979, that the two groups really came together. At least one of the constitutionalists, Shapur Baktiar saw dangers to constitutionalist ideals in a Khomeiny dominated regime and instead decided to accept, under strict conditions, the Shah's invitation to become Prime Minister.

During his formative years, Khomeiny is said by long-time acquaintances to have been impressed with Plato's 'Republic'. Some observers see him as living out the role of Plato's reluctant philosopher king (as religious guardian of Iran) within Plato's necessarily moralistic (in Khomeiny's case, Islamic morals) society.

He does seem reluctant to play a big role in day-to-day politics. He refused to support any particular Presidential candidate – and his office has issued a statement that he will no longer accept political petitions and letters.

Many observers believe that once the hostage crisis is over this reluctance to participate in day-to-day affairs will become more apparent. Under Iran's constitution, Khomeiny is the religious guardian of the country. This position has wide-ranging powers, including approval of Presidential candidates and appointment of the armed forces commander. Therefore the position, if carried out zealously could erode the role of President.

When Khomeiny dies, either another suitable religious guardian will have to "emerge" or the role will be carried out by a clergy-dominated guardian council. It is thought that such a council would be far less likely than Khomeiny to adopt a "reluctant" role. Instead it could become another Revolutionary Council.

On the surface it would seem that one word from the Ayatollah could end the American hostage crisis. Certainly the secular President Bani-Sadr would like the hostages released and the crisis over. But does Khomeiny suspect that the militant students may not obey an order to release the hostages? After all, Iranians en masse are enigmatic.

No tension in Teheran's life
From DAVID BALDERSTONE

'The Age', Teheran, April 29, 1980.

He was a little weathered old man dressed in a blue boiler suit and carrying a broom and dustpan. He didn't open his mouth, but communicated with an agile face and darting eyes.

He was sweeping the rubber-tiled floor of Teheran airport arrivals lounge this morning, and gathering dropped cigarette butts with his bare hands.

A Kuwait Airways Boeing 707 had just landed with a full load of Iranian workers. I was standing with them in one of several long queues leading to the passport officials.

The little old man swept his broom up, stopped beside me, and nodded his weathered face deliberately at me. Then he picked up my cabin case and typewriter and carried them past the head of the queue. He put them down carefully, turned towards me, and his face seemed to be nodding: "This will save you a lot of trouble."

Then, suddenly, a new passport official arrived and a new queue was about to start. The little old man dropped his broom and dustpan and raced back towards me stopping any Iranians starting the new queue. He then waved me forward into the number one position.

The odd thing was that no one objected. Instead, just four days after the abortive American hostage rescue bid, this reporter, whose fair hair betrays him as a non-Iranian, was ushered to the head of the queue by a group of Iranian workers.

Teheran is the centre of an international crisis which could bring the superpowers into conflict. But, on the surface at least, life goes on pretty much as usual.

Around the occupied US Embassy, where anti-American posters and placards bedeck Ayatollah Teleghani Avenue, the international crisis is obvious. Sporadic incidents between rival groups, who play politics sometimes with guns and bombs as well as placards, make it clear that Teheran is the capital of a country still going through the trauma of revolution.

But generally on the streets of Teheran, a city of around five million people, none of this intrudes.

Airport arrival procedures are more efficient than in most Middle Eastern countries. The pre-revolution sign saying each person is allowed to bring in a litre of spirits has been pasted over, and any alcohol found is seized. But Scotch whisky is available on the black market for anyone willing to pay $50 a bottle.

The most obvious sign that the economy lacks the confidence of pre-revolution days are the tens of idle building cranes towering over building sites, where no activity has taken place since 1978.

Iranians queuing for bread, eggs and meat reveal some food shortages. According to the Central Bank, wholesale food prices have risen 33 per cent since the revolution, and unemployment – mainly due to the collapse of the construction industry – is a real problem for the authorities.

But fresh fruit and vegetables seem to be plentiful. In the drizzling rain today, street stalls were doing a brisk trade in a wide range of produce.

As usual, the city hums with its notorious heavy traffic and suicidal youths on powerful motor cycles dart between cars and trucks. Life goes on in Teheran. And the little old weathered man at the airport keeps sweeping.

Hammer and sickle flies at the Caspian

DAVID BALDERSTONE 'The Age' Middle East correspondent, reports from Teheran on the Iranian crisis

'The Age', May 6, 1980

"Who is Bani-Sadr?" A young Iranian astride his idling Honda asked rhetorically, "Bani-Sadr is a nobody. He just occupies a title."

Here in the small city of Lahijan near Iran's Caspian Sea coast, there are only a few small poster pictures of Ayatollah Khomeiny and even less of President Bani-Sadr.

Instead, many banners carry the hammer and sickle, leaving nobody in any doubt about the political sympathies of the city's most vocal political group.

Ironically, the Caspian coast – once the playground of Iran's wealthy – is a stronghold of the Left and the communists. Beside the hammer and sickle, one banner reads: "Fight and shoot until reality becomes clear to you."

A senior member of the ruling Islamic clergy recently visited the area and returned shocked to Teheran where he said: "There were so many communist slogans; I thought I must have been in Russia."

From Teheran, the 325-kilometre road to Rasht, the largest town in the area, skirts the highest peaks of the Elburz range before descending to the subtropical plain beside the Caspian.

Rice paddies cover much of the rich agricultural land and there are 190 kilometres to Astara, the last Iranian city before the Soviet border.

Two weeks ago, Rasht was the scene of heavy fighting between the supporters of Iran's two main Leftist groups – the Mujahedin-e-Khalq and the Marxist Fedayeen-e-Khalq – and Islamic fundamentalists. Twenty people were killed and hundreds injured, and about 40 people remain in jail awaiting Islamic justice to take its swift course.

Old poplar trees with their new bright green leaves shade the streets of Rasht. Banners in support of the Mujahedin, Fedayeen and Tudeh (or Communist) Party bedeck most buildings.

In Rasht – like other towns in this area – the slogans do not directly attack Ayatollah Khomeiny or the Islamic Revolution. Some people say they don't have to: time is on the side of the Left and the communists.

With the revolutionary leaders losing their grip over Iran, and failing to solve their country's problems, it is only a matter of time before change comes. And the Leftists and communists don't intend to fight and lose control of the "revolution" a second time.

Even under the Shah's regime, the communist movement was strong underground in this area.

"About 30 per cent of the people in all the towns of this area are communists," Ali, an Iranian in his early twenties, estimated. Talking in the deserted Kebab restaurant in which he works, he said the communists were mainly young people. "The older people support the Mujahedin."

Asked why there were not more pictures of Dr Bani-Sadr in the streets, Ali said: "Every day people put them up, but the Leftists and communists tear them down the same night.

"A lot of people are not communists or Leftists, but they admire and sympathise with these groups because they are the people who have the guts to stand up and oppose the mistakes of the Islamic leaders."

Close proximity to the Soviet Union, and crystal clear reception from the medium wave broadcasts beamed from the Soviet side of the Caspian are obvious reasons for communist sympathies being strong in this area.

However, it goes deeper than this. In this area the workers tend to be highly educated by average Iranian standards and therefore more intelligently question Islamic Government or the rule of a monarch dedicated to capitalism – the only two systems of Government under which they have lived.

Driving east from Rasht with the Caspian on the left and the magnificent snow-capped and pine and poplar covered Elburz on the right, a reason for worker resentment becomes apparent. Behind high stone and brick walls and shrubbery stand the Caspian-side mansions of the wealthy. Many of them are deserted now – their owners having fled Iran during the revolution – but they remain as a reminder of the inequalities of capitalism, Iran-style.

A problem to haunt Iran
From DAVID BALDERSTONE in Teheran

'The Age', May 7, 1980

In the first few days after the fall of the Shah, Arabic-speaking Iranians in the port city of Khorammshahr tore down a brick wall built to hide the unsightly mud brick slums in which the Arabs lived.

It was a symbolic gesture which expressed clearly the fact that the Arabic-speaking Iranians in Iran's oil-producing province of Khuzestan, in the south-west, were no longer going to allow their problems and demands to be hidden.

In common with the Kurds, the Baluchis and Iran's other regional minorities, the Iranian revolution unleashed among the Arabs of Khuzestan the expectation that at last they would have a greater say in the running of their own affairs. Now 15 months after the revolution, they have found their expectations unfulfilled.

In May and June last year, fierce fighting between the Arabs of Khuzestan and the central authorities left several hundred dead. Hardly a week passes without Arab guerillas being blamed for sabotaging oil pipelines and facilities in the province.

The violent end to the siege of the Iranian Embassy in London by gunmen claiming to be Arabic-speaking Iranians has left three of the five terrorists dead. But the problems in Khuzestan faced by Iran's central authorities undoubtedly live on.

Although the sabotage of oil facilities is almost certain to continue, the central authorities have been fairly successful in putting down open violence in Khuzestan. Credit for this has gone to Admiral Madani, the former navy chief and Governor-General of the province, who directed military operations against the Arabs last year.

Since sabotage and violence broke out in the province shortly after the Shi'ite Moslem revolution, the predominantly Sunni Moslem regime in Bagdad has been blamed for stirring up trouble and supplying arms and explosives to the Arab guerillas. Therefore it was not surprising that the Iranian authorities put the finger on Bagdad for being somehow involved in the London siege, which certainly is not beyond the bounds of possibility.

Khuzestan, on the Iraqi border, not only contains most of Iran's oil fields. The country's largest refinery is at Abadan on the Shatt al-Arab – the disputed waterway which provides part of the border.

Traditionally the Arabs of Khuzestan – which the Iranian Arabs and the Iraqis call Arabistan – have been second class citizens. They carry out only the lowest jobs in the oil industry, which is manned predominantly by members of the Baktiar tribe from further north. They are mainly Shi'ite Moslems, but there are some Sunnis amongst them.

They are on average poorly paid and mostly live in slum conditions. They have every reason to feel the traditional Arab resentment towards Persians. They have never had any real representation on local government bodies.

Although the province's Arab leaders have spoken about wanting to take over control of its resources, their most consistent demands are less unacceptable to the central authorities, who quite obviously could not have a minority controlling the oil industry.

They want Arabic to be the principal language in their schools, and they want Arab culture and traditions respected. They want increased job opportunities and better housing. They don't want to be treated as second class citizens.

The Iranian authorities could well be right in blaming the Bagdad regime for trouble in Khuzestan. President Hussein has an interest in stirring up trouble in Iran. Because the Bagdad regime is seen to be a minority Sunni Moslem regime in a country where Shi'ites make up a slight majority, Mr Saddam Hussein is vulnerable to the same fate as the Shah – a Shi'ite revolution.

Therefore the more trouble the Iraqis can cause Teheran, the less likely it is that the Iranian revolution will be envied widely in Iraq.

The Arabs of Khuzestan tore down the wall hiding their slums. It is a sight the Iranian authorities will most likely have to live with for a considerable time.

Mullahs to decide fate of hostages

From a special correspondent in Teheran(Ed: this article did not carry David's by-line because it was during a journalists' strike in Australia, about which he knew nothing.)

'The Age', May 31, 1980

It has been a long day. At first light the fiat had climbed northeast out of Teheran across the Elburz mountains and sped along the Caspian coast to Gorgan, north central Iran.

After lunch of kebab and rice, and a failed attempt to see either the American hostages held in Gorgan or their captors, we were nearing the end of the return journey as darkness fell. The headlights had just picked up the sign: Teheran 30 kilometres.

Then, after a round trip of 750 kilometres, a rear wheel fell off, stranding the Fiat in the centre of the road.

The Iranian driver was in a state of despair. The traffic was brought to a standstill. But a band of helpful Iranians jumped from their cars and enthusiastically carried the Fiat to the side of the road.

We had not had time to think what to do next when a lorry fitted with a crane stopped. The lorry driver placed a railway sleeper through the front windows, hooked up the crane, and lifted the crippled car onto the truck. The driver muttered something about Allah being very good to us.

After the car was firmly secured, we climbed back inside. For the next hour as the lorry crept into Teheran, disco music blared out of the car-cassette player, and someone produced a drop of vodka.

Once the car had been unloaded outside a Teheran garage, the lorry driver asked our driver to translate something. "I would like you to know that we in Iran have nothing against foreigners. We like foreigners," he said. "We hope that the crisis is over soon."

He did not seem to mean it as a political statement. He was not passing judgement on whether the Americans should be released. He was not necessarily criticising the Islamic revolution.

Instead he was wanting to be friendly.

It is a sentiment expressed by a large cross-section of Iranians. During the heady days of the revolution – and especially since the hostage crisis – it has been a feeling obscured from the outside world by more newsworthy events.

Iran is a land of contradictions which has only ever been welded together by tough leaders. Since Cyrus the Great became King of Persia in 546 BC, the impressive leaders – in the main – have been those who took over when the previous ruling family had either been defeated in battle or degenerated.

This was the case when Reza Khan, the deposed Shah's father took over in 1925, and after initial thoughts of turning the country into a republic had himself proclaimed Shah.

From the Qajar dynasty, Reza Khan, who was known before the revolution as Shah Reza the Great, inherited a central authority which was virtually powerless over Khuzestan – the oil-rich province in South West Iran – and some of the northern provinces.

In the 1930s Reza Khan – with German help carved tunnels through the Elburz range mainly to enable his army to firmly control the northern provinces.

Today several of these long tunnels are without lights. No longer is it thought necessary to inspect carefully their cobbled linings to make certain the heavy traffic is not eroding their strength.

Given the fact that these road tunnels were built to aid unification of the country, their disrepair is symbolic of the gradual disintegration of Iran. Iran does not have a strong leader; instead power is divided.

Iran has Ayatollah Khomeiny. His leadership of the mass revolution that ousted the Shah was impressive. He remains widely respected.

"I am a middle class Iranian. I am educated. I am dubious about miracles," an Iranian businessman commented. "But when the might of the American army collapses in the desert near Tabas, can I say to the poor people of South Teheran that they are wrong to say Khomeiny is capable of miracles?"

Nevertheless, Khomeiny cannot be compared with strong leaders in the Persian tradition. His revolution has an army incapable of quelling the aspirations of the Kurds or protecting the vital oil pipeline system from sabotage.

Throughout Iran – particularly outside Teheran – it is difficult to know where authority lies.

Canadian and American journalists were apprehended by revolutionary guards in the north-eastern city of Mashad the other day.

They argued correctly that Mashad was back on limits for foreign correspondents. The local representative of the National Guidance (Information) Department supported the journalists. But the revolutionary guard commander said he did not take any notice of National Guidance because the department's minister was a spy.

This illustrates the central problem which has bugged Iran since the Shah's last Prime Minister fell in February. The problem has been a lack of central, unified authority. The seizing of the American hostages last November exacerbated this problem. The continued holding of the Americans has embroiled Iran in a crisis of its own making.

The ruling Revolutionary Council en masse did not have advance warning of the occupation of the US Embassy in Teheran last November. However, some members – almost certainly including Ayatollah Mohammed Beheshti – did know of the plan in advance.

The then Prime Minister, Mehdi Bazargan, did not know – and resigned out of frustration two days later.

The President, Mr Abolhassan Bani-Sadr, and the Foreign Minister, Mr Qotbzadeh, want the crisis over.

Nevertheless they cannot stand blameless. The hostage crisis has been the product of infighting within the continuing revolution which they support.

It is pretty clear that the main drive behind the hostage crisis was provided by Islamic fundamentalists, who feared that they would lose influence to the secular politicians.

The revolution was not a religious revolution. It was an anti-monarchy revolution. People of all classes and political leanings participated. The clergy played a major part because they had the only well organised, nation-wide political network – the mosques.

And Khomeiny was the property of the mullahs. They had spread his word, and he had delivered them from decades of repression under the Pahlavi dynasty – Reza Shah and his son, the deposed Shah. They tasted power – and enjoyed it.

In retrospect, it is difficult not to conclude that the American hostage crisis was engineered in a bid to prolong and enhance the power of the mullahs. If so, it has been successful.

By November last year, the revolutionary cycle was nearly over. The new constitution had been drafted; Presidential and parliamentary elections were in the wind. Through elections, the mullahs' power was about to be tested.

Intentionally or unintentionally the fundamentalists have benefitted by the hostage crisis. It has diverted attention of lower class Iranians away from inflation of at least 33 per cent since the revolution, high unemployment and food shortages. It has kept the attention of the poor people on the Islamic revolution.

This has resulted in the clergy backed "grand coalition" of nine Islamic parties dominated by Dr Beheshti's Islamic Republican Party winning control of 130 seats in the 270-seat Parliament or Majlis.

This is enough to give the grand coalition a majority because the election of 26 deputies has been indefinitely postponed because of trouble – mainly in the Kurdish region.

The IRP did lose out in the Presidential election in January. They nominated a little known candidate who – in any case – was disqualified shortly before the election because of doubts about his parents' Iranian nationality.

The IRP proposed another candidate, but it was too late. Abolhassan Bani-Sadr, a French-trained economist, won convincingly.

It was a defeat the IRP has not forgotten.

Working through their representatives on the Revolutionary Council, including Dr Beheshti, they stymied Dr Bani-Sadr's bid to centralise power, end the hostage crisis and appoint a Prime Minister.

In February, Khomeiny charged members of the Majlis with responsibility for deciding on the terms of the release of the American hostages.

Having won the right in the Majlis elections to choose a Prime Minister, it could be assumed that the Islamic fundamentalists have little more need for the American hostages.

If power was a predictable commodity in Iran, it could be assumed the Majlis would decide to release most of the hostages while putting the rest on trial.

One scenario is that the hostages put on trial – inevitably for being associated with the CIA – would be found guilty, but immediately deported.

The driver of the lorry mounted with a crane would be happy with that scenario. "I would like you to know that we in Iran have nothing against foreigners," he said.

High tension on the Left (sic) Bank
From DAVID BALDERSTONE in Amman

'The Age', June 13, 1980

It was far from being Bassam Shaka's only hope. But for someone who points the finger of blame at Israel for the booby trap bomb which cost him his legs, there was something poignant about it.

"A lot of individual Israelis were shocked by the bomb attacks just as our people were. Unfortunately these people are few and not influential in Israel. But we hope they will become more influential," he said.

Mr Shaka, who is mayor of the occupied West Bank city of Nablus, lost his legs after a booby trap bomb exploded in his car on 2 June. His friend, Mayor Karim Khalif of the West Bank town of Ramallah, lost his left foot when a similar bomb exploded in his car the same morning.

Doctors at the King Hussein medical centre in Amman, Jordan, say Mr Shaka is doing fine under the circumstances. Mr Shaka himself demonstrated he had lost none of his spirit for putting the Palestinian cause when he talked to 'The Age' yesterday.

"Hopefully what has happened will have opened the eyes of the world to what Israel is really about," he said. "The Israelis have always boasted about their so-called democratic traditions but what has happened is the opposite of democracy."

Mr Shaka, his family and the Palestinian Liberation Organisation blame Israeli authorities acting in co-operation with extremist Jewish settlers on the West Bank for the car bomb attacks.

This is not merely based on their hatred of the occupying force. The telephone at the Shaka home was cut about the time of the bomb attack, and when Mr Shaka was transferred to hospital the phones in the hospital went dead, family members said yesterday.

"Usually when a stone drops on the West Bank, the Israeli army comes to investigate," Mrs Eniah Shaka said yesterday. "But this time it took them several hours to come and inspect the car."

Wherever the blame lies, the co-ordinated bombings do indicate that the Israeli military authorities who consistently stress that they must be in control of security on the West Bank, paid little attention to guarding the homes of prominent officials at a time of severe tension between Arabs and Jewish settlers.

Mrs Shaka said Israel's former Defence Minister, Mr Ezer Weizman, had personally threatened Mr Shaka that his life would be in danger unless he co-operated with Israel.

Propped up in bed, a cage covering the stumps of his legs, Mr Shaka, an open supporter of the PLO, said the Israelis must realise that peace between Arabs and Jews could only be achieved through Israel's acceptance of the Palestinians' right to a State.

"The recent events prove that Israel fights the pressures for peace in the Middle East. They not only deport mayors, but threaten their lives as well. And this is not to mention the day-to-day harassment faced by Arabs in the occupied territories," he said.

"This all goes to show that Israel does not care for peace. Instead, Israel works for Zionist expansionism and against the Palestinians and peace."

Mayors in the West Bank are more than directors of municipal affairs. They are the resident political leaders, who – unlike their counterparts in Damascus and Beirut – speak out for Palestinian rights while under the thumb of Israeli military authorities.

Last month Israeli authorities expelled two mayors – Mr Fahd Qawasmi of Hebron and Mr Mohammed Milhem of Halhoul. On 2 June, the day of the attacks on Mr Shaka and Mr Khalif, the mayor of Al Bireh, Mr Ibrahim Tawil, had a narrow escape from a booby trap bomb attached to the door of his garage.

"These incidents make Palestinians think that peace will come only through force rather than negotiation," Mr Shaka said. A staunch opponent of Egyptian-Israeli-US negotiations on

Palestinian autonomy, he said, "hopefully these incidents will contribute to the failure of the Camp David process."

Middle East no closer to peace
From DAVID BALDERSTONE in Amman

'The Age', June 24, 1980

For once there has been a meeting of minds among Israel, Jordan, Irak and senior members of the Palestine Liberation Organisation.

They clearly agree on the purport of last week's European Economic Community statement on the Middle East: their differing reactions prove that.

Israel's Prime Minister, Mr Begin, condemns it as a "second Munich surrender"; Jordan, Irak and some members of the PLO say it contains "positive" elements.

For Israel's Government, it is a step in the wrong direction – a move towards wider pressure on Israel to withdraw from all territories occupied in 1967, and European recognition of the PLO.

For the Arabs, it is a major advance along the tortuous road towards a comprehensive Middle East settlement – a track along which they have been wandering in the wilderness now for 32 years.

By issuing the statement, which said growing Middle East tension rendered a "comprehensive settlement to the Israeli-Arab conflict more necessary and pressing than ever," the nine European leaders were serving notice that they believed the US-inspired Camp David peace process was running out of steam.

Since the Egyptian Presidential airliner touched down on Israeli soil on 20 November, 1977, the process has seen incredible highs and depressing lows. The so-called Sadat initiative has brought to the world stage such star-studded spectaculars as the Camp David accords, the Egyptian-Israeli peace treaty and the withdrawal of Israel from most of the Egyptian-Sinai territory occupied in 1967.

But it has not brought comprehensive peace closer because the Camp David process fails to tackle the crux of the Arab-Israeli dispute – the Palestinian problem.

Without a comprehensive settlement the peace treaty is worth little more than the paper it is written on. It is arguably dependent upon the survival of one man – President Sadat.

A map of the Middle East can be read many ways. The Israelis read it as showing their tiny country of 3.5 million in the midst of 150 million Arabs living from Irak to the Atlantic. The Arabs see it as showing a State – populated mainly by Jewish immigrants, many of whom have come from Europe – usurping a prime slice of the agriculturally rich "Fertile Crescent". For the estimated four million Palestinians living outside "Palestine", it represents homes lost and family ties broken.

Since Israel was created by the United Nations in 1948, there have been four major Arab-Israeli wars. In 1967, Israel occupied the now disputed territories – the West Bank and Gaza Strip.

Only one war – the 1973 war when Syria and Egypt surprised Israel on the holiest day in the Jewish calendar – can be considered in any way an Arab success. The Egyptians, who dub the 1973 war the "October victory", maintain they achieved a tactical victory which led to the return of the Suez Canal and provided that important element, Arab pride, enabling Mr Sadat to visit Jerusalem.

The task of settling the dispute was complicated further in 1974, when Arab leaders meeting in Rabat appointed the PLO the "sole legitimate representative of the Palestinian people". Therefore Jordan, which lost the West Bank to Israel in 1967, was no longer empowered to negotiate – even if King Hussein wanted to – with Israel over the return of the "Palestinian" West Bank in exchange for peace. The vicious circle was completed by Israel's refusal to sit down with the PLO.

Mr Sadat broke the circle in 1977 by visiting Jerusalem. In September 1978, at President Carter's retreat, Camp David, Egypt and Israel agreed to conclude within three months a peace treaty based upon UN Security Council resolution 242. They agreed also to negotiate an autonomy plan for Palestinians living on the West Bank and Gaza Strip.

Most Arab countries firmly united in opposition to what they saw as a sell-out by Mr Sadat. Their principal concern was that the accords had neutralised the biggest and militarily most powerful Arab country. Egypt had been withdrawn from the military equation.

The peace treaty was signed in March last year, but the autonomy plan was doomed even before serious negotiations between Egypt, Israel and the US got underway. West Bank leaders – most of whom are strong supporters of the PLO – rejected it. They wanted Israeli withdrawal from occupied territories, not Israeli-supervised "autonomy". Also, autonomy would do nothing for Palestinians living outside the occupied territories.

Nevertheless, the Camp David parties pushed on with negotiations in the vain hope – at least on the part of Egypt and the US – that West Bankers and people in the Gaza Strip would eventually play along.

By 26 May this year, the deadline set at the time of the signing of the peace treaty for conclusion of the negotiations, Egypt and Israel were a long way from reaching agreement on autonomy.

Although the deadline has passed, negotiators from Egypt, Israel and the US will sit down in Washington once again early next month to try to hammer out an agreement. The main differences involve the powers which should be granted to the envisaged Palestinian Council and whether East Jerusalem should be included.

East Jerusalem, which includes the main Christian, Jewish and Moslem holy places, was previously part of the Jordan-administered West Bank and therefore is considered by the international community to be still part of it. However Israel has unilaterally annexed the old city and says East and West Jerusalem make up the indivisible capital of Israel.

Behind the disagreement is that Mr Sadat envisages autonomy eventually leading to the establishment of a Palestinian State on the West Bank, whereas Mr Begin's Government wants to avoid this.

There seems little chance of next month's talks reaching agreement on the autonomy plan – and even if they do the Palestinians will not participate.

All along Arab opponents of the Sadat initiative have said the Camp David process would not solve the Arab-Israeli dispute. On the one hand, the Camp David philosophy born out of three decades of dispute has relied on a step-by-step approach leading eventually to comprehensive peace. On the other hand, Mr Sadat's Arab opponents believe that settlement is most likely to be achieved by unified Arab negotiating muscle (backed up by the threat of military clout) and pressure from Israel's supporters, mainly the US.

There is an unstated reason why Arab leaders do not like the step-by-step approach to peace: at each step another Arab leader becomes vulnerable to the wrath of the Arab world.

Since Mr Sadat visited Jerusalem there has been a hypothetical question which has remained unanswered. This is - what would have happened if King Hussein, President Hafez Assad of Syria, PLO chief Yasser Arafat and Lebanon's President Elias Sarkis had joined at the intial negotiations with Israel held at the Mena House Hotel in Cairo in December, 1977? Egypt claimed they were invited.

In the glare of publicity after Mr Sadat had visited Jerusalem would Israel have dared to leave the US-backed talks because the PLO was sitting at the same table? It was a no-lose situation for the Arabs.

Instead, Arab States and the PLO – spearheaded by the moderates, notably Jordan – embarked on a policy aimed at persuading EEC countries to adopt their own peace initiative to replace the Camp David process or pressure the US into talking to the PLO.

There is no doubt the EEC statement on the Middle East was important to the Arabs. It raised issues that meant a lot to them.

It went further than the controversial and ambiguously worded Security Council resolution on which the Camp David accords are based. First, unlike the resolution, it says the Palestinian issue is not simply one of refugees. Second the EEC leaders call on Israel to end its territorial occupation. This appears to call for total withdrawal and therefore goes further than the resolution, which is ambiguous.

The EEC statement also strongly criticised Israel's policy of establishing Jewish settlements in the occupied territories.

So where do the chances of Middle East peace stand now? Mr Begin says Jews have an inalienable right to settle throughput Eretz (greater) Israel (which, in Mr Begin's terms includes the occupied territories). The major guerilla group under the PLO umbrella, Fatah, recently reaffirmed its aim of liberating all of Palestine.

So the hardliners who hold power in both the Israel and PLO camps, hold apparently irreconcilable positions.

The rise in West Bank violence involving Arabs and Jewish settlers, and particularly the recent bomb attacks against two Arab mayors, have hardened the attitudes of moderate Arabs and further reduced the chance of compromise.

Conversely, turmoil in the Middle East – an ongoing revolution in Iran, serious unrest in Syria, and the Grand Mecca Mosque siege in Saudi Arabia – has made life easy for hardliners in Israel. They can say to the world and their countrymen: "Do you really want Israel to give back the West Bank so that a radical Palestinian State can be established on our doorstep?"

But the same turmoil seems likely to continue to push the US and the EEC towards policies aimed at ending the 32-year-old crisis.

An Arab-Israeli peace is as far away as ever. The only hope of compromise and eventual settlement lies in the EEC and the US recognising the PLO and then applying the strongest pressure to both sides.

Terrorism endangers Turkish democracy
From DAVID BALDERSTONE in Istanbul

'The Age', July 7, 1980

Students in the coastal city of Izmir, West Turkey had arranged a party following their university entrance examinations. By the end of the evening, five of them had been shot dead and, according to several surviving students, a Sergeant Hassan Dimici was treading in the blood, laughing, and shouting: "We have cleaned up the communists!"

Sergeant Dimici, who is a conscript in the Turkish army and a former architecture student from Istanbul, five other conscript sergeants, and a sub-lieutenant, have been arrested over the shootings that took place in the middle of June.

Four days after the Izmir massacre, a provincial chairman of Bulent Ecevit's Left-of-centre Opposition party, the Republican People's Party, was shot dead while shopping. A Party colleague accompanying the provincial chairman had ripped open his shirt, bared his chest, and pleaded with the gunmen. But both men were shot dead.

Never a day goes by without political killings in Turkey. Political terrorism is claiming up to 15 lives each day. So far this year, well over 1300 people have died at the hands of the extremists of Turkish politics – the splintered Leftist and communist groups and the neo-fascist Right.

It is widely thought that both the Left and the Right get help – and perhaps even directions – from outside the country. But what seems certain is that dissatisfaction over domestic problems is polarising the 48 million citizens and driving a constant supply of young Turks into the arms of extremist groups.

Faced with inflation of around 100 per cent a year, at least 20 per cent unemployment and millions of others greatly under-employed, more and more people are growing tired of the established order of Turkish democracy.

Partly due to deficiencies in the constitution, the two main parties, Suleiman Demirel's conservative Justice Party and the RPP, find it hard to gain an outright majority in national elections.

Therefore, the past decade has seen the odd spectacle of both the conservative Mr Demirel, and Mr Ecevit, a democratic socialist, at different times in coalition with the same small Right-wing National Socialist Party.

And the experience has been too much for both of them. Instead they have tried forming minority governments free from the inevitable compromises demanded by such a coalition.

Ecevit's flirtation with a minority government ended last November. Demirel is struggling along having survived a censure motion this week.

Further tarnishing the image of democracy is that the country's 450-seat National Assembly has tortuously voted in around 100 ballots during the past few months in a bid to elect a president. But Turkey – even after so many ballots – is still without a Head of State.

Although there are problems with the constitution, the blame for this sort of infighting among the elected politicians is widely seen to rest with the politicians themselves. People who want and respect democracy seem to feel the politicians are putting their own ambitions first, and failing to recognise the precariousness of democracy in Turkey.

On the other hand, the extremists of Left and Right delight in the failure of the politicians to cope with the democratic process. They, it seems, are hell bent on getting a dictatorship.

With political terrorism rife and problems with the democratic process, there is speculation that the army, an extremely powerful institution, might be on the verge of taking over.

Although the army is thought to be reluctant to take this step, there are precedents. The army staged a coup in 1960 and ousted the democratically-elected Government. And in 1971, following a long period of economic and political trouble, the army demanded the resignation of the Prime Minister, Mr Demirel.

Although the officer corps is considered to be conservative, the army is made up mainly of conscripts and therefore the polarisation in the community is reflected in the ranks. This is considered to be one main reason why the army would be extremely reluctant to take over again.

With parliamentary-approved martial law in force in 20 of Turkey's 67 provinces, the army has considerable power already in the main urban centres, including Ankara and Istanbul.

But while Turkey faces acute problems, it is the only predominantly Moslem country in the Middle East run along really democratic lines. It is a secular State in which the freedom of the Press, trade unions and political parties are guarded under the constitution.

Politically, it identifies itself with Europe rather than the Middle East. It is a member of NATO; it has long maintained diplomatic links with Israel.

One man, the great Ataturk, made Turkey what it is today. He was responsible for its secularism, its democracy, and its Westernisation – and a good deal of its problems.

Even today, 42 years after he died, Turks make what amounts to a pilgrimage to his lavish mausoleum in Ankara. They prostrate themselves, and some knock their heads against the stone floor, in praise of the founder of modern Turkey. "In some ways, Ataturk has replaced the Prophet Mohammed for Turks. One of the freedoms we don't have is the freedom to openly criticise Ataturk," a Turkish journalist explained to me.

Turkey's economic problems stem, at least in part, from Ataturk's extremely nationalistic, pro-Western attitudes. He was keen for Turkey to develop into an industrial nation, and agriculture was neglected. In fact the expansion of Turkey's already big agricultural exports is seen as a key to getting the Turkish economy, which suffers from an acute balance of payments problem, back on the rails.

The neglect of agriculture in favor of industry has driven millions of people from rural areas to the cities. Ankara is surrounded by the "gecekondu", makeshift shelters built by people moving to the industrial centres in search of a better life.

But a better life is not easily found by these people. Dissatisfaction drives many of them into the hands of extremist groups.

The Rightist view is that the Leftists are directed and armed from outside. A Turkish political scientist told me he believed aid was being given to the Leftists as part of a Soviet plot to gain control of Turkey. His argument was based on the importance of Turkey's geographical position – straddling the Bosphorus and the Dardanelles, and providing a Western buffer between the Soviet Union and the Arab world.

"Make no mistake about it. The Soviet Union wants the Bosphorus and intends to get it. In Turkey, it wants a friendly Government – a Government on the style of Babrak Karmal's in Afghanistan," the political scientist said.

Arms for Leftists, he believed, were coming from Sophia, capital of Bulgaria, and the Syrian capital, Damascus. While he may be correct in blaming Sophia and Damascus, it is widely thought that the arms do come from Eastern Europe and are shipped through small ports on the Turkish Aegean and Mediterranean.

Ironically, some of the people blamed for being behind political terrorism sit in Turkey's democratically elected Parliament. Therefore, it seems, Turkey – a country strategically important to the West and a probable target of Soviet designs – is being threatened from within its own admirably democratic institutions.

Arafat: enigma of the PLO
From DAVID BALDERSTONE in Beirut

'The Age', July 15, 1980

Yasser Arafat, the PLO chairman, was working steadily at his desk. He looked very much the bureaucrat as he dealt with his in-tray. He quickly read the papers before him and initialled them one by one.

He was dressed in the usual battle fatigues but his bald head was bare of the usual Arab kaffieh. He did not look up as we entered the air-conditioned office and moved to the conference table in the book-lined ante-room. The suite was too crammed with personal mementos and books to give any support to the theory that the Palestinian leader moves from office to office for security reasons.

It was after 1 am, but this floor of the apartment building in an area of West Beirut controlled by Palestinian guerillas was buzzing with activity. Outside Mr Arafat's office armed guards were roaming the corridors.

We sat down at the maple coloured table and after a couple of minutes Mr Arafat broke away from his papers and swept across to the head of the table. "Good evening," he said, his eyes darting around the room.

Yasser Arafat is an enigma. Israeli leaders and Israel's supporters staunchly oppose any dialogue with him because they point to PLO declarations expressing the aim of liberating all of Palestine. But Western politicians such as the Austrian Chancellor, Mr Kriesky, former West German Chancellor Mr Brandt, and now the Australian Opposition Leader, Mr Hayden, have come away from meetings with the impression that he and his PLO would be prepared in the future to recognise Israel's right to exist on its pre-1967 war borders.

During a 45-minute interview with 'The Age', the PLO chief confirmed that impression but at no time stated it directly.

During the interview Mr Arafat made two comments which supported the impression.

Firstly, he said the PLO was prepared to accept an independent Palestinian State on any part of Palestine from which Israel withdrew. This implies clearly that Mr Arafat is prepared to establish a State alongside Israel.

Secondly, he referred to recognition of Israel's right to exist as "my bargaining point". In other words he was not prepared to recognise Israel's right to exist until Israel and its Western supporters were prepared to recognise the Palestinians' right to a Sate. The point is Mr Arafat would not need a bargaining point if he was set on liberating all of Palestine.

Supporters of Israel could argue that these two points merely mean that Mr Arafat and the PLO are prepared initially to establish a State on any part of Palestine, but that then the aim would be to liberate it all. But there would be international safeguards for Israel if a Palestinian State were to be established. Also, Israel would continue to be militarily superior.

Mr Arafat said the last month's declaration by the largest of the Palestinian guerilla groups, Fatah, had been taken out of context. In the declaration, the Fatah congress looked forward to the establishment of a secular State in all of Palestine. This implied the elimination of the Jewish State of Israel.

"First of all, the Fatah communiqué was distorted," Mr Arafat said. "This was a lie distributed by the Israelis and Begin (Israel's Prime Minister) himself.

"We have declared that all resolutions decided and approved in the Palestine National Council are included in Fatah's political programme." (The PNC is in effect the PLO's Parliament-in-exile). "These resolutions are accepted on the Arab and international level, and include the resolution that we are prepared to accept a State on any part of Palestine, liberated or evacuated."

Did this mean that if the Israelis withdrew from the West Bank territory occupied in 1967 the PLO would establish a State on the West Bank, declare peace, and recognise Israel's right to exist?

"Is that an offer? Is that an offer? I cannot give away my bargaining point on one hypothesis, one big if," Mr Arafat replied. "The Israelis are only offering us more assassination, more oppression, more attacks.

"The Israeli leaders, the Israeli military junta have said they will continue their attacks, their aggression, their raids into Lebanon against the Palestinian people and the Lebanese people.

"They are attacking daily and using all the up-to-date American weapons against the Palestinian people in South Lebanon. They are even using cluster bombs and fragmentation shells."

Mr Arafat said Israel was not even following the Camp David agreements, which provided the foundation for the Egyptian-Israeli peace treaty. Israel was ignoring United Nations Security Council and General Assembly resolutions.

He blamed Israel's Prime Minister, Mr Begin, for the recent car bomb attacks on the West Bank. Mr Bassam Shaka, the mayor of Nablus, lost both legs in one attack and the mayor of Ramallah, Mr Karim Khalif, lost his left foot in another. "This is another example of officially organised terrorism. They can increase their terrorism against my people, but it is increasing our determination to continue our resistance against Israeli occupation," he said.

Mr Arafat was asked what effect the continuing turmoil in Iran had on Palestinian aims: "Although the PLO welcomed and helped the revolution in Iran, doesn't the continuing trouble there make it easy for Israeli leaders to say, domestically and internationally, 'Do you really want us to withdraw so that a radical Palestinian State can be established?'?"

Mr Arafat replied: "What you are saying is not fair, that is just one of the arguments put in the West against our rights. In 1969 we Arab Moslems and Christians offered that we were ready to live with the Jews in a democratic Palestinian State. The Israelis refused.

"So we offered another solution. We offered that we are ready to establish our State in any part of Palestine, evacuated or liberated. Also, they refuse it.

"What is it they offer? They offer new slavery to my people. I'm sorry but they are just full of excuses."

Amman July 18, 1980 (*To Mother and Aunt Ethel*)

As you would have seen, I met Yasser Arafat the other night. Funny thing is his mother was an Abu Seoud, although Mr Abu Seoud (*our landlord in Amman*) says he is only a distant relation. I knew this before last Saturday night's interview, but one of the PLO people confirmed it. I think I have told you before but the PLO gets all my stories sent to them. The young man who looks after their Australian interests and can quote everything about Australia said he was surprised to see me in Beirut.

"I thought you must have been living in Iran now. I particularly liked that story on the front page about the little Iranian man with a dustpan helping you at the airport." It was on the tip of my tongue to say that my mother's golfing friends liked that too.

I think I have been to Iran a couple of times and to Turkey since writing to you last. Turkey was great fun. I spent all the time in Ankara although as you noted, one of my stories was datelined Istanbul. Those unworldly people who edit 'The Age' probably think Turkey's capital is still Istanbul, which it hasn't been since just after the First World War. I am also angry with them for running the Hayden-Arafat meeting on page seven. But my biggest complaint is that they always refer to the West Bank as the Left Bank – it even appeared in a headline on my story about the mayor who lost his legs in an Israeli terrorist attack. The West Bank is in fact the right bank because the Jordan River as you know flows into the Dead Sea. Next time they ask me to do a story on Left Bank trouble I am going to catch the first plane to Paris!

I was eating a pleasant dinner in the Bulver Palace Hotel, Ankara one night. The Turks go for my favorites such as brains and sheep liver, which is perhaps not the wisest thing to eat in Ankara. But I did. I felt that a medicinal amount of wine would neutralise any bad things, and anyway it's always better to eat what you like. Back to dinner under the grand chandeliers of the Bulver Palace dining room. I had just finished dinner, had ordered Turkish coffee and a brandy, and this young man from the next table came over.

"You have been a matter of some speculation at our table", he said.

"Really", I replied.

"Yes, we cannot decide whether you are Scandinavian or German. We know you are not English because you are polite to the waiters. But we have been thrown into quite some confusion because West Germans and Scandinavians don't usually drink Turkish brandy."

I ended up having a drink with them in the hotel's pavement café.

In Iran last time I was lucky in getting a taxi driver who has become quite a good friend. He was a Lt. Colonel in the army under the Shah and was promoted to Colonel after the revolution. But he has since resigned because of the situation and is now driving taxis. I went to dinner at his place a couple of times and his family is very nice. I mentioned about his car breaking down in one of my stories, but you may not have seen it because it was during the Strike and by-lined "from a special correspondent in Teheran".

Khader N is very pleased with himself because he led a press walkout during the recent meeting of Arab foreign and economic ministers in Amman. I was away with Hayden (*the Australian Opposition Leader*), but facilities for the press were evidently very bad. After a press conference had been postponed twice and the press had been kept hanging around for six hours, Khader led the walkout. But the funniest thing was when the press was summoned to the Holiday Inn, where the meeting was taking place. Security, as always at these things was very tight and a soldier came up to Khader and said: "Is that your cigarette lighter?"

"Yes", said Khader.

"Light it", said the soldier.

"Why should I? If it is a bomb we will both die."

The time for travel
- DAVID BALDERSTONE

'The Age, Amman, July 19, 1980

Traffic in the Middle East became more impatient this week. Factory production plummeted and Government offices closed early.

Ramadan, during which all good Moslems fast from dawn to dusk, began last weekend.

The rise in Islamic fundamentalism and lingering fears that the Islamic revolution in Iran will spread have ensured tight Government regulations for the fast in most Arab countries. In Jordan it is illegal to smoke in the streets in daylight. Bars are closed. Shops are not allowed to sell alcoholic drinks.

During Ramadan, the world's 750 million Moslems are banned from eating, drinking, smoking and sex during daylight hours. "Allah……. desires you to fast the whole month so that you may magnify him and render thanks to him for giving you his guidance," the Koran says.

"It is lawful for you to lie with your wives on the night of the fast (and) eat and drink until you can tell a white thread from a black one in the light of the coming dawn. Then resume your fast until nightfall."

Ramadan, a month in the progressive Moslem lunar calendar, falls at the height of the Middle East summer this year. Temperatures in most of the region have been hovering about the 40-degree C mark this week. So it is an extremely difficult fast for good Moslems following the ban on drinking liquid between dawn and dusk.

According to Islamic tradition, the prophet Mohammed restricted his nightly diet during the fast to two dates and some milk. But these days it is common for large meals to be served after sunset. Many families hold all-night parties between the first meal, or Iftar, and the pre-sunrise "sun-hour" meal.

The Ramadan fast started with the sighting of the new moon and will finish at the end of the month with a large feast called the Eid Al Fitr.

Ramadan, particularly when it falls in mid-summer, causes medical problems. "After Ramadan we find patients coming to us with a dramatic increase in the incidence of kidney stones," said an Amman doctor who happens to be a Moslem.

"The tragedy is that the people who really suffer are the poorer people. They see it as having been told by the Prophet to fast and therefore go ahead and work with a pick and shovel all day digging up a road. Of course they get dehydrated and kidney stones develop.

"On the other hand, an educated Moslem, if he feels really thirsty, he will have a sip of water, or if he is extremely religious, go and lie on a bed. The point which some of the poorer people do not realise – and no one should expect them to realise – is that the body can only take so much."

Arab leaders, on the other hand, know how much the body can take. It is usual to find a great number of senior officials and Arab leaders travelling during Ramadan.

The reason? The Koran exempts travellers – and the aged and the sick – from fasting.

Sadat the successful
From DAVID BALDERSTONE, Middle East correspondent

'The Age', August 2, 1980

At 10.55 pm on 28 September, 1970, some hours after Cairo Radio had suspended normal programmes and begun broadcasting verses of the Koran, Anwar Sadat, the Vice-President, broadcast to the nation. President Gamal Abdul Nasser was dead.

Huge crowds of weeping and wailing Egyptians took to the streets of Cairo. Some people hit their heads against stone walls; some thumped passing cars, others tore at their hair. Crowds swelled along the corniche beside the Nile, and along Kasr El Nil, a main street. Everywhere there were people.

In the Press centre in the radio and television tower on the corniche, journalists gathered around the Middle East News Agency teleprinter. In the midst of reams of copy on Nasser's life and death, the agency put out a three paragraph story. It said simply that under the constitution, Anwar Sadat became provisional President.

Then ten years ago, the emphasis was on the "provisional". Few people thought Sadat, whom some of his competitors unkindly nicknamed "Nasser's poodle", would last.

This week, President Sadat, flanked by his own son and imperial Iran's Crown Prince Reza, led mourners at Egypt's State funeral for the deposed Shah of Iran. It was a classic performance by a man who has admitted he once wanted to be an actor.

He did it for an old friend who, as Shah, had provided massive financial aid for Egypt, particularly after the 1973 Middle East war. Sadat never wanted to forget as other world leaders did.

It was that kind of guts which took Anwar Sadat to Jerusalem in November 1977. It was that kind of guts with which he answered death threats made by opponents of his historic visit.

On his return to Cairo he shunned a bullet-proofed car and a helicopter. Instead he stood in an open car as it travelled slowly across Cairo through tens of thousands of cheering Egyptians. "Neither the Palestinians nor Gadaffi can deprive me of one hour of my life, if God doesn't accept it," Mr Sadat, a devout Moslem, has said.

Since then, he and Israel's Prime Minister, Mr Begin, have given many Press conferences together. The performance is so often the same. For example, after their summit in Haifa last year, they talked to the Press on a Mount Carmel hotel lawn overlooking the Mediterranean. Mr Begin repeated that Jerusalem would remain always the undivided capital of Israel – a concept unacceptable to Mr Sadat. But the Egyptian did not walk out. Instead, he drew on his pipe and stared motionless towards the sea.

Anwar Sadat was born into a large family in the Nile Valley village of Meit Abou El Kom, Lower Egypt, in 1918. In those days about 2000 people lived in the village of straw and mud houses and Nile-irrigated vegetation.

Although the village people of Egypt had suffered high inflation during World War I, Mr Sadat's early childhood corresponded with boom years. But the rich got richer and the poor poorer.

Officially, Egypt became independent from British protection soon after the war. But while the 1923 Constitution gave the king legislative powers and provided for a Parliament, Britain retained considerable power.

Amidst the threat of Mussolini's expansionist policies in Africa in the mid thirties, the British and Egypt's politicians were thrown close together. Under a 1936 Anglo-Egyptian agreement, Britain retained the right to station troops along the Suez Canal.

The treaty was detested by elements of Egyptian youth who were fiercely nationalistic, but the treaty and growing war clouds did bring about one reform which was to prove immensely significant later.

In a move designed to strengthen the Egyptian army, the elite military academy, which had been the domain of the sons of the wealthy only, was opened to all classes.

Gamal Abdul Nasser and Anwar Sadat were able to enter the academy under this reform in the mid thirties.

They and several other members of what was to become known as the Free Officers' Movement, graduated as second lieutenants in 1938.

In 1939 Mr Nasser was posted to the Sudan. During the next three years Mr Sadat, who was posted to Cairo, was to play a much bigger part in organising the still nascent Free Officers' Movement.

During this period, Mr Sadat made contact with the German headquarters in Libya. The main reason for this move seems to have been his nationalistic view of the German army as a means of liberating Egypt from British wartime "occupation".

In 1942, Mr Sadat was tried by two British judges and an Egyptian judge on a charge of conspiring against the security of the State in a time of war. Mr Sadat was sent to prison but escaped after two years. He was again imprisoned in 1946 and this kept him out of the Arab-Israeli war fought after Israel was founded in 1948.

In 1945, between imprisonments, Mr Sadat demonstrated ability for rash judgement, but was restrained by Mr Nasser. The British Ambassador, Lord Killearn (formerly Sir Miles Lampson) had refused to receive the Egyptian Prime Minister who had wanted to talk about Egypt's national interests. The ambassador's action caused widespread indignation.

"I went to see Nasser and put up a plan for revenge," Mr Sadat wrote in an early book, 'Revolt on the Nile'. "My idea was to blow up the British Embassy and everybody in it...Gamal listened attentively and then shook his head and said no. He reminded me of the terrible reprisals which had followed the murder in 1924 of Sir Lee Stack, Governor-General of the Sudan. The tragedy must not be repeated, said Nasser."

After the Arabs' humiliating defeat in the 1948 war, discontent with the rule of King Farouk spread. The royal court was seen to become even more corrupt, extravagant and incompetent.

On 22 July, 1952, the young Free Officers put their plans for revolution into action. But Mr Sadat, who had worked so long for this night, nearly missed the action. "I decided to give my children a treat and I took them to an open air cinema near my home," he wrote.

But Mr Sadat caught up with the revolution and was the officer who broadcast news of the coup over the radio.

He was made a Minister in the first post-revolution Government. He held various senior posts and was appointed a Vice-President in 1964. However the post was abandoned in 1968. He was made Vice-President again in 1969 – a year before Mr Nasser's death.

Mr Sadat has been married twice. After his first marriage ended in divorce, he married his current wife, Jihan Raouf, the 15-year-old daughter of Anglo-Egyptian parents, in 1949.

He is an extremely devout Moslem, and never drinks alcohol. He is observing the daylight hour fast during the current Islamic month of Ramadan. The fast must have been particularly difficult during Tuesday's funeral for the Shah.

In 1971 – the year after he was elected President after the initial term as provisional President – an attempt was made to overthrow him. After it was unsuccessful he became more secure and comfortable in the Presidency and has even been game enough to criticise some aspects of Mr Nasser's rule.

A firm believer in a mixed economy, he has encouraged domestic and foreign private investment.

Mr Sadat's decisions during the past ten years have led people to describe him as rash or impetuous. In 1972 he expelled the Soviets from Egypt. In 1973, he and Syria's President Hafez Assad attacked Israel. In 1977, he visited Israel. In 1979, he offered the Shah a home.

Were these the foolish decisions of an impetuous man? They seem more the decisions of a calculating leader who spends much of his time in contemplation.

Egypt, a poor country of more than 38 million people, needs peace. Before the war in October 1973, the road to peace was blocked. Mr Sadat went to war to achieve a limited victory and restore Arab pride. Although Israeli troops ended the 18-day war 45 miles from Cairo, the initial surprise attack had taken the Egyptian army deep into Sinai and shattered the Israelis.

The 1973 war paved the way to two Sinai disengagement treaties which enabled Mr Sadat to re-open the Suez Canal. By October this year the Canal will be earning Egypt close to $1000 million a year.

January 1977 was a bad month for Mr Sadat. Serious food price riots erupted in Cairo. The year did not improve, and after Mr Begin was elected in May, Egyptian generals warned Mr Sadat that Israel might launch a devastating pre-emptive strike against Egypt. Mr Sadat was frustrated with lack of progress towards an all-party Geneva peace conference, so he went to Jerusalem.

While there is no reason to doubt that compassion was the main force which drove him to offer the Shah a home, there were some plusses for him as well.

He may have calculated that he would win widespread public support, particularly in the US and Israel. He needs this support to pressure the Israeli Government to move towards an agreement on autonomy for Palestinians living in the occupied West Bank and Gaza Strip.

Also, to the vulnerable oil-rich kings and emirs of Arabia, he has proved himself to be someone who stands by his allies.

On the other hand, Egypt's peace treaty with Israel and the hosting of the deposed Shah have caused problems for Mr Sadat. Violence broke out in several centres when Islamic fundamentalists, who were already angered over Egypt's dealings with Israel, demonstrated against the Shah's presence earlier this year.

Egypt has been shunned by the Arab world since Mr Sadat visited Jerusalem. But although Egypt has lost millions in aid from oil-rich Arab States, the boycott of Egypt is not nearly as universally followed as the Arabs sometimes try to make out.

Opposition to the peace treaty with Israel and domestic and economic policies have forced Mr Sadat to crack down on opponents. This has disillusioned the middle class who supported his early political liberalisation. In the face of Islamic fundamentalism, he has taken measures to make Egypt more Islamic. This has angered Coptic Christians.

The "open door" economic policy has encouraged considerable foreign investment. Egypt benefits from the Suez Canal revenues and gets oil from the Sinai fields returned by Israel. But inflation is still about 30 per cent and average per capita income still only $350 a year.

Although Mr Sadat seems to remain popular with the great majority of Egyptians, discontent could spread unless the lot of the ordinary people improves. Unless this happens, his decisions could look more the work of an impetuous leader than part of a long term strategy worked out during long hours of contemplation.

Amman, August 8, 1980 (*To Mother and Aunt Ethel*)

We are off to Greece next Friday for two weeks holiday. We will spend a few days travelling on the mainland, and then intend catching a boat to Crete for five or six days. Then we will call in at a few of the smaller islands on our way back to Athens.

I saw Mrs Dajani walking up the street the other day and she asked when you were both coming back to Amman. I think she had told Mohammed before that you were probably returning this year, and by now believes her own story. "Not this year," I told her.

Susan has only one day more working at Sahab with the Yarmouk University archaeological team. As she has probably told you she has been getting up at 3.45 each morning, and is picked up around 4.10. They start work at 4.30 because it gets so hot. She is usually home by around noon. Today she is home because it is Friday.

Mohammed came yesterday and after he had cleaned the house I found him doing the clothes washing.

"Lady work every day so better she doesn't have to do washing on her holiday. No matter only take me short time," he said. He is not fasting for Ramadan because he became sick in the first week. You remember that Mohammed used to bring his boss' vacuum cleaner to our house. Well he now works for a new French couple across the road and they have a sparkling new steam iron. So he now brings that because he says it is better for the ironing. He said the couple said he could, but we must be getting a bit of a reputation as people who don't have any mod-cons.

Ill. 12. In the Greek Islands, August 1980

Turkish forces stage a reluctant coup
From DAVID BALDERSTONE

'The Age', Amman, September 12, 1980

Faced with the task of controlling political terrorism, which has claimed around 2000 lives so far this year, and irritated by haggling politicians, Turkey's military leaders reluctantly have taken over Government.

It was not an unexpected development. In fact, over the past few months, the Turkish leadership often has appeared hell bent on tempting the army to take over.

There are precedents for military rule and the Chief of the General Staff, General Kenan Evren, had issued two warnings to politicians in the past year that unless they stopped their haggling and got on with the job of governing, the army might take over.

Fraught with economic problems, Turkey is the weak link in the North Atlantic Treaty Organisation. On the other hand, Turkey – especially in the wake of the Shah's fall in Iran and the Soviet move into Afghanistan – is vitally important to the Western alliance.

It has the longest border with the Soviet Union of any of the 15 NATO countries, and controls the Bosphorus and the Dardanelles Straits which could, if closed, immobilise up to 250 Soviet ships in the Black Sea, according to Western intelligence sources.

In normal circumstances, it would be expected that a military takeover in Turkey would cause considerable embarrassment to the NATO allies.

But political terrorism has brought Turkey to the brink of civil war. Therefore, a military government could be considered by NATO members preferable to anarchy on the alliance's eastern flank.

Turkey is one of the few countries in the world where hints by military leaders who have just staged a coup that they intend returning the country to civilian and democratic government can be taken seriously.

After coups in 1960 and 1971, the military returned the country to democratic rule. And this time, there have been hints already that the military does not intend to rule permanently.

More than 20 people a day have been killed recently by terrorists from the splintered underground communist groups, and the neo-fascists. They are mainly carefully chosen targets with clear political affiliations.

It is believed that both the Left and the Right get help – and perhaps directions – from outside the country. Recently there have been accusations that the Left gets help from the Soviet Union.

But while terrorism may be aided from outside, here seems little doubt that domestic problems are polarising the 46 million inhabitants and driving young Turks into extremist groups. With 100 per cent inflation, 20 per cent unemployment and massive underemployment, Turks have become tired of the established order of Turkish democracy.

Partly due to deficiencies in the Constitution, the two main parties – Mr Suleiman Demirel's conservative Justice Party and Mr Bulent Ecevit's Republican People's Party – find it difficult to gain an outright majority in Parliament.

Therefore the past eight years have seen both men stumbling along leading minority governments or uncomfortable coalitions. Last month there was a chance of an early election which most observers thought would result in a clear majority for Mr Demirel.

It was a rare opportunity for Turkey to get a strong majority Government. But Mr Ecevit's men stymied the move.

Cues for conflict
From DAVID BALDERSTONE in Amman

'The Age', September 24, 1980

Iraq has embarked on a war with Iran which has thrown Iran's leaders face to face with reality, made nonsense of Islamic unity, threatened the survival of both the Bagdad and Teheran regimes, and dramatically increased the vulnerability of the West's vital oil supplies.

With Iraqi attacks deep into Iran, a long simmering border dispute which erupted into heavy border fighting a fortnight ago has brought prophecy about world war being fought over the Persian Gulf oil fields to the brink of reality.

Senior Western diplomats closely familiar with Iraq believe the Bagdad regime of President Saddam Hussein has the clear-cut aim of seizing a major slice of Iran's oil rich south-western province, Khuzestan.

Not only would this give Iraq, which is already the second largest Middle East oil supplier, access to at least some of Iran's potentially large oil exports, but something Iraq would like even more – Persian Gulf ports.

Iraq has only one rather inadequate port on the Persian Gulf. Access to this port, Basra, is through the Shatt al-Arab. Since 1975 Iran and Iraq have accepted the middle of this waterway as the border between the two countries. Although Iraq has traditionally claimed the whole of the waterway, Bagdad accepted the median line of the waterway in exchange for the Shah withdrawing his support for rebellious Iraqi Kurds in the north-east.

Although Iraq's President Hussein, who was then vice-president, negotiated the deal, he was never entirely happy with it. But Iran was then more powerful militarily.

Now the boot is on the other foot. Since the revolution, Iran's previously elite officer corps has been demoralised by purges of its most able battle commanders, and further weakened by a running battle with Iran's own Kurds in the north-west.

Iran is paying the price for its holier-than-thou hostility towards the United States. Its American-equipped armed forces are desperately short of spare parts, and – in any case – no longer have the help of American advisers and technicians who were always needed to keep the equipment in top working condition.

In this sense, the Iraqi-Iranian war has brought Iran's revolutionary leaders face to face with reality. After the revolution which ousted the Shah, the United States continued to supply spare parts and provide officer training. But this stopped with the seizure of the American hostages in November last year.

Although there have been minor clashes along the Iraqi-Iranian border for more than a year, the current fighting seems to have started on 4 September. With this fighting, Iraq renewed its claim to the whole of Shatt al-Arab waterway and some other small areas of disputed border territory.

But the scale of the fighting now indicates that the Iraqis are after much more than disputed border territory. By carrying out air raids on up to 10 Iranian air fields, Iraq stymied any chance of a negotiated settlement on the border dispute. Pride and face - very important currency in the Islamic world – are at stake now.

Ever since the border skirmishes started more than a year ago, some well-placed diplomats in the Arab world would have said Iraq had ambitions over Khuzestan, a province primarily inhabited by Arabic speaking Iranians. So, if there has been this lingering Iraqi ambition, why should President Hussein decide to move now?

Two factors seem to provide a clue. First the Iraqi military leadership has been for some time, in the words of a Western diplomat, "itching to go". It is believed the Iraqi military leadership feels it could win against its previously superior Iranian rival, and lift its own standing domestically and throughout the Arab world.

Secondly, it seems more than a coincidence that the fighting erupted around the time that Iran's new Prime Minister, Mr Rajai, came to a compromise agreement with Iran's President Bani-Sadr over the formation of a Cabinet. Most members of the Cabinet were Islamic fundamentalists.

The Bagdad regime would see a considerable advantage in increasing instability in Iran and reducing the effectiveness of its fundamentalist Islamic Government. This is because Iraq itself has a potential internal problem. Although the Bagdad regime is predominantly Sunni Moslem, more than 50 per cent of the population belong to the Shi'ite Moslem sect – the Iranian branch of Islam.

There are risks for Mr Hussein. Unlike all previous Iraqi leaders since the 1958 revolution which ousted the Hashemite monarchy, he is not a military man. Some diplomats do not discount the risk of an overconfident Iraqi general intoxicated with a victory in Iran turning his tanks around and heading towards Bagdad. There is also the risk that a war with Shi'ite Iran could provoke major discontent and strife within Iraq's Shi'ite population.

Assuming Iraq continues to hold the upper hand, Iran's revolutionary leaders face a much more immediate threat to their survival. In view of the fact that Iranians generally despise Arabs, any defeat by Iraq which involved the loss of territory might start widespread groundswell against the Islamic revolution. "If anyone wants to stage a military coup in Iran, a defeat could provide the opportunity of little mass opposition," a diplomat commented.

In the short term, the Iraqi-Iranian war should have a minimal effect on oil supplies because of the current glut on the market, but any long conflict would cause an increasing shortage as the northern winter approaches.

Western oil supplies could become critical very quickly if Iran pushes its claim to three islands near the entrance to the Persian Gulf. The islands, Abu Musa and Greater and Lesser Tumb, were seized by Iran after Britain withdrew from the area. Military action near the Persian Gulf entrance would discourage tankers entering the vital straits though which 40 per cent of Western oil supplies pass.

Big guns amid Bagdad's trees.
From DAVID BALDERSTONE, Middle East correspondent for 'The Age'

Bagdad, September 26, 1980

Dusk brings to Bagdad an uneasy silence. Darkness brings silhouettes of helmeted soldiers, anti-aircraft guns, military vehicles and fire engines lurking among the palm trees.

There are no street lights in the city, which has been bombed and gunned by Iranian aircraft for the past three days. Most houses are in darkness. Along the main roads there is a steady stream of headlights painted blue to make them less visible from the air.

Bagdad radio is broadcasting patriotic music and the television is screening latest film from the front. Iraqis are buoyed up by the firm belief that their forces are well on top of the battle with neighboring Iran. Five days have passed since Iraqi planes attacked military airfields deep inside Iran and lifted border fighting to all-out war.

Heavy fighting was reported today from Khorammshahr, one of Iran's two vitally important cities on the Shatt al-Arab waterway. Iraq yesterday claimed to have taken control of Khorammshahr but since then Iraqi military officials have said that the claim was premature.

In one of the latest military communiqués issued in Bagdad, Iraqi forces claim to have captured a complete Iranian army camp and taken 19 tanks and at least 100 Iranian prisoners. Iraq's military command said late yesterday that its ground forces were up to 75 kilometres inside Iran's oil-rich south-western province, Khuzestan. It seems clear that Iraqi forces are concentrating most of their attacks in this area, where the disputed Shatt al-Arab waterway provides the border.

About 170 kilometres north-east of Bagdad, Iraqi forces claim to have raised Iraq's green-starred red, white and black flag over the border towns of Qasr El-Shirin, Naft Shah and further south in

Mehran. Posters of Iraq's strong man, Saddam Hussein, have been pasted to buildings in these villages.

In what are portrayed here as mere pinpricks in Iraq's ever-rising morale, Iran continued air attacks against Iraqi cities, including Bagdad yesterday. Other targets included the two main cities of Iraq's oil-producing area, Kirkuk and Mosul, in the north.

And as dawn revealed once again today Bagdad's minarets and palm trees, there was no mistaking that the Iraqis were again ready for Iranian air raids. On many central Bagdad buildings, Soviet-made anti-aircraft guns can be clearly seen ready for action.

Iraq's military command has claimed further astounding success in shooting down Iranian planes. Yesterday Iraqis claimed to have shot down a total of 36 Iranian planes and they have followed up this claim today by saying a further nine Iranian aircraft have been shot down during morning battles.

The location of these battles is not known.

Iraqi success in shooting down Iranian aircraft seems to be mainly due to their Soviet-supplied SAM missiles. Informed Arab observers believe the Iraqis began a big thrust into Khuzestan yesterday. They confidently predict that Iraq will announce big gains in the area later today or tomorrow.

Iraq's deputy commander-in-chief, General Adnan Khatralla, said that Iraq's losses could not be compared with the far greater losses of military equipment and men inflicted on Iran since the all-out war started five days ago.

He said that unless Iran changed its mind and recognised Iraq's territorial claims, Iraq would continue the war.

He said that Iraq would not hesitate to ask for military support from other Arab countries if it was needed.

Although border clashes have been reported for more than a year since the Shah fell in Iran, the recent fighting broke out on 4 September. But it was not until Iraqi planes bombed deep into Iran on Monday and Iraq abrogated a treaty with Iran that full-scale war developed.

Under the treaty, signed in Algeria in 1975, Iraq agreed to accept the middle of the Shatt al-Arab as the border in return for the Shah's withdrawal of support for the Iraqi Kurds in the north.

The English language 'Bagdad Observer' today carried interviews with several of the hundreds of Iranian prisoners of war that Iraq claims to have captured since the fighting began.

The 'Bagdad Observer' said the prisoners were unanimous in describing the state of affairs in Iran as "terrible and deteriorating". One of the prisoners is quoted as saying that the only people who benefit now in Iran are Ayatollah Khomeiny's revolutionary guards.

The Iraqi authorities seem to have all but stopped foreign journalists arriving in Bagdad. I arrived late last night after an 800-kilometre bus trip from Amman. The usual 12-hour trip lasted 20 hours because the bus suffered a blow-out in the desert and then ran out of petrol.

Entering Iraq, there is little sign that the country is on a war footing. The desert highway is still carrying many trucks bound either for Bagdad or Amman.

It was not until the bus arrived at Ramadi, on the Euphrates River 120 kilometres from Bagdad that it became apparent the country was at war. Bridges across the river were heavily guarded and soldiers checked cars entering and leaving the town.

After the next town, Habbaniyah, missiles and anti-aircraft guns could be seen at the ready in the nearby sand hills. Further on, fishermen were trying their luck in marshes and children were minding flocks of fat-tailed sheep. They were grazing their sheep in lush pastures dotted with date palm trees. It was more like Mesopotamia than modern Iraq.

During the last 20 kilometres into Bagdad there were road blocks on every big intersection. At one point, police were stopping all vehicles and dousing headlights and taillights with blue paint, in accordance with blackout regulations.

The blackout was being observed most zealously in the military headquarters area of the city. There were no lights apparent from any of the buildings and soldiers were dotted 10 metres apart around the buildings. Fire trucks draped with palm leaves lurked in the shadows.

As dawn broke, air raid sirens wailed briefly throughout the city but today the Iranians did not launch one of the now common dawn raids on the capital.

A man who sees no borders
-DAVID BALDERSTONE

'The Age', Bagdad, September 27, 1980

Iraq's strong man, Saddam Hussein, goes to unusual lengths to keep in touch with his people.

In his days as Vice-President, ordinary Iraqis could telephone him with grievances. A special number was published in the newspapers. It was a direct line to Saddam Hussein.

Since becoming President he has been seen driving himself around Bagdad with minimal security. He calls unannounced into government offices and factories to talk to workers, hear grievances and check on efficiency.

That is one side of Saddam Hussein. The other side is a man who is uncompromisingly severe with political opponents.

Shortly after he became President in July last year, an alleged plot against the regime was uncovered and 21 senior members of the ruling Baath Party were executed.

Among those to die was a close personal friend of Saddam Hussein, the former Planning Minister Adnan Hussein.

Saddam Hussein was born in 1937 in Tikrit, which is beside the Tigris north of Bagdad. Although Tikrit is so small it can be missed by motorists driving from Bagdad north to Mosul, many of Iraq's power brokers come from this town.

A lawyer by training, he was educated in Bagdad and Cairo. He took part in an unsuccessful coup in 1958 and was forced to take refuge in Egypt. He returned to Iraq in 1963 and became active in the Baath Party.

Hussein played a leading role in the 1968 coup, which is called a revolution in Iraq, and was appointed vice-chairman of the revolutionary command council. A year later he became deputy to the President.

Although he is respected as extremely able and energetic, Hussein got a little help along the way. The man who became President in 1968, former president Ahmad Bakr, was a distant relative and also from Tikrit.

Although he became President only last year, when President Bakr stood down, he had long been considered Iraq's effective ruler.

A Baathist, he is a firm believer in pan-Arabism, the concept that the Arab world is one nation. It is widely thought that Mr Hussein wants Iraq to assume the leadership of the Arabs, a position effectively vacated by Egypt when President Sadat visited Jerusalem.

Iraq has considerable claim to this position. Not only is Iraq the second largest oil producer, but it has a resource most other Arab States crave – water.

Bagdad is hosting the next non-aligned summit in 1962. This is seen as a move by Mr Hussein to improve Iraq's prestige in the world.

Although oil has enabled Iraq to push ahead with development, it was not until the fall of the Shah that even Mr Hussein was able to envisage his country as the dominant power in the Persian Gulf.

Although several factors have driven Iraq to embark on a war with Iran, Mr Hussein's pan-Arab philosophy cannot be discounted as unimportant.

The main drive of the Iraqis has been into Iran's oil rich province, Khuzestan, which the Arabs call Arabistan. It is populated primarily by Arabs, who have been fighting for autonomy.

"Hussein is a pan-Arabist who sees no borders," a Western diplomat commented this week. "I am in no doubt that he wants to take control of Arabistan."

Rubble pile 22km inside Iran
From DAVID BALDERSTONE

'The Age', Bagdad, September 30, 1980

Just more than 22 kilometres inside Iran on the main Bagdad-Teheran highway, a pair of wrought iron gates lead to a short avenue of plane trees.

It was an imposing entrance, but all it leads to is a pile of concrete rubble now.

A rather impressive brigadier in the Iraqi tank corps pointed to the rubble, touched his moustache and said: "This was the Qasr El Shirin radio and television station. We detonated it because it used to broadcast Ayatollah Khomeiny propaganda."

I was among a group of journalists taken by the Iraqi army yesterday around captured Iranian territory at the northern end of Iraq's border thrust into Iran.

Dozens of pictures of Iraq's President Saddam Hussein had been raised over the entrances to buildings in the area and many poster pictures of Ayatollah Khomeiny had been daubed with a cross of white paint.

Some magnetic tape lay on the ground around the Qasr El Shirin TV station and one wondered whether it held the voice of some Iranian mullah calling for the overthrow of the Iraqi regime. A week ago, adjacent areas in Iraq would have received good reception from the station.

After the Shah fell in Iran early last year, Iraq made some initial overtures of friendship to the new Iranian regime. Iran replied with broadcasts calling up Shi'ite Moslems in Iraq, who make up around 55 per cent of the population, to rise up and overthrow the predominantly Sunni Moslem regime of President Hussein.

Although Iraq has said it went to war to regain disputed Iranian-held border territory, some Western diplomats in Bagdad believe the Iraqis had the secondary objective of further destabilising Iran and toppling the Khomeiny regime.

After leaving the bustle of Bagdad, the 150-kilometre road to the last major Iraqi town of Khanaquin leads through semi-desert dotted with mud brick villages.

A military convoy was coming from the front to Bagdad. Several American-made M-60 tanks captured from the Iranians were being trucked to Bagdad for display.

Once within 20 kilometres from the border the signs of war were clear to see. Half submerged in the trenches Iraqi tanks and artillery positions dotted the parched landscape. But this did not discourage an old Bedouin astride his donkey leading his sheep through the toys of war.

From Khanaquin it is about five kilometres to the Iraqi frontier village of Munthriya. The Iraqi border control post, which is now abandoned except for a few Iraqi soldiers, is just through this village.

A sign over one door read: "Passport Directorate". But there was no need for a passport check before crossing into these parts of Iraqi-controlled Iran.

The small Iranian border village of Khusrawil had been taken within a day. The Iranian passport control point had been heavily damaged by small arms fire. The records border officials in the Middle East tediously keep have been strewn around the building. The village itself seems to have received little damage. However a row of shops, which seem to be empty of all merchandise, have had their windows broken. Once through this village it is 10 kilometres by road to the first major Iranian town, Qasr El Shirin.

A poster of President Hussein has been posted to a road sign reading: "Teheran 547 kilometres". There is another road sign covered with a portrait of Ayatollah Khomeiny, which has been daubed with a white cross.

After 12 days, war leads to nowhere
From DAVID BALDERSTONE

'The Age', Basra (Iraq), October 3, 1980

Heading south from Basra, traffic gets scarce rapidly along the road on the Iraqi side of the disputed Shatt al-Arab waterway.

Iraqi 155mm artillery was sporadically pounding across the road into Iran when I and three other journalists took to the road yesterday.

To the left or Iranian side of the road which leads the hundred kilometres from Basra to the mouth of the Shatt al-Arab, Iraqi signal and division headquarters were dug in beside palm trees. To the right of the road heavy artillery and anti-aircraft guns were dug into the desert.

And deadly Soviet-built white surface-to-air missiles lay on their tracked khaki beds waiting for directions from their radar guidance system about a kilometre behind.

Across the Shatt al-Arab, smoke was still rising from the big Abadan refinery which was set alight during an Iraqi attack last week.

A tube of heavy smoke, mirroring the pall of smoke rising from the Abadan refinery, was rising from an Iraqi oil installation near Basra. At the most they were 45 kilometres apart and seemed symbolic of this Iraqi-Iranian war in which both sides have already become losers.

After 12 days of full scale war Iraqi ground forces have captured a lot of desert, but late in the week were having difficulty in capturing any of the larger cities of Iran's oil-rich province, Khuzestan.

For their part, the Iranians were resisting strongly in some strategic areas along the 600-kilometre front of the battle running inside Iran along the border. Also they were continuing to launch air strikes on targets inside Iraq.

On Wednesday the Iraqis offered a unilateral five day ceasefire, with certain conditions, and the Iranians immediately rejected the idea.

With Iraqi forces occupying large chunks of Iran's border areas, the Iraqis have to be considered to be on top still in the ground war. But equally it seemed rather obvious from here that Iraq's President Saddam Hussein had made a miscalculation when he escalated the border fighting to full scale war by bombing Iranian airfields on 22 September.

Iraqi clergy back Hussein

DAVID BALDERSTONE talks exclusively to two of Iraq's spiritual leaders

'The Age', Bagdad, October 8, 1980

One of Iraq's four Grand Ayatollahs – the men who apparently have given Saddam Hussein's war with Iran their blessing – is sitting cross-legged on the floor, roof fans stirring the heavily perfumed air.

He predicts that if the war continues, the world's Shi'ite Moslems will split. "Then there will be Persian Shi'ism and Arab Shi'ism," he says. "There will be a split along national boundaries."

I was visiting the Grand Ayatollah Sheik Ali Kashif al-Ghutta in his book-lined study in Najaf, world capital of the Shi'ite branch of Islam.

He and Iraq's three other Grand Ayatollahs are playing a crucial role in President Hussein's war strategy. They are the spiritual leaders of 60 per cent of the Iraqi population in a war against a predominantly Shi'ite enemy.

Their support is crucial because Iraq's Shi'ites, although the majority, must bow to the rival Sunni branch of Islam, which provides Iraq's political leadership.

They have ignored calls from Iran's mullahs since the late Shah's overthrow for Iraq's Shi'ites to rise up and overthrow President Hussein.

Iran's revolutionary leader, Ayatollah Khomeiny, lived in Najaf from 1964 until early 1978. He sought refuge there after being jailed in Iran in 1963 for his opposition to the Shah.

Najaf is a city of 350,000 built around the lavish mosaic and gold encrusted Mosque of Imam Ali, cousin of the Prophet Mohammed.

"When Ayatollah Khomeiny first established the Islamic Revolution in Iran, we welcomed it. Even the Iraqi Government welcomed the republic at first," Sheik Ali Kashif al-Ghutta said. But later on he became dissatisfied with the policies Khomeiny followed.

"Khomeiny used to be lonely here in Najaf. He did not like to socialise and preferred to stay in a single room. If you entered his house, you found it was modestly furnished. He was very generous and gave a lot of money to his students and followers."

Sheik Ali Kashif al-Ghutta's crossed legs were sheltering under a low desk on which a small reading lamp illuminated a book on Islamic law. The bearded Sheik fiddled with a bottle of eye drops, touched his white turban, and then talked about advice he had given to Khomeiny at Najaf.

"I told Khomeiny that he should make certain that the Islamic Republic of Iran, when it comes about, has good relations with its neighboring countries.

"Secondly, I personally advised him to make the son of the Shah (Crown Prince Reza) the constitutional monarch of Iran – a Shah without any political power. By doing this, the followers of the Shah would be with the Islamic Republic while Khomeiny would be the real leader."

I travelled the 160 kilometres south from Bagdad to Najaf yesterday. Up a small alley off Al-Rassul Street we knocked on the door of the house of an Islamic judge. The alley was lined with tailors and dry cleaning shops. Men were busy pedalling sewing machines.

The judge was not home. Suddenly, an Iraki security officer appeared and asked our driver what we were doing. He took down our names and asked us to wait in Al-Rassul Street.

After an hour and a half he reappeared with a man dressed in a green-mottled jungle camouflage uniform. In dusty central Najaf, where there are no trees, he provided the only greenery. "I am the deputy director of education in Najaf and a fighter in the people's army," he said in English.

For the next hour as women in black chadors and men dressed mainly in flowing galabias walked up and down Al-Rassul Street, the deputy director of education talked about Najaf, Khomeiny, and the people's loyalty to President Hussein.

To underline the point, he chased a small girl down the street and lifted her into his arms. "The children love Saddam Hussein and sing songs about him." He asked the little girl if she liked Hussein. She was overcome with shyness and no reply came.

Saddam Hussein is a Sunni Moslem and leads a predominantly Sunni Moslem Government. If you take away the Kurds of the north-east and the Christians, you are left with only about 30 per cent of the population of 12 million which could be considered mainstream Iraqi Sunni Moslems.

It is estimated that 60 per cent of Iraq's soldiers are Shi'ite Moslems. There has been speculation that if the war with Iran is drawn out over several months, and Iraq suffers high casualties, Iraq's Shi'ites may become disenchanted with the leadership of Saddam Hussein.

But there was no sign of the seeds of such disenchantment in Najaf yesterday. There were portraits of Hussein in most shop windows.

The deputy director of education confirmed that Khomeiny's eldest son, Mostafa and the father of Iran's President, Bani-Sadr were buried side by side in Najaf.

After midday prayers, the deputy director of education and another man led the way to the house of Sheik Ali Kashif al-Ghutta.

Wooden balconies were suspended above the narrow alleys which led to a heavy wooden gate about half a kilometre from the mosque. Inside there was a large courtyard from which a staircase led to the Sheik's library.

As we sat cross-legged around the room, Bedouin coffee, lemon juice and sweet tea were served. "I blame Khomeiny for this war," the Sheik said. "I do not think the Shi'ites of Iraq will go over to Khomeiny.

"There are not only Shi'ites in the army but Sunnis and Christians also. The Shi'ites are fighting for Iraq.

"President Hussein is very friendly to the Shi'ite ayatollahs, and the Shi'ites of Iraq follow their ayatollahs. When I fell ill, the President sent me a group of specialists to my house and they inspected me.

"And when I see him he asks me to explain Islamic philosophy to the world. He is a real Moslem character."

After an hour we got up to leave. The Sheik presented us each with a small bottle of perfume.

The Sheik's brother led the way across the courtyard to the gate. He pointed to some cushions on the ground, and said: "To my way of thinking, Khomeiny is a strange man. He used to sit on those cushions sometimes. He never said hello and never said goodbye and never smiled. Instead he would just get up and go. And although he speaks Arabic, he always wanted to speak Persian."

Five minutes' walk away was the house of Ayatollah Seyyad Kafae. He was a big happy man with a black turban.

It was wrong, he said, to say that there were problems because President Hussein was a Sunni Moslem governing a big Shi'ite population. "This is unreal and such speculation is not true. We here in Iraq are one nation and there are no divisions among the Iraqi people.

"When Khomeiny first came here I thought he would be a real Moslem leader and better than the Shah. But now I disagree with him."

Ayatollah Kafae said he did not agree with the Sheik that the war could cause a split in Shi'ite Islam. "I don't agree because when you look into the eyes of Iranians you see they love other Shi'ites and disagree with Khomeiny.

"It is a matter of how long Khomeiny lasts. And I don't think it will be long."

Ill. 13. Najaf, Iraq, October 1980

King steps up word war with Iranians
From DAVID BALDERSTONE

'The Age', Amman, October 14, 1980

King Hussein of Jordan last night accused Iran of having encouraged internal problems in Iraq and the Arab Gulf States. He accused Iran's leaders of "arrogance and high-handedness" and of having ambitions in Arab countries.

King Hussein made these comments while briefing members of the National Consultative Council on the reasons behind Jordan's decision to support Iraq in the war with Iran. He indicated that Jordan has supported Iraq so that Iraq would support Jordan in any future war with Israel.

"We in Jordan have acted on the basis of pan-Arab action. If we want our brothers to stand on our side, we must stand on their side," he said. "The Arabs should stand at the side of Iraq because Iraq has always stood at their side and never hesitated to support the Arab cause against Israel."

King Hussein last week pledged full support for Iraq. He said Jordan would not hesitate to provide "physical support" for Iraq if it were needed.

Since the fall of the Shah of Iran early last year, Iran's religious leaders have called upon Iraq's Shi'ite Moslems, who make up about 55 percent of the population, to rise up and overthrow the regime of President Hussein of Iraq, which has a predominantly Sunni Moslem leadership.

Also, some Iranian clergymen have said the Gulf island State of Bahrain should become part of Iran. This claim prompted a flare-up of trouble among Bahrain's Shi'ite population last year.

Statements by Iranian leaders also provoked trouble among Saudi Arabia's Shi'ite Moslems in November. The Shi'ite Moslems of Saudi Arabia live in the oil-rich eastern areas of the country.

Peace in the streets of a city at war
DAVID BALDERSTONE, 'The Age' Middle East correspondent, reports from Teheran, a capital at war

Teheran, October 23, 1980

War has not stopped Teheran living. Mossadegh Avenue, formerly Pahlavi Avenue, is still lined with street stalls selling Western-made jeans and pop music cassette tapes.

Well-decorated shop windows still display a better range of Western-style goods (many made in Iran) than any Arab capital except, perhaps, Beirut. Similarly by Middle East standards, Teheran street stalls are selling exceptionally high quality fresh fruit and vegetables, and stock a wide variety.

Iranians I spoke to yesterday said there was no serious shortage of food in the capital. "Eggs are sometimes short, but they have been for some time," a businessman said. This is not to say life is normal in Teheran a month after the Iraqi-Iranian war broke out. Petrol is rationed severely and heating fuels are scarce. And, if the shortage of heating fuel continues – as it almost certainly will – Iran's revolutionary leaders will have to face growing discontent as the winter snows fall upon the capital.

But, ironically, war has brought to Teheran a kind of order it didn't have before. Petrol rationing has meant fewer cars, and none of Teheran's notorious traffic jams. These days you can hear yourself think above the tooting horns.

Although the Iraqi invasion of Iran's border areas, including parts of the oil-rich province Khuzestan, has dented Iranian pride, I detected no hostility towards Westerners when I walked about parts of the city yesterday. In fact, if it had not been for an air-raid siren broadcast over the radio at 4.55 pm – the first for two days – it would not have seemed that daytime Teheran was a city at war.

After travelling – through hot sun in Turkey and rain, sleet and snow in Iran – along the only land route linking Teheran to Europe,

I arrived in the blacked-out capital in the early hours of yesterday morning. While waiting for baggage to be unloaded from the Turkish Airlines DC9 at Van, a city in Eastern Turkey, an Iranian asked me if I would like to share a taxi to the Iranian border. He was travelling with his wife, his two small children, his brother (an out-of-work architect), and a bazari – a member of Iran's traditionally important bazaar or merchant class.

Because the nearest border crossing to Van was closed, we had to take a three-hour drive along an unsealed border road north to the main crossing in north-west Iran at the Iranian border town of Bazargan. We had two cars and, at one stage, the car in which I was travelling bogged down in a creek flowing across the unsealed road. By some miracle, it started again after 15 minutes and dragged itself out.

It was dark by the time we arrived at the Bazargan border post. A large portrait of Ataturk – the father of modern Turkey who insisted upon secular government for that almost exclusively Moslem country – faced, across the customs hall, a portrait of Ayatollah Khomeiny, father of the Islamic Republic of Iran.

We were the only people entering Iran at the time. Several bus loads of Iranians – and a few Europeans – were fighting their way out of the country. "Why on earth are you going into Iran?" several of those leaving asked my Iranian companions.

The Iranian family insisted I should travel with them to Teheran. It was the kind of friendship and helpfulness I have found during eight trips to Iran since the revolution. These people just don't deserve the penalty of hostility they face in the West because of the actions of Iranian mobs and leaders.

A senior official at the border post said it would be unsafe to travel beyond Bazargan that night. He was not issuing a warning about the possibility of being caught in an Iraqi attack, but about the risk of being attacked by Iranian Kurds or Azerbaijanis.

Since the revolution, the central authorities have been in regular battle with the autonomy-seeking Kurds and, to a lesser extent, have faced problems with the Azerbaijanis. The official's warning revealed that although the authorities make out that all Iranians are united against Iraq, the problems still exist. The Iranian regime is not popular in this area of north-west Iran.

A man was washing his feet in the only basin in the Cina Hotel, Bazargan, when we checked in. The basin was in the hall outside the room I shared with the bazari and the weathered old hotel manager, who – it later transpired – wears his pyjamas all day underneath his baggy suit. A cat meowed outside the window most of the night but, for two dollars a night, one could not complain.

Seventeen kilometres on we stopped for breakfast. Boys grow into men early in this part of the world. A small boy of about 14, who was dressed in tie and shabby sports coat, was sitting at the head of one long table in the small restaurant. Elderly men would sit down for a while with him. They were not talking down to the lad: he was holding is own.

The 224 km-road to Tabriz, capital of Azerbaijan, mainly follows highland plains. The poplar trees were an autumn gold. Mud brick houses, haystacks, dung and peat stacks – fuel for the coming winter – dotted the plains…..there was already snow on the surrounding mountains. On this road to Tabriz, the mini-bus had the obligatory blow-out.

In Tabriz, there were queues of vehicles several kilometres long outside every petrol station. It was 3 pm by the time the mini-bus left Tabriz on the 10-hour drive to Teheran. For the first 300 kilometres light snow was falling against the windscreen of the unheated mini-bus.

Just before dusk we passed a truck sliced in half by an oncoming vehicle. The dead driver had been crushed backwards into his cargo of apples. A little further on we passed an overturned truck. The driver was the mini-bus driver's cousin. After a brief stop, our driver returned to report that the truck had been carrying lavatory ware and that all the toilets were broken.

By 8 pm the mini-bus was running short of diesel. In line with public transport regulations, the driver pushed to the head of the queue. Revolutionary guards pointed a gun at him and told him to move or they would shoot. He drove on.

At Qazvin, the last big town before Teheran, the mini-bus was stopped by more revolutionary guards. A truck stormed through the check-point going the other way. A guard fired into the air, but the truck driver did not stop.

As we approached Teheran, the mini-bus radio was tuned into Bagdad Radio. Messages from Iranian POWs to their families were being broadcast. Some ended their message with "Long live Saddam Hussein".

The bus groped its way through blackout Teheran. There was a very dim light showing from the entrance of the Intercontinental Hotel, but inside the hotel was functioning virtually normally. "Welcome back. It is good to see you," said the man at reception. Another echoed his greeting, but then asked, sadly: "And what are they saying about us Iranians outside Iran?"

Bazaaris flex muscles
From DAVIDBALDERSTONE in Teheran

'The Age', Teheran, November 12, 1980

It is not so much the pots and pans, bolts of cloth, pyramids of shoes, and Persian carpets that make it so exciting. No, the bazaar in Teheran is only partly about something so cold as merchandise.

Instead, it's the boys bearing trays of tea and Turkish coffee, the Jewish watchmakers squinting through eyeglasses, the men who beg you to change money, and , of course, the merchants or bazaaris themselves who make it what it is.

It is the centre of Teheran life: a place of enormous political influence. The deposed Shah and his father, Shah Reza, founder of the Pahlavi dynasty, tried to weaken its influence – and probably thought they had succeeded.

But when the scores went up at the end of the game and the weeping Shah left Iran "on holiday", few Iranians were in any doubt that the bazaaris' decision to pull down the shutters had played no small part in defeating the monarchy.

This week, the bazaaris were on the verge of deciding to pull down the shutters again. But it is less than two years since the Shah flew out so they haven't forgotten the enormous political consequences of closing the bazaar.

Although the bazaaris were strong supporters of the revolution, the deteriorating post-revolution economic situation in Iran has led to growing discontent in the bazaar.

But it was the detention for three days of the former Foreign Minister, Mr Sadegh Qotbzadeh that prompted the bazaaris to use their political muscle.

In the narrow alleyways covered by vaulted brick roofs, the bazaaris collected 300,000 signatures for a petition protesting against Mr Qotbzadeh's detention, and against moves undermining the position of Iran's President Abolhassan Bani-Sadr.

Mr Qotbzadeh was detained in his north Teheran home last Friday after he had said in a pre-recorded television debate that an atmosphere of anarchy prevailed in Iran's radio and television organisation and in other revolutionary organisations.

Behind Mr Qotbzadeh's criticism and three-day detention is a power struggle over whether the "liberal" politicians or the Islamic fundamentalists control not only television and radio but other Government institutions as well.

As businessmen, the bazaaris are interested in political and economic stability. While there remain some Jewish and Christian businessmen in the bazaar, most bazaaris are devout Moslems struggling to hold on to traditional values of Persian family life.

However, they tend to blame the Islamic fundamentalist bloc dominated by the clergy-backed Islamic Republican Party for many of Iran's economic problems.

In the past, the IRP has tended to claim the bazaar as part of its power base because of the bazaaris' devout Islamic beliefs.

However, a trend seems to be emerging that indicates that the bazaaris believe Iran's economic stability would be best achieved by the secular liberals led by Mr Bani-Sadr. Like Mr Bani-Sadr, who is a French-trained economist, most of the "liberals" are highly educated either in Iran or abroad.

"We strongly support the revolution. We don't want the Shah's son back or another monarchy," a bazaar merchant told me. "However we are beginning to think there has been a mistake made in this revolution. We want leaders who know how to run the country."

The political leaning of the bazaar towards the secular "liberals' is in part due to the ethnic make-up of the bazaar. A disproportionately high number of bazaar families come from the north-western provinces of East and West Azerbaijan.

Azerbaijanis see themselves as an elite – and have some claim to this boast. It is one of Iran's most prosperous areas, bordering Turkey and the Soviet Union. Prosperity has provided education. Proximity to Turkey and Russia has given Azerbaijanis access to political ideas other than those of either the ousted monarchy or the mullahs.

The people of Azerbaijan played a major part in the 1960 "constitutional revolution" during the Qajar dynasty. The first major anti-Shah riots took place in Tabriz, capital of East Azerbaijan. Iran's first post-revolution Prime Minister, Mr Bazargan and the now-disgraced first head of the oil company after the revolution, Mr Hassan Nazih, are among the prominent Azerbaijanis who fought for the overthrow of the Shah.

The deposed Shah had sought to weaken the political influence of the bazaar. He rebuilt the area, which is south of the modern centre of Teheran, with wider streets than previously, along a gridiron pattern. This made surveillance and security more simple. The Shah's regime built schools and welfare services outside the area to break down the concentration of influence.

Also, economic development and modernisation meant that much of the country's economic power moved to highrise buildings well north of the bazaar.

But the bazaar remains extremely important politically and economically. This week's 300,000-name petition could easily be the start of something more. The bazaaris have felt their political muscle once again.

A tenuous grasp of justice

'Age' man DAVID BALDERSTONE, the only correspondent in Teheran accredited to an English-speaking newspaper, reports on a crucial spy trial. It is one of the first such trials opened to Westerners.

'The Age', Teheran, November 13, 1980

A former political prisoner during the deposed Shah's reign, Mohammed Reza Sa'adati, 36, was explaining to the turbaned revolutionary Islamic judge his feelings about being arrested for spying for the Soviet Union less than three months after the revolution.

"In those days (during the Shah's reign) I didn't mind being charged as a subversive, but I did not expect to face these charges under the Islamic Republic of Iran," he said.

Ironically, Mr Sa'adati, an engineer and senior member of the Leftist Mujahedin Khalq organisation, was addressing a makeshift court in Teheran's notorious Evin prison – a jail where political prisoners were held during the Shah's reign.

Mr Sa'adati said that soon after his arrest on 25 April last year, he had written to Iran's Revolutionary Council that he did not consider himself a prisoner, but rather a guest of brother revolutionaries.

In a country where more than 1200 people have been executed since the revolution, Mr Sa'adati is just one man defending himself against a possible death sentence.

But, with Iran facing enormous economic and political problems, and as disenchantment grows over the rule of the Islamic mullahs, the trial has much wider implications.

The Mujahedin Khalq – one of the two main anti-monarchy terrorist organisations during the Shah's reign – is strong throughout much of the country. By supporters it is described as a "progressive Islamic movement". By opponents it is dubbed

"Marxist". The organisation's insignia is a rifle crossing a sickle, which at a quick glance can resemble a hammer and sickle.

The trial itself violates two and possibly three main articles of the new Constitution of the Islamic Republic of Iran. Just one of these is that Mr Sa'adati has been unable to take advantage of the constitutional right of all accused to have defence counsel.

After the trial started last week, people in the gallery shouted: "Death to the hypocrite!" and "Death to the spy!" When I attended the court this week, people in the court sniggered openly at the accused's comments – and one young man was able to make a statement in support of the prosecution from the gallery. Very democratic, one could say.

The prosecutor, Mr Lajvardi, who was in jail under the Shah and linked with an incident in which a bomb was thrown at the Teheran office of the Israeli airline, El Al, addressed the gallery, not the judge.

With a Dutch journalist and an interpreter, I attended the trial on Tuesday afternoon. It is one of the first revolutionary courts to be opened to foreign correspondents since the revolution.

The interpreter sat between me and the Dutch journalist. At one stage a man in a check sports coat, spotty tie and tartan scarf, left the row behind, noisily moved along our row, and forced himself between the interpreter and the Dutch journalist. He then talked and joked with the people he had been sitting beside in the row behind.

It was the fourth day of the trial. The court was a large rectangular room with cream walls roughly covered with brown felt to improve the acoustics. Quotes from a martyred revolutionary adorned the felt.

The revolutionary Islamic judge, Hojatoleslam Mousavi Tabrizi, also a member of Iran's Parliament, sat at a table covered with yellow felt. A red plastic jug of water was on the table. Four other court officials, including the prosecutor, sat in a row with the judge. The proceedings were recorded on a Sony video machine.

Mr Sa'adati sat in a chair to the right of the judge. A bright-eyed man with a moustache, he gave a warm smile to members of his family, including several women in black chadors, as he entered the court.

He is charged with having had "espionage relations" with the first Secretary of the Soviet Embassy in Teheran. The long indictment also accuses Mr Sa'adati of exchanging political, social, and military information with the Soviet Embassy.

The indictment says Mr Sa'adati admitted having secret relations with the Soviet espionage organisation, but he told the court he was under "psychological and physical" pressure during interrogation after his arrest.

Denying the espionage charge, Mr Sa'adati said that his job in the Mujahedin Khalq had been to gather details of the network of the US Central Intelligence Agency and to explain the nature of the Islamic revolution in Iran to the Soviet Union.

Article 168 of Iran's new constitution states that: "Investigation of political crimes and Press offences will be held in a public court with a judge and a jury".

A Teheran religious judge, Ayatollah Mohammed Gilani said in an interview on 19 December, 1979, that Mr Sa'adati faced a political charge. But the trial is being held before a judge sitting alone.

A prominent Iranian lawyer, Mr Abdul Karim Lahiji, said the trial was in breach of the constitution because the judge, as a Member of Parliament, was not allowed to act as a judge.

Mr Lahiji said he had written an open letter of protest about the trial to the 'Islamic Revolution' newspaper after getting no replies to letters to the Prosecutor-General dated 13, 20 and 22 September and 4 November last year.

The head of Iran's judiciary, Ayatollah Mohammed Beheshti, told a press conference yesterday there were problems in all revolutionary situations. "We must put up with limitations we are facing," he said.

Dr Beheshti, who headed the council of experts who drew up the constitution last year, said Iran did not have enough judges available who "knew deeply the revolutionary and Islamic system of ours".

He said it could not be expected "that in all regards and in all cases we'll act in line with criteria that we would like to see achieved". (*Ed: The accused was later executed.*)

Jordan-Syria border tense
From DAVID BALDERSTONE

'The Age', Amman, November 30, 1980

Jordan's armed forces remained on high alert today against possible attack from Syria. But Jordanian military and Government officials appeared to be trying to reduce tension between the two Arab nations.

While Damascus Radio continued to criticise Jordan at the weekend, Jordanian officials said little, apparently to avoid exacerbating the border tension.

But Jordan continued to strengthen and realign its forces in the north of the country in response to a continued Syrian troop build-up on the border.

While a senior Jordanian Government official expressed the view privately today that the border tension would not lead to a concerted Syrian attack, there were fears in Government and diplomatic circles that the troop build-up might spark a border clash difficult to halt.

Tension between Syria and Jordan, which has developed over the past 12 months, stems from Syrian allegations that Jordan has provided refuge to members of the fanatical Moslem Brotherhood organisation which has been waging a terrorist campaign against the Syrian regime.

However Syrian-Jordan relations have slumped dramatically since the Iran-Iraq war broke out in earnest nine weeks ago. Jordan has strongly supported Iraq in the war. Syria has leant towards Iran and is reported to have provided some aid to Ayatollah Khomeiny's Islamic Republic.

King Hussein of Jordan confirmed the Syrian troop build-up last week and pledged that Jordanian forces would defend every centimetre of Jordan's territory against any attack.

A senior Government official confirmed today that army leaders had decided they did not want to make any public comments about the force movements.

There have been reports that Syria has moved two divisions into the border area in the past week. But at least some of these troops may be part of a planned build-up of troops in the Golan Heights facing Israel.

Travellers from Damascus have seen several hundred Syrian tank transporters along the road leading to the main border crossing at Dera'a. Syria is believed to have moved about 400 tanks and several thousand troops to the border.

Jordanian forces, which are concentrated in the north of the country anyway, have been moved from a position facing Israel to one facing Syria since the Syrians built up their troops in the area. Other Jordanian troops have been moved to the north.

Since the start of the Gulf war, Jordanian Army reserves have been required to register.

Because of divisions in the Arab world stemming from the Gulf war, Syria led a boycott of the summit meeting of Arab leaders in Amman last week. Syria was joined in the boycott by Libya, Algeria, South Yemen, Lebanon and the Palestine Liberation Organisation.

Amman December 6, 1980 (*To Uncle Harold*)

Since the Gulf war broke out in earnest on September 22, life has been fairly hectic with two weeks in Iraq and then more than five weeks in Iran. Also, since I arrived back in Amman two weeks ago there has been the real risk of a war between Syria and Jordan. Even at a time of war, things in this part of the world are often hilarious. I arrived back in Amman by taxi from Damascus airport – about a three and a half hour trip. At the Syrian-Jordanian border at around midnight I was taken into a special room to be interviewed by a Jordanian Intelligence officer. This seems to be a new measure taken because of the Syrian-Jordanian crisis which stems from Jordan's support of Iraq and Syria's support of Iran in the war.

"What are the Syrians saying about Jordan", the Intelligence man asked me. I explained that I had come straight from Damascus airport and didn't really know. When he finally learnt that I had come from Teheran, he looked very suspicious and asked who was winning the war. At this stage I was not certain whether he was Syrian or Jordanian and therefore asked him.

"So", he replied. "If I say I am Syrian you will say Iran is winning and if I say Jordanian you will say Iraq." Indignantly he added: "I am a Jordanian secret policeman." Later I thought I should have replied: "Not any longer." Instead I complimented him on his English and he asked me where I had learnt such good English.

You might remember that Iraq captured Iran's oil minister while he was inspecting damage to oil installations near the front. I was in Iran at the time and the Iranians said that this kind of hostage-taking was in breach of every international regulation, which seemed a strange comment to come from Iran. I was having breakfast with a Swedish journalist, who said it reminded him of an incident during the Congo war. One side was furious one day and issued a fierce statement saying that the opposition had breached "every known international law by eating our colonel."

Amman December 11, 1980 (*To an Australian journalist colleague*)

Being in Jordan for Christmas reminds me of a story I was told from the days – before the 1967 war – when Jordan ruled over Jerusalem and Bethlehem. In those days, I am told, there was a sign as you entered Jordan from Syria. It read:

THIS IS THE HOLLY LAND
YOU ARE WELCOME TO IT

It is not there anymore - perhaps the Jordanians took it down after the Israelis took it too literally.

Amman December 14, 1980 (*To an Irish journalist colleague*)

Things got worse in Baghdad after you left – it became illegal to light cigarettes in the bar during an air raid. Of course I see their point – those Phantoms home in on the heat. In fact it makes one wonder how the Iranians have not killed more smokers during the war.

Since I returned from Iran, Jordan and Syria have been on the brink of war. My trusted advisor who sells stamps in the local post office – and sits in the local grocery when he gets tired of selling stamps – seems to know the full story about the reasons why the Syrians massed their troops on the border.

"Well, it's obvious", he told me. "The Syrians wanted to pull their troops out of Lebanon and had to find a face-saving way to do it."

It's business of war as usual in the Holy Land
From DAVID BALDERSTONE

'The Age', Amman, December 23, 1980

To achieve peace on earth and goodwill to all men in the Holy Land seems as difficult as ever this Christmas. Hopes are not high in the Middle East – home of the three great religions.

While an estimated 30,000 Christian pilgrims arrived in Bethlehem and Jerusalem, Christian militiamen and Syrian troops continued to be locked in battles early today in the mainly Christian Lebanese city of Zahle, 50 kilometres east of Beirut. A ceasefire was announced later, although an earlier one failed to hold.

In Bethlehem and the old city of Jerusalem, which are both in the West Bank territory occupied by Israel in 1967, Israeli troops were taking strict security precautions in case the cities should become the focus of a violent outburst of the tension in the West Bank. And a tense – almost certainly temporary – calm prevailed in South Lebanon where Israeli, Syrian and Christian militia forces were involved in heavy fighting last weekend.

Christians make up only a small minority of the populations in Israel, Egypt, Jordan and Syria. In Lebanon, the other Holy Land country with sites linked to the life of Jesus Christ – Christians make up between 40 and 50 per cent of the population.

Nevertheless, it is not only in Bethlehem and Jerusalem where the fact that it is Christmas is obvious. In the predominantly Moslem capitals of Amman and Damascus, lighted Christmas trees flicker from shops and homes. And Radio Jordan, whose listeners must be 90 per cent Moslem, has been wishing its audience a happy Christmas for days.

But, judging from events over the past two weeks, luck will have played a big part if Christmas celebrations are not punctuated by the sound of gunfire somewhere in the Holy Land on Christmas Day.

Most Middle East violence stems from the Arab-Israeli dispute. But the past six months has seen bitter clashes in Beirut and Zahle between the two main Lebanese Christian groups – the Falangists and former Lebanese President Camille Chamoun's National Liberal Party. Tension remains high between the two groups.

Although the Coptic Christians in Egypt have faced violent attacks from Moslem fundamentalists this year, there appears to be only limited violence directed against Christians for religious reasons in the rest of the area. Nevertheless, Christians often express fears about the rising tide of Islamic fundamentalism, and react to these fears by being chauvinistic about their religion.

This week's battle between Syrian troops and Falangist militiamen in Zahle is political rather than religious. It stems from Falangist opposition to the continued presence in Lebanon of around 30,000 Syrian troops, who entered the country in 1976 to bring the civil war to an end.

The latest violence in Zahle was sparked on Saturday when five Syrian troops were killed in the city. The Syrians responded by pounding the city with heavy artillery.

The first ceasefire came into effect yesterday. But last night the Falangist radio station reported that the Syrians had resumed their bombardment. It doesn't seem as though it will be a happy Christmas in Zahle.

1981
Holy war? Not exactly
- DAVID BALDERSTONE

'The Age', Amman, January, 31

Behind the decision of this week's Islamic summit conference to wage a holy war against Israel was a message to the new Reagan Administration and the West in general.

It is becoming increasingly urgent to bring closer a settlement in the Middle East.

Now that the leaders of Islamic countries and the Palestine Liberation Organisation have left the rarefied atmosphere of their mini-palaces in the luxurious conference centre on Taif hills, Saudi Arabia, Arab officials have provided an insight into what the pragmatic Islamic leaders mean by holy war or "jihad".

In the context of the Mecca declaration issued at the end of the summit, jihad, it seems, was not necessarily meant to mean hordes of Islamic warriors united under the green flag of Islam. Nor, it seems, does it mean that the Islamic world is about to wield the oil weapon.

Instead, according to Western diplomats and Arab officials in Amman, the call for a jihad served to forcefully remind the new Reagan Administration and the leaders of other Western countries of the potential power of Islamic countries whose patience over Israel's continued occupation of old Jerusalem and other Arab territories was fast running out.

The Mecca declaration announced the Islamic leaders' decision to wage a jihad "with all the means at our disposal" to liberate our occupied territories, liberate Jerusalem, and to achieve the right of Palestinians to an independent State in their homeland.

"Should Israel's leaders be scared of the decision to wage a jihad?" I asked a senior Jordanian official this week. "I don't think they are. Whether they should be is another question and I don't know the answer," he said.

Among Palestinians the decision to wage a jihad is unlikely to be received with too much hope. Jaundiced by 32 years of frustration, Arab rhetoric and promises, Palestinians are more likely to react similarly to the few I talked to this week. One rolled his eyes up into his head, and another said: "Talk, talk, talk."

The problem is that while about 900 million Moslems around the world have the potential for wielding enormous political clout, the Moslems in the Middle East are the first to realise that it is not a good time to talk about Islamic unity.

With the Gulf war continuing, Iran did not send a delegation to Taif because Iraq's President Saddam Hussein was there.

Relations between Jordan and Syria – two frontline States facing Israel – remain extremely cool. It is hard to find a voice in support of Colonel Gaddafi's intervention in Chad. And of course, President Sadat – leader of the biggest Moslem country in the Middle East – is out in the cold because of the Egyptian-Israeli peace treaty.

Nevertheless, the Mecca declaration proudly announced that "all Moslems, differing though they may be, in their language, colour, domicile and other conditions, form but one nation bound together in their common faith, moving together in a single direction."

However, a Western diplomat made the point that moderate Islamic States which participated in the conference have a case worth listening to.

"In the wake of the Soviet invasion of Afghanistan and in the face of further Soviet expansion, these States, which all look towards the West, want the US and the West to realise that their stability depends upon a solution to the Palestinian problems," he said.

"The Palestinian issue, and the occupation of Jerusalem, make up an extremely emotional issue in the eyes of Arabs and Moslems."

Syria 'sent soldiers to kill Jordan PM'
From DAVID BALDERSTONE

'The Age', Amman, February 26, 1981

A Syrian colonel, one of an alleged five-man hit squad arrested in Jordan late last month, said on Jordan television last night the brother of Syria's President Assad had ordered the squad's attempt to assassinate Jordan's Prime Minister.

During a two-hour programme, two other members of the hit squad said they had taken part in the massacre of more than 500 Syrian prisoners at a Syrian jail near the ancient ruins of Palmyra in June last year.

The Jordanian Government, in a statement broadcast during the programme, accused the Syrian regime of assassinating the Lebanese Druze leader, Mr Kamal Jumblatt, in Lebanon in 1977; a former Syrian Premier in Paris; prominent Arab journalist Salim al-Lawzi in Lebanon, and "many others in Lebanon and outside Lebanon".

The televised "confessions", which could have been seen in Jordan, Israel, much of Syria and northern Saudi Arabia, provided a damning indictment of the Syrian regime. They are likely to severely reduce President Assad's stature in the Arab world and among Western politicians.

One of Jordan's main aims in broadcasting the programme seems to have been to point up the heavy involvement of the Syrian President's brother, Colonel Rifaat Assad, in repressive actions.

Over the past three years the Assad regime has been combating a terrorist campaign aimed at toppling the President, who along with his most trusted advisers is a member of the minority Alawite Moslem sect. To combat this campaign, the regime has resorted to increasingly repressive measures.

Colonel Adnan Barakat, an Alawite officer in the Syrian defence companies controlled by Rifaat Assad, said he had received orders to lead a squad to kill the Jordanian Prime Minister Mr Badran, on 19 January. The orders were issued by Rifaat Assad.

Colonel Barakat said the plan had been to attack with hand grenades and Kalashnikov sub-machine guns Mr Badran's three-car convoy. The convoy was to be attacked at traffic lights near the Holiday Inn Hotel in Amman.

As it happened, Colonel Barakat was arrested near the Jordan-Syria border, and other members of the group were arrested near Amman.

Lebanon's barbaric 'saviour'
From DAVID BALDERSTONE in Metulla, Israel

'The Age', March 25, 1981

Major Sa'ad Haddad sees himself as saving Lebanon. The UN Security Council last week dubbed his actions as "barbaric". Israel supports him, and PLO chief Yasser Arafat hates him.

There is no one in the Middle East without a strong opinion about this renegade Lebanese Christian officer who controls Lebanon's southern areas bordering northern Israel.

The South Lebanon border area is commonly called the Christian enclave. But, in fact, 60 per cent of the people who live in the area, and support – and fight for – Major Haddad are Moslem.

And more curious than that is the fact that most of these Moslems belong to the same branch of Islam as Ayatollah Khomeiny. They are Shi'ite Moslems, led by a Christian and supported by Jews, fighting Palestinian guerillas and other mainly Moslem Arabs.

Late last week the Security Council condemned Major Haddad and described the actions of his militiamen as "barbaric". This latest condemnation of Major Haddad came after three Nigerian United Nations soldiers in South Lebanon had died after being caught by artillery fired by Haddad's men.

Major Haddad publicly regretted the incident and sent condolences to the UN troops. But how did it happen?

The background and the explanation are as knotted as the Middle East itself. Major Haddad was sent to South Lebanon by the Lebanese Government to control the area during the civil war.

When the scores went up at the end of the civil war, which was brought to an end by the intervention of a mainly Syrian Arab force, Major Haddad maintained control of the south.

However, the Palestinian guerilla groups held much of the area between Major Haddad and Beirut. And, predictably, they found Major Haddad a barrier to guerilla raids into Israel.

Because their access into Israel had been reduced by Major Haddad, the Palestinian guerillas made it nearly impossible for people living in the "Christian enclave" to move to and trade with Lebanon proper. So, instead, Major Haddad's area traded with, and got aid and employment from Israel.

Then, after a major Palestinian attack into Israel north of Tel Aviv, Israel invaded South Lebanon in March 1978 with the aim of destroying the Palestinian presence south of the Litani River, which flows an average of 25 kilometres north of Israel's border, but is only five kilometres from the border at one point.

After the Israeli invasion, the United Nations Interim Force in Lebanon (UNIFIL) was sent into South Lebanon.

The three Nigerians died last week when Major Haddad's forces fired on a position within the UNIFIL area being taken over by the Lebanese army, which is very weak and has been unable to take over sensitive positions in the rest of Lebanon.

Put simply, Israel and Major Haddad oppose the Lebanese army's move south because it changes the status quo, and could lead to greater Palestinian infiltration into the south.

The death of the three Nigerians brought to 59 the number of UNIFIL troops killed in South Lebanon in just under three years.

"No one sends messages of condolences when the PLO kills UN men. When I try to use peaceful means and send condolences, the Security Council condemns Haddad," Major Haddad said to me yesterday.

Looking genuinely bewildered, Major Haddad said: "I wonder why the world is putting pressure on me. The Soviet Union is trying to expand in the Middle East and the world worries about Sa'ad Haddad who is fighting to protect his country.

"We have struggled for five years. We are not going to give up now to Yasser Arafat or Hafez al-Assad (Syria's President)."

In the past year, Major Haddad's area has been able to trade with the rest of Lebanon. This is mainly due to the work of the UN troops.

Young militiamen dressed in Israeli-supplied uniforms are seen throughout the Haddad area. In Marjayoun – the "capital" of Major Haddad's area – Israeli and Lebanese currency is accepted.

Fresh fruit and vegetables grown in the area are plentiful and by day, life goes on as usual.

But over the past three nights, Palestinian guerillas have been firing rockets and artillery into the villages of the lush mountain fiefdom of Sa'ad Haddad. The Major has returned the fire using his heavy artillery and tanks mainly supplied by Israel, according to Western sources.

Although the area can now trade with the rest of Lebanon, the border enclave still receives its fuel from Israel. "This is the only place in the world where Jews supply petrol to Arabs," my Israeli army guide quipped.

An unlikely alliance
- DAVID BALDERSTONE

'The Age', Jerusalem, March 28, 1981

Hot on the heels of his reported meetings with King Hassan of Morocco and a brother of Jordan's King Hussein in London, Israel's Labor Opposition Leader, Shimon Peres, has suggested the formation of an alliance of Israel, Egypt, Jordan, and Saudi Arabia, to combat radicalisation in the Middle East.

It was a strange suggestion for Mr Peres to make in the run-up to Israel's elections on 30 June.

In a television interview this week, Mr Peres suggested that unofficial contacts with Arab leaders indicated that such an alliance was possible. In other words, Mr Perez said that Saudi Arabia, which led the recent call for a holy war to liberate Jerusalem from Israeli control, and Jordan, which has staunchly refused to join the Egyptian-Israeli-American Middle-East peace process, could be prepared to enter into an alliance with Israel and Egypt.

In the context of the election, it was a strange suggestion for Mr Peres to make for two reasons.

First, it is hard to see that many Israeli electors would believe the concept to be within the bounds of possibility.

And second, the suggestion can only focus attention on the issue on which the Prime Minister, Mr Begin can justifiably claim success: the Egyptian-Israeli peace treaty

To highlight the issue of improving Israel's position in the "hostile" Arab world – an issue on which Mr Begin can justly claim to have achieved more than any other Israeli Prime Minister – is even stranger because it diverts attention from the economic issue on which Mr Begin is pushing uphill to claim any success.

Recent opinion polls show that most Israelis believe inflation, which is running now at around 130 per cent annually, is the main issue.

"While we wish such an alliance could be achieved, Peres is talking about something that is not attainable whereas we can show what has been attained," the Prime Minister's spokesman, Dan Pattir, commented.

While it is difficult to see that Mr Peres' suggestion of such an alliance could be beneficial to him electorally, the explanation for the suggestion and the reported meetings with King Hassan and a Jordanian prince could be that Mr Peres wants to show that he is a statesman on a world scale. Traditionally, Israel's Prime Ministers have been strong on international statesmanship and have relegated social issues and the economy to relatively junior Ministers. This is one of the reasons the economy is in a mess.

To believe that an alliance between Israel, Egypt, Jordan and Saudi Arabia is possible, requires the belief that Arab leaders say one thing in public and another in private to be stretched to the limit.

In fact the impression gained from most people who talk privately with Saudi and Jordanian leaders is that both countries believe that radicalisation is more likely while the Palestinian issue remains unresolved. Therefore, it would appear, the last thing either country would seriously consider, is an alliance with the country which continues to occupy Arab lands won in the 1967 war.

Yemen troops crossed border: Oman
From DAVID BALDERSTONE

'The Age', Amman, March 30, 1981

There are increasing indications that the Soviet Union, through its ally South Yemen, is attempting to build up pressure against staunchly pro-Western Oman, which shares with Iran control of the Persian Gulf entrance. In a note submitted to the Arab League last week, Oman has alleged that on at least six occasions over the past five months, South Yemen troops "massed" on the border early this month, and that on at least one occasion, Yemeni armored vehicles opened fire on an Omani aircraft.

"These aggressive acts have been made with the massive support of Soviet, Cuban, and East German forces present in South Yemen," an Omani official said. The well-documented allegations appear to indicate that the Marxist South Yemen regime – with the approval of the Soviet Union – is attempting to rekindle civil war in the Oman province of Dhofar, neighboring South Yemen.

Sultan Qaboos announced victory over the Dhofar rebels in 1975 after British, Iranian and Jordanian troops had come to Oman's help. However, incidents continue to occur in the area. Tankers entering the Persian Gulf have to pass through Omani waters in the Strait of Hormuz. Therefore – with Iran still in turmoil – any internal instability in Oman would present a grave threat to Western oil supplies.

"The Omani note to the Arab League said the sultanate has at no time initiated any act of aggression against South Yemen," the Omani official said.

Begin's opponents have a big start
From DAVID BALDERSTONE in Jerusalem

'The Age', April 6, 1981

There was none of the glamour of the Israeli Prime Minister's meetings with Egypt's President Sadat. Instead Menachem Begin rose slowly from his chair to address a gathering of about 50 municipal officials.

He was dressed conservatively as always, in a grey suit and grey spotted tie. He spoke quietly and deliberately – so quietly in fact that everyone had to listen attentively for fear of missing anything.

And, of course, they didn't want to miss the Prime Minister telling them how glad he was to be back in their city, Ashkelon, and how important his Government saw the city's development within the wider aspirations for a better and more secure Israel.

The old campaigner, his heavy glasses sheltering his tired red eyes, and his wife by his side, was back on the campaign trail. And this day, it was pretty clear, Mr Begin was chasing the votes of oriental Jews, who helped him into Government in 1977, but – if the opinion polls can be believed – might desert him in the national elections on 30 June.

About 60 per cent of the 200,000 people who live in Ashkelon, a city on the coast south of Tel Aviv, are oriental Jews. Deputy Prime Minister Yigael Yadin's Democratic Movement for Change polled well in the city in 1977. But, with the DMC in the process of disbanding, Mr Begin is keen to minimize the drift towards the Labor Party led by Opposition Leader Shimon Peres.

After speaking to the inner group of senior municipal officials, Mr Begin walked across the road through a crowd of several hundred people, many of whom were waving small Israeli flags handed out by party workers.

Then the Prime Minister, who has secured Israel's peace treaty with the biggest Arab country, opened a memorial to Ashkelon's sons who had fallen in the country's four major wars with the Arabs, before opening a new low-income housing estate and a sports complex.

But Menachem Begin, 67, who waited 28 years to become Israel's sixth Prime Minister, is the underdog in the coming election.

While internationally it may be widely perceived that the Egyptian-Israeli peace treaty would give Mr Begin a formidable advantage in the June election, opinion polls show that most Israelis believe that inflation and the economy is the major issue in the election.

And no wonder. While Israel has never been a stranger to inflation, the coalition Government led by Mr Begin has overseen unprecedented inflation, which runs at the annual rate of slightly above 130 per cent.

Recent opinion polls show that Mr Peres' Labor Alignment would win twice as many seats as Mr Begin's Likud in elections for Israel's 120-seat Parliament, the Knesset.

A poll published this month by the English language 'Jerusalem Post' shows that the Likud would win only 25 seats against Labor's 52. However, while this gives Mr Peres a clear lead, it is not as significant as it might seem for two reasons.

Firstly, Israel has been traditionally ruled by coalition Governments, and with Labor highly unlikely to gain an overall majority, the formation of the next Government will depend very much behind whom the smaller parties will throw their support.

Secondly, this latest opinion poll showed that Mr Begin's Likud had picked up five seats since the previous poll six weeks before.

And there are three main reasons why Mr Begin is likely to narrow the gap even further in the three months before the election. It could be that Mr Begin will narrow the gap enough to prove the pundits wrong and be returned to office.

Firstly, in addition to reducing taxes on small cars, colour television sets and other major appliances, Mr Begin's Finance

Minister, Mr Yoram Aridor, has announced a ten per cent income tax reduction and a restructuring of income tax brackets, which will give Israelis an average of 23 per cent more disposable income from the beginning of April. The group to benefit most from this pre-election economic package is that of middle to low income earners, and that means oriental Jews. The impact on the electorate of this economic package could not be expected to show up in the polls until late April or early May.

Secondly, that old solder, Moshe Dayan, won't even fade away. This former Labor Alignment Minister, who deserted his former colleagues after the 1977 Labor defeat to become a Minister for two years in the Begin Government, seems certain to enter the political fray once again. Mr Dayan is almost certain to lead a new political party – or list of candidates, as he prefers to call it – which opinion polls show could win between four to 15 seats in Israel's proportional representation elections.

The most recent poll – a private survey commissioned for the Labor Party – showed a Dayan group would win 13 to 15 seats. It is thought that most people who would vote for the Dayan group would have formerly voted for either Labor or Yigael Yadin's disbanding DMC.

Even 10 seats could give Mr Dayan the opportunity to make Mr Begin or Mr Peres Prime Minister after the election.

Thirdly, the situation in South Lebanon north of Israel's border looks like deteriorating. This could lead to a closing of ranks behind the incumbent Prime Minister, and to the electorate feeling that the "security" issue was increasingly important vis-à-vis the economic issue.

While it would be hard to argue in favor of the Begin Government's handling of the economy, some observers believe that the economic issue has become more important to Israelis because the Egyptian-Israeli peace treaty has lessened concern on the traditional issue – security. The situation in Lebanon seems likely to deteriorate because the Lebanese Government (in a policy agreed with Syria) has decided to move regular Lebanese army units into the southern areas currently controlled by Israel's Lebanese ally, Major Sa'ad Haddad.

As a result of division within the Zionist groups – the smaller of which jealously guarded their chances of maintaining influence – before the formation of modern Israel in 1948, Israel's electoral system is one of proportional representation elections for a single constituency. This has achieved what the minority Zionist groups wanted – a lot of small parties and virtually no chance of a single party gaining a majority of seats.

The polls indicate that Mr Peres will become Prime Minister after the 30 June elections. But with Mr Begin's Likud gaining ground, and with the hard bargaining of putting together a coalition a long way ahead, it is too early to discount the Prime Minister in a grey suit and heavy glasses.

Rival powers shun peace for Lebanon
From DAVID BALDERSTONE in Beirut

'The Age', April 21, 1981

It was peak hour in Beirut, but the road was suddenly deserted. Just a kilometre back, cars, trucks and motorcycles had been battling each other, pedestrians and food carts.

But they had vanished as the road approached the so-called "green line", which divides predominantly Moslem West Beirut from Christian East Beirut.

The taxi driver stopped briefly at the Syrian army checkpoint, squeezed a smile for the young helmeted soldier, and then placed his foot firmly on the accelerator. The old Mercedes thundered along the road past burnt-out apartment buildings, which – during the past few days – had sheltered snipers playing a deadly game in a bid to keep the city divided.

After a couple of kilometres, the taxi stopped momentarily at a Lebanese army checkpoint sheltering under a couple of eucalyptus trees. Then another dash – this time to a checkpoint manned by young Falangist militiamen wearing Israeli army helmets, and carrying Kalashnikovs, and M-16 rifles.

We had crossed the "green line". There were only a few cars on the roads in East Beirut, which is controlled by the "Rightist" Christian Falangist militia. The area had taken a heavy pounding from Syrian artillery, and most of the shops were shuttered. Only 160,000 of East Beirut's 800,000-population remain.

Ironically, when the Syrians entered Lebanon in 1976, they brought the main civil war to a halt by supporting the Christian militias which were then being routed by forces of the Palestinian "Leftist" Lebanese alliance.

During the past three weeks, Syrian troops have routed Falangist forces defending the mainly Christian town of Zahle in the lush Beka'a Valley, 40 kilometres east of Beirut. From the Syrian point of view the Falangist presence in Zahle was an obstacle to their total control of the Beka'a which they perceive as necessary for their defence from Israeli attack.

The Syrians were angered that the Falangists were building a "military" access road from Christian strongholds in the Lebanon range to Zahle. But there are conflicting theories about what triggered the fighting.

At the same time, artillery battles ranged across the "green line" in Beirut between the Syrians and the Falangists.

Although the Syrians now control the areas surrounding Zahle, the Falangists believe they have won the international public relations war. And that is of paramount importance to them.

The Syrian force, which numbers around 30,000, is officially known as the Arab Deterrent Force and has a mandate from the Arab League. When it entered Lebanon, the mainly-Syrian force also included soldiers from other Arab countries which have since withdrawn their troops from the force.

When the force entered Lebanon, The Syrian objective was widely seen as attempting to balance power in the country.

Now, however, it is increasingly believed that the threatened Syrian regime of President Hafez Assad may be using the Lebanon force as a means of distracting attention from domestic problems, and as a way of controlling the Palestinian guerilla movement.

In addition, the continued presence of the Syrian force frightens many Lebanese – Christian and Moslems alike – into believing that Damascus intends to exert permanent influence over the country, which was once part of "greater Syria".

The Falangists view the Syrians as an "occupying" force, and believe that the recent fighting in Zahle and Beirut helped them sway some Arab Governments, as well as the US and some European countries, towards this view.

Although some senior officials in the Syrian regime are believed to have advised President Assad to withdraw from Lebanon, the more general view among Syrian officials is that if the force withdrew, the Lebanese civil war would merely break out again. This is also the view of some Western diplomats.

Because of this, the recent heavy fighting, which is continuing sporadically, prompted a flurry of diplomatic activity aimed at assessing what kind of force could replace the Syrians.

However, the idea of an alternative force has gone on the back-burner, mainly because few, if any, countries would be prepared to contribute troops to such a hazardous assignment.

The recent heavy fighting also cast some doubts on the theory that withdrawal of the Syrians would lead merely to renewed civil war between the opposing Lebanese and Palestinian factions.

Although some "Leftist" Lebanese leaders made a play for calling their militias onto alert, a senior Western diplomat noted that it appeared that the mainly Moslem "Leftist" forces and the Palestinians had been careful not to get involved in the fighting.

But the problem with Lebanon is that it is a microcosm of Middle East problems. Around 200,000 registered Palestinian refugees live in Lebanon and the country provides the only base from which guerillas are able to launch raids into Israel.

While the purely Lebanese factions may indeed be able to reconcile their deep differences under ideal circumstances, Middle East realities are unlikely to let this happen.

Divided Beirut is part of a divided country captive to regional and superpower forces, which have little concern whether Lebanon's system correctly divides power between Christians, Sunni Moslems and Shi'ite Moslems.

While the streets of East Beirut remain deserted, fashionable Rue Hamra in West Beirut is doing a roaring business. Boutiques and cinemas are open, and restaurants are providing the best food in the Middle East.

After spending the morning with the Falangists in East Beirut, I crossed back to West Beirut. On Rue Hamra, a weathered old man was selling day-old chicks from a trolley as the traffic moved bumper-to-bumper down past shops blaring out pop music.

He would place the fluttering chicks into plastic bags before handing them to the purchaser. Very hygienic, it could be said.

It could also be said that those fragile chicks, helpless against the weathered old man's hands, were symbolic of the Lebanese problem. No one has an interest in keeping their hands off once-beautiful Lebanon.

Iran slow to reopen 'hotbeds of dissent'
From DAVID BALDERSTONE

'The Age', Teheran, April 28, 1981

Demonstrators guarded by supporters on motorcycles, marched on Teheran University last week to protest about the continued closure of Iran's universities.

Fundamentalist Islamic zealots – some with shaved heads – clashed with the demonstrators and, according to local newspaper reports, two people died in the battle.

The authorities claimed that political groups, or "groupies" as they are dubbed by Iranian officials, had exploited the university closure in a bid to hold a demonstration in support of their own political cause.

As commonly happens at such demonstrations in post-revolution Iran, the zealots, or Hezbollahis (members of the "Party of God"), were stirred into action by statements made by members of the ruling fundamentalist clergy, who fear the universities could become a hotbed of political dissent.

About 175,000 students were thrown onto the streets when Iran's universities were closed a year ago. The official reason for the closure was that time was needed to "create an Islamic environment" within the universities.

However, it is common to find Iranians who believe that Iran's leaders noted the role played by university students in the revolution which overthrew the Shah, and are determined the student force will not be organised to undermine their position.

Last Friday a leading clergyman, Hojatoleslam Seyyad Ali Khamenei, told the main weekly prayer meeting in Teheran that the authorities "should not hurry with re-opening the universities". Closure of the universities, he said, did not mean closure of the doors of knowledge.

Hojatoleslam Khamenei said that universities under the Shah's regime served the affluent class, and did not serve the needs of the country.

Ironically, the affluent class still seems to be benefitting: the authorities still allow students to study abroad. About 60,000 Iranians are studying at universities outside Iran, and most of these students are in Western Europe.

This tends to support the theory that the authorities' main concern is political dissent in the universities, because presumably students in Western universities are not studying within an "Islamic environment".

However, like most issues in post-revolution Iran, there are two sides to the university issue. Higher education in Iran is under an organisation called the Cultural Revolution Council. A prominent member of this council, Dr Ali Shariat-Madari, argued persuasively that time had been needed to reorganise the university system in Iran after the revolution when I talked with him in Teheran this week.

Before the revolution, he said, there were 230 universities and higher education institutions in Iran. "The University of Shah Reza the Great at Babolsar beside the Caspian Sea had only 14 students. It was there so that academics could get allowances to go on holiday.

"When I was Minister of Higher Education in the (post-revolution) Provisional Government I joined it with four other institutions and called them the University of Mazandaran Province."

Dr Shariat-Madari said the aim of Iran's higher education system in the future would be to satisfy the needs of the country. Therefore, it was planned to reopen the university faculties of medicine, agriculture and engineering, and teacher training institutions at the beginning of the next academic year in September.

But the future for the humanities faculties is less certain. Dr Shariat-Madari said the Ministry of Education needed some graduates in humanities courses for teacher training. However, it seemed the humanities intake in the coming academic year would only cover students required by this ministry.

"In the past universities were not established with regard to the needs of the country as a whole," Dr Shariat-Madari said. "So we have had to revise teaching programmes, university administration and entrance criteria."

An aim of the Cultural Revolution Council is to organise higher education in such a way so that in future no area will be without doctors and agricultural scientists, for example. In the past, more backward provinces, such as Sistan and Baluchistan in south-east Iran, have tended to lack the level of medical services available to Iranians living in the more developed and prosperous areas of the country. This is given as one reason for the present unrest among the Baluchis.

Dr Shariat-Madari said the universities would make a special effort to take a few students from Baluchistan and other deprived areas into the medical and agricultural faculties because these students – once they graduated – would be more likely than city students to want to return to their areas and serve their people.

He said this would not necessarily involve a lowering of entrance standards. Instead, a special institution was being set up to provide special post-secondary education for such students before going on to university.

Dr Shariat-Madari was asked what was involved in creating an Islamic environment in the universities. He said first and second year students would have to take a course in Islamic culture and ideology. However, he claimed, Jewish and Christian students would not have to take this course.

While Dr Shariat-Madari, who taught in the US for several years, appears to be working sincerely to bring the country's university system in line with the needs of the country, other people will continue to suspect that the universities are closed for political reasons.

A bad deal after all
– DAVID BALDERSTONE

'The Age', Teheran, May 2, 1981

For the 52 Americans released in January after Iran and the US signed a complicated financial deal, the hostage crisis is over. But in Iran the legacy lives on.

It has become an issue in the political power struggle between the "liberal" politicians led by President Bani-Sadr and the clergy-backed Government of the Prime Minister, Mr Rajai.

In a damning attack on the incompetence of the Rajai Government this week, Dr Bani-Sadr described the deal as "the most expensive ever signed in history between America and Iran".

While the pro-Government newspaper 'Islamic Republic' headlined news of the deal when it was signed with "America on it knees", Dr Bani-Sadr said this week that the deal had delighted American bankers, and that the agreement was "designed to solve the hostage crisis in the interests of America".

Under the agreement, Dr Bani-Sadr said:

Iran had received only $2800 million of the $7900 transferred to Iran "on paper".

Iran had paid back to the Americans low-interest loans before they had matured, whereas Iran could have continued to make use of these advantageous loans.

Iran had repaid loans made by American banks to relatives and associates of the deposed Shah during the previous regime.

In a move to prove the incompetence of the Rajai Government, Dr Bani-Sadr is taking legal action against Mr Rajai and the Executive Affairs Minister, Mr Nabavi, for signing an agreement which allegedly violated Iran's constitution and went beyond the authority given to the Government by Iran's Majlis (Parliament).

Dr Bani-Sadr documented his complaints against the deal in a long letter to the Speaker of the Majlis.

In a sense, Dr Bani-Sadr, who was always critical of the hostage affair, is taking advantage of being able to afford the luxury of criticising the agreement now that the Americans have been released.

In other words, he is reminding Iranians that he was against the hostage affair, and adding that the fundamentalist Islamic politicians who prolonged the crisis could not even secure a good deal once they wanted one.

Syrians down Israeli aircraft
From DAVID BALDERSTONE

'The Age', Beirut, May 15, 1981

An Israeli pilotless reconnaissance aircraft crashed in Lebanon's Beka'a Valley today after being hit by a Syrian surface-to-air missile.

Israel's defence forces spokesman later confirmed that the "drone" was downed while on a "routine" reconnaissance mission over Lebanon.

The incident damaged hopes that US special envoy Mr Philip Habib would succeed in diplomatic efforts aimed at pulling Syria and Israel back from the brink of war.

It was the second time in two days that Syrian forces have claimed to have shot down an Israeli drone. Israel denied the first claim.

While Syrian troops manning and supporting their SAM-6 missiles in Lebanon's lush Beka'a Valley remained on high alert in case of an Israeli attack, crucial talks in Damascus today seemed likely to provide a clue to whether US diplomatic moves could succeed in easing the Syrian-Israeli crisis.

With Syria's State-run media continuing to suggest that Syria would refuse to remove the SAM missiles from the Beka'a Valley, Mr Habib rushed from Beirut to Damascus last night for a hastily arranged meeting with President Assad today.

Israel is demanding that Syria withdraw the missiles. The Syrians installed them after Israeli jets shot down two Syrian helicopters supporting Syrian peace-keeping troops in the valley last month.

Before travelling to Damascus, Mr Habib held talks in Beirut with Lebanon's President Elias Sarkis. He had arrived in the Lebanese capital from Israel by way of Damascus during the afternoon.

During his talks in Israel, the Prime Minister, Mr Begin, was reported as telling Mr Habib that while his Government was ready to give diplomatic moves every chance, Israel could not wait much longer.

Mr Begin disclosed to Israel's Parliament this week that he had ordered Israeli forces to destroy the Syrian missiles shortly after they were installed. However, he said, weather conditions prevented the action.

The downing of the Israeli drone today could increase Mr Begin's impatience with diplomatic moves aimed at resolving the crisis. The Right-wing Falangist radio in Beirut said the downed aircraft was one of three seen flying over the Beka'a Valley today.

The feeling that Mr Habib's shuttle diplomacy between Damascus, Beirut and Jerusalem had not run out of steam relieved tensions in the towns of the Beka'a Valley and in predominantly Moslem West Beirut yesterday.

Women in brightly coloured dresses and men with donkeys and tractors were tending the vines and crops when I drove through the valley on the way from Damascus to Beirut yesterday.

There was heavy traffic on the highway. Shops along the road were doing brisk business in soap powder, food and duty-free whisky and cigarettes. A stall selling fairy floss in the town of Chtaura attracted a large crowd of small children.

A human statistic in futile fighting
From DAVID BALDERSTONE

'The Age', Beirut, May 21, 1981

His face was blackened and wrinkled like a burnt pizza. He lay panting on the stained hospital bed. Abed Salim, a Palestinian militiaman, could hardly be said to be lucky to be alive as he slept through the 25th ceasefire within six weeks of fighting in Beirut.

Abed Salim lost his face and became a number in the list of people injured in the fighting across the "green line" dividing Beirut. This week alone at least 25 people have died and 125 people have been injured as Christian militiamen in East Beirut and Syrian troops in the west of the city rained mortars, artillery and rockets on each other.

Someone behind those guns on either side may know what the fighting this week achieved, but it appeared, as many times before, a futile exercise producing only casualty lists.

This week's fighting coincided with tension in Lebanon caused by serious doubts about whether US diplomatic efforts would succeed in drawing Syria and Israel back from the brink of war. The antagonists are Syrian troops, who make up the 30,000 strong Arab League deterrent force in Lebanon, and the Israeli-supported Christian Falangist militiamen, who consider the Syrians an occupying force.

During the lull in the fighting yesterday, I visited the Palestinian Red Crescent Society hospital on the coastal airport road just a few kilometres from the centre of West Beirut. The hospital is in the midst of Palestinian refugee camps, which the previous day had been hit by shells.

The Palestinian Red Crescent is an offshoot of the Palestine Liberation Organisation and this hospital is named Acre after the city in Israel, which Palestinians describe as occupied Palestine.

In two days of heavy fighting, which began last Saturday, the Acre hospital accepted 40 emergency cases caused directly by the fighting.

As well as Abed Salim, "numbers" on the casualty list included a 14-year old boy, who had been badly injured when a shell exploded near him as he was selling vegetables, and a nine-year-old Lebanese boy, who had been hit in the right eye by shrapnel. The scene would be similar in hospitals on the Christian side of the city, and in the clinics serving Syrian troops.

But this hospital, like other Palestinian Red Crescent hospitals in Lebanon, is on high alert because of the Middle East crisis. Some senior PLO officials believe that, regardless of whether the crisis over the Syrian missiles in Lebanon leads to a Syrian-Israeli war, Israel is planning a massive attack against the Palestinians in Lebanon. The view is shared by some Western diplomats.

The Acre hospital is the headquarters of Dr Fathi Arafat, president of the Red Crescent and brother of the PLO chairman, Mr Yasser Arafat. He was trained in Cairo and closely resembles his brother in appearance.

Over a cup of Turkish coffee, he said the Palestinian hospitals were prepared for a big influx of emergency patients.

Shells, probably fired by the Christian militiamen, fell close to the Acre hospital this week. Dr Arafat said he could not "exactly determine" whether they had been fired at the hospital.

"But there is a general determination on the part of our enemies to liquidate the Palestinians, so I think out medical centres may be a target," he said. A month ago a shell fell on the other major Palestinian hospital in Beirut.

"From the voices of these shells and bombs we are suffering very much. But at the same time it drives us to continue our revolution and struggle," Dr Arafat said. "We are sure of our victory."

He said that at last year's world assembly of the World Health Organisation in Geneva he had told delegates that only two delegates would not be returning to their homes after the conference.

"I said all delegates would return home except two – myself and the Minister of Israel's Public Health, who will return to my home."

In the midst of the Syria-Israel crisis and the related Beirut fighting, the PLO struggle for an independent Palestinian State continues. But Abed Salim with his scorched face and burnt-out eyes will never see Palestine, even if his friends do. Because this Palestinian militiaman has become a number on a casualty list from futile Beirut fighting.

Palestinians brace for attack
From DAVID BALDERSTONE

'The Age', Arnoun (Southern Lebanon), May 25, 1981

"This is the point of challenge," the Palestinian official said, pointing to the Crusaders' monument, Beaufort Castle, perched on a distant precipice.

"The Israelis want the village and Beaufort."

The official, Mahmoud Labadi, flanked by a few unshaven and weary Palestinian guerillas manning "forward military positions" in Arnoun said: "We may expect at any moment an attack or an invasion".

Israel's Prime Minister, Mr Begin, told the people of the northern Israeli town of Kyriat Shmona – about 15 kilometres from the Palestinian-held Beaufort Castle – that soon not one Palestinian rocket would fall on their town.

The castle is as strategically important today as it was in Crusader days. It commands a 300 metre cliff falling away to a bend in the Litani River.

On the other side of the river are the Israeli-backed "Christian" enclaves commanded by the renegade Lebanese officer Major Sa'ad Haddad. It is only seven kilometres north of Israel's northern-most town, Metulla.

Amid high tension caused by the crisis between Syria and Israel, Palestinian guerillas in Arnoun and the castle have exchanged artillery and rockets with Major Haddad's men on the other side of the ravine almost every day during the past six weeks.

When I visited Arnoun, sheep and goats were grazing among crops around the village, giving a deceptively peaceful feeling to the area. But the village's shell-damaged buildings and roads told the real story.

The evening before both the village and the castle had been shelled. There was no mistaking the fact that the Palestinian guerillas – some in helmets and some in Arab kaffiyehs – were expecting a resumption of the shelling at any time.

The Deputy Commander of Palestinian forces in the area, who described himself as "Brother Marwan", declared that his men would defend "advance positions in the face of Israeli attacks". He speculated that Israel could be planning something similar to the "Litani Operation", when Israel invaded Lebanon up to the Litani River in March 1978.

Palestine Liberation Organisation officials have interpreted Mr Begin's Kyriat Shmona statement as meaning that before Israel's elections on 30 June, Mr Begin intends to launch a massive attack against Palestinians in South Lebanon.

Many Western observers share this fear, and do not believe the risk will be diminished even if the Syria/Israel crisis is resolved peacefully.

Mahmoud Labadi, who is head of the PLO's information office and acting spokesman of the main guerila group, Fatah, said Israel was waging a "war of liquidation" against the Palestinian people. To underline his point, he took me and other correspondents to the Lebanese city of Nabatiyeh before going on the eight kilometres to Arnoun.

Before Lebanon's civil war, Nabatiyeh, which is 75 kilometres south of Beirut, had a population of around 75,000 Shi'ite Moslem Lebanese. It is a Palestinian guerilla stronghold now. Only about 20,000 Lebanese remain.

A combination of the civil war, which left the Palestinians firmly in control, and constant shelling and bombing by Israel and Major Haddad's militias ever since, drove the other Lebanese residents away.

Mr Labadi said Nabatiyeh was shelled by Major Haddad's militias almost every day. Certainly the buildings facing Major Haddad's enclaves had been hit by thousands of shells. "They fire blind to make sure no normal life can continue in the city," Mr Labadi said.

Last week a shell hit a car in the main street, killing three people. Bloodstains remain on a service station pavement where a bomb exploded, killing four, the next day.

Major Haddad, who views the Palestinians as well as the Syrian troops in Lebanon as an occupying force, probably has two objectives in firing blindly into Nabatiyeh. As well as trying to hit Palestinian emplacements, he possibly wants to turn the local Lebanese against the Palestinians.

Israeli raid dashes US peace hopes
From DAVID BALDERSTONE in Nicosia

'The Age', June 8, 1981

By attacking Iraq's nuclear reactors outside Bagdad, Israel has almost certainly made Iraq more determined to proceed with a nuclear programme, jeopardised Israeli-Egyptian relations and helped to unify the fractured Arab world.

Sunday's dusk raid, which the French Foreign Ministry has said destroyed one reactor but left the other unscathed, has killed once and for all the Reagan Administration's chance of persuading the Arabs that Soviet expansionism rather than Israel was the main threat to Middle East stability.

The Israelis, by using American aircraft and weapons, have undermined the US position in the Arab world, and all but completely dashed hopes that the US special envoy, Mr Philip Habib, could make any progress towards defusing the Syria-Israel crisis.

Undoubtedly, the Israeli action has further heightened Middle East tension at a time when Syria and Israel are already on the brink of war. But, in the short term at least, it is hard to believe that Iraq, which is bogged down in the Gulf war with Iran, could seriously consider any military retaliation against Israel.

Although Israel has always vehemently opposed Iraq's nuclear programme, Sunday's air raid marks the first time an Israeli Government has openly admitted carrying out an action aimed at destroying the programme.

However it is at least the sixth time that an attempt has been made to sabotage or delay the programme. A nuclear reactor bound for Iraq was sabotaged before being sent from France. In June 1980, the Egyptian scientist who headed the programme was killed in a Paris hotel.

During the first two weeks of the Gulf war, Phantom jets attacked the nuclear establishment on the edge of Bagdad. Although Iran's air force is equipped with Phantoms, Iranian officials denied any knowledge of the raid and Iraq's Defence Minister blamed Israel.

The Iraqis are reported to have captured saboteurs during attempts to penetrate the nuclear compound last December and in April.

Iraq has blamed Israel's intelligence service, Mossad, for being behind all attempts to delay the programme.

But none of the incidents has destroyed the programme. It remains a matter of speculation whether Sunday's air raid has done so.

It will certainly increase the determination of President Saddam Hussein of Iraq to proceed with a nuclear programme and Iraq – potentially the second largest Arab oil producer – could easily afford to replace equipment damaged in Sunday's raid.

However, the recent election of the French Socialist leader Francois Mitterrand, as President of France, will make it much more difficult – but not impossible – for Iraq to replace the nuclear equipment from France.

If President Giscard d'Estaing had been re-elected, Iraq almost certainly would have faced no problems in buying new nuclear equipment. But President Mitterrand, a close friend of Israel, has questioned the wisdom of the nuclear deal between France and Iraq.

On the other hand, the attack on the installation, which French officials said left at least one French technician dead, has shaken President Mitterrand's relationship with Israel.

French officials have refused to comment on whether the raid would affect President Mitterrand's trip to Israel later this year.

The Israeli Prime Minister, Mr Begin, has said that the reactors would have been operational within a month or two, and that Iraq planned to make nuclear weapons for use against Israel.

Whether or not this was Iraq's intention, a quick glance at the map of Israel and surrounding countries leaves the impression that it would be difficult for an Arab country to launch a nuclear attack against Israel without affecting major Arab population areas.

Because the raid took place while the Syria-Israeli missile crisis remained very much alive, the attack was a warning to Syria that Mr Begin's Government would not hesitate to take military action to protect what Jerusalem saw as Israel's security interests.

It has increased fears that unless the crisis over Syrian missiles in Lebanon's Beka'a Valley is resolved peacefully, Israel may act not only against the missiles, but against military installations in Syria as well.

Arab officials and some Western diplomats in Arab capitals have long held the view that Mr Begin would like to knock Syria's armed forces back a decade because Syria – following the Syrian-Soviet friendship treaty signed last year – is being supplied with more sophisticated Soviet weapons than ever before.

President Sadat of Egypt, who met Mr Begin in Sinai last week, was one of the first leaders to condemn the Israeli attack. Although it is unlikely to affect the Egypt-Israeli peace treaty, it could slow down the attempt to achieve normal relations between the two countries.

The Israeli action will hamper President Sadat's moves towards re-establishing relations with Arab countries, which condemned his peace treaty with Israel. And he was making progress.

Egypt has supplied Iraq with some military equipment since the start of the Gulf war, and last month Mr Sadat visited the Sudan – his first visit to an Arab country since he visited Jerusalem in November 1977.

Although relations between the rival Baath party capitals, Damascus and Bagdad, have been extremely strained for more than a year, the Syria-Israel missile crisis helped mend relations. On 13 May, Iraq's Foreign Minister, Mr Hammadi, said Iraq would aid

Syria in the event of war, despite Bagdad's conflict with the Damascus regime, which has supported Iran in the Gulf war.

That may have been rhetoric on 13 May. Following Sunday's air attack, it looks much more like a commitment.

Although Iraq seems unlikely to retaliate militarily, Sunday's raid has increased the risk of war in the Middle East. Bagdad is likely to loosen the reins on some of the more radical pro-Iraqi Palestinian groups operating in Lebanon.

And as the Syrian-Israeli crisis continues, just one dramatic Palestinian raid into Israel could spark the war fires. And these would be much more difficult to contain than the situation in Lebanon now.

Stay out of Sinai force, Arabs say
From DAVID BALDERSTONE

'The Age', Jerusalem, June 24, 1981

While Egypt and Israel would welcome Australia's participation in the multinational force for Sinai, Arab countries have increased their opposition to any Australian participation in the force since the Israeli attack on Iraq's nuclear plant.

Before Israel's 7 June attack on Iraq's nuclear facilities in Bagdad, Australian diplomats had been asked by Canberra to sound out officials in Jordan, Syria, Iraq and Saudi Arabia on the likely reactions if Australia should join the force.

These countries unanimously opposed Australian participation because of the force's association with the Egypt-Israel peace treaty, which they oppose. But, since the Israeli attack, using American-made planes, some Arab officials have intensified their opposition and are understood to have warned more strongly that Australian trade in the Arab world could be jeopardised.

This time the Arab opposition did not merely stem from the force's association with the Egypt-Israel peace treaty, but also because Australia would be linking itself clearly with the US in the Middle East at a time of strong anti-American feeling.

Judging from these Arab reactions, before and after the Israeli attack, it would be reasonable to assume that Arab opposition to Australian participation could become even more intense if an Australian officer was to become sole or joint military commander of the force.

In addition to the task of finding countries willing to contribute to the force, US-Israeli-Egyptian negotiations on the force remained somewhat bogged down this week over the question of the future United Nations role in Sinai peace-keeping.

The Egyptian-Israeli peace treaty envisaged that the UN would send a peace-keeping force to police Sinai after Israel's final withdrawal from the area next April. But a UN force became impossible because of Soviet opposition.

However, Egypt has continued to want the mandate of a multinational force, which has been formed as a replacement to the envisaged UN force, to state specifically that the force would be replaced by a UN force if that became possible.

While Israel is not against a possible future role for the UN, it insists that it must be made clear that any UN role would be part of the execution of the peace treaty. The Israeli point is that a UN role could be considered only if the UN first endorsed the peace treaty.

The Director-General of Israel's Foreign Ministry, Mr David Kimche, warned this week that negotiations over the force might not be concluded this week as hoped. "We hope we can conclude the talks, but we are by no means certain that we will be concluding the negotiations this time," he said.

It has been reported in the Israeli Press that Egyptian officials believe a specific mention in the force's mandate of a future UN role would encourage neutral and Third World countries to contribute to the multinational force, even though it was not a UN force.

A force to police Sinai after the final Israeli withdrawal from the area under the peace treaty has always been more important to Israel than to Egypt. Naturally, Israel has long considered the possibility that the situation in Egypt could change and that Sinai could become the route of an Egyptian military attack against Israel. The multinational force in Sinai would provide some protection against, and early warning of, such a possibility.

More of the same
- DAVID BALDERSTONE

'The Age', Jerusalem, July 4, 1981

Mr Menachem Begin's tenuous return to power this week cannot encourage any hope that the Israeli economy will improve, that ethnic divisions will be healed, or that any progress will be achieved towards a comprehensive Middle East peace.

After a bitter election campaign during which Mr Begin exploited the most basic emotions of Israelis and increased Israel's isolation in the world, the Government may have a majority of only two or maybe three seats in the Knesset.

This seems to mean that Mr Begin will not turn over a new leaf, but rather pursue his current policies.

Faced with the possibility that his Government could lose the confidence of the Knesset at any time, Mr Begin seems likely to run a continuous election campaign. He will follow the policies that brought him from certain defeat early in the year.

The big achievement during the four and a bit years of Mr Begin's first term was the peace treaty with Egypt, Israel's biggest and most powerful Arab neighbor. But it has to be noted that the process was started by the previous Labor Government and would not have ended in a peace treaty without Opposition support.

It was a Labor Government that signed the initial disengagement treaties with Egypt after the 1973 war. It was Labor that helped Mr Begin get the Knesset to ratify the treaty after half his own party deserted him on the issue.

But can peace between Egypt and Israel survive with Mr Begin at the helm again? The key to this question rests on progress being made in the negotiations on autonomy for the West Bank and Gaza Strip Palestinians as envisaged by the treaty's accompanying Camp David agreements.

Currently the accords are at a standstill, mainly because of the Begin Government's attitude towards the degree of autonomy and its objection to Arabs in East Jerusalem (unilaterally annexed by Israel after the 1967 war) being included in the autonomy plans.

With Mr Begin unlikely to change his attitude towards these issues, there is not much hope of real progress on these negotiations with Egypt.

Britain's Lord Carrington, who took over as the president of the EEC Council of Ministers on 1 July, had hoped to use his six-month term of office to get a European Middle East initiative off the ground. The aim was to build on what had already been achieved through the American-backed Egypt-Israel peace moves.

But with Mr Begin unlikely to be in the mood for anything with a whiff of compromise about it, Lord Carrington's move seems destined to failure.

While these issues may not have an immediate impact on the Israeli electorate, another term of a Begin Government handling the economy may well undermine support for the Prime Minister. After presiding over unprecedented inflation rising to 130 per cent a year, his government – in a pre-election gesture – handed out significant tax concessions.

Now Israel has to pay for these concessions, and that may give the Opposition a chance to bring down the shaky Begin Government and succeed where it failed this week.

More martyrs for Iran's revolution
From DAVID BALDERSTONE

'The Age', Amman, August 31, 1981

Once again opponents of Ayatollah Khomeini's rule in Iran have succeeded in hitting at the heart of the regime.

In June a bomb exploded killing the leader and major political tactician of the ruling Islamic Republican Party and 71 other party politicians. Now the regime's front men – the President and Prime Minister – are dead.

This latest bomb, which exploded in the Prime Minister's office while the country's Supreme Defence Council was meeting, has posed an inevitable question: how long can Ayatollah Khomeiny's regime last?

No simple answer to this question emerges from the web of Iranian intrigue. But given the history of the Iranian religion, Shi'ite Islam, and the course of the anti-Shah revolution which brought Ayatollah Khomeiny to power, this latest explosion may not have such a devastating impact on the survival of the regime as the saboteurs may have hoped.

Since the killing of the Imam Hussein in 1341, Shi'ite Moslems have been obsessed by the glory of martyrdom. This obsession contributed towards the fearless demonstrations against the late Shah. It has caused President Saddam Hussein's Iraqi army more than a little bother during the Gulf war.

Yesterday's bomb explosion in Teheran created two more prominent martyrs for Ayatollah Khomeiny's "revolution". That is how the deaths of President Rajai and the Prime Minister Bahonard will be portrayed by Iran's besieged rulers. Therefore, ironically, the deaths of these two leading members of the Government could provide a short respite at least to the problems plaguing Iran 30 months after Ayatollah Khomeiny's rise to power.

Nevertheless, with the main secular politicians still in Iran squeezed from power, the country's chronic brain drain which began before the revolution and the regime's shortage of skilled executive manpower, the absence of two more senior politicians will present great difficulties.

Mohammed Ali Rajai, the son of a poor shopkeeper, was born in Qazvin, north-west of Teheran, in 1933. He served in the Imperial Air Force before becoming an arithmetic teacher. He was jailed under the late Shah for counter-regime activities.

After Khomeiny returned triumphantly to Iran in 1979, Mr Rajai became Education Minister in the first Provisional Government. He was elected to Iran's first post-revolution Parliament and became Prime Minister last September.

He was elected President in the elections which followed the dismissal of former President Abolhassan Bani-Sadr two months ago.

Like Mr Rajai, Mohammed Javad Bahonard was virtually unknown in Iran before the revolution. The 47-year old clergyman was Prime Minister for less than a month.

He became head of the ruling Islamic Republican Party when the former head, Ayatollah Mohammed Beheshti, was killed in the June explosion. He became Prime Minister after Mr Rajai was elevated to the Presidency.

The most frightening thing for the clergy-dominated regime about the latest bomb blast inside the Prime Minister's office is that it seems to confirm what had been feared after the massive blast in June – that opponents of the regime have infiltrated the most trusted ranks of the Revolutionary Guard Corps.

In view of the nature of the revolution which ousted the late Shah this is not all that surprising. Despite Khomeiny's consistent and long opposition to the Shah, he was – up until his move from Iraq to Paris in 1978 – just one strand in the battle for change in Iran.

Another main stream was made up of constitutionalist politicians. There was also a strand made up of the two main guerilla groups which had opposed the Shah – the Mujahedeen el-Khalq and the Fedayeen. After the revolution youths and men of all walks of life, including alleged criminals who had been released from jail during the revolution, signed up for the Revolutionary Guards.

In addition to the main political power struggle which left the clerical fundamentalists on top and the secular politicians, notably Dr Bani-Sadr, without power, there were other fractures in the revolutionary power structure.

The Fedayeen split into a pro-Moscow majority and a more independent minority. The Mujahedeen el-Khalq gathered ground dramatically among middle-class youths, became a threat to the rule of the mullahs, and has been accused of acts of sabotage – including the June bomb explosion.

The infiltration is alarming for the Iranian rulers who, faced with major economic problems, rising unemployment, and the war with Iraq, will find it difficult to maintain what support they have in the coming months.

Judging by the regime's response to past "counter-revolutionary" acts, yesterday's explosion will draw massive reprisals. Alleged opponents – notably alleged members of the Mujahedeen – will be executed.

They too, will be martyrs.

Gulf war goes on.....a child dies
From DAVID BALDERSTONE

'The Age', Teheran, September 16, 1981

Eleven Iranian civilians were killed yesterday when long-range Iraqi artillery shelled residential areas of Ahvaz, the capital of Iran's south-western oil-rich province of Khuzestan.

For much of the world, the year-old Iran-Iraq war is something of a forgotten event. But for the people of Ahvaz, the war is a continuing nightmare.

Every couple of days, the Iraqis fire shells into the city.

At the front also, the war continues. A communiqué issued by the joint staff of the Iranian armed forces last night said that Iranian artillery had shelled Iraqi positions in several areas along the 600-kilometre battle front in the preceding 24 hours.

The communiqué said seven Iraqi aircraft had "invaded" Iranian air space yesterday, but had been forced to flee by Iranian anti-aircraft fire. An Iraqi aircraft had been seen flying near Tabriz, about 180 kilometres from the Iran-Iraq border.

Although the Iranian forces have pushed back slowly the Iraqi invading forces along much of the front, Iranian cities remain in reach of the long-range Iraqi artillery.

It would appear that the Iraqis are using their long-range artillery in a bid to demoralise the Iranian civilian population.

During a trip to the battle front, I witnessed continued frontline fighting, and the Iraqi shelling of Ahvaz and Abadan, the site of the world's largest oil refinery.

Four shells could be heard exploding on Ahvaz. Accompanied by Iranian officials, I visited a street in which one of the shells had landed.

A shell had made a crater in a road, an electricity pole had been broken, and ten people had been taken to hospital. A six-year-old boy was killed, according to an Iranian official.

Two hours later, while waiting for an Iranian military aircraft, I could hear the city again coming under Iraqi shelling. Iranian military officials said the shells were coming from Iraq's nearest positions 40 kilometres from the city.

The small group of foreign correspondents including myself saw no evidence of the invading Iraqi aircraft during a three day visit to the battle front.

However, as our Iranian military Fokker Friendship was about to taxi away from the Ahvaz terminal yesterday, the crew suddenly shut down the engines. A red alert had just been issued because invading aircraft had been detected in the area. The all clear was given 45 minutes later.

At the front line
From DAVID BALDERSTONE, in Teheran

'The Age', September 16, 1981

Like a rabbit into a burrow, the Iranian armored personnel carrier lurched into a hollow in the sand out of sight of the "enemy" mortar crews.

The Iraqi mortars, which had got progressively closer as the American-built APC dashed across the desert to the Iranian front lines, continued to fall around the tracked vehicle. We knew the "enemy" had lost us, but the heavy thud of his mortars kept falling around the APC like the angry footsteps of a hunter maddened by losing the game.

The amor-plating radiated heat and it was more than 50 degrees C inside the yellow and khaki cabin. But the suspicion lingers that it was not only the heat that was causing perspiration to drip from the faces staring at each other from the benches each side of the APC.

Only the young Iranian APC driver seemed cool. For him, it was just another day in the Iran-Iraq border war, which has claimed thousands of Iranian and Iraqi lives. A war that has now been going on for almost a year.

After a few long minutes, the thud of the hunter's footsteps moved away. The APC driver hoisted himself out of his round hatch, scrambled across the armor top and opened the heavy back hatch.

"This is where Saddam Hussein (Iraq's President) claims his troops defeated us two weeks ago by killing 5000 Iranians," said an Iranian army officer. "But you see it is still our front line in this area and Saddam's statement is nothing but a lie."

This front line was approximately 65 kilometres north-west of Ahvaz – capital of Iran's oil-rich province of Khuzestan in the south-west of the country.

After driving the Iraqis off desert rock and sand ridges, which the Iranians have named the Allah-o-Akbar (God is Great) heights, the Iranian army had driven a few metres further while the Iraqis retreated and dug in their new front lines in the heights around Bostan, about 20 kilometres from the Iran-Iraq border.

Here, as in other areas of the 600-kilometre front, the Iranians had slowly but surely pushed the Iraqi armored might back towards the border. The hollow in which our APC lurked was about 600 metres from the Iraqi front line. But the main fortifications of the "enemy" were 12 kilometres back and dug into the heights around Bostan.

Partly because the battle claims of both the Iranians and the Iraqis have been difficult to verify, the year-old Gulf war has become something of a forgotten war. After initial fears that the war might engulf the Persian Gulf countries in conflict subsided, much of the world's Press lost interest.

But this "forgotten" war remains very much an active battle. In addition to the front-line battles, long range Iraqi artillery continues to lob its deadly shells into Iranian civilian centres, such as Ahvaz; Iraqi MiG fighters penetrate Iranian air space, and the cost to both countries' economies has to be counted in millions of dollars.

Furthermore, while the chances of a direct superpower involvement appear slim, the war has implications for the strategic balance of the area. It is a very political war and the result could determine whether Iran eventually gets a pro-Soviet, pro-Western, or neutral Government.

Border clashes escalated into full scale war on 22 September last year, when Iraqi fighters bombed Iranian airbases, including Teheran airport. Iraq's publicly-stated objective was to regain sovereignty over the Shatt al-Arab waterway, which provided the border between the two countries in the south; a few islands in the Persian Gulf, and small pockets of land along the border.

The pre-war border had been negotiated by the late Shah of Iran and Saddam Hussein, who was then Iraq's Vice-President, in Algiers in 1975. In return for the Shah withdrawing support for

Iraqi Kurds battling the Bagdad regime for autonomy, Iraq agreed that the median line of the Shatt al-Arab was the border. Previously Iraq had sovereignty over all of the waterway and Iran merely had access to Abadan and Khorammshahr.

In addition, the 1975 agreement involved small adjustments to the land border. In 1975, the Shah was all powerful, and Saddam Hussein was criticised by other Arab countries for negotiating away Arab sovereignty over the Shat al-Arab and pockets of land.

But in September last year, Iraq appeared to be more powerful than Iran, whose armed forces had been purged during the revolution, and was short of spare parts. The boot appeared to be on the other foot. Therefore Saddam Hussein seems to have believed it was a good time to right the wrongs of the 1975 Algiers pact.

Clearly, Iraq had another objective – to teach Ayatollah Khomeiny and the Islamic clergy of Iran a lesson, and, ideally, bring the Islamic regime down. Saddam Hussein had a strong reason for wanting the fall of Ayatollah Khomeiny. Since the revolution which ousted the late Shah in Iran, Islamic clergymen had provocatively broadcast messages and sermons urging Moslems in neighboring countries to take a lesson from Iran and spread the Islamic revolution. Saddam Hussein was a target of Iranian abuse.

On paper, at least, he looked vulnerable to a popular uprising. President Hussein and most senior members of his regime are Sunni Moslem, whereas about 55 per cent of Iraq's 14-million population belong to the Shi'ite Moslem branch – the Iranian brand of Islam.

So, coinciding with the Iraqi air attacks, Iraqi tanks rolled into Iran and initially made good progress against the ill-prepared Iranians.

In the south, the Iraqis encircled the Iranian cities of Abadan and Khorammshahr on the Shatt al-Arab waterway, and established a major thrust towards Ahvaz. In addition, the Iraqis occupied pockets of land right along the 600-kilometre border war front, and penetrated deep into Iran through the Iranian border city of Qasr El Shirin, which is on the main Bagdad-Teheran road.

A year later the Iraqis continue to occupy tracts of Iranian border territory. But the Iranians – the underdogs of a year ago – are slowly but surely pushing the Iraqis back, and have rolled across the border into Iraq in the north of the country.

Miffed by the fact that the war is somewhat forgotten, and concerned that the Iranian victories were not getting much coverage, the Iranian army decided to take a small band of foreign correspondents including myself, to the front lines. The Iranian army, it transpired, was good to its word. The army had said front lines, and sure enough we saw front lines.

At 9.15am last Saturday, the Iranian army Fokker Friendship took off from Teheran's Mehrabad airport. An hour and a half later, the Fokker – buffeted by hot turbulent air – came down steeply and landed in Ahvaz, which, we learnt later, had been overflown by Iraqi MiGs earlier in the day.

After a two-hour bus ride in 45 degree heat, we arrived at the Allah-o-Akbar heights. As we sipped lemon juice in a headquarters bunker, an Iranian colonel said the area had been liberated by the Iranian 92nd Division nearly four months earlier. The Iraqi battalion, called the Alkendi battalion, had occupied the heights, but had been pushed off with the loss of around 250 soldiers and 70 tanks.

"Only three Iraqi tanks were able to escape," the colonel said. "No one from any of the international agencies came to identify the dead Iraqis, so we buried them according to Islamic law. About 100 bodies decomposed, so we buried them in their bunkers. We couldn't move them."

The front line was 10 kilometres from the Allah-o-Akbar heights, and the main Iraqi fortifications were 16 kilometres away at Bostan. "With the will of God we will move and reach the borders," said the colonel.

Because the Allah-o-Akbar heights were still coming under Iraqi shelling, we were divided into small groups and driven around the heights to see evidence of the Iraqi defeat. About 15 Iraqi Soviet-built tanks could be seen. Around a burnt-out Iraqi APC, the boots of Iraqi soldiers were lying in the sand. Open cases of Kraft cheese were in front of the APC together with a box of bread dried out by the hot desert sun.

We were then driven about four kilometres to an Iranian Red Crescent first-aid post where two APC vehicles were waiting. With a roar of the engine, our APC gathered speed for the run to the front line. The roof-hatch was open at this stage and the cameraman from Swedish television was filming the action. The first shell fell around two kilometres away. Good television stuff, that was. But as the shells fell closer and closer, the scene became more than merely good war footage. It was clear the Iraqis had the APC in their sights.

And their aim was improving fast. A mortar shell fell 500 metres away, but the next one exploded no more than 50 metres away. The roof-hatch was quickly closed, as the APC driver, who had seen it all before, dashed to the relative safety of a hollow in the sand. Memories of that burnt-out Iraqi APC kept coming back as we sat in the stifling heat inside the APC.

Earlier in the day, I was discussing with another reporter the relative advantages and disadvantages of a nine-to-five job in an air-conditioned office. It was a good time to bring up the subject again, and there was a consensus that a nine-to-five job had advantages.

Suicidal zeal fuels Iran war effort
From DAVID BALDERSTONE

'The Age', Teheran, September 17, 1981

The chant was familiar, but the surroundings were a bit odd. A motley group of men stood shouting: "God is great, Khomeiny is great, down with Saddam, down with America."

It was the Iranian front line near the oil refinery city of Abadan, on the disputed Shatt al-Arab waterway. The enemy troops of Iraq's President Saddam Hussein were dug in only 400 metres away. Despite the proximity of the Iraqi troops, a group of Iranian Revolutionary Guards, or Pasdars, took time off from the trenches to demonstrate their revolutionary and Islamic zeal for the group of foreign correspondents.

They were aged from 15 to 50. Some were shaven and some had beards. A few were bare-chested while others wore tee-shirts or old and grubby army shirts. They had one thing in common – they were all willing, even expecting, to become martyrs in what they see as a revolutionary and religious battle against Iraq.

The Revolutionary Guards, or Pasdaran Corps, have been an effective Iranian military weapon in the year-old Iran-Iraq war. Their almost suicidal zeal has contributed to the remarkable Iranian performance of slowly turning the war around and gradually pushing the Iraqi armed might back towards the border.

When Iraq invaded Iran a year ago, the Iraqi Government issued visas to several hundred foreign journalists. It was a clear indication that the tight-lipped Bagdad regime expected victory, and probably quickly. But victory has proved elusive for the Iraqis.

A mixture of military professionalism, Persian pride and determination, and Iranian revolutionary and Islamic fervour has contributed to Iran's ability to push the Iraqis back slowly.

On the other side of the coin, the Iraqi regime may be holding its army back in a bid to reduce casualties – and the political consequences of heavy losses. After all, although the Iraqis have been forced to retreat in most areas along the 600-kilometre battle front, they still occupy large tracts of Iranian land. And while they may not have achieved victory, they have not been defeated.

Last Sunday, the Iranian army took a group of foreign correspondents to Abadan, site of the world's largest oil refinery. From Ahvaz, we had to travel the long way around through Bandar Mahshar because the direct Ahvaz-Abadan road was in the war zone.

The Iranian cities of Abadan and Khorammshahr are on the eastern side of the Shatt al-Arab, which provides the border between the two countries in the south. The Iraqi port city of Basra is on the western side of the Shatt al-Arab, north of Khorammshahr.

When border clashes escalated into full-scale war on 22 September last year, an Iraqi armored column invaded Iran north of Khorammshahr, and after initially proceeding east swung south to encircle Khorammshahr and Abadan almost completely. The Abadan refinery and tank farm complex was badly damaged in the first days of the war, and is still burning.

We met the Revolutionary Guards at a flat, baked desert area at the front line. The monotony of the area is broken only by military earthworks which have created a maze of rock and sand ridges, which are used for cover.

Like 19th-century Englishmen spending a morning occupying ourselves in a folly in the grounds of a country mansion, we travelled around this maze of earthworks, never quite certain whether our army escorts knew the way to the cucumber sandwiches. The fear was we might be heading towards kebabs with the Iraqis instead.

Finally, we passed big posters of Ayatollah Khomeiny, and also the late President and Prime Minister of Iran, who were assassinated two weeks ago, and it was clear we were approaching the Revolutionary Guards' front line. [The Revolutionary Guards' lines are adorned with posters of members of the Iranian regime. There were no such posters in the army lines we saw during the three-day trip.]

Compared with the army bunkers further back from this front, the Revolutionary Guards' front line was a makeshift affair. While undoubtedly courageous fighters, the Guards appeared to be far less disciplined than their army colleagues.

The Revolutionary Guards were pleased to see the Western media arrive – particularly the television cameras. In a bid to make the scene more active they fired off machinegun rounds at the Iraqis dug into a parallel ridge 400 metres away. Then, a few of the Guards had an even better idea. Ignoring the protests of the reporters and a few of their own members, they moved a jeep-mounted anti-tank weapon into position and banged off a round at the Iraqis. The Guards responsible thought, it seems, that it would make better television if the Iraqis returned the fire. Luckily, they didn't.

Immediately the anti-tank weapon was fired, our army escorts rushed us to the jeeps and back to the safety of their lines.

A strong impression gained during the trip was that relations between the army and the Revolutionary Guards are at best cool. The Revolutionary Guards are very much the regime's men, and it was the regime which purged and weakened the army after the revolution.

Now, mainly due to the Iran-Iraq war, the army has re-established a strong command structure and, if the war was over, could be a power to be reckoned with in troubled Iran.

On the road to Abadan, the bus was stopped at a Revolutionary Guard checkpoint. The Iranian colonel refused to show his identification to the Revolutionary Guard on duty. He would show it only, he said, to the soldier on duty.

The soldier came aboard and the officer willingly showed his pass as the Revolutionary Guards retreated from the bus. It was symbolic of the army's widespread disdain for the Revolutionary Guards.

Divided opposition a Khomeiny asset

By DAVID BALDERSTONE, who has just returned to Amman from Iran

'The Age', Amman, September 29, 1981

Through a high-pitched crackle of radio interference, a patriotic Iranian martial tune came from the shortwave radio. Dusk was descending upon central Teheran, and a group of Iranians sat around the apartment living room listening to the "Voice of all against Khomeiny", which broadcasts from Iraq.

This and other opposition radio stations in Iraq and Egypt broadcast into Iran news about the country, statements by opposition leaders, political commentaries against Ayatollah Khomeiny's regime, and Iranian music banned in Iran since the Shah was ousted 31 months ago.

Like the now regular street clashes between opposition guerillas and the regime's Revolutionary Guards, and the wave of political assassinations of key figures in the regime, these radio stations raise expectations that the Khomeiny-led regime is about to fall.

Certainly, the regime is facing great problems. On top of the street clashes and assassinations the regime has other troubles it does not seem able to cope with – chronic economic problems, the highly political war with Iraq, and rebel activity in Kurdistan, Azerbaijan, and Baluchistan. Ayatollah Khomeiny's regime would appear to be plunging towards collapse.

But the Iranian opposition is deeply divided, and no group appears to have manoeuvred itself into a position of providing an alternative government, and seizing power.

Various Leftist groups have succeeded in causing civil disturbances on the streets, and have successfully launched a wave of political assassinations. The Right has hijacked Iranian gunboats on the high seas, and smuggled into Iran video tapes of the Shah's son declaring himself the new monarch. Rebels, some linked to the

Left and others probably aligned with the Right are stirring up trouble in Kurdistan and West Azerbaijan, two provinces in the north-west.

The imposition of ancient Islamic laws, the American hostage crisis, widespread executions and the sacking of President Bani-Sadr did not win support for the regime which, in part, rode to power by exploiting the late Shah's human rights violations.

Even in the Middle East Islamic heartland, where Ayatollah Khomeiny lives under the illusion that the majority of the people are itching for an Iran-style Islamic revolution, it is unusual to find people speaking in favor of the Islamic republic. And Iran's wavering alliances with Syria, Libya, and Algeria are far more political than ideological or religious.

The Khomeiny regime in Iran is protected by a Revolutionary Guard corps (the Pasdaran) of more than 100,000 armed men. If the street clashes developed into something akin to open civil war more than half the corps might defect and go into hiding. Some Western diplomats conservatively estimate that at least 25,000 Pasdaran would stay loyal to the regime – partly because their survival would be in jeopardy if the regime fell.

In addition to the Pasdaran, there are the Hezbollahis – self-appointed members of the so-called Party of God. These fanatics swell the crowd at regime gatherings, such as Friday prayers in Teheran, bully people allegedly not adhering to Islamic codes of dress and behaviour, and are willing participants in street clashes against the regime's opponents.

They tend to belong to the urban lower-middle class, and are widely believed to benefit from the regime's largesse.

Even after post-revolution purges, the army, air force, navy and police force include elements whose loyalty to the regime could be questioned. However the armed forces are preoccupied with the war against Iraq, and the new police chief, Colonel Hijazi, has taken steps to turn the police force into a loyal defender of the regime.

Teheran is in the eye of the gathering storm. The wave of assassinations against senior clergymen has left Teheran's avenues devoid of the mullahs, who two years ago used to proudly walk the city with a small entourage in tow. Powerful motor bikes, which used to be popular, have been banned following terror attacks and assassinations from motor cycles. Speed bumps have been installed across roads near revolutionary committee headquarters. And the Islamic Leftist guerilla group, Mujahedeen, regularly holds defiant anti-regime demonstrations at 4 or 5 pm.

But while people openly speak out about the regime, Teheran does not appear to be a city close to civil war. There is unemployment, food problems and dissatisfaction, but security is surprisingly relaxed – except around key Government buildings, such as the Parliament.

Apart from internal security and the war with Iraq, the economy is the major problem facing the regime. While the national wealth may not have filtered down to the people too well under the late Shah's regime, it would appear there is no wealth to filter down any more.

The Government originally unveiled a US$44,000 million budget for this financial year. With diminishing reserves, that was more than the Parliament's budget committee considered the country could afford, so, despite the war with Iraq, the defence budget was slashed by 36 per cent, and, despite the regime's ambition to develop Iran for Iranians, 26 per cent was cut from development spending estimates.

Even so, it appears the revised budget of US$37,000 million is too ambitious.

Although it seems unlikely that the regime can ever get its act together, there is a developing trend that may at least halt the tide of unpopularity and improve the management of the country.

The political assassinations have removed from the scene a number of politicians who could have been accused of being more interested in consolidating their power than in governing Iran.

Now the new Prime Minister Ayatollah Mahdavi Kany, is not a member of the ruling Islamic Republican Party, and is considered a "moderate' in terms of the regime. Similarly, Hojatoleslam Hashemi Rafsanjani, Speaker of the Parliament, is considered a comparatively pleasant and moderate man. Also, Ayatollah Khomeiny has appeared to have attempted recently to slow the tide of "revenge" executions of opponents of the regime.

But the biggest thing going for the regime could be the irreconcilable differences between its opponents. The Shah's last Prime Minister, Shapur Baktiar, has links with the Shah's son, but has called for the trial of former President Abolhassan Bani-Sadr, who is aligned with the exiled Mujahedeen leader Massoud Rajavi. There are other players in the opposition game, but it seems unlikely that a broadly based opposition to Ayatollah Khomeiny will develop in the near future.

So it would appear that the Khomeiny regime will bumble along for a while yet. But recent Iranian history has been full of surprises. After all, just a year before the Shah was forced to leave, President Carter proposed a champagne toast to the Shah at his Niavaran palace, North Teheran, and commented that Iran was an island of stability in the Middle East.

Regretful Ghali criticises Israelis
From DAVID BALDERSTONE in Cairo

'The Age', October 6, 1981

Boutros Ghali, Egypt's Minister of State for Foreign Affairs and the Egyptian bureaucrat most closely associated with nearly four years of Egyptian-Israeli talks, hesitated, as if wondering whether he should say what was on his mind.

He then went ahead in a tone of regret rather than bitterness, and said that he had found during the drawn-out talks that the Israeli side in general, had lacked "generosity" and "political imagination".

An academic by background, Dr Ghali was thinking back over the time since President Anwar Sadat visited Jerusalem in November 1977, a period which has produced the Egypt-Israeli peace treaty but has not resulted in agreement on Palestinian autonomy.

"I have suffered no personal frustration, because, since the first minute, I knew that this would be a long and difficult process," Dr Ghali said. "I disagreed with certain of my colleagues who had hoped the whole problem would be solved in a few months.

"I was hoping, however, that the Israelis would act with more generosity – at least to the Palestinians – and with more political imagination. Unfortunately, after four years, I find from their side neither generosity nor political imagination."

Little known outside academic circles until 1977, Dr Ghali became acting Foreign Minister just 48 hours before President Sadat visited Jerusalem. He was offered the job at this most sensitive time because the then Foreign Minister had suddenly quit in protest at President Sadat's dramatic initiative.

Boutros Ghali was born into a prominent Coptic Christian family in 1922. His grandfather, who was Prime Minister of Egypt from 1908 to 1910, had been assassinated by an Egyptian nationalist for allegedly collaborating with the British.

After graduating from Cairo University in 1946, he studied in Paris before returning to Egypt to become professor of political science at Cairo University. In the mid-fifties, he was awarded a Fulbright Fellowship and studied international law at Columbia University.

In 1963, he became head of the Academy of International Law Studies in The Hague, and in 1967 began a stint as a visiting professor at the Sorbonne. He has worked for the prominent Egyptian daily newspaper, 'Al Ahram'.

Since 1977 he has held the position of acting Foreign Minister, or Minister of State for Foreign Affairs, but has never been appointed Foreign Minister, mainly because he is not a Moslem.

Apart from President Sadat, Dr Ghali is considered to be the man in the Egyptian Government who has given the most thought to the implications of every move in the peace process, which is rejected by most Arab States.

In spite of the Egypt-Israel peace treaty, Dr Ghali acknowledges that "we are still at the beginning of the solution" to the Arab-Israeli crisis. This is not very different from the position of a growing number of Western Governments, particularly the west Europeans, who believe some new initiative will be needed unless agreement on autonomy for West Bank and Gaza Strip Palestinians is reached by April next year.

Next April, Israel is scheduled to complete its withdrawal from Sinai in line with the agreement with Egypt. However Egypt and Israel are far from agreement on the Palestinian autonomy issue, and it is widely believed that very little more can be achieved through the so-called "Camp David process", mainly because neither the Palestinians nor the other Arab parties to the dispute will participate.

To get out of this bind, the Soviet Union, which rejects the Camp David process, and Jordan have proposed that an all-party Geneva-style conference should be held.

"We never pretended to have full copyrights on the way to solve the Middle East crisis," Dr Ghali said. "We would be very happy to participate in any other kind of approach proposed by Saudi Arabia, Jordan or any country."

Dr Ghali then talks rhetorically with characteristic verve. "So you say the time is right for an international conference. We have no objection. But are the parties concerned ready to participate in this international conference? This is the question.

"Don't ask us to forget our approach, and don't say this is a bad approach before something else has been found. As long as there is no other alternative let us work on the basis of our tri-partite (Camp David) negotiations, even if the chances to reach an agreement are very limited."

Dr Ghali is surprisingly frank about his views on Jordan's failure to participate. He said that as long as the peace process remained at the "beginning of the beginning" of a solution to the Arab-Israeli crisis, he would, if he were an adviser to the Jordanian Government, advise the Jordanians "to just wait and see".

But he predicted that Jordan would participate in the process once the present approach produced "certain positive and tangible results" and began to work on the West Bank and Gaza Strip.

Looking ahead, Dr Ghali believes that a solution to the Arab-Israeli dispute could be achieved through a confederation of nations covering territory which in Ottoman times was Greater Syria. This would involve a confederation between "Lebanon, Syria, Jordan, Palestine and Israel".

But that, he stressed, was a plan for a long time in the future.

Death of a President
From DAVID BALDERSTONE

'The Age', Cairo, October 8, 1981

As troops maintained a heavy guard around Cairo's Nile-side radio and television complex and other traditional targets of coups d'état, the wheels of Egyptian Government turned – with impressive smoothness – towards appointing a leader to replace President Anwar Sadat.

But the crackle of machinegun fire, which cut Mr Sadat down at a military parade, left uncertainty echoing across Egypt, the Middle East, and the world. It could be no other way because Mr Sadat lived as dramatically as he died.

It could be no other way because Mr Sadat, who inherited a pro-Moscow Egypt from Gamal Abdul Nasser had – in 11 years as President – kicked out the Soviet Union, moved Egypt into the US camp and angered most of the Arab world by signing a peace treaty with Israel.

While fears of a major shift in Egyptian policy will persist in the West and in Israel for months, Vice-President Hosni Mubarak, who is in line to become Egypt's next President, wasted no time in pledging a continuation of Mr Sadat's controversial policies.

Reassuring as this may be, the new Egyptian leadership will inherit from Mr Sadat internal and international problems, which encouraged opponents of the regime and sowed the seeds of broadly based discontent.

Therefore, while there may be no dramatic shift in Egypt's policy over the coming months, it would be expected that the new leadership will begin to make subtle changes in a bid to placate some of Mr Sadat's critics and prevent discontent taking root.

Since Mr Sadat became President, his downfall had been predicted. Initially he was thought of as a stop-gap President. Just a year after taking office, he foiled a coup attempt. But it was his brave but controversial visit to Jerusalem in 1977 which built him into a target for assassination.

Mr Sadat's assassination came just over a month after he had carried out the biggest crackdown against alleged political opponents of his Presidency.

About 1500 people – mainly right-wing Moslem fundamentalists – were jailed during the crackdown, which Mr Sadat described as "electric shock treatment" for the nation.

He was deeply hurt by Western Press criticism of his action – especially criticism which questioned the necessity of the move. The Egyptian authorities insisted that is was necessary. There were suggestions that it would have taken place earlier, but that Mr Sadat had counselled restraint.

It is believed that Mr Mubarak told senior US officials in Washington last weekend that the Egyptian Government feared that sympathisers of Mr Sadat's arch enemy, Libya's Colonel Gaddafi, had infiltrated the armed forces. While it remains uncertain who was behind the assassination, the killing of Mr Sadat at a major military parade gives credence to the regime's fears.

Anwar Sadat was born into a large family in the Nile valley village of Meit Abou el Kom, Lower Egypt, in 1918. His father worked as a clerk in a nearby military hospital. His mother, originally from the Sudan, was illiterate.

When he was approaching the school-leaving age, the elite military academy, which had been the domain of the sons of the wealthy only, was opened to all classes. It was a move designed to strengthen the Egyptian army.

Nasser and Sadat were able to enter the academy under this reform in the mid-thirties. Nasser, Sadat, and several other members of what was to become known later as the Free Officers' Movement, graduated as second lieutenants in 1938. Nasser and Sadat, who joined the Signal Corps, were posted to Upper Egypt. Here the seeds of revolution, which were not to mature and overthrow the monarchy for another 14 years, were sown.

On 22 July 1952, the young officers put their plans to overthrow King Farouk into action. But Sadat, who had worked long for this night, nearly missed the action. "I decided to give my children a treat and I took them to an open air cinema near my home," he wrote in an earlier book.

"In the meantime, Nasser, who was summoning the conspirators himself, called for me in his famous little Austin car. He called again an hour later and finding me still out, left a note, which said quite simply: "It happens tonight. Rendezvous at Abdul Hakim's, 11 pm."

Sadat caught up with the revolution though, and was the man who announced, over Egyptian radio, King Farouk's overthrow.

The lesson of the success of the Free Officers' Movement in overthrowing the Egyptian leadership was learnt by young officers in other armies around the world. It was a lesson which may have inspired the soldiers who took part in Mr Sadat's assassination.

With most of Egypt's political and military top brass present at the military parade, which was staged to commemorate the start of the 1973 Middle East war, the plot could have been designed to wipe out the regime. It is wondered here whether the attack was to have been followed by a "Stage Two" which was shelved after the regime quickly asserted control.

Since the Egypt-Israel peace treaty was signed in March 1979 and Israel began returning Sinai to Egypt, a persistent question has been whether peace between Egypt and Israel depended on the survival of President Sadat. Israel's chief of staff, General Rafael Eitan, angered Mr Sadat by suggesting last month that it did.

The peace treaty stemmed from Mr Sadat's visit to Jerusalem in November 1977. It was his determination to push ahead – despite setbacks in the Egypt-Israel-US talks and mounting Arab criticism – that achieved the treaty and the continuing process of normalisation.

But while one man may have driven the Egyptian side to continue talking with the Israelis, the concept of peace between Egypt and Israel is widely popular in Egypt.

"You hear people complain about the food prices and the fact that the rich are getting richer and the poor poorer. But peace with Israel? People like the peace," a middle-class Egyptian said yesterday.

Nevertheless, there are problems with the continuing Egyptian-Israeli talks and Egyptian public opinion is hardly a stable commodity.

Israel is due to return to Egypt the remaining part of Sinai in April next year. Meanwhile, Egyptian-Israeli talks on autonomy for Palestinians living in the Gaza Strip and on the West Bank face great difficulties, mainly involving the degree of autonomy to be offered to the Palestinians.

The carrot of getting back the rest of Sinai in April next year would probably prove irresistible to the new Egyptian leadership.

But how much the new leadership would be prepared to fly in the face of Arab criticism and continue the autonomy talks and normalisation after that date is another question.

Certainly, the Israelis will have to play their cards much more carefully from now. The Israeli attack on the Iraqi nuclear reactor in Bagdad in June came just a week after Mr Sadat had met the Israeli Prime Minister Mr Begin, in Sinai.

The attack further damaged Mr Sadat's already tarnished image in the Arab world. Mr Begin, Egyptian officials felt, had made a fool of Mr Sadat, and this feeling was exacerbated when Israel bombed Beirut later that month.

It seems certain that the new Egyptian President, who will be struggling to establish his leadership, would lack the determination to proceed with the process of normalisation between Egypt and Israel if faced with a provocation on the scale of the Israeli attack on the Bagdad nuclear reactor.

Following Mr Sadat's death, the Arab world will make a concerted bid to draw Egypt back into the Arab fold. The major drive towards this goal seems likely to be made in the run-up to the next Arab summit meeting in Morocco next month.

While the new Egyptian leadership may be keen to re-establish relations with the other Arab States, the problem is how to achieve this without damaging what has been achieved already during the peace process. The moderate Arab States, spearheaded by Saudi Arabia and Jordan, are likely to attempt to get some formula, under which the Egyptian-Israeli peace process could be built upon rather than destroyed, adopted at the summit.

The fact that Mr Sadat has gone and a new Egyptian leadership is in power may make this a little more simple than it would otherwise have been for the Saudis – especially if they spread oil dollars around liberally.

The new Egyptian leadership is likely to place more public emphasis on domestic affairs than international relations. This could mean that the Egypt-Israel peace process will proceed in a less flamboyant manner – but proceed nevertheless.

Although Egypt has a reasonably good balance of payments position, domestic inflation is high and there is a growing disparity between rich and poor. Mass tourism and flamboyantly rich Egyptians have undermined traditional Egyptian values to a certain extent, and this angered the fundamentalist Islamic opponents of Mr Sadat.

Therefore, both on foreign and domestic affairs there are likely to be subtle changes in policy. But unless internal or exiled opponents of Mr Sadat manage to seize power in the coming months, the general course of his policies seems likely to continue – albeit discreetly.

Sadat plot linked to arrests
From DAVID BALDERSTONE

'The Age', Cairo, October 9, 1981

The brother of the apparent leader of the group which assassinated President Anwar Sadat had been arrested recently, the commander of Egypt's Republican Bodyguard, Major General Mahmoud Masri, disclosed today.

About 1500 people – mainly Right-wing Moslem fundamentalists – were arrested last month in the biggest crackdown on religious activists and political opponents of Mr Sadat's 11-year Presidency.

Although there has been some confusion about exactly how many men took part in the attack, General Masri and the Defence Minister, Abdel Halim Abu Ghazala, have disclosed that four men took part – only one of whom was a member of the regular army.

General Ghazala described the regular soldier as a "lieutenant named Khalid". General Masri said the regular soldier was "in his twenties".

"A brother of this man had been arrested in connection with recent incidents," General Masri said in an interview published in the Cairo newspaper 'Al Ahram' today.

In it General Masri said – in a statement raising serious questions about the adequacy of security at the military parade Mr Sadat was reviewing – that the soldier had arranged for the other three men to join the parade.

He said that whereas units taking part in the parade were not armed, the assassination squad had smuggled arms and explosives into their vehicle.

General Masri said that in the confusion leading to the attack, Mr Sadat – thinking the men in the group were loyal – had stood up to salute them.

A military vehicle and a motor cycle had broken down earlier in the parade so that when the vehicle carrying the assassins stopped in front of the reviewing stand it was thought that it, too, had broken down.

Three of the traitors came down from this vehicle, and President Sadat thought they would come forward to greet him, so he rose to return the salute," General Masri said.

"At this moment, the fourth man, who was still on the vehicle, opened fire and hit the President."

One of the group was killed in the attack. The other three were wounded, according to General Masri's version of events. The three had been operated on and were under interrogation.

Workmen were today continuing hasty construction of a tomb for Mr Sadat near Cairo's memorial of the Unknown Soldier. A mosque will later be built over the tomb.

Spectre of fanaticism
- DAVID BALDERSTONE

'The Age', Cairo, October 10, 1981

Faced with an increasingly angry tide of Moslem fundamentalism, the new Egyptian leadership may find it difficult to fulfil its pledge to follow President Sadat's policies.

The President-designate, Mr Hosni Mubarak, has blamed "Moslem fanatics" for Mr Sadat's assassination this week. If the new Egyptian leadership had any hope that serious trouble with Moslem fundamentalists might end with the assassination, this hope was dashed less than 48 hours later when Moslem fundamentalists clashed with police in the city of Assuit, 370 kilometres south of Cairo. The problem of Moslem fundamentalism, which has been fermenting below the surface for decades, will not die away.

Many of Mr Sadat's policies – such as decentralisation and birth control – were domestic issues of course. But the new leadership could exacerbate the Moslem fundamentalist problem if it is seen to pursue with vigour Mr Sadat's better-known policies such as the Egypt-Israel peace process and the open-door economic policy.

In view of the new leadership's pledge to continue these major policies, it may be correct to argue that the Moslem fundamentalist problem will become uncontrollable unless domestic policies succeed in increasing dramatically the standard of living of the Egyptian masses.

Otherwise, Islamic fundamentalism, which is vocal but has comparatively limited support in terms of Egypt's 41 million people, could gain support rapidly among the masses, who after all are mainly Moslem.

Compared with the Cairo of ten years ago, it is not difficult to see why fundamentalists oppose the open-door economic policy. While Mr Sadat's vision of a policy that would benefit all Egyptians may be correct in the long term, it does not escape anyone's view that the most obvious sign of this economic policy has been the construction of luxury hotels for tourists. Mass tourism on the current Egyptian scale not only highlights the disparity between rich and poor, but has subjected the ordinary Egyptian too suddenly to Western behaviour.

Although Mr Sadat cracked down heavily on Moslem fundamentalists a little over a month before he died, the record of his 11-year presidency indicates that he attempted to tread a careful line between Islamic fundamentalism and liberalism.

Within a year of coming to office in 1970, he released many political prisoners including members of the Moslem Brotherhood, which had been banned by his predecessor, President Nasser, in 1953.

Also, while continuing the ban on the Moslem Brotherhood, he encouraged the formation of Islamic societies – partly to try to counter the spread of Marxism.

At the same time, Mr Sadat, who was a devout Moslem and wrote that he had contacts with the Moslem Brotherhood in the 1940s, encouraged secular government and turned the rudder of Egypt towards the West.

In 1977 he cracked down on a fanatical Moslem group which sought to establish Islamic Government by force. Shortly afterward, his Government proposed laws (which in the end were not introduced) to placate Moslem fundamentalists. These laws would have made conversion from Islam a capital offence.

Last month about 1500 people – mainly Moslem fundamentalists – were arrested in the biggest crackdown of Mr Sadat's presidency. This action seems to have been due mainly to fears that the Moslem fundamentalists would unite with "Leftists" in an attempt to overthrow the regime.

Although many known Moslem extremist leaders remain in jail, the assassination and the problems in Assuit indicate that Egypt's new leadership will have to tread a careful course in a bid not to exacerbate the spectre of Moslem fundamentalism.

Anthony wooed on Sinai force
From DAVID BALDERSTONE, 'Age' Middle East correspondent

Cairo, October 12, 1981

Egypt has moved to keep alive Australia's interest in joining the Sinai peace keeping force. In a meeting with the Deputy Prime Minister, Mr Anthony at the weekend, Egypt's Foreign Minister, Mr Kamel Hassan Ali, gave assurances of Egypt's continued stability following President Sadat's assassination.

The Egyptian Minister sought the 30-minute meeting before Mr Antony's departure, to assure him that the leadership transition was taking place smoothly and that Mr Sadat's policies, especially the peace process with Israel, would continue.

The Egyptian Foreign minister was aware of reports that the chances of Australian participation in the Sinai force may have been further dimmed by the assassination.

Egypt is keen for Australia to join the multi-national force to police the Sinai after Israel completes its withdrawal from the area next April. The Government points out repeatedly that the force will police only the Israeli-Egypt border area and will not be linked to the United States rapid deployment force.

Mr Anthony met Mr Kamel Hassan Ali at the Heliopolis Sheraton after attending President Sadat's funeral It is understood that the Sinai force was not specifically discussed. Diplomats in Cairo point out that it would have been inappropriate for the Egyptian Minister to have raised a specific topic such as Australian participation in the force or bilateral trade just a few hours after Mr Sadat's funeral.

The Cairo daily 'Al Gomhuria', reported today that Mr Kamel Hassan Ali had discussed with Mr Anthony the "consolidation of bilateral relations between Egypt and Australia in all fields".

President Sadat's funeral was a sad and silent affair. Because of the security surrounding the world leaders present, ordinary Egyptians were kept away.

They had to watch the ceremony on television. The millions who had greeted Anwar Sadat when he drove through Cairo on return from Jerusalem in November 1977 were allowed no part in the funeral.

Nevertheless, white-uniformed paramilitary police – practised in restraining crowds – formed a human chain along the kilometre route of the funeral procession. The usual reporters' task of estimating the crowd on such occasions was made easy. There was no crowd.

In fact, the bugbear of security robbed the funeral of emotion. It was only when the late president's widow, Jihan Sadat, wiped tears from behind her dark glasses as the coffin was being lowered into its temporary grave that the tragedy of the occasion surfaced.

The body of Egypt's President for 11 years had been escorted by cavalrymen, military officers and dignitaries, and Egyptian officials to the temporary grave on the eastern outskirts of Cairo. The funeral began with prayers in the mosque at the Maadi military hospital, south of Cairo, where Mr Sadat died after being shot last Tuesday.

Sadat death opens new path to peace
From DAVID BALDERSTONE in Amman

'The Age', October 23, 1981

Just two weeks since President Anwar Sadat was assassinated, moves that could remove the roadblock on the path to overall Middle East peace appear to be under way.

It will be a tortuous path. But the Soviet Union's decision to grant to the PLO full diplomatic status, coupled with moves by moderate Arab States, could lead to a broadening of the Middle East peace process once Israel completes its withdrawal from Sinai in April.

The fact that the Soviet announcement on relations with the PLO quoted Mr Yasser Arafat as saying he backed the Soviet plan for an all-party Middle East peace conference, seems to underline the point that the upgrading of relations was not done to further polarise the Middle East but to get Moscow back into the peace process.

And, to achieve its long sought goal of getting back into the peace process, it could be argued that Moscow would have an interest in getting Mr Arafat's PLO to recognise conditionally Israel's right to exist, which is also the aim of the EEC countries.

Since President Sadat was assassinated, moderate Arab States – spearheaded by Saudi Arabia and Jordan – have moved fast to try to achieve some kind of Arab consensus on joint action which would gradually end the boycott on Egypt and build upon the Egypt-Israel peace treaty.

Egypt's new leadership seems to share this objective. Although Egypt's President Hosni Mubarak has pledged to continue the peace process with Israel, he has declared that there will be a halt to Egyptian verbal attacks on other Arab countries – even those countries most hostile to the Egypt-Israel peace treaty.

In spite of the tragedy surrounding Mr Sadat's death, his assassination removed an emotive figure. For the US

Administration Mr Sadat's death means a major pillar of their Middle East policy has fallen. For Israel, it raised fears again that Egyptian-Israeli peace depended on one man.

For the moderate Arab States, it created opportunities which had not existed while Mr Sadat was alive. It created the opportunity to build upon what had been achieved in the Egyptian-Israeli peace process without being associated with Mr Sadat.

"The assassination has removed the Arab objection to the image of the man who went to Jerusalem and signed the accords with Israel," a senior Jordanian official told me this week. "It has created new options, and the chance of renewed relations between Egypt and the Arabs." In other words, a new era had begun.

Most of the Arab world objected to the old era – the era of the Camp David accords and the Egypt-Israel peace treaty – because it neutralised Egypt's political and military muscle from the Middle East equation without achieving a major move towards a solution of the Palestinian problem, which is the crux of the Middle East crisis.

Some of the more hardline Arab States hope that Israel will not fulfil its commitment to withdraw from the rest of Sinai in April, and, therefore, undermine the whole Egypt-Israel peace process. Most Arab bureaucrats – including some in hardline States – concede that the Israelis will complete the withdrawal. Therefore most Arabs believe the Egypt-Israel peace treaty is a fact of life which should be built upon, not destroyed.

In August, Saudi Arabia's Crown Prince Fahd unveiled an eight-point peace plan, which implied recognition of Israel's right to exist by stating that: "all States in the region should be able to live in peace". Crown Prince Fahd's plan also said Israel should withdraw from all territory occupied during the 1967 Six Day War, and said that an independent Palestinian State should be set up with (Arab East) Jerusalem as its capital.

As it stands, the Saudi plan is unacceptable to the Israelis as well as the Syrians and Libyans. Israel's Prime Minister, Mr Begin, has said "no" to total withdrawal to 1967 borders, "no" to the establishment of a Palestinian State and "no" to the division of

Jerusalem, which was unified after the Israelis stormed East Jerusalem during the 1967 war.

And, again, as it stands at present, the Israelis will not have to budge from those three objections. This is mainly because the PLO has not publicly recognised Israel's right to exist so that Israel refuses to deal with the organisation, which it says pledges its destruction.

Britain's Lord Carrington, who is president of the European Council of Ministers, has talked – since Mr Sadat's death – of the need for the PLO to recognise conditionally Israel's right to exist.

The EEC Venice summit declaration issued last year said the PLO must be "associated" with the peace process. Former US Presidents Gerald Ford and Jimmy Carter said after attending Mr Sadat's funeral that the PLO would have to be involved in the Middle East peace process if a solution was to be achieved.

Early next month, King Hussein of Jordan will visit President Reagan in Washington. It is reliably believed that his main message will be that Washington must talk with the PLO if the process towards peace is to progress, and that the Arabs do not share the US Administration's view that the main risk to instability in the Middle East is Soviet expansionism. Instead the king is likely to tell Mr Reagan that the Arabs believe that the main risk is the failure of the US to address itself to a solution of the Palestinian problem.

But it is the Soviet move in upgrading the PLO's status in Moscow that is really interesting. If it wants to be involved again in the Middle East peace process, the Soviet Union would probably be realistic enough to believe that the PLO should conditionally recognise Israel's right to exist.

Moscow has the power to persuade the PLO leadership to go out on a limb and conditionally recognise Israel's right to exist. More than anything else, it has the power to minimise hardline Palestinian opposition to such a move.

Similarly, it has the influence to make Syria – with whom it has a friendship treaty – toe the line.

Parliament vote shows split in Iran leadership
From DAVID BALDERSTONE

'The Age', Amman, October 24, 1981

The members of Iran's Parliament, in an unexpected move this week, appear to have demonstrated that there are major divisions even within the ruling elite in Iran – about the style of government needed in the current difficulties.

This indication surfaced yesterday when the Majlis, or Parliament, rejected the nomination of a hardline Islamic fundamentalist for the post of Iran's new Prime Minister.

Dr Ali Akhbar Vellayati, who is American educated, had been nominated for the post of Prime Minister by Iran's new president, Hojatoleslam Khamenei. However the Parliament voted 80 to 74 against Dr Vellayati's nomination. Thirty-eight members of the Majlis abstained, according to the official Pars newsagency.

Dr Vellayati is a hardline fundamentalist and should have been expected to win approval as Prime Minister from the Parliament which is dominated by members of the fundamentalist Islamic Republican Party. This is especially so because he was nominated by President Khamenei, who is head of the IRP.

The Majlis' vote appeared to indicate there is still a power struggle going on in Iran between hardline fundamentalists and "moderates" in the Iranian hierarchy.

However, more interesting than this is the fact that the vote indicates that members of Parliament, who were previously staunch supporters of the IRP, may be drifting away from a position of loyally supporting the party line.

When Iran's first post-revolution president, Dr Abolhassan Bani-Sadr was sacked by Ayatollah Khomeiny in June, it appeared that the so-called fundamentalist politicians had won victory over the "moderates" or "liberals" in Iran's internal power struggle.

However, the sacking of Dr Bani-Sadr unleashed internal unrest within the country. Guerillas belonging to the Islamic Leftist organisation, Mujahedeen Khalq demonstrated on the streets. Then a massive explosion wrecked the headquarters of the IRP and killed the party head, Ayatollah Beheshti, and 71 other party politicians.

This explosion was followed by another blast early in September which killed the Prime Minister and the man who had succeeded Dr Bani-Sadr, President Mohammed Ali Rajai.

Initially a presidential council headed by the Majlis' Speaker, Hojatoleslam Rafsanjani, took over the role of the President. The council appointed a long-time friend of Ayatollah Khomeiny, Ayatollah Mohammed Reza Mahdavi-Kany to fill the post of Prime Minister.

Subsequently, Hojatoleslam Khamenei was elected Iran's new President, and last week Mr Mahdavi-Kany resigned amidst criticism that he was too moderate to hold the post in such difficult circumstances. Mr Mahdavi-Kany was not a member of the IRP.

This week's vote by the Majlis indicates that a majority of members may believe that Iran needs a moderate to head the Government at present.

A lot of criticism can be levelled at Iran's Majlis. But the members come from different parts of the country, and are people who would be in touch with rampant dissatisfaction within the community.

It can be assumed that they would hear criticism of the high number of executions (particularly of Mujahedeen Khalq members), and the economic and unemployment problems throughout the country.

In Bonn, the West German Justice Minister, Mr Juergen Schmude decried the spate of executions in Iran.

AAP-Reuter reports that Mr Schmude told members of the United Nations Human Rights Committee meeting: "The unbroken chain of execution oppresses us.

"That parents are even asked to denounce their children and that minors are executed is a terrible offence against the spirit and letter of the human rights agreement."

Ayatollah Khomeiny said in a recent broadcast that it was a religious duty for parents to denounce their children to the authorities if they were involved in anti-Government violence.

Saudis arm PLO, Iraq, says Israel
From DAVID BALDERSTONE

'The Age', Jerusalem, November 10, 1981

Israel's Defence Minister, Mr Sharon, yesterday alleged that Saudi Arabia was transferring American-made weapons to Iraq and had become one of the main sources of weapons for Palestinian guerillas based in Lebanon.

He said Saudi Arabia, which he described as the "most corrupted regime in the near East", was becoming a "military factor" in the Middle East.

Mr Sharon said Israel had passed to the United States information about the transfer of American-made arms from Saudi Arabia to Iraq. However, he indicated that he believed the US was already aware of the transfer of arms.

Mr Sharon, who was giving his first Press conference for foreign journalists since his appointment as Minister after Israel's 30 June election, said Saudi Arabia's supply of weapons to Iraq and the Palestinians was "a beginning – a dangerous beginning."

Mr Sharon's allegations against Saudi Arabia appeared to be designed to discredit the kingdom at a time when Saudi Arabia's eight-point Middle East peace plan, which Israel rejects, is being conditionally welcomed in Western Europe and by some US politicians.

Conflicting statements by the US Administration had made it "very hard" for Israel to know what the US policy was at the present time, he said.

"Voices we hear from Washington and Europe do not encourage us. They make us think we must be much more careful."

Mr Sharon's comments followed a statement by Israel's Foreign Minister, Mr Shamir, that Israel might be forced to "reassess its attitude" towards the peace process because of the West's failure to appreciate Israel's concessions and its misguided reliance on Saudi Arabia.

However, Mr Sharon said Israel intended to abide by the Camp David Accords and the Egypt-Israel Peace Treaty. It would complete its withdrawal from Sinai on schedule next April, and still hoped that Egypt and Israel would sign an agreement on autonomy for West Bank and Gaza Strip Palestinians by that date.

The Camp David Accords were the only chance of peace, Mr Sharon said.

Israel disputes the widely held view that the Saudi peace plan implies recognition of Israel's right to exist. Israel is concerned about the plan because it calls for the establishment of a Palestinian State and calls for the right of Palestinians to return to their homes within Israel proper (not just the occupied territories).

Israeli leaders are furious that Britain's Foreign Secretary, Lord Carrington has welcomed parts of the Saudi plan. Israel has reacted by stating that it might reject Britain's participation in the multi-national force which will police the Egypt-Israel border after Israel completes its withdrawal from the area next April.

Mr Sharon said that if EEC countries continued to "stick" to the community's Venice Declaration, which said the Palestine Liberation Organisation should be "associated" with the Middle East peace process, or supported the Saudi plan, then they would not be accepted in the multi-national force.

He said Saudi Arabia was the main source of PLO income and "becoming" one of the main sources of PLO arms.

The only target of these weapons was Israel, he said. "We will treat Saudi Arabia exactly as we will treat any confrontation State."

In printed material released by Mr Sharon after the Press conference, it was alleged that Saudi Arabia had "mediated" the supply of US-made 105 and 155 mm artillery guns for Iraq.

On the subject of Lebanon, Mr Sharon alleged that the PLO had violated the ceasefire in Lebanon 21 times since the ceasefire came into force in July.

He also expressed concern about the continued presence of Syrian surface-to-air missiles in Lebanon's Beka'a Valley.

He said he hoped the situation in Lebanon and between groups in Lebanon and Israel could be solved politically. But, he warned, if a political solution was not found, "Israel would have to act".

Sinai 1982: Will the Diggers be back?
DAVID BALDERSTONE of 'The Age' reports from Jerusalem

'The Age', November 14, 1981

The sparsely vegetated desert ridges, which only an hour ago had looked golden, were turning grey as dusk descended. On the outskirts of Rafa, the light sea breeze tickled the leaves of the gum trees, which draw life out of the harsh Sinai Desert where Australian soldiers have served and died during the past 65 years.

The bright sun had gone, but the Rafa town lights had not come on. So the ugliness of the shoddy concrete houses and Seven Up and Pepsi advertisements was not obvious. Instead, there was something of a timeless quality about the place as brightly dressed Bedouin women pushed their goats and sheep slowly back to the town at the end of another day.

A donkey cart carrying an Arab couple and their three children clip-clopped along the road. But it was the distant sound of the pounding hooves of a cantering horse which turned the clock back from 1981 to 1917.

At dusk on 9 January, 1917, Australian Light Horsemen helped capture Rafa from the Turks. The soldiers had ridden all the previous night; the horses were without water. Victory came at nightfall after a series of long, sustained charges with fixed bayonets in the face of Turkish riflemen and German machine-gunners. "Rafa was a grim, deadly fight, waged up to the moment when our exhausted, but still excited troopers jumped down on the Turks in their trenches," H S Gullett wrote in 'Australia in Palestine', published in 1919.

Sixty-five years later, members of the Australian armed forces may be going back to Rafa as members of the 2500-strong multi-national Sinai peace force. When Israel returns the rest of Sinai to Egypt next April, the Egypt-Israel border will run through the southern outskirts of Rafa, just inland from the Mediterranean coast.

Egypt and Israel want Australia to participate in the force, which will police the border area after Israel completes its withdrawal in line with the peace treaty. For Egypt and Israel Australia is a trusted, friendly country.

It is easy for a Government to say that a country is "trusted and friendly". Far more important is the fact that Egyptians, Palestinians and Israelis remember Australian troops this way as well.

Perhaps it all began in that bleak January of 1917: "The spirit of mercy which has distinguished so many Australian fights was shown here (Rafa) at is best," Gullett wrote. "The Turks, who had shot at our men mercilessly and effectively until they charged home into the very trenches, then dropped their rifles and held out their hands – to have them warmly shaken by the Australians."

Gullett notes that the night march from Al Arish, which is described today as the capital of Sinai, to the outskirts of Rafa, had taken the Australians from the desert to the "fringe of Palestine". "Travelling all night through the heavy sand, they came just before dawn, on sounder going for their horses, and daylight showed them a wide, rolling landscape gay with brilliant winter flowers – the fringe of Palestine."

At 1 pm on 25 April next year, Israel is scheduled to have completed its withdrawal from Sinai. Then Rafa will mark the "fringe" or border between Egyptian Sinai and the Gaza Strip territory, which Israel will continue to occupy.

At that time, the multi-national peace force will begin policing the border. The force will maintain checkpoints and observation posts, and conduct reconnaissance patrols to make certain Egypt and Israel observe the provisions of the peace treaty and the Camp David accords, which ended 30 years of hostilities between the two countries.

Also, part of the multi-national force will be stationed at Sharm el-Sheikh at the entrance to the Gulf of Aqaba to ensure freedom of navigation through the Strait of Tiran. Israel has bitter memories of the run-up to the 1967 Middle East war, when Egypt's President

Nasser blockaded the strait and prevented ships sailing up the Gulf of Aqaba to Israel's southern port, Eilat.

On 22 October the Australian Prime Minister, Mr Fraser, announced that Australia would participate in the multi-national force if Britain and Canada also contributed troops. Since then, he has indicated that the Government might drop the condition of Canada's participation.

Early this week it looked increasingly doubtful that Britain would take part after Israel's Prime Minister, Mr Begin, threatened to reject British participation. Mr Begin's threat followed a statement by Britain's Foreign Secretary, Lord Carrington, that if Britain took part it would be on the basis only of "seeing the return of Arab territory to the Arabs".

Israel made the point that the multi-national force would assume its duties after Israel has completed its withdrawal from Sinai and would play no part in supervising Israel's withdrawal.

However, as the week progressed, diplomats in Washington, Cairo, Jerusalem and London worked to resolve differences between Britain and Israel. The pendulum began to swing back towards likely British participation.

In turn, therefore, Australian participation looks likely. Mr Fraser said on 22 October that the Australian contribution under consideration "comprises elements of an air transport unit, equipped with helicopters and fixed-wing aircraft, and probably involving some 200-300 personnel". It is thought in the Middle East that the Australians would be based in the Rafa area – probably at a nearby abandoned Israeli airbase.

The multi-national force is necessary mainly because of Israeli nervousness about returning Sinai, which it occupied in 1967, to Egypt. This withdrawal, which is more than half completed already, is the third time Israel has pulled back from Sinai. In 1949, Israel withdrew from a small area which it had occupied during the "war of independence". In March 1957, United States and United Nations pressure forced Israel to withdraw again from Sinai, which it had occupied the previous year during the Suez crisis.

In return for peace with Egypt, Israel is giving up the strategic depth of Sinai, four air bases, the Abu Rudeis and Alma oilfields on the Gulf of Suez, and a number of Israeli settlements and tourist resorts.

Although the Israeli Government repeated this week that it is firmly committed to withdrawing from Sinai on schedule next April, a substantial section of the Israeli community is nervous about the move and a smaller group is flatly opposed to returning Sinai to Egypt. This group includes ultra-nationalists, who see Sinai as part of historic Israel, and Israeli settlers, who have struggled to build a home in the area since 1967.

Driving south from Rafa along the road to Al Arish, palm trees and gum trees, which were imported from Australia after World War I, gradually give way to desert scrub and sand dunes. About 11 kilometres from Rafa, a turn-off to the right leads to one of the Jewish settlements. Called Yamit, it is a well-established town of concrete and stone, built behind a palm grove on the edge of the blue Mediterranean.

Some of the 500 families who lived in Yamit have already left. Others intend staying on – some in the desperate hope that even at this late stage Israel will not complete its withdrawal.

Three weeks ago, 23 ultra-nationalistic families moved into the Yamit motel as a protest at the withdrawal. They intend to stay until the Israeli army comes to evict them. The motel was being considered as the initial headquarters of the peace force.

Nechama Hershkovitz and her husband moved their family into the motel three weeks ago. Originally an immigrant to Israel from the United States, Mrs Hershkovitz lived in Rehovot, near Tel Aviv, previously.

"We paid for the first two weeks and then they decided to close the motel," Nechama Hershkovitz said. "We are against returning Yamit to the Egyptians and feel that if it is full of people it will be harder to do so. Some of the people here are members of nationalistic groups. Others just don't want to give back territories. There are people of both the major political parties here.

"A lot of people are here because they are against giving back any part of Israel, although we feel peace with Egypt is very important." She seemed to question whether the peace would last. "We just think that giving back Yamit means that the next war will start closer to the centre of Israel.

"It is not the first time we have given back this land. All our husbands are in the reserve, and they don't want to fight for this land over and over again."

Nechama Hershkovitz said she did not expect violence when the Israeli authorities finally came to evacuate Yamit. "It is a peaceful protest. Nobody is thinking of fighting at all. I'm not saying people will just walk out, but people will not use any weapons."

Between the town of Yamit, which is adorned with Israeli flags, and the sea shore, a small Arab village is built among the palm trees. Two small fish restaurants stand on the edge of the 200-metre wide beach of golden sand. Bright blue rollers were pounding the beach as a few Israelis enjoyed one of their last chances to swim at Yamit before the withdrawal.

Inland from the town is the agricultural settlement of Sadot. Here the Israelis have made the desert bloom. With the help of drip irrigation, tomatoes and melons were growing out of the sand around the town, which houses 70 families.

"When we came here it was desert," commented Yousi Mass, who is a leading member of the Stop Sinai Withdrawal campaign. "With my friends, I made this settlement what it is and I think it is a disaster for all the settlements of Israel when the government destroys settlements.

"We think that if peace depends upon this Yamit area, which makes up only 1 per cent of Sinai, it is not peace. We don't argue with the Egyptians. We argue with the Israeli Government."

Mr Mass said Sadot and Yamit had been built by Israel as a barrier against Palestinian guerilla infiltration into the Gaza Strip, which has been the home of Palestinian refugees since Israel's creation. The Stop Sinai Withdrawal campaign was against the

Camp David peace process. "We say that the withdrawal should be stopped so that a reassessment can be made," he said.

Mr Mass said the situation in the Middle East had changed since Sadat visited Jerusalem in 1977. The Shah had been deposed in Iran, the Soviet Union had invaded Afghanistan, the Gulf war had erupted, and Sadat had been assassinated.

He admitted that on the day of Sadat's murder the people of Sadot thought that withdrawal might be stopped. "We thought that Sadat's death might stop the withdrawal, and maybe it still will. Look, Sadat's death was a tragedy but if it stops the withdrawal… We are happy to stop the withdrawal."

But with Egypt's new President Hosni Mubarak, pledging to continue the peace process with Israel, that does not look likely.

Australian troops fought in the Sinai area during both world wars. From 1976 to 1979, the RAAF had a contingent stationed in Ismailia on the Suez Canal as part of the United Nations emergency force, which observed the Egypt-Israel disengagement agreements.

Some of the Australian soldiers who died during both world wars are buried in the Commonwealth war cemetery at Gaza, north of Rafa. The cemetery is an island of peace on the outskirts of squalid, bustling Gaza. Opposite the Seven Up bottling plant, a narrow avenue of Cyprus pines leads to the cemetery which has more than 3000 Commonwealth graves.

The head gardener, Ibrahim Rabie Jaradeh, 43, has worked at the cemetery for 23 years. We sat down to tea in his living room. The wall is adorned with two colourful Australian tea towels on which "Greetings from Hargraves, NSW" is written. One shows outback scenes, and the other depicts a map of Australia and a kangaroo.

"The people of Gaza like the Australians," Ibrahim said, apologising for his English. "They knew him from the 1940s. They knew him and they like him very well. All the people of Gaza like the Australians because all of them are kind."

He then talks about his work of which he is justifiably proud. "The human is the human. If he does good, he finds good. If he does bad, he finds bad."

I asked Ibrahim what he thought about the fact Israel will continue to occupy the Gaza Strip after it withdraws from Sinai next April. "This problem is bigger than my head. The whole world is involved," he said.

Ibrahim leads the way to the cemetery nursery, where he has winter seedlings thriving. On the way, he draws attention to the graves of 22 Canadians, who died while peace-keeping in Sinai in the 1960s. They had not died during hostilities, but the graves still provide a lesson that peace forces suffer casualties.

Ibrahim pointed up at a Jacaranda tree, and then observed that Palestine was like Australia. "There is much desert and much green. Australia is beautiful, I am told."

His mind then drifted back to the multi-national peace force. "I heard that some people from Australia might come. We like them visiting Gaza. I hope they come."

On 23 August, a group of Israeli soldiers visited the war cemetery. "The garden is very beautiful and take caring good. But life is better," they wrote in the visitors' book. A few weeks later some other Israelis visited the cemetery. Their English was more fluent. "The garden is very beautiful, but life is better," they wrote.

Summit failure lifts tension in Mideast
From DAVID BALDERSTONE

'The Age', Fez, Morocco, November 26, 1981

Arab leaders left here today after their aborted summit meeting giving no indication that the serious differences over Saudi Arabia's Middle East peace plan could be resolved quickly.

The summit meeting broke up late yesterday, less than five hours after the official opening while the delegations were discussing the eight-point Middle East peace plan unveiled by Crown Prince Fahd in August.

The host and conference chairman, King Hassan of Morocco, warned that the failure of the talks left a "very serious and very gave" situation in the Middle East. There would be wide-ranging repercussions in the area because of the breakdown of the summit, he said.

The summit's failure leaves the Arab world as divided as it ever has been. It is likely to leave for a long time bitter wounds and divisions between the moderates led by Saudi Arabia, and hardliners, including Libya and Syria.

There is already speculation that these divisions could erupt into violence in Lebanon, which unwillingly hosts militia representing most factions in the Arab world.

It also places a question mark over Saudi Arabia's willingness to continue to support financially Syria and Libya.

The summit broke up when Crown Prince Fahd, who had listened with irritation to criticism during the debate on the Saudi peace plan, declared abruptly: "I don't want any more of this nonsense."

Officials said that immediately delegates stood up and began leaving the conference room.

King Hassan later announced formally that the conference had been indefinitely postponed.

In what appeared to be a limp, face-saving device aimed at making the best of the fiasco, the king added that a follow-up committee would study ways of resolving differences over the peace plan.

Despite this, Arab observers here believe there is little prospect of resolving the differences in the near future.

Although the Saudi peace plan implies recognition of Israel's right to exist, it calls for Israeli withdrawal from all Arab territories occupied in 1967 and for the establishment of a Palestinian State with East Jerusalem as its capital.

A last-minute development which led to the failure of the summit was the announcement that Syria's President Hafez Assad would not attend.

President Assad has strongly criticised the Saudi plan, but has left the door open to enable Syrian reconsideration of it.

Some Arab observers here believe that the summit's failure indicates that the hardline Arab States still hold the upper hand in Arab world politics. "It proves that despite Saudi oil wealth President Assad is still more important than Crown Prince Fahd when it comes to the question of the Arab-Israeli dispute," an Arab journalist said.

Ever since Crown Prince Fahd unveiled the peace plan in August, it has drawn differing reactions from the Arab world.

While the Palestine Liberation Organisation leader, Mr Yasser Arafat, has expressed support for the plan, other elements in the PLO have rejected it. Libya and Iraq have rejected it also.

The summit began with a colourful opening ceremony in a royal place near Fez.

Throughout the opening ceremony Mr Arafat looked pensive, rocking gently on his leather swivel chair.

Some observers believe he has a lot to look pensive about. Some go as far as to say that he has put his job on the line supporting the Saudi plan – especially as Arab hardliners have now succeeded in stymying the plan.

Before the summit finally broke up the Saudi delegation made it clear they would accept no compromise on the plan. It is understood the Saudi delegation felt that if they allowed it to be watered down so that consensus could be achieved, it would lose all meaning.

It is believed the Saudi delegation was extremely disappointed about the failure of the summit.

They paid for the staging of the summit and in return asked the Moroccans to ban sales of alcohol in the Fez district during the summit.

Middle East Encounters 511

Ill. 14. Fez, Morocco, November 1981

Long distance battle for Iran
From DAVID BALDERSTONE in Paris

'The Age', December 15, 1981

In one of the grand apartment buildings lining the Boulevard Raspail, near the centre of Paris, the battle for Iran is being fought.

Former Prime Minister Shapur Baktiar's National Resistance Movement is one of several Iranian opposition groups operating from Paris. The other main group is a coalition led by Iran's first post-revolution President, Abolhassan Bani-Sadr, and Mr Massoud Rajavi, the leader of the Islamic Leftist guerilla group, Mujahedeen Khalq. But there is no collaboration between Dr Bani-Sadr and Dr Baktiar, who was the Shah's last Prime Minister.

Dressed in a grey suit and a dark brown tie, lawyer Arfa Zadeh, a founder of Dr Baktiar's National Resistance Movement and a council member of the exiled Iranian National Front, talked about the movement's hopes for the future of Iran. However, with refreshing realism, he suggested that the time was not yet ripe for an uprising against Ayatollah Khomeiny's regime.

"We don't think that if Khomeiny dies this Government will fail," Mr Zadeh said. "It has become a system. If the present Government falls before the appropriate time, it will keep its roots. But if we wait it will show its total incompetence, and will facilitate its own fall without keeping any roots."

Dr Baktiar's National Resistance Movement aims to establish democracy in Iran one day. Mr Zadeh said some elements in the movement favored a republican system for Iran, whereas others favored a constitutional monarchy. However, they were united in believing that democratically elected representatives must decide the form of Government.

Mr Zadeh claimed that Dr Baktiar and the movement had the greatest support and influence within Iran of any of the opposition groups. While it is difficult to prove the accuracy of this claim, I have found – during 10 visits to Iran since the revolution – rapidly increasing support for Dr Baktiar within the country.

With widespread disenchantment with Ayatollah Khomeiny's Islamic Government, Iranians inside Iran seem to have reappraised Dr Baktiar, the man who persuaded the Shah to leave Iran "on holiday".

Although he was Prime Minister for little more than a month before Ayatollah Khomeiny took firm control of Iran in February, 1979, Dr Baktiar had in that short time engineered the Shah's departure, ordered the release of political prisoners and the dismantlement of the dreaded secret police organisation, Savak.

"Many Iranian intellectuals have another view about Dr Baktiar now," Mr Zadeh said. "They have found out that he was right and they were wrong about Khomeiny."

However, it is one thing to identify the fact that the Khomeiny regime has dwindling support, and quite another to speculate about its downfall. The Khomeiny regime is protected by a Revolutionary Guard corps (the Pasdaran) of up to 100,000 men. If street clashes developed into something akin to open civil war, more than half the corps might defect and go into hiding. However, Western diplomats conservatively estimate that at least 25,000 Pasdaran would stay loyal to the regime – partly because their survival would be in jeopardy if the regime fell.

Mr Zadeh was vague about how exactly the National Resistance Movement believed a changeover in power in Iran would happen: "There are many ways…..we can't talk about it."

But then he was a little more forthcoming. He said there would be a simultaneous uprising within Iran and outside Iran. He claimed contacts had already been established with tribal leaders, representatives of ethnic groups, and some military officers.

A few prominent Islamic clergymen, who were disenchanted with the Khomeiny regime, would play an important part.

Mr Zadeh said a provisional Government would rule Iran for a limited period during which parliamentary elections would be held under the provisions of the 1906 constitution, which was based on Belgium's constitution. It envisages a constitutional monarchy.

Mr Zadeh said the 1906 constitution, with the exception of the five articles dealing with the monarchy, would be used during the period of provisional Government. It would be up to the new Parliament to draft a new constitution and make a decision about whether the country should be a republic or a constitutional monarchy.

Mr Zadeh was very firm on the idea that the Parliament or the people directly should decide whether the country should be a republic or a constitutional monarchy. This appears to be the National Resistance Movement's main difference with the other opposition groups in exile, who have firm stands on the system of Government.

Mr Zadeh did not have too much to say in praise of other Iranian opposition figures in exile. Dr Bani-Sadr was an "opportunist"; Mr Rajavi, the Mujahedeen leader, would take Iran into the Soviet camp; the Shah's twin sister, Princess Ashraf, who he called "Mrs Ashraf", was "corrupt".

Mr Zadeh confirmed that Dr Baktiar had been in contact with the Shah's son, Crown Prince Reza, who lives in Cairo and who has declared himself the new Shah. Mr Zadeh said he did not consider the prince the Shah because the Shah would have to be approved by Parliament.

"The people must make their decision again." There could not be a monarch unless the people decided they wanted one. "We cannot close our eyes and pretend that nothing has happened in Iran."

Mr Zadeh was jailed five times during the Shah's reign. He was forced into exile by the Khomeiny regime. He, like so many others, continues the fight for Iran. Asked about his apparent lack of security, he shrugged and commented: "We can only die once."

Golan move puts peace in danger
From DAVID BALDERSTONE in Amman

'The Age', December 16, 1981

The decision of Israel's Government effectively to annex the Golan Heights provides new Egyptian President, Mr Mubarak, with the first major test of his ability to continue Egyptian-Israeli normalisation under Israeli provocation.

The decision of the Begin Government was made on the very day that the first official Egyptian delegation to visit the Israeli-occupied Golan Heights was touring the heights.

That timing by the Israeli Government was reminiscent of the timing of Israel's June bombing raid on Iraq's nuclear reactor, which came just a few days after the Israeli Prime Minister, Mr Begin, had held a summit meeting with President Sadat in Sinai.

The attack further damaged Mr Sadat's already tarnished image in the Arab world. Mr Begin, Egyptian officials felt, had made a fool of Mr Sadat, and that feeling was exacerbated when Israel bombed Beirut later in June.

Just a few hours before the Israeli Cabinet's decision was announced, the leader of the Egyptian tourism delegation visiting the heights was quoted by Israel radio as saying there was nothing political about the visit. It is extremely doubtful that he thought that way later in the day.

It is not suggested that the Begin Government deliberately set out to embarrass the Egyptians as there are other reasons why the Government might take such a decision at this time.

But, undeniably, it illustrates how insensitive the Israeli Government is to the feelings of the new Egyptian regime at a time when the Egyptian-Israeli peace process is a very tender seedling. In short, it was an undiplomatic and unfriendly gesture.

Israel occupied Syria's Golan Heights during the Six Day War of 1967. Israel's argument that the heights, which look down over the Sea of Galilee, are strategically important to Israel cannot be dismissed. However, for 14 years, Israel has occupied the heights without feeling the need to annex the area.

Along with the Golan Heights, Israel occupied East Jerusalem and the West Bank (previously held by Jordan), and the Gaza Strip and Sinai (previously held by Egypt) during the 1967 war.

The only part of these occupied territories previously annexed by Israel was East Jerusalem, which Israel considered part of its indivisible capital. Israel's annexation of East Jerusalem has not been recognised by any other country. The Israeli Government's decision effectively to annex the Golan Heights seems also unlikely to be recognised by any other country.

Commentators in Israel have speculated that Mr Begin, who left hospital just before the special Cabinet meeting, may have decided to annex the Golan Heights now for domestic reasons. According to this theory, Begin believed it would help the Israeli Government persuade Israeli settlers in Sinai to leave the area peacefully before Israel completes its withdrawal there in April next year in line with the Egyptian-Israeli peace treaty. The Government, according to theory wanted to offer some evidence that no other territories would be handed back to the Arabs.

While it may be kind to give Mr Begin the benefit of the doubt that he was merely playing cynical domestic politics, the fact remains that the decision to annex the Golan Heights has serious implications for the Middle East. The already unstable area has been brought closer to catastrophe through the Begin Government's decision.

Quite naturally, Syria was among the first Arab countries to react with hostility to the Israeli decision. After all, the Golan Heights are still Syrian territory under international law.

However, the danger is that the Syrians will be unable to stop with rhetoric. President Hafez Assad of Syria, like Mr Begin, has to face domestic political considerations.

The immediate problem is the continuing dispute between Syria and Israel over Syria's deployment of surface-to-air missiles in Lebanon's Beka'a Valley. Will the stand-off continue, or will the Syrians feel obliged to flout the missiles' presence more aggressively and even attempt to bring down an Israeli fighter violating Lebanese air space?

It could well be that Lebanon will once again be the focus of a serious escalation of Middle East tension which undeniably has been exacerbated by the Begin Government's decision about the Golan Heights.

However, the longer-term implication could be more serious. Currently, there is a United Nations observer force separating Israeli and Syrian military positions on the Golan Heights. The mandate was extended for another six months two weeks ago.

But it is difficult to see that Syria could extend the mandate of the force again now that the "occupying force" on the Golan Heights has annexed the area. That would be tantamount to recognising the annexation.

And without the UN force, the Syria-Israel front line could once again become active.

The Israeli decision also has depressing implications on the question of furthering the peace process started by the Egypt-Israel peace treaty.

As the abortive Arab summit in the Moroccan city of Fez proved, the Arabs were having trouble enough gaining consensus on the Saudi Arabian peace plan, which is considered to imply recognition of Israel's right to exist.

Syria was one of the main stumbling blocks to acceptance of the plan, which also calls for the establishment of a Palestinian State with East Jerusalem as its capital.

Now, it will be all the more difficult for the Arabs to get Syria to accept the plan. (Syria's position on recognition of Israel's right to exist is confusing, in fact, because although it has been half-hearted about the Saudi plan, it is on record as accepting UN Security

Council Resolution 338, which implies recognition of Israel's right to exist.)

Another big loser from the Begin Government's decision will be the United States. Although Washington has said it was taken by surprise, it will not be seen that way in the Middle East. This is partly due to Arab paranoia about Israel's bankroller, but also because it comes at a time when US prestige in the Middle East is at a particularly low ebb.

But the major loser from this Israeli Government decision is the Egyptian regime led by President Mubarak. The Egyptians were among the first to criticise the move. They rejected it, and said it contradicted the Camp David agreements upon which the Egyptian-Israeli peace treaty was based.

It was a sad decision for anyone believing in Israel's right to exist. It was far, far more sad for anyone wishing that Israel could live in peace.

Bahrain, a land of problems
From DAVID BALDERSTONE in Amman

'The Age', December 23, 1981

In the months after the fall of the Shah in 1979, Iran's new Islamic leaders renewed a historical claim on the Persian Gulf island state of Bahrain.

In those heady days after the Iranian "revolution", some Iranian religious leaders – convinced that they could rule Iran better than the deposed Shah – talked about the importance of exporting the Islamic revolution outside Iran's borders.

The immediate reaction of the Sates bordering the Gulf, which, with the exception of Iraq, were all dominated by ruling families, was that of anger laced with more than an insignificant bout of the jitters. But as the situation in Iran deteriorated, and it became widely seen that Ayatollah Khomeiny was not very successful at ruling Iran, the Gulf States gradually relaxed.

Last week the authorities in Bahrain – acting on a tip-off from Dubai – arrested 60 people for allegedly planning to stage a coup d'état to coincide with the State's Independence Day. The authorities said the people belonged to a pro-Iranian group called the Islamic Front for the Liberation of Bahrain.

The authorities claimed that some of the people arrested had received training in Iran. The authorities claimed Iran had been behind the plot – a charge quickly denied in Teheran. On the one hand, the denial by Teheran does not mean all that much because power is so divided in Iran at present that the officials issuing the denial may not have been in a position to be aware that some branch of Iranian Government was behind the abortive plot.

On the other hand, the Bahrain authorities' accusation against Teheran does not mean all that much because the Islamic Republic of Iran is not known for its firm grasp of diplomatic niceties and the idea of non-interference in another country's affairs. And, in any case, whether or not Iran was involved in the alleged Bahrain plot, Bahrain does have problems likely to fuel a proportion of the population's desire for change.

About half Bahrain's 335,000-population belongs to the Shi'ite branch of Islam – the branch to which most Iranians belong. These Bahraini Shi'ites – many of whom have close family links with Iran – tend to be worse off economically than Bahrain's Sunni Moslems. Bombarded by Iranian radio day and night, it is not surprising that some members of the Bahrain Shi'ite community see advantages in the Shi'ite Islamic revolution in Iran.

Another problem facing Bahrain stems from the fact it has become a major business centre in the Gulf region. Therefore, a lot of Western and Arab businessmen live in Bahrain. Western ideas, dress and behaviour are common. At this time of a resurgence of Islamic ideas, many Moslems become offended sincerely by Western dress and some Western behaviour. When it is linked to frustrations over a disparity between rich and poor, it becomes a major irritant.

Iran has dropped, or shelved its claim to Bahrain. It remains uncertain whether Iran was involved in last week's alleged coup d'état. But it would be surprising if it marked the end of Bahrain's internal troubles.

1982
Persecuted people
- DAVID BALDERSTONE

'The Age', Amman, January 18, 1982

The reported execution of another eight prominent members of the Baha'i faith in Iran once again raises the question of religious persecution of members of the faith in the Islamic Republic of Iran.

Although these alleged executions provoked further condemnation of Ayatollah Khomeiny's regime this week, there seems little, if any, chance that Baha'is will find safety in Iran in the foreseeable future.

Although representatives of the regime deny that Baha'is are systematically persecuted, they cannot deny that the Baha'i faith was the only major religion ignored when the Islamic republic's new constitution was drafted. Whereas the constitution provides for the Zoroastrian, Jewish and Christian communities to have a representative each in the country's 270 seat National Assembly, the Baha'i were not given this right (in fact the Jewish representative was disqualified after his election).

Although acts of violence against the Baha'is and the faith's buildings catalogued by international Baha'i communities over the past three years indicate systematic persecution since the Iranian revolution, persecution of the Baha'i community in Iran is nothing new. Outbreaks of violence against members of the faith occurred in 1905 during the Qajar dynasty and in 1955 during the reign of the late Shah.

However, persecution began the day that Siyyid Ali Mohammed, known in the faith by the title "Bab", declared in Shiraz in 1844 that he was a prophet of God and that his task was to pave the way for the appearance of the "great prophet, the promised of all ages". The Bab was executed in 1850.

In Bagdad in 1863, Mirza Husayn Ali, after being banished from Persia because he declared the Bab's teachings were true, proclaimed that he was the great prophet. To the Baha'is he is known as Baha'u'llah (the glory of God).

Despite the tragedy of the persecution, the origins of the religion provide the key to understanding the reason for the consistent persecution.

The point is that the appearance of these two Baha'i prophets was – and continues to be – extremely sensitive in Iran where the majority religion is Shi'ite Islam, which teaches that its missing twelfth Imam will re-appear in the last day of judgement as the Mahdi, or guided one.

There are two other factors which may have contributed towards persecution of the Baha'is in Ayatollah Khomeiny's Iran.

First, the Baha'i world centre is in Haifa, Israel. Although it was there more than 50 years before the establishment of modern Israel, it is probable that it is not easy for Baha'is in Iran to get that point across when local revolutionary guards find correspondence and money transfers addressed to somewhere in Israel.

Second, Baha'is are taught to obey the government of the country in which they live and not participate in politics. In the early post-revolution days, this could have been interpreted by "revolutionary" Iranians that the Baha'is did nothing to protest about the excesses of the late Shah, and did nothing to bring about his downfall.

None of these points excuses persecution of the Baha'is. But they do point to the likelihood that the Baha'is will not find safe refuge in Iran in the near future.

Divided by peace
- DAVID BALDERSTONE

'The Age', Jerusalem, January 30, 1982

When Israel completes its withdrawal from Sinai in less than three months, Rafa, an Arab city dotted with palm and gum trees, will be divided once again. Ironically, Rafa was united by war and will be divided by peace.

Somehow, despite the honking horns, clip clopping donkey carts, and the electronic muezzin calling from the mosque's minaret, Rafa beside the Mediterranean is peaceful enough this week.

Arab men sit along the main shopping roads sipping Turkish coffee and talking.

What they are talking about most these days is the border fence that will cut Rafa in two once Israel completes its withdrawal from Sinai on 25 April.

The Egyptian-Israeli border, which stretches from the Gulf of Aqaba to the Mediterranean, runs through Rafa under an agreement signed in 1906 between the Ottoman Empire, which ruled Palestine, and Britain on behalf of Egypt. Technically Rafa is half in Sinai and half in the Gaza Strip, but Israel is retaining the Gaza Strip under occupation.

So far only a few metal pegs mark the border across the city of Rafa. But from the eastern edge of the city, bulldozers have cut a 40-metre wide strip of land through cactus and orchards. The strip stretches as far as the eye can see towards a point on the gulf just south of Eilat.

But it does not enter the city of Rafa. In fact, the Israeli authorities have assured residents that they do not intend to demolish any of the city's buildings and that the border strip will not cross the city.

Nevertheless, there will be a border fence and the residents believe that some demolition will take place. This is because since 1967 some buildings have been built across the line of the old border fence which demarcated Egyptian Sinai from the Egyptian administered Gaza Strip before 1967.

"The Government said they would not destroy any houses," said Dr Ziyat Shaat, a municipal councillor. "But I can't believe that they will let the border just pass over the roofs of houses."

The Rafa issue is just one of the problems faced by the Israeli and Egyptian authorities as they re-establish their border after 15 years. But it is the major problem and because it is so political the people of Rafa are to pay a considerable price. "Rafa is paying the price of the peace between Egypt and Israel," Dr Shaat said.

After the 1906 border agreement was signed, two twin cities developed – Rafa Sinai and Rafa Palestine. After the creation of the modern state of Israel, Egypt kept both cities separate even though it had control over the Gaza Strip. The border did not come down until Israel occupied Sinai and the Gaza Strip during the Six Day War of 1967.

Since 1967, a great number of Rafa's 80,000 people started farming land or creating businesses on the other side of the "border". Some people from Rafa Sinai went to live in Rafa Palestine and vice versa.

However, people will have to return to their own sides when the border is re-erected. Egyptians will live in Rafa Sinai and the Palestinians, who are officially refugees, will live in Rafa Palestine.

A Rafa bookseller, Hassan Mohammed Ramadan, said the border was going to create a lot of problems. "You may take this as a joke," he said very seriously. "But one of our municipal councillors has a wife and a house on each side of the border. What is he going to do?"

The problem is acute for 500 Palestinian refugee families who were settled in the "Canada camp" on the Egyptian side of the border after 1967. It looks certain they will be moved back into the Gaza Strip because they are not Egyptian nationals.

Senior Israeli officials have floated the idea that the problem could be solved by the whole town being taken over by Egypt or Israel.

But such a border change would be politically difficult for the Egyptians. If they left the city in Israeli hands, they would not be able to tell the Egyptian people they had reclaimed the whole of Sinai. If Egypt took over the whole of the city, they would be accused of usurping Palestinian land.

"The Egyptian Government does not want one metre of Sinai to remain in Israeli hands," Dr. Shaat said. "If it did they could not tell their people that they got all Sinai back."

The Egyptians and Israelis are studying different ways of solving the problem. An Israeli idea is that the border should skirt buildings blocking the border line. But Israeli police are reported to be concerned that this could lead to Rafa becoming a smuggling centre.

And one local resident said he believed the Israelis would have only to suspect that one "terrorist" bomb had crossed the border for there to be a 40-metre border strip cut through the town within days.

Jordanians heed king's call to fight for Iraq
From DAVID BALDERSTONE

'The Age', Amman, January 31, 1982

Hundreds of Jordanians began enlisting yesterday in the volunteer force being raised by King Hussein to fight for Iraq in the Gulf war.

At recruitment stations around the country men signed up and the Government last night announced that civil servants who volunteered would retain their rights and pay during their absence.

In a televised speech on Thursday night King Hussein announced the formation of the force and said he would serve in it. He said he hoped to be able to spend as much time as possible at the front.

At a recruitment station I visited in Amman yesterday about 60 volunteers had signed on. Some were immediately taken by army bus to begin training at a base near Amman.

"I am an Arab and I am going to Iraq to help because Iraq is an Arab country," said Zuheir Youssef, a 28-year-old Jordanian seaman who has previously served in Jordan's army.

"We want peace. We don't like to fight because many people will die. But Iran doesn't like peace. Khomeiny is a crazy man. He talks about Islam but just fights and kills all the time."

Most of the volunteers said they saw the war as an Arab cause, not merely a war involving Iraq. King Hussein placed a heavy emphasis on his belief that the Iraqis' battle against Iran was an Arab cause when he announced the formation of the force.

"If danger threatens part of the Arab nation, it is a threat to the whole nation," he said.

"The duty of the nation in this case is to rise and confront this danger and neutralise it."

The king has been Iraq's most vocal supporter since the outbreak of full scale war with Iran in September 1980. Since then Jordan has allowed Iraq access to the Jordanian port of Aqaba.

Western diplomats in Amman believe that King Hussein may have been prompted to form the volunteer force because of recent Iranian gains against Iraq on the battle front. Some diplomats believe the recent attempted coup in Bahrain, which the Bahrain authorities alleged was organised in Iran, could have been another factor influencing the king's decision.

A war just waiting to happen
From DAVID BALDERSTONE

'The Age', Beirut, March 13, 1982

Before the Lebanese civil war, Damour – a town about 20 kilometres south of here – was populated mainly by Lebanese Christians. The war changed all that, and now only a few Christians remain.

Palestinian guerillas now control the town. Palestinian refugees and Lebanese refugees from troubled southern Lebanon have taken over many of the apartment blocks.

Damour, which overlooks the Mediterranean, is no stranger to trouble. Palestinian gun positions have been bombed several times by the Israelis since the civil war.

This week the town is bracing itself for another attack. With increasing expectations that Israel is about to attack Palestinian positions in Lebanon, Palestinian leaders have predicted that Damour, rather than Palestinian positions in the south of the country, could be the main target of the Israelis.

Once again Lebanon is the victim of the fact that it is the battleground for Middle East disputes. Whereas some people use a board on which to play war games, Middle East interests use Lebanon.

For several months, Israel has been threatening to strike at Palestinian positions in Lebanon. Although the US special envoy, Mr Philip Habib, at least contained tension during his latest two-week mission, there are fears that the risk of an outbreak of fighting will increase as the date of Israel's scheduled final withdrawal from Sinai approaches.

At this time an Israeli thrust into Lebanon would have repercussions far beyond the borders. It could spark a direct clash between Israel and Syrian forces in Lebanon. It would strengthen the positions of hardline elements within the Palestine Liberation

Organisation. It would undermine efforts by moderate Arab Governments to get Arab agreement on the Saudi Arabian Middle East peace plan.

Israel's Defence Minister, Mr Sharon, has said that Israel had no plans to invade unless action by Palestinian guerillas provoked an attack. But the Israelis have made it clear that they could consider any Palestinian guerilla action either across the Jordanian or Lebanese frontiers or from within Israel as provocation.

But this threat raises the question of whether or not the Palestinian guerilla leadership can control all actions by all guerilla groups. One action against Israel carried out by a radical splinter group could be enough for the Israelis to consider the seven-month ceasefire broken, even if the PLO leadership had no part in directing it.

How could Israel's Sinai withdrawal have anything to do with the possibility of an Israeli attack against Palestinian positions in Lebanon? The answer may be a reflection of growing cynicism about the actions of the Israeli Government. Nevertheless, there is a view shared widely not only by the Palestinians and Arab Governments, but by Western diplomats as well that Israel would like to attack Lebanon not only for the sake of delivering a hard blow to the Palestinian guerilla machine.

Apart from a direct military objective, there are three main reasons why the Israeli Government could consider an attack before its final Sinai withdrawal as beneficial.

First, in view of the fact an attack would strengthen the position of hardline Arabs; it would undermine the chances of rapprochement between the Arab States and Egypt. The likely thinking of the Arabs would be that they could not move closer to Egypt after a war between the Palestinians and Egypt's peace partner.

The Israeli Government has shown signs already that it would not welcome Egypt returning to the Arab fold. For one thing, it would be at the expense of the continuing normalisation process between Egypt and Israel.

Second, a Palestinian-Israeli battle at this time would undermine current moves by conservative Arab States to get an Arab summit to adopt the Saudi Arabian peace plan once the Sinai withdrawal has been completed.

The eight point plan is considered to implicitly recognise Israel's right to exist, although the Saudis themselves have made contradictory statements on this point. Adoption of the plan by an Arab summit, which would include the PLO, would lead almost certainly to an improvement in relations between the PLO leader, Mr Yasser Arafat, and European Governments – and maybe even the American Administration.

Third, a Palestinian-Israeli battle would halt the gradual improvement in relations between the United States and the Arab world. That is considered by many Arab officials and some Western diplomats to be a major objective of the present Israeli Government.

A senior Jordanian official told 'The Age' this week that he believed Israel did not want relations between Arab Governments and the US to improve too much. "They don't want the US to be influenced by Arab thinking on the Arab-Israeli dispute," he said.

He believed that this was a significant reason why Israel was so strongly opposing the possibility of the Americans supplying mobile Hawk missiles and F-16 warplanes to Jordan. He said Jordan was no threat to Israel. As evidence, he mentioned the multi-million-dollar Jordan Valley irrigation project along the border between Jordan and the Israeli-occupied West Bank territory. This project would almost certainly be destroyed if there was a war between Jordan and Israel.

The same official said that moves to get the Saudi peace plan approved by an Arab summit would "really get underway" once the Sinai withdrawal had been completed. He added that "all the Arabs" wanted rapprochement with Egypt.

Israelis join West Bank protest
From DAVID BALDERSTONE

'The Age', Jerusalem, March 28, 1982

Major disturbances continued on the Israeli-occupied West Bank yesterday as thousands of Israelis demonstrated in Tel Aviv against the Israeli Government's policies in the territory.

Israeli soldiers were reported to have used tear gas to disperse demonstrators in West Bank towns.

With Arab demonstrations planned for Tuesday there appears little likelihood today of an early end to the violence, which was sparked by the dismissal of a pro-PLO West Bank mayor 10 days ago.

In a new development, hundreds of Israeli Arab youths demonstrated in the Israeli city of Nazareth. They burned car tyres and stoned a bus in an expression of solidarity with Palestinians living in the occupied territories. Most of the Nazareth Arabs hold Israeli nationality.

With tension still high on the West Bank yesterday, the Australian Minister for Foreign Affairs, Mr Street, toured the old city of Jerusalem, where many shops stayed closed because of a general strike by Arab shopkeepers.

Although Israeli soldiers always patrol the old city, which was occupied by Israel in 1967, it appeared there was increased security yesterday because of the disturbances.

Several Israeli soldiers accompanied Mr Street during his visit to the old city.

After the Jewish Sabbath holiday, Mr Street began the official task of his tour to Israel today by laying a wreath at Yad Vashem, the holocaust museum.

Later, he was taken by helicopter to northern Israel before having his first working session with Israel's Foreign Minister, Mr Shamir.

Thousands of Israelis – supporters of the Peace Now movement – demonstrated in Tel Aviv yesterday. They were protesting against the Government's handling of affairs in the West Bank and Gaza Strip.

Israeli authorities yesterday placed under house arrest the dismissed West Bank mayor of El Bireh, Mr Ibrahim Tawil. Mt Tawil's dismissal 10 days ago sparked the violence on the West Bank and Gaza Strip, which has left eight people dead.

Mr Tawil's sacking was followed by the dismissal of two other West Bank mayors – Mr Bassam Shaka'a of Nablus and Mr Karim Khalim of Ramallah.

Although under house arrest, Mr Tawil came to the front gate of his house in El Bireh to talk to journalists while Israeli soldiers confining him to the house looked on. He said he feared Israel might annex the West Bank.

Israeli authorities dismissed Mr Tawil because as mayor of El Bireh he refused to cooperate with the so-called civil administration on the West Bank.

He said that when Israeli soldiers came to tell him that he was under house arrest yesterday they kicked at the door and abused his wife.

Palestinian rights key issue: Street
From DAVID BALDERSTONE

'The Age', Jerusalem, March 29, 1982

The Australian Minister for Foreign Affairs, Mr Street, said last night Israel would need courage to make further territorial compromises and accept Palestinian rights if Middle East peace was to be achieved.

Speaking at a dinner hosted by Israel's Foreign Minister, Mr Shamir, Mr Street strongly implied that he believed growing tensions in the area – particularly on the occupied West Bank – stemmed from the failure of the Egyptian-Israeli talks on Palestinian autonomy to "proceed any distance" towards meeting the aspirations of the Palestinians.

Mr Street called for the establishment of a Palestinian homeland alongside Israel.

Although the idea of a Palestinian homeland has been a theme of Australia's Middle East policy, the form and geographic location of this homeland have not been spelled out.

The Israeli Government is aware that the idea of a homeland is part of Australian policy, but the fact that Mr Street reaffirmed the call in front of Mr Shamir heavily underlined the idea. Israel rejects the concept of a Palestinian State being established on the West Bank, which it occupied in 1967.

Earlier during a meeting with Mr Shamir, Mr Street expressed Australia's concern about the outbreak of violence on the occupied West Bank – violence which has left eight people dead over the past 11 days. It is believed that during the meeting Mr Street criticised recent Israeli actions on the West Bank.

While Mr Street reassured Mr Shamir of Australia's strong support for Israel, it is believed that he said recent Israeli actions had made it very difficult for Australia and other countries friendly to Israel – in the international arena.

During the dinner attended by senior Israeli officials, Mr Street praised the courage of Israel's Prime Minister, Mr Begin, in committing Israel to withdraw from Sinai.

"The late President Sadat recognised the essential truth that peace in the Middle East would remain a mirage until the reality of Israel's existence was accepted as a fact," Mr Street said.

"Prime Minster Begin's courage in turn accepted the fact that territory alone does not guarantee peace.

"The demands for courage, however, do not stop at the borders of the Sinai. For if it is an essential truth that the only path to peace in the Middle East lies in accepting Israel's right to exist, it is equally true that the same path must traverse the reality of Palestinian aspirations."

Mr Street re-affirmed that Australia would not recognise the Palestine Liberation Organisation unless it recognised Israel's right to exist. He also said the legitimate rights of the Palestinians included the right to a homeland alongside Israel.

Mr Street said Australia remained unequivocal in its support for Israel and would continue to oppose all attempts to expel Israel from international organisations. However, he said Australia would also continue to voice its concern about the Palestinian problem.

Mr Shamir praised Australia's support for Israel. "In international forums and organisations where Israel is often faced with a large hostile coalition, Australia has stood up, again and again, in support of Israel's cause," Mr Shamir said.

Earlier yesterday Mr Street was flown by helicopter to a kibbutz on the Lebanese border. He was briefed on the security situation in Lebanon and the importance of Israel retaining the Golan Heights.

A senior Israeli army officer, Brigadier-General Bar-am Amos, told Mr Street that Israel could never withdraw even a metre from the Golan Heights.

Australia-PLO contact encouraged
From DAVID BALDERSTONE

'The Age', Cairo, March 31, 1982

Egyptian leaders appeared likely today to encourage Australia to increase contacts with the Palestine Liberation Organisation.

Just before his arrival in Cairo last night, The Minister for Foreign Affairs, Mr Street, said that Australia's policy towards the PLO could change if the organisation recognised Israel's right to exist.

A senior aide to the Egyptian Minister for Foreign Affairs, Dr Boutros Ghali, told 'The Age' today that Egypt encouraged countries to have contacts with all Palestinians, including the PLO. Such contacts enhanced the peace process, he said. However, he stressed, that it was up to the Australian Government to decide whether or not to recognise the PLO.

Last year the late President Sadat urged the United States to talk to the PLO. Egyptian leaders recently confirmed that Egypt still had contacts with the PLO despite the public break in relations following President Sadat's visit to Jerusalem in 1977.

Currently only Australian diplomats below ambassador level have contacts with the PLO in Beirut, Damascus and Amman.

Mr Street said last night that Australia's policy towards the PLO "could change" if it recognised Israel's right to exist. But he stopped short of saying that PLO recognition of Israel would automatically lead to Australia recognising the PLO.

"If the PLO made a decision – and stated it publicly – to recognise Israel then that would be a major breakthrough," he said.

It could "open doors" in the peace process that have so far remained closed because of the PLO's failure to recognise publicly Israel's right to exist, he said.

Israeli raid near, Lebanon fears
From DAVID BALDERSTONE

'The Age', Beirut, April 11, 1982

Israeli warplanes flew over Beirut today, drawing anti-aircraft fire as President Sarkis of Lebanon continued crisis talks aimed at averting a threatened Israeli attack into Lebanon.

As tension mounted along the Israel-Lebanon border today, an Israeli military spokesman announced that Israel had captured two Palestinian guerillas after they had crossed into Israel from Jordan.

The spokesman said the two guerillas belonged to Fatah, the Palestinian guerilla group headed by the Palestine Liberation Organisation chairman, Mr Yasser Arafat.

This announcement further increased fears of an Israeli attack against Palestinian positions in Lebanon because Israel has been warning for some time that it would retaliate against alleged violations of the eight-month old ceasefire which applies primarily to the Israel-Lebanon border.

Amid increased weekend tension, President Reagan appealed to all sides to show restraint.

President Sarkis summoned the US Ambassador to Lebanon, Mr Robert Dillon, to the presidential palace yesterday and sought US guarantees and assurances that Israel would not invade Lebanon.

A Lebanese Government spokesman said Mr Sarkis had told the ambassador that Israel had massed two divisions totalling 40,000 men on Israel's northern border in readiness for a big attack against Palestinian positions in Lebanon.

Although reports from Israel indicate that Government officials are describing the claim that two divisions have been massed along the border as exaggerated, sources in Israel have confirmed that there has been a large call-up of Israeli reservists over the past week.

The Israeli Cabinet met today and discussed the security situation in the north of the country.

Fears of an Israeli attack against Palestinian positions in Lebanon increased last week after an Israeli diplomat was assassinated in Paris. Israel's Foreign Minister, Mr Shamir, warned after the assassination that Israel would strike without mercy at the Palestinians.

In addition, there is concern in Beirut that Israel could be inclined to take an early opportunity to attack Syrian surface-to-air missiles, which the Syrian "peace-keeping" force in Lebanon installed in the country's Beka'a Valley just under a year ago.

An Israeli attack against the Syrian missiles could lead to an Israel-Syria military confrontation, which would escalate the current crisis to a level not seen since the 1973 Middle East war.

Syrian troops and Palestinian guerillas have been placed on high alert. A US-negotiated ceasefire involving Israel and Palestinian forces has been in force over the past eight months.

After initially meeting President Sarkis yesterday, Dr Dillon returned to the presidential palace four hours later to assure the Lebanese President that the US was doing its utmost to make certain the ceasefire was maintained. Mr Sarkis also met the Soviet Ambassador to Lebanon yesterday.

Officials of the PLO confirmed today that Mr Arafat had warned supporters at the weekend that Israel would invade south Lebanon within "48 hours". Similar fears were expressed by Western diplomats during discussions with 'The Age' in Amman yesterday.

Lebanon's State Radio has reported that Palestinian forces opened fire on Israeli ships.

Millions strike over killing of Moslems
From DAVID BALDERSTONE

'The Age', Beirut, April 14, 1982

Millions of Moslems went on strike in the Middle East today to protest against Israeli actions in the occupied territories, including the Old City of Jerusalem.

In most Arab capitals, shops remained shuttered, airlines ceased operations, and telephone operators were refusing to connect calls.

The unprecedented strike was called by Saudi Arabia's King Khaled yesterday in response to last Sunday's incident in Jerusalem when an American immigrant to Israel opened fire on people visiting the mosques on the Temple Mount. Two Palestinians were killed and rioting broke out.

Ironically, worker-initiated strikes are illegal in many Arab countries.

In predominantly Moslem West Beirut shops on the main shopping street, Rue Hamra remained closed. Palestinian and Lebanese Leftist militiamen were patrolling the area to make certain that shops were closed.

Most Arab countries responded to King Khaled's call by ordering that Government offices remained closed today. But, Christian political leaders in Beirut have criticised the Sunni Moslem Lebanese Prime Minsiter, Mr Wazzan, for ordering the closure of Government offices.

The former Lebanese President Mr Camille Chamoun said the Government was not a trade union and that the strike set a "serious precedent".

In the Syrian capital, Damascus, the Government newspaper, 'Tishrin', criticised the Arabs for not taking more forceful measures against Israeli actions in the occupied territories.

The newspaper said Arab Governments had been content with making statements and speeches.

Last Sunday's incident in the Old City of Jerusalem – an incident deplored by the Israeli Government – followed several weeks of violence on the occupied West Bank.

The violence erupted after the Israeli civilian administrator of the occupied territories sacked the Palestinian mayor of El Bireh. This sacking was followed by the sacking of two other West Bank Palestinian mayors.

The Washington Post reports that Israeli troops firing on Arab demonstrators in the Gaza Strip yesterday killed a seven-year-old boy and wounded at least 17 other people as protests against the mosque shootings continued to sweep the occupied territories.

Palestinian youths tried to break into an army base near a Gaza Strip refugee camp and were driven back by a fusillade of gunfire that left 21 protesters injured, 11 of them with gunshot wounds. Four Israeli soldiers were injured, one seriously, by rocks thrown in the melee.

In the centre of Gaza town, six more Palestinians were shot when Israeli troops opened fire on a rock-throwing crowd.

The Gaza mayor, Mr Rashid Shawa, said it was the worst day of Arab-Israeli clashes in the territory since the riots of 1971-72, when the Israeli army bulldozed large sections of the refugee camps in an effort to curb a wave of attacks against Israeli troops.

Early yesterday morning, the army command announced Israeli security forces confronted two Palestinian guerillas who tried to infiltrate the West Bank from Jordan, and drove them back across the Jordan River. The guerillas threw a hand grenade at the Israeli army patrol, but there were no injuries, the spokesman said.

Mr Shawa and other Palestinian sources said 50 demonstrators had been wounded by gunfire in yesterday's unrest in the Gaza Strip alone.

M-E peace a mirage after Sinai handover
From DAVID BALDERSTONE

'The Age', Amman, April 23, 1982

Despite last minute hitches, Israeli flags seem certain to be lowered over the Sinai Peninsula on schedule this weekend. It will be the second time that 33-year-old Israel will have completed withdrawal from Sinai.

Unlike Israel's previous departure from Sinai in 1957, this withdrawal marks the completion of Israel's return of territory in exchange for peace with Egypt. But the architects of the Camp David accords, which paved the way to the Egypt-Israel peace treaty, envisaged this hand over of territory to mean much more.

The Camp David accords envisaged that by this time – three years after the peace treaty was signed on the White House lawn – West Bank and Gaza Strip Palestinians would be enjoying full autonomy for a transitional period not exceeding five years. At the end of this transitional period, Egypt, Israel, Jordan and Palestinian representatives would have decided the final status of the West Bank and Gaza Strip.

The accords were described as a framework for peace in the Middle East. But, now, as Israel completes its withdrawal from Sinai, there is no agreement on Palestinian autonomy; the transitional period has not been entered, and comprehensive Arab-Israeli peace is as far away as ever.

This weekend's handover of the remaining third of Sinai under Israel control is expected to be a sombre affair. This will contrast dramatically with Israel's return of the first two-thirds of Sinai to Egypt in May 1979.

The late President Sadat and Israel's Prime Minister, Mr Begin, were in the Sinai capital, Al Arish, for the handover and met Egyptian and Israeli war invalids. Tears streamed down the cheeks of the Israeli Prime Minister as he kissed the badly mangled face of an Egyptian veteran from the 1967 war, which left Sinai in Israel's control.

As Mr Sadat and Mr Begin toured the small city in their extravagantly long motorcade, the front of the motorcade caught up with the back at one stage.

It was moving and amusing, but above all, there was a spirit of real peace at that 1979 ceremony.

But this weekend will be different. So much has happened, it could be no other way. Leaving aside the rights and wrongs of Jewish settlement in occupied territories, Israeli soldiers will have just completed the task of forcibly removing settlers from Sinai. For most Israelis – no matter what they think of the settlers – the sight of Israeli soldiers fighting Israelis is a traumatic affair exacerbating anxieties about the durability of peace with Egypt.

It is difficult to be in any doubt that the new Egyptian leadership and moderate Arab States want rapprochement – even though the Egyptians continually stress that it would not be at the expense of Egypt's peace treaty with Israel.

Although Israel fears that rapprochement between Egypt and the Arab world will undermine its normalisation process with Egypt, the chance of this reconciliation provides the best hopes of further steps towards comprehensive Middle East peace.

In a sense, it could give the Arabs a second chance at the opportunities they missed immediately after Mr Sadat visited Jerusalem in November 1977.

A month after that visit, Mr Sadat convened talks between Israeli and Egyptian officials at the Mena House Hotel near the Pyramids just outside Cairo. Egyptian officials insisted that the other "confrontation" partners to the Arab-Israeli dispute – Jordan, Syria, Lebanon and the Palestine Liberation Organisation – were invited to attend, but in Arab circles the "invitation" is still disputed.

If the other parties had attended, the whole peace process since Mr Sadat's Jerusalem visit could have been much different. But the Arabs chose not to attend. And therefore, they gave up their ability to influence events, which led to the signing of the Camp David accords.

Instead, they closed ranks, some more reluctantly than others, in opposition to the whole Sadat initiative. In the Arabs' eyes, he was to be condemned for recognising Israel's right to exist on its pre-1967 borders by his action of addressing Israel's Parliament in Jerusalem.

It was this Arab opposition to Mr Sadat's "recognition" of Israel's pre-1967 borders that confused the world's perception of the Arabs' stand towards Israel so much. And no wonder, because Jordan and Syria were then seen to be "opposing Israel's recognition", whereas in fact they had both previously implied recognition of Israel's right to exist.

Despite this implied recognition, the Arabs intensified their anger against Mr Sadat for having recognised Israel by visiting Jerusalem.

And, they lost control of events. The Camp David accords were drafted, and the peace treaty was signed.

But the Camp David formula for peace in the Middle East has not worked either. There are four main reasons.

First, the accords ignored the realities of Arab politics. They ignored the fact that Jordan, Syria, the PLO and Lebanon would not participate individually.

Each party has so much influence on the others' survival that there is safety only in moving en bloc.

Secondly, the accords held out little hope that Syria would ever get Israel to return the Golan Heights.

Thirdly, the accords provided no role for the Soviet Union. This is despite the fact that a Soviet role in an eventual solution to the Arab-Israeli crisis is essential if for no other reason but the fact that Moscow has enormous capacity to cause trouble if it is not included.

Fourthly, the accords failed to mention the PLO, which at the Rabat Arab summit of 1974 had been appointed the sole legitimate representative of the Palestinian people.

But despite the Arabs' objections to the Sadat initiative, the Camp David accords, and the Egypt/Israel peace treaty, the Arabs have come up with some positive ideas which indicate that they want peace with Israel.

Arab summits have repeatedly reaffirmed the Arab nations' obligation to a just peace based upon full Israeli withdrawal from all Arab territories occupied in 1967. Can this resolution signed by Arab leaders, including the PLO chairman Mr Yasser Arafat, mean anything else but the fact that the Arabs accept Israel's right to exist on its pre-1967 border?

Also, Saudi Arabia's eight-point peace plan, which was unveiled last year, implied recognition of Israel's right to exist.

The most important fact in relation to this plan was that senior aides to Mr Arafat hoped to draft it.

But the Arabs have failed to adopt this plan for exactly the same reasons that they have been reluctant to move towards peace with Israel.

There can be little hope that Arab consensus on moves towards peace will be achieved in the immediate wake of Israeli actions such as the bombing of Iraq's nuclear reactor; last year's bombing of Beirut; the annexation of the Golan Heights; continued Jewish settlement in occupied territories, and recent events on the West Bank.

The Arabs, not unreasonably, think Israel is not interested in peace.

So Israel is scheduled to complete its withdrawal from Sinai this weekend. Peace between Israel and the biggest Arab country, Egypt, will seem secure. But the overall Arab-Israeli peace seems as far away as ever.

PLO keeping the peace
From DAVID BALDERSTONE

'The Age', Amman, May 3, 1982

Despite Israeli allegations to the contrary, most Western diplomats and independent observers in the Middle East believe that the Palestine Liberation Organisation has generally kept the nine-month-old Palestinian-Israeli ceasefire.

It can be further argued that this Palestinian restraint gives the lie to the often-put allegation that the PLO, and Mr Yasser Arafat in particular, if given the opportunity to run an independent Palestinian nation could not control radical and fanatical elements in the admittedly diverse organisation.

In other words, this Palestinian restraint could be taken as an indication that the PLO could provide responsible leadership for a Palestinian nation. This is an argument as consistently put by PLO officials as it is denied by Israel.

Since Israel's recent big bombing raid against three Palestinian "positions" in Lebanon, Israeli officials have been privately expressing the view that the Palestinians would retaliate.

First, police in northern Israel were put on alert, and many residents of northern Israeli settlements slept in air-raid shelters for fear of Palestinian rocket attacks. But nothing came.

Then Israeli officials expressed fears – allegedly based on intelligence – that the Palestinians would mount a big, or dramatic, attack on 25 April, the day of the Sinai handover. But the day passed without any big attack.

Then there were fears that the attack would occur on Israel's Independence Day. But again, the day passed peacefully.

The Palestinian-Israeli ceasefire was negotiated by the US special envoy, Mr Phillip Habib, last July after several months of tension in the Middle East battleground, Lebanon, which culminated in Israel's heavy bombing of predominantly Palestinian areas of Beirut.

After the Israeli bombing raid, Israel's Foreign Ministry described it as a counter-attack, launched in retaliation for Palestinian violation of the ceasefire.

Since the ceasefire came into force, the Ministry said, the "terrorists" had launched 32 attacks along the Lebanese border, 81 "actions" against United Nations soldiers in South Lebanon, four guerilla incursions from Jordan, 35 "actions" inside Israel, 57 "actions" in the occupied territories, and 20 "actions" abroad.

These 229 actions, the Ministry said, left 23 people dead. Only two of those killed were Israeli soldiers. In one hour of bombing over Lebanon more died than the Palestinians had allegedly killed in 229 "violations" of the ceasefire spread over nine months. Lebanese police said at least 25 people died in the raid.

Western diplomats in Tel Aviv, who consistently study Israeli allegations of Palestinian violations of the ceasefire, said they did not believe the violations of the ceasefire amounted to very much.

Western diplomats in Beirut and Amman go further and say they believe the PLO has generally maintained the ceasefire.

Admittedly, assessing violations of the ceasefire is a difficult task because details of the agreement have not been revealed.

Throughout the ceasefire, Israeli warplanes have maintained regular reconnaissance flights over Lebanon, Jordan, and sometimes Saudi Arabia. These violations of the airspace of neighboring nations may not be violations of the ceasefire technically, but they are certainly provocative.

Also, the Israel Defence Forces said that it had launched the bombing raids because of the Palestinian violations culminating in an incident in which an Israeli soldier was killed by a landmine in South Lebanon. What right do Israeli soldiers have to be inside Lebanese territory?

Israeli troops have been providing assistance to the Christian border enclaves commanded by the renegade Lebanese officer Major Sa'ad Haddad since Israel's 1978 invasion of South Lebanon. After this invasion, Israel ignored a United Nations demand that its positions be handed over to United Nations soldiers in the area, and instead handed border positions over to Major Haddad and his militia.

Israel has warned that it will retaliate heavily against any Palestinian attack, and no one doubts these words. But for the time being, the PLO appears to be keeping the peace.

'Jerusalem offensive' gives Iran initiative in Gulf war
From DAVID BALDERSTONE

'The Age', Teheran, May 8, 1982

Without blindfolds or bindings, 2250 Iraqi prisoners of war sat cross-legged on a grass sports ground beside Teheran's railway station. For them the bloody, 20-month Iran-Iraq war was over and despite a little understandable nervousness, they looked quite relieved about that.

They were among more than 5000 Iraqis captured during Iran's latest attack, code-named the "Jerusalem offensive". This enabled Iranian forces to raise once again the Islamic Republic's green, white and red flag along part of a crucial strip of the Iran-Iraq border, from which they were pushed when Iraqi tanks rolled in on 22 September, 1980.

The offensive provided them with a dilemma as well – whether to advance into Iraq for strategic reasons or continue to doggedly flush the Iraqis out of every square metre of Iranian territory.

But the crucial political decisions being taken in Teheran and Bagdad at this important stage of the war were far from the minds of the POWs sitting cross-legged on the playing field. Their minds were set on survival during what could be a long time in a prison camp.

Defensively, it seemed, some clutched posters of Iranian political-religious leaders as Iranian soldiers and Revolutionary Guards (Pasdars) stood guard. Loudspeakers mounted near a large portrait of Ayatollah Khomeiny chanted out: "Our way is the right way... martyrdom is so good... It is the way of righteousness".

Then, with a Revolutionary Guard leading, they jogged to buses to be driven to prison camps. As they reached the perimeter of the sports ground, a group of Iranians led the prisoners in a chorus of 'Death of Saddam'. With some reluctance it seemed, but with the idea of survival paramount in their hearts, the prisoners joined in the chant demanding the death of Iraq's President Saddam Hussein.

Indeed, it is difficult to believe that President Hussein could not be in severe political trouble. After 20 months of war, he has achieved nothing. The war has crippled Iraq's economy and slashed oil exports from 2.5 million barrels a day in 1980 to around 500,000 barrels now.

After months of sporadic cross-border artillery duels, Iraq escalated the conflict in September 1980 by bombing several Iranian air bases – including Teheran's civil and military airport – and occupied large areas of Iranian border territory, particularly in the oil-rich south-western province of Khuzestan.

Iraq succeeded in occupying much of Iran's port city of Khorammshahr on the disputed Shatt al-Arab waterway. However Iraq failed to occupy the oil refinery city of Abadan, just south of Khorammshahr. Nevertheless Iraqi attacks severely damaged the world's largest oil refinery in Abadan and Iraqi tanks initially succeeded in almost completely surrounding the city.

Now Iraq is left with the major part of Khorammshahr and little more than what could be described as pockets of Iranian territory along the border from Khorammshahr to Qasr El Shirin around 500 kilometres to the north.

Before escalating the conflict, President Hussein abrogated the Algiers Pact he had signed with the then Shah of Iran. In return for the Shah withdrawing support from Iraq's autonomy-seeking Kurds, this pact marked the border along the median line of the Shatt al-Arab waterway. Previously, Iraq held sovereignty over the whole waterway.

The official reason for the Iraqi escalation of the conflict was that Iraq believed it had been cheated out of pockets of border territory; wanted sovereignty over two islands held by Iran near the mouth of the Gulf and demanded complete sovereignty over the Shatt al-Arab.

However, it is no secret that President Hussein, a Sunni Moslem, wanted to bring down the Shi'ite Moslem regime of Ayatollah Khomeiny in Iran and stop the Iranian revolutionaries fermenting trouble amongst Iraq's Shi'ite Moslems who make up 55 per cent of Iraq's population.

Due to a serious Iraqi miscalculation that a short, sharp war would bring Iran to the negotiating table if not to its knees, the boot is on the other foot now.

Although Iranian forces are concentrating on removing the Iraqis, the Teheran regime makes no secret of the fact that it hopes – and expects – that Iranian battle successes will bring about the downfall of President Hussein.

The latest Iranian victories have sent shockwaves through the capitals of moderate Arab countries. Moderate leaders assume, perhaps wrongly, that an Iranian victory would lead to the spread of the Iranian revolution.

Gulf victories 'according to plan'
From DAVID BALDERSTONE

'The Age', May 11, 1982

Iran's most senior military officer leant forward in his chair and remembered the first bitter weeks of the Iran-Iraq war 20 months ago: "The world said Iran was dead. Even some elements in Iran said Iran was defeated."

He then opened his brown briefcase and drew out a folder containing Iraq's war strategy which had been drawn up two months after the start of hostilities in September 1980.

As he traced through the pages with his finger, he read sections out aloud. He then asked proudly: "Who could have imagined that our forces would be able to follow this strategy with less than 1 per cent error?"

It was a statement rather than a question. In the wake of Iran's most recent battle victories, the head of the Joint Chiefs of Staff, General Ghassem-Ali Zahir-Nedjad, was explaining why Iran was slow to get going, and how it had turned defeat into almost certain victory.

In an exclusive interview with 'The Age' – one of the few he has given to the foreign Press – General Zahir-Nedjad, who is also Deputy (to Ayatollah Khomeiny) Commander in Chief, said it would be militarily simple for the Iranian forces to advance into Iraq and cut off the only port city, Basra, from the rest of Iraq. "It would be as easy as drinking a glass of water," he said.

But he stressed that, up to now, Ayatollah Khomeiny had not allowed Iranian forces to advance into Iraq. "He has even warned us that not even one civilian should be wounded on the other side of the border," he said.

The interview took place in the general's wood-panelled office in Teheran. A portrait of Ayatollah Khomeiny was hanging on the wall. Outside fountains played in the perfectly kept barracks gardens, which were blooming with red roses.

The general said that at the start Iran had only 45 per cent of the military personnel it needed. This was mainly because national service had been cut from two years to one after the revolution which ousted the Shah.

He also said only 20 percent of the army's equipment was in good condition "and almost all of it was being used in domestic conflicts.

"At the beginning of the war, Iraq was strong, but we were weak. We knew we could not achieve victory in the short run, but we knew that in the long run we would achieve it.

"When Iraq started the attack on Iran, the Iranian armed forces were not well prepared and we were not in a good condition to fight the war. Also the Pasdaran (Revolutionary Guard) and the people's forces were not prepared for fighting the Iraqis."

Although the army came under pressure to act quickly to oust the invading Iraqis, General Zahir-Nedjad said the military took into account these realities and coolly developed a three-stage strategy which had been followed faithfully throughout.

During the first stage, the objective was to keep the Iraqis as close to the border as possible and prevent them making further advances. "Also at this stage, we were preparing our force – the armed forces and the popular people's forces – to maximise the army's abilities," he said.

During the second stage, the objective was to carry out small offensives on a local basis, while the third stage objective was to throw the enemy out of the country.

"This strategy was written down and given to all units," he said. "This is why you saw that two months after the war began, Iranian victories started to increase day by day."

In addition to this strategy, General Zahir-Nedjad said there were other factors why Iran had been able to turn early defeat into almost certain victory. "We were defending our country, whereas the Iraqis had aggressed against us. It was not only the armed forces which were insulted. The emotions of the whole nation had been injured.

"We were defending our dignity, integrity, our belief in the revolution and our country." On the other hand "the Iraqi soldiers don't know what they are fighting for…the Iraqi nation does not know why it is sacrificing so many soldiers and sacrificing so many resources".

Another factor which had helped in the long term was that Iran had greater manpower. Iran's population is nearly three times greater than Iraq's.

"In the short term an Iraqi soldier could handle a heavy burden but not in the long run," he said. "Recognising this, we tried to damage Iraqi personnel and Iraqi experts or try to arrest them. That is why we have up to 10 times more prisoners of war than they do.

"Last night I was listening to the Iraqi radio and the Iraqis were announcing that they felt sorry that the Iranians had sent 16 and 17-year-olds to fight and that they don't want to kill them," he said.

"But Iraq has sent its 15 and 16-metre missiles into our cities and killed children and their parents. They have killed these families as they lie asleep at night and they have even hit hospitals," he said with emotion.

He then hesitated, touched his dark moustache, and swept back his grey, balding hair, before going on. "I feel sorry for those who feel sympathy with the so-called peace calls of Saddam Hussein."

Opposition lives on in the Majlis
From DAVID BALDERSTONE, who recently visited Teheran

'The Age', May 27, 1982

Since Abolhassan Bani-Sadr escaped from Iran after being sacked as Iran's first post-revolution President last June, there has been an impression outside Iran that opposition voices inside the troubled country have been all but completely silenced.

Certainly, the regime-controlled Press does not publicise the views of critics of the regime. Iran's first post-revolution Prime Minister, Mehdi Bazargan, is rarely heard of, and Ibrahim Yazdi, a former post-revolution Minister, quietly goes about his business as a member of the Parliament, or Majlis.

The Foreign Minister during most of the American hostage crisis, Sadegh Qotbzadeh, is in Teheran's Evin prison accused of being involved in a plot to overthrow the regime.

Although criticism of the regime can be heard easily in private, it appears that the urban guerilla group, Mujahedeen Khalq, and other Leftist groups provide the only people opposing the regime. And their way is not with words, but with guns and bombs.

But, despite this impression abroad, there remains a small band of lonely opposition voices in the Majlis. There are about 30 "Opposition" deputies, overwhelmingly outnumbered when they sit among the 240 Majlis deputies.

They are often abused in the Government-controlled Press. For fear of being misunderstood, they rarely give interviews to the few foreign journalists in Teheran these days. The risks of being misunderstood are just too great.

Ezzatullah Sahabi, a Minister in Mr Bazargan's post-revolution Provisional Government, is one of these "Opposition" members in the Majlis. As he talked to 'The Age', he carefully weighed every word, and at the end pleaded: "Be careful".

He talked about his differences with the regime, the mistakes of Mr Bazargan's Provisional Government, and the differences within Iran's Islamic clergy generally, and within the ruling clergy itself.

"A coup d'état may take place but it could not last", Mr Sahabi said. The situation in Iran was different today to what it had been in 1953, when the Central Intelligence Agency helped oust the nationalist Prime Minister, Dr Mohammed Mossadegh, and restored the late Shah to the throne.

"Today, the masses of people are with the regime and especially with the Imam (Ayatollah Khomeiny), Mr Sahabi said. "Today people are armed and the past three years of conflicts and especially the war with Iraq have trained people and given them a militant revolutionary attitude."

An electrical engineer by training, Mr Sahabi spent more than 10 years in jail under the Shah's regime for political activity against the monarchy.

A devout Moslem, he is a supporter of the Islamic republic and the revolution. His differences with the ruling clergy-dominated elite are mainly over the manner in which it controls the political and bureaucratic machinery.

Turning the clock back to the heady days after the Shah was ousted early in 1979, Mr Sahabi said the Provisional Government – and particularly Mr Bazargan – had made many mistakes.

Although Mr Bazargan was "sincere" and "worked hard", he failed to comprehend the revolutionary atmosphere of the society – "and didn't want to understand either".

Mr Sahabi divided the opposition inside Iran into three groups. First, he said, there was the "radical left", including the Mujahedeen Khalq guerilla group. Second, there were "democrats and liberals". Third, there was a group not aligned with either of the first two, but opposed to the manner in which the regime ruled. He included himself within the third group.

"If the war with Iraq ends, criticism of the manner in which the Government is governing will intensify. Because of the war and special problems facing the revolution, the Opposition – except the radical Left – is not fighting the Government."

Mr Sahabi said the traditional Islamic clergy in Iran had differences with Ayatollah Khomeiny. He was extremely worried that the traditional clergy might attempt to impose an extreme Rightist regime in Iran once Ayatollah Khomeiny left the scene.

News Diary
DAVID BALDERSTONE in Amman

'The Age', May 31, 1982

The hi-fi word of Allah

The electronic muezzins, which save mullahs the bother of climbing minarets to call the faithful to prayer, have become louder and louder here in the Jordanian capital, Amman, during the past two weeks.

Is this a result of the spread of revolutionary Islam? After all, many have read – and some of us have written – the journalistic cliché about shockwaves being sent through moderate Arab capitals by the recent victories of Ayatollah Khomeiny's forces in the war against Iraq.

And, Amman is a moderate Arab capital, and Jordan is Iraq's closest ally.

The answer is no. Annually, at this time in the Islamic year, when the fasting month of Ramadan is just a few weeks away, the pre-recorded muezzins boom across the city.

It is not so noticeable in central Amman, which is literally downtown, being in a valley between the residential hills, or Jebels. Down town, the electronic muezzin has to compete with the cacophony of horns as traffic dodges hordes of pedestrians, including the bearers of sweet mint tea and Turkish coffee.

But up in the treed area of Jebel Amman, where life is more sedate, a Moslem would have to be stone deaf to miss the call.

Ramadan, especially as it falls in the height of summer at present, is a time to leave Amman. Smoking in the street during the daytime is forbidden, bars are closed, and restaurants will not serve wine.

And little can be achieved because the public service, which collectively suffers the pains of fasting from dawn to dusk (even though many officials do not fast) works at half pace, and that in some departments appears close to backwards.

Most ambassadors to King Hussein's Hashemite Court take leave during Ramadan, but with the uncertain political situation in neighboring Iraq, some European ambassadors are being told to stay put this year. Because of the shockwaves, that is.

Down to basics

While the approaching month of Ramadan may be to blame for the shouting electronic muezzins, there are signs of a growth of Islamic fundamentalism in Amman.

An increasing number of women are wearing the Islamic headscarf and a long, drab coat, with a solemn face to match. But, according to reliable sources, at least some of these women are wearing the Islamic garb merely because they are paid by a fundamentalist group to do so.

Therefore, it would seem that Western analysts are not alone in considering the cost of the spread of Islamic fundamentalism. Some people make money while others fear financial loss.

Flight of fancy

Since their recent victories in the Gulf war, Iranian leaders have an air of superiority about the righteousness of their cause.

But an analysis of Iran's superiority in the air, during the conflict, would have to take account of the considerable number of Iranian Air Force pilots who have taken off on sortie, and flipped off across the border – to what they see as freedom.

"Have you got a gun?" the young Iranian pilot asked a German correspondent, as we boarded a transport plane in Teheran, heading to the war front.

"No," replied the German.

"What a pity," said the pilot. "If you had a gun you could force me to fly to Cairo."

At the end of the battle front trip, as we waited for a plane back to Teheran, another Iranian Air Force pilot asked: "And how is Australia?"

Without waiting for a reply, he asked: "Can you help me get a visa?"

Then a French correspondent came up, and asked the pilot about the Iranian Air Force's problems with spare parts. But the Frenchman's English was not too clear and the pilot shook his head questioningly.

"What our French colleague means," a man from 'The Times' of London, elaborated, "is if a wing falls off one of your aircraft do you have another wing to place upon it?" To me this did seem, at that time, an overstatement of a spare parts problem.

The young Iranian pilot's attitude immediately changed. Whereas he had been talking softly and confidentially, he was now almost shouting.

"You Europeans think you are the only people who can make wings," he began in reply. "Well, we Iranians are just as clever as you Europeans, and we can make wings. If a wing falls off an aircraft we make another and fit it to the aircraft."

The correspondents stood, stunned. But then the Iranian pilot came close again, and resumed talking confidentially. "I had to say that stupid thing because someone was listening," he said, alluding to "revolutionary ears" being about the place. "Of course, we can't make wings," he declared.

Old diggers

Since Australian troops helped capture Amman from Ottoman rule in 1918 during World War I, Australians have been involved in developing the area, which became part of British mandated Palestine, and then the Hashemite Kingdom of Jordan.

An Australian team of archaeologists and architects has just begun work on a multi-million dollar development of the Roman city of Jerash, 50 kilometres north of Amman.

Jerash and Amman, which were known in Roman times as Gerasa and Philadelphia, were two of the cities of the Roman Decapolis – the 10 outpost cities of the Roman Empire in the Middle East.

The aim of Jordan's Department of Antiquities is to develop Jerash, which is one of Jordan's most impressive archaeological sites.

The task of the Australian team is to excavate an unexplored area of the city, and to help in the reconstruction of the city's second theatre, which seated about 3000.

The team has been organised by Professor Basil Hennessey, of Sydney University, who has excavated in Jordan for many years.

Ill. 15. Clearing the North Theatre, Jerash, 1982

Israel invades Lebanon: Tanks roll over border for strike at PLO
From DAVID BALDERSTONE in Beirut

'The Age', June 6, 1982

Israeli mechanised ground forces led by tanks advanced into Lebanon today on the third day of heavy Palestinian-Israeli fighting.

The Israeli tanks entered Lebanon by coastal roads and advanced towards the port city of Tyre, a Palestinian stronghold about 25 kilometres north of the border, according to a United Nations official and other witnesses.

The Israeli invasion came on the third successive day of heavy bombing raids into Lebanon by Israeli planes during which an Israeli F-16 was shot down.

President Reagan has urged Israel to refrain from further action that could widen conflict in the Middle East.

It is believed the Israeli ground forces advanced through lines of the UN peace-keeping force in southern Lebanon on a route which appeared to be heading to Palestinian positions around Tyre.

The UN Security Council late last night called for a ceasefire.

It is believed that before Israeli ground forces entered Lebanon today, the Palestine Liberation Organisation had ordered its forces to halt the shelling of settlements in northern Israel.

The fighting began on Friday with Israeli planes bombing Palestinian positions in Beirut and southern Lebanon in retaliation for the attempted assassination of Israel's Ambassador to Britain, Mr Shlomo Argov on Thursday night.

There was some speculation that Israel's Cabinet, which met in Jerusalem today, might have ordered an invasion of southern Lebanon – a development which would push the conflict to the level of Israel's invasion in 1978.

In addition to the Israeli plane which Israel's military command confirmed had been shot down over southern Lebanon, Palestinian officials in Beirut claimed that an Israeli military helicopter had been shot down.

The pilot parachuted to the ground near Nabatiyeh, about 15 kilometres from the border, and was captured by Palestinian guerillas.

It is the first time since 1974 that the Israelis have admitted losing an aircraft in conflict.

Last night the Security Council unanimously called for a ceasefire to come into effect just after dawn. The call had no effect. State-run Beirut Radio reported that Israeli planes bombed a southern Lebanese village soon after dawn.

Israeli planes appeared to be concentrating their bombing today on Palestinian targets around Nabatiyeh and the southern Lebanese ports of Tyre and Sidon.

Despite Israeli bombing as close as 40 kilometres away at Sidon, Beirut airport opened at dawn today. It has been closed for several hours over the past two days.

A few airliners took the opportunity and took the flight path over the Mediterranean beyond Beirut harbour and descended to the airport across areas of the city bristling with anti-aircraft weapons manned by jumpy gunners.

The airliners flew almost directly over the Camille Chamoun sports stadium, which was the main target of Israeli bombing raids around Beirut on Friday.

The Israelis claim the stadium was used by the Palestinians as a major munitions depot. The broken and mangled upper tiers of the reinforced concrete grandstands were drooping precariously today as rescue workers continued to sort through the rubble.

Nearby, and throughout much of West Beirut, helmeted gunners scanned the sky with anti-aircraft guns.

The fighting has finally brought an end to the shaky 11-month Palestinian-Israeli ceasefire, which was negotiated by the US special envoy, Mr Phillip Habib. Mr Habib is due back in the Middle East this week.

Although the Palestine Liberation Organisation has denied responsibility for the assassination attempt, Israel says it was the latest on the list of more than 150 Palestinian violations of the ceasefire.

Syrians bring in more armor
From DAVID BALDERSTONE, 'The Age' Middle East correspondent

'The Age', Beirut, June 8, 1982

Mechanised Syrian armored reinforcements were seen entering Lebanon today as fierce land and air battles continued on the third day of the Israeli invasion.

Truck loads of Syrian troops and rocket launchers moved in on the main Damascus-Beirut road last night and early today.

Witnesses said they were heading south through the Beka'a Valley in which Syria installed surface-to-air missiles last year.

It was not clear late today whether the reinforcements were designed to defend Syrian emplacements in between the coastal Lebanon Range and the parallel Ante-Lebanon Range further inland, or for use in major action against the Israelis.

There were further reports of clashes between Israeli troops and the Syrian and Lebanese armies.

The risk of full-scale Syrian assault against the Israeli forces remained high.

Israeli war planes continued heavy bombing raids against targets just south of Beirut. The capital shook to the sound of anti-aircraft fire most of the day as Israeli jets streaked over the city in support of advancing troops.

Military authorities in Tel Aviv claimed its jets shot down two Syrian MiGs in dogfights near Beirut, and the port city of Damour, 21 kilometres south of the city.

The air attacks followed the heavy attacks on the Palestinian Liberation Organisation headquarters south of Beirut last night.

There were unconfirmed reports today that Abu Jihad, military deputy to the PLO chairman, Yasser Arafat, had been killed during last night's bombing raids.

Mr Arafat last night urged his forces to continue the battle and to inflict heavy damage on the Israeli forces.

Late today Sidon was reported surrounded by Israeli forces.

An Israeli ground force was believed to be advancing north of Sidon to link up with another Israeli force just south of Sidon, which landed from the sea two days ago.

The regional command of the PLO is based in Sidon. Palestinian positions on the hills behind Damour have been consistently bombed by the Israelis over the past two years.

The road from Beirut to Damascus was deserted when I drove along it last night. Anti-aircraft military vehicles were strategically placed along the route. The road had been broken today by Israeli bombing north of Damour.

Israeli ground forces, supported from the sea and air, invaded Lebanon two days ago on the third day of intensive bombing raids against Palestinian positions in South Lebanon.

The initial intensive bombing began last Friday after the attempted assassination in London of Israel's Ambassador to Britain, Mr Shlomo Argov, who remained in a serious condition today.

Israel says its aim is to drive the PLO and Lebanese militia 40 kilometres north of the Lebanon-Israel border, to prevent them from shelling northern Israeli settlements.

Reports of casualties during the invasion have differed widely.

Israel has claimed that about 500 Palestinians have been killed for the loss of 25 Israeli soldiers.

However, the PLO today claimed that 400 Israeli troops had been killed or wounded.

Palestinian officials and their Lebanese Leftist allies were using loudspeakers atop Mosque minarets and roving vehicles to appeal for blood in predominantly Moslem West Beirut today.

The appeals indicated that the Palestinian forces had suffered heavy casualties.

Israel has responded to a United Nations Security Council call for a ceasefire by stating that Israeli forces would stay in Lebanon until the Lebanese internal situation changed so that Palestinian forces could not use the country as a base for attacking Israel.

The sky over Beirut was ablaze with red tracer last night as anti-aircraft gunners tried to hit Israeli aircraft.

War casualties cram hospital
From DAVID BALDERSTONE

'The Age', Beirut, June 9, 1982

The Lebanese doctor, his green medical suit heavily bloodstained, emerged from the operating theatre and described his patient's condition: "His colon and small intestine had burst out of his body."

Dr Adnan Diab then placed two bloodstained pieces of shrapnel he had removed from the patient on a tissue on his desk, leaned back wearily, and lit a cigarette.

The patient, a Palestinian fighter, had been severely wounded early today as the Israeli forces moved closer to Beirut.

The scene was the Palestinian Red Crescent's Acre Hospital next to the Sabra Palestinian refugee camp on the southern outskirts of Beirut.

With other reporters I visited the hospital today. It is near targets of recent heavy Israeli bombing over the past six days. No one was hiding fears that the area could be bombed later today as Israeli forces continue their thrust north towards the capital.

To get to the hospital we drove south along the Beirut Corniche – once a haven for sun and fun in the Paris of the Middle East – past truck-mounted anti-aircraft weapons pointing skywards. Earlier today, they had sent volleys into the air when Israeli warplanes were detected.

Despite the conflict so close to the city, many shops lifted their shutters along the fashionable Rue Hamra in central West Beirut today. People were sipping Turkish coffee as they listened to radios blaring the latest news.

But while there was an air of normality in the centre of the city, war felt very close at the Acre Hospital. One Palestinian fighter with a shrapnel wound in his arm had walked for four hours to the hospital after he had been wounded in the battle around Damour, the Palestinian stronghold town, 21 kilometres south of Beirut yesterday.

Dr Fathi Arafat – brother of the Palestine Liberation Organisation's chairman, Yasser Arafat, directs the Palestinian Red Crescent and was in a defiant mood today, despite heavy Palestinian casualties suffered since the Israelis invaded Lebanon on Sunday.

"We are in high spirits. We always declare that our revolution will have its victory," Dr Arafat told us as we talked in his book-lined office in Acre Hospital.

"We don't think about how many casualties we have suffered. We are facing a war aimed at killing all Palestinians."

Dr Arafat said he believed there had been thousands of casualties on both sides. More than 90 per cent of casualties on the Palestinian side had been civilians, he said.

Beirut about to fall: Israel

From DAVID BALDERSTONE, 'The Age' Middle East correspondent

'The Age', Beirut, June 10, 1982

Israeli planes today dropped leaflets on Beirut warning that Israel was about to capture the city.

The leaflets told Syrian forces in Lebanon to leave Beirut within a few hours.

The warning came after Israel had made saturation ground, sea and air attacks on Palestinian areas of southern Beirut, near the international airport.

As the Israeli navy continued shelling and Israeli planes bombed Beirut's southern suburbs, the rumble and scream of Israeli jets could be heard continually over the city.

The naval and air bombardment began at dawn. The headquarters of the Palestinian Liberation Organisation is in southern Beirut.

Israeli tanks were trying to approach the city along the coast road from positions established near the coast town of Damour, 21 kilometres south of the city, according to the Lebanese Christian radio station, 'Voice of Lebanon'.

The few shopkeepers who had courageously opened for business this morning later brought down the shutters. Fights broke out as people queued for increasingly scarce commodities, particularly bread.

The Israeli leaflet, addressed to the Syrian commander in Lebanon, said: "We shall capture the city in a short period."

It was signed by Israel's northern commander, and included a map showing two routes which could be used by the Syrians for a few hours to withdraw from the city back to Syria.

"We have committed a large part of our air, naval and ground forces, including a huge number of tanks, for the area of Beirut city," the leaflet said in Arabic.

"These forces can outgun and outnumber all your forces.

"As an experienced general, who lacks no wisdom, you must know that any attempt to throw your forces against the defence army (Israel Defence Forces) is tantamount to suicide.

"Since we do not want to fight the Syrian army, we have issued orders to our forces to let you and your forces leave the city."

Palestinian and Leftist Lebanese militiamen moved around the city and gathered as many leaflets as they could from the rubbish-littered gutters and pavements.

They also broadcast appeals over loud-hailers for the leaflets to be ignored.

State-run Beirut Radio reported today that Israeli forces had tried to land today at Beirut international airport, which was closed two days ago. The radio reported that the landing had been repulsed.

Heavy fighting was reported to be going on between Israeli forces and Syrian troops in the Beka'a Valley.

As news of heavy civilian casualties in southern Beirut reached central Beirut today, the Palestine Liberation Organisation's description of the Israeli invasion of Palestine as an annihilation campaign looked more and more apt. Palestinian refugee camps are located in southern Beirut.

Some Western diplomats have privately described the Israeli operation as a "final solution".

Israeli gunboats could be seen off the Beirut coast this afternoon. Smoke was rising from where the shells and bombs landed on southern Beirut. Over the centre of predominantly Moslem West Beirut, puffs of smoke could be seen in the sky behind Israeli warplanes.

Israeli ground forces, supported from the sea and air, invaded Lebanon last Sunday on the third day of intensive bombing raids against Palestinian positions in southern Lebanon.

The intial intensive bombing began last Friday after the attempted assassination in London of Israel's Ambassador to Britain, Mr Shlomo Argov.

The invasion, which has been widely condemned internationally, has cost Israel heavy casualties. An Israeli military spokesman told correspondents in Jerusalem today that in the 24 hours to midnight last night (8 am Melbourne time Thursday), 13 Israeli combatants had been reported killed. This brought to 45 the number of Israelis killed in the operation so far. In the same 24 hours, 27 Israelis had been seriously injured, 44 moderately injured and 93 slightly injured.

Although there were no reliable figures on Palestinian and Lebanese casualties, a senior Palestinian official said yesterday the invasion had left 8000 people dead, injured or missing.

Israel claimed last night that its planes destroyed Syria's surface-to-air missile system in the Beka'a Valley in a massive air attack yesterday.

Syria, which has about 25,000 Arab league-mandated "peace-keeping" troops in Lebanon, installed the missiles in the Lebanese valley last year after Israeli jets had shot down a Syrian helicopter over the valley.

Israel looks set for a long stay
From DAVID BALDERSTONE

'The Age', Beirut, June12, 1982

With the rumble of battle in the background, a small unshaven man sat behind his flower stall on West Beirut's main shopping street, Rue Hamra, early today. The white flowers he was selling looked exquisite laid out on a rough table beside the dirty gutter.

He wasn't doing much business. Perhaps this was because many people were queuing for bread 20 metres down the street. While he waited for customers, he held a small radio to his ear and listened to the latest news from the battle front just a few kilometres away.

This poignant early morning scene – the beautifully fresh flowers, the latest transistorised news, the dirty street and the sound of battle – provided an aptly contradictory scene early on the sixth day of Israel's invasion of Lebanon.

It was a scene of hope and despair. For many Lebanese that is the contradictory way in which they view the current crisis.

The thoughts of hope are directed along the probably erroneous line that the Israeli invasion may lead to a situation in which Lebanon's problems can be resolved once and for all. The thoughts of despair are obvious: once again Lebanon is being used as a playground for Middle East conflict.

Of course, the Israeli invasion has consequences far beyond the borders of the country. It is difficult to see that the invasion has solved any of Israel's problems. In fact the invasion means that Israel will live in an even more hostile, and unstable, area of the world.

The invasion has provided an indication that the present Israeli Government has decided to ignore attempts to resolve the crux of the Arab-Israeli dispute – the Palestinian problem.

In addition, the invasion is likely to further radicalise the Middle East, seriously undermine American influence, and jeopardise the stability of moderate regimes. It calls into question the role of the United Nations peace-keeping troops in this area. In short, it is bad news for the West.

With the sound of battle in the background, it is difficult to take an optimistic view. But amid the despair, there is a slim possibility that the Israeli invasion could lead to a resumption of Lebanese Government authority over the country, and – after initial radicalisation of the Palestinian movement – lead to an alignment with Jordan's King Hussein and the weakened PLO, which could jointly negotiate peace – in return for territory – with Israel.

The Israeli invasion, which has been widely condemned internationally, indicates that the present Israeli Government believes that the Palestinian problem can be resolved if Palestinian guns are out of range of Israel and Lebanese sovereignty – presumably under Christian rule, can be restored over Lebanese soil.

Palestinian guerilla forces, which were originally founded in Lebanon in the late 1960s, moved into Lebanon in force after being routed by King Hussein's army in Jordan in 1970-71.

This move of the Palestinian forces to Lebanon was merely an exacerbating element, rather than a cause, of the Lebanese civil war, which has raged on and off since 1975.

The basic cause of the civil war was the fact that Lebanese Moslem communities felt they were second class citizens in a country in which the Maronite Christian community enjoyed power and wealth under a system established when the Christians made up more than 50 per cent of the population.

Under this system, Lebanon's President must be a Maronite Christian, the Prime Minister a Sunni Moslem and the third ranking official – the Speaker of the Parliament – a Shi'ite Moslem.

The Palestinian presence exacerbated the underlying problems because the Palestinians provided armed clout to the Lebanese Leftist or Moslem militias.

In recent months however, the Palestinian Moslem alliance has come under severe strain.

Therefore there are moves underway aimed at achieving an anti-Palestinian Lebanese alliance to take over control of Lebanon in the event of an Israeli withdrawal.

It is doubtful that this could be achieved for anything but the briefest short term because the underlying problems behind the civil war are still present. And the Maronite Christian political front seems unlikely to compromise at all at present as it feels in a strong position in the wake of Israeli action against their arch rivals, the Palestinian forces.

Instead, Israel looks set for a long occupation of the areas they have captured. Otherwise they will have achieved nothing except a temporary weakening of the PLO through their costly invasion.

Israeli armor traps PLO in Beirut
From DAVID BALDERSTONE

'The Age', Beirut, June 15, 1982

Israeli armored columns and Lebanese Christian militia have combined to complete the encirclement of Palestine Libration Organisation positions in Beirut.

As the Israelis drove into the hillside suburb of Hadath, welcomed by Lebanese Christian inhabitants, fighting continued with Palestinians entrenched around Beirut airport on the coast.

The airport, damaged in several days of intense fighting between Israelis and Palestinians, was paralysed. Israeli gunboats were patrolling offshore and checking all ships moving into and out of Beirut. With the last escape roads cut, the PLO leaders were bottled up in their enclave in Moslem West Beirut.

Local residents were fleeing to the relative security of Christian parts of the city because they were expecting the Israelis to mount a final assault to crush the PLO positions.

The Israelis had thrust ahead after the collapse of a short-lived ceasefire with the Palestinians yesterday. Their armored columns skirted around the capital and made no immediate attempt to enter the city centre.

Only at the beach resort of Khalde, near the end of the main runway of Beirut airport, was their advance stopped by fierce Palestinian resistance.

A huge column of smoke could be seen rising above Khalde – 13 kilometres from the heart of the city – where Israeli fighter-bombers unleashed a barrage of bombs on Palestinian tank and artillery positions over the weekend. By mid-morning no new airstrikes were reported.

Meanwhile, at an urgent Cabinet meeting, the Lebanese President, Elias Sarkis, formed a seven-man salvation committee today to cope with the "grave situation" following the encirclement of the PLO.

State-run Beirut Radio said the salvation committee would be made up of politicians and factional leaders under the chairmanship of President Sarkis.

Apart from President Sarkis and the Prime Minister, Mr Wazzan, the board will include: the Foreign Minister, Mr Fuad Butros; Nasri Maarouf of the Rightist Christian National Liberal Party, Nabih Berri, leader of the Shi'ite Moslem paramilitary organisation AMAL; Bashir Gemayel, commander of the Right-wing Christian "Lebanese Forces", and Walid Jumblatt, leader of the Leftist alliance known as the National Movement.

As well as being spread across the political spectrum the members represent the main religious denominations in Lebanon.

The urgent Cabinet meeting has taken place at the Baabda Presidential Palace – with Israeli tanks parked only 200 metres away.

The tanks, nestling under pine trees, had a clear view of the mountain-side palace and of Palestinian areas in West and South Beirut.

Some of the Israelis had their boots off and were drinking fruit juice.

They were uneasily enjoying the calm, having arrived in the picturesque area overnight in the move that had completed the encirclement of Beirut.

A young Israeli soldier told me he had not expected to be in Beirut. "It's not so comfortable, but it's okay," he said.

The compound around the palace was guarded by units of the Christian-officered Lebanese army, which has remained on the sidelines of Lebanon's factional conflicts.

An Israeli armored personnel carrier, its crew sitting in the open, was seen driving past the Lebanese army guards outside the palace without any show of hostility between them.

After heavy air bombardment of Palestinian gun positions around Beirut late yesterday, the Israeli tanks and armored personnel carriers had stormed into Baabda village, about eight kilometres from the centre of West Beirut.

Israel's Defence Minister, Mr Sharon, met Christian political leaders overnight, Israel Radio reported today. The radio said the Christian leaders had agreed with the Israeli military operation into Lebanon.

A Lebanese army officer in Baabda told me today that Mr Sharon had swaggered into Baabda and asked the chief of the local Lebanese paramilitary police to arrange 12 rooms for the night for the officers accompanying him.

Today, Lebanese paramilitary forces were still mingling with the Israelis in Baabda, and traffic was proceeding a little nervously past the Israeli tanks.

Some of the tanks had fluorescent orange markers on top so they could be seen by Israeli warplanes.

Although this area was peaceful, fighting was continuing south of the city. Traffic streaming out of Moslem West Beirut to Christian East Beirut showed there were major fears that the Israelis were about to launch a final assault on Palestinian positions in West and South Beirut.

Palestinian guerillas around the city were bracing themselves for an attack aimed at destroying the political and military infrastructure of the PLO.

PLO chairman Yasser Arafat was attempting to negotiate a ceasefire with the Israelis and has appealed to Egypt to act as an intermediary.

The Israeli Foreign minister, Mr Shamir, confirmed that Cairo had been asked by the PLO to use its influence to get Israel to halt fighting.

The message was passed on by Egypt's ambassador in Tel Aviv, Saad Mortada.

In Cairo, the Minister of State for Foreign Affairs, Mr Boutros Ghali, told reporters the message was part of Egypt's contacts with all concerned parties to halt the fighting in Lebanon and to bring about a withdrawal of Israeli troops.

This was the first time the PLO had asked the Egyptians to mediate on its behalf since Egypt signed a peace treaty with Israel in 1979.

The move was interpreted by Israel Radio's political commentator Shimon Schiffer as a sign of the PLO's desperate position in Beirut.

Israeli officials have been reported as saying they would not agree to stop hostilities because Palestinian fighters had broken the ceasefire which came into effect on Saturday night. However, they said Israelis would not fire unless fired upon.

But with the fighting going on just south of Beirut, there seemed little chance of any kind of informal ceasefire bringing an end to the Israeli-Palestinian war.

Many Western embassies in Beirut that had not already offered their citizens safe conduct out of Lebanon published advertisements today in Lebanese newspapers, asking their citizens to contact them.

The Irish, Spanish, Swedish and Swiss embassies published appeals, while the US embassy repeated its advice of last week that US citizens should leave Beirut until the fighting abates around the city.

The evacuation of French, Italian and some British citizens along with United Nations personnel was taking place today and tomorrow in boats leaving Junieh.

The 'Los Angeles Times' reports from Jerusalem that the Israeli Cabinet will demand that the PLO be prevented from rebuilding its military infrastructure in southern Lebanon as part of the price for withdrawal of Israeli troops, Cabinet sources said.

As a long-term demand, Israel will seek the removal of all "foreign forces" – specifically those of Syria and the PLO – from Lebanon, the sources said.

US special envoy Philip Habib was expected to return to Damascus today with Israeli proposals for ending the strife in Lebanon.

Mr Habib, who helped arrange the ceasefire, has called on Israel not to fire back at Palestinian positions in Beirut.

He arrived in Israel from Damascus last Friday and conferred with the Prime Minister, Mr Begin, yesterday. Israeli officials said they believed he would return to the Syrian capital today.

The officials said Mr Begin had complained that the guerillas had continuously violated Saturday's ceasefire and fired on Israeli forces.

Israeli forces withheld fire "as long as possible but then had to reply to protect our soldiers," the Israeli Deputy Chief of Staff, Major-General Moshe Levy, told Israel Radio last night.

Israel guns batter PLO
From DAVID BALDERSTONE

'The Age', Beirut, June 18, 1982

Fighting broke out again today between Israeli forces and Palestinian guerillas on the southern outskirts of Beirut, as talks involving the Palestinian Liberation Organisation continued in a bid for a ceasefire.

After a day of contradictory comments from the PLO, the State-run Beirut Radio suggested that the PLO leader, Yasser Arafat, was prepared to accept a new form of Palestinian presence in Lebanon.

The radio said Israeli gunners shelled the Palestinian camp at Bourj al-Brajneh close to Beirut airport, from hill positions. The Palestinians and their Lebanese Leftist allies returned the fire.

The two sides agreed to a ceasefire last week, but Israeli forces have since made slow but steady encroachments on Palestinian positions.

Israeli troops yesterday captured part of the Lebanese University science faculty building near the airport after fierce fighting in which the Palestinians said they killed 12 Israeli soldiers.

Beirut residents said Israeli troops spent the night dropping flares over the airport and south Beirut to pinpoint Palestinian positions and movements.

Palestinian sources said Israeli troops, now in the 12th day of their invasion, appeared to be aiming for the Palestinian strongholds of Chatila and Sabra, both just north of the airport.

Lebanese newspapers showed photographs of earth ramparts built by Palestinians in the southern suburbs in anticipation of an Israeli assault on their remaining positions.

The guerillas have vowed they will fight to the last man if the Israelis try to force their way into West Beirut.

There were no reports of fighting on the eastern flank of West Beirut, where the Palestinians and their allies face Right-wing Christians friendly to Israel across the "green line" dividing the city.

Beirut Radio said the Lebanese army was taking up new positions and manning new roadblocks in the mainly Christian eastern part of the city.

Israel and the United States are pressing the Lebanese Government to send the army into West Beirut to disarm the guerillas, diplomatic source said.

The report of Mr Arafat's views on a new status for the Palestinians in Lebanon – although obscured somewhat by PLO statements later in the day – raised a number of political possibilities.

Coming after the Israelis had occupied most of the PLO strongholds south of Beirut and had tightened their grip on the organisation's headquarters of west and south Beirut, it appeared to indicate merely that the PLO leader was accepting the obvious.

On the other hand, it also followed quotes from a senior aide to Mr Arafat that Palestinian guerillas might lay down their arms in exchange for recognition by the United States – which would indicate that the PLO was leaning towards a fundamental political compromise.

In a United Press International report yesterday, the aide indicated that Palestinian guerillas would be prepared to lay down their arms under certain conditions.

Mr Hani Al Hassan, a member of the central committee of the biggest Palestinian guerila group, Fatah, was reported as saying the PLO was ready to discuss everything, including laying down its arms, provided the talks were held directly with the United States.

Later however, PLO spokesman Mahmoud Labadi said Mr Al Hassan had been misquoted.

However, the PLO has long sought US recognition, and it is conceivable that part of the PLO leadership may have considered the US would reconsider its position towards the organisation if it meant a halt to the bloodshed.

There is also speculation here that Mr Al Hassan was quoted correctly and was "flying a kite" to test US reaction, but when the US State Department reaffirmed that the US would not talk to the PLO until it recognised Israel's right to exist, the PLO denied Mr Al Hassan's comments.

Consultations continued today between the Lebanese authorities and the PLO.

Lebanese political sources said efforts to convene a meeting of a National Salvation Board to deal with the invasion crisis were beginning to gain ground.

The Lebanese President, Mr Elias Sarkis, named seven board members last Monday but only one turned up for the first meeting and two pro-Palestinian nominees were hesitant to participate.

Mr Walid Jumblatt, leader of the Leftist National Movement, at first called for a more representative board but yesterday was showing greater willingness to take part, political sources said.

Mr Nabih Berri, leader of the Shi'ite paramilitary organisation, AMAL, had also dropped his intial objections and the board could hold its first meeting within a week, the sources said.

The Israeli Prime Minister, Mr Menachem Begin, phoned his Cabinet from New York yesterday and told them to do what is necessary "for the sake of the security of Israel," – even if this causes the cancellation of his scheduled meeting on Monday with President Reagan.

He was reacting to reports that his meeting with President Reagan may be cancelled if Israel "does not behave". Mr Begin also plans to meet with the Secretary of State, Mr Alexander Haig, at the United Nations.

These reports referred to the concern of American officials that, despite contrary assurances, Israel's army intends to invade Beirut to annihilate the PLO leaders surrounded there.

The Government in Jerusalem announced that Mr Begin called Mr Simcha Ehrlich, acting Prime Minister in his absence, shortly after it was reported that Israeli commandos, with the help of artillery fire from Lebanon's Falangist militia, had captured a strategic building only a mile from Beirut airport.

Meanwhile, Israeli Defence Foreign Ministry and other officials met yesterday to develop ways to achieve the basic conditions Israel has said it will insist upon before its army withdraws from Lebanon.

The planners are charged with drafting position papers to be presented to a seven-member ministerial committee headed by Mr Begin.

The ministerial committee will make Israel's final decisions in what are likely to be tough, prolonged negotiations with Syria and Lebanon, and possibly the United States and other countries which might contribute peace-keeping troops, as well as – but only indirectly – the PLO.

Blood and mystery follow Israel's drive to Beirut
From DAVID BALDERSTONE in Beirut

'The Age', June 19, 1982

Through the shattered glass littering a deserted road they ran carrying their baby. He was wearing khaki military pants and a white tee-shirt. It was difficult to say later how the woman was dressed because the tears pouring down her face distracted attention from what she was wearing.

The baby looked injured, perhaps even dead. As they ran, Israeli shells continued to fall occasionally on the West Beirut residential area the couple had just left. It was an agonising war portrait which did not portray a scene of blood and bodies on a footpath but of people just coping.

"We should have asked them whether we could help, whether we could take them to a hospital in our taxi or something," my colleague said. But we hadn't, and the couple had gone now. When shells are falling, albeit further away than usual, minds glaze and don't always tell you what you should do.

We may not have even been able to help, but at least we would have found out who the couple were and what had happened. Perhaps his khaki pants indicated that he was a Palestinian, or more likely a Lebanese Leftist militiaman because we were in a Lebanese Moslem residential area of the city.

It does not matter really that these questions remained unanswered. This bloody Palestinian-Israeli war which has brought Israeli troops to Beirut has left a long list of questions unanswered.

The taxi driver had driven off and glided his taxi into the protection of the garage of a highrise apartment building. We inspected the damage caused to an apartment block where an Israeli shell had hit the day before. Several people had been killed and two floors of the building were destroyed. But there were no people around so seeing the damage did not give a feeling of this war.

It is people that many of the unanswered questions revolve around – the future for the people of Lebanon, the Palestinians and the future security of the people of Israel.

It will be a long time before the full implications are known of the war, which has left an unknown number of Israeli soldiers dead and thousands of Lebanese and Palestinians either dead, wounded, missing or homeless.

Certainly the political and military infrastructure of the Palestine Liberation Organisation has been severely damaged. Lebanon has been the PLO's main base since the troops of Jordan's King Hussein drove Palestinian guerillas out of Jordan in 1970-71. But the infrastructure has not been completely destroyed because it continues to exist in the Syrian capital, Damascus, and to a lesser extent in the Jordanian capital, Amman.

The Israeli invasion began three days after Israel's ambassador to Britain was shot by anti-PLO Palestinian extremists in London. Initially the Israeli move appeared to give Lebanon a new chance for national reconciliation but following the fierceness and extent of the fighting, it is doubtful that this will be achieved.

At the same time, it must be said that the Israeli invasion, which has left Israeli troops occupying the coastal area of Lebanon from the Israeli border to Beirut, has given Lebanon the best opportunity for reconciliation since its civil war began in 1975.

For seven years, the Palestinian guerillas and Leftist militias have had their main military positions in these areas. Now the Israelis intend to withdraw only if they can hand them over to the control of the Lebanese Army supported by an international peace-keeping force.

During the civil war, Palestinian military forces provided the clout the Lebanese Leftist forces needed to fight for more rights for Lebanese Shi'ite and Sunni Moslems in Lebanon's complicated confessional system of government. During the months before the Israeli invasion, this Palestinian-Leftist alliance began to come unstuck, mainly because the traditional residents of the area –

particularly the Shi'ite Moslems – became weary of Palestinian guerillas occupying their land.

Therefore by crushing the Lebanese Leftist militias and the Palestinian guerillas, Israel has converted this weariness into a real chance of reconciliation between the various political and religious factions in the country.

"Ninety per cent of the Lebanese people want an end to the crisis," a Sunni Moslem businessman from Lebanon's northern port of Tripoli told me this week. "As a Sunni Moslem, I couldn't care less if the Lebanese President has to be a Maronite Christian. We just want an end to crisis. We want Lebanon back." In speaking of a Christian President, the businessman was referring to Lebanon's confessional system, under which the President has to be a Maronite, the Prime Minister a Sunni Moslem, and the Speaker a Shi'ite. This system, which is based on a no-longer valid census which showed Maronites making up more than half the population, permeates the whole society.

"I feel sorry for the Palestinians." The businessman went on. "But I don't want them occupying my country." Among the Lebanese, this attitude has been very strong during the Israeli invasion. The Israelis were doing what the Lebanese themselves had not been able to do – evict the Palestinian guerillas. Nevertheless, the casualties among Lebanese and Palestinians are likely to lead to more extremism among the poorer people which will complicate the chances of long-term national reconciliation.

Because the Palestinians have nowhere to go, it's likely the Palestinian war machine will be built up again. Palestinian officials said this week that many of their fighters had been six and seven-year-old Palestinian "cubs" during the Jordanian civil war. Similarly this war will create new recruits.

An example of this savage method of recruiting is not hard to find. A television cameraman was filming damage around the Sabra Palestinian refugee camp in South Beirut when a Palestinian boy placed a beer carton down beside him and removed a hessian cover. The boy, who was about nine, pointed down to the box, which contained chunks of human flesh that he had gathered together after a shell had struck his home.

Judging by previous onslaughts against the Palestinians, that boy is likely to be a prime target for recruitment into a Palestinian guerilla organisation.

But the war has brought out dissatisfactions among the Palestinian and Leftist groups, including a widespread feeling of desperation with the Arab leadership. Alluding to the lack of any significant support for the Palestinians during the crisis, a 22-year-old Shi'ite Moslem from South Lebanon told me: "Arab leaders are just full of talk."

Until three years ago, when he was seriously injured during factional clashes, this young man had been a fighter in a communist militia. But when he was injured, "no one even sent me a flower. No one visited me," he said angrily.

"They need you while you are alive and can fight. But then they thought I would die, so they didn't worry about me anymore." He noted that Israeli officers, including a general, had been killed during the fighting. "Have you ever heard of a Palestinian general being killed in fighting? None of the leaders are ever killed. This is what is wrong with Arab leaders – they don't fight for their people."

Driving around the war-hit areas of Beirut, it becomes obvious that thousands of millions of dollars will be required to repair the damage. Shells have left craters in many of the roads of South and West Beirut as well as heavily damaging buildings. Drains have burst, and power lines have been brought down.

Despite power failures, emergency services including hospitals have held up to the strain reasonably well. I stood in the forecourt of the American University of Beirut Hospital in central West Beirut as ambulances arrived during a day of particularly heavy fighting.

Stretchers were lined up waiting, and patients were admitted to casualty wards quickly. The ambulances which belonged to the various militias usually arrived with an armed fighter aboard to guard the vehicle.

Whereas most shops were closed in West Beirut, the scene was different in Christian East Beirut. Shops there were open and the streets clean. While there were mixed feelings about the invasion in West Beirut the Christians of East Beirut generally welcomed the conflict as a means of achieving national reconciliation under a strong Maronite Christian.

Westerners warned to quit Beirut
From DAVID BALDERSTONE

'The Age', Beirut, June 22, 1982

Israeli warplanes screamed over Beirut today as fierce fighting continued between Syrian and Israeli forces in the east of the city and an Israeli gunboat shelled Syrian military positions on the West Beirut seafront.

The United States, British and French embassies advised their nationals to leave Beirut yesterday. A British ship evacuated British and Commonwealth citizens from Junieh port in the Christian sector, just north of the capital today.

One senior Western diplomat said last night that the Americans had reluctantly advised their nationals to leave because the US Secretary of State, Mr Haig, had not been convinced that Israel's Prime Minister, Mr Begin, had grasped the message that the US Administration was against Israeli forces entering the besieged city.

There is a strong feeling in this sector of the city that Israel is about to launch a heavy attack against the guerillas. A portent of this came today – staff of the Commodore Hotel where I am staying put protective tape on the windows.

The all-out Israeli attack could come after the special US envoy, Mr Habib, leaves Beirut today. He was due to go to Jerusalem.

The renewed heavy fighting, which broke out less than a day after the latest Syrian-Israeli ceasefire had been proclaimed, further reduced hopes of a political solution to the crisis.

Throughout the day the rumble of high-flying Israeli warplanes could be heard over Beirut and sporadic explosions rocked the city during the day.

Sirens wailed as ambulances rushed to the scene of the explosions in the west side of the city where around 6000

Palestinian and Lebanese Leftist fighters have been trapped by Israeli forces.

Today's fighting was centred around Syrian positions near the Beirut-Damascus highway to the east of the city. Israeli forces appeared to be trying to tighten their grip on the road.

Two massive blasts – presumed to be car bombs – rocked West Beirut late yesterday. Twenty-five people are known to have died in the explosions in the seafront area, which was largely destroyed in the so-called "Battle for the Hotels" during the 1975-76 civil war. Another 125 people were wounded.

An Israeli Defence Forces spokesman in Tel Aviv blamed Syrian forces for starting the fighting today.

The Lebanese Christian radio station "Voice of Lebanon" said today that one Syrian MiG fighter had been shot down during the fighting.

Israeli warplanes made some low passes over Beirut and drew heavy anti-aircraft fire from Palestinian positions and Leftist militiamen in the western sector of the city.

Meanwhile, political consultations aimed at finding a peaceful solution appeared to be failing. While the Lebanese Cabinet met in emergency session today, there were only slight hopes of a political solution emerging from talks between members of the new National Salvation Council. The council, representing the country's religious and political faction leaders, has been talking for several days.

The talks revolve around the idea of the Lebanese Army being deployed in West Beirut and the Palestinian guerillas withdrawing into the Palestinian refugee camps.

In return there are demands that the Israeli forces should withdraw from positions around Beirut.

Mr Habib is believed to have sought clarification about the future presence of the Palestinian Liberation Organisation in Lebanon, during meetings with Lebanese leaders yesterday.

PLO evacuation hitch
From DAVID BALDERSTONE

'The Age', West Beirut, June 28, 1982

Five Egyptian frigates left Alexandria harbour yesterday and headed towards Beirut, leading to speculation that they were being sent to evacuate the 6000 Palestinian guerillas trapped in besieged West Beirut.

However, it is believed that a tentative plan to evacuate the guerillas and the Palestine Liberation Organisation leadership was abandoned early today.

President Mubarak of Egypt had said he would welcome the PLO as a political, but not a military, organisation based in Egypt.

But it is believed that the PLO is not prepared to give up its arms and leave by sea. Late today, it was believed that the Palestinians were insisting on leaving Beirut by road to Syria carrying their arms.

With Israeli armor maintaining its tight grip around West Beirut, the PLO earlier today appeared to be edging towards a political deal which would avert a final battle for the city.

However hopeful signs were mixed with gloom as Palestinian and Lebanese Leftist fighters continued to stand by on full alert in the shell-shattered rubble around the approaches to the city.

After a day of increased fighting in West Beirut, President Sarkis of Lebanon said last night Beirut was facing "imminent and certain disaster".

"In these difficult hours, the Lebanese are holding their breath expecting dangers that threaten the city of Beirut with total and fatal destruction," Mr Sarkis said in a statement broadcast on TV last night.

Despite hardline public statements by the PLO today, it appeared that political talks aimed at resolving the crisis were making progress.

Despite Israeli demands that Palestinian guerillas should be disarmed and the PLO's leadership removed from Beirut, it is believed today that the PLO has continued to demand a "symbolic and regular" military presence in Lebanon.

The word "regular" is important in this context because it draws a distinction with the irregular fighters who have been an important force in West Beirut since Lebanon's civil war.

It appeared toady that the PLO was looking for a military presence in Lebanon similar to that in Jordan, where Palestinian guerillas were routed by King Hussein's army 10 years ago.

In Jordan, units of the Palestine Liberation Army are based under the firm control of the Jordanian Army.

As these tortuous negotiations – involving the PLO, Lebanese authorities, and the special US envoy, Mr Philip Habib – continued today, it appeared that a main reason why the negotiations were taking so long was the trapped PLO's need to save face.

Saving face is a factor which delays most negotiations in the Arab world.

Hardline statements by PLO officials today have to be read in this context. A PLO official said today the Palestinian forces would fight on.

"The decisions by the Palestinian leadership have always been, since the Zionist-American invasion, for steadfastness and victory," the official said.

However there were fears that increasing Israeli impatience would run out before a political deal involving the PLO had been worked out.

Arafat plays a game of brinkmanship
From DAVID BALDERSTONE

'The Age', West Beirut, July 8, 1982

In the Palestinian headquarters area of besieged West Beirut the street was almost deserted. There were sandbags, rubble from a bombed building, broken glass, and a few lightly armed men.

Suddenly, a small car followed by a Mercedes turned the corner and pulled up outside one of the apartment buildings. Mr Yasser Arafat stepped out of the small car, and the street came alive.

Armed guards jumped from the Mercedes, and surrounded the chairman of the Palestine Liberation Organisation. His eyes darting and twinkling, Mr Arafat shook hands with the PLO fighters and workers.

For a man under the siege of Israeli armor, he seemed extremely relaxed. For the leader of an estimated 6000 guerillas trapped in West Beirut, he gave no impression that he felt he was defeated.

Instead, Mr Arafat said the struggle for Palestine would go on. "There is one choice for Palestinians – death or victory. The solution for the Middle East problem is for the Palestinians to return to their homeland."

These were the kind of words Mr Arafat has been uttering more and more frequently since the Israeli forces invaded Lebanon on 6 June.

In a sense he has had to. While negotiating the almost certain evacuation of the PLO from Beirut, and a future for the organisation, he has had to keep up the morale of the fighters.

In order to get the best possible deal from the American-spearheaded negotiations, Mr Arafat has had to be able to demonstrate that if Israel took the military option and moved into West Beirut, the operation would cost a lot of lives in the street to street fighting.

With another reporter, I went to the PLO headquarters area yesterday. We didn't expect to meet Mr Arafat. The very few people who know his movements keep them to themselves. He is a wanted man.

After he arrived at the building we were ushered into a dingy back room. First Mr Arafat sat down, and then he stood up. Then he darted into the next room, and then he returned.

A few hours earlier, the Soviet Union had warned the United States against landing marines in Beirut.

"This is a very important statement. It means more and more elements and factors are entering into the equation," Mr Arafat said.

Pressed on the point that the statement did not go as far as the PLO might have wished, he said: "That's enough on this topic."

This response appeared to reflect the growing disenchantment with the Soviet Union in the Arab world.

Although the US – as Israel's main economic supporter and arms supplier – has taken the brunt of public criticism, the Soviet Union has been strongly criticised for failing to do anything of substance to try to halt the Israeli invasion.

In the superpower context, the current negotiations over the probable evacuation of the PLO have important implications.

Although the US continues to refuse to recognise the PLO until the organisation recognises Israel's right to exist, the US has had to accept the PLO as a "negotiating partner" in an attempt to prevent a final battle for Beirut.

The negotiations have not been face to face. Mr Arafat has not met the special envoy Mr Philip Habib. But Mr Habib has had to seek Mr Arafat's views through intermediaries.

This relationship could develop further if, as expected, Mr Arafat and the mainstream PLO leadership end up in Cairo – capital of the US's closest Arab ally and Israel's peace partner.

Although the Israeli invasion has severely crippled the PLO's political and military infrastructure, it could turn the PLO into a force which will be hard to ignore.

With the PLO mainstream likely to go to Cairo, Mr Arafat will find himself free from Syrian control and hardline Palestinian influence. He may turn out to be a much more free agent than he has been in the past – a man who can lead the PLO into a peace process which will lead – through diplomacy rather than rockets and bombs – to the establishment of a Palestinian State.

On the other hand, the PLO could collapse in flames and rubble in the next few days. Mr Arafat is playing the game of brinkmanship to the limit. Many people think he has already gone too far in this dangerous game.

After agreeing in principle to the evacuation of the PLO, he has appeared to toughen his stand on the type of international force which should come into West Beirut to supervise the evacuation.

He appeared to indicate yesterday that he would only accept a United Nations force. But like so many of his comments, which have led to confusion in the past, he only appeared to "indicate". He said the PLO's proposal was for a United Nations force.

Did this mean he would not accept a United States, French and Lebanese multinational force? He merely repeated that the proposal was for a UN force.

This reminded me of his statement that the PLO believes in a just peace based on full Israeli withdrawal to 1967 borders. This statement implies recognition of Israel's right to exist. But he has never explicitly said the PLO recognises Israel's right to exist.

Mr Arafat left as quickly as he had arrived. His guards asked us not to take photographs of his small car, which had ski racks on the roof. The ski racks could mean Mr Arafat is on a slippery slope. Then again, the racks could mean he intends to drag on the negotiations until snow begins to fall on the Lebanese mountains in four months' time.

Guns open up again in Lebanon
From DAVID BALDERSTONE

'The Age', Beirut, July 11, 1982

Fierce artillery and rocket duels broke out today as diplomatic efforts to end the Lebanon crisis intensified.

The fighting, which followed a night of sporadic gunfire, was concentrated around the Palestinian stronghold areas in the southern suburbs of West Beirut.

It was believed that Palestinian gunners were returning fire against Israeli positions on the Christian east side of the city's dividing line around the Presidential palace at Baabda in the hills above Beirut.

The rumble of missiles streaking out of positions near the centre of West Beirut rolled across the city, punctuated by the sound of incoming shells.

Earlier, the Palestine Liberation Organisation welcomed Syria's refusal to accept the Palestinian fighters trapped in West Beirut.

A PLO spokesman, Mahmoud Labadi, told me the organisation was very pleased about the Syrian decision because it meant there was nowhere except Palestine for the guerillas to go.

On Friday night the official Syrian newsagency quoted a senior official saying Syria was – under normal circumstances – a homeland of the Palestinians and the Arabs as a whole.

"But under the prevailing circumstances there is no room for the Palestinian fighters to move from Beirut to Syria because their natural place is where they are at present pending the recovery of their legitimate rights," the official said.

The Syrian statement, which was repeated today, stymied a plan for the guerillas to be evacuated overland from Beirut to Syria. An earlier plan envisaged at least some of the guerillas being evacuated by sea from Beirut to the Syrian port of Latakia.

It is understood the Syrians made the decision because the Damascus regime felt slighted by the belated US decision to involve it in negotiations.

However, there could be a change of Syrian attitude when Syria's Foreign Minister, Mr Khaddam, visits Washington later this week.

The US Deputy Assistant Secretary of State, Mr Morris Draper, who returned to Beirut from Damascus at the weekend, today briefed the US special envoy, Mr Habib, on his mission.

Mr Habib today continued his against-the-clock struggle to achieve a political solution to the crisis.

One positive point emerged out of the confused political situation at the weekend when Greece said it was willing to provide naval vessels to evacuate the trapped guerillas if the PLO requested it.

The Papandreou Government's offer added credibility to the proposed multinational force, which would be made up of US marines, French troops and units of the Lebanese Army.

Ships of the US Sixth Fleet arrived off the Lebanese coast late last week.

Witnesses have reported two French naval vessels in the Cyprus harbour of Larnaca. Sailors told a reporter now in Beirut that the ships were standing by for a request to come to Beirut.

French troops attached to the United Nations force in South Lebanon are also ready to come to Beirut.

Begin peace pact plan gets rebuff
From DAVID BALDERSTONE

'The Age', West Beirut, July 18, 1982

Lebanon's Prime Minister, Mr Wazzan, has rejected the idea of a peace treaty between Lebanon and Israel.

Mr Wazzan's statement was published today - less than 24 hours after Israel's Prime Minister predicted that such a peace treaty would be signed before the end of the year.

"I am certain that Lebanon will not sign a unilateral peace treaty with Israel," Mr Wazzan said in an interview published in Beirut's 'Monday Morning' magazine.

"All local, Arab and international efforts and the efforts of all peace-loving forces, must henceforth focus on achieving comprehensive peace which eliminates all the tragedies of the region, foremost among which is the tragedy of the Lebanese and Palestinian peoples," he said.

Mr Wazzan's statement came as negotiations aimed at evacuating the Palestine Liberation Organisation from besieged West Beirut remained deadlocked.

At a mass rally in Tel Aviv last night, Mr Begin said the PLO had less than a month in which to leave West Beirut.

In addition to predicting the Lebanon-Israel peace treaty, Mr Begin offered to discuss with King Hussein of Jordan peace between their countries.

Mr Begin proposed a confederation between the two. He said Israel would provide Jordan with a free port at Haifa in exchange for a peace treaty.

Similar suggestions by Mr Begin in the past have been rejected out of hand by Jordan.

But a number of factors which have placed increased pressure on King Hussein probably provide the reason why Mr Begin renewed the offer at this stage.

King Hussein is being pressured from two sides – Islamic fundamentalism and Palestinian political developments in the wake of Israel's invasion of Lebanon.

Iran's invasion of Iraq last week is sure to concern King Hussein, as it might force Iraq's President Saddam Hussein from power. Jordan has been Iraq's strongest ally in the Gulf war, having received millions of dollars of aid from Iraq.

Along with other moderate Arab leaders, King Hussein has expressed concern about the consequences of Iranian victory in the Gulf war, which would provide another boost for Ayatollah Khomeiny's brand of Islamic fundamentalism.

On the other hand, the removal of the PLO from Lebanon could place pressure on the monarchy in Jordan – which has a Palestinian population of more than 50 per cent.

Despite these pressures, King Hussein will be rather cynical of Mr Begin's offer. Understandably, since Mr Begin's Defence Minister, Mr Sharon, has regularly expressed the view that Jordan is a Palestinian State.

News Diary
From DAVID BALDERSTONE in Amman

'The Age', August 2, 1982

The only way to travel

If a Lebanese taxi driver will not take you, no one will. He will drive, and charge, like a wounded bull, but he will go almost anywhere.

It was with several of this curious breed of men that I travelled from besieged West Beirut to the Jordanian capital Amman. In normal times there would be nothing so strange about that as taxis are a way of life in the Middle East, where it seems, many people have never quite adjusted to the invention of the aeroplane.

But at present, the direct Beirut to Damascus route takes you through the no-man's land between Israeli and Syrian forces in the Lebanon ranges to the east of the Lebanese capital.

There is another way – dubbed the scenic route by journalists – through the northern Lebanese port of Tripoli and the central Syrian city of Homs. But this takes seven hours, and if the intelligence network run by the taxi drivers declares the direct route safe it is preferable, as it takes only three hours.

True to his word, my driver was in the lobby of the Commodore Hotel, West Beirut at 6 am, and well entrenched in a political discussion over Turkish coffee when I emerged at 6.30.

First we travelled to his home, an obligatory gesture apparently, to show the wife that her husband is really going where he said he was.

Then we crossed the "green line" dividing the city, farewelling the last of the trapped Palestinian guerillas and their bunkers, passed the Christian Lebanese and Israeli checkpoints and headed for the Beirut-Damascus highway. We had to stop for petrol, of course, and five minutes later for a sandwich breakfast. In five years, I have not known a Middle East driver who was not hungry.

All went well as we charged up the mountain and through the village of Bhamdoun, where shattered buildings remained as a monument to heavy Syrian-Israeli fighting. But as we approached the Israeli front line, a tinge of concern crossed the driver's face. He stopped the few drivers coming the other way, sought intelligence about the state of the road, and shook his head with deep concern. "You will have to change drivers," he declared.

So, when we reached the Israeli line and the coiled barbed wire across the highway, I farewelled the driver. Another was immediately on hand to help carry my baggage to his cab on the other side of the barbed wire.

Evidently the highway was dangerous – some said mined – so we detoured through a series of villages lying between the Israeli and Syrian lines, and rejoined the highway near the village called Sofar. With Israeli parachute flares drifting down overhead, there was only one thing comforting about this stage of the journey: the driver had his two young sons with him. Surely it could not be dangerous if this man took his young sons along, could it?

At the first Syrian checkpoint, a Syrian soldier had "I love you" scratched in felt pen on his webbing belt. A few kilometres on we stopped at a café; the driver was hungry.

It was only 9 am but three Syrian soldiers were drinking beer. Time has no meaning during war – or at least that's what I told myself as I ordered an arak. The flares continued to drift down overhead.

A few kilometres further drivers had to be changed once again. It seems the driver with the two young sons specialised on the between-lines stretch, where understandably, the fare was highest.

The third driver drove across the lush Beka'a Valley, through the Lebanese and Syrian border posts, and on to Damascus. I don't recollect him having to stop to eat, but he did have to stop for a box of lemons.

Don't shoot

During the early days of the crisis, the management of the Commodore Hotel decided it was inappropriate to have the pianist playing in the bar while the Israelis were invading.

So poor Anwar Maatouk was out of work. But not for long. He was hired by a television cameraman – who was short of a soundman, those extraordinarily brave people who carry the equipment into battle with the cameraman. The soundman is joined by an umbilical cord. If the cameraman is brave – and this veteran of wars is – so is the soundman.

In his own right the pianist was brave – some say because he went out to battle as high as a kite on something or other well known in Lebanon.

"All you have to do is push these buttons and turn on the machine when I tell you," the cameraman instructed the pianist.

Shells were falling all around. The cameraman was tracking an approaching Israeli plane through his lens. The cameraman shouted: "Hit the machine." He meant of course, turn it on.

The Israeli plane continued its deadly dive towards it target. The cameraman got a gentle tap on his shoulder, and the pianist asked: "What will I hit the machine with?"

After his short-lived career as a soundman, I can claim some credit for getting him his rightful job back as a pianist. With a colleague singing, I took to the keyboard one night after dinner with a broad repertoire spearheaded by 'Waltzing Matilda' and 'Land of Hope and Glory'.

The Commodore's manager, Fouard Saleh, rehired the piano player that night.

Top secret

Crossing the Syrian-Jordan border en route to Amman, I had to pass through the usual checks by internal intelligence officers of both countries. This always reminds me of the experience a friend, a British archaeologist, had in northern Iraq.

He and his team had to pass through a small village every night from their archaeological site to their accommodation. One night, a plain-clothed man stopped their car as they entered the village.

"Passports please," the man requested.

"Why should we show you our passports?" the archaeologists asked.

"Because I am the secret policeman of the village."

"How do we know you are the secret policemen?"

"Ask anyone in the village," the secret policeman said. "They all know."

Know-alls

After seven weeks in West Beirut, Amman appears to be a great city. People complain about the lack of night life, but laughs during the day make up for it.

Mohammed, our trusted man who cleans the flat and calls every day to make sure everything is in order, was first on the scene at 7.30 the morning after I arrived back in Amman.

"How is Beirut?" he asked. I was given about 10 seconds to answer before he launched into his explanation about the geopolitical situation in the Middle East.

Then the gas man delivered another cylinder for the stove and sought an opinion on the Beirut situation. Then the rubbish man arrived and asked the same questions.

Exhausted, I went to the local store for some milk. Suleiman, the owner's assistant, emerged from behind the cornflakes and said he had prayed for me every day during Ramadan.

Unlike the others, he was honest enough not to seek my opinion about Beirut before launching into his version of events.

"I told you, Mr David, something was going to happen this summer, and sure enough something did," he declared.

I remain sceptical about whether Suleiman knew any more than me about what was going to happen this summer.

Hussein's reputation for survival tested
From DAVID BALDERSTONE

'The Age', Amman, August 7, 1982

If it were not for the fact that King Hussein – aged only 46 – had survived as ruler of Jordan for a staggering 30 years, it could be argued that the current crisis in Lebanon and its implications for the area had numbered his days on the Hashemite throne.

As a ruler in the turbulent Middle East, he has survived many crises – and even more assassination attempts. Nevertheless, members of the Hashemite court are known to be extremely concerned at present because King Hussein is being squeezed from two sides – the risk of creeping Islamic fundamentalism from Iran and implied Israeli threats to turn Jordan over to the Palestinians as their sought-after State.

On the other hand, he is older, wiser, and more experienced now than when he survived a major coup attempt at 22; lost the West Bank, including East Jerusalem, to Israel in 1967 at 31, and survived a civil war at the age of 36.

Although it is understood King Hussein is sometimes miffed when oil-rich Saudis make political moves behind his back, and, although he has poor relations with his neighbor, President Assad of Syria, a survivor is greatly respected in the Arab world. And one thing is not in doubt – King Hussein is a survivor.

The king has been Iraq's closest supporter during the Iran-Iraq war. Therefore, until the final outcome of the war is known and while the future of Iraq's President Saddam Hussein remains uncertain, there is concern in Jordan about the possibility of a major change in Iraq, which could affect Jordan.

Although there is nothing to indicate that King Hussein is under threat at present from the rise of Islamic fundamentalism in Jordan itself, there are worries that the fall of Saddam Hussein – if it happened – could lead to internal disenchantment with the king in

Jordan. This would be mainly because of his close association with Saddam Hussein.

However, the problems caused by the threat of instability in Iraq were compounded by Israel's invasion of Lebanon – and Israel's subsequent determination to oust the Palestine Liberation Organisation from Lebanon.

Suddenly, for many Jordanians, it looked as though Israel was intent on changing the facts on the ground to turn its oft-put argument that Jordan is the Palestinian State into reality. Most alarming for many Jordanian officials is the fact that this argument is most regularly espoused by Israel's hawkish Defence Minister, Ariel Sharon.

Jordanian officials take seriously a theory – implicitly supported by Mr Sharon's statements – that the Lebanon invasion is merely stage one of a plan of moving the Palestinians from Lebanon, destabilising the Hashemite throne and handing Jordan to the Palestinians as their State.

The idea is a far too simplistic means of solving the Palestinian problem.

But with his army bogged down in the quagmire of Lebanese and Palestinian politics for eight weeks, few people – apart from his hawkish supporters in Israel – give Mr Sharon much credit for being anything but simplistic.

His actions in Lebanon and on the West Bank and Gaza Strip betray him as a man who prefers to use military might rather than face the crux of the undoubtedly difficult Palestinian question.

A senior Jordanian official told 'The Age' this week that Jordan took seriously the threat that Mr Sharon might turn his tanks on Jordan as a means of turning it into a Palestinian State.

While some Western diplomats in Amman believe that the Jordanians were concerned that the United States – particularly when Mr Haig was Secretary of State – was leaning towards Mr Sharon's ideas about Jordan, the official put a different slant on the question of US support for Jordan.

"We don't think the US has any doubts about the sovereignty and integrity of Jordan," he said. "But should Sharon attack Jordan, the question is how much would the US fight for Jordan?"

The most common Israeli criticisms of the present status quo in Jordan is that the country covers more than 70 per cent of the territory which was originally British mandated Palestine; the Hashemites do not come from the area, and that well over 50 per cent of the population is Palestinian (ie. from West of the Jordan River). These bald facts are indisputable.

But for some Israelis and their supporters abroad – many of whom compensate for their guilt about not living in the "Jewish homeland" by financial aid and writing letters to newspapers – to state that Jordan makes up 70 per cent of mandated Palestine ignores the fact that two-thirds of Jordan is unusable gibber desert.

Although the Hashemite family came to Jordan after being deposed as rulers of the Hejaz area of what is today Saudi Arabia, both King Hussein's father and grandfather preceded him as kings of Jordan.

If the Hashemites were to answer both, they would point out that only one (Yitzhak Rabin) of Israel's seven Prime Ministers was born in Palestine/Israel. And if Israel's other six Prime Ministers gained legitimacy from the fact they were descendants of the Israelite tribes, then it could be pointed out equally that Hashemite tribes wandered into what is today's Jordan from their bases around Mecca and Medina.

Fifty per cent of Jordan's population – including a number of Cabinet Ministers – is Palestinian because much of the Palestinian population or their parents were driven from, or fled their homes when Israel was created in 1948, or during the 1967 Six Day War.

King Hussein's grandfather, King Abdullah, can be severely criticised for annexing the West Bank after the 1948 war instead of handing it over to the Palestinians for their homeland as envisaged in the 1947 United Nations partition plan.

Although King Hussein ruled the West Bank until the 1967 war, it is generally agreed that he has no desire to rule over the area again. "If you are king of the East Bank of the Jordan River, you probably say that is fine," a Western diplomat said this week. "Why bother to risk your throne by taking on the West Bank again?"

Arabs share Beirut blame
From DAVID BALDERSTONE in Amman

'The Age', August 10, 1982

As the Beirut crisis continues, a considerable amount of blame for what is happening in Lebanon can be levelled at the Arab League – that gaggle of Arab States stretching from Iraq in the east to Morocco beside the Atlantic Ocean.

The League's failure in the past to come to grips with a peace process aimed at resolving the Arab-Israeli crisis has created the political environment which goes some way to explaining – but not excusing – Israel's invasion of Lebanon.

Since 1978, it has been on the tip of the League's collective tongue to state that it recognised Israel's right to exist.

But due to the jealousies between Arab leaders and feuds between States – most of which were totally unrelated to the Arab-Israeli dispute – the League could never quite bring itself to say that explicitly.

If the Arab League, which includes the Palestine Liberation Organisation, had taken such a step it could have led to a broadening of the Egypt-Israel peace process and perhaps US-PLO talks.

At the very least, it would have made it much more politically unacceptable for Israel to move its tanks into Lebanon in a bid to break the back of the PLO.

Although Israel has suffered badly in terms of world opinion as the full extent of the invasion and its destruction has become known, it would have suffered from the very first day, 6 June – if the Arab League had been seen as willing to recognise Israel.

Ironically, all Israel's neighbors – Egypt, Jordan, Syria and Lebanon – have long implied recognition of Israel's right to exist.

Furthermore, even though the 1978 Arab summit meeting in Bagdad was held in anger caused by the late President Sadat's peace initiative, it still came close to recognising Israel.

The summit's final communiqué, which was signed by Yasser Arafat and other Arab leaders, said in part: "The summit confirmed the Arab nations' obligation towards a just peace based on full Israeli withdrawal from all territories occupied during 1967."

This implied that the Arab League was prepared to live in a "just peace" with Israel – if Israel withdrew from the occupied territories, including Arab East Jerusalem.

But the communiqué did not go that extra bit and explicitly recognise Israel's right to exist.

This communiqué was reaffirmed at the Tunis summit in 1979, and the Amman summit in 1980.

If the League had been able to bring itself to recognise Israel's right to exist, the hand of Mr Arafat and other politically moderate PLO officials would have been strengthened if they had attempted – as they almost certainly would have – to get the Palestine National Council (the PLO's Parliament) to ratify the decision and amend the organisation's controversial covenant.

The Arab League's next attempt to imply recognition of Israel's right to exist was at last year's abortive summit in Morocco. Then, the eight-point Saudi Arabian peace plan, which was drafted by senior aides of Mr Arafat and implied recognition of Israel's right to exist, was due to be discussed. But Syria did not think the timing was right; its President, Hafez Assad failed to attend, and the summit was cancelled. That was ironic because Syria had implied recognition of Israel when it signed the 1974 disengagement agreement between Syrian and Israeli forces. This agreement is based on United Nations Security Council Resolution 338, which implies recognition of Israel through its call for the implementation of Security Council Resolution 242 in all its parts.

Jordan and Lebanon recognise Resolution 242 directly, and therefore, recognise Israel's right to exist. Egypt of course, has a peace treaty with Israel.

Resolution 242, which was adopted after the 1967 war, calls for "withdrawal of Israeli armed forces from territories occupied in the recent conflict" and guarantees the "territorial inviolability and political independence of every State in the area".

Because there is no "the" before the word territories, it is often argued that it merely calls for Israeli forces to withdraw from some of the territories occupied in 1967 – the West Bank, the Gaza Strip and the Golan Heights.

Deliberately, the resolution was written vaguely.

But this is an erroneous argument if the resolution is read in the context of the preamble, which emphasises the "inadmissibility of the acquisition of territory by war".

There is widespread Arab disenchantment with the failure of the Arab League to do anything concrete to halt the Israeli invasion of Lebanon. Most people talk of the Arab failure to impose an oil embargo against the United States.

Israel accepts US Beirut peace plan
From DAVID BALDERSTONE

'The Age', Jerusalem, August 11, 1982

The Israeli Government today approved in principle a United States-initiated plan which could see Palestinian guerillas begin to leave besieged West Beirut within days.

It appears certain – more than nine weeks after Israeli forces rolled into Lebanon – that the Beirut crisis is nearly over.

The Israeli Cabinet met today to consider the US plan, presented to the Israeli Government by the United States late last night.

The plan, hammered out by US special envoy, Mr Philip Habib, was also presented to the Lebanese Government and the Palestine Liberation Organisation late last night.

After today's Cabinet meeting a Government spokesman said that the Israeli Cabinet approved in principle Mr Habib's plan.

However, Cabinet had some suggestions on the plan. These had been presented to Mr Habib, who is in Beirut, the spokesman said.

Meanwhile Beirut Radio reported today that Israeli forces had been strengthened around Beirut. This was interpreted as a move designed by the Israelis to keep the military options open in case Mr Habib's plan falls through.

After a heavy day of fighting yesterday, Beirut was reported quiet today.

It is understood that under Mr Habib's plan the first group of Palestinian guerillas would leave Beirut within a few days, or at most within a week. The plan has been hammered out by Mr Habib after more than 50 days of discussion with Lebanese and Israeli leaders.

Mr Habib also heard the views of the leader of the Palestine Liberation Organisation, Mr Yasser Arafat, through Lebanon's Prime Minister, Mr Wazzan. Typed copies of the plan were presented to Israel, the Lebanese Government and the PLO last night.

It is believed that under the plan 200 to 300 French paratroopers would arrive in West Beirut a few hours before the first group of Palestinian guerillas leave the Lebanese capital. They would be the intial group of a multinational force which would remain in West Beirut for 30 days.

It is believed that the PLO and the Lebanese Government agreed to the plan after hearing it detailed. It is believed that the first group of guerillas to leave Beirut might use Cyprus and the Syrian port city of Latakia as staging points before being sent to Arab countries. The guerillas are to go to Jordan, Iraq and Syria. However, it is believed that Mr Habib hoped that Egypt would accept some of the guerillas once the plan was accepted.

Although a lot of intrigue has been going on behind the scenes, this hope was undermined slightly last night when the Egyptian Presidential adviser, Mr Osama El Baz, repeated that Egypt would accept guerillas only if the evacuation was a step towards an overall settlement to the Palestinian problem.

Mr Begin discussed the plan today with United States Ambassador to Israel, Mr Samuel Lewis.

The multinational force would comprise United States marines, and French and Italian troops. The bulk of the force would not be deployed in Beirut before most of the Palestinians left the city. Troops of the Lebanese army would also be deployed in the city.

A committee of military officials of the United States, Lebanon and Italy have already discussed deployment of the multinational force in Beirut. It is understood that the initial group of guerillas would go to Iraq and Jordan. The Palestinian guerillas would hand over their heavy weapons to the Lebanese Army on the second last day of the evacuation.

Come and see for yourself, Begin challenges Fraser
- *DAVID BALDERSTONE*

'The Age', Jerusalem, August 11, 1982

Israel's Prime Minister, Mr Begin, has challenged Australia's Prime Minister, Mr Fraser, to visit Israel and Lebanon. The challenge follows Mr Fraser's criticism of Israel's military actions in and around besieged West Beirut.

"I invite Fraser to come over and visit Israel and Lebanon so that he can see for himself," Mr Begin said in an immediate reaction. "He will change his mind, as others did before him."

Although Mr Begin's reaction was hasty, there were signs today that the Israeli Government was taking Mr Fraser's criticism extremely seriously.

Although preoccupied with a Cabinet meeting on the Beirut crisis this morning, Israel's Foreign Minister, Mr Shamir, was due to study the full text of the Australian statement today.

Mr Fraser's statement was covered prominently on Israel radio, and was carried in English language and Hebrew language newspapers.

In his intial reaction, Mr Begin said he had not been previously aware that Mr Fraser was the sort of person who preached to Israel.

"I do not know just how wise a man Fraser is, but since he is a Prime Minister he is undoubtedly wise – present company excepted," the Israeli Prime Minister said.

A full text of Mr Fraser's criticism was presented to the Israeli Foreign Ministry by Australia's Charge d'Affairs in Israel, Mr Mark Pierce, yesterday.

While condemning the unwillingness of the Palestine Liberation Organisation to recognise Israel's right to exist, Mr Fraser criticised Israel's military actions around Beirut.

"Despite the provocations Israel has received, its present actions in persisting with the use of its formidable military strength in Beirut, long after achieving its initially declared objective, are short-sighted and foolish," Mr Fraser said.

Australia's Leader of the Opposition, Mr Hayden yesterday "applauded" the Prime Minister's Monday statement.

"The Labor Party agrees with the Prime Minister that Israel's action in Lebanon runs the risk of forfeiting support from its traditional friends who have since Israel was founded, admired the tenacity with which it has maintained its democratic system in extremely adverse circumstances," Mr Hayden said.

Israel threatens to shell Syrians
From DAVID BALDERSTONE

'The Age', Jerusalem, August 22, 1982

Israel has warned Syria about the dangers of allowing Palestinian guerillas into Syrian-controlled areas of Lebanon to launch attacks against Israeli troops.

The warning came as the evacuation of guerillas from West Beirut got underway yesterday.

The warning about continued ceasefire violations underlines the fragility of the situation in Lebanon, despite the evacuation of PLO guerillas. Israel's Defence Minister, Mr Sharon, delivered the warning through US special envoy, Mr Philip Habib, during a meeting in Beirut yesterday.

The warning followed an implied threat earlier by the Israeli Foreign Minister, Mr Shamir that Israel was prepared to use military moves in a bid to remove Syria's forces from Lebanon. He said that Israeli forces were within artillery range of Syria's capital, Damascus.

In the latest alleged ceasefire violation, three Palestinian guerillas were killed overnight when they attempted to infiltrate Israeli lines east of Beirut.

Announcing the incident, an Israeli defence force spokesman said no Israeli soldiers were injured.

The alleged violation in the "Eastern sector" of the Lebanon war front was believed to be one of the main subjects discussed at today's meeting of Israel's Cabinet. It is believed there are between 3000 and 4000 Palestinian guerillas operating behind Syrian lines in Lebanon. Like the 25,000 Syrian soldiers in Lebanon, the guerillas are not covered by the American drafted evacuation plan, which covers guerillas in West Beirut.

The Israeli Cabinet also discussed the failure of the Lebanese authorities to check the identities of the guerillas who began leaving Beirut yesterday.

Israel last week insisted that the identities of the guerillas be checked because it is concerned that the PLO allegedly has planned to keep up to 2000 guerillas in West Beirut under cover of false identity papers.

Israel's Government views the evacuation of Palestinian guerillas from West Beirut as merely the first stage of a plan to remove all foreign forces from Lebanon. Mr Shamir reaffirmed at the weekend that Israeli forces would not leave Lebanon until Syrian forces, and the remaining Palestinian guerillas left Lebanon.

"The evacuation of the terrorists from Beirut is the important first step," Mr Shamir said in an Israel radio interview.

The Cabinet was scheduled to discuss the removal of Syrian forces today. Israeli officials have said that while Israel would prefer the Syrians to agree to leave through negotiations, Israel has a military option.

Syrian forces entered Lebanon in 1976 as the main contingent of the "Arab deterrent force", which was sent in by the Arab League to try and bring an end to Lebanese civil war. However, since then other Arab countries have withdrawn from the force and the Arab League this year refrained from renewing the mandate.

Israeli peace treaty gets Beirut rebuff
From DAVID BALDERSTONE

'The Age', Jerusalem, September 30, 1982

As Beirut airport reopened to civilian traffic today following the withdrawal of Israeli troops from the city, internal Lebanese developments indicated Israel had failed in its attempt to establish a pro-Israel Government in Lebanon.

Instead, it appeared likely that the new Government would seek a working relationship with Syria and distance itself from Tel Aviv, dashing Israeli hopes of a peace treaty in the near future.

The likelihood of the new Government seeking closer ties with Damascus increased yesterday after a pro-Syria former President threw his support behind Mr Gemayel's Presidency.

Former President Suleiman Franjieh, who has a blood feud with the Gemayel family, supported Mr Gemayel's Presidency.

Despite this, Mr Franjieh has vowed revenge on the Gemayel family since his son Tony Franjieh, and his family were killed in 1978. Mr Franjieh alleges that the killing was carried out at the orders of Bashir Gemayel – the President-elect who died in a bomb blast two weeks ago.

Although it is not known who was behind Mr Gemayel's assassination, the family feud has been mentioned as a possible reason for the blast.

In view of Mr Franjieh's close relationship with President Assad of Syria, it seems Mr Franjieh's support of Mr Gemayel is linked to a Syrian desire for a good relationship.

Israel's Defence Minister, Mr Sharon, yesterday blamed Syria for the assassination of Mr Gemayel, who had a long association with Israel.

Begin's coalition still far ahead in popularity polls
From DAVID BALDERSTONE

'The Age', Jerusalem, October 1, 1982

Despite widespread anguish in Israel over its association with the Christian massacre of Palestinians in Beirut, Israel's coalition Government would be returned to power if elections were held now. (*Ed. Following the evacuation of the Palestinian guerillas, and the assassination of Bashir Gemayel, Israeli forces advanced on West Beirut in mid-September, surrounding the Sabra and Chatila Palestinian refugee camps, which they then invited the Right-wing Christian militias to enter. There the militias massacred the inhabitants – somewhere between 800 and 2000 people.*)

An opinion poll taken after the massacre – and the subsequent calls for the resignation of the Prime Minister, Mr Begin – has indicated that Mr Begin's Likud bloc would do substantially better now than it did in last year's election.

Also, the opinion poll published in today's English language 'Jerusalem Post' indicated that while the Opposition Alignment Grouping was able to organise Israel's largest political rally last weekend it would in fact do worse than it did in last year's election.

The poll supports another poll published earlier in the week which showed that Mr Begin and his hawkish Defence Minister, Mr Sharon, were by far the most popular politicians in Israel.

The polls have given comfort to Mr Begin, who is reported to want an early election to be held as soon as the full judicial inquiry set up this week into the massacre is completed.

The polls also provide comfort for Mr Sharon, whose resignation has been demanded repeatedly by his opponents. Not that comfort is something the determined Mr Sharon, who supporters hailed as "King of Israel", appears to need.

The 'Jerusalem Post' poll today indicated that if elections were held now Mr Begin's Likud bloc would win 60 seats – compared with 48 in last year's election – in the 120-seat Knesset.

Mr Begin's current coalition partners would give the Government a comfortable majority.

On the other hand, the Opposition Alignment Grouping, which won 47 seats in last year's election, would win only 39 seats now, according to the poll.

The opinion poll does show that Mr Begin's Likud bloc has lost support since the first heady weeks of Israel's invasion of Lebanon, dubbed the "Peace for Galilee" operation. Mr Begin then was enjoying an all time high in popularity.

Mr Begin's position has been enhanced by problems in the Opposition, which are largely due to continued rivalry between the Opposition leader, Mr Peres, and the former Prime Minister, Mr Rabin.

However, while the polls provide reassurance for Mr Begin in the face of domestic and international criticism of Israel's association with the massacre in Beirut, a lot could happen before the next election.

The elections will not be held until the judicial inquiry into the massacre is completed. It is not expected to start work for several weeks, and may not be completed in under a year. Mr Begin's Government belatedly set up the inquiry this week.

In a year's time, economic problems exacerbated by the cost of the war in Lebanon and growing dissatisfaction with the war could turn the tide of support against Mr Begin.

Inside the refugee camps of Lebanon
From DAVID BALDERSTONE in Tyre, South Lebanon

'The Age', Tyre, October 11, 1982

Amid the twisted rubble of the Palestinian refugee camp devastatingly damaged by Israeli bombing; amid the fetid stench of open drains; amid the eeriness of a community noticeably robbed of most of its men, the situation was laced heavily with irony.

An Israeli officer was surrounded by a group of bright-eyed, olive-skinned, and colourfully-dressed young Palestinian children - another generation made homeless by the 34-year-old Arab-Israeli dispute.

But the children were not shouting in anger. They were shouting: "Shalom," and asking the officer: "How-are-you" in their stilted English. The Israeli was returning the greeting with the few words of Arabic that he knew.

The Israeli reserve officer hopped back into our car, and as we drove off, he drew heavily on a cigarette, and said: "I can't understand it. I didn't expect that." He spoke quickly as if fearing his voice would crack, and then fell silent, pondering.

Four months after Israel's invasion of Lebanon, that incident in the Ein Hilwe camp in Sidon, about 35 kilometres south of Beirut, is not an isolated one in refugee camps still occupied by Israeli forces.

In the wake of the Christian massacres in Chatila and Sabra refugee camps in Beirut, Palestinians widely see the Israelis – the force which turned their houses and lives upside down within a few days of the 6 June invasion – as their greatest protection against further massacres.

It would be wrong to suggest that the Palestinians remaining in the camps like the Israelis, and want them to stay. It is merely they fear the Right-wing Christian forces more, and feel another massacre is less likely while the Israeli soldiers remain in the area.

They would prefer international protection. (*Ed. At this stage, not many were aware of the role the Israelis played in the Sabra and Chatila massacres, which was not that of protection.*)

But another massacre seems possible – even probable – in the horrendous jungle of political violence in Lebanon, where blood feuds and revenge killings are part of life.

"No one has come here, but we are very afraid," Heyat Mohammed, a young Palestinian girl studying architectural drawing, said. "We want Israel to give us back our men, who are in prison, because we haven't any young men to look after us.

"We are only women and children here," she said in the schoolroom which has served as home for three families since Israeli bombs destroyed their camp homes in June.

Their men – held in the Israeli built prison camp at Ansar in South Lebanon – feel the same way. Mahmoud, a Palestinian held by the Israelis at Ansar, said the Palestinian prisoners feared their families would be massacred or terrorised while they were away. "A lot, a lot, we fear this might happen."

Without radios and newspapers, news of the Chatila and Sabra massacres filtered into the Ansar prison camp only when new prisoners arrived at the prison.

Mahmoud, a 37-year-old English teacher, could not find the exact words to describe the feeling in the prison when the news spread. But his emphasis, his soft tone, and his falling eyes said what was unsaid. "It was…you imagine the feeling. Some prisoners had families in Chatila and Sabra, and just imagine what it was like."

The Ansar prison camp has been bulldozed out of the rocky knolls to the east of Nabatiyeh. A three-metre high earth mound surrounds the prison compound, where tents are arranged in sections. Each section is capable of holding about 400 prisoners. It is understood there are only 7000 prisoners at present.

Coiled barbed wire, a security fence and mines surround the prison compound, which is circled by arc lights and watch towers spaced every 50 metres.

Although the two prisoners interviewed by me and another reporter appeared in good health, the sight of the compound set in isolated terrain set the mind wondering what Israeli survivors of the Holocaust would think. But then, this war is full of irony: not the least being that Israel has been allied to the Lebanese Falangist, or Kataib – a party partly inspired by admiration of Nazi Germany and Spain's General Franco.

Last week, bulldozers were working on the construction of an adjacent earth-walled compound which will almost double the size of the Ansar prison. Although the Israelis have already released several hundred prisoners – mainly Lebanese – the construction of the new camp indicated that the Palestinian women's hope of getting their men back in the near future may be in vain.

In fact, it would appear to indicate the opposite: that more men will be rounded up and more women left alone. An Israeli officer at Ansar would say only that the prison was being extended in case it was needed, and to enable some people from the existing compound to be transferred to the new compound.

Prisoner Mahmoud was born in Acre, Palestine, but has lived in Lebanon since the creation of the State of Israel in 1948. He was arrested in Sidon on 9 June after "someone had said I was a member of the PLO".

In preparation for the coming winter, Mahmoud said the Israelis had replaced the original summer tents with tents suitable for winter. Pullovers had been issued.

As Mahmoud talked, our Israeli escort officer handed the other prisoner, Hassani Bedowi, aged 18, a cigarette. Hassani, a tractor driver, had been born in Sidon of Palestinian parents, but had lived – and been arrested – in the southern Lebanese port of Tyre, formerly a stronghold of the PLO.

Mahmoud, the "leader" of the 400-man Section One of the prison, said the prisoners had been provided with chess sets and other games. "In my section we have planted some herbs, and started to decorate the camp with some posters. I found some of the other prisoners were illiterate so started a class, a little school. They (the Israelis) gave us holy books – the Holy Koran and the New Testament."

He said when prisoners were released "we are able to say goodbye". When asked whether he would like to see peace between Israel and the Palestinians, he said it was a broad question. But he then offered a line: "I would like everybody to live in peace." The prisoners prepare their own food, and Mahmoud said it was "quite good". He then qualified that with an understatement: "Of course, we are not at home now."

As well as the doctors among the prisoners, International Red Cross doctors and Israeli military doctors treat the prisoners.

In the Palestinian camps of South Lebanon, the refugees face two main problems: the possibility of further massacres or terror attacks and the approaching winter. After nearly four months of delay, bulldozers began levelling the devastated Ein Hilwe camp in Sidon last week in preparation for the erection of tents.

According to officials of the United Nations Works and Relief Agency, up to 60,000 Palestinians have been made homeless by the fighting. In Ein Hilwe camp, which previously housed 25,000 refugees, about 8000 to 10,000 people remain, grabbing shelter in the rubble, in burnt-out and damaged buildings, and in the few remaining rooms which remained unscathed.

A few Israeli soldiers, who arrived at the camp for the first time during our visit, expressed shock at the devastation. It appeared that television and press coverage had inadequately conveyed the extent of the damage.

An UNWRA official said he did not know how well the tents would protect the refugees during the winter. He said UNWRA's experience with tents was limited to 1948, when Palestinians first found themselves in refugee camps.

Despite the rubble, despite the horror, the resilient Palestinians are building up their lives again. Amid the devastation, stalls selling a wide range of fruit and vegetables have sprung up. Brightly coloured dresses are on sale in the midst of broken concrete. This tends to belie the problems caused by a temporary water supply, and the makeshift toilet arrangements.

UNWRA has formally requested the United Nations Secretary-General to provide observers or an armed force to improve the virtually non-existent security arrangements in the camps. At present the camps, which would be easy to infiltrate, are haphazardly patrolled by Lebanese soldiers, Lebanese police and Israeli border guards.

As dusk descended, a large crowd of Lebanese and Palestinian families gathered near an Israeli military post in Tyre, where groups of prisoners from Ansar prison camp are released. The Israelis do not release a list of prisoners who will be released on any particular day, which causes emotional strain among the families.

The families gather merely in the hope that their fathers and brothers will come home tonight. For many, every day is a harrowing disappointment. Ali, a Lebanese Shi'ite Moslem was standing in the crowd waiting for his father. "They (the Israelis) said yesterday some would come, but they didn't come. We wait until about 7.30 at night," he said.

"I believe my father – he's a butcher – is in there praying every day. There are many innocent people. He was taken two and a half months ago."

After breaking away for a few minutes, Ali returned, and in a tone of confidentiality said: "I forgot to say, I should have said…. They change the food every day in the prison. They (the prisoners) play cards every day…

"…But it would be better for them to come home to us."

News Diary
From DAVID BALDERSTONE in Amman

'The Age', October, 1982

Two sides of a weary war

Dusk was descending over the port in Tyre, Lebanon's southernmost coastal city.

Just over four months ago Palestinian guerillas and Leftist Lebanese militiamen were wandering the streets carrying their small arms. It was something out of the Wild West in those days. Now, in the wake of Israel's invasion of South Lebanon, the gun-toting militiamen have disappeared.

The Lebanese shopkeepers are repainting their shops. Rubble is being cleared. There is a lot of work still to be done as the city pulls itself back together in the wake of the Palestinian defeat. At dusk, the Phoenician port looks serene. The fishing boats are back in the bay, which is surrounded by the mellowed stone buildings of the Ottoman period.

The soft light hides the fact that many of the red-tiled roofs of buildings have been destroyed or severely damaged in artillery duels, mainly between Palestinian forces in Tyre and the guns of the renegade Lebanese officer, Major Sa'ad Haddad, in the border enclaves.

As we sat in a café overlooking the port, the proprietor did not want to take Israeli shekels for the beer and coffee. While, perhaps, quite glad that the Israelis had rid Tyre of militiamen, he had fast learnt that with Israel's 100-plus per cent inflation, shekels needed to be changed quickly, otherwise the margin of profit on a cup of coffee evaporates quickly.

As we sat drinking, there was the isolated gun shot. Someone was shooting pigeons, but it was suggested jokingly that the people of Tyre could not sleep at night without the sound of gunfire. After all, they have put up with it for seven years.

As we talked, I commented to our Israeli escort officer that I hadn't been to Tyre since the old management – meaning the Palestine Liberation Organisation – had left.

"We are told they are terrible people, terrorists," said the officer, who when not doing reserve duty is an academic. "What are they like?"

The other reporter and I hesitated. Then he, based in Jerusalem, said: "They are like people in the Israeli Defence Forces – some are impressive and some unimpressive".

Fighting fresh

Long before Israel's 6 June invasion of Lebanon, the Lebanese forces – the umbrella organisation of Lebanese Christian militias led by the Phalange militia – had been supplied with Israeli military uniforms.

But while both Christian militiamen and their unofficial allies, the Israelis, wear almost identical uniforms, there is a distinct difference – as a generalisation – in their appearance.

While no one could doubt the superb courage and training of the Israeli Defence Forces, Israeli soldiers often appear to go out of their way to appear unsoldierly. "Spit and polish has never been a big thing in the Israeli army," commented an Israeli officer. "It probably could be no other way in view of the fact virtually every Israeli has to serve in the army."

On the other hand, the mainly svelte Christian militiamen swagger around East Beirut and the Christian-controlled areas of Lebanon in the narcissistic style of people who are confident they were born to rule.

Their neatly pressed, spotlessly clean uniforms, sometimes matched with the fragrance of a high quality after-shave, often make the militiamen appear like models for the latest khaki fashions.

After the Israeli forces stormed all the way to Beirut without any fighting help from the Christian militiamen, most Israeli soldiers got their first glimpse of their unofficial allies.

Now, many Israeli soldiers have dubbed their Christian allies "the eau de cologne soldiers".

Fruity logic

Trade between Israel and the Arab world has long been a hush-hush affair. In addition to the Arab produce of the occupied West Bank territory, some Israeli-made goods slip across the Jordan River bridges into Jordan, and other Israeli good are re-packed in Cyprus.

But Israel's invasion of Lebanon has led to a significant amount of Israeli goods being exported to Lebanon.

With another colleague, I watched Israeli bananas and avocados being transferred from an Israeli lorry to a Lebanese truck just inside Lebanon, near the border with Israel the other day.

We were curious whether such a large quantity of bananas and avocados were destined for Lebanon alone or if they were destined for other Arab countries.

"They are just for the Beirut market", said the Lebanese businessman, long practised in dealing with the trading intrigues of the Arab world.

Suddenly his face dropped. An official of an Israeli export agency came up and said: "Really, I must ask you not to write the story about the fact that a lot of these goods are being transhipped to other Arab countries. The Lebanese are worried that if the Syrians find out about it, they will cause trouble."

"You understand?" What we understood was that we had confirmation of what we had suspected, but not had confirmed.

Begin bristles

While it is easy to have mixed feelings about the wisdom of Menachem Begin's political decisions – especially in the wake of Israel's invasion of Lebanon – no one can deny the toughness and stamina of Israel's Prime Minister.

In addition to the problems of guiding a country at war, especially in the wake of the Christian massacre of Palestinians in Beirut, Mr Begin has had another problem as well. It is a problem which many observers believe is draining energy from the wily political fox more than anything else – including the calls for the resignation of his Defence Minister, Mr Sharon.

Mr Begin's wife, Aliza, has been in a serious condition in hospital suffering from chronic asthma. Her condition remains serious.

The English-language 'Jerusalem Post' reported this weekend that senior officials of Mr Begin's party have said the Prime Minister has been in an "extremely bad mood" since the massacre, and his wife's sickness.

New offensives in a forgotten war
From DAVID BALDERSTONE in Amman

'The Age', November 4, 1982

With the weather about to break along the Iran-Iraq war front, the latest Iranian offensive is likely to be the last before the 36 month war goes into hibernation for winter once again.

By launching a new offensive this week the Iranians are considered to have taken advantage of the weather before the heavy rains bog down the tanks and cripple supply lines – particularly on the Iranian side.

While both Iran and Iraq have again issued somewhat contradictory accounts of the fighting, both military commands have confirmed heavy fighting in the central sector of the 650-kilometre war front.

After several days of artillery bombardment aimed at softening up Iraqi positions, Iran claimed yesterday to have recovered two small oil fields close to the international border to the west of the Iranian air base city of Dezful, which is 200 kilometres north-east of Basra. On the other hand, the Iraqis claim to have repulsed the latest Iranian offensive.

Since the conflict began in earnest in September 1980, the fortunes of war have swung like a pendulum between Bagdad and Teheran. At the start it appeared likely that the invading Iraqi army would achieve its objectives within a few weeks, and the Iraqi regime expected the conflict to end in glorious negotiated victory. Things didn't turn out that way.

Instead, the Iranians – through careful planning, religious zeal, and outrage that Iranian territory was being invaded – halted the Iraqi advance, and by late last year began pushing the Iraqis back steadily towards the border.

In the face of this pressure, and in the hope of a negotiated end to the war, Iraq made a series of "tactical" withdrawals, and by the middle of this year had withdrawn from all but a few pockets of Iranian territory.

The pendulum was pointing towards Teheran. For domestic reasons and the obsessive hatred of the mainly Sunni-Moslem Iraqi regime, the Shi'ite Moslem leadership in Teheran pushed on. And, for a time, it looked quite likely that Iran would succeed in its attempt to bring about the downfall of Iraq's President Saddam Hussein.

But after a series of costly offensives the Iranians have failed to make any major headway into Iraq, President Hussein looks increasingly more secure, and the pendulum appears to be inclined towards Bagdad again – albeit a little hesitatingly.

The Gulf war has become a somewhat forgotten war: a conflict overshadowed by events in Lebanon.

Nevertheless, the implications of the conflict remain of the utmost importance. The long- term survival of both the Teheran and Bagdad regimes – at least in their current form – remain very much in the balance.

Gulf security and Western oil supplies continue to be at stake. The Soviet Union stands to add to its so-far modest gains in Iran.

Also, because everything is intertwined in the jungle of Middle East politics, further moves towards an Arab-Israeli settlement could be severely jeopardised if President Hussein were to fall from power.

A changeover in leadership in Iraq could easily lead to oil-barren Jordan being robbed of a second source (in addition to Saudi Arabia) of support and finance. In view of the fact that Jordan's participation (either with or without an association with the Palestine Liberation Organisation) in future peace negotiations is vital if any progress is to be made, any lessening of financial support for Jordan's King Hussein would further reduce the chances of the politically cautious king making any bold move.

Also, the fall of Saddam Hussein's Sunni Moslem regime would stoke fears of the spread of Iranian-style Islamic fundamentalism in the capitals of the Arabian peninsula. This would mean Arab rulers would be all the more cautious about moves regarding the religiously emotional Arab-Israeli dispute.

Following the failure of Iran's major offensive early last month, sporadic fighting has continued in several areas of the front. The fighting has been centred around Iraq's southern port city of Basra, and around Nafti Shah, about 40 kilometres to the north. Also, Iraq has used its recently regained air superiority to bomb Iranian oil installations and Dezful.

Iraq's most staunch Arab supporter, King Hussein, was given an unsolicited demonstration of Iraq's regained aerial prowess when he visited Iraq recently. As the royal Boeing 727 flew across Iraq, Iraqi Soviet MiG-23s converged as a wing-tip to wing-tip escort. It is understood some members of the royal party, while impressed that Iraq had its sophisticated MiG-23s in the air, would have preferred to have merely taken President Hussein's word. The MiGs were a bit close for comfort.

Saddam Hussein's fortunes appear to have improved since Iran first attempted to carry the war into Iraq territory. With the so-called "Arab homeland" having been under attack, Iraq has secured more Arab support – particularly, in the form of troops, from the Sudan – and on the other hand, Iran has lost most of the limited Arab support it had.

Although Iran appears to be a long way from achieving its goal of bringing down Saddam Hussein, the Teheran regime, while somewhat divided, appears to be continuing to reject mediation efforts.

Iran's President Khamenei this week dubbed the latest Islamic peace mission as "US-inspired".

With mediation attempts continuing to fail, and the winter rains approaching, there appears little likelihood of an early end to the crisis. "Both sides appear ready and able to sustain the conflict," a Western diplomat said.

New opportunities open up for PLO after defeat
From DAVID BALDERSTONE

'The Age', Amman, December 4, 1982

Behind the growing co-operation between Jordan and the Palestine Liberation Organisation is a web of intrigue which could determine whether the PLO is able to snatch the political opportunities opened up by its military defeat in Beirut.

Eleven years after Palestinian guerillas were driven from Jordan, this week's decision by King Hussein and PLO chief Yasser Arafat to establish a joint political committee to study peace moves could lead to a breakthrough in the Middle East peace process.

But the odds are stacked firmly against it. However, Mr Arafat's willingness – at the very least – to explore further Palestinian-Jordanian co-operation could enable the PLO to make real political gains.

The evacuation of fighters and the subsequent massacre of Palestinians in two of the city's refugee camps underlined in Washington and European capitals the necessity of finding a solution to the Palestinian problem if Arab-Israeli peace is ever to be achieved.

On the other side of the coin, the poor showing of Soviet arms – used both by the Syrians and the Palestinians – plus Moscow's failure to do anything except mouth empty statements of solidarity in support of the Palestinians, underlined to much of the PLO leadership that progress towards their aspirations for a State rested with Washington.

Furthermore, Mr Arafat was fully aware of the significance of the negotiations to end the Israeli siege of Beirut. The US special envoy, Mr Philip Habib, had to listen to Mr Arafat – albeit through intermediaries. Political progress was being made during military defeat.

Following its loss in Lebanon of a military base within artillery range of Israel, the PLO mainstream – led by Mr Arafat – has looked more and more towards political means of getting a Palestinian State on the Israeli-occupied West Bank.

The military defeat served the PLO "moderates", who might better be described as pragmatists, in two ways. First it put paid to the notion, which provided strength for radical Palestinians, that the PLO's tenth rate army could ever be a match for Israel's Defence Forces. Significantly, and as the continuing deaths of Israeli soldiers in Lebanon appear to substantiate, the loss of the PLO's "State within a State" has been achieved without loss to the Palestinians' guerilla capability.

Secondly, despite many political mistakes in the past and the prospect of many still to come, Mr Arafat and others appear to have twigged that the Beirut siege and the massacres gained their cause considerable world sympathy worth building on politically.

But knowing the importance of making political progress is simpler than achieving it. For the PLO to make real progress with Washington, it would have to recognise Israel's right to exist. The US Administration has said repeatedly it would not consider talks with the PLO unless it recognised this right.

Such a watershed in PLO policy would require two-thirds majority approval from the organisation's parliament-in-exile, the Palestine National Council. This would be no easy matter, especially as Syria directly, and Israel indirectly, can have enormous influence over PNC decisions.

The Syrian influence is direct in that Syria plays host to, and has enormous clout over, many PNC members. The Israeli influence is indirect in that it has demonstrated in the past that actions – such as repressive measures in the occupied territories or an attack against Palestinian guerillas still in Lebanon – on the eve of Palestinian decisions, serve to strengthen the position of Palestinian hardliners.

Last week's meeting of the PLO's central committee, a 66-member body representing the main factions within the PNC, demonstrated how difficult it would be to get a two-thirds majority of the PNC in favor of recognising Israel's right to exist, or another main issue, the question of "confederation" with Jordan.

The central council criticised but did not reject, President Reagan's peace initiative, which falls short of supporting the PLO's demand for a Palestinian State, and instead calls for a Palestinian homeland in federation with Jordan.

President Reagan's initiative, which was rejected by Israel, is one of two "peace plans" to have been brought forward since the Lebanon crisis. The other was the Arab summit plan adopted at Fez, Morocco in September. This plan called for the establishment of a Palestinian State under PLO leadership with East (Arab) Jerusalem as its capital.

News Diary
DAVID BALDERSTONE in Amman

'The Age', Amman, December 13, 1982

Christmas, Jordan style

Christmas decorations decking out the shops, carols broadcast regularly by Radio Jordan, and turkeys and plum puddings in the supermarkets belie the fact that only around 7 per cent of Jordan's population are Christians.

Many Moslems as well as Christians enter into the spirit of Christmas in Jordan, the country that ruled the Christian sites in Jerusalem and Bethlehem before the Israeli occupation in 1967.

At Amman's leading Chinese restaurant, run by a Christian Chinese, the recorded background music the other night included a medley of carols. 'Born is the King of Israel', boomed the chorus to 'The First Noel'.

The private lives of the royal family are kept at discreet distance. It is known that King Hussein, whose family ruled the Moslem holy places of Mecca and Medina until World War I, sends Christmas cards to prominent politicians around the world each year. A cynical view would be that the gesture is not a bad PR move.

Members of the royal family, although Moslem, have a traditional Christmas dinner each year.

All this is not surprising, as Moslems say Jesus Christ was a prophet. Even the regime of Ayatollah Khomeiny in Iran allows considerable television time for Christmas programmes.

Amman is often described correctly as a desert capital. For nine months of the year there are water shortages.

But at 840 metres the city gets very cold during the winter. It snows most years, sometimes heavily. The chilly December we have had so far could point to a white Christmas.

Unhelpful

In the Middle East it is often a futile exercise to telephone a hotel and ask for a guest unless you know the guest's room number.

A Danish colleague staying in the Ramses Hilton in Cairo recently rang the hotel switchboard to ask the room number of another journalist in the hotel. The switchboard operator assured the Dane that the other journalist was not staying in the hotel.

Frustrated, the Dane rang the switchboard again and this time asked which room he himself was staying in. Again the operator said there was no one of that name at the hotel.

"But that's me, and I'm staying in this hotel," the Dane fumed.

"Well, sir, why are you trying to ring yourself?" the operator asked.

Chauvinism

A year ago, a big topic of conversation over mulled wine at pre-Christmas diplomatic parties was the impending arrival of a woman, Ms Victoria Kingsmill, to head the Australian Embassy in Amman (as Charge d'Affairs).

Although diplomatic receptions inhibit many people from having strong views about anything, the prevailing view of those who dared to speak their minds was that it was a very courageous move to send a woman to head a diplomatic mission in a Moslem country. But the word "courageous" was used in the context that it would not work.

"First woman I have ever heard of heading a diplomatic mission in the Arab world," I remember one diplomat saying. A woman would not have the same access to Jordanian officials, some said.

Of course it was all nonsense. Ms Kingsmill has had no more difficulty seeing senior Jordanian officials than her male colleagues from other embassies.

There were some advantages. At some top-level dinners she was noticed because she and Jordan's only woman Minister, Mrs Inam Mufti, were the only women present. But Ms Kingsmill could not take part in the fiercely male domain of expressing condolences upon the death of prominent men.

Ms Kingsmill's husband Don was formerly Australia's ambassador to Saudi Arabia. He has taken two years off from the Department of Foreign Affairs to be in Amman with his wife.

Although no reflection on her successful performance, Ms Kingsmill is in the process of being eclipsed as head of the Australian Embassy. Due to an upgrading of relations between Jordan and Australia, Mr Richard Gate, formerly Australia's Ambassador to Burma, has arrived in Amman as Ambassador to Jordan.

Scotched

In the face of potential instability in the Persian Gulf, the United States and Saudi Arabia agreed just over a year ago that US-manned Airborne Surveillance Aircraft (AWAC) would keep watch over the Saudi skies.

In the wake of Ayatollah Khomeiny's revolution in Iran, the prime concern was to halt the spread of Islamic fundamentalism. As it turns out, the AWAC – maintaining their almost constant watch over oil-rich Arabia – have done the Islamic fundamentalists a favor. They have made it almost impossible to get a bottle of Scotch in Saudi Arabia.

Scotch whisky, like other alcohol, has long been illegal in Saudi Arabia. But, before the AWAC arrived it was available at a price: up to $70 a bottle. It used to be smuggled in on desert routes.

Now the AWAC spot the smugglers' "trains". The desert-boot-clad Saudi National Guard use the intelligence from the AWAC as a good training exercise, despatch a patrol, and often enough collect the smuggled Scotch.

Concession may follow PLO talks in Jordan
From DAVID BALDERSTONE

'The Age', Amman, December 14, 1982

Jordan's King Hussein may be able to tell President Reagan later this month that the PLO is seriously considering allowing non-PLO members to represent Palestinians at future peace negotiations.

The Chairman of the Palestine Liberation Organisation, Mr Yasser Arafat, is meeting senior officials in Amman today and the main topic of talks will be a proposal to send a joint Jordanian-Palestinian delegation to any future peace talks.

Mr Arafat arrived in Amman yesterday on his third visit to Jordan since Palestinian fighters were evacuated from Beirut earlier this year.

During today's talks, which are in the framework of the recently established Palestinian-Jordanian committee, consideration was expected to be given to the idea of non-PLO representation.

King Hussein is expected to be able to tell President Reagan that the PLO is seriously considering the idea, when they meet in Washington on 21 December.

However no firm PLO statement on this issue is expected to be released after this week's talks in Amman.

King Hussein is abroad and not expected to return to Jordan before going to Washington. The PLO leadership is considering the idea of allowing non-PLO Palestinians to participate in peace talks because of Israel's refusal to deal with it.

PLO sources said last night the Arabs basically wanted to demonstrate flexibility to the US Administration.

They said that while the organisation might approve non-PLO negotiators, they would have to be sympathetic to the PLO and would be expected to report back to the PLO leadership.

A semblance of security returns to Beirut
From DAVID BALDERSTONE in Beirut

'The Age', December 22, 1982

The dusk scene wouldn't have been surprising in too many capitals of the world. But the taxi driver pointed excitedly at the commuters travelling from West to East Beirut in a modern bus. "Bus, very good," he declared.

It was a symbol of unity in Lebanon's so-recently divided capital. It was a symbol of security in West Beirut where so recently people ran the risk of being caught in the crossfire between rival militias.

But behind the Christmas tinsel decking out Beirut's main streets, behind the hordes of workmen feverishly repairing bombed and shelled buildings, behind the Levantine extravagance oozing from restaurants and nightclubs, there is a growing air of pessimism.

It is not so much that Beirut is the capital of Lebanon. Beirut is Lebanon.

With about 30,000 Israeli troops dug in over most of South Lebanon, an even greater number of Syrian troops occupying the Beka'a Valley and other areas, Palestinian guerillas sticking to their guns, and rival militias still very heavily armed, the authority of the Lebanese Republic extends only a little beyond Beirut.

A Lebanese diplomat was congratulated recently on his ambassadorial posting. He shrugged and said it was not a great honour to represent two square miles.

After a summer of violence, snow has fallen on the Lebanese ranges heralding a winter of protracted US-led negotiations aimed at removing all foreign forces – Israeli, Syrian and Palestinian – from Lebanon.

Although the negotiations have led to some agreement on a partial withdrawal of forces, there are likely to be serious hiccups during the continuing negotiations.

In fact, with the Israeli military making preparations to stay up to a year, and the Syrian regime making only on-again off-again signs of withdrawing their troops, there are increasing fears of a serious Syrian-Israeli war taking place in the spring – in March or April.

Western military analysts note that the Israelis have already moved heavy equipment into Lebanon in readiness for the possibility of war with Syria.

But although it is difficult to be an optimist about Lebanon's future, the Lebanese of Beirut are working hard to prove the pessimists wrong. Four months after the last of the Palestinian fighters left the city after the summer siege, shops are packed with Western goods and damaged buildings are being repaired.

Shanty shops, which sprang up during the civil war around the West Beirut Corniche blocking out views of much of the city's coastline, have been removed. Streets are being paved.

"Even the police are handing out parking tickets these days," said a taxi driver. "But very few people are bothering to pay the fines."

While a kind of normality is returning to Beirut, Lebanon's second city – the northern port of Tripoli – provides an instant reminder of what West Beirut was like until four months ago. Also it provides a warning of how wafer-thin the veneer of normality is.

In Tripoli, where rival militias aided by Syrian troops and Palestinian guerillas have clashed heavily recently, gunmen roam the streets.

Even in West Beirut, there are fears that the security situation could easily deteriorate. Although the gunmen of the "Leftist" Lebanese militias put away their guns when their Palestinian allies were evacuated, the militias still hold some medium and light weapons in the city.

There was an ominous sign after the assassination attempt earlier this month against the Druze political leader, Mr Walid Jumblatt. Gun-toting members of his militia established road blocks around his West Beirut residence without any interference from the Lebanese Army, which is meant to stop such things happening.

There are fears that similar attacks against "Leftist" leaders or officials could provoke open clashes and sectarian strife. Diplomats are dubious whether the Lebanese Army – although supported morally at least by the multinational force – would have the will and be powerful enough to halt a serious outburst of violence.

In Christian East Beirut, the Christian "Lebanese Forces" remain fully armed, although they have removed most of their heavy weapons into the mountains. There is little hope of the "Lebanese Forces" disarming before the Christian political grouping has been convinced that the Lebanese Army has the will and the clout to enforce its authority – and that could take a very long time.

Although Israel and Syria were on the verge of beginning a partial withdrawal of troops this week, the American-led negotiations aimed at removing all foreign forces from Lebanon will be protracted.

With Israeli artillery within range of Damascus, the Syrian regime will agree to some withdrawal of its troops to coincide with a corresponding Israeli withdrawal of forces. There has been speculation recently that the Soviet Union has encourage Syria to drag its feet in withdrawal negotiations for fear that the American-led negotiations would lead to another US success after the successful US negotiations to remove the Palestinian fighters from Beirut.

As far as the Israelis are concerned, it is feared the Israeli Government wants to delay withdrawal of its forces until it is certain that the Middle East peace initiative of President Reagan is dead. Israel has rejected this initiative, which calls for the establishment of a Palestinian homeland linked to Jordan.

It can be argued that with American efforts concentrated on negotiating withdrawal of all foreign forces from Lebanon, the US Administration will be diverted from the broader issue of Arab-Israeli peace, therefore the Israeli Government – if it wants to stymie broader peace moves which would involve some long-term withdrawal from the West Bank – can delay withdrawal from Lebanon for up to a year. By that time President Reagan will only be a year away from Presidential elections and more conscious of the power of the Jewish lobby.

The question of withdrawal of Palestinian forces from Tripoli and the Beka'a Valley also presents many problems.

After the massacre of Palestinians in two Beirut refugee areas in September, the leadership of the Palestine Liberation Organisation will be extremely reluctant to accept US guarantees that Palestinian civilians will not be harmed if the fighters are withdrawn.

The over-riding problem of foreign forces has tended to obscure Lebanon's internal political problems. After eight years of civil war, the vast majority of Lebanese merely want to live in peace. But the underlying problems involving Lebanon's' confessional system of Government remain.

Under this system, the President has to be a Maronite Christian, the Prime Minister a Sunni Moslem and the third-ranking official, the Speaker, a Shi'ite Moslem. Although it is generally agreed that this distribution of power no longer reflects the sizes of the various communities, the re-emergence of the Maronites as the strongest, if not biggest, group, has resulted in the Maronites showing no willingness for political compromise.

"As the Maronites see it, they won the civil war so why should they compromise," a Western diplomat said.

1983
Sharon resigns post, but stays in the Cabinet
From DAVID BALDERSTONE

'The Age', Jerusalem, February 11, 1983

Israel's controversial Defence Minister, Mr Sharon, resigned today in a move that probably saved the Begin Government from an early election.

Mr Sharon telephoned his resignation to the Prime Minister, Mr Begin, today after spending several hours considering a Cabinet decision that he should resign.

Mr Sharon was expected today to remain in the Cabinet as a Minister without portfolio. Mr Begin is expected to take over the Defence portfolio – at least temporarily.

Mr Sharon's resignation followed a Cabinet decision yesterday that the findings of a judicial Commission of Inquiry into last September's Beirut massacre of Palestinians should be accepted. The commission had recommended that Mr Sharon should give up his portfolio.

While the Cabinet was meeting, a demonstrator was killed and nine people were wounded when a hand grenade exploded at a rally of a few thousand "Peace Now" supporters outside the Prime Minister's Office in Jerusalem.

Opposition figures accused the Government of creating a dangerous climate, and Mr Begin made his first live broadcast appearance in months to appeal for calm.

"The heart weeps for the young man who was thus murdered," Mr Begin said.

Mr Sharon, like Mr Begin, draws a great deal of support from Israel's Oriental and Sephardic community – which makes up more than 50 per cent of the country's population.

Mr Sharon's resignation followed a Cabinet meeting late last night during which his colleagues voted 16 to 1 that all the Commission of Inquiry's recommendations into the massacre be accepted and implemented.

It is believed that Mr Begin himself recommended that the inquiry's recommendations should be accepted. The inquiry, among other things, recommended that Mr Sharon should resign or be dismissed.

During the Cabinet session, Mr Sharon challenged Mr Begin to sack him, according to reports from Cabinet Ministers and Israel radio.

The radio quoted Mr Sharon as telling the Cabinet: "I lay my head before you. I won't chop it off myself. You will have to bring down the guillotine."

Although his political future remained in doubt today, Mr Sharon could count on a great deal of support if he decided to pursue his political career. Despite the report's findings on the Beirut massacre, no one could discount Mr Sharon as a future Prime Minister of Israel.

The Israeli Chief of Staff, General Eitan, who had been severely censured by the commission, issued a statement late last night supporting the Cabinet decision to implement the inquiry's recommendations.

"The military echelon will carry out the decision of the Government, as is customary in a functioning democracy," he said.

"Israel's defence forces will learn the lessons of the inquiry commission's findings," he said. He praised the Israel Defence Forces' performance.

"The IDF (Israel Defence Forces) will prove that it has the ability to withstand criticism and to draw painful conclusions from it," he said. But other military officers censured by the commission warned the Cabinet of the jarring effect the report would have on army morale.

According to a report on Israel Television, the officers sought to persuade the Cabinet not to adopt all the commission's recommendations.

The report called for the sacking of the Military Intelligence Chief, Major-General Yehoshua Saguy, and the barring of Brigadier General Amos Yaron, commander of Israel's forces in Beirut at the time of the massacre, from command positions for three years.

General Saguy described what he called "the beginnings of frustration" among his officers, who he said felt the report was unjust.

General Saguy, whom the report condemned for "breach of duty" in failing to warn of the danger of a massacre, told the Ministers that the recommendations could have the same dampening effect on Israeli intelligence as during the aftermath of the 1973 Arab-Israeli war.

He was referring to the shock the army suffered in 1974 with the dismissal of its then commander, General Eli Zeira, for failing to warn the Government of the Egyptian-Syrian Yom Kippur attack.

Jordan king may try to climb the minaret
From DAVID BALDERSTONE

'The Age', Amman, February 26, 1983

Back in November 1977, when the late President Sadat of Egypt first announced his intention to visit Jerusalem, an Arab colleague of mine shrugged and said: "We have a saying in Arabic…When the donkey climbs the minaret".

He was not likening Mr Sadat to a donkey. Instead, jaundiced after 29 years of stalemate in the Arab-Israeli dispute, he was sceptical about whether Mr Sadat would really make such a courageous move. He was likening the chances to those of a donkey being able to climb to the top of a narrow minaret.

Two days later, the Egyptian presidential Boeing 707 airliner lowered its undercarriage and touched down at Lod international airport.

The donkey had climbed the minaret.

Understandably, there is similar scepticism today amidst growing indications that Jordan's King Hussein – with at least tacit approval of the chairman of the Palestine Liberation Organisation, Yasser Arafat, is moving rapidly towards a decision as significant, if not as spectacular, as Mr Sadat's 1977 move.

Arab leaders understandably hold their cards close to their chests and therefore a lot remains in the realm of speculation.

"After 30 years on the throne," a Western diplomat observed this week, the king knows more about Middle East politics than any diplomat or foreign correspondent. If the king tells the British or American Ambassador something, it cannot be assumed that he is telling everything, or, indeed, believes everything he is saying."

Nevertheless, by assembling a montage from official statements, PLO and Jordanian background briefings, and pessimistic and optimistic speculation, a possible scenario emerges.

If all goes well, King Hussein and Mr Arafat could decide within a month on the formation of a joint Jordanian-Palestinian delegation, which could be dispatched to peace talks with Israel. Because Israel refuses to deal with the PLO, the Palestinians would not be known members of the PLO. It would probably be led by a Jordanian Minister, possibly Mr Adnan Abu Odeh, King Hussein's Palestinian Information Minister.

Mooted as a possible venue for the talks is Jericho, the Biblically important West Bank city just a few kilometres inside the current "boundary" between Jordan and Israeli-controlled territory.

King Hussein would not take part in initial talks. Therefore, presumably, the Israeli side would be led by a Minister, or senior civil servant. In other words, the talks would be at a similar level to the Lebanon-US-Israel talks on the withdrawal of foreign forces from Lebanon.

The two main delegations would be joined by delegations from the US and Egypt. So much for the scenario, which may never see the light of day. While all this remains within the realm of possibility, it is interesting to note that the speculation that Jordan might join peace talks comes not only from the Arab side. An Israeli newspaper reported this week that Israel's Prime Minister, Mr Begin, had been speedy in appointing Mr Moshe Arens as Defence Minister in succession to Ariel Sharon because he believed King Hussein might move soon to join peace talks.

Mr Arens, although a hardliner who previously refused the Defence portfolio because he opposed Israel's withdrawal from Sinai in exchange for peace with Egypt, is respected by the US Administration for the way he carried out his job as Ambassador to Washington.

Israel's 'Jerusalem Post' has published a story from an Israeli diplomat about how Mr Arens reversed the opinion of US Senators at a Senate hearing on the advisability of the US supplying F-16s to Jordan.

Mr Arens unemotionally explained why the supply of the aircraft would be dangerous not only for Israel, but for the Jordanians as well.

"And the best thing about it," the diplomat went on, "is that he never once mentioned the Bible, the Holocaust, or the Soviets". That kind of man, Mr Begin could reasonably think, is exactly the kind of man the Israeli Government will need in the front line if King Hussein takes the plunge. Because, inevitably, such a move by King Hussein would increase US pressure on Israel at a time when relations between the two allies are at a low ebb.

Indeed for there to be a chance of a Jordanian-Palestinian negotiating team materialising at all will require US pressure on Israel to at least temporarily halt Jewish settlement in the West Bank and Gaza Strip.

Although Mr Arens believes that the occupied territories should always remain under Israeli control, Mr Arens, as Ambassador to Washington, criticised Mr Begin's Government last September when it rejected President Reagan's peace plan and answered it by establishing three new Jewish settlements.

It remains to be seen what Mr Arens would advise Mr Begin if a halt to Jewish settlements became the only stumbling block to a Jordanian-Palestinian dialogue with Israel.

Jordanian officials say that King Hussein wants to join the peace process now because he fears that with Jewish settlement on the West Bank proceeding at such a pace it might be his last opportunity.

It appears that Mr Arafat cautiously leans towards this view and it is thought the latest meeting of the PLO's Palestine National Council has left him enough room to manoeuvre to sanction a Jordanian-Palestinian delegation, which in any case would report back to him.

Also, the feeling amongst the people of the West Bank and Jordan is as favorable towards a courageous move now as it is ever likely to be. The undoubtedly arguable observation can be made that – following last summer's siege of Beirut – the people feel something has to be tried. Things cannot go on as they have for the past 35 years.

A moderate member of the Palestine National Council told the Press after resigning from the council last week: "If that (the battle of Beirut) was a victory, then all we need is a series of victories and we will be holding the next PNC meeting in Fiji." He was damning Palestinian rhetoric and commenting on the fact that the PNC was meeting for the first time in a country – Algeria – not bordering Israel.

The reactions of Saudi Arabia and Syria will have to be taken into account before King Hussein would make a move. Jordan requires Saudi aid, and would not want inevitable Syrian hostility to such a move to extend beyond angry rhetoric. "The Saudis are part of the moderate camp and can be pressured by the Americans – especially at this time of slumped oil prices and the ongoing Iran-Iraq war," a Jordanian official told me, perhaps a bit too hopefully.

"And the Syrians are bogged down in Lebanon … We are not concerned about the Syrians." Again, it may have been too hopeful a sentiment.

"But why would King Hussein make a move which could backfire and leave him with nothing? He is extremely fatalistic. Also he is a seasoned politician."

That was an understatement. After all, after 31 years on a throne in arguably the most unstable area of the world, King Hussein is only 48 years of age.

News Diary
DAVID BALDERSTONE in Amman

'The Age', February 28, 1983

Jordanians met "next PM"

While Bob Hawke's sympathy for Israel is well recorded, he also has close links with Jordan, having visited Amman twice as the guest of Crown Prince Hassan, King Hussein's brother.

"This is Bob Hawke, the next Prime Minister of Australia", Jordanian businessman Raouf Abu Jaber said as he introduced Mr Hawke at parties he gave during the visits in 1978 and 1980.

Even in 1978, Mr Hawke gave no hint of denying the introduction, and most guests – some probably oblivious to the present Prime Minister's name – accepted it with polite smiles. "Maybe", the Australian guest uttered to the Jordanians who pursued the possibility.

The visits stemmed from a trip Crown Prince Hassan made to Australia in 1977. Knowing Mr Hawke to be a supporter of Israel, the crown prince decided that the best way to try to influence Mr Hawke's views would be to invite him to Jordan. There's no point always preaching to those sympathetic to the Arab cause, the prince believed.

The normal practice is for the Jordanians to put such a guest into a hotel at Government expense. But according to palace aides, the crown prince thought about this and decided it would be better for Mr Hawke to stay with a Jordanian family. It would give Mr Hawke a better feel of the country.

So Mr and Mrs Abu Jaber were asked to host Mr Hawke in 1978. They were thought to be a particularly suitable choice because Mr Abu Jaber is a Jordanian and his wife a Palestinian. Therefore to some extent they represented the viewpoints of the Jordanian and Palestinian communities that make up the country's population.

It evidently worked well, and Mr Abu Jaber asked Mr Hawke to stay again in 1980.

"I think I remember Mr Hawke writing to the crown prince and admitting that his views had changed slightly because of his visits to Jordan," a former palace aide recalled at the weekend.

TV reform

When it comes to criticism of Government run television channels the situation is not the same the world over.

In Jordan the question of political bias does not arise. Not too surprisingly, no one demands equal time with King Hussein.

Here the criticism is directed towards the moral tone of certain programmes. Jordan's appointed parliament, the National Consultative Council, decided last week to cancel some programmes which "are hostile to Jordanian traditions and culture. The aim was to strengthen the national identity of our citizens".

Jordan TV, which is designed to win hearts and minds in Israel as well as providing viewing in Jordan, shows a good mix of British and American programmes on its English-language station.

It even puts out a surprising number of Australian programmes – 'Bluey', 'Against the Wind', 'Sara Dane', and 'Ned Kelly' to name a few. They are sub-titled in Arabic by JTV.

In its wisdom, the Consultative Council decided that there should be more Jordanian-made programmes. No one could blame them. But, judging from recent experience, the Jordanian ego demands that an extraordinary amount of time be devoted to titles.

Whereas, through some miscalculation of timing, most foreign programmes lose half or all the concluding credits, a recent 15 minute Jordanian-made English magazine programme was taken up with five minutes of credits.

In view of awareness about rising Moslem fundamentalism it is not surprising that the Consultative Council in this conservative country has acted. For example, a spy film shown during prime time the other night included the four-letter word that got 'Boys in the Band' into trouble, plus a drawn-out close-up of a man's throat being cut – in full colour.

Desert snow

Struggling to change the tyre of my car the other day with snow underfoot and still falling, it occurred to me that the Press, by so often describing Amman as the "desert capital of the Hashemite kingdom", conjured up the wrong impression of this city.

The locals often complain about the Western Press description of their hilly city of medium-rise apartment blocks where donkeys and camels are hardly ever seen jostling with the Mercedes and BMWs. They see it as another demeaning way the Press identifies the Arab people with, to use their phrase "derogatory Arab stereotypes".

Of course, to describe Amman as a desert capital comes close to the truth – at least for seven months of the year. Amman is on the edge of the desert, and for seven months it never rains, and the desert dust clings to the trees.

But most years it snows in Amman, which is about 800 metres above sea level. This year there have been three heavy snowfalls.

Ironically, in one respect Amman is more identifiably Arab in winter than it is in summer. In winter, a significantly higher proportion of the male population wear the traditional Arab headdress, the kaffiyeh. This cotton headdress, designed to protect against sun and dust, is hardly suitable for rain and snow, but is worn all the same.

Whereas in summer, our loyal man Mohammed arrives in open neck shirt and slacks, he looks quite formal in sports coat and kaffiyeh in winter. A bit of a ceremony takes place as he spreads his damp kaffiyeh over the heater to dry before settling down to coffee.

In summer we talk politics over coffee, in winter, weather and politics. The slightly exasperating thing about all this is that as well as knowing with absolute certainty everything about Middle East politics, he equally knows where each storm has come from and is going to – and why.

Protocol

Of course to diplomats, it was a deadly serious question of protocol, and there was no hint of a funny side to it at all. Richard Gate, Australia' s new ambassador to Jordan, was not able to stand at the door and greet guests as they arrived at the Australia Day party in Amman last month.

The problem was that while he had been in Jordan for more than a month, the Jordanians had not found an opportunity for him to present his credentials to King Hussein.

Therefore, strictly speaking, he was not the ambassador.

So Mr Gate's number two, who in terms of protocol was probably still number one, had to receive the guests. Of course, Mr Gate had a much better time just mingling. But that's not the point.

The following day Mr Gate was able to present his credentials.

New hope of a solution to Cyprus problem
From DAVID BALDERSTONE

'The Age', Amman, March 14, 1983

In the nine years since Turkish troops landed in Cyprus following the Athens-inspired coup against the late Archbishop Makarios, there has been little reason for optimism about a settlement of the Cyprus problem.

The strategic interests of the big powers have been more important than the plight of close to 250,000 refugees – Cypriots displaced within their own country.

But now, more than at any time since the Turkish army occupied the northern third of the island, there is glimmer of hope that progress may be made towards a solution.

When the talks between representatives of the strategic island's Greek and Turkish communities resumed last week after a two month hiatus caused by the presidential election, there was hope that the regional factors in the East Mediterranean area could lead to some progress.

There is hope based on signs, albeit tenuous, that the US Administration – concerned about Lebanon and the wider Israeli-Palestinian issue at a time of some gains by the Soviet Union in Iraq and Syria – is showing more interest in a solution to the Cyprus sore.

But any real progress towards a solution is fraught with problems. While the inter-communal talks taking place in divided Nicosia's grand old Ledra Palace Hotel are important, it is difficult to escape the view that the future of Cyprus will be decided in Washington, London, Moscow, Athens and Ankara.

The bustling harbour at Limassol, the Britons turning lobster red during their package tours to Paphos, and the Scandinavians bathing topless on the golden beaches at Ayia Napa belie the country's political and economic problems.

President Kyprianou's decisive victory – with the help of the Communist Party – in last month's presidential election had given Cyprus the opportunity of five years of domestic political stability, which could allow the Government to tackle controversial issues, including the Greek-Turkish Cypriot problem.

It was the first open and competitive presidential election since independence in 1960. In 1977 the Cyprus Parliament elected Mr Kyprianou to complete Archbishop Makarios' term of office, and the following year Mr Kyprianou was elected unopposed. Last month's election, however, reflected the spectrum of politics on "Greek" Cyprus.

Mr Kyprianou won almost 57 per cent of the vote, with about two thirds of his support coming from the Communist Party, Akel.

Mr Kyprianou, who describes his own Diko Party as "a perfect combination between pure Centre and progressive Right", was quick to rule out the possibility of any Communist Party members becoming members of the Government. "I have no intention of bringing communism to Cyprus," he said.

The problem for those wanting a solution to the Cyprus dispute is that the issue has not caused anyone but the Cypriots themselves any major discomfort. No shot is ever fired across the dividing line. Unlike the Arab-Israeli dispute, it has not provided a threat to the stability of the region, although it does exacerbate historical tensions between Athens and Ankara. The British maintain their sovereign military bases with only occasional calls for their removal.

Carter raps Israel over Palestinians
From DAVID BALDERSTONE

'The Age', Amman, March 15, 1983

Former US President Jimmy Carter – architect of the Camp David accords – last night strongly criticised the Israeli Government's ideas on Palestinian autonomy.

But he softened his criticism by noting that Palestinian representatives had refused to take part in talks on autonomy for Palestinians in the West Bank and Gaza Strip.

The negotiations envisaged in the Camp David accords, which paved the way to the Egypt-Israel peace treaty, were to have been a key factor in moving towards settlement of the Arab-Israeli dispute. But the negotiations have become bogged down.

Mr Carter, speaking in Amman, where he met Jordan's King Hussein, said: "The present definition of autonomy as expressed by (Israel's) Prime Minister Begin has no relationship to the definition of full autonomy which I understood at Camp David and which President Sadat understood.

"It is a very limited, almost meaningless, degree of autonomy," he said, noting that Palestinians living in (Arab) East Jerusalem were excluded by Israel from joining the autonomy process.

"I think Prime Minister Begin's proposals on autonomy have been very poor and very short of what is reasonable. On the other hand he is not seeing the Palestinians come forward and negotiate."

Mr Carter said he hoped that King Hussein and West Bank Palestinians would "initiate conversations" with Israel and Egypt, and perhaps the US, to further the peace process.

However, he said that for King Hussein to join the peace process without the support of moderate Arab States and the Palestinians would be "pointless, even counterproductive".

Mr Carter left Amman for Saudi Arabia last night on the next leg of his Middle East tour, during which he met members of the Palestine Liberation Organisation.

PLO divided on mandate for Jordan
From DAVID BALDERSTONE

'The Age', Amman, April 8, 1983

King Hussein of Jordan appeared to be facing today an increasingly lonely decision on whether to join the Middle East peace process with a joint Jordanian-Palestinian delegation.

Judging from statements by two hardline senior officials of the Palestine Liberation Organisation, the PLO will refuse to authorise the king to negotiate on behalf of the Palestinians. However a final decision may be known this weekend when the PLO chairman, Mr Yasser Arafat, is scheduled to return to Amman for a further round of talks with King Hussein.

Hopes that the king would be able to make the politically dangerous decision to join the process under the cover of a PLO mandate and an Arab summit mandate seemed to be fading rapidly. And without this political cover from the PLO and the Arab League, a positive response by King Hussein to President Reagan's request for Jordan to join could leave the king in a dangerously isolated position in the Arab world.

However, a special envoy of President Mubarak of Egypt was expected in Amman this weekend in a bid to persuade the king to at least keep the door open for a decision to join peace talks.

The Head of Information, Mr Yasser Abu Rabbo told Reuters in Kuwait last night: "The PLO has refused to authorise King Hussein to negotiate." And another senior official, Mr Saleh Khalaf, who is also known as Abu Iyad, said: "it is impossible to authorise anyone to speak or negotiate in the name of the PLO." Both these officials are known to lean towards Syria, which is hostile towards the idea of King Hussein joining the peace process. Therefore their comments may reflect political jockeying within the PLO hierarchy rather than being statements of fact on a final PLO decision.

M-E Plan still alive

David Balderstone, 'The Age' Middle East correspondent reports from Amman

'The Age', April 11, 1983

Arab politics appear to demand that, despite obstacles and setbacks, the door should be left a little open in case another miracle occurs in the Holy Land.

While making it clear that the Jordanian-PLO talks had broken down, the Jordanian statement left the door to the future ajar by stating that Jordan still believed progress could be made through a confederal agreement between Jordan and the PLO.

"We believe, and continue to believe, that this aim (progress towards peace) can be achieved through an agreement between Jordan and the PLO on the establishment of a confederal relationship that would govern and regulate the future of Jordanian and Palestinian peoples," the statement said. The Jordanian-PLO talks had centred on finding a bridge between President Reagan's proposals and last September's Fez Arab summit proposals, which called for the establishment of an independent Palestinian State.

There is no doubt, however, that Jordan's decision has dealt a heavy blow to President Reagan's peace proposals and strengthened the position of Palestinian hardliners.

It has also opened the door to further Soviet advances in the Middle East, giving Moscow its first chance since the late President Sadat of Egypt went to Jerusalem in 1977 to get involved once again in the peace process.

With time running out before next year's US Presidential elections, Jordan's decision means there is little prospect of any dramatic moves in the search for Middle East peace in the foreseeable future.

The Jordanian decision has been welcomed by the Syrian Government, which is supported and armed by the Soviet Union and which has considerable political clout over PLO hardliners.

The breakdown indicates once again that Mr Arafat has opted for consensus leadership of the organisation at the possible expense of political gains for the Palestinian people.

Just a month ago, Jordanian officials were optimistic enough to predict that the PLO would give Jordan a mandate to join the peace process with a delegation of Jordanian officials and non-PLO Palestinians.

Jordan's Information Minister, Mr Adnan Abu Odeh, said Jordan would continue to have normal relations with the PLO. He said PLO offices in Jordan would continue their "normal work" and that Palestine Liberation Army forces would remain in the country.

"Our decision to abandon talks with the PLO leadership on joint political moves for Middle East peace in no way means that our present relationship will be weakened," he said.

War clouds darken Lebanon's summer
From DAVID BALDERSTONE in Damascus

'The Age', Damascus, April 27, 1983

A young man dressed in a dark suit led the mourners up the steps to the ancient monastery of Seydnaya, 30 kilometres north of Damascus.

Ceremonially, he carried a portrait of the dead man – a young Syrian officer killed a few days earlier in Lebanon. A Syrian general arrived in a black Mercedes to pay his respects. The village mourned, as a chill wind blew off the nearby peaks of the Ante-Lebanon range, which provides the border between Syrian and Lebanon.

The martyr's funeral and the chill wind may have been symbolic of what is likely to be a dangerous summer for the Syrian forces facing the Israelis in Lebanon's Beka'a Valley.

Unless the US Secretary of State, Mr Schultz, who is visiting the Middle East this week, achieves a breakthrough in the drawn-out talks on the withdrawal of Israeli troops from Lebanon (which would probably lead to a Syrian withdrawal as well) war looks a distinct possibility.

Such a war, which is widely expected in Damascus, would provide a severe test for Syria's newly supplied Soviet weapons. But, more important, it could determine whether the Soviet Union, which is using Syria as a foothold in the Arab world, continues to make gains in the Middle East.

Despite the view of most military observers that Israel would come out on top in a military conflict with Syria, it would be wrong to assume that Moscow would attempt to pull Damascus back from the brink of war.

While a conflict might reflect badly on Soviet arms and equipment, a Syrian-Israeli war would almost certainly stop once and for all the Reagan Administration's vain attempts to broaden the Middle East peace process.

It would also strengthen the position of the so-called hardliners opposing a broadening of the peace process under present circumstances.

Therefore, Moscow could believe that even a military defeat for Syria could further open the door to expanding Soviet influence in the Middle East.

But there are dangers for Moscow. Although the Soviet Union's relationship with Damascus has been built slowly, steadily, and above all, cautiously, Moscow's bid to use Syria as a foothold for strengthening ties in the Middle East is fraught with risks.

While Moscow is building bridges again with Cairo and Bagdad, Kremlin advisers would be wise if they were reminding the new Soviet leader, Mr Andropov, of Moscow's experiences in Egypt, the Sudan and Iraq – three leading Arab countries, whose previously strong relations with the Soviet Union were cooled overnight at the whim of the countries' leaders.

With Syria, Moscow is playing for high stakes against high risks. With no real ideological sympathy in Damascus for communism, the Moscow-Damascus connection is very much merely a matter of necessity for Syria.

Without access to American arms, and without the money for European weapons, Damascus has been forced to turn to the Soviet Union.

The best thing going for the Soviet Union in relations with Syria has been the US Middle East policy, which has all but ignored Syria.

This month, President Reagan attempted to correct this situation by reassuring Syria's President Assad that he wanted Middle East negotiations aimed at securing Israeli withdrawal from the Syrian Golan Heights as well as the West Bank and Gaza Strip.

President Reagan's Middle East peace plan, which Mr Schultz will attempt to revive this week, is based on UN Security Council

Resolution 242. This resolution, passed after the 1967 war, calls for Israeli military withdrawal from territories occupied during the war – the West Bank, Gaza Strip and the Golan Heights (*Ed. - and Sinai – which was subsequently returned to Egypt*).

Understandably, the Syrians resent the fact that the Golan Heights are often forgotten when attention is paid to the West Bank and Gaza Strip. (In any case, Israel immediately rejected the American statement by saying Israel would never withdraw from the Golan.)

As well as replacing all the military equipment lost by Syria during the war in Lebanon last year, the Soviet Union has installed long range SAM-5 missiles near Damascus and Homs, approximately 150 kilometres north of the capital.

The range of these missiles, which are manned by Soviet forces, covers Lebanon and Northern Israel. Therefore, they are a potential threat to Israeli air operations. It is the first time the missiles have been supplied to a country outside the Warsaw Pact.

Because of this threat to Israeli air operations, there remain considerable fears that Israel might attempt to knock out the batteries. This would be likely to start a direct Syrian-Israeli clash in Lebanon and with Soviet troops manning the missiles run the risk of drawing Moscow into the conflict. The dangers are immense.

Syria has up to 30,000 troops stationed in Lebanon's Beka'a Valley. Syrian troops originally entered Lebanon in 1976 as the major component of the Arab "deterrent" force aimed at quelling civil war violence.

Damascus has said it will withdraw its troops from Lebanon when Israel withdraws its forces. However, the Syrian position is deliberately ambiguous and Syrian intentions remain somewhat of a mystery.

Diplomats in Damascus are divided in their views on Syrian withdrawal. While some believe the Syrians do want to withdraw, one Western diplomat said he believed the Soviet Union would not want the Syrians to pull out. The diplomat believed that Moscow would be justifiably fearful that the US would fill the "influence" vacuum left by Syrian withdrawal.

Therefore, a long, hot summer looks likely in Lebanon. With Syrian and Israeli troops only a few hundred metres apart in some places, it would not be difficult for either side to find provocation for a clash.

With Israeli artillery in range of Damascus, and with Soviet troops manning the SAM-5 missiles, it could prove difficult to contain the clash or a limited conflict.

News Diary
DAVID BALDERSTONE in Amman

'The Age', May 2, 1983

Khalil Wazir was here

When Palestinian fighters and leaders were scattered among various Arab capitals after the siege of Beirut last year, our sleepy street in treed Jebel Amman got a new resident.

Khalil Wazir, better known as Abu Jihad (Father of the Holy War), deputy commander (to Yasser Arafat) of the Palestinian commando group Fatah, moved into the big house across the road from our front gate.

Now, he appears to have left as suddenly as he arrived. Although Khalil Wazir continued to travel a lot to other Arab capitals, he spent a considerable amount of time in Amman as he was involved heavily in Mr Arafat's talks with King Hussein on possible PLO-Jordanian co-operation in the peace process.

There was something of a conspiracy of silence among the street's other residents, some of whom never miss a chance to gossip. Perhaps there was a realisation that, as effectively Fatah's day-to-day commander, Khalil Wazir had a security problem.

Mind you, even without the gossip, it was not difficult to tell that someone of considerable importance had moved in.

His BMW and an accompanying Mercedes retained their Lebanese number plates. And a group of young men hovered around the garden day and night when he was in town.

Inadvertently, the driver revealed his holster whenever he bent over to polish the hub caps.

Over coffee in his living room, Khalil Wazir indicated that he missed the political life of Beirut in the days before the PLO evacuated the city. He said there was "very light" political life in

Amman, whereas Beirut had had "political life and everything was moving".

His son and daughter arrived home from school while we were talking and he went to considerable lengths to introduce them to his Australian neighbor. He was proud of how well his children spoke English.

Then, this month on the day the Jordanian Government announced that its talks with the PLO had broken down, Khalil Wazir packed some belongings and left town. He hasn't been seen at the house since.

Jordanian officials insist that he is still in Amman. But Khalil Wazir may have another reason for leaving the house in Amman. Residents of the street believe that the royal family was paying the rent. Perhaps Khalil Wazir doesn't feel comfortable about accepting the king's largesse after the breakdown in the talks.

Celebration

After the strain of the drawn-out and now moribund talks with the PLO, King Hussein looked considerably more relaxed this week as he celebrated the birth of his tenth child – a girl.

The baby girl, who has been named Princess Iman (Faith), is the third child of King Hussein and his American wife, Queen Noor. The queen, who is the king's fourth wife, was formerly Lisa Halaby and lived in Sydney for some time before moving to Amman.

In typical style, King Hussein, 48, who became king at the age of 18 in 1952, took the steering wheel to drive his new daughter and the queen home from hospital.

Last month, as the Jordan-PLO talks had reached a crucial stage, the king himself had spent a short time in hospital. The strain of the talks had brought on a heart condition.

Odd customs

A usually reliable source was telling a story in Amman this weekend that has a distinct ring of truth about it for anyone who has spent years coping with customs officials in the Arab world.

On the other hand, it might seem apocryphal to those fortunate enough not to have to cope with over-zealous, suspicious, bloody-minded and Kafka-like Arab customs.

The story goes like this: An American military adviser was sent to oil-rich Saudi Arabia to train Saudi soldiers in the art of parachuting. All went well. The Saudi troops coped admirably as they drifted down over the Arabian deserts, and the American went home satisfied his mission was completed.

Shortly after the American officer left, the Saudis plucked up courage and undertook another exercise in parachuting. Again, even without the American's help, the Saudis drifted down and landed safely.

But, while the jump had gone well, the Saudis were a bit uncertain how to refold the parachutes. So they decided to send them to the American officer in the US for refolding. The American obliged and sent them back with a Saudi courier. When the Saudi arrived at Riyadh airport in Saudi Arabia, the customs officials looked suspiciously at the folded parachutes, and exclaimed that anything could be inside those packages.

So the customs officials unfolded them again.

Name calling

While on the topic of customs, the details required never cease to amaze me. Driving from Amman to Damascus the other day, about an hour's worth of paperwork was involved at the Syrian border post clearing my Jordan-registered car into Syria.

One detail needed to complete the customs declaration for my car was my mother's first name.

Of course, passport officials in the Middle East love these sorts of details. To be asked for father's first name is common, but sometimes they even ask for grandfather's first name. Of course, they don't have any easy way of checking whether the names provided are correct.

In any case, I don't really know how important names are. Over the years I have been registered at Middle East borders as David Robert (Robert being my second name), David Robert Bal, David Bal, and sometimes even correctly.

Media power

Although not too many people in Arab capitals would join me in regretting openly the fact that from the weekend Israel Radio's English-language broadcasts will not be as easily heard, it is known that a lot of people in Arab capitals religiously tune in. And these people include most senior Arab officials.

Therefore, it seems incomprehensible that Israel, which has always been credited with a certain brilliance in public relations, is reducing the powers of its English-language output because of other demands on its powerful transmitters.

While Arab-language Israel Radio broadcasts will continue, it seems, at full strength, a point the Israeli authorities should have borne in mind is that Arab officials are quite aware that the English-language broadcasts give a better flavour of what the Jerusalem Government is thinking. This is because briefings to journalists in Israel are given in English or Hebrew.

Meanwhile, Jordan Television has announced that it has boosted the power of its transmissions and can now be picked up throughout Israel, the West Bank, Syria, and as far away as Cyprus. It would seem the Jordanians, who put out a good proportion of American, British and even Australian programs, also know something about public relations.

Another milestone on the road to nowhere
From DAVID BALDERSTONE in Amman

'The Age', May 12, 1983

When Israeli armor rolled into Lebanon last June, the Israeli Government named the war "Peace for Galilee operation".

It was, Israel said, to protect the people of northern Israel from Palestinian rockets, artillery, and a growing hang-glider-equipped air force.

But the code name was something of a misnomer as Galilee was enjoying almost undisturbed peace because the Palestine Liberation Organisation in South Lebanon was, more or less, observing an unofficial ceasefire.

Now, 11 months and 481 dead Israeli soldiers later, and with 20,000 Israeli troops still deployed in Lebanon, the Prime Minister, Mr Begin, can claim he has brought even more peace to Galilee.

On the other hand, Mr Begin is left with his troops on the brink of a full-scale war with Syria (a war which could involve the Soviet Union directly); the West is left with the fact that the war has enabled Moscow to make gains in the Middle East, and the Lebanese are left with their country closer to long-term partition than at any time since the outbreak of civil war in 1975.

If, as some people claim, Israel is the West's only real friend in the Middle East, it can be observed that with Mr Begin's Government as a friend, the West doesn't need enemies.

"Peace for Galilee" was a misnomer not only because Galilee was enjoying a virtual peace, but because the Israeli invasion of Lebanon was a grand plan aimed at destroying the PLO's military infrastructure and serving Israel's security and business interests (and, perhaps water needs) in one of two ways.

First, and preferably, the Israelis believed the operation might lead to the establishment of a reunified Lebanon with a Government that would look kindly upon good relations – including an open border for trade with Israel.

Second, if this failed, Israel was prepared – perhaps reluctantly – to maintain its interests in Lebanon by a policy which would lead to virtual partition.

Indeed, during the first months of the invasion, it looked as if the Palestinian war machine had been dealt a near-fatal blow. With the evacuation of Beirut, Palestinian fighters were dispersed to other Arab capitals.

But with the latest intelligence reports that 2000 Palestinian fighters have recently slipped across the Syrian border to join the guerillas behind Syrian lines, the PLO's war machine cannot be described as dead.

However, what can arguably be described as dead are President Reagan's Middle East peace plan – unveiled after the Israeli siege of Beirut – and (short of something close to a miracle) the bid by US Secretary of State, Mr Schultz, to negotiate a withdrawal of foreign forces from Lebanon.

After Israel's Cabinet approved Mr Schultz's plan last Friday, he declared it as a "milestone". Two days later, after the Syrian Government reacted unenthusiastically, it looked like a milestone on the road to nowhere.

Apportionment of blame for the plan's failure to get off the ground has been confused by the breakdown of protracted talks between Jordan and the PLO.

Jordan had hoped the talks would lead to the PLO giving King Hussein some kind of mandate to form a joint Jordanian-Palestinian delegation for negotiations within the framework of the Reagan plan. However PLO hardliners (backed by Syria) rejected the idea.

But it was not Jordan, not the PLO and not Syria, that rejected the Reagan plan when it was unveiled last September – it was Israel, the US' wayward dependent and the "West's only stable friend in the Middle East".

Furthermore, while it is a disappointment that the PLO did not give King Hussein an opportunity to test the water with a joint delegation, Israel did nothing to help.

In fact it hindered the chances of the talks succeeding by continuing the policy of Jewish settlements on the West Bank and delayed talks on the withdrawal of foreign forces from Lebanon.

It is fair to say that some elements within the PLO don't appear to want peace. It is equally fair to say that Israel's settlement policy doesn't conjure up the vision of a craving for an overall settlement.

Since Mr Schultz met President Assad of Syria last weekend, the Government-controlled Syrian Press has maintained a torrent of criticism about Mr Schultz's plan for the withdrawal of foreign forces from Lebanon.

While President Assad did not reject the plan, it looks extremely unlikely that Syria will agree to withdraw its estimated 30,000-plus troops from Lebanon.

Only Saudi financial persuasion, Soviet influence, or that rare commodity in the Middle East, plain good sense, might persuade Damascus to pull out its troops.

Syria's past record of taking Saudi money, but not always the covering advice, makes Saudi influence a doubtful element. And it is arguable whether Moscow would see a Syrian withdrawal as being in its strategic interest.

This is because Moscow and Damascus would fear that the vacuum left in Lebanon by a Syrian departure would be filled by American influence.

Israel has said it will not withdraw unless the Syrian and Palestinian forces pull out simultaneously.

Therefore it looks very much as if foreign forces will remain in Lebanon, with the ever-increasing risk of a Syrian-Israeli war – a conflict which would be likely to involve the Soviet troops manning Syria's recently installed SAM-5 missiles.

With an increasing, but significant, number of Israelis opposing the invasion of Lebanon, Mr Begin's Government might not consider it politically practical to deploy the number of troops required to drive the Syrians out.

On the other hand, Mr Begin, who, unlike President Assad has to face elections, must be counting the cost of brinkmanship into which his "Peace for Galilee" operation has drawn him.

A majority of the split Shi'ite Moslem community of South Lebanon which cheered the advancing Israeli troops 11 months ago are now demonstrating in protest against the Israeli occupation.

And for the first time since Mr Begin came to power in 1977, opinion polls are beginning to show that he would lose an election held now.

But, naturally, Mr Begin could assume he would do well in northern Israel – because he has provided peace for Galilee.

Amman May 14, 1983 (*To an Australian journalist colleague*)

We were on Cyprus ten days ago, and the house in Kakopetria is looking really good. It will be finished by the middle of June. It has lost any resemblance to the chooks' house that it was. It is much larger than it used to seem. The builder that Susan got to do the job is very good, and doing the work more as a work of art than a task of renovation. Despite the help of a Linguaphone, the architect (Susan) and the builder still carry on as if they are two inmates at the Royal School for the Deaf and Dumb, and any serious translation has to be carried out at the Maryland by John.

*****

As you may know, I resigned from The Age in February (actually not that long after I returned from Australia) and am finishing up at the end of June. Basically I want a change, but the reasons given were accumulation of six years wear and tear on my nerves, cost of living here, and twenty weeks of travelling away from Susan last year. Because of budget problems, Creighton says they are not replacing me this coming financial year. At the end of June we are moving to Kakopetria.

Susan will either get a job in Nicosia, or do the conservation course at York University, in which case I will go there for most of the nine months.

PLO chief faces military revolt
David Balderstone reports from Amman

'The Age', May 16, 1983

Syria was treading a tightrope between hostile rhetoric and a war with Israel today as the Lebanese and Israeli Governments prepared to sign the Syrian-opposed agreement for the withdrawal of foreign forces from Lebanon.

With 20,000 Israeli troops facing about 30,000 Palestinian-supported Syrian troops in Lebanon, tension has risen dramatically with the leaders of Syria and the PLO closing ranks against the agreement. Israeli, Lebanese and American negotiators met in the Israeli city of Netanya and finished work on drafting the agreement, which covers the withdrawal of Israeli forces from Lebanon.

However, Israel has said it will not withdraw its forces unless Syria and the PLO agree to withdraw their forces simultaneously. Mr Arafat's warning about war was closely echoed by the Government-controlled Syrian Press, which speculated that civil war would break out if Lebanon signed the troop withdrawal agreement.

Mr Arafat's visit to Lebanon was the first since he left Beirut with the evacuation of Palestinian fighters last year. The real risk is that his fighting rhetoric could easily lead to war. With sporadic incidents across the lines dividing Syrian and Israeli troops in Lebanon, either side could seize at any time the excuse of provocation to launch a major attack.

Mid-East: new tack needed
From DAVID BALDERSTONE in Amman

'The Age', May 30, 1983

Syria's continued refusal to end its opposition to the Israel-Lebanon agreement on the withdrawal of foreign forces from Lebanon highlights once again the shortcomings of the United States step-by-step approach to Middle East peace moves.

Furthermore, Syria's firm stand plus the spectre of Soviet gains in the area focuses attention on the question of whether Moscow should be involved in the peace process.

And the answer is probably yes.

Because, without the full involvement of the Soviet Union, Moscow's tacticians have too much scope to cause trouble among the major parties and the myriad factions in the Arab-Israeli dispute.

The idea of the Soviet Union being fully involved in the peace process is not new or radical. It is merely different to the approach followed since President Sadat visited Jerusalem in 1977.

Early in October 1977, less than two months before Mr Sadat visited Jerusalem, the US and the Soviet Union, in a statement issued simultaneously in Washington and Moscow, said jointly that a Geneva-style conference chaired by both superpowers was the only way to solve the Arab-Israeli dispute.

When the Egyptian presidential airliner touched down at Lod airport near Tel Aviv on 20 November, 1977, the world was amazed, the Israelis stunned and overjoyed – and the hardline Arabs fumed.

Perhaps more significantly, Mr Sadat's courageous move prompted President Carter to throw the idea of a joint US-Soviet approach to solving the dispute out the window.

Instead, the US moved towards the step-by-step approach: chiselling away at the problem by dealing with one of Israel's neighbors at a time.

And, undoubtedly, it brought dramatic results – the Camp David accords leading to the Egypt-Israel peace treaty. But it didn't bring an overall solution, which requires a compromise settlement of the Palestinian question, any closer.

President Reagan has pursued the step-by-step approach. The Secretary of State, Mr Schultz, negotiated a troop withdrawal agreement between Lebanon and Israel – and then referred it to Syria.

Syria remains unenthusiastic (to put it mildly), and Israel's agreement to withdraw, which was conditional upon Syria and the Palestinians agreeing to pull out their troops looks valueless.

The lesson, which was obvious to many from the start, is that the step-by-step approach has a basic flaw.

This is that it leaves too many people with a right of veto.

In the case of the Camp David accords, which repeatedly call for Jordan to join the now-stalled negotiations on Palestinian autonomy, Syria, the Palestine Liberation Organisation, and other hardline Arabs held the right of veto over a broadening of the peace process.

In the case of the Schultz-negotiated troop withdrawal agreement, Syria, the PLO and the Soviet Union hold a right of veto.

In both cases, the US failed glaringly to consult directly other parties.

Former President Carter has admitted that he erred in not keeping Jordan's King Hussein informed of progress in the Camp David talks, which repeatedly called on Jordan to join the process.

When recently shuttling between Jerusalem and Beirut in the run-up to the Israel-Lebanon troop withdrawal agreement, Mr Schultz failed to take the time to visit Damascus to keep the Syrian Government informed of progress.

Bearing in mind that courtesy is highly important in dealing with the Arabs, it was a fundamental error.

Mr Schultz was snared in the same trap that caught Mr Carter. The odd thing about American diplomacy in the Middle East is that US diplomats are amongst the most intelligent, realistic, and sensitive in the area. Obviously, successive Administrations have taken scant notice of their advice.

In the wake of Israel's conditional decision to withdraw its troops (if Syria and the PLO do the same) from Lebanon, most attention is focused on Syria.

This ignores a further complication – that the PLO has something akin to a right of veto over any Syrian decision to withdraw troops.

And hardline Palestinians – especially in the wake of the threat to the leadership of the PLO chairman, Mr Arafat, from advocates of armed struggle within his own Fatah group – will almost certainly end up dictating the final PLO line on troop withdrawal.

But why does this affect the Syrians and the Soviet Union? Syria and Moscow have succeeded in gathering the PLO leadership in Damascus in the wake of last year's siege of Beirut. Damascus demands that Syria be seen as the only real protector of the Palestinian cause.

In view of this, Damascus would find it difficult to agree to withdraw its forces from Lebanon – a move which would leave the remaining PLO forces vulnerable.

The US step-by-step approach to peace negotiations has produced a peace treaty and an Israeli-Lebanon troop withdrawal accord for legalistically minded Israel to wave at the United Nations, the International Court at The Hague, and in capitals of friendly countries like Australia.

But it hasn't brought an overall settlement any closer, and the peace treaty with Egypt could turn out to be nothing more than a piece of paper unless the overall Palestinian issue is addressed.

Stable as it may be at present, even Egypt is not immune to the conniving of Moscow tacticians and hardline Arabs.

There was some wisdom in what President Carter agreed with Moscow in October 1977.

PLO leader appeals for backing
From DAVID BALDERSTONE

'The Age', Amman, June 22, 1983

Yasser Arafat has appealed to Saudi and other Arab leaders to help save him from a revolt in Palestinian guerilla ranks which he now alleges is Syria-assisted.

From a refugee camp base near Tripoli in northern Lebanon, Mr Arafat, head of the Palestine Liberation Organisation, sent urgent messages last night to Arab leaders and some other Heads of State, calling for international support.

The Palestinians' WAFA newsagency reported that Mr Arafat said Syrian tanks helped his hardline opponents in clashes with his men in the Syrian-held Beka'a Valley in eastern Lebanon.

WAFA said Mr Arafat had sent a message to the Syrian President Mr Assad, about Syrian forces' "serious change of stand".

Libya had publicly endorsed the mutiny that started in Mr Arafat's guerilla movement early in May, but this was the first time Mr Arafat had alleged Syrian intervention.

The dissidents said that overnight from Monday to Tuesday they routed Arafat "saboteurs" from eight posts in the Beka'a Valley to control the highway from Damascus, the supply route for Mr Arafat's retreating supporters in eastern Lebanon.

WAFA said an Arafat aide flew to Moscow with the PLO chief's appeal.

Mr Arafat, 54, has become a world-wide symbol of the Palestinian struggle to wrest a homeland from Israel. He co-founded Fatah in the late 1950s and became PLO chairman in 1969. But Fatah, biggest of its eight guerilla groups, is his PLO power base.

If Syria continues to support the rebels, Mr Arafat and his supporters will find themselves trapped in northern Lebanon.

Mr Arafat's usual access to this area is through the Syrian land border. His other alternatives would be a difficult departure by sea, or a seemingly impossible escape south through areas controlled by the Lebanese Christians and the Lebanese Government.

Syria's involvement in Fatah's internal battles yesterday – an involvement confirmed by independent observers – must be seen as reducing pressure on Israeli forces facing Syrian troops in Lebanon.

In a sense it means Syria has begun employing the tactic of brinkmanship on two fronts – one against the Israelis and one against Mr Arafat's mainstream Fatah.

If Syria intends to pursue its support of the Fatah dissidents, who basically oppose Mr Arafat's leaning towards diplomacy, Damascus will find it difficult to withdraw its troops from Lebanon.

To survive, Mr Arafat may have to adopt more of the dissidents' policies. This would probably mean he could not negotiate a withdrawal of Palestinian guerillas from Lebanon.

As Syria clearly wants to be seen as the custodian of the PLO it could not withdraw its troops from Lebanon – leaving the Palestinians uncovered – without a lot of policy backtracking.

Mr Arafat has survived crises before – the last was the Israeli siege of Beirut last year. He could well survive again.

Where to from here?
From DAVID BALDERSTONE in Amman

June 27, 1983

Like cats ready to pounce, they sat in the shade peacefully but alert. They clutched their guns as they sat guard outside a few drab offices on the ground floor of an apartment building.

There was a feeling of déjà vu. I had never been to this office of the Palestine Liberation Organisation in a refugee camp on the hills above the northern Lebanese port of Tripoli, 80 kilometres north of Beirut.

But things looked so familiar: a couple of desks with clerks bureaucratically administering finances, a revolutionary poster stuck to the wall, tables with small cups holding the dregs of Turkish coffee and saucers with cigarette butts.

It could have been a PLO office in West Beirut a year ago, or in Amman during the civil war in 1970, or a Palestinian office in Nablus just before Israel occupied the West Bank in 1967.

There was a difference of course.

For the Palestinians, there had been glory in the siege of Beirut a year ago. For weeks on end, the PLO was able to taunt and tease the might of Israeli armor as the terms of evacuation were laboriously negotiated.

The people in the Tripoli office were again under siege. But there was not much glory because the people laying siege were dissident colleagues in the Fatah commando group – the PLO's biggest guerilla group.

The Fatah rebellion has provided Israel's Prime Minister, Mr Begin, with a major political achievement at a time when he was facing mounting criticism at home over the year-long war in Lebanon. With or without the Israeli invasion of Lebanon, the rebellion may have occurred. But Mr Begin doesn't have to worry about that minor detail when he speaks to the Israeli people.

But even if the wash-up of the rebellion leaves a divided PLO, or a PLO firmly under Syrian control, the Palestinian problem remains unresolved. It may give Israel and the world a short respite, but the Palestinian problem will remain the crux of the Middle East problem.

"I was evacuated from West Beirut on the ships last year," said a young official in the Tripoli office. "I went to Tunis, but it was too far away so I came back to Lebanon."

More practised in the art of providing a quotable line, Ahmad Abdul Rahman, a member of Fatah's revolutionary council, said: "The PLO is like a wounded bird soaring over the Mediterranean looking for a tree on which to land."

The vision of Mr Rahman's wounded bird provides an excuse for describing the smallness of the area which is the centrepiece of the Middle East dispute. It is the smallness which makes the problem so difficult to solve: a smallness which provides both Arab and Israeli propagandists with graphic arguments.

The route has changed now, but up until a couple of years ago, soaring by airliner on the direct Amman-Cairo flight gave an illustration of the area. Due to the need to avoid Israeli airspace, the plane would take off from Amman and skirt Israel by flying north over Damascus, north-west over Beirut, and then turn south-west for Cairo. The point is the flight took less time than a Melbourne-Brisbane non-stop flight.

Laid over a map of Victoria, the smallness of the area is even more dramatic perhaps. In approximate terms, and by treating Melbourne as Amman, Damascus would be placed just north of Wangaratta, Beirut just west of Numurkah, and Jerusalem at Ballan.

Mind you, the state of the roads, mountainous terrain, border bureaucracy, the odd armed checkpoint, and the coiled barbed wire dividing Syrian and Israeli battle lines in Lebanon, would convince the keenest Sunday driver that this illustration is relevant in terms of kilometres only.

Outside this centrepiece area are 17 Arab countries, all with an opinion on the dispute, and a few with the clout, either financial or through arms, to influence the Arab factions to the dispute, particularly the PLO and not many of the countries with clout urge moderation.

Now back to Mr Rahman's wounded bird looking for a tree. First the PLO found its tree – a state within a state – in Jordan. Then during bloody battles in 1970, the Palestinian fighters were driven out and gradually regrouped in Lebanon.

Last year's Israeli invasion of Lebanon destroyed the PLO's state within a state in South Lebanon and the fighters and headquarters officials were evacuated by sea from West Beirut. But only the most optimistic, or naïve, believe that was an end to the Palestinian problem.

After the evacuation from West Beirut, with the siege of Beirut still fresh in the West's mind, it can be argued the PLO should have built on world sympathy and firmly grasped the political option by formally recognising Israel's right to exist.

But it didn't, and that's not all that surprising since the Palestinians have missed just about every opportunity since the first world Zionist congress, convened by Theodor Herzl, proposed the idea of a Jewish State in Palestine in 1897.

"It is often said that the Palestinian question is a chronicle of missed opportunities," Jordan's King Hussein wrote a few years ago. "This is partly true, though not entirely.

"…..It is my considered opinion that the Zionist thrust and avalanche could have been blunted, but not entirely thwarted.

"The tragic undoing and dismantling of the Palestinian people, to which their leadership unwittingly contributed, was that they adamantly refused to accept this unpleasant but elementary fact of life," King Hussein wrote.

Palestinians are many things. They are refugees living in camps in Arab countries and Israeli-controlled occupied territories. They are Israeli citizens in Israel proper. They are millionaires sipping cocktails at parties in Amman. They are scattered throughout a worldwide Diaspora. They are bureaucrats in the Gulf countries.

Some are fighters. Some live happily in Arab countries and throughout the Diaspora.

Defeated by the dim light in an Amman bar as I waited for a friend, I put down the 'Economist' I was reading. "Thought you'd be struggling to read in this light," came a voice from the shadows. "Where you from?"

"Australia," I replied.

"Strike, so am I....emigrated there from Palestine 20 years ago," the voice continued.

Reluctantly, I asked how he enjoyed being back in the Middle East. "Well, mate, bit disappointed really. There I have been fighting for the Palestinian cause tooth and nail in Sydney for 20 bloody years, and what do I find when I come back?

"I find my family living in a bloody big mansion in Amman and they don't even want to go back to Palestine."

It is difficult to generalise about Palestinian aspirations, but most commonly Palestinians say they want their own State – in a sense, to prove there is a Palestinian identity.

Judging by the upsurge of Palestinian nationalism amongst the Arabs who took up Israeli citizenship after the creation of the State of Israel in 1948, this sentiment would appear to apply just as much to Israeli Arabs as those living in the occupied territories and the Diaspora.

In fact, rightly or wrongly, it doesn't matter what the aspirations of a majority of the world's six million Palestinians are. It doesn't matter because there is a huge reservoir of Palestinians ready to fight to keep the Palestinian sore open.

After six years talking to ordinary Palestinian civilians and PLO officials, some impressive, some distinctly unimpressive, I am sceptical the Palestinian problem can ever be resolved.

Some people live comfortably with the fantasy that if the Palestinian problem would just go away, the Middle East would become a peaceful place. But the Levant is an area of jealousies between sects, tribes and villages, where for so often, and for so long, the gun has been the arbiter.

An unresolved Palestinian problem exacerbates these problems.

Lebanese romantics, of whom there are many (something to do with the mountains and the sea, Phoenician heritage, and east Mediterranean macho), firmly dispute the fact that a major reason for the civil war was religious differences. In part they are right, but only in part.

They are a bit like many Palestinians who take the broad brush approach to wiping out historical incidents, and firmly declare, even believe, that "we Arabs and our cousins the Jews used to live happily side by side before Israel was founded".

Some truth to it of course, but one has to ignore a lot of feuds and fighting to be categorical about it.

In Lebanon, there is very little religious intolerance in terms of freedom of worship. Some families are linked across religious lines. The Christians are able to point to Moslems within their militias, and vice versa.

Nevertheless, the underlying cause of the civil war stems from dissatisfaction with Lebanon's traditional confessional system of government – the system under which power (and, in effect, wealth) is shared. Under this system, the President has to be a Maronite Christian, the Prime Minister a Sunni Moslem and the Speaker a Shi'ite Moslem. The system has tended to permeate the whole society.

The system is based on a 1943 census, which showed that the Maronites were the biggest community, with the Sunnis being the second biggest group and the Shi'ites the third.

The influx of Palestinians after Israel's creation in 1948, after the 1967 Six Day War, and again after the 1970 civil war in Jordan, exacerbated Lebanon's confessional problems and the PLO guerilla groups provided added clout for the Lebanese Leftist militias drawn mainly from the Moslem and Druze communities, when civil war broke out in 1975 – a war between the haves and have nots.

If, as some Lebanese claim, the Press was wrong to generalise by categorising the warring sides during the civil war as "Christian Rightist" and Moslem Leftist" forces, it was equally misleading for the Press to portray the Christians as a firmly united alliance.

There were two main Christian militias: the Falangists led by Bashir Gemayel, who was assassinated just before he was to become president last year, and the Tigers militia led by Dany Chamoun, son of former Lebanese President Camille Chamoun. They were supported in general terms by two other Christian militias, the Guardians of the Cedars, and the group representing former President Suleiman Franjieh.

In bitter fighting in 1980 after the main civil war had ended, the Falangist militia defeated Dany Chamoun's Tigers and both militias were amalgamated into the "Lebanese Forces".

In the extensively damaged headquarters building of Chamoun's National Liberal Party in East Beirut, I asked Dany Chamoun if he was confident that civil war would not break out again if all foreign forces – Syrian, Israeli and Palestinian – were withdrawn from Lebanon.

Dany Chamoun is a confident, dashing man, who – although he has no government position – remains highly influential within Lebanon's somewhat feudal political system.

It was the only question in an hour long interview which he did not answer immediately. Instead he hesitated before saying: "A hundred percent I am not sure....To be honest with you, I am not sure of it.

"This is why from the moment I came back (to Lebanon) in January, I have been pressing for the creation of some form of organisation next to the President in which the representatives of the confessional groups could work together to produce political change.

"I have always said there is a Lebanese problem," he said, in an apparent reference to those who argue that all Lebanon's problems stem from the Palestinian presence.

"Lebanese society has undergone tremendous changes since 1943. Education has brought about tremendous changes. There have been changes in habits, ideas.

"Everyone has the same openings for education now, so, therefore, we must be realistic and modify our political system.

"To ignore them, yes, I think we would have problems."

Dany Chamoun and Lebanon's President Amin Gemayel have something very fundamentally important in common. Whereas Dany's brother Dory, and Amin's brother, Bashir, were political hardliners (Bashir moderated his position as he moved towards assuming the presidency), Dany and Amin are consensus men. They angered some Christian hardliners by maintaining dialogue with Moslem and Palestinian leaders within the Lebanese political spectrum.

Dany Chamoun said relations with the Gemayel family were "proper, perfect". "I have never had any problem with President Amin Gemayel....for a very short period there was a problem with Bashir, but that was patched up before Bashir died.

"If you lived the way we lived from 1975-82 you are bound to have friction. The abundance of weapons; militias get beyond the control of two persons even though they want to be on the best of relations."

It is often said the Israeli invasion of Lebanon restored the Maronite Christians to a position of supremacy in Lebanon. So do the Christians want change?

"Everybody wants a change. The Christians want a change, the Moslems want a change. The traditional method of balancing confessional power within the civil service and other institutions does not really represent the confessional balance of power."

Under the present system, he said, squabbles over whether a Christian, Sunni, Shi'ite – to name the three main groups – should fill a particular position often stopped the process of government.

"Sometimes in the public service we have a directorate, which doesn't have a director because we are still squabbling over who this director should be.

"(There are) stupid institutions like we can't have a Sunni ambassador to Paris, can't have a Maronite ambassador to another country because the Sunnis have that position.

"Just by putting someone as head of the Directorate of Civil Aviation, for example, or another as Director of Public Works, doesn't give you a balance of power.

"Even the commander of the army being Christian does not provide any sanctuary for the Christians."

On the question of long term relations between Lebanon and Israel, Mr Chamoun said: "To be realistic, we want to live in peace. The Israeli State is there: nobody is going to destroy Israel. We want to develop our country; we want to live in peace with Israel."

Mr Chamoun said the Christians had fought the Palestinians because they were "imposing themselves on Lebanon.

"There is a Palestinian problem in the Middle East. Some will be accommodated in the Arab world; some are being accommodated in Israel. Eventually we all have to share the burden for a number of displaced persons. But the main factor is that we reach a situation for which there isn't any armed struggle – where the arms impose themselves as a state within a state."

As the Lebanese Government, through American mediation, attempts to free the country of foreign forces, including the Palestinians, there is mounting speculation that if the Palestinian fighters are expelled from Lebanon they will merely drift back to Jordan, from whence they came in 1970-71.

"I don't think so. Jordan has gone through bad experiences with the Palestinian armies," Dany Chamoun said. "I don't think it is going to permit a resurgence of this...the king and country don't want to go back to having an armed struggle.

"Really, it is not our worry, except that we have a friend in King Hussein and would not like to see his country in trouble."

Most commonly, there are three ways of solving the Palestinian problem put forward. First, autonomy for Palestinians living in the Israeli occupied West Bank and Gaza Strip territories. Secondly, the creation of a Palestinian State on the West Bank. Thirdly, the emergence of Jordan as the Palestinian State.

The autonomy idea as envisaged in the Camp David accords, which paved the way to the Egypt-Israel peace treaty, has been rejected by West Bank Palestinian leaders, the PLO, Jordan and most Arab countries. In my view they were short sighted in their rejection as the Camp David process provided for autonomy for a transitional period of five years only, after which the final status of the occupied territories would have been negotiated.

On the other hand, the autonomy plan gave nothing to Diaspora Palestinians, and in any case the Egypt-Israel negotiations on the issue are stalled.

The idea of Jordan being the Palestinian State has often been advocated by Israeli leaders, particularly Israel's former Defence Minister, Ariel Sharon.

Well over 50 percent of Jordan's population is Palestinian, and perhaps as much as 90 percent of public sector business is controlled by Palestinians. So why not?

For one thing, the rest of the population is not Palestinian, controls the army, and would fight against Palestinian domination.

Secondly, Jordan – with severe economic problems and always dependent upon foreign, mainly Saudi Arabian, aid – is unlikely to ever become viable. Despite some intensive agriculture on the east bank of the below-sea-level Jordan Valley, and cropping and grazing on the Jordanian hills, over 75 percent of Jordan receives less than 100 millimetres of rain a year. Jordan does not produce oil. It is mainly desert.

Rainfall maps of the area show that Israel, Lebanon and parts of Syria hold most of the area known traditionally as the "fertile crescent".

So what about a Palestinian State on the West Bank?

Such a State – particularly if it was linked to Jordan economically – would probably satisfy the majority of Palestinians, even though most would not want to live there. But Israel has repeatedly said "no" to a Palestinian State on the West Bank – for security reasons, and because the present Government considers it to be part of the Biblical land of Israel.

With the West Bank territory cutting Jerusalem in half, and stretching down the coastal plain to within 15 kilometres of Tel Aviv, Israel's security considerations cannot be ignored.

But in an area where most conversation centres on the Arab-Israeli dispute, and where a multitude of schemes abound, I offer an idea. It is an idea which depends on the cultivation of trust between Arabs and Israelis, rather than the maintenance of bigger and bigger armies.

The plan requires both the Arabs and the Israelis to compromise courageously. On the one hand, Israel has to accept in principle the idea of returning the West Bank to Arab sovereignty over a long time scale. (In fact, Israel implied this when it accepted UN Security Council Resolution 242, which calls for withdrawal of Israeli forces from territories occupied during the 1967 war.)

On the other hand, the Arabs have to agree to treat Jewish settlers on the West Bank as Diaspora Jews. They can remain in their settlements under Arab sovereignty. No big deal about this really, as there are Jewish communities in Syria, Egypt, Morocco and other Arab countries.

Having agreed on these principles, the Arabs and Israelis have to agree on a drawn-out time scale for Israeli withdrawal from the West Bank. Because of security problems and the need for building of trust, a three year time scale – as was the case with the withdrawal from Sinai – would be unsuitable. A time-scale of around 20 years would have to be looked at.

The fact that the settlers could remain would work to both Israeli and Arab advantage. For the Israelis it would alleviate the heart wrenching scenes which accompanied withdrawal from Sinai, and would enable fundamentalist Jews to remain in Eretz Israel. For the Arabs, such a plan would send all but the most hardy or fundamentalist Jews scurrying back to Israel proper.

After six years of talking to Arabs and Israelis, I feel fairly confident this plan will never be implemented. There's not much compassion or faith in the Holy Land.

But the consequences of failure to resolve the Palestinian problem could be grim indeed – both for the Arab States neighboring Israel, Western interests, and Israel itself.

Although Iran has gone out of the news somewhat, the growth of Islamic fundamentalism remains a real thing. The continuing failure of existing forces, including the PLO, to alleviate the crisis could lead to a further growth in Islamic fundamentalism. Young Palestinians and other Arabs, disillusioned at the failure of the existing forces, are likely to turn to Islam as a liberator.

Already this has begun to happen amongst young Palestinians on the West Bank, where pro-PLO students have clashed with Islamic fundamentalists.

This would not only destabilise the Arab regimes, but also could infect Israel's own Arab population.

In view of Israel's limited Jewish population growth, this could exacerbate widespread Israeli fears that they will be outnumbered in their own State by considerably faster breeding Arab Israelis. Some statistics show this could happen within 50 years.

Furthermore, Arab States ruled or heavily influenced by Islamic fundamentalism would never recognise Israel's right to exist, and could back track on the implied recognition already demonstrated by Syria and Jordan.

Now back to the scene in the PLO office in Tripoli, Lebanon. Ahmad Abdul Rahman is drawing on a cigarette as he talks about the dissidents, or mutineers, within Fatah's ranks.

Referring to the dissidents, who oppose diplomacy in favor of armed struggle, he said: "The problem is we have a lot of romantics within the revolution.

"After all, it is difficult to be realistic in the Palestinian Revolution. That's why we have so many dreamers."

Kakopetria, Cyprus July 4, 1983 (*To Mother*)

We arrived here last Thursday…

We hired a car in Larnaca (airport) and drove to Kakopetria. The main street is just suitable for one car and as we stopped at our lane we were greeted by the village women dressed in black. Most stood back and were just welcoming, but one old one decided to help carry our cases…. All of which were too heavy of course. She settled for the typewriter, an excuse for coming into our lovely house, and then called in her daughter, who must be around 50. She showed her daughter the shower, her eyes all alight.

I had thought the old people of the old village (even though the new village, tourists, restaurants, etc. is only 100 metres away) may have resisted our coming to Kakopetria. (*Ed: it was a stronghold of Cypriot activism against the British before 1960.*) I was quite wrong. I think they feel that if foreigners like their village then their sons and daughters will appreciate it also. I rather guess that the old people have written to their families living in the Cypriot Diaspora this week saying: "So you are doing well in Canada/ Britain/Australia, but we need a shower and proper lighting in our house. Don't tell us the houses are too old; this Australian architect has everything in the house. Send cheque soonest."

I interpret by the way you ask "when are we leaving for London; how long are we staying in Cyprus," that you cannot exactly imagine that the house is suitable to live in. From the pictures we showed you originally, I don't blame you. But the house is magnificent; incredible if you bear in mind what it was like. You remember Clovelly, Cornwall? Well, as the village is renovated (it is all under an Antiquities order) the whole village will be just as impressive.

Ill. 16. In the kitchen, Kakopetria house, July 1983

Kakopetria, Cyprus July 12, 1983 (*To Mother and Aunt Ethel*)

I am writing from the desk in our upstairs living room. I am looking out through a window at the pine-covered Troodos Mountains – Mount Olympus to be exact. It is dusk and the lights around the British white radar surveillance balloon can be seen a few miles away. In winter the mountain is covered in snow.

We have been here almost two weeks now and the house is very good. A donkey walks past our bedroom every morning about 6 am on the way to the fields and arrives back about 5 pm. Church bells from the white church about 50 metres away wake us some mornings. Not as often as the call to prayer from the mosques in Amman.

Our bank manager, who is in fact a refugee from the Turkish occupied section of the island, is very nice. His brothers and sisters all moved to Australia after the Turkish invasion. His family keep asking him to visit them in Melbourne, but he explained that they are such a close-knit family he doesn't want to go just yet because it would upset him leaving his family. His family in Australia, I mean. With him almost in tears, we talked about his family.

He said he had heard that we had renovated a very nice house in the old village, and I invited him for a drink. He is going on holiday and will come after he returns – but only, he said, on condition that he can take us out to dinner in return.

Living here is a bit like living in a museum as every day people come to admire the village and our house.

Ill. 17. Main street of Old Kakopetria, Cyprus

Kakopetria, Cyprus August 25, 1983 (*To Mother*)

We are leaving here on 16th September. We are taking the car on a ship to Venice, and then driving straight across Europe, and will be in York on Thursday 22nd September.

On Tuesday Susan went to Nicosia for the day as UNESCO was running a seminar on archaeological conservation. Susan had met the organiser, a Brit who we met with Crystal, at the Cyprus Department of Antiquities and he invited her. The heads of all the Mediterranean antiquities departments were there – including Adnan Hadidi, the Jordanian head. Last night they all visited Kakopetria at the end of a day tripping around Cyprus. All thirty of them came through our house. Adnan was very impressed and stayed for a beer with the British organiser. The Israeli came too, and I made him feel at home with a friendly "Shalom".

The builder's daughter is getting married next Sunday and we have been invited. It is going to be a little difficult as there will be a language problem.

Thanks to me, we are well in with the priest, who turns out to be married with four children. I bought him a beer at The Mill the other day. To cut a long story short, he expressed interest in our house, saying people said it is very good. He is renovating his at the moment, so I invited him to come and see ours. He's very impressed and wanted Susan to help him. In my mood of expansive generosity, I agreed. Problem is he wants to add a room, which Susan thinks he should be allowed to, but the Department fiercely opposes.

Heslington, York October 9, 1983 (*To Mother*)

Perhaps the time had come for us to leave Kakopetria when we did. Because, we had the bank manager to drinks a few days before we left. After he sat down, he said to me: "I suppose most of your work is in the winter." He must have noted me wandering the village for nearly two months. The next night he took us out to dinner at a restaurant at the junction of the Kakopetria to Nicosia road with the one to Morphou. The latter is now blocked because of the Turkish occupation of the north, but it is close to the Green Line and is the closest he can get to his former home.

As well as the comment about my winter work, there was another laugh, this time about Susan. We met a travel agent in the Rialto Hotel in Kakopetria, and Susan asked him about student fares between Britain and Cyprus. Susan pushed him on how old a student could be, but did not disclose that she was returning to university.

"Well, couldn't be over thirty….no-one's a student after thirty." Susan changed the subject.

*****

We moved into our "cottage" on Oct 1 as scheduled. It is very good and quite big. It is in a row built about 10-12 years ago. The living room has double doors opening onto a small garden overlooking farmland. It belongs to a dairy farmer, and the cows come and look in when we have the lights on at dusk. Except in peak traffic, it takes about eight minutes only to drive to the King's Manor (where Susan's course is held) from here. It is quite amazing being so close to the centre of the city and still having an unspoilt view of English countryside. Tulip and daffodil bulbs are on special at present so I have bought them for planting in the garden.

Heslington, York October 27, 1983 (*To Mother and Aunt Ethel*)

Last Thursday, in London, the editor of The Spectator, Alexander Chancellor, who visited Amman and spent a lot of time with us, invited me to the magazine's fortnightly lunch. You know the type of thing – a thinkers' lunch with plenty of red wine. About twelve were there – including the owner, Lord Grimond, Alexander, and Barry Humphries, who is currently doing a promotion for them. Sitting at the other end of the table, I didn't have a lot to say to him, but as he was leaving, he said to me: "Any relation of John Balderstone.... I remember him clearly from Camberwell Grammar."

"Glory be", I said. "He's my brother....older brother.

"Yes, about my age", said Barry.

Kakopetria, Cyprus Christmas Day 1983 (*To Mother*)

We have had a very funny Christmas Day. Two days ago, a man called Dinos, who used to run the Co-op supermarket and is awaiting a more highly-paid job in Saudi Arabia, asked me for a drink at 9.30 am after church on Christmas Day. We used to have the occasional beer together during the summer. I was just out of bed today when Dinos called – at 9 am – insisting that we had arranged to have breakfast with his family. As I was dressed in night attire only Susan answered the door, and she and Dinos arranged to meet on the bridge in thirty minutes. Dinos was most insistent that it had all been arranged. So we were on the bridge within half an hour. Soon after we were sitting at their dining table in the new side of Kakopetria – their house would be about 50 years old – with all Dinos' family. His father-in-law was there, and his wife, and all his children and their husbands. There were about twelve in all. Father-in-law asked Susan what she would like to drink. She thought and said: "Maybe tea."

"Are you sick", responded father-in-law? They had offered whisky, wine, beer etc. and were quite taken aback by Susan's attitude. I had seen the corks being removed from the wine bottles so I, once again saved the day, by saying I would like wine. Although there was dry red, Susan, I and Dinos opted for Pink Lady rose, which is semi-sweet and fairly heavy. At first I couldn't think why it seemed so appropriate for twenty to ten on Christmas morning but then it dawned: it resembled communion wine. To eat we were served a famous Greek soup with egg and lemon juice, then liver and chicken and fruits. Another bottle of wine arrived at five to ten. It was a good breakfast.

*****

We have heard it has been very hot in Melbourne over Christmas. A man who runs a kebab restaurant near the Maryland in the new village has a family in Sydney and as I walk past each day he gives me an account of weather in Australia. He seems to speak to Australia every second day.

*****

We stayed one night this week in Nicosia as I am doing a feature on The Cyprus Question for 'The Age'. I talked with Klafkos Clerides, a former president and head of one of the main Greek Cypriot parties one day, and then crossed to the occupied side the next in order to talk with the head of Turkish Cyprus.

1984
Heslington, York February 28, 1984 (*To David Wadham*)

Since we got back from Kakopetria I have been working steadily on a novel based in Amman, Jerusalem and Damascus and I think it's going rather well. At least it's going well word wise, and it's a matter of waiting and seeing whether any publisher will think it is any good quality wise.

I feel I must push on with the novel because for the first few months after "retirement", I worked on the first few chapters of a factual book on the Middle East. I found the going tough, even though an agent in London had shown interest in looking at it. In the end I didn't even send it to him as I didn't think I could finish it. Therefore, I want to finish the novel.

The problem with my characters in the novel is they have an unquenchable thirst for gin and tonic. And they are so realistic that whenever they have one I feel like one too. Actually I've thought that Schweppes might be interested in publishing it.

Heslington, York June 20, 1984 (*To Mother and Aunt Ethel*)

My garden could be described only as "A Picture". The daffs and tulips have now gone, but the petunias are flowering very nicely. I have grown them all from seed, but some were from Australia and they are doing much better than the English variety. However the Australian ones are rather baffled by the weather. For the past two days it has been very hot, but previously it has been cold – although the overnight frosts have stopped at last. The rabbits play in the paddock at dawn and dusk, and the cuckoos are singing all the time. It now doesn't get dark until 10.30 pm and it's fully light again by 4 am. Some change from winter when it used to get dark at 4.30 pm!

We are going out folly hunting again tomorrow. It's an all day trip up the north Yorkshire coast. Which reminds me, about two weeks ago Dr Derek Lindstrum, the course director, invited us to dinner at his house in Leeds. He is very proud of his house and justifiably – we saw his library, Persian rugs etc. We were shown into every room, but it was frowned upon when I wanted a cigarette. Of course, I explained – knowing more than him about Iran – that the Persian carpets were suffering from withdrawal symptoms. Everyone knows, of course, that those carpets are made by smokers for smokers and they become limp and dull in smoke-free surroundings.

I am madly retyping my book, which contrary to earlier advice, is a novel set in the Middle East. I have to retype it myself to change names used which might otherwise have led some people to erroneously believe they were the characters involved. (*Ed. This eventually became 'A Road from Damascus' published in 1992.*)

Ill. 18. Petunia display, Heslington, June 1984

Heslington, York, September 5, 1984 (*To Mother and Aunt Ethel*)

How time flies! We are leaving here tomorrow for our trip back to Cyprus via Greece. Not only has the year been "challenging and rewarding", but also we have emerged from it as very well-rounded people. It's my excellent cooking and English beer.

We changed our route plans completely today after Susan read a story in 'The Guardian' about shipping and petrol strikes in Italy. We are now driving to Luxemburg, and then dashing across West Germany to Austria. From there we will drive through Yugoslavia to Greece. We catch the MV Sol Olympia at midnight of the 20th for Cyprus via Crete and arrive in Cyprus on 22 September.

Gasthof Drachenwand, near Mondsee, Austria
September 12, 1984 (*To Mother and Aunt Ethel*)

The ferry arrived in Zeebrugge, Belgium last Friday morning and we drove to Luxemburg for the first night. For lunch in Belgium I found a great restaurant, which served mussels all different ways. We had them cooked in white wine – the way we do them. I was a bit put out because Susan said she would order as my French – the little I know – is made up of old-fashioned courteous phrases that no one uses any more. In short my French is too polite. It was quite lucky I found the restaurant as Susan was a little hot around the collar because I had managed to direct her into the centre of Brussels rather than out onto the ring road (she was driving). My eyes seem to pick up signs like "Moules" better than destinations.

*****

I should have mentioned that I had to take over ordering food again in Luxemburg, where they speak French as well as their own obscure language. I had to take over because Susan's French relies on the waiter being able to lip read. I said to Susan that what needed to be done was to say in a loud voice "Pardon Monsieur, der beera, silver plate." She said "you do it then." And I did, loudly. And she said I asked the wrong man. But it arrived. He was obviously impressed by old-fashioned courtesies.

Perhaps I didn't ever tell you, but covering the Arab summit in Morocco a few years back was a nightmare. Moroccans speak only Arabic and French. To get a call to 'The Age' I had to use the phrase book to get all the numbers. But my reward came when I heard 'The Age' copy taker saying to the editor: "It's David Balderstone and he is speaking French to the operator."

The End

Postscript

The Iran-Iraq war finally ended in 1988, and Ayatollah Khomeiny died in 1995. The Soviet Union collapsed in 1989. Iraq's invasion of Kuwait in 1990 was repulsed by the American-led "Desert Storm". Jordan and Israel signed a peace treaty in 1994, following the first Oslo accord between the Palestinians and Israel in 1993 and the establishment of the Palestinian Authority. The second Oslo accord in 1995 led to election of a Palestine Legislative Council and the fragmentation of the West Bank into numerous enclaves amongst Israeli settlements. A Lebanon-Syria ceasefire was finally achieved in 2000. Saddam Hussein was removed from power following America's invasion of Iraq in 2003. Since then the area has become a maelstrom of conflicting aspirations and violence.

During the unfolding of these events in the years since 1984, the Palestinian presence on the West Bank has been eroded to the extent that it now appears on the map as non-contiguous patches surrounded and interspersed by Israeli settlements, from which they are separated by a high concrete wall. Gaza has become a stronghold of Palestinian Islamic militarism under Hamas, with frequent outbreaks of violence to the sorry detriment of the civilian communities on both sides. It has become even clearer now that Israel will never allow an independent Palestinian State on the West Bank and Gaza Strip. The current apartheid situation of the West Bank and Gaza Strip seems likely to continue indefinitely, while the Palestinian areas in the West Bank territory continue to be eroded by new Israeli settlements and punitive incursions and Gaza continues to be eroded by military destruction.

Meanwhile, following the overthrow of the Shah and the emergence of the Islamic Republic of Iran as a Shi'ite Muslim power, other Shi'ite Muslim groups, for so long the downtrodden, impoverished communities within the surrounding Arab countries have increased in population and found their voice. Their sectarian conflict with the ongoing extremist Sunni Muslim sects together with secular movements for democracy has overwhelmed the previous dominance in the Arab world of the struggle for Palestinian rights.

The consequences of the division of Arabia by the Western powers after World War I have been dire indeed. As David noted in his piece 'Once again the West carves up the East' of February 11, 1980:

"Poor old Hussein (great-grandfather of today's King Hussein of Jordan) thought Britain intended to grant the Arabs independence as a reward for helping crush the Ottomans. Instead Britain and France carved up the area, drew borders with an incredible lack of sensitivity, and paved the way for the creation of Israel on the area's prime land (which is something, presumably, the Ottomans would never have done)."

He went on to point out that: "Any strategy designed to maintain the West's interests in the Middle East, and the Gulf particularly, should be based on the assumption that all the Gulf leaders are vulnerable to revolution." He proposed "three issues which cannot be ignored if a successful 'people policy' is to evolve. They are the Palestinian question, self-restraint on doubtfully needed exports to the area, and being careful that any military strategy for the protection of the Gulf is not seen by the people of the area as a threat to independence".

He considered that: "Real moves towards a solution to the Palestinian problem are important because it is modern Islam's most tangible grievance against the US and other supporters of Israel."

However subsequent Western military interventions in the Gulf have perhaps eclipsed the Palestinian cause as modern Islam's most tangible grievance, in so far as they threatened Arab independence. His point regarding doubtfully needed exports is also playing out: "Did Iran, the Middle East's largest potential producer of oil and gas, need to embark on a deal costing up to $US14,000 million on two nuclear reactors? While the argument is often put forward that an exporting country cannot help it if a ruler or his Government wants to buy, it is interesting to note that the former Shah himself once wondered aloud whether the Americans were supplying so many arms to Iran for the protection of their strategic interests, or for the sake of their arms industry."

Today the Palestinian issue is just one of many factors that have contributed to the chaos in the Middle East. As David noted in his final piece from Amman, "the Levant is an area of jealousies between sects, tribes and villages, where for so often, and for so long, the gun has been the arbiter".

The removal of Saddam Hussein paved the way for a Shi'ite takeover of the Government of Iraq. While this is not an Iran-type Islamic regime, its lack of attention to the interests of the Sunni communities and minority groups, just as has that of the Assad Government in Syria allowed the Sunni fundamentalist forces fighting as "Islamic State" to promote their particular form of religious intolerance. These IS proponents of an Arab caliphate in Syria and Iraq have the intention no doubt to one day cover the whole of Arabia. In this context it is worth remembering that the idea of Arab independence under an Arab caliphate as discussed between Sharif Hussein and the British at the start of WWI covered the whole area, from southern Turkey to the Indian Ocean - including Syria and Iraq, and the Arabian Peninsula including Yemen, Oman, the United Arab Emirates, Qatar, Bahrain and Kuwait.

As Patrick Steel concluded in his Introduction to the 1986 edition of *The Struggle for Syria*: "To ignore the reasons for local tension and its history, worse still to drive local forces to the wall, is to unleash the demons of terrorism against which even the mightiest have no adequate defence".

Susan Balderstone, Parkville, July 2015

Other books by David Balderstone

A Road from Damascus
The Poppy Press Australia 1992
ISBN 0-646-11440-9 (paperback)
Kindle e-book 2010
ISBN 978-0-646-11440-8

The Baghdad Chameleon
The Poppy Press Australia 2012
ISBN 978-0-646-57495-0 (paperback)
Kindle e-book 2011
ISBN 978-0-9943464-1-4

Shining the Boot of a Nation:
a Portrait of Egypt after Nasser
The Poppy Press Australia 2015
978-0-9943464-2-1 (paperback)
Kindle e-book 2014
ISBN 978-0-646-92445-8

Dead Reckoning: a play in two acts
The Poppy Press Australia 1998
Kindle e-book 2014
ISBN 978-0-646-93349-8

www.davidbalderstone.com